Central and Eastern Europe

Central and Eastern Europe: The Opening Curtain?

EDITED BY

William E. Griffith
Massachusetts Institute of Technology

Westview Press
BOULDER, SAN FRANCISCO, & LONDON

Published in 1989 in the United States of America by Westview Press, Inc., 5500 Central Avenue, Boulder, Colorado 80301, and in the United Kingdom by Westview Press, Inc., 13 Brunswick Centre, London WC1N 1AF, England

Library of Congress Cataloging-in-Publication Data
Central and Eastern Europe: The opening curtain?
Includes index.
1. Europe, Eastern—Politics and government—
1945– . 2. Europe, Eastern—Economic conditions—
1945– . 3. Europe, Eastern—Foreign relations
1945– . I. Griffith, William E.
DJK50.C46 1989 947 88-27974
ISBN 0-8133-0773-2
ISBN 0-8133-0774-0 (pbk.)

Printed and bound in the United States of America

The paper used in this publication meets the requirements of the American National Standard for Permanence of Paper for Printed Library Materials Z39.48-1984.

10 9 8 7 6 5 4 3 2 1

Contents

About the Contributors

Wolfgang Berner is the former deputy director of the Cologne-based Federal Institute of East European and International Studies. Since his retirement in February 1988, he has worked as a free-lance researcher and writer. He has written and edited books, articles, and research papers on Soviet foreign policy, West German–East European relations, and international communism.

Seweryn Bialer is the Robert and Renee Belfer Professor of Social Science and International Relations at Columbia University and director of the university's Research Institute on International Change. He has written and edited a number of books including, with Michael Mandelbaum, *The Global Rivals* (1988), a companion book to the public television series; *Gorbachev's Russia and American Foreign Policy,* edited with Michael Mandelbaum (Westview, 1988); and *Politics, Society, and Nationality Inside Gorbachev's Russia* (Westview, 1989). He is an expert in international politics, particularly U.S.-Soviet relations.

J. F. Brown is a visiting lecturer at the University of California, Berkeley. He has written extensively on East European affairs, and his latest book is *Eastern Europe and Communist Rule* (1988). At present, he is working on a study of the Balkans and superpower relations.

Charles Gati is a professor of political science at Union College and a senior research fellow at Columbia University's Research Institute on International Change. He is the author of *Hungary and the Soviet Bloc* (1986); *Soviet–East European Relations: An Introductory Essay* (forthcoming); and numerous books and articles on Soviet and U.S. policies toward Eastern Europe.

William E. Griffith is Ford Professor of Political Science at the Massachusetts Institute of Technology. He is the author and editor of many books and articles on Europe and the Communist world; his most recent book is *Superpowers and Regional Tensions: The USSR, The United States, and Europe* (1981). He is an expert in Communist and international affairs.

Dale R. Herspring is a foreign service officer who has served in the U.S. missions in Berlin, Warsaw, and Moscow, and he will soon return to the U.S. Embassy in Moscow. His most recent book, with Robbin Laird, is *The*

Soviet Union and Strategic Arms. He is a specialist on Communist political and military affairs.

Michael Mandelbaum is the director of the Project on East-West Relations and a senior fellow at the Council on Foreign Relations. His most recent books are *The Fate of Nations: The Search for National Security in the 19th and 20th Centuries* (1988); and, with Seweryn Bialer, *The Global Rivals* (1988). His areas of expertise include international politics, security affairs, and East-West relations.

Paul Marer is a professor of international business at the School of Business at Indiana University. His most recent books are *Dollar GNPs of the USSR and Eastern Europe* (1986) (a study done for the World Bank); and *Creditworthyness and Reform in Poland* (1988), which he coedited. His specialty is the economies and trade of Eastern Europe.

Vojtech Mastny is a professor of international relations at Boston University and is currently at the Netherlands Institute for Advanced Studies until July 1989. He has written widely on the history of World War II and the immediate post-1945 period. His most recent book is *Helsinki, Human Rights, and European Security* (1986). His area of expertise is diplomatic history during and after World War II.

Viktor Meier is the Balkans correspondent, stationed in Vienna, of the West German newspaper *Frankfurter Allgemeine Zeitung.* He is one of the leading Western authorities on the countries of Eastern and Southeastern Europe, about which he has written and published extensively.

Dominique Moïsi is associate director of the French Institute of International Relations, Paris, and editor of *Politique étrangère.* He is the author of many articles on international politics, most recently "French Foreign Policy: The Challenge of Adaptation," *Foreign Affairs* (Fall 1988). He is a political analyst and a foreign policy expert.

Mark Palmer is a foreign service officer who is presently the U.S. ambassador to Hungary. Previously he was deputy assistant secretary of state for European affairs (1982–1986). His special interest is the Soviet Union and Eastern Europe.

Robert Sharlet is a professor of political science at Union College, Schenectady, New York. In addition to a number of articles and chapters on Eastern Europe, he has published five books on the USSR, the most recent a coedited volume, *P. I. Stuchka: Selected Writings on Soviet Law and Marxism* (1988). He is a specialist on Soviet and East European law, politics, and human rights.

H. Gordon Skilling is a professor of political science, emeritus, University of Toronto. He is the author of several books on the Soviet Union and Eastern Europe, including *Czechoslovakia's Interrupted Revolution* (1976) and *Samizdat and Independent Society in Central and Eastern Europe* (in press). His special interest is Czechoslovakia.

Angela Stent is an associate professor of government at Georgetown University and a research fellow at Harvard University's Russian Research Center. She is the author of *From Embargo to Ostpolitik* (1981); *Technology Transfer to the Soviet Union* (1983); and "Gorbachev and Western Europe," *Europe* (1987). Her special interests are East-West relations and Soviet–West European relations.

Sarah Meiklejohn Terry is an associate professor of political science at Tufts University and a fellow at Harvard University's Russian Research Center. Her most recent book, as editor and contributor, is *Soviet Policy in Eastern Europe* (1984). She has written numerous articles on contemporary Polish and East European politics and Soviet–East European relations. Her current research focuses on the impact of leadership change on bloc cohesion.

John Van Oudenaren is a policy analyst in the political science department of the RAND Corporation. He was previously a research scholar at the Kennan Institute for Advanced Russian Studies and a member of the Policy Planning Staff of the State Department. He has written *Soviet Policy Toward Eastern Europe: Options for the 1980s and Beyond* (1983). He is a specialist on Soviet foreign policy.

Preface

The East-West Forum, located in Washington, D.C., and New York, is a research and policy analysis organization sponsored by the Samuel Bronfman Foundation. The Forum aims to build a bridge between scholarship and policymaking. It brings scholars and policymakers together in seminars, briefings, and conferences and in the production of books. Through this process it hopes to generate reliable information and high quality analyses that will prove useful to those engaged in the debates that shape and will shape U.S. policy during this period of significant changes in East-West relations.

As with the Forum's earlier works, the authors of the chapters in this book subjected their work to a series of critical editorial workshops sponsored by the Forum. Aside from the authors, the participants of the workshops were Timothy Garton Ash, Vernon Aspaturian, Istvan Deak, Pierre Hassner, Hanns-Dieter Jacobsen, Ross Johnson, Karl Kaiser, Melvin Lasky, Paul Lendvai, Kerry McNamara, John Michael Montias, Edwina Moreton, Robin Remington, Joseph Rothschild, Volker Rühe, Jutta Scherrer, Enid Schoettle, Rudolf Tökés, and Sharon Wolchik.

The East-West Forum would like to extend its thanks to Stephen E. Herbits, Executive Vice President, Joseph E. Seagram & Sons, Inc.; William K. Friedman, Trustee of the Samuel Bronfman Foundation; Seweryn Bialer, Chairman of the East-West Forum; David E. Morey, the Forum's Associate Executive Director; and Thomas Sherlock, the Forum's Rapporteur.

The Forum plans to continue providing useful information and analyses. The continued participation and help of these individuals and others will be invaluable.

James M. Montgomery
Executive Director
East-West Forum

Acknowledgments

I could never have completed the editing of this volume as rapidly and as well as has happened without the assistance of my administrative assistant, Gerti Gillen, and of several doctoral candidates in the Department of Political Science of the Massachusetts Institute of Technology: my principal research assistant, Susan Sanders, and my other research assistants, Richard Deeg, Jennifer Nupp, Harry Ozeroff, and Norbert Rabl. My warmest thanks to them all.

William E. Griffith

Introduction

For more than forty years the West has lived in the shadow of danger from the East. Enormous sacrifices, tragedies, and outlays have been a part of the heavy cost borne by the United States and the Atlantic Alliance in the face of the Cold War. Today, however, there is a new Soviet leader in the East and the possibility exists that changes in his country will affect and perhaps even interrupt the harsh pattern of East-West relations that has unfolded during these four decades.

In its first two books, *Gorbachev's Russia and American Foreign Policy* and *Politics, Society, and Nationality Inside Gorbachev's Russia,* the East-West Forum sought to illuminate the potential for change in today's Soviet Union. In this, its third volume, the Forum's objective is to understand and analyze—in both political and Western policy terms—perhaps the greatest non-Soviet challenge to General Secretary Mikhail Gorbachev's *perestroika:* Central and Eastern Europe.

Eastern Europe has always been at the heart of the forty-year-old pattern of East-West relations. Indeed, historically the region has for decades been a birthplace of unpredictable and dangerous events. The Cold War, after all, started in Eastern Europe; if it is going to end, it has to end there.

These are extraordinary times in Eastern Europe. We see there more political flux and uncertainty than at any time since 1956. The current mixture of political uncertainty, economic difficulty and Soviet–East European tensions may place the region on a more volatile footing than at any time since the Cold War began.

Today, the people of Eastern Europe want their own *perestroika* because their systems—like the USSR's—are simply not working economically. In fact, Gorbachev's arrival on the political scene and the accompanying reforms he has ushered forth are a main catalyst for the flux and uncertainty in Eastern Europe. The Soviet Union and its General Secretary remain the major influences on the region. Although Gorbachev's reforms, given fundamental historical and cultural distinctions, affect Eastern Europe and the Soviet Union differently, *perestroika* has a much greater potential for implementation in Eastern Europe than in the USSR itself.

At present, Soviet policy toward Eastern Europe, like Moscow's policies toward other parts of the world, is driven by an overriding emphasis on internal reform. As a result, the Soviet leadership's goal in Eastern Europe is a negative one: to avoid crisis. Gorbachev seems to realize that, as has happened in the past, an explosion in the region could derail his reform efforts at home. Historically, there has been an important if shadowy interrelationship between reform in the Soviet Union and in Eastern Europe. The efforts of Alexei Kosygin, the yearning of Czechoslovakia, the spark of Solidarity, and the arrival of Gorbachev's *perestroika* were and are all connected even if the nexuses are difficult or impossible to sketch out. Leonid Brezhnev and the interim leadership that followed him could not see and benefit completely from this historical lesson. Gorbachev can.

Perhaps as a result, Moscow is permitting the individual ruling parties in Eastern Europe more latitude now than they enjoyed in Brezhnev's day. Indeed, Soviet spokesmen sometimes point out that their nation cannot be held responsible for what happens in the region because it does not completely control the local parties. That is true. The recent and relatively "conservative" behavior of the Czechoslovak and East German parties can hardly be to the General Secretary's liking.

Yet Moscow, for all this new tolerance, will not be infinitely flexible in Eastern Europe. The Soviet empire there remains vital for a variety of reasons—ideological, national and strategic. Some Soviet spokesmen say the Brezhnev Doctrine has been repealed and that Soviet troops will never again invade a neighboring Communist country to enforce ideological orthodoxy. Western policymakers, however, cannot be certain of this even if those making such statements are. The limits of Soviet tolerance remain unclear. Perhaps events like those that occurred in Czechoslovakia in 1968 are now tolerable, but an uprising of the kind we saw in Hungary in 1956 would not be. In any case, Moscow will insist no country leave the Warsaw Pact; and the Kremlin may be determined, too, that the various Communist parties retain their monopolies of effective political power throughout Eastern Europe.

At the bottom of this is the fact that Soviet attitudes toward Eastern Europe are changing. What is unacceptable now may become acceptable five years hence—assuming that the process of reform remains. Thus, as in the past, the Soviets' sense of what is permissible in the empire is closely tied to what they seek, and what they are willing to tolerate, in their own country. Soviet reformers optimistically say they can build a socialist system that is humane, just, prosperous, and different from capitalism—one that the peoples of Eastern Europe will welcome. History and reality, however, argue that such a vision of socialism is unachievable and that any system that comes from the East will leave the peoples of Eastern Europe discontent.

There is also a second fundamental reason for the turmoil in Eastern Europe: Each of the regimes there is in crisis. Importantly, in every case, the root of this crisis is the political illegitimacy of the Communist governments of the region. All were imposed by the Soviet Union. None has ever won genuine acceptance. It is one thing to tolerate a Communist regime when standards of living are rising; it is quite another when the economies of Eastern Europe are, to one extent or another, failing.

The failure of communism in Eastern Europe is a broad one. It is a failure not just of particular policies, but of the systems themselves. It includes not only Poland and Romania, but also the postwar "success stories"—Hungary and even the German Democratic Republic (GDR). Moreover, this failure is not just economic. It is political.

There is another feature common to all of the region's countries: the rise of nationalism. Some regimes, such as the GDR, have used this development to try winning legitimacy. Others, as in the case of Bulgaria's treatment of its Turks and Romania's governing of its Hungarians, have attempted to exploit the resentment of ethnic minorities for their own ends. Most dramatically, in Yugoslavia, nationalist passions threaten the very structure of the state.

Thus, as the eighteen following chapters attest, the individual states of Eastern Europe find themselves at a political crossroad. In Poland, probably the country closest to explosion, there exists today a mobilized population and a weak government that favors reforms but is so distrusted it cannot implement them.

In Hungary, a nation far less divided than Poland, the old leadership of János Kádár has been retired. Economically, the living standard of Hungarians is better than that of the Poles. Yet the country carries a heavy external debt, and the economy, never as thoroughly reformed as the West generally believed, is lagging. Today, there is strong pressure for change and even talk of a multiparty system.

In Czechoslovakia, by contrast, official policies run largely counter to the prevailing currents in Moscow. Prague's leadership is conservative. The closest thing to a reformer in its ranks, former prime minister Lubomír Štrougal, was recently removed. And the Czechoslovak people are still in great measure traumatized by the events of 1968 and afterward. Nonetheless, slowly, they are beginning to show signs of political life, as was evidenced in August 1988 by the extraordinary demonstration in Prague during the twentieth anniversary of the Soviet invasion.

For the GDR's part, there has always been an important element differentiating it from the rest of Eastern Europe: its relationship with West Germany. This relationship includes massive West German economic subsidies that help stabilize the GDR. Furthermore, East Berlin's leadership is conservative, has publicly scorned *perestroika*, and is, in turn, privately disliked in Moscow. Also, it should be noted, that leadership is old. Prospective successors are reportedly more flexible.

In Romania, Nicolae Ceauşescu is likely to fail continually in his attempt to establish socialism in one family. When he leaves the scene, so will his relatives; this will itself be an improvement. Yet the outlook for Bucharest, with its economy ruined, is bleak.

In Yugoslavia, one of two Eastern European states not a member of the Warsaw Pact (Albania is the other), the government is also experiencing the exhaustion of its own modified version of socialism. Yugoslavia's deep ethnic, religious and national cleavages—long suppressed but never eradicated by Marshall Tito—have taken on a new centrifugal and politically explosive quality. With public life increasingly revolving around these divisions, particularly the reassertion of Serbian nationalism, Yugoslavia risks slipping back into the bloody and contentious pattern of politics it followed in the prewar period.

What, then, should be Western policy for the region? As is pointed out in the final section of this volume, both the peoples and governments of Eastern Europe want more Western ties—but for different reasons. East European peoples identify with Western values and institutions. Their governments seek economic resources to stave off political turmoil. Nevertheless, the actual record of Eastern European governments in using economic assistance is poor. Loans have been wasted, most dramatically in Poland. What is needed is not more money, but sweeping internal reforms so that existing resources are used more productively.

Thus, reforms of specific policies are needed, such as an end to the wasteful subsidies these governments provide for food, clothing and shelter. Changes of economic strategy are also in order—for example, an end to the overemphasis on heavy industry. Most important, changes in and of the economic system itself are required, including the use of real prices, the introduction of market mechanisms and the drastic dilution of the power of central planners.

This change will be difficult. Removing subsidies could trigger political unrest; this has been the pattern in postwar Poland. Moreover, needed economic changes could limit the power of the party, which Eastern European Communists will not be anxious to permit.

Another important element in the West's promotion of East European reform involves targeting nongovernmental bodies, of which there are several in Poland. Joint ventures with Western firms enjoying majority control is another way to drop reform behind the Iron Curtain.

Ultimately, the Federal Republic of Germany will be one of the most important Western countries for Eastern Europe. Geography and history explain this; part of Germany has been part of Soviet Eastern Europe. For twenty years, the West German presence in Eastern Europe has grown steadily, if unobtrusively.

West Germany, therefore, practices a particular policy toward the East. Above all, Bonn is motivated by a concern for Germans—in the GDR and elsewhere; it tries to increase contacts with Eastern Germans as much as possible, in pursuit of the Federal Republic's stated goal of preserving a single German nation. Of course, the Communist governments of the region can shut off these contacts. This is why West German policies, invariably, emphasize conciliation.

This policy is supported across the West German political spectrum. It does, however, at times put Bonn at odds with Washington and with its own European allies. U.S. policy toward Eastern Europe often stresses security and politics; West Germany's emphasis is on economics as a means to bring about political change. Washington tries often to deal directly with the peoples of these nations; Bonn is more willing to work through the regimes. Washington and Paris tend to emphasize human rights; Bonn tends to be more concerned about influencing East European governments in their de facto behavior toward the human beings they control. Finally, in the past, Washington has been far more willing to practice policies of pressure, leverage and conditionality than have West Germany and its European allies.

Thus, together, the arrival in today's Soviet Union of *perestroika* and the new and complex volatility present in each of the Central and Eastern leadership circles pose a serious and unprecedented challenge for Western scholars, opinion leaders and policymakers. A region that has always lain at the heart of East-West conflict but has seldom rested near the top of the policy agenda is today being thrust front and center. What will be the pace and form of Central and Eastern European reforms? How will the Soviet leadership—with its "new thinking"—adjust to these regional changes? Is there an "opening" in the Iron Curtain Winston Churchill described as having descended upon a postwar continent? Finally, can the West coordinate its policy toward the region?

Edgar M. Bronfman
President, East-West Forum

Central and Eastern Europe

1

Central and Eastern Europe: The Global Context

William E. Griffith

The global high-technology revolution and the inability of Communist leaders of Central and Eastern Europe to cope with it are driving these countries, and the Soviet Union, into further decline vis-à-vis the Western developed world. Their relative decline is the worse because for the first time since 1945 this revolution centers outside Europe, in East Asia and the United States, against which this decline must now be measured. The economic and technological revival of Western Europe, especially of the Federal Republic of Germany (FRG), the only state with a compelling political as well as a traditional economic interest in Central and Eastern Europe, and the European Community's (EC) revived move toward unity make the EC, and most of all the FRG, an increasingly important economic, financial, and technological partner for these Communist countries. Even so, despite Mikhail Gorbachev's probable inability to catch up with the West in high technology, the Soviet Union will still keep its predominant influence over its key strategic allies, the German Democratic Republic (GDR) and Poland. Nevertheless, continuing Soviet technological backwardness will intensify the decline of Central and Eastern Europe.

The high-technology revolution has other negative consequences for Communist Central and Eastern Europe, as it does for other declining countries, including much of the Third World. The more important high technology becomes for economic growth, the more economies require better educated and skilled personnel, more emphasis on meritocracy, and therefore less on egalitarianism. Communist ideology and working-class sentiment oppose this. So does the ruling Communist political-bureaucratic intelligentsia, the *nomenklatura,* because massive replacement of ideologically but not technologically qualified managers is one precondition for success in high technology. Finally, this revolution, like the first Industrial Revolution, increases disparities between and among more and less developed states: in Central and Eastern Europe, for example, between East Germany and Poland and between Slovenia and Macedonia.

The high-technology revolution is primarily an information revolution based on the extremely rapid acquisition, processing, and retrieval of immense quantities of data made possible by microelectronics and computers. (This is also true of its other main component, biotechnology.) Its fundamental impact is to render national borders, and thus national sovereignty, inconsequential for many economic activities.[1] It is the more rapid because it is the first one in which two relatively equal, meritocratic states, the United States and Japan, are competing so fiercely that they are driving each other forward much more rapidly than either would forge ahead on its own.[2] Thus, Communist Central and Eastern Europe is falling even more rapidly behind than was the case in the first Industrial Revolution.

The Soviet Union is only a military superpower. Its attractiveness as a political, economic, or cultural model has collapsed, most of all in Central and Eastern Europe, where Soviet technological backwardness has become a future to be feared, not a model to be imitated. But the high-technology revolution also has great military implications. The 1982 Israeli destruction of the Syrian air force and air defenses showed what Western military high technology can do. Because military high technology, nuclear and conventional, feeds on nonmilitary high technology, Gorbachev and the Soviet military need nonmilitary microelectronic high technology in order not to become what they fear the most: a second-rate military power.

To understand the crisis in Communist Central and Eastern Europe we must first analyze the causes, contents, and probable results for Moscow's allies of Gorbachev's changes in the Soviet Union. The main causes of the crisis have been the decline in Soviet economic growth; the USSR's increasing technological backwardness; its accelerating social strains, notably alcoholism and rising mortality rates; its massive corruption; the bureaucratic antireformism of its *nomenklatura;* and its overextension and self-engendered isolation in foreign policy.

Gorbachev's revolutionary "new thinking"—*perestroika* (restructuring), *glasnost'* (openness), and *demokratizatsiya* (democratization)—is a consequence of his view, new to Marxism-Leninism, that the economic base and political superstructure of Soviet society have become major obstacles to, rather than instruments for, the advancement of socialism. Therefore, he holds, the USSR must be qualitatively revolutionized from above under continued Communist party leadership, albeit without violence and not against a class enemy (although Gorbachev hints that the *nomenklatura* is that). This, he hopes, will include the establishment of a partial rule of law; the passage of some, but not decisive, power from the Communist party to elected state organs; moves toward a market economy; and a greater emphasis on the human factor, that is, a shift from class to individual interests and incentives.

In the Soviet Union, as in Central and Eastern Europe, the working class has been the chief mass beneficiary of Communist egalitarianism. But the high-technology revolution rewards achievement, intensifies social stratification, and downgrades unskilled labor. It makes full employment—that is, concealed overemployment—a greater enemy of productivity and economic growth. When to this is added the traditional passivity of the working class in most underdeveloped countries, such as most of the Soviet Union, plus the total distrust of their Communist masters by the post-Solidarity Polish working class, the obstacles in the Soviet Union and in Communist Central and Eastern Europe to modernization (rising productivity, economic growth, and technological innovation) are immense indeed.

Soviet foreign policy's "new thinking," according to Gorbachev, also requires modernization, given the dangers of nuclear war and ecological catastrophe, north-south tensions, and Soviet external overextension and resultant isolation and encirclement. It follows that there can be no victory in nuclear war; that there is no possibility of military superiority; and that Karl von Clausewitz's dictum that war is the violent extension of politics is invalid. These require that Soviet foreign policy emphasize Soviet-U.S. and Sino-Soviet détente, interdependence, and mutual security rather than international class struggle against imperialism even at the risk of war. Nuclear deterrence and parity must be replaced by "reasonable sufficiency" and by a gradual transition to a nonnuclear world and to the nonuse of force to solve international conflicts, while preserving strategic stability by arms control agreements. An operationally defensive strategy must replace an offensive one, and *glasnost'* must be extended to military postures (that is, by intrusive verification). Soviet expansion in the Third World must no longer be judged, as Leonid Brezhnev did, by East-West geostrategic considerations but by regional ones, and therefore such expansion must be abandoned or cut back when it has been unsuccessful or has interfered with détente. The Soviet Union must also become more active in international organizations such as the U.N., GATT, and UNCTAD to help Soviet modernization and increase Soviet influence in them.[3]

Western sceptics maintain that all this is at worst disinformation to lull the West into lack of vigilance and at best merely a pause (*peredyshka*), the better to resume the advance later on. Such scepticism has recently been proven false with respect to the Soviet-Yugoslav break and the Sino-Soviet dispute, and the present relatively open Soviet criticism of Joseph Stalin's and Leonid Brezhnev's foreign policy makes its current falsity likely.

The Soviet need for major economic reforms was clear several years before Brezhnev died. But had, say, Viktor Grishin, not Gorbachev, been elected General Secretary when Konstantin Chernenko died, he would not soon, if ever, have introduced the major reforms that Gorbachev has. Thus, the personality of the new leader was a major factor in at least the timing of this great change in Soviet domestic and foreign policy and its consequences for Communist Central and Eastern Europe. The converse might become true, but probably only partially so, if Gorbachev were to be removed or feel compelled to reverse his reforms, but neither seemed likely in late 1988.

Ronald Reagan reciprocated Gorbachev's détente policy primarily because U.S. public opinion came to favor détente, and so eventually and largely for that reason did he. After the 1975 fall of Saigon, according to U.S. public opinion polls, most Americans gave first priority to strengthening U.S.

military capability. This continued until the early 1980s, when public sentiment began to focus instead on arms control negotiations with the Soviet Union, although most Americans still deeply distrusted Moscow. Reagan's victory in intermediate nuclear forces (INF) deployment; his triumphal reelection in 1984; his increasing concern with the destructiveness of nuclear weapons and with history's verdict about his administration; his support of the Strategic Defense Initiative, which he hoped would become a shield against Soviet nuclear attack; and the urgings of Secretary of State George Shultz pushed him in the same direction. Thus, the timing of Gorbachev's coming to power and Reagan's turn toward détente was nearly simultaneous.[4]

Historically, in Central and Eastern Europe, except in interwar Czechoslovakia, nationalism won over modernization, and the region thereby remained semideveloped.[5] But today popular support for each reinforces the other because Soviet domination means economic backwardness, political repression, cultural stagnation, and foreign domination. In addition, for the more developed Central European states, the Soviet demand for more and better quality exports interferes with their hard-currency purchases of Western technology by means of exports to the West and thus accelerates their declining export competitiveness and their differentiation.[6]

The latter is in large part the result of the reassertion of traditional historic patterns. Thus, "Central and Eastern Europe" has lost much of its relevance. (Do East Berlin and Tirana, Weimar and Priština, belong to the same region? A historical absurdity!) Of the three westernmost countries, East Germany, Czechoslovakia, and Hungary, the export competitiveness of the first and the last is threatened by the Pacific Rim states, whereas the second is barely waking up to this danger. Conversely, Poland and Romania are rapidly sinking into the Third World. The southern and eastern parts of Yugoslavia are threatened with the same fate, from which Albania has not yet escaped, whereas Bulgaria is becoming developed.

The impact in Communist Central and Eastern Europe of Gorbachev's reforms is different, greater, and more destabilizing than in the Great Russian half of the Soviet Union. (It is not necessarily less destabilizing than in the other nations of the Soviet Union, as we have seen in the Baltic republics, Armenia and Azerbaijan, Kazakhstan, and the western Ukraine.) This is the result of the post-1953 Central and East European "destabilization syndrome": reform in the Soviet Union; nationalist unrest among the non-Great Russians; the decline of fear and the consequent rise of dissidence among the intelligentsia; the release of nationalist discontents; the advanced age of several of the Central and East European leaders and the consequent likelihood of succession struggles; and the historically demonstrable probability that "appetite grows with eating," that political decompression from above after tyranny is likely to get out of the control of the decompressors. In Communist Central and Eastern Europe, especially in Poland, East Germany, and Hungary, the economic situation worsened after at first improving, another classic cause of political destabilization. Moreover, most of these countries have always thought themselves culturally superior to, if unfortunately dominated by Russia. The impact in the region of Gorbachev's revolution is also likely to be greater than that of Nikita Khrushchev's reforms because Gorbachev's go much farther, as does his acknowledgment of Soviet backwardness and the consequent Soviet delegitimization.

Gorbachev's policies toward Communist Central and Eastern Europe are contradictory and therefore counterproductive. On the one hand, he favors reform and détente, which in the past have neither succeeded nor stabilized the region but have done the contrary. This policy implies greater ties with the West, from which credits and high technology can be secured, but these ties bring political influence, as does exposure to popular Western culture. On the other hand, Gorbachev wants to stabilize, at a somewhat lower level, primary Soviet influence in Central and Eastern Europe and to have the region contribute to the modernization of Soviet society. His policies there are thus risky indeed.

Although the Hungarian and East German opposition to Soviet INF counterdeployment and the breaking off of arms control negotiations probably played a minor role in Western calculations, public opinion in East Berlin and Budapest supported their leaders' resistance and Gorbachev's and Reagan's renewed détente because these publics had no taste for annihilation without representation. Moreover, their leaders knew that only renewed détente, especially with West Germany, would increase the flow to them of Western credits and technology, which they needed because of their own technological backwardness, the increasing competition of the Pacific Rim states, and the rising Soviet demand for more and better quality exports from them.[7]

Gorbachev and his colleagues have said less that is new about Communist Central and Eastern Europe than about any other region of Soviet foreign policy. The main point that he has made, notably in the spring 1988 Soviet-Yugoslav communiqué, is that there will no longer be Soviet military intervention there. Yet most Western analysts prudently think it probable that Moscow would intervene to prevent at least East Germany and Poland from going the way that Imre Nagy tried to go in Hungary in 1958: withdrawal from the Warsaw Pact, military neutrality, and a multiparty system.

But Gorbachev has tolerated much greater autonomy of these states than Brezhnev or Chernenko did. In Hungary, the recent replacement of János Kádár by Károly Grósz was probably the result of pressure from below in Budapest, not of Gorbachev's initiative. In East Germany, he has tolerated public opposition by Erich Honecker to his reforms that was unparalleled, except in semiautonomous Romania. In contrast to Brezhnev's 1971 removal of Walter Ulbricht and Chernenko's 1984 veto of Honecker's trip to Bonn, Gorbachev did not object to Honecker's 1987 trip there. Gorbachev changed his policies toward Hungary and East Germany to tolerate not only their autonomous but also their contrasting policies: Grósz pushed reform, but Honecker resisted it.

The impact in Communist Central and Eastern Europe of Gorbachev's reforms is likely to be far greater than the impact of Khrushchev's in 1956.

Reformists and dissidents in Eastern Europe, particularly in antireform East Germany, Romania, and Czechoslovakia, think Gorbachev much more attractive than their own leaders, not only because of his program but also because of his background and style. Like them, but unlike their leaders, he is a member of the intelligentsia, and his program promises to raise their status and ease their repression.

With respect to Western Europe, the Soviet Union opposes Franco–West German cooperative military arrangements primarily because it fears West German access to French nuclear weapons. In view of the declining Bundeswehr demographic prospects, this even more exaggerates than Moscow usually does "the German danger." Gorbachev wants to improve relations with Bonn and thus help get more credits and technology, but he also wants to prevent a major increase in West German influence in Central and Eastern Europe.

The current revival there of the concept of "Central Europe" *(Mitteleuropa)*, which Moscow also dislikes, originated among Czech and Hungarian dissidents and has gained considerable popularity in Austria and in the two German states. It calls for the revival of the cultural, not the political, concept of Central Europe in the cultural area of what was the Austro-Hungarian Empire, to which Prague and Vienna, Budapest and Kraków, and Ljubljana and Zagreb all belonged. It is not, and cannot be, a successful political concept because without Germany, divided or united, it would be too weak to maintain its independence, but with Germany the Germans would dominate it—hardly the aim of its Czech and Hungarian authors.

Nor should *Mitteleuropa* be confused with another idea, "the Europeanization of Europe," which would require the military evacuation of Eastern Europe by the Soviet Union and of Western Europe by the United States—a goal that no government in the North Atlantic Treaty Organization (NATO) or the Warsaw Pact favors. This concept, which originated in West Germany, was originally put forward by Peter Bender, Social Democratic party (SPD) *Ostpolitik* ideologist,[8] and has been developed by Egon Bahr. Although the Bender-Bahr versions are very unlikely to be adopted by the West European governments, they do have some similarity, although more differences, with Charles de Gaulle's foreign policy ("beyond Yalta") and with President John Kennedy's concept of a European "second pillar" for NATO.

The West German Aspect

The FRG is the Western country that will most increase its influence over Communist Central and Eastern Europe. As this subject is discussed at length in Chapter 14, only a few key points need be made here. Germany has historically always been the European country that has had the most influence in Central and Eastern Europe as a conqueror, developer, and, under Hitler, exterminator. But his Thousand Year Reich lasted only twelve years. By 1988, West Germany, stable, democratic, prosperous, and the most powerful advocate of West European unity, was again expanding its economic and technological influence in Communist Central and Eastern Europe. Its influence is different, and in one respect stronger, than Imperial or Nazi Germany because West Germany is the only Western country that has an impelling political reason, as well as traditional economic ones, for doing so: what Willy Brandt once said was the bottom-line objective of West German *Ostpolitik*, "to maintain the substance of the [German] nation." This requires that Bonn's relations with East Berlin, and therefore with Moscow, be those of détente rather than of tension and that Bonn therefore must pursue what Egon Bahr long ago labeled "change through rapprochement" (*Wandel durch Annäherung*). That the present Center-Right CDU/CSU-FDP government in Bonn (Christian Democratic Union, the [Bavarian] Christian Social Union, and the Free Democratic Party) has taken over the SPD's *Ostpolitik*, hardly without change, shows that this policy enjoys such a broad consensus of support that it has become a part of West German *raison d'état*. That the policy's ultimate objective is indeed change, however much its instrument is encouragement of stability, worries its Eastern neighbors, but their immediate need is more West German credits and technology. That such change enjoys little genuine, as opposed to rhetorical, support among Bonn's Western allies helps limit Eastern fears.

The Declining Importance of East-West Relations

Western priorities are rapidly changing from East-West relations, be they of confrontation or of détente, to concern with other problems. The two most important of these are economic and environmental. The main reasons for this change are two. First, as has been set forth previously, Gorbachev is withdrawing from military confrontation with the United States because there is no other way for the Soviet Union to avoid becoming a second-rate power than to concentrate on the modernization that the high-technology revolution demands. Second, the United States is reciprocating Gorbachev's policy of détente not only because its people's mood has turned against confrontation with the Soviet Union, in part because Gorbachev seems to many of them to be foreswearing it, but because they believe that the United States has other, more important problems. Western Europe and Japan have never wanted confrontation anyway, Deng Xiaoping's China does not either, and the Third World is too exhausted by its low economic growth and its many destructive wars to do anything else but concern itself with its own decline.

The Soviet empire seems likely to continue declining and therefore will be less able or inclined to play a major international role in economic or environmental problems. These problems are thus likely to concern primarily the developed West (including Japan), a China that is trying to enter the world market, and such newly industrializing countries as the Pacific Rim states, Brazil, and those states with important natural resources for export, be they petroleum or labor or, like Mexico, both.

The principal economic problem is the growing asymmetry between the economic interdependence, particularly in financial markets, and the lack of significant political interdependence of the developed world. This asymmetry is fostering the growth of economically counterproductive but psychologically probable protectionist nationalism. The main example of this is the Japanese-U.S. trade rivalry, made even worse psychologically by mutual incomprehension of language, culture, and race, plus memories of the bloodshed in World War II and mutual feelings of superiority and lack of experience in foreign trade. The result has been a growth of protectionist sentiment in the United States, coupled with and fanned by Japan's traditional unwillingness to have its market penetrated by foreigners. The situation is made even worse by another, double asymmetry: Japan relies overwhelmingly on the United States for its security and in return finances much of the massive U.S. budgetary deficit, but Japan also uses its enormous trade surplus to buy up assets in the United States, thus further increasing U.S. resentment against it. Indeed, Japan is increasingly convinced of something that the U.S. public only talks about: that the United States is in irreversible decline. Whether this is the case is something we can hardly yet know, but that the Soviet Union is in decline seems probable.

Closer to Communist Central and Eastern Europe, the revival of the EC's move toward unification, now symbolized by "1992" when all remaining economic and social barriers within the community are scheduled to disappear, has one principal cause: the West European fear that the United States and Japan will pull so far ahead in high technology that Western Europe will no longer be able to compete effectively in world markets. This move toward unification, particularly Austria's decision to apply for entry into the EC while remaining, like Ireland, neutral, has greatly increased the desire among Eastern Europe's more developed parts to have closer economic relations with the EC and their greater resentment at the less developed parts of the region and against the Soviet Union for, they think, making this goal less attainable. The Eastern European attraction to the EC was further encouraged by the Council for Mutual Economic Assistance (Soviet) decision in spring 1988 to establish diplomatic relations with the EC, thereby implicitly abandoning Moscow's previous refusal to recognize West Berlin as a part of the EC.[9]

The more the EC unites and remains protectionist, and the longer it so remains dependent on the United States for security, the more it, only less so than Japan, will be seen in the United States as a security profiteer and an economic menace. Conversely, the longer the United States maintains such enormous budgetary and foreign trade deficits in order that its citizens can live so much beyond their means, the more Japan and Western Europe will resent the resultant high U.S. interest rates and the export of U.S. inflation that these deficits require.

Protectionism, history teaches, is counterproductive. Yet the pressure for it by the U.S. trade unions and even more by EC and U.S. farmers shows the seriousness of the problem. It is becoming, in the judgment of many experts, the principal problem for the United States and the rest of the developed world and will increasingly take priority over declining Soviet-

U.S. tension. Yet it can be, as it should be, successfully controlled. Jagdish Bhagwati, for example, suggested that trade disputes be resolved by more impartial bilateral or multilateral commissions, which would penalize frivolous petitions and thereby limit harassment and hostilities. He also suggested that adjustment assistance programs be strengthened in order to ease the decline or exit of firms and then retrain workers.[10]

Protectionism will also make the situation of Communist Central and Eastern Europe even worse, and thus accentuate its decline, because protectionism will make it more difficult for Eastern Europe to export to the hard-currency countries in order to buy their high technology. Protectionism will also make Eastern Europe even more dependent on the Federal Republic, will favor East Germany over the other Communist Central and Eastern countries, but will not do so enough to prevent even the GDR from further relative decline.

The Environment

By "environment" I mean not only ecological problems but the priority that is given, or should be, by Western countries to such problems as epidemics (especially AIDS), hunger, pollution, and erosion of the ozone layer.[11] To at least a growing minority of the developed world, these increasingly seem to be more pressing than declining Soviet-U.S. tension. As the Chernobyl disaster demonstrated, such a catastrophe can greatly intensify their effect, but the fact that, for example, its effect was much greater in West Germany than in France also showed how great differentiation can be in this respect as well.

The effect of the apparent withdrawal of the Soviet Union from several regional crisis areas, and the likelihood that its Central and Eastern European allies will withdraw with them, will be paradoxical. On the one hand, the withdrawal will limit the effects of bloody conflicts, as it may do in Afghanistan, but on the other hand it reflects a Soviet disillusionment with the Third World that makes it even less likely that Moscow will participate effectively, for example, in Third World famine relief.

The Soviet Union and the Communist Central and Eastern European countries are among the world's greatest polluters of the atmosphere. This is especially true of Poland, East Germany, and Czechoslovakia, where the use of coal without ecological safeguards has already destroyed much of their forests (and West Germany's) and has made some areas almost unlivable.[12] But the more these countries decline, the fewer opportunities they will have to reverse their ecological catastrophe.

AIDS is becoming a threatening global epidemic, not only in Africa where it reportedly appeared first and largely afflicts heterosexuals, but increasingly in the United States and to a lesser extent in Western Europe. In the United States its rise among male homosexuals has leveled off, but it continues to rise among ethnic minorities, primarily as a result of infection through use of unclean needles by drug addicts. When we realize that in the United

States alone this disease will likely infect several million and kill perhaps one-quarter million by 1991, we can see that this catastrophe also is bound to distract attention from East-West relations.[13] Although the disease is only beginning to spread in Europe, there is not soon likely to be a cure, and therefore Europe, including Central and Eastern Europe, also will be involved in this growing catastrophe.

* * *

Why, then, this book, and why now? Its readers will, I hope, realize that Communist Central and Eastern Europe is once again, as it has intermittently been since World War II, a crucial potential area of crisis. Moscow might well again intervene militarily, at least in Poland or East Germany, to crush an uprising. This could be a serious, perhaps politically fatal blow to Gorbachev and to East-West détente, which is a possibility that concerns West Germany even more than the United States. The latter has other reasons to be concerned about the region: the large percentage of its citizens whose ethnic origin is there and the probable continuing global and European rivalry between the Soviet Union and the West. For all these reasons we need to understand this region, the problems it poses for the Soviet Union and the West, and what we in the West can and should do about them.

Notes

1. W. Michael Blumenthal, "The World Economy and Technological Change," *Foreign Affairs* 66, no. 3, (Winter 1987-88), pp. 529–550.
2. "Clash of the Titans," *The Economist*, August 23, 1986, pp. 1–18.
3. Seweryn Bialer and Michael Mandelbaum, eds., *Gorbachev's Russia and American Foreign Policy* (Boulder, Colo.: Westview Press, 1988).
4. William E. Griffith, *The Super-Powers and Regional Tensions* (Lexington, Mass.: Lexington Books, 1982), pp. 5–8, 17–19.
5. Andrew C. Janos, *The Politics of Backwardness in Hungary: 1825–1945* (Princeton, N.J.: Princeton University Press, 1982); and Andrew C. Janos, "The One-Party State and Social Mobilization: Eastern Europe Between the Wars," in Samuel P. Huntington et al., eds. *Authoritarian Politics in Modern Society: The Dynamics of Established One-Party Systems* (New York: Basic Books, 1970).
6. Jürgen Nötzöld, András Inotai, Klaus Schröder, "East-West Trade at the Crossroads," *Aussenpolitik* (English ed.) 37, no. 4 (1986), pp. 400–412; András Inotai, "Probleme der Wirtschaftsbeziehungen der Europäischen RGW-Länder mit dem Westen," *Stiftung Wissenschaft und Politik* (Ebenhausen), no. AZ 2515 (April 1987); András Inotai, Jürgen Nötzöld, Klaus Schröder, eds., *Ost-West Wirtschaftsbeziehungen am Scheideweg* (Baden-Baden: Nomos, 1987).
7. Nötzöld et al., ibid.
8. Peter Bender, *Das Ende des Ideologischen Zeitalters* (Berlin: Severin & Siedler, 1981).
9. *The Economist*, February 13, 1988, pp. 11–12, 45–49; Andreas Khol, "Von der Süderweiterung der EG zur EFTA-Erweiterung? Die Vorreiterrolle Österreichs," *Europa Archiv* 43, no. 13 (July 10, 1988), pp. 359–370.

10. Jagdish Bhagwati, *Protectionism* (Cambridge, Mass.: MIT Press, 1988); see also Robert Gilpin, *The Political Economy of International Relations* (Princeton, N.J.: Princeton University Press, 1987).

11. "Effects of Changes in Stratospheric Ozone and Global Climate," vol. 1 (Washington, D.C.: United Nations Environment Program and the U.S. Environmental Protection Agency, August 1986) and F. Sherwood Rowland, "Can We Close the Ozone Hole?" *Technology Review* 90, no. 6 (August-September 1987), pp. 51–58.

12. Christine Zvosec, "Environmental Deterioration in Eastern Europe," *Survey* 28, no. 4 (1984), pp. 117–141.

13. Jeffrey E. Harris, "The AIDS Epidemic: Looking into the 1990's," *Technology Review* 90, no. 5 (July 1987), pp. 59–65.

2

Eastern Europe and the West in the Perspective of Time

Vojtech Mastny

Eastern Europe's place in the world is largely determined by the West's adversarial relationship with the Soviet Union. Because Moscow has seen the preservation of its hegemony in the region to be a vital interest, any infringement on that hegemony worsens East-West relations. Nevertheless, these relations, although still uncertain, now look brighter, and as a result the role of Eastern Europe is likely to change. Is the change to be for the worse or the better? Historically, the region has generated international instability. Two world wars originated there; so did the cold war. Although no catastrophes have occurred since, Eastern Europe has produced a sequence of crises, none accurately anticipated, that prompted the only hostile interventions the continent has experienced since 1945. Nor has this sequence necessarily ended.

History can guide as well as deceive—nowhere more than in a region, like Eastern Europe, of exalted historical consciousness bred by a singularly traumatic past. What in the legacy of the past portends the future? How does Eastern Europe affect Western interests, and what, if anything, should be done about it? Any answer to these questions is inevitably subjective; however, the resulting uncertainty may be reduced by adopting a historical perspective.

The Formative Traditions (to 1918)

A glance at the map of Europe shows that its eastern part is more land than sea oriented and more vulnerable than the western part to invasion. Yet apart from the great division between Western and Eastern Christianity—which is not coterminous with today's political division of the continent—for centuries eastern Europe did not pose any special international problems. Not only were communications then severely limited, but for a long time few significant differences in the level of development distinguished Europe's East from West, and those that did often favored the East. The medieval kingdoms of Bulgaria, Serbia, Poland, and Bohemia, not to speak of the Byzantine Empire, matched or exceeded in achievement their western contemporaries. This relative homogeneity of Christian Europe did not last, however. For several reasons, its two parts began to diverge.

By the end of the Middle Ages, the growth of the cities, the Renaissance, and the Reformation greatly accelerated the development of western Europe. These great movements did not entirely bypass eastern Europe, but their impact there was much more limited and uneven. The Ottoman expansion, culminating in the fall of Constantinople in 1453, contributed to the shift of economic gravity from the Mediterranean to the Atlantic. The Turkish conquest of the Balkans led to the ascendancy of an alien political culture in a substantial portion of the continent. Farther north, the Thirty Years' War (1618–1648), the most devastating of the wars of religion, subsequently retarded the development of Germany and its eastern neighbors.

By then, the retrogressive phenomenon sometimes called the "second serfdom" had already taken effect in most of eastern, but not in western, Europe. Because of the greater strength of the landowning nobility and the relative weakness of royal power and city-based middle classes, the spread of production for market in agriculture tightened the peasants' bondage rather than progressively emancipating them. Because the overwhelming majority of Europeans were still peasants, this had profound social, economic, and political consequences detrimental to freedom in eastern Europe that lasted well into the twentieth century.

The Western idea of freedom rested on the acceptance of individual freedom as a given right. Institutions were created to secure that right. Farther east, freedom was more likely to be derived from membership in a social, economic, religious, or ethnic group and was often asserted at the expense of other groups. The scarcity of indigenous institutions to uphold it made freedom more precarious.

The Influence of the Empires

That multinational empires, rather than nation-states, became prevalent in the east, further accentuated the divergence between the two parts of the continent and created greater obstacles to the assertion of national identity once nationalism became the chief organizing principle of statehood following the French Revolution. Because of Eastern Europe's greater intermingling of ethnic groups, clear lines of nationality were more difficult to draw, and the attempt to do so was more likely to encounter resistance. Both reasons, compounded by the later spread of nationalism and its coincidence with the economic and social upheavals generated by the Industrial Revolution, caused the greater virulence of nationalism in eastern Europe and gave birth to the distinction between the characteristically eastern European–German concept of a nation as a quasimystical living body and the more prosaic Western concept of a nation as a political entity.

The impact of the empires varied. Initially, the condition of the Turkish sultan's European subjects compared favorably with the situation in much of contemporary Europe. But their degradation proceeded apace once the empire's decadence set in during the seventeenth century and persisted for another three hundred years. Habitual violence, contempt for human dignity, and the corrosive venality permeating Ottoman public life remained hallmarks of the militaristic Ottoman political culture long after they ceased to be acceptable in the West and hindered the development of modern institutions and economic growth.

Incorporation into the staunchly Catholic Austrian Empire of the Habsburgs did not necessarily benefit those lands of eastern Europe that became part of it, particularly not their Protestant inhabitants, but at least it helped prevent them from falling under Ottoman rule. In addition to its historic role as Europe's main defender against the Turks, the Habsburg Empire, which possessed extensive territories in the west as well, provided a vital link between the two parts of the continent and ensured the continuing Western orientation of the predominantly Catholic Czechs, Hungarians, Croats, and Slovenes. Even after the Turkish threat had receded and the Habsburgs had lost their western possessions, loyalty to the emperor was a sufficiently strong unifying idea to keep Austria's diverse populations together—for the lack of better alternatives, if for no other reasons.

To those eastern Europeans who became subjects of the Orthodox Russian Empire during the eighteenth and nineteenth centuries, neither defense against a common enemy nor a link with the wider world could justify their subordination, especially not among the mainly Catholic or Protestant Poles, Lithuanians, Latvians, Estonians, and Finns. Moreover, all these peoples tended to regard themselves as culturally superior to the ruling Russians, for whom they served as a barrier against real or imagined foreign enemies and as intermediaries with the more advanced parts of Europe. The resulting ambivalence gave them leverages that were not always sufficient to promote national self-assertion but were sometimes quite sufficient to exert disruptive influence on Russia proper. (Radical socialism was one such influence.)

The Polish Commonwealth

Before its demise at the end of the eighteenth century, the Polish commonwealth had acquired Western traits unparalleled elsewhere in eastern Europe. Although one of the largest European states, this aristocratic republic was an anachronism in the age of state absolutism. In its practice of a religious and ethnic tolerance extraordinary by the standards of the time, the Polish gentry—a very large minority—acted as a harbinger of the future. The Poles went to extremes in creating institutions to protect the rights of the individual against abuse by state power—a concern of impeccable modernity.

Unfortunately, this supremacy of social self-organization over state organization facilitated the country's (Russian-masterminded) dismemberment by its neighbors at the end of the eighteenth century—a disruption of the European order that many contemporaries took more seriously than they did the French Revolution. Yet the same qualities that doomed Polish independence helped the nation, now separated from the state, to survive and even thrive in adversity. The Poles preserved a strong sense of national identity and a capacity to find substitutes for state institutions, even to the extent of conducting something of a foreign policy through their agile émigré community. In upholding the nation's identity, as well as its pronounced Western orientation, the Catholic church in Poland assumed a preeminent political and institutional role comparable only to its role in Ireland and Quebec.

In conformity with Jean-Jacques Rousseau's pertinent admonition that "if you cannot prevent your enemies from swallowing you whole, at least you must do what you can to prevent them from digesting you,"[1] the Poles successfully made their independence a durable European question. The adage "For Your Freedom and Ours," given substance by their participation in liberation struggles around the globe, proclaimed a concept of the nation's larger mission, which poets gave an extreme expression by likening Poland's sacrifice to that of a new Messiah. The message that Europe could not be secure unless Poland was free proved of lasting relevance.

No other eastern European issue evoked so much Western sympathy as did the plight of the Poles in the hands of the partitioning powers—Russia, Prussia, and Austria. Yet policies to alleviate it were always in short supply. Napoleon quite cynically used Polish soldiers to advance his imperial designs from Russia to Haiti. When the Poles revolted in 1830, the beneficiary was Belgium, which the British helped to erect as a model liberal kingdom while the Russian tsar was crushing the Poles. Nor did Napoleon III, among nineteenth-century rulers the foremost advocate of national liberation, try to apply it in eastern Europe. As a result, the West's impact on the East consisted less in policy than in influence, which, however, was enormous and included the spread of the formidable ideas of liberalism, nationalism, and industrialism.

Germany and Eastern Europe

Of all modern nations, Germany had the longest, deepest, and most contradictory relationship with eastern Europe. Not only had Germans frequently invaded it; they had also maintained there large, prosperous, and unassimilated settlements since the Middle Ages. German culture set the standards that eastern Europeans widely imitated. German romanticism inspired their national aspirations more than did any other intellectual current.

The rise of Bismarck's unified German Reich put an end to the Germany of small states, which had been generally hospitable to those aspirations. The unification did not immediately increase German involvement in eastern Europe except in Prussian Poland; Bismarck himself deprecated the Balkans as "not worth the bones of a Pomeranian grenadier." Instead, the exclusion of Austria from German affairs drew that country ever more deeply into entanglements with the explosive nationalisms of the East. By the twentieth century, however, Germany's stake in the integrity of the Habsburg Empire as its only valuable ally, besides the imperialist proclivities of Bismarck's successors, posited its leading role in eastern Europe. This role was ultimately derived from the German quest for world power status.

A German-sponsored international order need not have infringed on the well-being of the peoples of central and eastern Europe; Friedrich Naumann's influential concept of *Mitteleuropa,* for example, was built on liberal, not authoritarian, premises. The eventual rise of the German menace was largely due to an inflation of German ambitions during and after World War I—an avoidable catastrophe no one wished and hardly anyone anticipated. Nor was it preordained that, barring that catastrophe, the peoples of the region had to seek the fulfillment of their national aspirations in its complete restructuring.

Nationalist Aspirations

This was particularly true about the Czechs of Bohemia and Moravia, who had lacked a state of their own since the Middle Ages but whose lands were indispensable to the survival of the Habsburg Empire. After the Czech nobility had been destroyed in an abortive revolt against their Habsburg foreign rulers in the seventeenth century—the last such revolt in Czech history—there developed from a peasant base a large and prosperous middle class that set the tone of Czech politics. Although possessing a religious myth that linked Czech nationalism to the struggle of the medieval Hussite heretics against the universalism of the church of Rome, they were in fact the most secularized of all eastern Europeans. The Czechs gained steadily in politics, economy, and, especially, public administration at the expense of the local Germans and thrived within the large Austrian entity. Prior to World War I, Prague was a cosmopolitan center where Czech and German cultures flourished side by side. No Czech political grouping of any stature aimed at national independence.

In contrast to the Czechs, the Magyars of Hungary boasted an uninterrupted continuity of statehood for a thousand years, along with a view of themselves as a buffeted island in a sea of ethnically alien neighbors. The Magyar gentry, which was almost as large as its Polish counterpart, was a vigorous bearer of ethnic identity and derived self-confidence from its well-established local autonomy. Unlike Poland, Hungary was never totally deprived of its state institutions; its parliament, in particular, survived as a mighty symbol of the country's resistance against foreign encroachments.

In 1848–1849, Hungary enjoyed a brief moment of glory when it seized independence from Vienna in an armed struggle inspired by Western liberal ideas. It failed when a Russian army, invited in by Austria, administered the Magyars a crushing defeat, which excited much of contemporary western Europe and even the United States. Nevertheless, twenty years later the vanquished Hungarians managed to take advantage of Austria's defeat by Prussia to become accepted by their erstwhile oppressors as co-equal. Thus, courage, persistence, and skillful timing paid off, although possibly too much for the nation's good.

Having acquired an influence on the Dual Monarchy's policy, especially on its foreign affairs, that was far in excess of their numbers, Magyar nationalists tried to assimilate rather than respect the many ethnic groups that they dominated but that outnumbered them—a prescription for disaster. Nor did the Magyars modernize their political and social institutions, which enabled the impoverished lower nobility to fill the ranks of the bureaucracy, the assimilated Jewish community largely to substitute for the middle class, and the peasantry to subsist in a squalor hard to be found in any other country claiming Western heritage. Although these were Hungary's own problems rather than the result of the Habsburg rule, the Magyars never felt quite satisfied with their status in the monarchy, the considerable economic benefits they derived from it notwithstanding.

What sealed the fate of Hungary, as of the entire Habsburg monarchy, was the inability of leading politicians to contain the ethnic conflicts of southeast Europe, which embroiled them in World War I. The region's propensity for generating conflict stemmed from what contemporaries called the "Eastern Question," the one aspect of eastern Europe about which the major powers did have definite policies. At issue was the management of the Ottoman Empire's irreversible decline, which, because of the extreme fragmentation of its unruly peoples implied in the term *Balkanization,* took much longer than the empire's weak central power would have otherwise justified.

Great Britain took the lead in opposing a precipitous dismantling of the Turkish realm lest Russia substitute for it in the strategically important eastern Mediterranean. But although this British policy was determined by larger imperial interests rather than by solicitude for the Balkan peoples, concern for their well-being was not totally alien to Europe's foremost liberal nation. Indeed, William Gladstone's campaign against the Turks' "Bulgarian atrocities" deserves to be remembered as an early attempt to make foreign policy compatible with "human rights." Although unsuccessful, it at least introduced the issue into the domestic political debate. For the same reason that Britain was loath to see the Ottoman Empire disappear too quickly, it also preferred the familiar certainty of Austria-Hungary to the unknown perils of its dismemberment.

Nor did the French, despite their opposition to Austria-Hungary as Germany's ally and their sympathy for the national aspirations of the Poles, Magyars, and Czechs, go so far as to seek the empire's demise until almost the time when its self-destruction in 1918 made this inevitable. Similarly, the presence in the United States of growing numbers of citizens of eastern European ancestry did not cause Washington to deviate—until that late date—from John Quincy Adams's advice that the nation should "be the well-wisher to the freedom and independence of all" but "champion and vindicator only of its own."[2] Of all the great powers of the time Italy, which entertained territorial claims against Austria-Hungary, was the first to make its replacement by fully independent national states an unambiguous goal of policy by sponsoring in Rome the blatantly subversive congress of the empire's "oppressed nationalities" in 1917.

Until the denouement at the end of World War I, the future of eastern Europe was uncertain. The extent of the great powers' restraint, more than any excess of interference, fostered this uncertainty. Their diminishing ability to manage the problems of the region, singly or collectively, gave its peoples growing opportunities to assert themselves—for better or for worse. The first to succeed were Serbia and Montenegro—the former by getting autonomy from the Turks as early as 1816, the latter by never entirely losing it. A hundred years later, the Serbs forced the issue of self-determination that touched off World War I.

Of those two remote principalities, both of which were pro-Russian on ethnic and religious grounds, Serbia experienced the longest period of statehood with leadership pretensions. But Serbia's statehood was too troublesome and its pretentions too heavy-handed to appeal unequivocally to other southern Slavs, even the most closely related Croats and Slovenes, whose Catholic faith and Western orientation made them different. Unlike the fiercely independent Serbs, the Slovenes and Croats were not so averse to living under foreign rule, particularly the tolerable Austro-Hungarian variety. Throughout the nineteenth century, discord among southern Slavs cast doubt on the desirability or viability of their unification under Serbian auspices. But neither could an integration of so disparate an ethnic agglomerate on the basis of a mutual recognition of equality be easily accomplished, which proved to be the crux of the structural problem of later Yugoslavia.

In 1878, the Bulgarians achieved national independence, at once rather than in stages, at a higher level of economic development, with decisive foreign help, and amid temporary satisfaction of exalted territorial ambitions. This last accomplishment crumbled almost immediately, which led to recurrent territorial claims against neighboring states and recurrent failures. But the crucial Russian military role in the liberation of Bulgaria and the initial Russian support for its expansionism had lasting consequences. They shaped the myth of the country's exclusive Russophilism, despite its people's pro-German orientation, which was the strongest in the Balkans.

This was evident not only in the Bulgarian preference for importing a German dynasty—a rule rather than an exception in that part of Europe—but also in the country's pro-German political alignments at critical times. The Bulgarians earned the sobriquet of the "Prussians of the Balkans." To be sure, their reputed brutality stemmed more from their Ottoman experience than from anything German; also the structure of their peasant society, the most egalitarian in the region, differed from Prussia's. Yet Prussian virtues could be seen in the Bulgarians' respect for education, work ethic, and predilection for rational economic enterprises—all of which distinguished them from their neighbors. Although relative, these virtues suggested an eye for modernity rare in the Balkans.

The contrast applied particularly to Romania, the most Ottomanized of the countries that gained full independence before World War I. Having been formed out of the autonomous principalities of Moldavia and Wallachia, Romania had suffered a uniquely retrogressive experience during the eighteenth century—which elsewhere in Europe brought enlightenment and progress. Romania suffered unbridled, institutionalized corruption under the rule of the Phanariot princes, to whom the Turkish sultan farmed out the provinces to be run for personal profit. Modern Romania possessed the dubious distinction of maintaining what was perhaps Europe's sharpest cleavage between a destitute peasantry and an upper class singularly aloof, socially irresponsible, culturally pretentious, and morally ambivalent. In 1907, the peasantry erupted in Europe's last jacquerie, whose excesses perpetuated the cleavage.

Despite these handicaps, the building of the Romanian nation-state was in important ways more successful than its counterparts in Bulgaria and Hungary. Romania emerged with a large territory, well endowed with natural resources and further enlarged as a result of alliance with the victors in World War I, Romania's unimpressive military performance notwithstanding. Nevertheless, the incorporation of the huge Magyar minority in Transylvania, which—like the Germans in Czechoslovakia—was the former ruling nationality and therefore chafed under its second-class citizenship, justified questions about whether Romania's successes, like Hungary's before, had not been too great for its own good.

The Turkish legacy, which proved so detrimental to Romania, did not lack redeeming features in Albania, the most primitive as well as ethnically alien part of the Balkans. Having been, besides the Bosnians, the only Europeans to embrace Islam extensively, the Albanians benefited from it most, particularly those who made (sometimes spectacular) careers in the Ottoman establishment and beyond. A disproportionate number of the grand viziers were of Albanian origin, as were the founder of modern Egypt, Mehmet Ali, and an eminent Italian prime minister, Francesco Crispi. Whether these extraordinary outlets for the most enterprising individuals or the absorption of the others in ubiquitous tribal strife mitigated Albanian nationalism, it proved the least disruptive. In 1912, the country was the last in the Balkans to form a state, and even then it occurred only at the prodding of outside powers. Indeed, the newly formed state was only an autonomous one within the crumbling Turkish empire. Although formal independence followed soon, its origins did not augur well for its affirmation.

Albania apart, the Balkan peoples' growing ability to pursue their aspirations outside of the great powers' tutelage was the single main reason World War I started as it did at the time it did. In 1914, to be sure, these peoples and their leaders did not foresee the disastrous consequences of their actions any more than did the much more experienced politicians of the rest of Europe. The eastern Europeans saw themselves breaking their bonds and moving toward greater freedom, and in some ways they were. Yet whether the freedom they would acquire could last was another question. From today's perspective, the forty years that followed, culminating in the imposition on most of eastern Europe of a rule more effectively repressive than any of its predecessors, seem more of an aberration than a sound alternative to the condition only temporarily superseded in the aftermath of World War I.

Independence Gained and Lost (1918–1953)

The aftermath of World War I in eastern Europe was made exceptional by the power vacuum. All the regional great powers—Russia, Germany, Austria-Hungary, and the Ottoman Empire—had been defeated either outright or through disintegration (or both in the case of Austria-Hungary). Yet the vacuum did not immediately draw in other aspirants. Preoccupied with its imperial problems and faltering economy, Great Britain remained aloof while France became involved *à contrecoeur* and *faute de mieux*. In seeking an alignment against Germany, France would have preferred one with Russia had the Bolshevik Revolution not ruled this out. Only as a poor second choice did the French align themselves with the weak, untested, and quarrelsome "successor" states—Poland, Czechoslovakia, Romania, and Yugoslavia. The alignment differed from the *cordon sanitaire* that some French leaders, notably Marshal Ferdinand Foch, had hoped to create as a barrier against the spread of Soviet communism (the idea never left the drawing board). In any event, the loose French organization of eastern Europe served neither its integration nor its security.

To the extent that outside powers determined the postwar settlement, the formative influence was less French than American. This marked an unprecedented commitment by the great trans-Atlantic democracy, which had long been stirring the imagination of eastern Europeans as the land of freedom, opportunity, and prosperity but had never before been an actor on their local scene. At the end of World War I, by far the most popular foreign leader in the region was President Woodrow Wilson. His concept of national self-determination, enforced by an international organization to maintain security, responded best to eastern European aspirations. Although the application of the concept at the Paris peace conference fell short of the ideal and the United States eventually withheld its backing, at least one accomplishment of the peacemakers withstood the test of time remarkably well: Today's boundaries of eastern Europe resemble closely those they drew, with but two significant exceptions. These are the shifting of Poland from east to west and the extinction of the three Baltic states' independence—changes enforced unilaterally by the Soviet Union during World War II that the peoples concerned did not regard as an improvement.

The securing of durable state entities broadly expressive of the wishes of the majority of their inhabitants was no negligible accomplishment of the peacemaking of 1919; it was also the only major one. The domestic stability and external security of the new states rested on precarious foundations. Never before or after have there been more democracies in eastern Europe. Yet because they were superimposed upon largely nondemocratic social and economic structures without the cement of necessary political experience, within a decade these democracies succumbed to either outright dictatorships or authoritarian regimes of some sort.

Not even Czechoslovakia, usually singled as an exception because of its high degree of social pluralism, political tolerance, economic prosperity, and plain civility, was a genuine exception. Maurice Beaumont, the French historian, alluded to the *dictature du respect* of the country's paternalistic president, Tomáš G. Masaryk, who possessed such a moral authority that his judgment was not seriously questioned.[3] Moreover, interwar Czechoslovakia pretended to be a nation without ever successfully integrating its numerous ethnic groups, particularly not its two supposedly ruling nationalities, the Czechs and the Slovaks, who had lived under different governments for a thousand years. As the most artificial of the "successor states," Czechoslovakia could not count on the loyalty of too many of its citizens when its integrity came to be threatened in 1938. The decision to compromise it was then made solely by Masaryk's handpicked successor, Edvard Beneš, while the people and their elected representatives acquiesced, however unhappily. Having gained their independence in 1918 mainly by skillful diplomacy, the Czechs lost it without a fight twenty years later.

Whatever the shortcomings of democracy in Czechoslovakia, they paled in comparison with its plight in interwar Poland. There Marshal Józef Piłsudski, exasperated by the country's brief parliamentary experience, established a personal authoritarian regime in 1926. Unlike Masaryk's, Piłsudski's authority rested largely on military accomplishment—Poland's liberation by force during World War I and the remarkable national exertion that in 1920 stopped the Soviet armies marching on Warsaw and into Europe. Rather than the pluralistic traditions of prepartition Poland, Piłsudski epitomized the exaltation of military virtues, which thereafter sustained his compatriots.

His authoritarianism aside, Piłsudski was a leader of powerful vision whom lesser successors have been vainly trying to approximate ever since. Not only was he the rare person who had predicted accurately the course of World War I and acted accordingly; he also had a clear concept of Poland's place in Europe, which he pursued consistently if unsuccessfully. Rightly regarding Russia as a greater long-term threat than Germany, he tried to revive the old Polish commonwealth as an anti-Soviet association of eastern European peoples under Polish leadership. Faced with the rising threat of Nazi Germany, he resorted without illusions to the alternative of accommodation with Adolf Hitler. Four years after Piłsudski's death, the accommodation failed; it had not prevented vigorous resistance against the attacking German army.

In the end, the Poles did not manage to preserve their independence any better than did the Czechs; but they at least preserved their self-respect. It is difficult to imagine how they could have saved more; indeed, they could have saved much less. The defects of Piłsudski's policies were the defects of Poland's predicament. Even apart from an impossible geopolitical situation, a miracle would have been required to integrate into a functioning democracy no less than three legacies of oppressive foreign rule—Russian, Prussian, and Austrian. An economy capable of meeting the needs of eastern Europe's largest nation was never created, and too many disaffected minorities sapped the vitality of the state.

The reverse minority problem plagued Hungary, whose postwar territorial amputations—the worst in the region—consigned too many Magyars unwillingly to the neighboring states. Poland was not immune to delusions of grandeur as a quasi-great power, while Hungary suffered from the complex of a victim. Punished far more than it deserved, it became the most bitter of the revisionist nations dedicated to undoing the postwar settlement. This overwhelming preoccupation diverted its attention from the long overdue reform of its political and social structures.

The experience of 1919, when Hungary gave birth to eastern Europe's only authentic Communist revolution and provided it with a largely Jewish leadership, provoked a backlash of right-wing lawlessness and anti-Semitism. Like Poland, the other nation that prided itself on being the bastion of the West in the East, Hungary remained singularly un-Western in its politics and social organization. But unlike Poland, Hungary failed to produce any leader of more than local stature. Although enlightened conservatism remained in short supply, the Right in interwar Hungary was more typically reactionary than radical.

The latter variety figured prominently in Romania. Its Iron Guard evolved into eastern Europe's strongest Fascist movement, unique in deriving its strength from its appeal to the impoverished peasantry. Centrist alternatives were available in the liberal and peasant parties, but there was not enough middle ground to make their leaders sufficiently confident to act. Even so, the country was making progress toward a more equitable political system; its notorious elections, in particular, were getting less rather than more rigged. But whatever the chances of improvement, they were lost once the imposition of the king's dictatorship led to a relapse into more corrupt and cynical manipulation of power.

Although corruption and cynicism were far from unknown in Bulgaria, they were less conspicuous than were violence and recklessness. Both the Right and the Left, including a Communist party more intimate with Moscow than any other, were guilty of appalling atrocities. The military interfered in politics more often than anywhere in Europe, and the Bulgarian police maintained their reputation as the most vicious in the region. In the interwar years, the country served as a foremost haven of international terrorism, which Bulgarian governments frequently deployed in pursuit of their revisionist aims.

The chief target of these activities was Yugoslavia, the microcosm of eastern Europe's ethnic diversity. Unified under Serbian domination, it failed to set the much-needed example of equilibrium and tolerance. Inequities in power-sharing among its different nationalities fueled violence, which in turn prompted King Alexander to impose his personal rule, only to fall victim to assassination forthwith. When the hour of reckoning struck in 1941 in the form of Hitler's threat to Yugoslav independence, the upsurge of patriotism that the anti-German coup of Serbian military officers elicited in Belgrade was deceptive of the state's true condition. More revealing of the widespread indifference of its nationalities to its survival was the inglorious collapse of the Yugoslav army, the southern Slavs' legendary martial prowess notwithstanding.

Lest the distressing picture of independent eastern Europe between the two world wars appear overdrawn, it ought to be emphasized that its defects were due not to any lack of talent or character but rather to the enormity of problems characteristic of a particular stage of development. These were not dissimilar to those that many Third World countries faced after World War II except that the international climate was far less hospitable. In particular, no comparable Western assistance was available to the new states, which, carved out of the defunct empires, struggled to establish viable economies only to have the Great Depression set them back.

The Penetration of Eastern Europe by the Fascist Powers

Germany was eastern Europe's natural trading partner. Its economic penetration of the region in the 1930s foreshadowed Hitler's subsequent bid for political domination. As the flourishing of agriculture oriented to the German market indicated, the connection could have been mutually beneficial if only different regimes had been in power in Germany as well as in Italy. The rise there of Fascists bent on destroying the established international order made the crucial difference.

As in 1917 under a liberal government, a decade later under Benito Mussolini's dictatorship Italy again took the lead in making the disruption of eastern Europe a national policy by sponsoring international terrorism in its southern part and by other means. Hitler's Germany subsequently proved more effective in targeting the northern part, particularly by fomenting unrest there among German minorities. With their independence threatened, the eastern Europeans proved not totally incapable of sorting out their problems—as the incipient rapprochement of revisionist Hungary and Bulgaria with its neighbors as late as 1938 indicated. But eastern Europeans acted too little and too late.

Nevertheless, the problems of the region, although numerous and grave, were not getting appreciably worse during the 1930s until the two Fascist powers, for their own deplorable reasons, chose gratuitously to aggravate them. This made the road to World War II fundamentally different from that to World War I. Compared with 1914, the factors that precipitated war in 1939 were transparent. Eastern Europe was an object rather than a subject of destabilization. The course of events was also predetermined to a far greater degree, although in ways so unique that they diminish considerably the value of any lessons to be drawn.

The demise of independent eastern Europe followed from the lack of interest in it by anyone except expansionist Germany and Italy. While isolationist United States chose to remain absent, France and Britain were preoccupied with domestic and imperial problems and handicapped by a correct self-perception of weakness. The Soviet Union's self-inflicted weakness was the result of its revolution and Joseph Stalin's bloodletting. In striving to prod the Western powers to defend eastern Europe against Hitler without sharing the risk, the Soviet leader gave no indication of an intention to compete for its control in any foreseeable future.

The 1938 Munich agreement meant Western acquiescence in German and Italian domination of the region, even though the Western powers assumed this could provide a new framework for international stability. Instead the dictators, who wanted more, proceeded to redraw the map to promote instability, of which they hoped to be the arbiters and beneficiaries. In view of impending German attack on Poland, Britain's partial reversal of appeasement by extending to Poland a guarantee of integrity created for Moscow an unexpected opportunity. Hitler's willingness to share the spoils with Stalin in order to keep the West at bay opened the door to Soviet penetration into eastern Europe.

The Soviet Expansion into Eastern Europe

The Stalin-Hitler pact of August 1939 made history by implementing the new Soviet concept of security by imperial expansion—which was more threatening, because more viable, than the previous concepts of security by world revolution or partial collaboration with the West. The consequences—Stalin's grab of eastern Poland, his war against Finland, his quashing of the Baltic people's independence, his forcible annexation of Bessarabia from Romania—were catastrophic for eastern Europeans as well as for the image of the Soviet Union as an acceptable hegemonial power.

His territorial aggrandizement did not give Stalin the security he craved and instead provoked in eastern Europe a struggle for clients desperately clinging to remnants of their independence. In this struggle, Germany, despite its own tarnished reputation, could offer more and gain more than its Communist rival. By nourishing Hitler's aggressive proclivities, which culminated in his final decision to attack the Soviet Union, eastern Europe thus played a crucial role as a catalyst of the war's expansion rather than as a cause of its original outbreak.

Although his concept of security by empire proved counterproductive in 1941, Stalin did not abandon it; he did the opposite. He insisted on keeping the fruits of his collaboration with Hitler and sought more territory—not necessarily by annexation or even by indirect control through subservient Communist regimes, if subservient non-Communist ones could be had. The manner of Moscow's control was at issue once the Soviet armies began to pour into eastern Europe toward the end of the war. Eastern Europe's future depended in varying degrees on the vicissitudes of the military operations, Stalin's perceptions of Soviet security interests in each country, Western tolerance of those interests, and the conduct of the eastern Europeans. Stalin strove for a sphere of influence but acted as if neither the limits of the sphere nor the nature of the influence was firmly fixed in his mind.

As so often happens, Poland was an exception. Unable to resolve the German question without Western cooperation and mindful of the bitter Polish hostility, to which he had so outstandingly contributed, Stalin chose to regard a subservient Poland as the key to Soviet security. The country's future was thus predetermined as soon as he could enforce his will. It was sealed in 1944 when the Poles valiantly but vainly tried to wrest their independence from the Germans during the Warsaw uprising. While the Red Army stood by as the Poles were being slaughtered, the last chance of Polish-Soviet reconciliation may have been lost. Nor could armed resistance against the Moscow-installed regime, more widespread and protracted in Poland than anywhere in eastern Europe, reverse the verdict of superior Soviet power.

Yet the Polish tragedy did not mean total loss; it even brought significant gains. So unequivocal had been the nation's will to shape its destiny that even the Polish Communists, although thoroughly dependent on Moscow, were swayed; they, too, after all, had been purged by Stalin worse than other East European Communists had been. Although forced to acquiesce in the surrender of the country's eastern territories, they obtained from a reluctant Stalin assent to more compensation in the west than he had originally contemplated. This ensured a substantially undiminished and economically more valuable territorial base for Poland, which, because of the depredations by its enemies, also emerged for the first time in history as an ethnically nearly homogeneous state.

Next to Poland, Stalin initially attached the greatest strategic importance to Romania and Finland. Yet he suppressed the Romanians, whom he despised, the most and the Finns, whom he respected, the least. Not only had Romania been Hitler's most willing ally in the war against the Soviet Union, establishing there a record of atrocities second only to the German one; it had also later betrayed the Germans by switching sides. In contrast, Stalin was the one who had treacherously attacked the Finns in 1939. For their part, the Finns subsequently showed much ingenuity in matching resistance with reassurance, thus shaping Soviet interests in conformity with their own.

In assuming that those interests were flexible rather than fixed, the Finns succeeded better than the Czechs, although Czechoslovakia, rather than deflecting Moscow, attracted it. This was not because Soviet troops overran most of the country in 1945, for by the end of that year all of them had left, as had all the U.S. troops. More important was the Communist victory in free elections the following year—the only such victory anywhere in eastern Europe. The most pertinent factor, however, was Czechoslovakia's quest to become Moscow's favorite protégé—a policy pursued by President Beneš with the support of even the non-Communist parties in its ruling coalition.

Czechoslovakia sought Soviet backing for the expulsion of its German as well as its Magyar minorities—an extreme project put into effect amid excesses both distressing and puzzling to admirers of the country's prewar democracy. The deterioration of its body politic was suggestive of the demoralizing impact of the Nazi occupation, which, although universally hated, had brought less physical deprivation than elsewhere in the region.

There had been less visible resistance and more invisible collaboration; yet Czechoslovakia ranked among the victor nations.

Whereas political opportunity shaped the Soviet interest in Czechoslovakia, military opportunity mattered more in Bulgaria and Hungary. Although historic links and geography foreshadowed Moscow's preponderance in Bulgaria, only the Romanian turn to Moscow prompted the Soviet decision to occupy Bulgaria. The subsequent speed of its Sovietization, however, was more the result of the Bulgarian Communists' ability to capture control of the underground and seize power by a coup d'état even before the Soviet arrival. Certainly the slaughter of their political enemies, which was unparalleled in scope and violence, was justified more by Bulgarian custom than by Soviet interest.

Hungary's case was different. Stalin repeatedly indicated that he wished the West to share in Hungary's liberation, but Britain and the United States demurred for military reasons. Moreover, they unnecessarily signaled to him that their political interest in the country was limited, even more so than in Bulgaria. Once in control of Hungary, Stalin nevertheless exercised restraint. He introduced a multiparty system and directed the Communists to respect it without any time limitation, their electoral defeat notwithstanding. His restraint in less important Hungary served to foster Western acquiescence in the subjugation of the more important Poland.

Stalin thus acted as if he would have preferred to attain control of Eastern Europe with, rather than against, his Western Allies. Whether this gave them more bargaining power than they thought is an intriguing but moot question, for their interests were not sufficiently involved to make them use it; besides, the Allies wanted Soviet cooperation, particularly in the treatment of Germany. In the end, Stalin's inability to obtain in Eastern Europe the kind of security he wanted by methods compatible with Western preferences led him to act in a manner that made the West wonder where, if anywhere, were the limits of Soviet security. This caused the United States to draw a line in Germany and Western Europe, which in turn led Stalin to conclude that nothing short of the establishment of full-fledged Communist regimes in his sphere of influence could give him enough security in the mounting confrontation. The turning point was reached in 1947 with the establishment of the Cominform as the coordinating agency for Eastern Europe's Sovietization.

The Limits of Sovietization in Yugoslavia, Greece, and Finland

The imposition of communism did not depend entirely on Soviet will. Yugoslavia on its own had already patterned itself after the Soviet model. The Communists under Marshal Tito had been sufficiently strong to seize power without Soviet help; they had done this by winning a civil war through domination of the wartime resistance. They promoted communism elsewhere in the Balkans, planned to incorporate Albania, and took the lead in supporting the Greek Communists' bid for power.

Although not the cause of the historic split between Stalin and Tito, the Yugoslavs' assertiveness enabled them to preserve their independence after the split occurred for other reasons. The Yugoslav Communists at first anticipated even closer association with the Soviet Union, perhaps even as one of its constituent republics, and tried to coordinate their policies with Stalin's. At issue in the confrontation that Stalin gratuitously precipitated was not anything they did wrong but rather a change in his own policies. Subservience without any semblance of partnership was now required from even the most loyal—and especially from them in order to maximize its effect. Moreover, by 1948 the expansion of communism in the Balkans became more risky after the United States had backed the Greek government.

Tito took great pains to appease Stalin before rallying his people to resist and then reluctantly seeking support from the United States. It was an act of remarkable U.S. statecraft to provide Tito with support at the height of the cold war on the assumption that Communist Yugoslavia had become a viable national state capable of resisting Soviet expansionism. Although the proof of its viability lay in the future, the preservation of Yugoslav independence has remained an axiom of U.S. security policy—an unparalleled U.S. stake in any part of Eastern Europe.

Although Stalin did not consider a Communist bid for power in Greece worth the risk of aggravating the cold war, no such consideration seemed to apply in Czechoslovakia. Nor was effective resistance to be expected from a country that, like Yugoslavia, had made friendship with Moscow the lodestar of its policy but, unlike Yugoslavia, lacked the resources to reverse it if necessitated by intolerable Soviet behavior. In 1949, the Communist coup in a country so obliging harmed Soviet interests by bolstering Western Europe's willingness to rally behind U.S. leadership. This unintended effect may have provided the critical margin of restraint that subsequently led Stalin to desist from a similar subjugation of Finland.

Thus, Yugoslavia, Finland, and Greece, largely through their own efforts but also as a result of Washington's policy of containment, were spared the Sovietization that all but obliterated the last vestiges of independence in the rest of Eastern Europe. Except for East Germany, whose integration was delayed by the unresolved German question, the nations of the region were now molded into little replicas of the Soviet Union—an unprecedented and quixotic attempt to make unity out of diversity in a traditionally heterogeneous part of the continent. In fact, even in the heyday of Stalinism, significant national differences persisted. They influenced the pattern of the Stalinist purges, which, as witchhunts for largely nonexistent enemies, assumed notably more vicious forms in the most loyalist Czechoslovakia and Bulgaria than in notoriously anti-Soviet Poland.

Stalinism destroyed the old social structures, which led to a general social and cultural leveling, the growth of a "new class" of the system's beneficiaries notwithstanding. The leveling added to the impact of World War II, which had reduced substantially the region's minorities; in particular, the Holocaust and emigration all but eliminated Eastern European Jewry, although not anti-Semitism. Stalinism also transformed the predominantly agricultural economies into industrial ones in a manner that facilitated immediate growth but hampered long-term growth. Most important, Moscow acquired a vital stake in the maintenance of the new order in a part of Europe that it chose to regard as the main safeguard of its security but that bore the seeds of its insecurity.

For the West, the region during the cold war assumed importance as the Soviets' Achilles' heel—or so it seemed in 1949 when the U.S. and British secret services infiltrated agents to overthrow the regime in Albania, the weakest link in the chain of Moscow's power. They failed, but the vulnerability persisted, keeping hopes for Western liberation high among Eastern Europeans. By the time of Stalin's death in 1953, this was the only part of the world where much, perhaps most, of the people ardently wished for another war to regain freedom. Yet 1953 was not 1914, nor was there any likelihood of a return to the extraordinary conditions of the interwar period during which Eastern Europe had gained and lost its freedom. Instead, the subsequent developments highlighted the renewed relevance of the experience antedating World War I.

Reassertion of Diversity (Since 1953)

Eastern Europe since 1953 has seen a gradual but irresistible reassertion of an old, as well as a new, diversity and Moscow's reluctant yet genuine adaptation to it. As early as 1945, George Kennan foresaw the outcome when, pondering the birth of the Soviet empire, he wondered rhetorically whether it could possibly last.[4] Aside from the region's heterogeneity, he alluded to the awkward predicament of an imperial power compelled to rely mainly on force to maintain mastery over countries in important ways more advanced than itself and potentially more subversive. But the inevitable end of the Soviet empire, as of all empires, merely provides a necessary long-term perspective rather than unequivocal guidance in assessing its dynamism at any given time.

The first anti-Soviet rebellions after Stalin's death marked the end of an era rather than its beginning. The insurgents' militant identification with the West—most visible in the streets of East Berlin but best symbolized by the U.S. flag raised over the captured party headquarters in the Czechoslovak city of Plzeň—and the use of Stalinist methods to crush them pointed to the past. The Soviet investment in propping up the Communist regime in East Berlin marked the German Democratic Republic's (GDR) transition from an expendable to an integral part of the Soviet empire. This reduced the GDR's differences from the rest of Eastern Europe.

The GDR's Status in the Soviet Bloc

The main remnant of East Germany's special status—its partly open border with the West—disappeared in 1961 after the construction of the Berlin Wall. This made possible the remarkable transformation of the Soviet bloc's most artificial and precarious state into its economically soundest and internationally most influential member. Surpassing all others in economic accomplishment and political stability, the GDR alone has made the Soviet system work with only minor modifications. Thus, the regime most dependent on Soviet backing—the only one in Europe that keeps on its territory more foreign than national troops—has nevertheless established the best conditions for forming with Moscow a relationship based on partnership rather than on mere subordination.

Erstwhile pariahs of Eastern Europe, the East German leaders have pursued this goal purposefully and persistently. They made themselves especially useful to Moscow as its best suppliers of quality goods and most willing accomplices in assorted Third World ventures. Eventually, these leaders even claimed to shape common policy in such important matters as relations with West Germany and the deployment of missiles in central Europe. In 1984, the GDR sought rapprochement with Bonn and reduction of the intermediate-range nuclear forces (INF) crisis while the wary and weak Kremlin leaders were doing the opposite. Yet no sooner did a strong leader, Mikhail Gorbachev, replace them than these policies were vindicated by being adopted as Moscow's own. In turn, East Berlin could afford *not* to follow the latest Soviet example of greater openness at home.

The GDR has managed to assert its separate identity with, rather than against, the Soviet Union. There has been a nineteenth-century air about this accomplishment. It was made possible by a partial reversion to the condition prior to the German unification when several German states had maintained their distinctiveness in the shadow of major powers while entertaining with one another a multitude of relationships based on mutual convenience and respect, although not necessarily affection. Indeed, the supposedly forward-looking Communist German state has even acquired in the West a specious reputation as a quaintly provincial preserve of the German past. More to the point, its rulers and their subjects alike have been cultivating a nostalgia for the glories of its Prussian and imperial heritage rather than for its more equivocal post–World War I legacy.

The reassertion of East Germany's Protestant Prussian values has accentuated the historic cleavage between Germany and Poland, the most Catholic nation of Eastern Europe. The GDR's ascendancy has challenged Poland's status as the Soviet bloc's second most important member—a distinction derived as much from the vital service its rulers performed by keeping Europe's most profoundly anti-Soviet people subdued. The permanence of this accomplishment, however, remains in doubt.

Poland's Differences

In 1956, the Poles were the first to break the Stalinist mold by creating their version of "national communism," which combined reassurance of Moscow with the maintenance of such specifically Polish features as renewed private agriculture and the privileged position of the Catholic church. The availability at that critical time of leaders capable of impressing this alternative on the skeptical Kremlin, as well as the nation's willingness to give them the necessary minimum of trust, suggested a break with the romantic Polish tradition of valiant but hopeless struggle against impossible odds.

The break added relevance to Poland's other nineteenth-century tradition—that of "organic work," small steady gains within resented but accepted foreign empires. Acceptance of Moscow's supremacy did not prevent the Poles from repeatedly toppling their oppressive and incompetent governments while avoiding armed Soviet intervention—a feat without parallel in Eastern Europe. Not even the rise of Solidarity in 1980, which led to the Soviet empire's most severe crisis, proved an exception. The growth of this remarkably disciplined, sophisticated, and spontaneous grass-roots movement testified to the evolution in Poland of a vital civil society. Its strength contrasted with the weakness of the country's interwar democracy but was only too consistent with the deeper traditions of tolerance and social self-organization dating back to the old commonwealth.

But inherent in those traditions was the presence in the loosely structured body politic of special interest groups willing and able to seek advancement in league with a foreign power—the common denominator of both the eighteenth-century confederates of Targowica and the military clique responsible for Solidarity's suppression in 1981. Conceivably, the availability within the Polish party of a leadership ready to stand up to Soviet pressure as in 1956 would have made the cost of Soviet intervention prohibitive, thus compelling Moscow to accommodate itself to Poland's pluralization as best as it could.[5] The absence of such a leadership was suggestive of the depth of demoralization within a corrupt elite increasingly isolated from society. Yet the weakness of the oppressors also ensured that Poland remained, despite its setback, the Soviet bloc's most pluralist nation. Maneuvers calculated to enable the church to rule on the propriety of the regime's actions presage the possible course of further pluralization.

Hungarian Moderation

In 1956, the popular upheaval contained in Poland broke loose in Hungary, which lacked the sobering fresh memory of a great struggle and a great defeat. The ensuing suppression of the national insurrection by Soviet force provided such an experience, bringing the people to a point of despair and hopelessness no other Eastern Europeans knew. Yet this was also a state of mind uniquely responsive to a capable, moderate, and farsighted leadership, which, unlike in the interwar period, became available in the person of János Kádár.

Hungary's subsequent development was reminiscent of events more than a century earlier after another seemingly total defeat, also inflicted by Russian arms. Once again the nation soon compensated for its defeat by achieving a privileged position within the empire, although not with any love for it. Thus, the people that risked the most in an uneven struggle gained the most, even though the Hungarians utilized their gains in ways less conducive to pluralism than did the Poles.

Hungary's modus vivendi with the Soviet Union entailed a substantial measure of freedom to shape internal policies without infringing on either the party's monopoly of power or its basic loyalty to Moscow in foreign affairs. The result was a mixture of relative freedom and relative prosperity that made the country the most livable in Eastern Europe. Hungary's foreign policy, notably its quest for rapprochements between smaller countries on both parts of the ideological divide, was carefully calculated to promote its national interest yet to be compatible with the Soviet one.

Having been the envy of Eastern Europeans for three decades, the Hungarian model at last faltered because of its excessive dependence on the skills of one aging man and the bad performance of a hybrid economy. The model, which had gone the farthest in combining the Soviet command system with laissez-faire, generated expectations that could not be fulfilled and severe social problems, especially a widening gap between the rich and the poor. They were aggravated by the regime's inability to improve the plight of the Magyar minority in Romania, Europe's largest. Compounded by perhaps exceptional susceptibility to despair—if Hungary's history of high suicide rates is an indication—the outcome has been the most pervasive case of malaise in the region.

Romanian Autonomy

In the worsening Hungarian-Romanian conflict regarding the Magyars in Transylvania, ethnic rivalries that antedated World War I and had not been adequately managed since now reasserted themselves. Evocative of still more distant reminiscences has been the conduct of the autocratic regime of Nicolae Ceauşescu, which has been responsible for reigniting the problem. The regime's exalted nationalism, rife with extravagant historical claims, has had an air of the nineteenth-century era of nation building rather than of a higher stage of political maturity. In word and deed, Ceauşescu has invoked historical predecessors, particularly those Romanian princes who by cajoling and placating their Ottoman superiors were able to expand their room for maneuver as well as for license. The antecedent of the eighteenth-century corrupt Phanariot rule has been especially applicable.

Once the most thoroughly subjugated of Stalin's satellites, Romania has acquired—for its rulers although not for its people—the greatest measure of autonomy from Moscow. This was made possible by the relatively low strategic importance for the Soviet Union of a country lacking borders with any member of the North Atlantic Treaty Organization. But neither has Romania been sufficiently important for anyone else to add weight to its example. Nor has its attractiveness increased as a result of the Ceauşescu regime, which presides over the lowest standard of living and the worst human rights abuses in the Soviet bloc.

Czechoslovak Conformity

The nationalist Romanian model of Communist autocracy has not been any less suitable for emulation than has been the more internationalist

Czechoslovak model of Communist democracy postulated by the abortive reform movement of 1968. Unlike Solidarity in Poland, this movement proceeded from above rather than from below, thus recalling the paternalistic traits of Czechoslovakia's interwar democracy. Otherwise, however, the zealotry of its Marxist proponents, who cast themselves as harbingers of a renaissance of communism anywhere, including the Soviet Union, lacked modern precedents in Czech history—unless modernity is stretched so far as to include the medieval Hussite heresy. Their ideological zeal proved the movement's undoing by provoking Moscow's intervention—the reason for uncertainty about whether their faith in its viability suggested that it was not.

The reversion of Czechoslovakia, unlike Hungary after a comparable military incursion, to the previous patterns of dependence on Moscow and domestic repression makes the 1968 events appear a historic deviation. On the one hand, the Prague rulers' eager toeing of the Soviet line conformed with Czechoslovakia's post–World War II reputation as the most willingly obedient Soviet satellite. On the other hand, the most thorough depoliticization of the body politic to occur anywhere in Eastern Europe indicated continuities with the pre–World War I era, when cultural and economic concerns overshadowed politics, rather than with the exceptional years of Czechoslovakia's interwar independence.

At least the Czechoslovak Communists, in contrast to their democratic predecessors, dispelled doubts about the country's viability as a state. They succeeded in equalizing the Slovak and Czech levels of economic development, but this did not instill in the two peoples much love for each other. A lively and stubborn, although small and largely isolated, community of dissidents persisted more in the Czech lands than in Slovakia. Dedicated to strictly legal methods of political struggle, the dissidents built on preindependence traditions. They were products of a culture that, unlike the Polish one, has never produced grand political designs but has inspired some of Eastern Europe's most admired absurdist literature and film-making, both of which are particularly incisive in rendering the mind of the "small man."

Bulgarian Modernity

In the ascendancy throughout Eastern Europe of indigenous determinants of development, Bulgaria has been no exception, its misleadingly Russophile reputation notwithstanding. Its superficial calm and stability under Todor Zhivkov, by 1987 the longest-lasting Communist ruler in the region, belied the reassertion of its earlier traditions, including its propensity for violence and its quest for modernity. Alone among Europe's Communist nations, but otherwise much in keeping with its own past, Bulgaria experienced in 1965 a military conspiracy against the regime in power. Less characteristically, the unsuccessful conspirators escaped with relatively lenient punishment. They had not been challenging friendship with the Soviet Union; rather, they were seeking a more genuine partnership that, as in the nineteenth century, would not preclude the country from maintaining other friendships. By the 1980s, Germany had emerged as Bulgaria's other foreign friend, and commercial and cultural ties with both German states flourished.

Like the GDR, Bulgaria has been asserting itself with, rather than against, Moscow. In promoting a cult of its medieval grandeur, Bulgaria has been raising disruptive claims against neighbors occupying much of its historic territory, particularly Yugoslavia. No less disruptive, although otherwise only too consistent with past antecedents, has been Sofia's conspicuous involvement in international shady dealings—drug traffic, arms peddling, assassinations—and especially its brutal campaign to forcibly assimilate the country's large Turkish minority. Bulgaria's modernizing bent, as manifested in an infatuation with automation as a key to economic growth, has distinguished it not only from its Balkan neighbors but also from the Soviet Union. In response to Gorbachev's call for restructuring, Sofia briefly went the farthest in suggesting a reduction of the party's economic and political responsibilities.

Albanian and Yugoslav Nonalignment

The separate non-Soviet, even anti-Soviet, identities of the nonaligned communist countries of Eastern Europe—Albania and Yugoslavia—have assumed new dimensions. Postwar Albania's ability to defy its successive protectors—Yugoslavia, the Soviet Union, the People's Republic of China—signified a lasting reversal of the dependency that had marked its brief statehood since 1913. The ruthless and cunning regime of Enver Hoxha demonstrated the same capacity to deflect overbearing foreign rulers that had enabled the remote tribal society to survive the Ottoman hegemony largely intact, but at the cost of persisting backwardness.

As in the Ottoman times, Albanians continued to project themselves abroad in diverse special ways. Their pose as the world's revolutionary vanguard, translated into practice mainly in broadcasts by Radio Tirana, may be dismissed as an amusing eccentricity. But there has been nothing trivial about the result of the Albanians' spectacular demographic growth at the expense of the once predominant Serbs in Kosovo—eastern Europe's most intractable minority—an irredentist problem that threatens the integrity of Yugoslavia.

Yugoslavia best epitomizes the direction in which Eastern Europe has been moving. Pluralism and independence now appear to be the more lasting results of Tito's long rule, even though he used to be prematurely praised for his "solution" of the country's nationality problem. Again, the relevant antecedent is not the Serbian-dominated interwar Yugoslavia but rather the pre–World War I diversity in search of a solution—a legacy germane to the problems of the region as a whole and indeed to the Soviet Union. There, too, economic impasse seems insoluble without radical political restructuring. Further devolution of power in what is still a one-party state suggests the direction of the change in Yugoslavia, while mounting nationality conflict threatens its orderly course.

The Reassertion of the Pre-1914 Legacy

Does the wide-ranging reassertion of Eastern Europe's pre-1914 legacy presage a relapse into Balkanization, with all the ominous implications for international order? The area has now for more than forty years been the all but exclusive preserve of the Soviet Union. By comparison, all others have been bystanders whose impact could not possibly compare with that of the region's internal dynamics. Yet Western interests have been involved, particularly those of the United States. Washington has borne the brunt of the global competition with Moscow, and at the same time the United States has enjoyed extraordinary popularity among the region's peoples.

Western acceptance of Moscow's Eastern European empire has not precluded recurrent efforts to loosen it, but without any operational policy based on the expectation of its dissolution. U.S. policies have ranged from subversion at the height of the cold war to selective engagement with the regimes in power and promotion of direct contacts with their peoples. As a result, the state of relations with Washington has become an important factor in determining the rulers' legitimacy in the eyes of their subjects. Among the second-rank powers, Britain has been handicapped by its historic lack of interest in Eastern Europe and by the overall narrowing of its foreign commitments because of its imperial decline. De Gaulle's premature advocacy of a Europe "from the Atlantic to the Urals" in the 1960s created a stir but few lasting results, although the idea has since grown more topical now that improved conditions exist for overcoming the continent's cold war partition.

In fostering those conditions, smaller Western nations with historic interests in the area have sometimes been effective out of proportion with their power, despite their more tarnished past. Italy, once the troublemaker in the Balkans, has regained influence on potentially crucial developments there—on Albania's opening to the world as its foremost trading partner and on the management of Yugoslavia's integrity through the special relationship between the Italian and Yugoslav communist parties. This relationship is believed to be discreetly steered by the Rome Foreign Ministry. Nor have vestiges of an unredeemed Nazi past prevented neutral Austria from becoming an immensely attractive model for Eastern Europeans because of its economic, social, and political success.

The contrast of that role with Austria's pitiful condition between the wars has again highlighted the greater relevance of the more distant historical experiences. This applies not so much to the nostalgia of Hungarian and Czech intellectuals for Habsburg central Europe, but to the stature that the Austrian remnant of the once cosmopolitan empire has attained as a vigorous advocate of human rights and a premier haven for refugees from Eastern Europe. In a very different allusion to the nineteenth-century, Austria has also provided the model of an alternative German state, thereby usurping the foremost ambition of the GDR.

The historic German role in Eastern Europe has been resumed by West Germany, which now functions as the key nation for the region's further development. The West Germans have overcome the crippling legacy of their past—which was never too great an obstacle with their former allies Hungary, Romania, and Bulgaria and eventually declined in Yugoslavia, Czechoslovakia, and even Poland. Since the 1960s, the affirmative engagement of Bonn's *Ostpolitik* has created in Eastern Europe a growing West German presence with tangible results that are sometimes more than its architects were prepared to handle. The GDR's special economic accomplishment and its special permeability to Western influences have been largely of West German making. In Poland, Bonn took the lead in unwittingly forging the fateful link between the huge credits extended to Warsaw by Western banks and the Polish regime's mismanagement of the bonanza that triggered the 1980 Solidarity crisis. The Federal Republic remains the indispensable supplier of the modern technology on which Eastern Europe's future decisively hinges. To help its peoples enter the twenty-first century, German technology has become as crucial for their self-assertion as German culture used to be in the nineteenth.

Conclusion

What has changed since the peak of Eastern Europe's Stalinist integration was achieved in 1953 is more pertinent than what has remained the same. More and more the salient issues in the politics of the different countries have been of their own, rather than of Soviet, making. The Soviet Union has not ceased to be the oppressive hegemonic power, but the nature of its hegemony has been changing. More decisions of substance are apt to be made in the national capitals rather than in the Kremlin, whether by the latter's choice or its default. More reluctant to uphold its hegemony by force, Moscow has been adapting to change by redefining—more implicitly than explicitly—what hegemony means.

The many similarities between Eastern Europe's present predicament and its pre–World War I predicament do not preclude the possibility of explosions disruptive of international stability. But enough dissimilarities exist to reduce substantially the probability of a major catastrophe. The quest for statehood, which used to breed so much nationalist passion, has been fulfilled. No state now maintains territorial claims against another. Even in the areas of the fiercest ethnic conflict, such as Kosovo and Transylvania, at issue is self-determination within the existing state system rather than the creation of new sovereign entities or the redrawing of boundaries by force.

These changes suggest the degree of political maturity the peoples of the region have achieved despite, or precisely because of, their experiences with precarious independence and with the Nazi and Stalinist tyrannies. Although nationalism has again been rising, it has not been the same parochial version, born of ignorance and isolation, that led to tragedy before. Despite persisting barriers, Eastern Europeans have been moving about the region more freely and in larger numbers than they have ever been. They have been getting to know and respect, although not necessarily love, each other. They have also become better informed about the wider world because the Western mass media have been able to penetrate ever more extensively the artificially closed region.

Today's Eastern Europe is not the playground of several approximately equal great powers. Rather, it is the stage on which the gradual but irreversible decline of one of the superpowers is being enacted, with other countries posing as interested but not eager spectators. Nevertheless, interest is bound to increase as the transformation of the established European security environment proceeds.

Progress in the reduction of nuclear armaments has already focused attention on the necessary next stage—the adjustment of the conventional forces that have been the ultimate props of the Yalta system of partitioned Europe. Any reduction of these forces, which have been the mainstay of Soviet power, would then inevitably accentuate the nonmilitary aspects of security—those political, economic, social, and other assets that, in turn, are a Western strength. If implemented, the process presages Eastern Europe's eventual integration into Europe as a whole and the effective, although probably unstated, termination of the Soviet empire as history has known it. The apparent compatibility of the impending security realignment with Gorbachev's "new thinking" on foreign policy gives this process an air of plausibility that was not present before.

Notes

1. Quoted in Norman Davies, *God's Playground: A History of Poland,* vol. 1 (New York: Columbia University Press, 1982), p. 369.

2. Walter LaFeber, ed., *John Quincy Adams and American Continental Empire: Letters, Speeches, and Papers* (Chicago: Times Books, 1965), p. 45.

3. Maurice Beaumont, *La faillite de la paix (1918–1939)* (Paris: Presses Universitaires de France, 1946), p. 430.

4. George F. Kennan, *Memoirs, 1925–1950* (Boston: Little, Brown, 1967), p. 533.

5. In the opinion of an insider involved in the preparations for the military coup: Ryszard Jerzy Kukliński, "Wojna z narodem widziana ot środka," *Kultura* (Paris) (April 1987), p. 16.

3

The Economies and Trade of Eastern Europe

Paul Marer

Eastern Europe is a geopolitical rather than a geographical term. The region denoted by this term comprises the eight small and medium-sized Communist countries in Europe: Albania, Bulgaria, Czechoslovakia, the German Democratic Republic (GDR), Hungary, Poland, Romania, and Yugoslavia. The total population of these countries is about 140 million, and the total gross national product (GNP) is roughly the same as that of France or the People's Republic of China. The region is a mosaic of peoples and cultures of ancient and different origins whose varied historical experiences were often marked by bitter conflicts. At the same time, Eastern Europe is a historical entity in the sense that since the Middle Ages its economic development has lagged behind Western Europe's, and there have been long periods of cooperation among some of its component units. Today, the countries of Eastern Europe are united by the fact that they have Communist political and economic systems, modeled, at least initially, on those of the USSR. In all but two of the countries, communism was introduced—and today is ultimately still maintained—by Soviet armed forces. The two exceptions are Albania and Yugoslavia, where communism was established by their own guerrilla forces in the wake of World War II, civil war, and revolution, which is perhaps the reason these two countries later succeeded in becoming independent of the USSR. The other six states function as members of the Council for Mutual Economic Assistance (CMEA) and the Warsaw Pact and as individual actors on the world stage.

For the six Eastern European members of the CMEA, close cooperation with the USSR is partly a political imperative and partly an economic necessity. But this has worried even their leaders, who ultimately depend on the USSR to stay in power. The closer they cooperate and the deeper they are economically integrated with the USSR, the more likely they will be dominated by Moscow.

Nevertheless, there is surprisingly little economic or political integration among the Eastern European countries, for several reasons. First, as a group, they have no deep historical tradition of regionwide economic or political cooperation. Second, the Soviet Union discouraged close cooperation among the Eastern European states. Stalin did so decisively,[1] and subsequent Soviet leaders did so more subtly. Third, development levels differ widely from one country to the next. When World War II ended, the region was made up of industrialized nations (the GDR and Czechoslovakia); countries at an early stage of industrialization but with some developed industrial sectors (the USSR, Hungary, and Poland); and very poor, essentially agricultural societies (Romania, Bulgaria, Yugoslavia, and Albania). The less developed countries wanted to become industrialized through policies that gave priority to import substitution and self-sufficiency over international specialization—the same policies the USSR pursued in the 1930s and after the war.

In spite of tremendous diversity, that seven of the eight Eastern European countries still have a "traditional" (Soviet-type) or "modified" centrally planned economy (CPE) (however much these differ in detail) makes broad generalizations possible about the economic and trade situations of Eastern Europe. Even Yugoslavia, whose economic system is different, has inherited so many legacies from its earlier CPE system that many of these findings are valid for it also.

This chapter focuses on the six Eastern European members of the CMEA, with only occasional references to Yugoslavia because it does not always "fit" with the rest of Eastern Europe. Albania is not included, except for an occasional mention, because of its lesser importance, because little information is available on it, and because some of its policies also do not "fit" with the rest of Eastern Europe.

Measuring and Interpreting Economic Performance

A realistic understanding of what specialists do and do not know about the comparative economic performance of each Eastern European country—that is, comparative within the region and to a group of market economy countries—requires a brief discussion of the conceptual and measurement problems of assessing the economic performance of CPEs. Economic performance is multidimensional. The five indicators economists most often use to measure performance in a given country over time and to compare countries are the growth rates of aggregate output, production efficiency (how much input is used to produce a unit of output), the standard of living and distribution of income (including inflation experience), the level of unemployment, and export competitiveness.

Comparatively good performance in one area may be achieved at the expense of a concurrent or postponed weaker performance in some other area. For example, large foreign borrowing can accelerate a country's growth rate to impressive levels for some years, but servicing a large debt later can drag down future growth rates if the resources borrowed were invested unwisely.

Statistical measures of CPE economic performance have two major sets of problems. One is that the data are often insufficient or of exceptionally poor quality. The other is the difficulty of interpreting the data, owing to the CPEs' unique systemic features.

Problems of Measurement

An objective assessment of Eastern Europe's economic performance based solely on official data is virtually impossible because the statistics use different definitions of many economic concepts than those customary in market economies and because the data are "politicized" in various ways and for a variety of reasons. Although the Eastern European countries differ widely in this regard, published primary data are generally scarce, and much information is published on a selective basis. For instance, publication may include only those index numbers whose derivation may not be documented and, in some countries, that do not meet commonly accepted international standards.

Take, for example, the most frequently used measure of performance, the rate of economic growth. The CPEs' national accounts are based on the net material product (NMP), which differs from the GNP used in market economies in that NMP excludes depreciation and much of the net value added in so-called nonproductive services. The official NMP growth rates are then computed with distorted prices and according to methods of index number construction that (in almost all cases) tend to yield varying degrees of upward bias. A few years ago, I coordinated the work of a team of independent experts to investigate this and related issues for the World Bank. We concluded that for many CPEs the degree of bias has been so substantial that their official growth rates cannot be compared meaningfully with the GNP growth rates of market economies.[2]

CPEs rely on the double-deflation method: Both the value of gross output and the value of material purchases and depreciation are deflated separately by the relevant price indices.

$$\text{NMP} = (\text{output} \times \text{output price index}) - (\text{inputs} \times \text{input price index})$$

Gross value (output × output price index) is typically overstated, not only because the physical quantity of production tends to be overstated by producers (who are evaluated on whether they fulfill or overfulfill their taut physical output plan), but also because the price indices used to deflate production are downwardly biased, so that the resulting constant-price series will be upwardly biased. CPE output price indices are downwardly biased primarily because of the method of introducing "new" products. Enterprise plan fulfillment is measured in "constant" prices of latter years. Products are often redesigned slightly, labeled new products, and then introduced at significantly higher prices, so that constant-price output will have an inflated value. More generally, new products tend to be priced at higher introductory prices rather than at lower serial-production prices. At the same time, there is less of an opportunity, or need, to misstate physical inputs and their price indices. Under *glasnost'* (openness), this problem is now openly acknowledged even in the USSR.

> Careful calculations, based on about 100 different types of machinery and equipment, showed that while during 1976–83 the physical quantity of these goods increased by 9%, their constant ruble value increased by 75%. Officially, only the latter statistic exists; it is the basis for evaluating the rate of growth of the machinery sector. Although the speed of growth is impressive, it is not clear where this huge increment in production has disappeared. The answer: the machinery simply does not exist.[3]

If statistics on the rate of growth of output are not dependable, measures of productivity will also have problems because they relate the growth of inputs to the growth of output.

Official price indices are also unreliable. Producer price indices are problematic for the reasons already stated. Consumer price indices tend to be biased as well because in many countries the authorities prefer, for political reasons, to hide the true extent of inflation.

To be sure, there are significant differences among the CPEs regarding the presence and importance of statistical problems. In terms of the amount of information released and of its usefulness, Western experts judge Hungary, Poland, and Yugoslavia "good," Czechoslovakia "satisfactory," Bulgaria and the USSR "poor," and the GDR and Romania "extremely poor." It is ironic that East Germany is ranked at the bottom of the group because it may well have the best statistical system in the region. Nonetheless, little of the GDR's data is released, probably because the political leadership fears that if the economy is shown to lag behind that of the Federal Republic of Germany (FRG), that would be grist for the mill of Western propaganda, whereas if the economy is shown to be performing well, the GDR might have to carry greater burdens in the CMEA.

In terms of the reliability of published statistical information, Hungary's is the "best," approaching or on a par with Western standards. Poland, Yugoslavia, and (with areas of exception) the GDR follow with a "satisfactory" ranking. Bulgaria and the USSR are judged "low to satisfactory." Romania is the worst; it publishes grossly inflated and quite implausible production and living standards statistics.[4]

Problems with the official CPE growth rates and other statistics have prompted considerable efforts in the West to develop alternative measures. These use official data exclusively but replicate as much as possible commonly accepted standards of valuation and index number construction. Regarding growth rates, the basic Western approach is to aggregate the official physical output series into branch, sector, and GNP indices, using weights constructed from official data and adjusted for known distortions. But the implementation of this alternative approach is hindered by serious gaps in published data for some of the countries. This generally leaves researchers with no alternative but to rely on official "constant-price" indices to estimate the growth rate of certain branches, a practice that may give an upward bias to the recomputed indices as well.

Problems of Interpretation

Even if accurate economic statistics can be obtained or reconstructed, interpreting them is problematic. For example, growth rates of output do not reveal that a significant and perhaps growing share of production of presumably "tradable" goods and services is not salable on the world market. Nor do these rates reveal that a large share of output would not be purchased by domestic producers (as inputs) or by domestic consumers (as final products) if users had access to the better-quality goods and services readily available in much of the rest of the world or if the economic system would motivate enterprises to be cost-conscious. This is now recognized even by Mikhail Gorbachev and his key advisers, one of whom wrote, "A significant share of goods produced [in the USSR] does not satisfy social requirements and is, consequently, superfluous. . . . While we produce twice as much metal as the USA, we buy rolled metal in other countries. The USSR produces 4.5 times more tractors than the USA, though we have a smaller grain-growing area. . . . Eliminating this wasteful production is the key task in restructuring the economic mechanism."[5]

Or take statistics on unemployment. The percentage of workers without jobs is uniformly low in all Eastern European countries except Yugoslavia. The wiping out of open unemployment is perhaps the most significant economic and social achievement of the postwar regimes in Eastern Europe. But these economies suffer from disguised unemployment. The expansion drives that characterize them at both national and enterprise levels create such a high level of aggregate demand that there is overemployment at the macro level and underemployment at the micro level, as enterprises hoard and hide their labor surpluses (as they do other inputs) and use workers inefficiently. Until recently, practically all blue-collar and white-collar workers were guaranteed employment as well as their current jobs. In earlier years, staying at the same place of work was enforced; more recently, it is rewarded, although not necessarily through the wage system. Open unemployment in many capitalist countries and disguised unemployment in all CPEs are alternative forms of inefficiency, although with quite different outcomes for income distribution.

Consider inflation. Both CPEs and market economies are subject to inflationary pressures, but these typically manifest in different ways. Market economies are characterized mainly by open inflation. CPEs suffer repressed inflation, whose symptoms are chronic shortages, queues, inefficiency in the distribution system, and widespread corruption. In such economies it is common to impose price controls; to open "commercial" or "hard-currency" shops where goods not available in the regular retail outlets are sold at substantially higher prices (as in the GDR) or only for foreign currency (a practice especially widespread in Poland); and to trade many goods and services at higher prices in the "second economy" under conditions that range from the officially sanctioned to the illegal. These practices keep open inflation under "control" but hurt consumers in ways not revealed by the statistics.

The standard of living and income distribution are further aspects of economic performance about which it is difficult to make statistically meaningful comparative assessments. In CPEs, publicly supplied goods and services, such as nominally free health care and education, subsidized housing, public transportation, and many basic food items, are a much larger share of a family's consumption than is the case in comparable market economies. Wide differences among the Eastern European countries in the availability of consumer goods and services is another difficulty in comparing living standards.

Interpreting income distribution data is also problematic. Wage and salary incomes are significantly more equally distributed in CPEs than in market economies, although insufficient differentiation—based on education, skill, and effort—creates problems. Moreover, in CPEs the elite have a wide range of economic privileges, so that income distribution is much less equal than it would appear from published statistics. This is an especially important consideration in countries in which the availability of consumer goods and services through normal distribution channels is deficient (less so in Hungary than, say, in Romania or Poland) and in which travel to the West is restricted (less the case in Hungary and Poland). The economic value of privileges, such as ability to obtain desirable housing quickly, access to well-stocked special stores, and permission to travel to the West with a hard-currency allowance, can exceed the recipient's money wages.

A problem not unique to CPEs, but one that hinders cross-country comparisons both within Eastern Europe and between CPEs and market economies, is activities in the "second economy," which I define as all forms of private economic activity, legal or illegal. In each country, a part of the second economy's output is included in the official statistics on output; another part is not reported. The latter includes some of the output produced in the private agricultural sector, a significant share of privately financed construction of residences, and services of all kinds rendered privately. The exclusion from gross national product or gross domestic product of a portion of output, and of input, resulting from private economic activities causes an understatement of the output and the standard of living. The consensus of Western experts is that such activities are exceedingly important in Hungary, Poland, the GDR, and Yugoslavia, are beginning to assume importance in Bulgaria, and are modest in the USSR, Romania, and Czechoslovakia.

There are special problems as well in interpreting data on CPEs' trade and balance of payments. Whereas the CPEs' trade with the West is conducted at Western prices and is settled (mostly) in convertible currencies, trade with the other CPEs is conducted at different prices and is settled (mostly) in transferable rubles (TR), which are neither convertible nor transferable. Moreover, each CPE sets its exchange rate vis-à-vis the currencies of the individual Eastern European countries differently (and apparently, for the most part, arbitrarily). The result is that trade and payment flows, as well as assets and liabilities, denominated in TRs or in their Eastern European domestic currency equivalents are not comparable with those denominated in convertible currencies or with the domestic currency equivalents reported in Eastern European statistical publications.

Roughly half of the USSR's and (on average) Eastern Europe's trade is with the West (including the developing countries), and much of the rest is with members of the CMEA. Trade shares cannot be computed accurately because prices and price levels in trade with the West often differ substantially from those in trade with the East and because the exchange rates are arbitrary. We know a great deal about Eastern Europe's trade, balance of payments, and debt situation vis-à-vis the industrial countries, but there is much we do not know about corresponding magnitudes and trends in commerce with the East and with the developing countries. Thus, a great deal of caution must be exercised in making performance comparisons among the Eastern European countries or between them and market economies.

Eastern Europe's Comparative Postwar Economic Performance

Physical Indicators: Methods and Results

An ingenious way of getting around the measurement problems as far as comparable levels of development and growth rates are concerned is through the use of the physical indicator method. This method takes a set of physical indicators of the annual *flow* of current production (such as bushels of grain and barrels of oil) and the *stock* of the country's accumulated wealth (such as standardized dwelling units or the number of hospital beds per thousand persons) for market economies for which meaningful dollar per capital GNPs can be obtained through official (and by and large market-determined) exchange rates. For all the countries in the sample, each physical indicator is plotted against each country's dollar per capita GNP. The curve fitted to the resulting graph points reveals the systematic relationship between the level of a physical indicator and corresponding dollar per capita GNP in market economies. From this relationship one can estimate the dollar per capita GNP for a CPE on the basis of its physical indicators, on which published figures tend to be more reliable than other kinds of data. As many independent estimates of a CPE's dollar per capita GNP can be obtained as there are physical indicators (as few as twenty-five or as many as seventy-five have been used in various studies). An average (usually unweighted) of the independent estimates then serves as an estimate of a CPE's per capita dollar GNP, which is comparable with similarly obtained estimates for other CPEs and market economies.

One such computation, involving thirty-two countries—including all the Eastern and Western European nations plus the United States, Japan, and five Latin American nations—was made by a Hungarian economist for 1937, 1960, 1970, and 1980, based on forty-nine physical indicators.[6] The summary results are given in Appendix 3.1. Although the computations establish only levels of per capita dollar GNPs, shifts in the relative levels of development among countries are strongly suggestive of which countries had relatively fast or relatively slow rates of growth. On that basis it is possible to evaluate the relative growth performance of the Eastern European countries vis-à-vis each other and to compare them with selected market economies.

Several caveats are in order. An important shortcoming of the physical indicator method is that it cannot take into account the often large differences among countries in the quality and assortment of their products and services. The physical indicator method also may not reveal the inefficiency of production or whether the technology gap is growing. For these reasons, some experts believe that the physical indicator method yields dollar per capita GNP estimates for CPEs that are upwardly biased. My own view is that any bias is not likely to be so large as to invalidate the broad trends revealed. This conclusion is supported by a comparison of the average 1980 development levels of six *groups* of countries, including the Eastern European CPEs plus Yugoslavia, relative to that of the United States (Table 3.1). The physical indicator method finds that in 1980 the average level of development of the seven Eastern European countries was approximately three-fifths that of Western Europe and about the same as that of Greece, Spain, and Portugal. These results do not suggest that the method has an unacceptably large upward bias for the CPEs.

Relative levels of development may not match relative standards of living. For certain countries, the former may be higher during periods of relatively high capital-formation levels in order to catch up with more advanced countries. Development levels may also be high because resource allocation is lastingly less efficient so that to keep up with other countries, the inefficient must invest more per unit of GNP. Or high levels may result from significant investments made for purposes other than to satisfy public and private consumption needs in the future, such as the greater glory of the state.[7] For CPEs, the share of investment in GNP seems to be significantly higher than the average for comparable market economies (probably for all three of the aforementioned reasons), which means that CPE consumption levels are significantly lower than those suggested by their relative levels of dollar per capita GNPs.

One computation, based on the physical indicators method, compared the estimated 1965 levels of the individual Eastern European countries' and the Soviet Union's (1) investment per capita and (2) private plus public consumption per capita with average Western European levels of (1) investment per capita and (2) consumption per capita, respectively. In every CPE, relative levels of per capita investment were higher than relative levels of per capita consumption, as shown in Table 3.2. The difference was the largest for the USSR and the smallest for Hungary.

Although one should not exaggerate the degree of accuracy with which such computations can be made, the results are broadly plausible and

TABLE 3.1. Economic Development Levels of Groups of Countries in 1980

Country or Group of Countries	Per Capita GNP in 1980 (average weighted by population)	
	$/capita	U.S. = 100
United States	11,580	100
Scandinavian countries[a]	8,650	75
The original Common Market "Six"[b]	6,970	60
All European market economies[c]	5,837	50
Southern European market economies (excluding Turkey)[d]	3,623	31
Eastern European Seven[e]	3,476	30
Less developed European market economies[f]	2,504	22
South American countries[g]	1,596	14

[a]Finland, Norway, Sweden
[b]Belgium and Luxembourg, France, the Netherlands, the FRG, and Italy
[c]Austria, Belgium and Luxembourg, Denmark, United Kingdom, Finland, France, Greece, the Netherlands, Ireland, Norway, the FRG, Italy, Portugal, Spain, Switzerland, Sweden, and Turkey
[d]Greece, Spain, and Portugal
[e]Bulgaria, Czechoslovakia, Poland, Hungary, the GDR, Romania, and Yugoslavia
[f]Greece, Spain, Portugal, and Turkey
[g]Argentina, Brazil, Chile, Mexico, and Peru

Source: Eva Ehrlich, "Absolute and Relative Economic Development Levels and Their Structure, 1937-1980" (Budapest: 1987, unpublished), Table 2, p. 10.

revealing. The USSR has had the highest discrepancy between relative levels of investment and consumption. Although in 1965 the USSR's level of per capita investment was 79 percent of that of a sample of Western European countries, the Soviet level of per capita consumption was only 52 percent—a difference of 27 percent. Comparisons of per capita GNP levels (a weighted average of per capita investment and consumption levels) would show the USSR level at about 60 percent of Western Europe's. The size of the investment-consumption discrepancy may be the result of a strong preference for investment over consumption, a low investment efficiency, and the reporting of significant military expenditures (supposedly included in public consumption) as "investment."

Among the CPEs, Hungary's level of investment was relatively modest. This may have been an element of János Kádár's policy of "reconciliation"

TABLE 3.2. 1965 Per Capita Levels of Investment and Consumption of the CMEA Countries Relative to a (Weighted) Average of Germany, France, and Belgium

	Investment (percent)	Consumption (percent)	Difference (Inv.-Cons.) (percent)
USSR	79	52	27
Czechoslovakia	98	74	24
GDR	95	76	19
Poland	69	51	18
Bulgaria	61	46	15
Romania	50	36	14
Hungary	63	56	7

Source: Jan Winiecki, "Four Kinds of Fallacies in Comparing Market-Type and Soviet-Type Economies" (Stockholm: Institute for International Economic Studies, July 1987), Table 10, p. 60.

with the population in the wake of the "events of 1956." To be sure, Hungary's level of investment was still higher than "justified" by the level of development of the country, based on comparisons with market economies at comparable development levels.

The much lower level of consumption in the CPEs relative to market economies at comparable development levels also derives from the inability of comparisons of living standards to take into account, or do so adequately, the pervasive shortages and poor sophistication, quality, reliability, and "circumstances of sale" of the goods and services provided to the population. One observer noted, "How often and how fast does this bus run? Electricity is cheap, but how often are there power cuts? How old are these eggs? How often is the elevator out of order?"[8]

To illustrate further, the basic small car in the GDR is the Trabant. It is, with only slight exaggeration, an uncomfortable plastic box that pollutes heavily and breaks down often. The basic small car in the FRG used to be the Volkswagen Beetle; today it is the Golf. Both models are incomparably better than the Trabant.

New apartments in the CPEs are notoriously poor in quality. For example, they often need replastering even before the first tenant moves in. Residents spend large efforts and typically wait for a long time for (often temporary) solutions to maintenance problems. Moreover, much of new apartment construction is gray, drab, and barracks-like.

Shopping involves much searching, queuing, forced substitutions, crowded conditions, discourteous service, poor packaging, rejects, and a high proportion of spoilage. Routine bribing of those who sell consumer goods and

TABLE 3.3. Development-Level Ranking of the Six Eastern European Countries and Yugoslavia Among a Group of Thirty-Two Countries in 1937, 1960, 1970, and 1980

	1937	1960	1970	1980
GDR	7-8	16	17	17
Czechoslovakia	19	17	19	19
Hungary	24	22	23	22
Poland	25	23	24	24
Romania	30	31	31	28
Yugoslavia	31	32	29	27
Bulgaria	32	25	27	23

Source: Derived from data in Eva Ehrlich, "Absolute and Relative Economic Development Levels and Their Structure, 1937-1980" (Budapest: 1987, unpublished).

provide services to the population is practiced in all the CPEs. It is the consumer's way of trying to remedy, on an individual basis, these problems.

Although the features of consumption enumerated here can be found in all CPEs, their degree and relative importance vary greatly from country to country. Eyewitness accounts (including my own, having recently traveled in each of the six Eastern European countries and in the USSR) suggest that these problems are relatively less severe in Hungary and are of overwhelming importance in Romania. A further characteristic of CPEs that depresses their standard of living is the relative neglect of investment in infrastructure (housing, roads, telephones). Although these matters are difficult to quantify, it is undeniable that the standard of living in the CPEs is significantly lower than is suggested by per capita GNP comparisons with market economies. But the extent of the difference varies considerably from country to country.

If we keep the aforementioned caveats in mind and turn back to revealed development levels measured by per capita dollar GNPs, we see that changes in the relative positions of the Eastern European countries and Yugoslavia between 1937 and 1980 are highlighted by benchmark-year shifts in their rankings among the thirty-two countries. The most revealing comparisons are between 1937 and 1960 and between 1960 and 1980 (see Table 3.3).

Between 1937 and 1960, the most dramatic shift in relative positions involved the GDR, which moved down from eighth to sixteenth place, probably because of the heavy burden of reparation payments and other unpaid resource transfers to the USSR, the absence of Marshall Plan aid, and the loss of skilled labor through emigration until the Berlin Wall was built in 1961.[9] In contrast, Bulgaria improved significantly, moving up from thirty-second to twenty-fifth place, probably because the country made fewer economic policy mistakes than did the other Eastern European countries[10] and received preferential treatment from the USSR. The other five countries were more or less able to keep their prewar rankings. Between 1960 and 1980, the relative positions of three of the more developed countries deteriorated (Czechoslovakia's by two places, the GDR's and Poland's by one place); those of three of the less developed countries improved (Yugoslavia's by five places, Romania by three places, and Bulgaria by two places); and Hungary's remained unchanged.

The results are influenced by the reference countries included in the comparisons. If more Latin American and African countries were included, Eastern Europe's relative performance would appear to be better; if more of the successfully industrializing Asian countries were included, it would seem relatively worse. Therefore we limit our more detailed comparisons to Europe.

Comparing Eastern and Western Europe

Even more than physical indicators data, demographic statistics, such as life expectancy and infant mortality, circumvent problems of data accuracy and valuation because birth and death statistics are readily available in most countries. Health conditions, especially mortality, are directly shaped by many of the same economic and social conditions that determine the standard of living.

Eastern Europe and the USSR enjoyed rapid health improvements in the 1950s and 1960s. During these two decades, the (unweighted) life expectancy at birth of the Eastern European countries rose by six years; the corresponding improvement in Western Europe during the same period was three and one-half years. Whereas in the early 1950s, life spans were about six years longer in Western than in Eastern Europe, by the late 1960s, the gap had narrowed to about two and one-half years. Since then, however, the gap has again widened, so that by the early 1980s, life spans were about five years longer in Western than in Eastern Europe. Among the latter group of countries, only the GDR continued to record steady, although modest, gains in life expectancy during the most recent decades.[11]

If we turn back to the evidence revealed by dollar per capita GNP comparisons based on the physical indicators method, in both Eastern and Western Europe the revealed trend is that of the relatively less developed countries reducing the gap. Between 1960 and 1980, France, Finland, Austria, Italy, Spain, and Greece each advanced by several places among the thirty-two countries, while the United Kingdom moved down (by nine places), as did Denmark (by six) and Switzerland (by three).

As there appears to be an inverse relationship between development level and performance irrespective of economic system, the per capita income levels of the individual Eastern European countries are compared, for four benchmark years, with selected Western European market economies at comparable levels of development in 1937 or 1960 (Table 3.4). An increase in the ratio of the estimated per capita dollar GNP of an Eastern European

TABLE 3.4. Changes in Relative Positions of the Eastern European Countries and Yugoslavia in Bilateral Comparisons with Market Economy Countries, 1937, 1960, 1970, and 1980 (ratios x 100)

	1937	1960	1970	1980
GDR/FRG	100[a]	70	71	64
GDR/France	128[a]	84	83	72
GDR/U.K.	77[a]	60	66	80
Czechoslovakia/Austria	90	91	78	70
Czechoslovakia/France	64	84	74	66
Czechoslovakia/U.K.	39	60	59	73
Hungary/Austria	63	56	51	52
Hungary/Italy	89	86	70	74
Hungary/Spain	126	128	96	90
Poland/Austria	53	54	47	45
Poland/Italy	74	85	64	63
Poland/Spain	105	125	88	77
Romania/Spain	85	85	58	60
Romania/Greece	88	100	78	78
Romania/Portugal	87	100	88	109
Yugoslavia/Spain	84	82	63	62
Yugoslavia/Greece	87	97	83	81
Yugoslavia/Portugal	86	97	94	112
Bulgaria/Spain	79	104	75	84
Bulgaria/Greece	82	122	100	110
Bulgaria/Portugal	81	122	113	153

[a]See note b to Appendix 3.1.

Source: Calculated from Eva Ehrlich, "Absolute and Relative Economic Development Levels and Their Structure, 1937-1980" (Budapest: 1987, unpublished), Table 5, p. 15.

to that of a Western European country (multiplied by 100) means that the Eastern European country has improved its performance relative to the market economy (its economy apparently grew more rapidly in real terms); a decline means that that country has fallen behind.

GDR. During the early postwar period, the GDR fell significantly behind the main Western European countries. During the 1960s, the gap did not increase further, but during the 1970s it did, except vis-à-vis the United Kingdom. The heavy armaments burden of the GDR relative to that of the FRG may have been a factor.

Czechoslovakia. This nation appears to have done quite well during the 1950s (about as well as Austria and much better than France or the United Kingdom), but then did relatively poorly during the 1960s and 1970s, except vis-à-vis the United Kingdom.

Hungary. Although it is compared with nations that have done much better than average among the market economies, Hungary appeared to hold its own between 1937 and 1960. Since then it has not quite kept up with Austria and has fallen significantly behind Italy and Spain.

Poland. Against the same countries as Hungary, Poland did relatively well until about 1960 but has not kept up since then.

Romania. The country did well between 1937 and 1960, did not keep up during the 1960s, but did so again during the 1970s, especially against poorly performing Portugal.

Yugoslavia. Against the same group of countries as Romania, its story is essentially the same.

Bulgaria. Relative performance was outstanding between 1937 and 1960, lagged significantly during the 1960s, and then came back during the 1970s.

These comparisons suggest the following broad trends and interpretations. Between 1937 and 1960, six of the seven Eastern European countries did as well or better in terms of growth rates than did the comparable Western European market economies; the GDR was the exception. In terms of pace of development, Eastern Europe did well because of the fast tempo of its postwar reconstruction and the often brutal, military-like resource-mobilization campaigns its leaders pursued after the CPE system was introduced.

During the 1950s, the authorities mobilized unemployed and underemployed labor and other resources, increased investment in human and physical capital at a rapid pace, and got the resources needed to finance these activities by imposing a high rate of forced saving on the population and by neglecting infrastructure. The authorities deployed the large increases in inputs into sectors of relatively high productivity, such as industry and construction, and thereby quickly achieved impressively high rates of growth of output. Eventually, however, the rapid forced mobilization of the economy had to be moderated as the growth of inputs slowed, more and more bottlenecks appeared, and the populations expressed, in various ways, their resentment about these policies. In all countries, these problems led to periodic crises that in some cases triggered political upheavals.

During the 1960s, the development gap between Eastern and Western Europe appears to have increased, except against some of the poorly performing market economies, such as the United Kingdom and Portugal. The GDR was again the exception; it was able to keep up. The tempo of Western European development picked up after 1958, when the main countries achieved the full convertibility of their currencies and the Common Market was formed. By then, Eastern Europe's engine of growth (the rapid mobilization of domestic capital, labor, and other inputs, which supported the industrial takeoff) had begun to slow down.

During the 1960s and early 1970s, Eastern Europe's emerging problems (which a growing number of their own experts began to attribute, some as early as the second half of the 1950s, to the shortcomings of the CPE system) were held in check by two factors. One was the temporarily improved performance brought about by limited economic reforms (prompted either by a severe economic and political crisis or by the example of the Liberman-Kosygin reforms in the USSR). The other was the benefit the Eastern European countries derived from bilateral economic "integration" of a special kind with the USSR. This took the form of a rapid expansion of trade. Eastern Europe obtained growing quantities of cheap energy, raw materials, and energy- and material-intensive semimanufactures in exchange for products of the light industries, foodstuffs, machinery and equipment, and other manufactures. Moreover, cheap Soviet energy and raw materials facilitated the development of metallurgical and standard manufactured products, some of which were exported to the West, where they earned convertible currency. This made it possible for Eastern Europe to put aside its worries about obtaining crucial supplies of input or finding markets for their rapidly growing and often poor quality output.

But this was only temporary. The USSR became less and less able and willing to continue integration along these lines. The Eastern Europeans began to realize that the short-term benefits of this type of integration were offset by their long-term costs. Integration with the USSR helped create and sustain an outdated industrial structure and mode of production that were excessively wasteful of inputs. For example, the steel industry, which was not built or expanded in Eastern Europe until the 1950s, was for the rest of the world a modern "engine of growth" only during the early decades of the century. During the 1960s, the rapid development of Eastern Europe's chemical industries improved the region's industrial structure, but subsequently, with its lagging high-tech industries, Eastern Europe fell behind considerably. The switch to high-tech industries—a necessity for the GDR and Czechoslovakia as early as the 1960s, for Hungary and Poland by the 1970s, and for the southern-tier countries during the 1980s—is greatly impeded by the economic system and policies of traditional central planning.

During the 1970s, five of the seven Eastern European countries were able to halt or reverse the earlier trend of falling behind Western Europe (where performance deteriorated), at least as far as the growth rates were concerned. Not so the GDR and Czechoslovakia, the two most developed countries, which could not keep up with the better-performing countries of Western Europe. These two countries were the first to exhaust growth based on a rapid increase in inputs. The GDR certainly always had fewer such possibilities than did the other countries. Also during this decade, the Eastern European countries found a new source of growth: the rapid expansion of trade with the West, a significant part of it supported by large Western credits.

* * *

By the late 1970s and early 1980s, the Eastern European countries could count on none of the three support mechanisms they enjoyed during the previous decades: rapid mobilization and deployment of inputs, integration with the USSR, and Western credits. The rate of growth of complementary domestic inputs (capital and labor) slowed greatly and in some countries came to a complete halt. The share of investment in national income could not be increased any longer at the expense of consumption. Practically all who could be employed were already in the labor force, and all who could be shifted from less to more productive sectors were transferred. At the same time, more and more serious bottlenecks appeared in agriculture, material supplies and intermediate goods, components and spare parts, modern technology—generally convertible-currency imports—and in infrastructure and the service sectors. These bottlenecks precluded the earlier possibility of redeploying increasingly scarce resources into sectors with quick payoffs in terms of growth of output. They also revealed that something was fundamentally amiss with Eastern European economic policies and systems.

Concurrently, Eastern Europe's economic connection with the Soviets and the other CMEA partners became less and less dynamic. Their terms of trade vis-à-vis the USSR worsened, and the purchase of "hard goods" (energy and raw materials) and the sale of "soft goods" (manufactures) became increasingly difficult. By the early 1980s, the Soviets were willing to increase their deliveries only against convertible currencies or "hard goods." These difficulties were the result of fundamental problems in the domestic economies of the Soviet Union and Eastern Europe, as well as in the CMEA's trade and financial mechanisms.

During the early 1980s, Eastern Europe (including Yugoslavia) suddenly found itself unable to borrow further large sums from the West with which to finance a net inflow of resources from abroad and was saddled with interest on a large outstanding debt, whose payment required a substantial net resource outflow. This could be realized only by a drastic cut of imports from the West, which in turn had all kinds of adverse short- and long-term economic consequence. The tension in the Eastern European countries' convertible-currency balances of payments, which used to occur periodically, now became chronic.

During the early 1980s, Eastern Europe's large debt and inability (in some cases also unwillingness) to get large additional credits required these countries not just to generate multiyear export surpluses with the West but to maintain such surpluses at a time when their terms of trade with the

USSR were deteriorating and the quantity of their Soviet imports stagnated or declined. Whereas the stagnation or decline of Eastern Europe's imports from the West was forced upon the region by its shortage of convertible currency, the decline or stagnation of imports from the USSR could be traced to a slowdown in the growth of production in key sectors of Soviet exports. The shortage of convertible currency made it impossible for Eastern Europe to replace Soviet imports with purchases from the West.

To summarize: The burden of debt service to the West and the deterioration in the terms of trade with the USSR have prevented the Eastern European economies from resolving the severe tensions in the balance of payments. Whereas in previous decades this could be managed by reining in investment or consumption for a year or two, thereafter resuming economic growth, today Eastern Europe no longer has this possibility and thus faces a "permanent stagnation" crisis, which is not fully revealed by the countries' economic statistics.[12]

Economic Integration with the USSR and Intra-CMEA Relations

Economic relations among a group of CPEs are fundamentally different than those among a group of market economies, such as the European Community. Much international commerce in the West is conducted by private firms seeking profit opportunities, so that a reduction of barriers to the movement of goods, factors of production, and money across national borders helps to integrate their economies. In contrast, in countries with central planning all movement of goods and production factors across national borders requires explicit action by the governments. Agreements about specialization are difficult to reach, as is finding a workable mechanism to implement them.[13]

During the first postwar decade, the Soviet concept of regional economic "integration" was that each Eastern European country should carry out Soviet instructions. The orders given by the USSR under Joseph Stalin were demonstrably exploitative. My rough computations show that through various channels, ranging from war reparations to joint stock companies to unfair prices in trade, the Soviets obtained an estimated $14 billion in resources from the six Eastern European countries, with the GDR bearing the brunt of the burden. This was roughly the same as the amount spent by the United States in Western Europe under the Marshall Plan.[14]

Soviet economic policy toward Eastern Europe began to change after Stalin's death, as the high political cost of economic exploitation and pervasive direct interference was brought home by the defection of Yugoslavia (after 1948) and the uprisings and revolts in East Germany (in 1953), Hungary, and Poland (both in 1956). Nikita Khrushchev's discrediting of certain aspects of Stalin's dictatorial methods also played an important role. The Soviet Union's post-1956 policy was to move its trade with Eastern Europe toward a more equitable, commercial basis by agreeing to pricing and negotiating rules acceptable to all members and then adhering to those rules even if they temporarily disadvantaged the USSR. The Soviet Union also has tried to find a new, more voluntary basis for regional integration. Suggestions for CMEA integration have ranged from Khrushchev's proposal in the early 1960s for a supranational authority that would extend the traditional institutions of central planning to the regional level, to Hungarian and Polish proposals favoring greater reliance on market mechanisms. Khrushchev's proposal brought to the surface Eastern Europe's fear that bloc integration under a supranational authority would mean even greater domination by the USSR. The most uncompromising stand against this supranationalism was taken by Romania.[15] Perhaps recalling that earlier pressures on Yugoslavia and Albania had contributed to those countries' assertion of their independence from the bloc, the USSR decided not to press its proposals.

Nevertheless, during the 1960s economic "integration" in the CMEA proceeded. This included technical decisions involving large, bloc-wide infrastructure projects, such as electricity grids and oil pipelines, for which engineering considerations provided the rationale. These projects were supplemented later by joint investment projects, most of them located in the USSR, exploiting and transporting its natural resources. But economic relations remained largely bilateral, even though the political superstructure of the CMEA was formally designed to be multilateral. Of key importance during the 1960s was the Soviet willingness to export increased quantities of energy and raw materials in exchange for Eastern European manufactured products.

In the 1950s, exchange of primary products for Eastern European manufactured goods was advantageous for the USSR because its partners were able to supply machinery and other manufactures denied to the Soviets by the Western embargo, and because there was no world shortage of energy and raw materials and therefore no strong demand for Soviet supplies of them. By the 1960s, the pattern of Soviet trade with Eastern Europe had become ossified. But there was no great economic pressure on the USSR to alter the trade pattern because it was able to expand energy and raw material production rapidly and at a reasonable cost.

During the 1970s, circumstances began to change. The Soviet Union's rapid expansion of trade with the West increased its opportunity cost as a large net supplier of "hard goods" to Eastern Europe, as did the rising domestic cost of extracting and transporting these commodities from increasingly remote Siberian regions. The Soviet Union began to complain that some of its trade with Eastern Europe was disadvantageous, even though the disadvantages were mitigated by the large windfall gains the USSR enjoyed from improved terms of trade with the West, the rising price of gold, and the Soviet ability to tap into the Organization of Petroleum Exporting Countries' (OPEC) surplus by selling military hardware to OPEC. During 1973–82, these windfall gains yielded the USSR tens of billions of dollars, thereby enabling it to increase its hard-currency export revenues almost as rapidly as its hard-currency imports (that is, without having to incur a large foreign debt). Thus, the opportunity cost of supplying increased amounts of energy and raw materials to Eastern Europe, even at subsidized prices, did not appear to be a crushing burden. Moreover, the USSR obtained at least partial compensation, which took the form of Eastern European investment contributions to Soviet projects and subsidies to the non-European members of the CMEA (Mongolia, Cuba, and Vietnam) and selected Third World countries. These resource flows from Eastern Europe served to support the Soviet Union's global political and military objectives.

The rate of growth of the volume of Soviet "hard-good" exports to Eastern Europe declined steeply during the 1970s and stopped growing altogether in the early 1980s. Because a significant part of Eastern Europe's exports to the West is composed of Soviet energy and raw materials transformed into intermediate products, such as ferrous and nonferrous metals and chemicals, Soviet actions constrained Eastern Europe's ability to increase the sales of these traditional products to convertible-currency markets. At the same time, the sharp deterioration of Eastern Europe's terms of trade with the Soviet Union during 1975–1985 required significant increases in the quantity of their export to the USSR. These developments forced the Eastern Europeans to step up purchases from the world market, which in turn increased the pressure on them to earn or to borrow the needed hard currency.

Toward the end of the 1970s another factor became increasingly important in Soviet calculations: the growing economic weaknesses of the Eastern European countries and the related political instability, actual or potential. This prompted the Soviets to proceed cautiously in raising export prices too steeply or in curtailing energy and raw material shipments too precipitously.

Different mechanisms are employed by the CMEA countries in trade with each other and with the West. With partners outside the bloc, they trade at current world market prices. In intrabloc trade, prices are linked by an agreed formula to Western world market prices of an agreed earlier period, currently a five-year moving average. Western prices are used because each CMEA country sets its domestic prices and exchange rates differently and arbitrarily, so that no country is willing to accept the prices of the others for valuing exports and imports.

CMEA prices can be determined relatively easily for primary products, that is, for standard commodities traded on the world market at published prices. Between 1973 and 1982, the world prices of energy and many raw materials rose sharply. CMEA prices, because of the price rule, rose more slowly. Thus, during this period the USSR, as a net exporter of energy and raw materials, sold these goods to Eastern Europe at less than world prices, which meant implicit Soviet subsidies. In recent years, these subsidies have declined and may have disappeared because world energy prices dropped while intra-CMEA prices continued to rise because of the pricing formula.

For most manufactures there is only a world market price range for similar but often not identical products. There is little accurate information on intra-CMEA prices of manufactures. What there is suggests that in the

1960s, prices used to be relatively high, but since then their rate of increase has lagged behind price increases on the world market. Depending on the assumptions one makes about the prices at which manufactures are traded in the CMEA and what they might be "worth" on the world market, one may conclude that the Soviet Union, as a large net importer of manufactures, has been providing further large implicit subsidies to Eastern Europe[16] or that there is insufficient basis to say so, much less to estimate specific subsidy amounts.[17]

Be that as it may, there is agreement among those who take the Soviet perspective that Eastern Europe has benefited from Soviet willingness to have a surplus in primary products and a deficit in manufactures and that for about a decade (1973–1983) Eastern Europe gained from the inertia built into the CMEA price mechanism. Some Western experts argue that the implicit economic subsidies were calibrated and granted purposefully by the Soviets as an instrument of policy.[18] Others hold that Soviet policymakers did not intend to make the transfers, but that certain considerations led the Soviets to accept them.[19]

The Eastern European perspective on this issue is different from the Soviet perception or from certain Western interpretations of this Soviet largesse. Eastern Europeans point out that the benefits of Soviet price subsidies are offset, at least in part, by Soviet insistence on composition and quantities of imports and exports different from those that would prevail if Eastern Europe chose its own imports and exports freely at prevailing prices. This is not to deny that the Eastern European countries would face tremendous difficulties if they were forced on short notice to reorient their trade from the CMEA to the world market. But they nevertheless note that this "cost" was imposed on them with the Soviet-type economic system and development model. Moreover, their region's political-military alliance with the USSR has forced the East Europeans into an adversary relationship with the West that has denied them some technology and other trade benefits.

Many Eastern Europeans also note that the Soviet market's willingness to absorb poor quality goods and obsolete equipment is an advantage to the seller only in the short run. In the long run, this reduces the pressure and incentive to innovate and produce "for the market," thereby causing Eastern European firms to fall further and further behind competitors on the world market. This cost appears to burden mainly the more advanced CMEA countries; the "bill" is presented when they must expand their manufactured exports to the West to pay for goods and services unavailable on the protected CMEA market. Thus, I agree with Vojtech Mastny that adoption of the Soviet model facilitated the immediate but hampered the long-term development of Eastern Europe.[20]

Eastern Europeans also complain about the large "joint investment" contributions they have been pressured to make in projects located in the USSR. These involve substantial credits to the Soviets, granted at 2 percent interest, mostly in the form of exports produced in part from large convertible-currency imports. During 1984–1985, the Eastern European countries have been squeezed by the substantial deterioration in their terms of trade with the Soviet Union. This required them to increase the *volume* of exports to the USSR considerably faster than they were able to increase the volume of imports. Increased exports paid for the lion's share of the terms of trade loss; credit by the Soviets (in the form of Soviet trade surplus) covered the rest. Eastern Europe's indebtedness to the USSR thus increased.

Although comprehensive data are not available, the following statistics are revealing. The deterioration of four Eastern European countries' terms of trade with the USSR from 1978 until 1983 or 1984 (as available) were:[21]

Bulgaria (1978–1984)	27 percent
Czechoslovakia (1978–1983)	17 percent
Hungary (1978–1984)	14 percent
Poland (1978–1983)	13 percent

Between 1978 and 1984, the terms of trade of the USSR with the CMEA countries as a group improved by 33 percent.

Owing to the reduced ability and willingness of the USSR since the late 1960s to export energy and raw materials to Eastern Europe, and the improvement in its terms of trade, the average annual increase in the *volume* of Soviet exports to the CMEA was as follows:[22]

1966–1970	11 percent
1971–1975	7 percent
1976–1980	5 percent
1981–1985	0 percent

The Soviets' single largest export earner in the CMEA as well as in the West is oil. In 1982, when the Soviets faced production difficulties and a weakening world market price, they cut the export of crude oil to Eastern Europe to levels less than those set under the medium-term agreements for 1981–1985 and increased the delivery to the West (partly through increased reexporting of Middle East oil). During early 1985, when domestic production again dropped, the export cuts fell primarily on deliveries to the West (40 percent) and only secondarily to Eastern Europe (7 percent).[23]

Between the mid-1970s and the mid-1980s, the volume of Eastern European exports to the USSR had to increase considerably faster than the volume of imports. This in turn required more hard-currency imports and also preempted some goods that could have been exported for convertible currency and was thus a factor in the region's growing indebtedness to the West.

On developments since 1987, we have information only on Hungary, whose experience—experts in the CMEA countries tell us—is not atypical for the rest of Eastern Europe. Since 1987, when Hungary's terms of trade with the USSR began to improve (owing to the earlier decline in world energy prices and the CMEA formula), a new situation has arisen. Keeping trade bilaterally balanced requires that Hungary's (Eastern Europe's) exports to the USSR decline, that its imports from the USSR accelerate, or that some combination of adjustment in the growth of export and import volumes occurs.[24] This has created new tensions. During earlier periods, Hungarian enterprises got used to the authorities supporting rapid expansion of exports to the USSR, even though exports were not allowed to increase as rapidly as Hungarian firms would have liked. In recent years, because the USSR has not been willing to sell more of the commodities Hungary would like to import, and the machinery and other manufactures it offers to sell are typically not of good quality or the kinds of products Hungary needs, something of an impasse has developed in Hungarian-Soviet (and, presumably, in East European–Soviet) trade relations.[25] In an attempt to resolve it, Hungarian authorities are now encouraging Hungarian firms to find additional products that can be imported from the USSR so as to avoid a faster-than-planned repayment of Hungary's Soviet debt. Hungary's TR debt stood at 1 billion TR at the end of 1987, down from 1.4 billion TR in 1983 (1 TR is about $1.40). Slower repayment means that Hungary can more easily maintain consumption and investment levels.

Imports from Eastern Europe, especially machinery imports, are important for the USSR. Published Soviet figures suggest that during the first half of the 1980s about a third of all equipment investment was imported, with Eastern Europe providing more than three times as much in value terms (between 20 and 25 percent of the total equipment investment) as the West.[26] Thus, a strong Soviet interest in closer technological cooperation with the Eastern European countries is understandable. So is its desire to obtain more and better quality capital goods from its trade partners.

The purpose of each of the priority specialization programs adopted by the CMEA has been to harness the intellectual-technical capacities of the individual Eastern European countries to assist the Soviet Union in catching up with and maintaining its economic independence from the West. This was the purpose of the specialization program in computers adopted during the early 1970s, the electronic parts and components program instituted during the late 1970s and early 1980s, and the comprehensive program of cooperation in science and technology adopted at the forty-first (special) meeting of the CMEA in December 1985. The last program envisages priority cooperation and progress in electronics, automation, nuclear energy, new materials and technologies, and biotechnology through the creation of mutually compatible technologies and increased specialization and trade throughout the CMEA. A key provision of the program emphasizes direct relations between enterprises and scientific institutes.[27]

There is no reason, however, to believe that Gorbachev's economic objectives vis-à-vis Eastern Europe can be realized more successfully than was the modest and limited success the Soviets had with previous CMEA programs. In fact, the obstacles to Soviet–Eastern European technological and trade cooperation have increased as Eastern Europe's technological and export capabilities have declined because of prolonged deep cuts and stagnation in investment; the severe curtailment in technology, equipment, and component imports from the West; and the region's inability to overcome the systemic problems that also hinder innovation and technological progress in the USSR. Furthermore, Eastern Europe's precarious economic situation means that Soviet pressure or economic leverage is not likely to be effective and may even be counterproductive. Thus, however genuine the Soviet desire to get "more" out of Eastern Europe, objective factors stand in the way of its realization.

Economic Relations with the West

Throughout the 1960s and 1970s, East-West trade increased rapidly. During the early 1970s, the leaderships in the USSR and Eastern Europe tried to reverse the secular decline in growth rates of output and productivity and the growing technological gap vis-à-vis the West by accelerating the import of Western technology. To be sure, there were significant differences in implementation. For example, while Poland imported Western machinery, equipment, and licenses rather indiscriminately, Czechoslovakia was much more cautious. Nevertheless, the decision and implementation of the policy of "staking on the West" were facilitated by the emerging détente between the Soviet Union and the West. With the help of imported technology, the CMEA countries intended to modernize their industries and increase the competitiveness of their exports in Western and CMEA markets. But much of the new capacity created with Western technology was invested in the wrong sectors, or the capacity came on stream with such long delays that in the meantime competitors had already captured the targeted markets.

The accelerated importation of Western technology forced a rapid expansion of complementary imports from the West to operate the new capacity because many needed inputs were not available in sufficient quantities or quality from domestic or CMEA sources. Between 1973 and 1979, Eastern Europe's imports from the Organization for Economic Cooperation and Development (OECD) countries grew from $10 billion to more than $20 billion; the USSR's from $5 billion to more than $20 billion; and the CMEA's from about $15 billion to nearly $45 billion, computed at current values (Figure 3.1). During the same period, the value of the USSR's exports expanded at approximately the same rate, while that of Eastern Europe increased much more slowly (Figure 3.2). Thus, a significant portion of Eastern Europe's imports from the West during the 1970s was obtained on credit.[28]

After 1973, when the Eastern European countries faced the first energy price explosion (Poland and Romania, as net energy exporters at the time, did not suffer) and the ensuing Western recession, their policymakers concluded that the domestic economy should be shielded from these "temporary" adverse developments in the world economy. Most countries compounded this mistake by concluding that the appropriate response to the external shocks was to maintain or accelerate their already rapid growth rates of domestic production, and they did so without adjusting the structure of output to post-1973 scarcities on the world market. Simultaneously they

FIGURE 3.1 OECD Exports to the CMEA, the USSR, and Eastern Europe, 1974–1986 (billions of U.S. $)

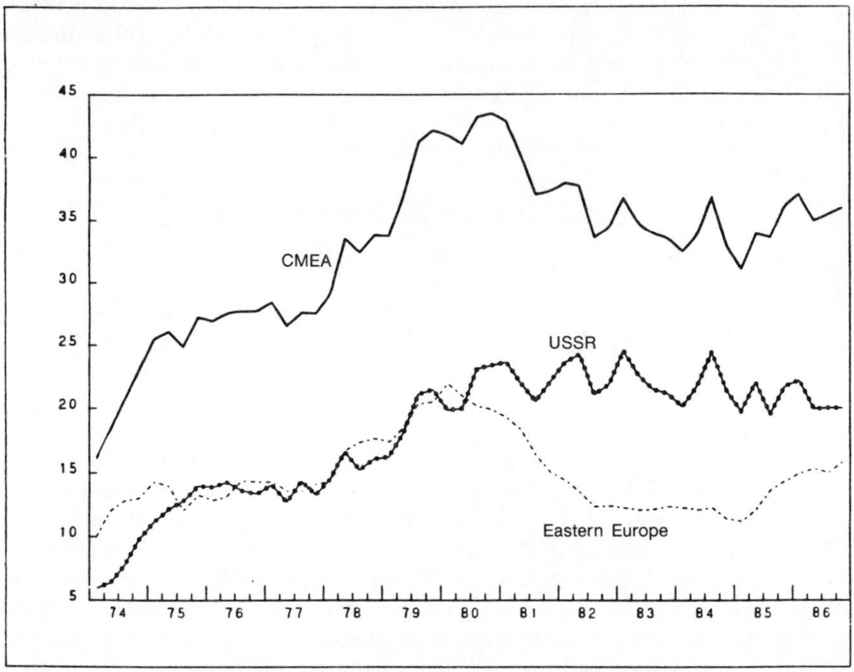

Source: Jan Stankovsky, "Ost-West-Handel 1985/87: Wachsende Probleme zu Beginn des neuen Fünfjahresplanse," Forschungsberichte no. 120 (Vienna: Wiener Institut für Internationale Wirtschaftsvergleiche, August 1986), p. 66.

also tried to maintain the growth of domestic consumption. As a consequence of these policies, the total gross debt of the six Eastern European countries and Yugoslavia to the West increased from $9 billion in 1970 to $84 billion by 1980 (Figure 3.3).

Eastern Europe's large trade and current-account deficits were caused by a combination of bad policy decisions, systemic inefficiencies, and adverse external developments. The shortcomings of the economic system included enterprise incentives to give priority to output rather than profit maximization; a "soft budget constraint" that enables inefficient producers to prosper through government subsidies (which means that efficient producers must bear excessive tax burdens, which limits their expansion); and distorted prices that give the wrong allocation signals. Insufficient attention to costs encourages hoarding and excessive use of materials so that imports are higher than necessary. Desire for output maximization at all levels (producers, planners, political leaders) and soft budget constraint, which engender too many investment projects and the wasteful use of inputs, swell imports. Lack of effective domestic and import competition hinders product innovation

FIGURE 3.2. OECD Imports from the CMEA, the USSR, and Eastern Europe, 1974–1986 (billions of U.S. $)

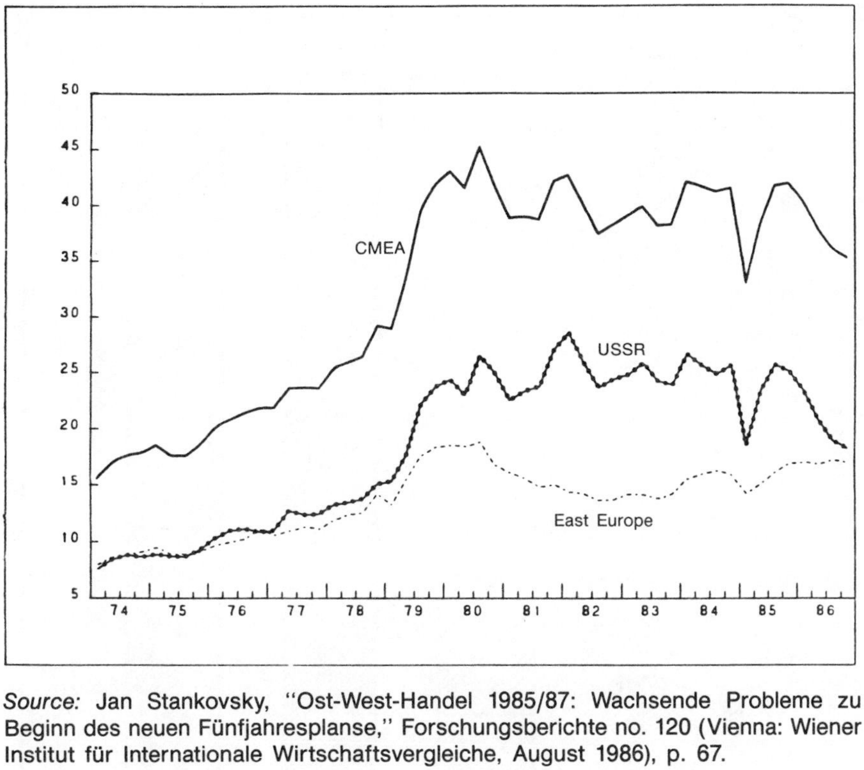

Source: Jan Stankovsky, "Ost-West-Handel 1985/87: Wachsende Probleme zu Beginn des neuen Fünfjahresplanse," Forschungsberichte no. 120 (Vienna: Wiener Institut für Internationale Wirtschaftsvergleiche, August 1986), p. 67.

and flexible adaptation to customer preferences. How can producers of manufactures compete successfully on the world market (and to some extent also on the regional CMEA market) if they have not mastered the competitive skills in their domestic markets?

The Eastern European economies were also adversely affected by changes in their terms of trade, sluggish demand conditions in the markets of their main Western trading partners, and the rising cost and (during 1982–1984) suddenly reduced availability of foreign credits. Some combination of these factors has led all of the Eastern European countries, including Yugoslavia, to accumulate large debts and has eventually pushed several into balance-of-payments crises. There were notable differences, however, in how the countries reacted when the problem reached crisis proportions.

Three countries were forced to reschedule, but with important differences. Poland waited until it had no choice in the matter; it has rescheduled each year since 1981, in the midst of chaotic domestic conditions, and has tried each time to work out the best arrangements for the short run. Romania shared many similarities with Poland until its crisis peaked; thereafter

FIGURE 3.3. Gross Hard-Currency Debt of the Eastern European Countries, Year End, 1970, 1975, 1980, 1983 (billions of current $)

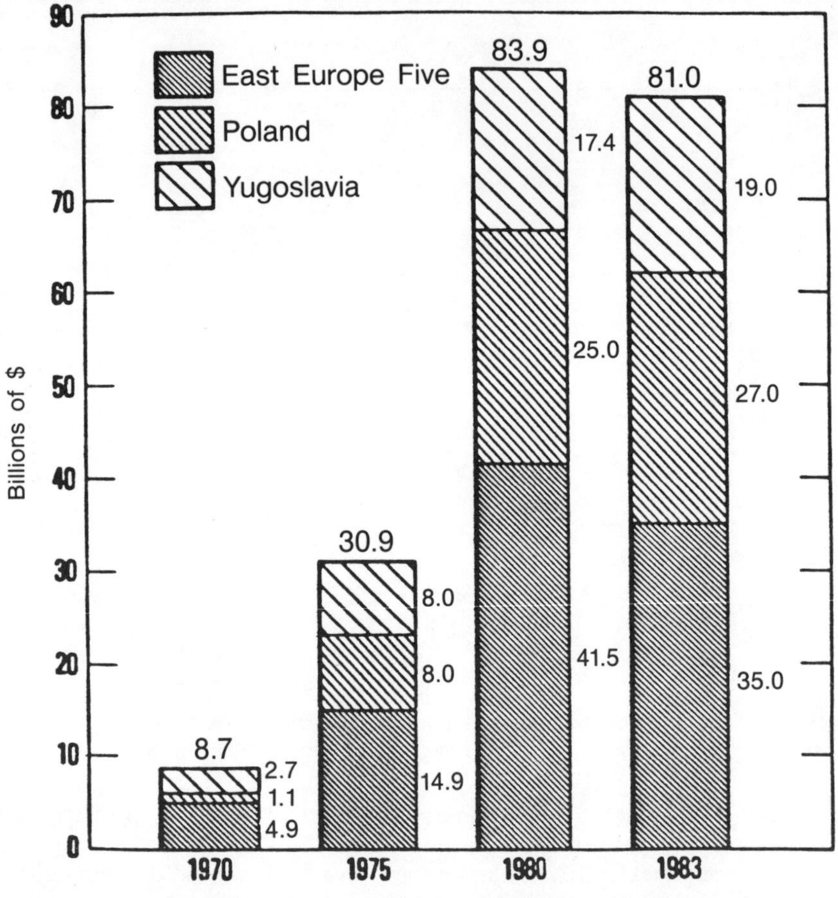

Source: Compiled by the author from various official sources.

Nicolae Ceauşescu decided to substantially reduce the debt, and he cut domestic consumption to the bone in order to do so. Yugoslavia's reschedulings have been more orderly and have been accompanied by substantial new credits. These partly reflect the Western consensus that helping to stabilize Yugoslavia's economy is a way to help it preserve its independence. The task of stabilization is daunting, however, given the extraordinarily high degree of politicization of economic decisions (or their absence) at the macro as well as micro levels. In my view, this factor, more than the system of self-management, is basically responsible for the rapid deterioration of Yugoslavia's economic performance.

Three countries tapped special relationships forged throughout the years to help them manage the crisis. Bulgaria, whose net convertible-currency debt in 1978 approached $4 billion (as a percentage of exports, one of the highest in Eastern Europe), reduced its debt by slowing the growth of its economy, cutting back the output of selected import-intensive products, and by occasional reexport of Soviet oil.[29] Similar domestic adjustments were made several years later by the other Eastern European countries. In addition, West Germany helped the GDR by providing bridge credits. During 1982–1983, Hungary turned to the International Monetary Fund, the World Bank, and the Western financial community to obtain bridge financing, at a time when new credits were not generally available to Eastern Europe. The debt burden of Czechoslovakia was not so substantial as to force the country into a payments crisis.

Eastern Europe's severe payments crisis—not unlike that faced by many Third World countries—dispelled once and for all the earlier conventional wisdom that CPEs can fully control their balances of payments. The crises have also shown that there is no all-encompassing Soviet credit umbrella over Eastern Europe, although the umbrella may be opened to provide some protection, to a few countries, under certain circumstances. The crisis and response also underscored that the Eastern European countries should not be treated as an undifferentiated bloc.

Yet certain broad generalizations can be made. If a country wants to improve its external payments, or is forced to do so because continued deficits cannot be financed, it must improve its "current account." If the country has large outstanding debts on which interest must be paid, the trade deficit must be turned into a trade surplus. Two interrelated policy decisions must then be made: First, a combination of export expansion and import reduction; second, decisions on the components of domestic "absorption" (sum of consumption and investment) that are to be held down to save on imports and to free output for exports.

Eastern European policymakers have had little choice but to rely mostly on cutting imports because they have no surpluses in primary products and a large part of their manufactures are not competitive on world markets. Between 1980 and 1986, neither the Eastern European countries nor the USSR was able to increase the value of exports to the OECD (Figure 3.2), although the volume of their exports grew considerably (Figure 3.4, first pair of inset charts). But they drastically cut the value of their imports from the OECD during 1980–1982, maintained imports at those reduced levels during 1983–1984, and permitted only a modest increase during 1985–1987.

The first pair of inset charts shows that during 1975–1987 the rate of growth of the volume of Eastern European exports was unable to keep pace with the average rate of growth of the volume of Western imports from all sources. The USSR was more successful because of its large energy exports.

The second pair of inset charts shows that whereas Eastern Europe was forced to drastically curtail the *volume* of its imports from the West after 1979, the Soviet Union was able to expand its purchases rapidly until 1984,

FIGURE 3.4. Trade and Payments of Eastern Europe and the USSR with Market Economies, 1975–1987

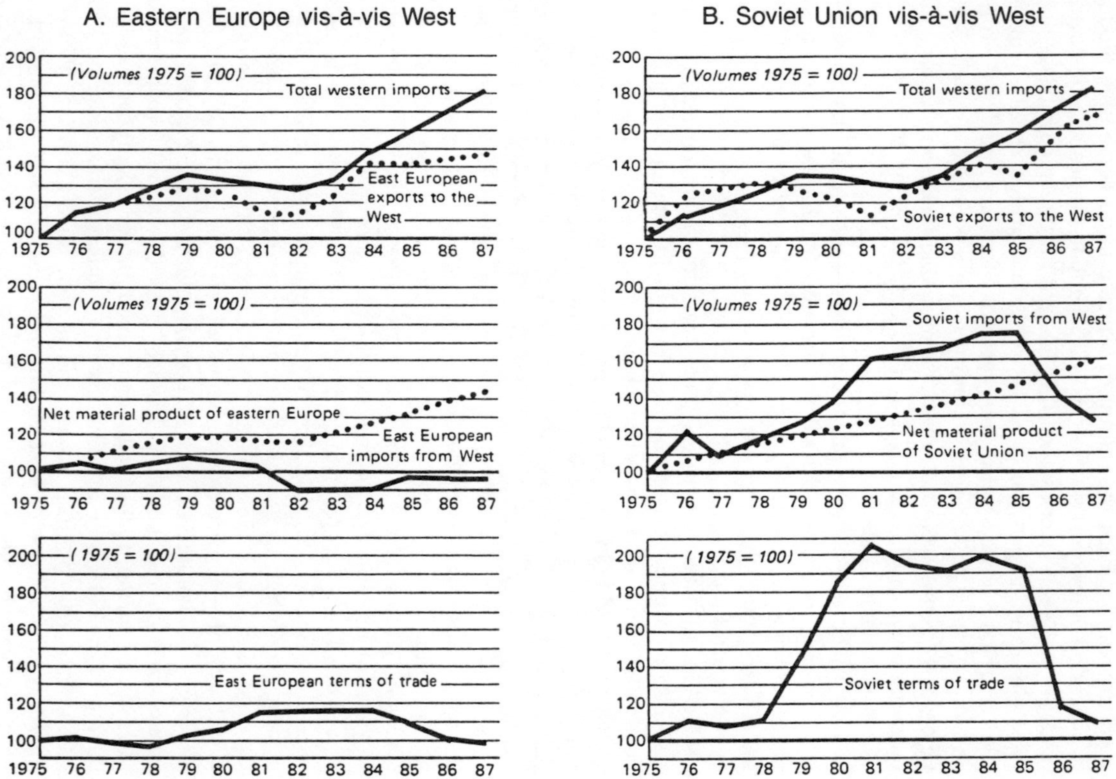

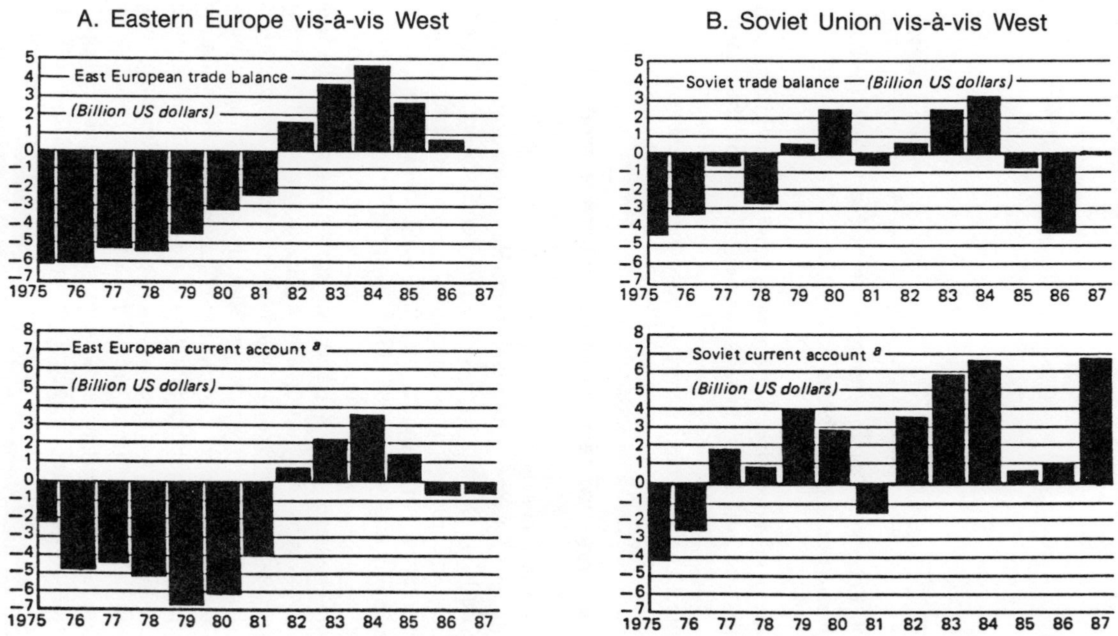

Source: United Nations, Economic Commission for Europe, *Economic Survey of Europe in 1987–1988* (New York: U.N., 1988), p. 290.

TABLE 3.5. Current-Account Balances of Eastern Europe and Romania, 1982-1987 (billions of current $)

	Eastern Europe Six	Romania	Eastern European Five
1982	0.7	0.7	0.0
1983	2.2	0.9	1.3
1984	3.7	1.5	2.2
1985	1.4	0.9	0.5
1986	-0.7	1.4	-2.1
1987	-0.4	2.0	-2.4

Source: United Nations, Economic Commission for Europe, *Economic Survey of Europe in 1987-1988* (New York: U.N., 1988), p. 359.

but thereafter it made deep cuts also. (The reader should not give much significance to the statistics on NMP growth, which represent the biased official figures.)

The third pair of inset charts clearly distinguishes Eastern European trade trends from those of the USSR. Whereas during 1985–1987 Eastern Europe's terms of trade with the West did not change significantly, those of the USSR went on a roller coaster ride, owing to large fluctuations in world energy prices.

The fourth pair of inset charts depicts trade balances with the West. Throughout the 1970s, the Eastern European countries were running large and persistent trade deficits. During 1979–1981, the deficits were reduced, and by 1982–1985 they had turned into substantial yearly trade surpluses. But the more rapid increase in imports that followed nearly eliminated Eastern Europe's trade surpluses by 1986–1987. During the same period, Soviet trade balances with the West exhibited a much more erratic pattern.

The last pair of inset charts shows trends in current-account balances with Western trading partners, including developing countries. (A deficit means that the country is a net borrower vis-à-vis the group of countries depicted; a surplus, that it is a net lender or that its outstanding debt is being reduced.) The total for Eastern Europe hides large differences among the countries. In some years, Romania alone ran a larger current-account surplus than did all of Eastern Europe, so that although Romania was reducing its outstanding debt, the cumulative debts of several other Eastern European countries increased. Hungary's performance was notably poor; it had a significant current-account deficit each year during 1985–1987. Poland, because of large interest obligations on huge outstanding debt, also had a negative balance each year during 1980–1987.[30] Table 3.5 shows that Romania has run a large current-account surplus each year since 1982, which it has used to implement its declared policy of paying interest on outstanding obligations fully and eventually to eliminate its external indebtedness. The sacrifices this policy has required of the population have been so enormous that a large spontaneous demonstration by workers in Braşov erupted in November of 1987, despite the fact that Romania is one of the world's most repressive police states.

The Soviet current-account balance appears favorable, but much of the trade surplus probably reflects the large credits the USSR has been extending for years to developing countries in connection with the sale of arms, factories, and machinery. Presumably, a substantial share of those loans are "soft"—that is, full servicing and repayment are not likely.

Eastern Europe's substantial cut of imports from the West has had severe adverse consequences for its economies. As shown in Figure 3.4 (the second pair of insets), the volume of Eastern Europe's imports in 1987 was still less than the volume of its imports in 1975. Reorienting trade from West to East, or substituting domestic production, was generally not possible because imports from the West were purchased in the first place when the goods were not available from domestic or CMEA sources.

The need to achieve a significant improvement in the current-account balance when debt service obligations are high, when large new credits are not available or not prudent to obtain, and when capacity to increase exports is limited leaves the Eastern European countries no choice but to limit imports from the West. This causes problems and bottlenecks in domestic production. The need to generate an export surplus requires that the real level of domestic "absorption" (spending) remain even less than the level of output, which itself may be growing slowly, stagnating, or declining.

The basic choice is therefore between altering consumption or net investment. The former is difficult for political reasons; the latter, because it tends to reduce future economic and export potential (unless planners succeed in abandoning projects that are uneconomical, in which case output and efficiency may increase). In all of the Eastern European countries except Romania, the largest cuts were made in investment, although in most countries significant reductions were made in consumption as well. The consequence was a deterioration in capital stock throughout Eastern Europe. Today a high percentage of production capacity is made up of aging machinery and obsolete technology.[31] This partly reflects and partly reinforces these economies' system-determined weaknesses for technological innovation. The planners' and enterprise managers' habitual concern with gross output as a key indicator of economic performance, plus the absence of competitive pressures for equipment renewal, accounts for a tendency in CPEs to keep machinery and equipment operating much longer than it would be economical to do so. This is now reinforced by these economies' reduced ability to import Western technology and results in an increasingly obsolete industrial base in Eastern Europe. This in turn contributes to Eastern Europe's declining competitiveness in international markets, as well as to a slowing if not a stagnation in the growth of productivity. Unless these trends can be reversed through fundamental economic reforms, I do not see how continued stagnation or decline in consumption (a significant part of which is subsidized) can be avoided.

Political Implications and the Reform Imperative

Can the traditional or modified CPEs in Eastern Europe, and Yugoslavia with its unique system, avoid continued decline or stagnation in consumption? Can these countries weather a crisis, either internally or externally induced? Fundamental improvement requires that six sets of problems be attacked successfully and more or less simultaneously: macropolicy, sectoral, structural, environmental, systemic, and political reforms.

Macroeconomic policy problems require a two-part reform effort. The first part comprises the maintenance or reestablishment of equilibrium in the domestic economy; the avoidance of "overheating" caused by overambitious plans; a guarantee that the money income of the population is covered by an adequate supply of the right kinds of consumer goods and services; and (once a workable, economy-wide market mechanism is operating), the pursuit of tax, interest rate, and exchange rate policies that provide appropriate incentives. The second is the gradual liberalization of imports and the opening up of the economies to import competition. I believe that Eastern European policymakers are mistaken when they contend that their severe balance-of-payments problems force them to curtail imports. In fact, if producers do not have prompt access to imports (at appropriate exchange rates), they cannot become or remain competitive in world markets with manufactured exports.

The two most important *sectoral* problems are the deterioration in the physical infrastructure and, in several countries, the neglect of agriculture. Rapid industrialization and the wasteful use of inputs were financed throughout the region by holding down personal consumption and by neglecting infrastructure. This now constrains the region in two ways. The outdated infrastructure hinders the adoption of some essential modern technology, such as computer networking, and also causes a growing dissatisfaction in the population, which is unable to gain access to quality goods and essential services (housing, telephones, a good education, and decent medical care). Furthermore, much of the limited investment in infrastructure is concentrated in the cities, which makes even slower any improvements in the quality of life in the countryside.

The poor performance of agriculture and the neglect of food processing create costly imbalances. Although in several countries agriculture absorbs a disproportionately large share of total investment and labor, many countries face shortages of certain kinds of food product that put a strain on the balance of payments and further stir up public discontent. Even in Hungary, where agricultural output has risen impressively since the early 1960s, the neglect of the food processing industries is causing serious problems.

Structural problems derive from the unwavering priority given to rapid expansion of the production of energy-intensive and raw material–intensive investment goods. Four decades of such an "industrial policy" has created a production structure that is no longer adapted to the present and future needs of economic development and external competitiveness. Although the decisionmakers have realized this for some time, so far they have not demonstrated the political will, nor have they designed an appropriate mechanism of investment decisionmaking, to deal with the problem in a meaningful way.

The *environmental* problem—rapid deterioration in the quality of the environment—is becoming increasingly serious throughout Eastern Europe. In the midst of sustained economic crises, the authorities appear unable to effectively manage the problem. This contributes to the growing political tension between the authorities and the population.

The *systemic* problems manifest themselves in the low level of labor productivity and increasing capital intensity throughout the region. To solve them, the six countries must find an ideologically and politically acceptable model of a socialist yet efficient economic system. In my view, such a model does not yet exist, which is not to say that significant and sustained improvements in performance may not be possible, with or without major alterations in the economic system. Systemic reforms must proceed on two parallel tracks: the permanent expansion of the scope and operational freedom of the private sector and the "marketization" of the operations of state-owned enterprises (a much more difficult task).

The *political* problem the regimes face is the almost complete absence of legitimacy in some countries and inadequate legitimacy in the others. This constrains economic performance and the prospects that reforms can improve it. The absence of political legitimacy generates widespread cynicism and apathy in the economic sphere as well. In my view, the most feasible solution may not lie in the introduction of a Western-type democracy with a multiparty system. Rather, the solution may lie in increasing the separation between the party and the economy; in finding ways for political leaders to be accountable for their actions; and in developing institutionalized means to air and resolve inevitable conflicts among interest groups, many of which are economically based.

Although the introduction of fundamental reforms of the kind sketched here is clearly imperative, their implementation faces severe obstacles. One is that the more comprehensive the reforms, the greater the opposition to them by vested interests. For example, significant cuts in subsidies are painful, as are, for some, the discontinuation of preference for enterprises in the heavy industries (which have powerful lobbies) in favor of light industries and the service sector. The distorted wage structure will have to be rectified by raising the relative income positions of professionals, such as scientists, engineers, and educators. Labor discipline will have to be improved significantly and across the board. For a time, inflation and unemployment may rise, and income distribution will become less egalitarian. Disturbances of these vested interests are sure to create political tensions that are exceedingly difficult to manage. Another serious obstacle is the exercise of political power. Will the Communist parties in these countries be willing to exercise power differently? Will the parties significantly reduce their pervasive role in economic decisions and transfer considerable political power, say, to Parliament? Will those members be competitively elected?

It is not surprising that Eastern Europe's aging leaders are especially reluctant to face these new political risks. Nevertheless, the Gorbachev-initiated discussion of some of these issues in the USSR means that authorities in the Eastern European countries now also have a freer hand to tackle them. This was demonstrated by the unceremonious replacement in May 1988 of Hungary's seventy-six-year-old leader, János Kádár, by Károly Grósz which at least suggested that implementation of the kinds of major reform Kádár was unwilling to endorse might now be possible. Sooner or later, the other Eastern European countries must do likewise, but the reform strategies, their timing, and the outcomes will still be country specific.

Acknowledgments

I thank J. M. Montias for permission to incorporate the valuable comments he made on an early version of this chapter, William Griffith for his suggestions and editorial assistance, and the following colleagues for their comments on an early draft or for insights on particular points: Tamás Bácskai, Tamás Bauer, Seweryn Bialer, György Enyedi, Charles Gati, Eva Ehrlich, Iván Major, Hanns-Dieter Jacobsen, Michael Mandelbaum, Vojtech Mastny, Catherine Sokil, and Angela Stent. I also thank Eva Ehrlich for permission to cite the results of her computations of the dollar per capita GNP levels of countries.

Notes

1. I. Berend, "The Problem of Eastern European Economic Integration in Historical Perspective," in I. Vajda and M. Simai, eds., *Foreign Trade in a Planned Economy* (Cambridge: Cambridge University Press, 1971), p. 17.
2. Paul Marer, *Dollar GNPs of the U.S.S.R. and Eastern Europe* (Baltimore, Md.: Johns Hopkins University Press for the World Bank, 1985).
3. V. Selunin and G. Hanin, "Can We Trust in Our Production Statistics?" (in Russian), *Novy mir* (Moscow), no. 2 (1987), p. 3.
4. Jan Vanous, "The Soviet Economic Information System and Its Impact on Economic Reform." *PlanEcon Report* 3, no. 46 (November 12, 1987), pp. 3–7.
5. A. G. Aganbegyan, "Problems in the Radical Restructuring of Economic Management in the USSR." (Moscow: August 1987, unpublished), p. 3.
6. Eva Ehrlich, "Absolute and Relative Economic Development Levels and Their Structure, 1937–1980" (Budapest: 1987, unpublished).
7. Jan Winiecki, "Four Kinds of Fallacies in Comparing Market-Type and Soviet-Type Economies" (Stockholm: Institute for International Economic Studies, July 1987). This is the source of much of my information on the problems of measuring the standard of living.
8. Peter Wiles, quoted in ibid., p. 26.
9. To be sure, my assumption that in 1937 the two parts of Germany were equally developed may be incorrect, so that some gap in favor of the western part of Germany may have existed before the war as well. If so, the GDR's "slide" between 1937 and 1960 was less than here indicated.

10. Gur Ofer, "Growth Strategy Specialization in Agriculture, and Trade: Bulgaria and Eastern Europe," in Paul Marer and J. M. Montias, eds., *East European Integration and East-West Trade* (Bloomington: Indiana University Press, 1980), pp. 283–313.

11. Nick Eberstadt, "Health of an Empire: Poverty and Social Progress in the CMEA Bloc," in Henry Rowen and Charles Wolf, Jr., eds., *The Future of the Soviet Empire* (Santa Monica, Calif.: Rand Corporation, 1988), pp. 227–228.

12. Tamás Bauer, "Crisis Instead of Cycles?" (in Hungarian), *Közgazdasági szemle* (Budapest) 34, no. 12 (December 1987), p. 1423.

13. Paul Marer and J. M. Montias, "Theory and Measurement of East European Integration," in Marer and Montias, eds., *East European Integration*, pp. 5–16.

14. Paul Marer, "Soviet Economic Policy in Eastern Europe," in John P. Hardt (ed.), *Reorientation and Commercial Relations of the Economies of Eastern Europe* (Washington, D.C.: U.S. Government Printing Office, 1974).

15. Details can be found in J. M. Montias, *Economic Development in Communist Romania* (Cambridge, Mass.: MIT Press, 1967).

16. Michael Marrese and Jan Vanous, *Soviet Subsidization of Trade with Eastern Europe: A Soviet Perspective* (Berkeley: Institute of International Studies of the University of California, 1983), pp. 52–60.

17. Paul Marer, "The Political Economy of Soviet Relations with Eastern Europe," in Sarah M. Terry, ed., *Soviet Policy in Eastern Europe* (New Haven, Conn.: Yale University Press, 1984), pp. 171–186.

18. Marrese and Vanous, *Soviet Subsidization*, pp. 145–149.

19. Franklyn D. Holzman, *The Economics of Soviet Bloc Trade and Finance* (Boulder, Colo.: Westview Press, 1987), pp. 187–197.

20. See Chapter 2 in this volume.

21. Bauer, "Crisis Instead," pp. 1418–1420. No information is available for the GDR and Romania.

22. Ibid., p. 1424.

23. Philip Hanson, "Soviet Foreign Trade Policies in the 1980s" (Cologne: Bericht 41-1986 des Bundesinstituts für ostwissenschaftliche und internationale Studien, 1986), pp. 27–28.

24. As the currencies of the CMEA countries are not convertible, neither are any trade surpluses that may be generated, unless there is a special agreement to settle a balance in convertible currency. Therefore, it is not in the interest of any CPE to permit surpluses with other CPEs to develop or to repay credits faster than necessary.

25. András Köves, "A New Situation in Hungarian-Soviet Trade: What Is to Be Done?" (Paper presented at the Conference on the Challenge of Simultaneous Economic Relations with East and West, Bellagio, Italy, March 1–4, 1988).

26. Hanson, "Soviet Foreign Trade Policies," pp. 27–28, 61.

27. United Nations, *World Economic Survey, 1987* (New York: U.N., 1987), p. 126.

28. Jan Stankovsky, "Ost-West-Handel 1985/87: Wachsende Probleme zu Beginn des neuen Fünfjahresplanse," Forschungsberichte no. 120 (Vienna: Wiener Institut für Internationale Wirtschaftsvergleiche, August 1986).

29. J. M. Montias, "Industrial Policy and Foreign Trade in Bulgaria" (unpublished manuscript, 1987).

30. United Nations, Economic Commission for Europe, *Economic Survey of Europe in 1986–1987* (New York: U.N., 1987), p. 21.

31. This is documented for Poland, and its effect on the country's trade is elaborated in K. Poznanski, "The Competitiveness of Polish Industry and Indebtedness," in P. Marer and W. Siwinski, eds., *Creditworthiness and Reform in Poland: Western and Polish Perspectives* (Bloomington: Indiana University Press, 1988), pp. 45–57.

APPENDIX 3.1

Ranking by Development Levels and Changes in Relative Positions of Thirty-Two Countries, 1937, 1960, 1970 and 1980 (in current U.S. $ of the corresponding year)

Countries in order of 1937	National Income/SNA $/capita	
	1937	
	Rank	U.S. = 100
United States	1	100
United Kingdom	2	77.2
Australia	3	75.2
New Zealand	4	71.9
Sweden	5	70.2
Canada	6	62.5
FRG[a]	7-8	59.6
GDR[b]	7-8	59.6
Denmark	9	59.6
Belgium and Luxembourg	10	57.9
Switzerland	11	56.1
The Netherlands	12	53.7
Norway	13	52.6
France	14	46.5
Argentina	15	38.6
Finland	16	37.5
Austria	17	33.3
Ireland	18	31.6
Czechoslovakia	19	29.8
South Africa	20	27.2
Chile	21	26.3
Italy	22	23.7
Japan	23	23.7
Hungary	24	21.1
Poland	25	17.5
Spain	26	16.7
Portugal	27	16.3
Greece	28	16.1
Mexico	29	15.3
Romania	30	14.2
Yugoslavia	31	14.0
Bulgaria	32	13.2

[a]Reduced to present territory.

[b]The scholar who did these computations, Eva Ehrlich, did not make any assumption about the prewar per capita income of the present territory of the GDR relative to the rest of Germany and did not rank order the GDR. I, however, assumed that the territory that presently constitutes the GDR had the same level of per capita income in 1937 as did the part of the country that presently constitutes the FRG. Computations by Paul Gregory and Gert

APPENDIX 3.1 (*continued*)

Countries in order of 1937	Dollar GNP Per Capita					
	1960		1970		1980	
	Rank	U.S. = 100	Rank	U.S. = 100	Rank	U.S. = 100
United States	1	100	1	100	1	100
United Kingdom	6	58.3	8	59.0	15	57.7
Australia	4	65.1	4	67.0	3	78.5
New Zealand	5	63.9	7	59.5	14	59.2
Sweden	3	67.6	2	76.0	4	77.8
Canada	2	84.5	3	72.0	2	87.4
FRG[a]	9	50.0	11	55.0	6	71.2
GDR[b]	16	35.1	17	39.0	17	45.9
Denmark	8	51.0	5	60.0	13	60.2
Belgium and Luxembourg	11	47.9	12	53.0	7	70.3
Switzerland	7	55.8	9	58.0	9	69.0
The Netherlands	12	45.0	6	60.0	11	60.5
Norway	10	49.0	10	57.0	8	69.9
France	13	41.3	13	47.0	10	63.8
Argentina	21	22.7	21	28.0	26	22.5
Finland	15	37.6	14	47.0	5	73.4
Austria	14	38.0	15	45.0	12	60.4
Ireland	18	27.3	18	35.0	20	36.3
Czechoslovakia	17	34.7	19	35.0	19	42.3
South Africa	24	20.2	25	19.0	30	17.4
Chile	27	15.7	30	14.0	31	16.2
Italy	20	24.4	20	33.0	18	43.1
Japan	19	24.8	16	43.0	16	56.8
Hungary	22	21.1	23	23.0	22	31.7
Poland	23	20.7	24	21.0	24	27.3
Spain	26	16.5	22	24.0	21	35.4
Portugal	29	14.0	28	16.0	29	19.6
Greece	30	14.0	26	18.0	25	27.2
Mexico	28	14.5	32	13.0	32	13.2
Romania	31	14.0	31	14.0	28	21.3
Yugoslavia	32	13.6	29	15.0	27	21.9
Bulgaria	25	17.1	27	18.0	23	29.9

Leptin ("Similar Societies Under Differing Economic Systems: Case of the Two Germanies," *Soviet Studies* 29, no. 4 [1977]) show that in 1936 the territory that is now the GDR had per capita GNP equal to 98 percent of that of the present territory of the FRG. But they also show that by 1948 the eastern part's income level was 17 percent lower than the western part's, presumably because war damage was greater, postwar reconstruction was slower, and reparation deliveries had to be made to the USSR. Some experts do not accept that the two regions were comparably developed before the war. Indeed, although Saxony and the area around Berlin were quite developed, the eastern part of Germany as a whole was more agrarian and possessed less heavy industry than did the other part of Germany.

Source: Eva Ehrlich, "Absolute and Relative Economic Development Levels and Their Structure, 1937-1980" (Budapest: 1987, unpublished), p. 15.

4

Technology Transfer to Eastern Europe: Paradoxes, Policies, Prospects

Angela Stent

As we approach the twenty-first century, a country's level of technological development will increasingly determine its political, military, and economic influence in the world. The United States is concerned about its technological prowess compared to that of Japan; and Western Europe realizes that it is technologically behind the United States in some microelectronic fields. Yet, from an Eastern European perspective, both the United States and Western Europe are more advanced technologically than is any member of the Council for Mutual Economic Assistance (CMEA) and, as Eastern Europe is aware, the technology gap is growing. These facts of international economic life form the basis of Eastern and Western policies. The West wants to maintain its technological lead over the East, although there is disagreement within the North Atlantic Treaty Organization (NATO) about how great that lead is and should be. The East, however, tries to acquire as much Western technology as possible, by legal or illegal means, but its economic performance continues to decline. The subject of technology transfer to Eastern Europe is therefore characterized by conflicting pressures and policies between the two alliance systems and within them.

Western technology transfer policies toward the Communist world have been characterized for four decades by internal debate and a tendency toward inconsistency. These policies have provoked arguments within NATO because there is no consensus about their impact on Eastern Europe. The allied disputes highlight the problems in postwar Western policy toward Eastern Europe that go beyond economics. Quite simply, both the United States and Western Europe have historically pursued a policy toward Eastern Europe that is primarily determined by their relations with the Soviet Union, although their declaratory goal has usually been to encourage greater Eastern European autonomy from Moscow.

The Federal Republic of Germany (FRG) is the only Western country that has consistently pursued an active policy toward one Eastern European country in the postwar era, the German Democratic Republic (GDR). Indeed, much of the FRG's policy toward the Soviet Union has been determined by Bonn's *Deutschlandpolitik,* instead of the other way round. This policy, which once tried to isolate the GDR, is no longer directed toward that or toward loosening Moscow's ties with East Berlin. The FRG also has the largest economic stake in Eastern Europe. Recently, the FRG and other Western European countries, whose interests are largely regional, began to develop a more differentiated policy toward Eastern Europe. The United States, whose interests and responsibilities are global, remains preoccupied with the Soviet Union, its chief antagonist, and continues to regard Eastern Europe as an extension of the Soviet Union, particularly for purposes of technology transfer.

Overall, the United States and its allies have disagreed on the role of economic ties in East-West relations. The United States, which is far less dependent on trade for its economic viability than is Western Europe or Japan, and which has virtually no historic trade ties to Eastern Europe, has tended to regard trade with CMEA as economically marginal and politically and morally questionable. Successive U.S. administrations have stressed that because the USSR is the country's chief antagonist, and because much of the defense budget is spent on protecting it from the Soviet threat, it makes no sense to strengthen CMEA economies, which are weaker than those of the Western alliance. On the other hand, some business groups and other sectors of the population, occasionally supported by the administration, have argued that East-West trade is economically and politically beneficial because it can improve relations between the two superpowers. These groups have been criticized by organized labor and various ethnic groups that oppose doing anything to support Communist governments. The whole subject, therefore, remains controversial.

In Western Europe and Japan, particularly among those countries with long historical ties to Eastern Europe, trade with CMEA is a normal, desirable aspect of international commerce. Indeed, Western Europeans prefer to separate politics and trade and reject economic sanctions as an acceptable means of pursuing Western interests in Eastern Europe and the USSR. The United States, on the other hand, encourages the politicization of East-West trade, particularly through the use of sanctions and other legally based foreign policy controls. Both tactics are largely a response to domestic lobbying groups.

The United States and Western Europe would have a variety of technologies to offer Eastern Europe if there were no restrictions on technology exports; but a range of export controls limits the nature of the East-West technological exchange. The United States is the only Western nation that has a more or less clearly defined technology transfer policy enshrined in national law. These national controls also affect Western Europe because they form the basis of the multilateral controls imposed by the Coordinating Committee

(COCOM) in Paris, whose members include all NATO countries and Japan (but minus Iceland).

This chapter will analyze Western technology transfer policy in light of a complex mosaic of national and multilateral policies. Although the real target of U.S. policy is the Soviet Union, the U.S. attempt to pursue a policy of economic and technological containment of the USSR has affected Western and Eastern Europe. Moreover, Western debates about technology transfer have intensified as East-West trade has slackened in recent years. This chapter will outline the nature of the Western debate about technology transfer; survey the postwar development of technology transfer policies; discuss the impact of the 1982–1983 pipeline crisis on Western policy; examine Eastern Europe's technological needs; and discuss the current state of the debate and prospects for future changes. This chapter will show that Eastern Europe's consciousness of the need to catch up with the West is growing as the region is falling further and further behind technologically. But as long as Western policy remains restrictive, it will deny Eastern Europe the wherewithal to become a technological equal to the West.

Of course, Eastern Europe, like the Soviet Union, pursues an active policy of illegal, although now more visible, technology acquisition and technological espionage in the United States and Western Europe. These activities indicate how important Western technology is to CMEA countries. But this chapter will not detail these activities because of lack of data in the public domain. It will examine the relationship of technology transfer to domestic economic organization and highlight a further significant point: Without thoroughgoing structural economic reform, even unrestricted imports or theft of Western technology would probably not solve Eastern Europe's economic problems or overcome its technological backwardness. The answer to Eastern Europe's technological problems lies not in the West, but primarily in the East.

Technology Transfer: Definition, Measurement, Classification

Definitions of Technology

Much has been written about technology transfer from West to East, often in highly partisan terms. Yet very rarely do its proponents or opponents produce a clear definition of technology. This reflects a lack of agreement within the Western alliance on what constitutes technology and on how to measure its international flow.

According to one authoritative definition, technology involves the "application of scientific knowledge to practical purposes."[1] Most analysts agree that technology comprises tangible products (embodied technology) and intangible knowledge (disembodied technology). Although one can attempt to control the flow of the former, it is virtually impossible to control the latter. Anyone can purchase Western scientific and technological publications that contain a wide variety of technological information.

When we speak of technology transfer, therefore, we are dealing with the transfer of capability, an inherently difficult process to quantify. The Organization for Economic Cooperation and Development (OECD), which has published the most comprehensive studies of East-West technology transfer, focuses on embodied technology (products, licenses, and some forms of industrial cooperation) in its statistical studies because disembodied technology transfer is nearly impossible to measure. Thus, any data involved in quantifying technology transfer can become the subject of dispute. The U.S. government has attempted to classify high technology by issuing periodic statistics on East-West technology transfer using categories drawn from Standard International Trade Classifications. This classification scheme summarizes trade information by organizing commodities into different groupings. No U.S. ally has officially adopted this means of definition.

In 1976, the United States adopted a restrictive definition of technology when it issued a Department of Defense (DOD) report entitled *An Analysis of Export Controls of U.S. Technology—A DoD Perspective,* commonly known as the Bucy Report. This report differentiated "evolutionary" from "revolutionary" technology and advocated severe restrictions on the export of design and manufacturing know-how combined with a lessening of controls on certain machinery. The Bucy Report proposed that the transfer of "critical technologies" to CMEA nations should be carefully controlled. The critical technology approach assumes that "one can select the subset of technologies of significant military value on which our national military technology superiority can be presumed to be most dependent."[2] As a result of this report, DOD produced a *Militarily Critical Technologies List,* which runs 700 pages in its classified and 150 in its unclassified version. This list, which is embodied in U.S. national export control laws, is the only official definition of technology for the purpose of making licensing decisions. The United States' COCOM partners are skeptical about how one can implement such a comprehensive list in concrete export licensing decisions. Nevertheless, all NATO members accept that they should not export the latest microelectronic technology to CMEA, but they disagree on how to define high, as opposed to low and medium, technology.

Civilian Versus Military Technology

Another major area of Western disagreement is the distinction between civilian and military technology. All COCOM members agree that they should not sell nuclear missiles or tanks to the Soviet bloc; but whereas the United States has in the past argued that certain washing machines should not be exported because their electronic controls contain technology whose application in military spheres would strengthen Communist power, the Europeans and Japanese consider this definition of "dual-use" technology far too broad and unenforceable. Moreover, those in the United States who favor strict export controls argue that the USSR and Eastern Europe are able to turn civilian technology into military uses. Europeans are generally more skeptical about CMEA's ability to utilize these technologies for either military or civilian purposes in any way that threatens Western security.

The United States defines a security threat as anything that can contribute indirectly to the Warsaw Pact's military might. At its broadest, this would include any technology that strengthens any part of the CMEA industrial base. The U.S. allies favor a narrower definition—military technology is anything that has direct application to the conduct of war. As microelectronic chips, for instance, become smaller, cheaper, and more powerful, the question of the difference between civilian and military use, particularly in the computer sphere, will become increasingly cloudy. Moreover there is also the unresolved question of which civilian technologies that are exported to Eastern Europe could ultimately enhance Soviet military might.

How Does One Define National Security?

Underlying these debates is a fundamental transatlantic disagreement on what enhances or threatens national security. The U.S. concept of security has tended to be primarily military, whereas that espoused by the Western Europeans and the Japanese is economic as well as military. As a leading European proponent of East-West trade has written, "It is impossible to prove—with the exclusion of a few high technology areas—that East-West trade adds more to Soviet power than it contributes to the well-being of Western economies."[3] From the European point of view, a healthy economy with a strong export sector ensures domestic sociopolitical stability and thus contributes to national security. If technology exports to the East provide more jobs, then they enhance Western security. The United States has tended to emphasize the dangers to national security arising from exporting to the Warsaw Pact nations, probably because its own economic ties with these nations are far less important than those of Western Europe. Washington argues for a broader definition of what threatens national security and a narrower definition of what enhances it than does either London, Paris, Bonn, or Tokyo. A systematic debate about the relationship between economics and national security has only recently begun in the United States.

How Important Is Western Technology for CMEA Economies?

Any viable technology transfer policy should be based on a NATO consensus on the impact of Western technology on these economies. But there is no agreement in the West on this central question for two reasons: The CMEA countries provide inadequate statistics; and, even if one had the data and could agree on how to define technology, it is conceptually very difficult to measure the contribution of Western technology to the economic growth rate or productivity rate of any particular sector or of a national economy as a whole. Most Western studies on the impact of Western technology have focused on the Soviet Union. (The OECD has published studies on selected Eastern European countries, but the information available on these economies is incomplete.) The literature about the USSR, however, reflects many of the arguments about Eastern Europe. The essential question is: How efficiently can CMEA countries, with socialist economic systems and political cultures so different from the West and which are years behind the West technologically, absorb and diffuse Western technology, which is the product of a capitalist economic system?

On one end of the political spectrum, Anthony Sutton, in his voluminous study *Western Technology and Soviet Economic Development, 1945 to 1965,* argued that all technology exports to the USSR have fueled Soviet military might. "It is the availability of Western technology that makes Soviet industry more efficient—The Soviet Union and its socialist allies are dependent on the Western world for technical and economic viability—We have constructed and maintain a first-order threat to Western society."[4]

Sutton's words of warning have since been echoed by all those opposed to trade with CMEA, from the public and private sectors. His conclusions, however, have been refuted by many Western economic specialists on CMEA. Most recent analyses of the impact of Western technology on the USSR and Eastern Europe argue that it has been marginal but not irrelevant. Active technology transfer mechanisms—that is, joint ventures and other arrangements whereby Western firms participate directly in production—are more successful than passive mechanisms, such as the purchase of licenses. Although Western equipment has probably retarded further economic decline and enhanced economic growth by removing bottlenecks in certain sectors, it has not been able to solve the major economic difficulty of these countries—their lack of export competitiveness—because their systems cannot absorb and diffuse Western technology efficiently. Indeed, the cost of some technology imports may have been more than the benefit. Analyses of selected Eastern European countries emphasize that unless these countries introduce significant economic reforms, they cannot fully benefit from Western technology imports, particularly in their export sectors. The information revolution provides an instructive example here. Even if a CMEA country were able to manufacture or import all the personal computers it desires, it could probably not make optimal use of these computers because its entire socioeconomic system is inimical to the free flow of ideas and information and to innovation in general. Western technology that is a product of Western political culture and the market economy cannot be fully effective in a state-controlled, centralized economy with a more authoritarian political system. Indeed, the very factors that hinder the efficient utilization of Western technology also hinder the development of indigenous technological capability in Eastern Europe.

What Is the Linkage Between Technology Transfer and International Politics?

Any nation that participates in East-West technology transfer recognizes that it cannot be divorced from the overall economic and political climate. Nevertheless, Eastern and Western Europeans agree that trade and technology transfer policy should be insulated from political interference as much as possible because it is economically too important to be jeopardized and provides one channel of nonantagonistic communication. The United States, by contrast, has always regarded its economic ties with CMEA as inherently political because they are economically marginal. U.S. legislation enables the president and the Congress to restrict trade for national security and for foreign policy purposes—for instance, to respond to the Soviet invasion of Afghanistan or to the imposition of martial law in Poland. But this causes problems with the allies, who point to a basic inconsistency: If technology transfer decisions are to be made on technical grounds related to national security, then a nation should not suddenly change these criteria in response to political events. Interfering with trade policies for ad hoc political reasons means that policies are inherently inconsistent and unpredictable. If it is permissible to sell oil drilling equipment to the Soviets because the technology does not threaten Western security, then the treatment of dissidents should not alter this judgment, as it did during the Carter administration.

The United States has used economic sanctions to punish the Soviets—or Poles—retroactively for activities of which it disapproves or as a deterrent to future undesirable actions. U.S. allies do not have legislation that empowers them to impose such foreign policy controls on their exports. They reject the use of economic sanctions for political reasons. They accept the possibility of using economic incentives for political purposes, but prefer to separate their economic and political relations. The United States has also politicized trade policies by differentiating between some Eastern European states—Romania, Poland, and Hungary, for instance—and the USSR in granting most favored nation (MFN) status. Hungary receives special treatment because of its relative domestic liberalization. Poland and Romania have, at different times, received MFN for domestic or foreign policy reasons. Western Europe grants MFN to all CMEA nations. But the U.S. policy of differentiation does not apply to technology transfer because Washington assumes that any technology sold to Eastern Europe could find its way to the USSR. In COCOM, only the People's Republic of China (PRC) now receives special treatment as a "friendly, less developed nation," and the United States introduces the lion's share of COCOM exception requests for Beijing. This position is viewed by most other COCOM members with a healthy dose of skepticism. They suspect that the United States is ostensibly using political criteria—the PRC's rapprochement with the West—to gain commercial advantage.

On the other hand, former assistant secretary of defense for international security policy, Richard Perle, had another explanation for this phenomenon: "If anyone doubts my skepticism about how our allies administer and enforce the rules, consider this: the U.S. has 15 times as many licenses as Japan awaiting COCOM review for sales to China. Either we are doing 15 times as much business as the Japanese in high-technology exports to China or the Japanese aren't bothering even to request licenses."[5]

The Evolution of Western Policy

The United States

The United States has always led in shaping multilateral Western policies. Immediately after 1945, there was some debate about whether to encourage trade with the USSR. After the Soviet takeover of Eastern Europe, the United States adopted a policy of economic warfare toward the Soviet Union and its partners. Because it was thought possible that the Soviet bloc might go to war with the United States, it made no sense to trade with the bloc. The 1949 Export Control Act imposed severe restrictions on the export of all goods to Communist nations. The 1951 Mutual Defense Assistance Control Act (known as the Battle Act) empowered the president to terminate all forms of military, economic, and financial assistance to any nation that sold embargoed goods to a prohibited destination. This enabled the United States to impose sanctions on its allies, most of whom were receiving Marshall Plan aid, if they violated the Export Control Act. The premise behind U.S. policy was that the West could weaken the Soviet economy and retard the growth of the Soviet military-industrial strength by denying it machinery exports.

U.S. policy remained unchanged until the Kennedy administration, which began to retreat from economic warfare by selling grain to the USSR. Technology transfer remained severely restricted, however, as the 1963 allied dispute about the construction of the friendship oil pipeline showed. (In this dispute, Washington tried to get its allies to cancel exports of large-diameter pipe to the USSR. Only the FRG complied.) This dual agricultural/industrial policy continued under President Lyndon Johnson who, in 1965, created a special committee on U.S. trade with Eastern Europe and the Soviet Union. Johnson's policy of "bridge building" was the first explicit U.S. attempt to differentiate between Eastern Europe and the Soviet Union economically and thus to encourage Eastern European autonomy from Moscow through the use of trade incentives. Nevertheless, technology transfer was still excepted from this liberalization.

Since the 1960s, the basic dilemma for U.S. policy has been how to reconcile the desire to encourage Eastern European independence from the Soviet Union with the conviction that Eastern Europe must be treated as indistinguishable from the Soviet Union for national security reasons. As a result, the United States policy of liberalizing trade with Eastern Europe is limited to nontechnological areas.

The major change in U.S. policy toward the USSR and Eastern Europe came under the Nixon administration, which introduced the first large-scale liberalization of export controls. The 1969 Export Administration Act, which replaced the Export Control Act, was based on the assumption that trade and technology transfer to CMEA countries should be encouraged, unless it could detrimentally affect U.S. security. The act placed the burden of proof on the opponents, rather than on the proponents, of commerce with Communist nations.

Although the Democratic-controlled Congress passed this act, it was determined to assert its right over the Nixon administration to make foreign policy in other areas, which was a response to the period of the Vietnam War when the powers of the Congress had been eclipsed by the presidency. Congress therefore refused to accept the Nixon-Kissinger economic détente and instead passed the Jackson-Vanik amendment in 1973, which denied the Soviet Union and Eastern Europe MFN status unless they liberalized emigration policies. Subsequently, in 1974, the Stevenson amendment set a low limit on official credits for the Soviet Union, irrespective of its behavior on human rights questions. After 1976, three Eastern European nations were granted MFN—Poland (since 1956), Romania and Hungary (in 1976)—although this required annual waivers under the terms of Jackson-Vanik.

President Jimmy Carter, with his strong commitment to human rights, began by encouraging trade with the USSR and Eastern Europe. Yet he later imposed sanctions on the Soviet Union for its treatment of dissidents and embargoed grain sales after the invasion of Afghanistan. Nevertheless, Eastern Europe remained largely untouched by these actions. Under President Ronald Reagan, a tighter technology export policy combined with encouragement of grain sales to the USSR revived debates about the utility of economic warfare. As a response to the imposition of martial law in Poland, the Reagan administration imposed trade sanctions against the Soviet Union and Poland. East-West trade policy became more restrictive under the Reagan administration, and the DOD was given more power over licensing decisions.

A perennial difficulty in formulating any coherent East-West technology export policy (or any other aspect of foreign policy, for that matter) is the cacophony of inputs from the various branches of the U.S. government, not to mention the Congress, domestic lobbies, and other interest groups. There is no single national U.S. policy because different branches of the government espouse contrasting views on the subject. There is rivalry within the executive branch, especially between the Department of Defense, which favors a highly restrictive policy and is disinclined to differentiate among various East European countries, and the Departments of Commerce and State, which favor a more flexible, less restrictive policy and do differentiate among Eastern European countries. (There were also disagreements within these departments during the Reagan administration.) These bureaucratic squabbles are exacerbated by Congress's desire to shape policies and by its tendency to politicize East-West economic relations. There are also various lobbying groups—in particular, ethnic groups (Jewish and Polish) and organized labor in the AFL-CIO—that are deeply involved in policymaking and often favor sanctions or restrictions. All these conflicting pressures hamper the pursuit of a consistent, effective national policy. Of course, East-West trade is an attractive target for politicization because it is economically marginal (See Table 4.1).

TABLE 4.1. U.S. High-Technology Exports to the Communist Countries and to the World, 1982 (U.S. $ in millions)

	Total exports	Manufactured exports	High-technology exports	High-technology exports as percent of total	High-technology exports as percent of manufactured
Cuba	$1.0	$0.9	--[a]	3.7	3.9
PRC	2,904.5	1,066.7	$165.3	5.7	15.5
Yugoslavia	490.0	200.4	55.3	11.3	27.6
Bulgaria	106.5	35.4	6.7	6.3	18.9
Czechoslovakia	83.6	20.5	5.7	6.8	27.7
GDR	222.6	13.9	6.5	2.9	46.7
Hungary	67.8	58.9	13.8	20.4	23.5
Poland	292.6	65.5	8.2	2.8	12.6
Romania	223.2	51.6	20.6	9.2	39.8
USSR	2,589.0	598.4	32.1	1.2	5.4
Total Communist countries	6,997.5	2,112.5	314.4	4.5	14.9
World	206,044.7	140,323.2	38,461.3	18.7	27.4

[a]Negligible

Source: Department of Commerce from U.N. Series D data.

Western Europe

Because Eastern Europe is more important economically to Western Europe than it is to the United States, Western Europe has a less restrictive policy on technology transfer than does the United States. There is also a domestic consensus on East-West trade in every country. The last European politician to support a restrictive East-West trade policy was Konrad Adenauer, who criticized the first U.S. grain sales to the USSR by saying that "only the most stupid cows choose their butchers."[6] CMEA is an attractive market for the Western European steel, machine-tool, and chemical industries and has become increasingly important in the past decade as these industries have been in decline. Indeed, CMEA keeps alive some of the old, smokestack industries in Western Europe. Western Europe complies with COCOM policies on export controls but, unlike the United States, has few nationally originated technology controls of its own.

In the immediate postwar era, when Western Europe was devastated economically and dependent on the United States for Marshall Plan aid, it

TABLE 4.2. USSR Sources of Industrialized West, High-Technology Products (in million $)

	1970		1975	
	High-technology exports to USSR	As percent of total	High-technology exports to USSR	As percent of total
Canada	$0.2		$14.4	0.9
United States	12.5	3.1	219.2	13.5
Japan	43.5	10.8	169.2	10.4
Belgium-Luxembourg	5.9	1.5	26.5	1.6
Denmark	4.8	1.2	13.4	.8
France	58.5	14.5	223.7	13.8
FRG	92.9	23.0	519.8	31.9
Ireland			.3	
Italy	69.6	17.3	155.7	9.6
Netherlands	1.1	.3	20.6	1.3
United Kingdom	56.0	13.9	51.7	3.2
Austria	5.6	1.4	27.4	1.7
Finland	6.3	1.6	35.9	2.2
Norway	.1		13.4	.8
Sweden	22.3	5.5	51.3	3.2
Switzerland	23.6	5.9	83.0	5.1
Total	402.9	100.0	1,626.0	100.0

[a]Negligible
[b]Estimated

Source: U.S. Department of Commerce from U.N. Series D trade data.

complied with stringent U.S. national export restrictions to Eastern Europe. Since the 1960s, Western Europe has had more active economic relations with the USSR and Eastern Europe and has essentially let the United States set the limits for technology controls. Like the United States, Western Europe has sought to encourage Eastern European autonomy through trade links, using positive, not negative, levers. But Western Europe has also been wary of provoking the Soviet Union through the actions that appear to encourage too much Eastern European autonomy vis-à-vis the Soviet Union. In general, however, Western Europe's economic relations with Eastern Europe, especially in the field of high technology, are modest, with the exception of the FRG.

TABLE 4.2 (*continued*)

1980		1981		1982	
High-technology exports to USSR	As percent of total	High-technology exports to USSR	As percent of total	High-technology exports to USSR	As percent of total
$27.5	1.2	$0.4	0	$0.4	0
84.7	3.6	56.5	3.2	32.1	1.5
400.2	17.2	366.0	20.0	378.2	17.6
18.0	.8	12.1	.7	15.4	.7
23.1	.1	17.9	1.0	21.8	1.0
341.3	14.8	204.7	11.5	191.6	8.9
727.2	31.6	501.8	28.3	563.9	26.3
.2	-[a]	0	0	.3	0
222.2	9.6	156.3	8.8	238.8	10.9
6.1	.3	10.0	.6	8.7[b]	.4
125.7	5.5	132.5	7.5	96.9	4.5
48.2	2.1	30.4	1.7	47.4	2.2
86.2	3.7	121.8	6.9	375.6	17.5
12.3	.5	6.5	.4	9.6	.4
71.1	3.1	77.3	4.4	63.7	3.0
136.4	5.9	80.0	4.5	106.5	5.0
2,330.0	100.0	1,774.4	100.0	2,145.7	100.0

West Germany is the most important supplier of high technology to the USSR and Eastern Europe and has been so for some time. It has always had a special interest in the CMEA region (see Table 4.2). Because it is a central European nation with long historical ties to Eastern Europe, the FRG's policy is determined mainly by its desire to keep open the German question and to make life more tolerable for people who live in the other Germany and for ethnic Germans living in other Eastern European countries. In the early postwar years, West Germany maintained close economic links with East Germany but, following the U.S. lead, adopted a restrictive policy toward the rest of CMEA. After Adenauer's departure, the FRG pursued an active economic policy toward Eastern Europe as a substitute for political ties. But only after the inauguration of the new *Ostpolitik* and *Deutschlandpolitik* in 1969 was the Federal Republic able to develop a more successful policy toward Eastern Europe. Bonn then accepted that this had to be done on the basis of primary ties to the GDR and the Soviet Union, instead of encouraging Eastern European independence from the Soviet Union and isolating the GDR from the rest of the world, as the FRG had previously tried to do. Its goal was to offer trade inducements in return for political concessions—mainly the emigration of ethnic Germans from Poland and other countries—and also to secure markets for German manufactures. The growth of *Osthandel* (trade with the East) was seen in the FRG as a prerequisite for improving political ties with the area. The FRG was willing to comply with U.S.-originated controls to the East if these directly contributed to military power; but it refused to impose controls on a broader range of goods. Moreover, it would not go along with sanctions against Poland in 1981. By way of explanation, the FRG cited its special historical responsibility in Polish history and claimed that economic sanctions would be regarded in Poland and abroad as aggressive and would not achieve much.

The FRG believes in using trade incentives, not sanctions, in pursuit of its objectives in Eastern Europe. West Germany has been remarkably successful in gaining humanitarian concessions from East Germany, which, however, come with a high pricetag. In return for a series of loans to the GDR, it has secured not only the emigration of East Germans, but also, in 1987, an unprecedented 3 million visitors from the GDR to the FRG, 1 million of whom were younger than sixty-five. The FRG has also been successful in Hungary. In 1987, Bonn guaranteed a 1 billion DM loan to Budapest and in return signed an agreement with the Hungarians to improve conditions for ethnic Germans in Hungary. In 1987, 78,523 immigrants from Eastern Europe arrived in the FRG, the third highest number since 1950. Sixty percent of these immigrants were from Poland, and 18 percent were from the USSR. Thus, Bonn has a unique political agenda toward Eastern Europe, backed by economic largesse.

Multilateral Policy

In view of the different Western interests in political and economic ties with Eastern Europe and the inherent difficulties in formulating clear guidelines for technology transfer policies, it is not surprising that COCOM, which is responsible for multilateral technology transfer policy, is beset with contradictions. COCOM is an informal organization, its deliberations are secret, and its powers of enforcement are limited. Yet it has been generally effective in coordinating allied technology transfers because there is a genuine desire to restrict exports of technology to CMEA that could pose a direct security threat to the West. The problem is that COCOM was designed as a technical, not a political, organization, but the United States under the Reagan administration sought to turn it into a forum that was more political than Washington's partners were willing to accept.

COCOM, which was founded in 1949, has delegates who are appointed either by member countries' foreign ministries or economic ministries. Its delegates serve a limited term and meet weekly in an annex to the U.S. Embassy in Paris. Its deliberations are secret, as are its lists. But a careful perusal of the national export control lists of member countries gives a good idea of what is controlled multilaterally. COCOM has no strict basis in treaty law and therefore has a somewhat anomalous status. COCOM has three tasks: to develop lists of technologies and products (triannually re-negotiated) that will be embargoed, controlled, or monitored; to hold weekly consultations on applications for exceptions to these lists (most exception requests are approved); and to ensure that COCOM regulations are enforced by a process of consultation. Decisions must be unanimous, although there are no means for punishing countries that violate its rules. The applications for exceptions are generated by different branches of member governments, depending on the country. Washington complains that in most COCOM countries, ministries of defense do not have enough input into decisionmaking. Since the 1960s, the list of embargoed goods has shrunk, with the focus increasingly being on high technology products. Whereas rules for the PRC have been liberalized significantly, Eastern Europe is treated more or less like the Soviet Union, although recently European and U.S. firms were given permission to export previously prohibited civil aircraft to the GDR and Poland. Since the invasion of Afghanistan, there have been no exception requests for the Soviet Union, but there were some for Eastern Europe. The USSR, of course, imports a larger volume of high technology than do its Eastern European partners.

In recent years, disputes within COCOM have centered on how to define dual-use technology; whether COCOM should alter its lists to respond to political developments; whether COCOM should have a special military committee; how to enforce COCOM rules; and how to secure the cooperation of nonmember states such as Switzerland, Austria, or Singapore. The United States has also tried to use COCOM to impose general restrictions on industrial trade with CMEA, which its allies have rejected.

In 1982, after a decade during which COCOM members seemed to give low priority to the organization, COCOM's role was upgraded with the first ministerial-level meeting in twenty-five years because events in Afghanistan and Poland signaled the end of the détente of the 1970s and because there was increasing NATO, and especially U.S., concern about Soviet and Eastern European industrial espionage and theft of technology. In January 1988, another high-level COCOM meeting reaffirmed the need for controls to maintain Western leads "in strategically sensitive technology essential to their security." COCOM agreed to enhance its coordination in order to rationalize export control lists and decontrol items that are no longer strategically significant; strengthen cooperation with third countries; strengthen national controls; and encourage intra-Western technology transfers. COCOM also pledged to have annual high-level meetings in the future.[7] This January meeting was in part a response to the Toshiba-Kongsberg actions, in which

Japanese and Norwegian firms illegally supplied multiaxis milling machines to the USSR that can greatly reduce submarine propeller noise. The object of the meeting was to have lists that are shorter but better enforced. On August 1, 1988, a new computer list was introduced, allowing previously barred small computers to be exported to CMEA.

Most participants and observers agreed that this meeting was successful. But some of the Reagan administration's greatest hawks on this issue remained highly critical of the organization, and they tried to move it in a more military direction. Former Assistant Secretary Perle charged that all of the COCOM allies had resisted U.S. efforts to strengthen the organization: "The last thing on their minds is the security of the Western alliance."[8] Despite its inevitable shortcomings, however, COCOM is the one Western forum in which technology transfer policies can be coordinated and in which the technology transfer status of the latest scientific advances can be multilaterally discussed. It will continue to be the single most important Western mechanism for controlling exports of high technology to Eastern Europe.

Lessons of the Pipeline Crisis

Transatlantic disagreements about East-West trade and technology transfer recently came to a head when the United States sought to prevent its allies from selling compressor components manufactured under U.S. license for the construction of a Soviet natural gas export pipeline from Urengoi to Western Europe. The pipeline crisis involved a Soviet project, although sanctions were imposed as a response to the declaration of martial law in Poland. Yet it is instructive to examine the implications of this dispute because they affect overall East-West technology transfer policy. The U.S. attempt, in 1982, to impose extraterritorial sanctions on the export of compressor parts failed when France, Britain, Italy, and the FRG went ahead with their exports. The sanctions were lifted later on that year, after George Shultz, who was on record as opposing "light switch diplomacy" that turned sanctions on and off, replaced Alexander Haig as U.S. secretary of state and decided that these sanctions were not worth the trouble they had caused within the alliance.

During the pipeline dispute, there was a fundamental disagreement about Western objectives toward the USSR. In the Reagan administration's view, it was not in the West's interest to assist Moscow in the development of its energy sector by exporting energy technology to the Soviet Union because a stronger economy would mean a more formidable military opponent. The Europeans challenged this view, arguing that it was in the general interest to have more, rather than less, hydrocarbons in the world. They also disputed the view of some members of the Reagan administration that it was desirable to have weaker, as opposed to stronger, CMEA economies. This applied particularly to Poland, in which the United States focused on not aiding the Jaruzelski government economically, whereas the Europeans focused on supplying material help to the Polish population.

A second area of disagreement concerned the compressor components. As these were not on the COCOM lists, the Europeans argued, they could not be construed as high technology and their export could not be prohibited. When the Reagan administration then argued that the reason for prohibiting their export was political—to punish the Soviets for Polish martial law—the Europeans again demurred, arguing that economic sanctions were not an appropriate response to Soviet or Polish political action. If the pipeline did not constitute a security threat, it should be built.

The transatlantic disputes involved different definitions of security. The major U.S. security concern was that the Soviet economy would be strengthened through the increased hard-currency revenues from new gas sales and that this would threaten Western security. The chief European security concern was to diversify supplies of natural gas and thereby reduce dependence on the Organization of Petroleum Exporting Countries (OPEC).

The pipeline dispute also involved West-West disputes that were only indirectly related to East-West problems. The Western Europeans challenged the validity in international law of the extraterritorial application of U.S. legislation. They also viewed these sanctions—as did many in the U.S. DoD—as sanctions against Western Europe rather than against the USSR. Indeed, the United States has traditionally used disputes about East-West economic ties to try imposing its policies on a wide range of East-West issues on its allies. The pipeline sanctions came at a time when there was a lively debate about arms control and the stationing of U.S. intermediate-range missiles in Europe, and the sanctions strengthened criticism of Washington's policies in some sectors of European public opinion. Thus, a dispute regarding a relatively minor economic issue had major repercussions on alliance unity, which led French Foreign Minister Claude Cheysson to warn of a "progressive divorce" between the United States and its allies.

Secretary Shultz persuaded the president to lift the sanctions when it was clear that they had not succeeded in preventing the export of compressor components and after the Europeans had agreed to take a fresh look at technology transfer questions. After the lifting of the U.S. sanctions, both sides made an attempt to improve their coordination of East-West trade policy. Four studies on East-West trade—one done at COCOM, one at the OECD, one at NATO, and one at the International Energy Agency—were undertaken, with positive results. In COCOM, the lists were revised and shortened, focusing on the most up-to-date microelectronic technology. The computer list, which was ten years old, was revised. Member states agreed to encourage a greater input on licensing decisions from their ministries of defense. COCOM's secretariat was upgraded, its budget increased, and its equipment updated (until then it had functioned virtually without computers). Member states also agreed to restrict their technology exports to neutral countries that might reexport them to CMEA.

The other studies involved an agreement in NATO to discuss the security aspects of economic ties with the Warsaw Pact more extensively than before; an agreement in the International Energy Agency that Western Europe should not become overly dependent on Soviet gas; and an OECD agreement, in 1982, to reclassify the Soviet Union and Eastern Europe for the purposes of credits. The USSR, the GDR, and Czechoslovakia are now classified as advanced countries that have to pay the highest rate of interest; Bulgaria, Hungary, Poland, and Romania were raised to the next highest category. This tightening of COCOM regulations and of credit terms to some extent satisfied the United States while allowing the Europeans not to look as if they had capitulated to U.S. pressure.

Nevertheless, as a result of this dispute, the United States tightened its efforts to halt illegal technology transfer through espionage and limited the sharing of technology and scientific information with its allies for fear that this knowledge will be leaked to the East. The United States has, for instance, prevented West German scientists from participating in U.S. conferences whose material was deemed to be sensitive. Concerns about East-West technology transfer have led to a retrenchment in West-West technology transfer.

Technology Transfer: Eastern European Perspectives

As Western technology transfer policy has vacillated between more or fewer restrictions in the 1980s, Eastern Europe's technological needs have grown. Not only does CMEA require more Western technology for the improvement of its own economic performance; the Soviet Union has increasingly pressed its allies to export high-quality technology to the USSR under new bilateral and CMEA agreements. Because oil prices and the dollar have fallen, Soviet hard-currency earnings have been slashed by one-third. It has therefore become more difficult to import Western machinery, and so the Soviet Union has made more technological demands on its own partners. Western Europe is the key to Eastern European technological development, if Eastern Europe is to meet Soviet technological demands, which have grown since the introduction of Mikhail Gorbachev's ambitious *perestroika* (restructuring) program. Eastern Europe must improve the competitiveness of its export sector if it is to grow economically.

This section will examine the technological needs and potential of Poland, Hungary, the GDR, and Czechoslovakia. Romania is omitted because it is the least developed CMEA nation, its economy is in catastrophic shape, and reliable data are hard to come by.

Bulgaria provides a different perspective on these issues because it has embarked on a successful economic reorganization and its electronics exports have become increasingly important to the Soviet Union, acting as a substitute for Western technology. Indeed, although other areas of the economy have been less productive, Bulgaria has done better than most CMEA nations in technological terms. For instance, when each CMEA country decided to become self-sufficient in microchip production in the late 1970s, Bulgaria, unlike any other socialist country, chose to produce Motorola microchips, which are particularly useful for "high-end" computers designed for en-

TABLE 4.3. Destination by Country of Communist High-Tech Imports from the Industrial West (in percentage)

	1970	1975	1981	1982
USSR	34	35	31	40
PRC	9	13	19	15
Bulgaria	2	3	4	4
Czechoslovakia	8	6	6	6
GDR	4	2	4	4
Hungary	5	4	6	6
Poland	7	13	6	6
Romania	9	7	4	3
Yugoslavia	19	14	17	15
Other	3	3	3	2

Source: J. Martens, "Quantification of Western Exports of High-Technology Products to Communist Countries," in *East European Economies: Slow Growth in the 1980s*, Joint Committee Report (Washington, D.C.: U.S. Government Printing Office, March 1986).

gineering uses rather than simple accounting and calculating. Moreover, since 1972 Japanese companies such as Hitachi and Toshiba have worked closely with the Bulgarian computer industry and in 1982 set up a center for Japanese specialists to train Bulgarians. Japan and Bulgaria also cooperate in electronics, robotics, and other fields.[9] However, Bulgaria has not been the subject of any thorough Western study on technology transfer thus far. The Bulgarians have only recently begun to release the trade data necessary to make a thorough study of technology transfer. Moreover, Bulgaria's foreign trade is overwhelmingly with the USSR and the other CMEA countries.

Poland

Poland's severe economic problems in recent years have stemmed from its excessive borrowing in the 1970s, the product of a strategy to overcome technological backwardness and to improve economic performance by turning to the West. Poland took 7 percent of Communist high-technology imports from the West in 1970, 13 percent in 1975 (the highest of any Eastern European state), and 6 percent in 1982 (see Table 4.3), thus significantly increasing its Western technology imports in the 1970s. Like all other CMEA states, Poland primarily needs Western technology to improve the quality of its exports; enhance its export competitiveness in Western markets so as to reduce its level of indebtedness; and fulfill intra-CMEA technology-sharing obligations. Poles also hope that this technology will help to raise the standard of living.

After 1968, Poland's economic strategy focused on the development of selected branches of industry and groups of commodities in which Poland was expected to specialize. Until the early 1970s, imports from the West were mainly needed for the relatively quick removal of bottlenecks, rather than as an element of a long-term development strategy. Thereafter, conscious of the need to modernize and build a viable export sector, the government relied on readily available Western credits in the early détente era and greatly increased its foreign indebtedness in order to import more technology. After the 1975 "new economic maneuver," the import intensity of production increased. From 1972 to 1979, Western technology played a role in Polish investment in the chemical industry, small printing, metallurgy and other sectors. But the strategy failed to produce harmonious, balanced growth. A major study of the impact of Western technology on the Polish economy concluded that it is difficult to say if Western embodied technology transfer had any impact on the economic performance of any particular sector. In general, the sectors that received the higher proportion of Western imports did relatively better than others. Yet in terms of foreign trade, the chemical and light industries, which received the highest allocation of Western embodied technology per unit of investment outlays, did very poorly. Western technology therefore had a very limited impact on the expansion of Poland's exports to nonsocialist countries, although Poland did utilize Western technology to expand its exports to CMEA.[10]

The statistical evidence suggests that Poland's sudden acceleration of technology imports from the West in the 1970s was excessive in relation to the limited capacity of the economy to absorb and diffuse the technology in such a short time, as well as to pay for it. Western technology imports may, however, have somewhat reduced the rate of decline in capital and labor productivity. Poland's problem is that in order to reduce its foreign debt, it has to depend on production in traditional export sectors that were not the main recipients of Western technology. Those sectors that did receive the bulk of Western technology were not able to enhance their export performance because of problems inherent in the Polish economy.

Although the Polish economic situation has improved somewhat since 1982, economic performance remains lower than the levels of the late 1970s. Poland needs Western technology to enhance its export performance but lacks the hard currency to import large quantities. Even if Poland could import as much as it wanted to, its economic structure would be resistant to the efficient utilization of this technology.

Czechoslovakia

Czech economic performance has traditionally been superior to that of Poland, and Czechoslovakia is more highly developed technologically than is Poland. Indeed, prior to its incorporation into the Soviet bloc, Czechoslovakia was one of Europe's technological leaders. It has accounted for 6 percent of Communist high-technology imports from the industrial West since 1970. Since the mid-1970s, economic performance has fluctuated, but there has been a decline in efficiency in all sectors of the economy. Czechoslovakia has lost market share in engineering products since 1965, even within CMEA. In the late 1970s, Czechoslovakia increased its exports of industrial consumer goods and gained in market share in chemical exports. In 1972, it was the first country to formalize rules for East-West industrial cooperation, but so far, there have been no joint ventures with the West. Only 2 percent of the country's total trade with nonsocialist countries is classified as industrial cooperation.

Czechoslovakia seems to have absorbed and diffused Western technology more efficiently than has Poland, perhaps because the former starts from a higher level of development. But the lack of thorough economic reform, hard-currency constraints, and the declining technical level of Czech industry will complicate the prospects for any future increases of these imports and their effective absorption.[11]

Hungary

Hungary has the most market-oriented system of any CMEA country, and its economic performance has in the two decades since the introduction of the New Economic Mechanism (NEM) been quite respectable. Yet Hungary, too, has not been able to use Western technology optimally, nor has Western technology had any major impact on its domestic and external economic performance. Hungary accounts for another 6 percent of total Communist high-technology imports from the industrialized West, and the Federal Republic of Germany is its main Western long-term supplier, as is the case of all other CMEA nations.

At the beginning of the 1970s, Hungary was a medium-developed country, compared to other CMEA economies. It raised its technological level by a series of cooperative agreements with other CMEA nations, for instance with the Soviet Union in the area of petrochemicals. From 1971 to 1978, imports of machinery from the West more than doubled in real terms. Since then, purchases have declined in absolute value. Most of Hungary's exports to the West consist of raw materials and semimanufactures. Relative to the size of its economy, Hungary participates more actively in East-West trade than do other Eastern European countries, but its participation is less pronounced in technology-related than in non-technology-related products.

Hungary's export performance since the introduction of the NEM compares favorably to that of other CMEA nations. But its ability to utilize Western technology efficiently has been hampered by the persistence of systemic problems and the constraint of the external economic environment, which means that obsolete technology has been replaced too slowly and there has not been enough effort domestically in applied research and development. Hungary would like to import more Western technology, but Hungary will be constrained in the future by its hard-currency debt and by the need to tackle yet further systemic problems by way of reform.[12] The 1987 West German 1 billion DM loan has alleviated the most urgent repayment problems, but the debt issue persists. Moreover, Budapest will be increasingly challenged by the countries of the Pacific Rim, whose manufactured exports have become more competitive with those of Hungary.

The German Democratic Republic

The GDR is technologically the most highly developed CMEA country. It also has consistently had the highest growth rates of the Soviet bloc, although it has one of the most centralized economic systems in CMEA. It has greatly benefited from its unique economic relationship with the FRG. Because West Germany, for political reasons, does not treat East Germany as a foreign country, inter-German trade is considered to be domestic trade, which has made the GDR a de facto member of the European Community. Moreover, it does not have to expend a pfennig of hard currency in its trade with the FRG. The currency used in inter-German trade is an accounting unit (*Verrechnungseinheit* [VE], where 1 VE equals 1 DM), and imports and exports are settled in a clearing process. Despite these advantages, which no other CMEA nation enjoys, and despite its relatively advanced technology sector, the GDR has also had problems with hard-currency shortages and systemic economic difficulties that have hampered the import and utilization of Western technology. Precisely because the GDR is technologically the most advanced CMEA nation, it is most threatened by the newly industrializing countries of the Pacific Rim, whose ability to produce highly efficient, cheap microelectronic goods is a direct challenge to the GDR's ability to compete on world markets. A recent example highlights the challenge: KDW, the giant West Berlin department store, recently switched from using GDR to using Korean computers. Moreover, the recent relaxation of COCOM computer controls also means that the GDR will have some Western competition in CMEA computer markets.

The GDR's economic situation has improved in the last few years. It has managed to reduce its hard-currency debt by sharply cutting back on hard-currency imports and boosting hard-currency exports in the early 1980s, at the expense of domestic consumption and investment. It is questionable whether the GDR can boost investment in high technology in the future, unless it introduces more reforms. In the current five-year plan (1986–90), the priority sectors for investment are microelectronics, robot technology, and information technology. The GDR has been concentrating on high-tech industries—the inclusion of computer-aided processes in manufacturing—since the early 1980s. Because its technological level is far greater than that of other CMEA states, its most desirable partners are in the West, particularly the FRG. Nevertheless, inter-German trade has not solved the GDR's technological problems. In 1987, the GDR economy grew by 3.6 percent, although many branches of industry failed to achieve their growth targets. The electrotechnical and "key technologies" branches, such as microelectronic components and computers, did relatively well by contrast. Yet, according to one expert, despite the success in these technological fields, unless the entire economy becomes more productive, the contribution of these industries will not be enough to stimulate long-lasting economic growth.[13]

The GDR's ability to optimize its international participation in such a way as to maximize its competitiveness is hampered by its need to supply the Soviet Union with technology. It is the USSR's most important trading partner, and in the next five-year plan exports to the USSR are slated to rise by 20 percent over the previous period. The Soviets are trying to intensify their technological cooperation with the GDR through special enterprise-to-enterprise links, much to the dismay of their East German ally, which realizes that it has nothing to gain and much to lose from this form of cooperation. But because it depends on Moscow for its economic and political survival, the GDR has no choice but to go along with these plans.

The GDR accounts for about 4 percent of Communist high-technology imports from the industrialized West. It is the only CMEA nation that does not have legal provisions for joint ventures, and it is only moderately interested in East-West technological cooperation. Some sectors have been targeted for greater industrial cooperation in order to enhance export competitiveness, as evidenced by the GDR agreement with Volkswagen to produce automobile engines. Nevertheless, the major reason for the GDR's lack of interest in joint ventures and other forms of industrial cooperation is probably that it does not need them because of inter-German trade.

There is relatively little data on inter-German technology transfer, a subject of great concern to the FRG's allies, especially the United States. Because of the FRG's desire to secure political and humanitarian concessions from the GDR, it is willing to make significant economic concessions, including direct and indirect financial transfers that amount to 2.5 billion DM a year. Some U.S. officials fear that these concessions include less stringent controls on technology transfer from the FRG to the GDR. These suspicions are compounded by the fact that inter-German trade is covered by legislation that is separate from the *Aussenwirtschaftsgesetz* (foreign trade law) that covers all other foreign trade. According to one study, however, high-technology items constitute a relatively small percentage of West German exports to East Germany. Investment goods amounted to around 28.3 percent of deliveries in 1976–1980 and went down to 16 percent in 1984. The decrease in mechanical engineering products is even greater, falling to 8.8 percent in 1985 (see Table 4.4).[14] These statistics suggest that the GDR is not particularly dependent upon Western technology imports for its own economic performance. But undoubtedly, inter-German trade as a whole, including financial transfers and the interest-free annual 850 million DM swing credits, has helped the GDR to prosper as much as it has.

Certainly, the FRG is interested in increasing technological cooperation with the GDR for political reasons. Recently, inter-German discussions on their similar *Technik-Kultur* (technical culture) have begun. These focus on common historical and current approaches to scientific education and also on possible future joint initiatives on technology in international organizations. Some GDR citizens have also applied to participate in the Western European Eureka high-tech project, in which the FRG will play a leading role in telecommunications.

TABLE 4.4. Deliveries by the Federal Republic of Germany[a] in Inner-German Trade, 1971-1985

Products or Product Groups	1971-75[b]	1976-80[b]	1981	1982	1983	1984	1985
			(DM million)				
Total	3203	4653	5576	6382	6947	6403	7903
			(percentage shares)				
Products of the basic materials and production goods industries[c]	53.8	52.4	55.7	56.9	57.6	59.8	58.3
Oil	2.5	6.0	12.4	10.9	9.7	10.3	8.9
Iron and steel[d]	12.8	9.8	7.1	10.9	15.9	12.8	11.8
Chemical products[e]	23.2	20.4	19.7	21.7	20.1	22.4	19.6
Products of the investment goods industries	23.8	28.3	25.5	20.0	18.2	16.0	18.7
Mechanical engineering products	17.3	19.5	17.4	13.9	11.1	9.9	8.8
Products of the consumer goods industries	9.5	7.5	7.5	7.4	6.8	7.5	8.8
Textiles and clothing	6.1	3.9	4.1	4.2	4.0	4.2	3.8
Products of agriculture[f] and of the foodstuff and semi-luxury industries	11.7	10.6	10.0	14.5	16.3	15.5	13.3
Feedstuffs (oil cakes and meal)	5.1	2.9	3.6	4.9	6.7	7.1	5.1
All products[g]	100	100	100	100	100	100	100

[a]Including Berlin (West)
[b]Five-year average
[c]Including mining products
[d]Including foundry products and products of wire making, cold rolling mills, and steel reduction
[e]Including products made from synthetic materials and rubber products
[f]Including hunting, forestry, and fisheries
[g]Including nonclassified products

Source: Hanns-Dieter Jacobsen, "Security Implications of Inner-German Economic Relations" (Paper presented at Wilson Center, Washington, D.C., August 27, 1986), p. 44.

Current and Future Prospects

This analysis of the role of Western technology imports in Eastern European economies shows that there was a significant increase in Western embodied technology imports by Eastern Europe in the early 1970s; they doubled from 1970 to 1975, a product of the détente era and the West's willingness to extend large-scale credits to CMEA. From 1975 to 1983, as the Eastern European debt grew, the world economy deteriorated, and détente waned, Western technology imports declined by almost 50 percent. Only the GDR has been able to improve its export performance in OECD markets since the late 1970s, and that involved a potentially problematic cutback in domestic investment. The data show that most Western technology was used in nonexport sectors, and the areas in which it was most productive were chemicals and iron and steel. Since the 1970s, CMEA countries as a whole have become less competitive in Western markets. The relatively weak impact of Western technology was mainly the result of the systemic problems of these Eastern European economies. Current CMEA five-year plans stress the development of indigenous technologies and intra-CMEA technological cooperation.

The picture from the Eastern European side, therefore, looks fairly sobering. If current trends continue, the technological gap between the two halves of Europe will widen, and Eastern Europe will fall far behind. Even the most advanced state, the GDR, will be eclipsed by the newly industrializing countries.

Under these circumstances, the fact that the West cannot agree on an East-West technology transfer policy might seem unimportant. After all, if the Eastern Europeans can neither afford nor utilize Western technology, why spend so much time arguing about it? There are good reasons to do so, despite all the evidence marshaled so far. The debate about East-West technology transfer goes beyond the narrow technological issues to the broader question of what Western policy toward Eastern Europe should be. There are differences between Western Europe, particularly the Federal Republic of Germany, and the United States in this area. West German policy is explicitly oriented toward increasing technology transfer to Eastern Europe. Foreign Minister Hans-Dietrich Genscher has argued that the West should try to narrow the East-West technology gap and develop more sophisticated forms of East-West cooperation, including joint ventures and direct investment in Eastern Europe. The FRG has broadened its influence in Eastern Europe as it has increased its economic largesse. For instance, the 1987 loan to Hungary enabled Budapest to avoid rescheduling its hard-currency debt in 1987, and there is talk of granting a new 4 billion DM loan to the GDR. Bulgaria has become increasingly interested in importing West German electronics components and in broadening economic ties with the FRG. Following Genscher's visit to Warsaw and Chancellor Helmut Kohl's to Prague (the first visit by a West German chancellor since 1973), there was more talk of increasing economic ties with Poland and Czechoslovakia. From Bonn's point of view (and this position cuts across all political parties), the goal is to strengthen and stabilize Eastern European economies and to make life in a divided Europe more tolerable by improving the living conditions of all citizens of Eastern Europe, not only of ethnic Germans and citizens of the GDR.

No other Western European country has as intense an interest in Eastern Europe as has the Federal Republic, but France is generally supportive of higher living standards there and endorses West German policies. In the Gorbachev era, when the Soviet general secretary speaks about Europe as "our common house" and the European Community and CMEA have at last signed an agreement, there is greater Western European interest in a more active dialogue between the two halves of Europe.

The United States, as a global superpower largely responsible for the defense of Western Europe, has a different perspective. On the one hand, Washington supports the FRG's policy on inter-German relations and on improving conditions for Eastern European populations. On the other hand, some in Congress and the administration have argued that the GDR's support for Soviet activities in the Third World, which takes the form of training the secret police in countries under Soviet influence and providing arms and training to groups hostile towards the United States, should decrease the U.S. interest in economic ties with the GDR. This, plus the Berlin Wall, is why the GDR, for instance, does not receive MFN. Washington is also concerned about other Eastern European activities that challenge the U.S. international role.

There is no automatic assumption in Washington that the West should strengthen Eastern European economies. If the United States does not trade with them, it forfeits any potential influence over these states. But too much trade with Eastern Europe helps shore up the region's economies, postpones necessary reforms, and keeps in power governments that are unpopular domestically. But one could also argue that if the West did contribute to greater economic efficiency, then the regimes of Eastern Europe might be willing to forfeit some of their political control over their populations in return for better economic performance. Because all Western countries are dealing with unknowns in relation to Eastern Europe, it is particularly difficult to come to definite conclusions in any of these key issues.

A common Western goal, arguably, should be to improve the economic and political situation in Eastern Europe as much as is necessary to prevent widespread popular unrest that might trigger Soviet military intervention. But the West does not necessarily have a stake in supporting the economies of Eastern Europe in such a way as to facilitate Soviet domination or domestic repression. There are indications that Gorbachev has begun to rethink traditional Soviet policy toward Eastern Europe and may be willing to tolerate somewhat more internal diversity if this promotes more efficient CMEA economies. It is too early, however, to judge how much diversity Moscow will permit, and therefore at the moment these are the difficult parameters within which the West will have to make choices. It would be desirable to have a common Western policy toward Eastern Europe, but this is unlikely for the foreseeable future. West Germany's stake in a stable, prosperous Eastern Europe is not necessarily the same as is the U.S. interest in the area, and so the two sides will continue to agree to differ.

As long as this situation prevails, the United States will continue to argue with its allies about technology transfer. Although the United States developed a somewhat more active policy toward Eastern Europe during the second Reagan administration, its technology transfer policy remained Moscow oriented and restrictive. Infighting among the various branches of the executive for control of this policy continues. Congress is considering legislation to amend the 1979 Export Administration Act that would tighten multilateral controls over technology exports, simplify licensing procedures within this country, reduce the size of the control list, and define more clearly the role of the various U.S. government agencies.

This process of reconsideration will undoubtedly continue for some time, as various causes célèbres, such as the Toshiba-Kongsberg case, hit the headlines, with calls by the U.S. media and U.S. politicians for stricter controls and sanctions against U.S. allies. Meanwhile, an influential 1987 Academy of Sciences study of U.S. export controls concluded that export controls are essential if the technological lead that the West currently enjoys over CMEA is to be maintained. But the study argued that a cumbersome mechanism that attempts to control too much ends up by weakening U.S. security. While recommending the strengthening of multilateral controls on dual-use technologies, the study criticized the political use of technology sanctions and stressed the importance of maintaining U.S. technological strength and allied unity: "The executive branch has failed to implement the existing provisions of the law in a coherent, effective manner, which has in turn created uncertainty, confusion and criticism both at home and abroad. In the absence of appropriate corrective measures, these continuing problems will exact even higher tolls—on both Western economic viability and innovative capacity and on the military security of the United States and its allies."[15] The study was welcomed by the U.S. business community and by the NATO allies. It remains to be seen whether the administration will act upon it.

In the future, the United States will face a more complex trading environment. Since the devaluation of the dollar, U.S. exports have become more competitive, but basic questions about the U.S. trade structure remain. Moreover, in response to the problem of export competitiveness, protectionist tendencies have grown, and the whole question of the government's role in international trade has become more controversial. The debate about the damage done to the United States' competitive position by inconsistent government policies may have a salutary effect on East-West trade policy by making the policy more predictable.

The United States may well adopt a more open policy toward Eastern Europe in the next few years, but prospects for increasing transfers of high technology are very limited. Eastern Europe will remain economically marginal to the United States, and the United States will have only limited economic significance for Eastern Europe, although its economic impact on Eastern Europe is far larger than Eastern Europe's on the United States.

Western Europe will remain critical of the current U.S. policy on export controls; especially when tighter West-West controls are imposed in the name of East-West security. If there were to be a recession, Eastern Europe would appear a more attractive market for West European industrial exports. Technology transfer to the East will remain a subject of contention within the Western alliance.

I conclude, therefore, with a paradox. Disputes about East-West technology transfer increase friction within NATO. But neither Eastern Europe nor the Soviet Union seem to have been able to take advantage of this friction to any significant degree. They have neither the financial wherewithal to purchase all the technology they need nor the systemic ability fully to benefit from it. They cannot even gain political advantage from these NATO quarrels. In the next few years, the political climate for East-West European trade will probably be the most favorable that it has ever been, with the possible exception of the early 1970s. But because of the economic problems of Eastern Europe and the likely absence of real, thoroughgoing economic *perestroika,* CMEA will probably not be able to take full advantage of this opening. As one specialist in the USSR put it, "By the year 2000, there will be two economic axes: U.S.-Japan, the high-tech, microelectronic axis, and Western Europe and Eastern Europe, the low-tech, traditional, complementary axis." From the Soviet Union's perspective, this scenario may have some appeal. But neither Eastern nor Western Europe can contemplate this prospect with anything but apprehension.

Acknowledgments

The author gratefully acknowledges Carla Krüger's research assistance.

Notes

1. J. F. Bucy, "Technology Transfer and East-West Trade: A Reappraisal," *International Security* (Winter 1980–1981), p. 134.

2. R. M. Davies, "The Department of Defense Statement on Critical Technology for Export Controls," Statement before the Subcommittee on International Economic Policy and Trade, Committee on Foreign Affairs of the United States House of Representatives, March 22, 1979.

3. Giovanni Agnelli, "East-West Trade: A European View," *Foreign Affairs* (Summer 1980), p. 1027.

4. Anthony Sutton, *Western Technology and Soviet Economic Development, 1945 to 1965* (Stanford, Calif.: Hoover Institution Publications, 1973), pp. 399–400.

5. Richard Perle, "Making Sure Our Technology Stays Ours," *Wall Street Journal,* July 22, 1987, p. 20.

6. Cited in Angela Stent, *From Embargo to Ostpolitik: The Political Economy of West German–Soviet Relations, 1955–80* (New York: Cambridge University Press, 1981), p. 123.

7. U.S. Department of State Press Release, "Results of the Senior Political Meeting on Strengthening the Coordinating Committee on Multilateral Export Controls (COCOM)," January 29, 1988.

8. Perle, "Making Sure," p. 20.

9. Ana Ivanova, "Bulgaria's Growing Technological Importance to the USSR," (*Radio Free Europe Report,* Bulgarian SR/7, July 29, 1988).

10. Zbigniew Fallenbuchl, *East-West Technology Transfer: Study of Poland* (Paris: Organization for Economic Cooperation and Development, 1983).

11. Friedrich Levcik and Jiri Skolka, *East-West Technology Transfer: Study of Czechoslovakia* (Paris: Organization for Economic Cooperation and Development, 1984).

12. Paul Marer, *East-West Technology Transfer: Study of Hungary, 1968–1984* (Paris: Organization for Economic Cooperation and Development, 1986).

13. Doris Cornelsen, "Die Lage der DDR—Wirtschaft zur Jahreswende 1987/88," Deutsches Institut für Wirtschaftsforschung, *Wochenbericht* 5, (1988), pp. 59–67.

14. Hanns-Dieter Jacobsen, "Security Implications of Inner-German Economic Relations" (Paper presented at Wilson Center, Washington, D.C., August 27, 1986).

15. National Academy of Sciences, *Balancing the National Interest* (Washington, D.C.: National Academy Press, 1987), p. 177.

5

The Soviet Union and Eastern Europe: New Prospects and Old Dilemmas

John Van Oudenaren

Since he became General Secretary in March 1985, Mikhail Gorbachev has repeatedly addressed the theme of Soviet power and its future. In sharp contrast to his predecessors, all of whom displayed the historical optimism characteristic of Marxist-Leninist leaders, Gorbachev is haunted by the specter of economic, technological, military, and political lag and decline. His program of *perestroika* (restructuring) is aimed at reversing current trends and at ensuring, as he remarked in a speech several months before his predecessor's death, that "the Soviet Union enters the millenium in a manner worthy of a great power."[1]

Gorbachev has never offered a systematic exposition of the role he expects Eastern Europe to play in helping to accomplish the ambitious goals he has set for his own country. But in such major policy pronouncements as his report to the Twenty-seventh Congress of the Communist Party of the Soviet Union (CPSU), his November 2, 1987, speech marking the seventieth anniversary of the Bolshevik Revolution, and his book *Perestroika,* he has stressed the strong relationship between developments in the Soviet Union and in the broader "socialist system," the core of which is Eastern Europe. That a new Soviet leader should stress this relationship is not surprising. Gorbachev's fundamental interest is power, and few factors in Soviet and indeed Russian history are more closely bound up with the vicissitudes of the Soviet Union's position in the world than developments in Eastern Europe.

Historically, Eastern Europe has been an *indicator of* and a *factor determining* Russia's relative position in Europe and by extension on a global basis. Russia's emergence as a great power during the eighteenth century was associated with the decline and eventual disappearance of an independent Poland and with the steady rise of Russian influence in the Balkans. Tsarist influence in Eastern Europe reached its height during the first half of the nineteenth century when, under the norms established at the Congress of Vienna, the tsar acted on behalf of the concert of powers to preserve the domestic status quo in the region. Conversely, Russian power in Europe reached a low point in 1917, following internal collapse and forced withdrawal from World War I, which led to the creation of an independent Polish state and the three Baltic republics.

The Stalinist Legacy

Joseph Stalin's main foreign policy achievement was to restore the Soviet Union's traditional position in the region. As a result of the Hitler-Stalin pact and the Soviet Union's victory in World War II, the Baltic states were abolished, the USSR's own borders were pushed westward, and a whole group of formally independent but Soviet-dominated states was formed. Most importantly, the USSR had reasserted its traditional position in Poland and extended its control over a third of Germany. The Soviet Union thus was assured a voice in any postwar decisions regarding either reunification or permanent partition of the German nation.

Having established Soviet preeminence in Eastern Europe, Stalin had to decide how to organize the "social systems" of these countries. Until 1948, Sovietization of the "peoples' democracies" proceeded rather slowly, thus raising the question of whether Stalin might have had an alternative order in mind that was later aborted by the deepening cold war, or whether he might have been willing to tolerate more pluralism in some countries (Hungary and Czechoslovakia) than in others. But whatever Stalin's original intentions, by 1948 he insisted that the local Communist authorities replicate as closely and as rapidly as possible the Stalinist model in each country of the bloc.

With the partial exception of Poland, collectivization along Soviet lines was pressed in each country. National armies were established under the close supervision of Soviet advisers and, in the Polish case, under the direct control of officers who had served in the Red Army. All countries began programs of rapid industrialization. Meanwhile, the USSR removed huge quantities of capital and machinery from the region and established an exploitative system of joint stock companies through which Eastern European resources could flow to the Soviet Union.

Stalin's policies probably were appropriate to the conditions as he saw them. Faced with the immense task of reconstruction and the "inevitability" of another war with the West, Stalin imposed the Soviet model as rapidly as possible once it became clear that Soviet gains in Western Europe would be thwarted by the direct application of U.S. political, economic and, eventually, military power. But these policies, whatever their rationale at the time, led to the creation of a complex and interlocking set of dilemmas that has plagued all subsequent Soviet leaders, up to and including Gorbachev.

These dilemmas have persisted on three levels: the national, the intrabloc, and the East-West. On the national level, the imposition of complete

Communist party hegemony deprived the Eastern European governments of any real political legitimacy in the eyes of their own populations. Henceforth, to be an Eastern European leader was to be, in effect, the agent of a foreign power. This basic lack of legitimacy, combined with poor economic performance, has meant that domestic upheavals have occurred at roughly ten-year intervals in Eastern Europe and have affected all countries except Bulgaria and Romania.

On the intrabloc level, the imposition from above of the Soviet model of centrally planned "socialism in one country" made genuine economic integration infinitely more difficult to achieve. It meant that each country developed a similar industrial structure with a strong emphasis on heavy industry and its own centralized economic organization with a largely vertical flow of information and decisions. This economic structure prevented the spontaneous development of horizontal intrabloc patterns of trade and cooperation that might have replaced the prevailing East-West patterns of trade (mainly with the Federal Republic of Germany, or the FRG) of the pre–World War II period. It ensured that the Soviet Union would not be able to achieve steady, self-sustaining progress toward integration, which in turn helped to worsen economic performance and thereby further undermined domestic stability and regime legitimacy in individual countries.

Finally, on the East-West level, Stalin's Sovietization of Eastern Europe resulted in a deep East-West cleavage and the permanent emplacement of U.S. power on the continent. Consolidation of the U.S. position in Western Europe was not only directly detrimental to Soviet security interests but contributed, in Soviet eyes at least, to the perpetuation of an unstable situation within the Soviet bloc. In the cold war period, the U.S. presence made possible the Western "position of strength" policy, which was based on a refusal to recognize the legitimacy of the postwar order in the East. Although the Brezhnev leadership attributed historic significance to the European "settlement" of the early 1970s and saw the Helsinki Final Act and West Germany's bilateral treaties with Poland, the German Democratic Republic (GDR), Czechoslovakia, and the USSR as evidence of the West's acceptance of postwar realities, it was clearly disappointed, especially after 1980, that this international legitimation did not contribute more to Eastern Europe's internal stability and did not lead to greater Western restraint in backing Solidarity and other "subversive" forces in the bloc.

The Importance of Eastern Europe

Notwithstanding the failures of Soviet bloc policy during the past four decades, no Soviet leader has seriously contemplated a *fundamental* rethinking of Soviet policy toward the region. This inherently conservative approach reflects both caution (never risk what one already has for the prospect of achieving something better) and optimism (with enough tinkering somehow the situation can be put right). It also reflects the enormous importance all Soviet leaders have assigned to Eastern Europe.

Eastern Europe is important to the Soviet Union for four reasons. First, Eastern Europe serves as a defensive military glacis, thereby ensuring that in anything short of global nuclear war the Soviet homeland will be spared the devastation it underwent in World War II. It could be argued that in the nuclear age, this buffer role has lost its former significance. This is not, however, and never has been the prevailing Soviet view. Early in the postwar period, Soviet military planners suggested in their writings that they could win a war with the United States by quickly overrunning the whole of Europe before the United States could bring its nuclear monopoly into play.[2] A forward presence in Eastern Europe was vital to making such a strategy work.

The "revolution in Soviet military affairs" that took place after 1953 resulted in a change of strategy, but, with the possible exception of a brief period in the late 1950s (when Nikita Khrushchev appeared ready to stake everything on long-range missiles), did not lead to a downgrading of Eastern Europe's strategic importance. Throughout this period, the Soviet Union devoted both its defense and its political-arms control policies to attempts to neutralize the U.S. nuclear deterrent. With the "deterror deterred," conventional warfare became more rather than less important, and the strategic value of Eastern European territory was enhanced rather than diminished. This situation is unlikely to change under Gorbachev. To the extent that there is a grain of seriousness in his rhetoric about creating a nuclear-free world (with a nuclear-free Europe a vital first step), Eastern Europe may even gain in strategic significance.

Second, Eastern Europe serves as an ideological buffer that protects the Soviet Union from subversive influences emanating from the West. The seriousness with which the Soviet leadership regards this role was demonstrated in 1968, when developments in Czechoslovakia caused concern among the leaders of the neighboring Ukraine, and again in 1980–1981, when the crisis in Poland had spillover effects in the Baltic republics, especially Lithuania.

Third, Eastern Europe provides the Soviet Union with a base from which to exercise political influence over those parts of Europe not under direct Soviet control. Here again, it could be argued that this view is obsolete and that the Soviet presence and the recurrent upheavals in the region act as barriers to rather than as facilitators of increased Soviet influence in Western Europe. From the Soviet perspective, however, control of Eastern Europe is the only way of guaranteeing that a fundamental change in the European security order, if it occurs, takes place in a direction favorable to rather than destructive of Soviet interests. Only this presence (in the northern tier countries if not necessarily in the Balkans) can rule out absolutely the creation of a reunified Germany, which, even if it were neutral, could still pose a formidable threat to the Soviet Union.

With reunification not an option (as all significant political forces in West Germany now realize), the Soviet Union can concentrate on trying to manipulate the intra-German relationship and the broader symmetries and parallelisms between the two halves of Europe, thereby hoping to entice the West into a new security arrangement on terms favorable to the East. Such a policy is inevitably a "second best" alternative to the direct advance of Soviet influence in a Europe stripped of U.S. protection, but seen from Moscow this alternative is infinitely preferable to a "third best" approach that would entail risks of a strong Germany and evoke memories of the two world wars.

Fourth, Eastern Europe contributes directly to Soviet economic, military, and political capabilities and thereby strengthens the Soviet Union in its rivalry with the United States and "world imperialism." But it is true that Eastern Europe is an economic burden on the USSR and is seen as such by both the leaders and the population of the Soviet Union. This burden grew dramatically in the 1970s, as the USSR came to subsidize the region by providing below-market-cost energy and natural resources in exchange for substandard industrial goods.

From the Soviet perspective, however, these growing costs of empire have been an unintended side effect of Soviet and Eastern European policies and of world economic developments. These costs are not a permanent structural factor. With the right policies, it is hoped in Moscow, more of these resources can be put at the Soviet Union's disposal for the global competition. All of the Eastern European states, and especially East Germany, contribute to Soviet technological achievements, and Moscow hopes that these contributions in particular can be increased in the coming years.

In addition, Eastern Europe makes symbolic, nonmaterial contributions to the Soviet Union's global standing. Leadership of a group of medium-sized industrial powers that automatically supports the USSR on nearly all international issues bolsters the Soviet claim to co-equal status as a superpower at the head of an alternative "world system." Perhaps more importantly, control of Eastern Europe assures the USSR a place in European affairs and allows it to be seen as a full-fledged European power—something that traditionally has mattered a great deal to tsarist and Soviet elites.

Overcoming the Stalinist Legacy

In view of the contributions that Eastern Europe makes to Soviet power, Stalin's successors all have come to share the view that they have no choice but to try overcoming the contradictory and inherently unstable features of the Stalinist model without endangering the basic Stalinist achievement—namely, a strong bloc essentially committed to the same international goals and organized around the same fundamental economic and political principles as the Soviet Union.

Khrushchev's Socialist Community

Khrushchev mounted the first sustained effort to square the circle of maintaining control while overcoming the negative effects that come with it. Establishing a pattern that has since been followed in one form or another by all Soviet leaders, Khrushchev adopted policies that combined recognition of a degree of legitimate national diversity with the pursuit of closer bloc integration. He reversed Stalin's drive toward artificial uniformity but at the same time introduced the idea of a "socialist community" gradually moving toward unity. Whereas Stalin's Eastern Europe had been uniform but atomized, Khrushchev's was to be both diverse and integrated.

Some of the measures toward the recognition of diversity, such as the re-adoption of traditional military uniforms, were largely symbolic but nonetheless politically significant. More importantly, Hungary, Poland, and other bloc members also were allowed a certain latitude to pursue their separate national "roads to socialism." Among the acceptable "roads" was what Khrushchev later called "goulash Communism," which attempted to base its legitimacy not on ideological fervor but on the promise of rising personal consumption.

To promote the process of integration, Khrushchev tried to transform the Council for Mutual Economic Assistance (CMEA), which originally had been little more than a paper scheme that was founded to counter the Marshall Plan and to help isolate Yugoslavia, into an organization with real power. Khrushchev hoped to endow CMEA with supranational authority to adjust plans and to allocate investment throughout the bloc.

In the military sphere, he sought to use the Warsaw Pact to promote integration and standardization. At its founding in May 1955, the Warsaw Pact was important mainly as the East's political reply to the rearming of West Germany and, following the Austrian State Treaty and the withdrawal of Soviet troops from that country, as a means to provide a legal justification for the continued stationing of Soviet troops in neighboring countries. The pact did not play much of a role in fostering Soviet–Eastern European military cooperation, which was efficiently managed through a tight network of bilateral links. But under Khrushchev's prodding, the pact gradually began to play a more substantive role. The Political Consultative Committee (PCC) and several subsidiary organs laid the basis for closer military and foreign policy coordination. In 1961, the first military maneuvers were held. The Soviets also began to press their allies to upgrade their military forces by purchasing large amounts of Soviet hardware.

Despite some progress toward his goals, in the final analysis Khrushchev's policies were not successful. Ultimately, he could not strike a stable balance between an acceptable degree of national diversity and sustained movement toward unity. The latter ran into increasing resistance, while the former raced ahead and ultimately culminated in the Prague Spring of 1968. His plans for economic integration were strongly resisted by some of the Eastern Europeans, who rightly feared that supranationality would entail complete subordination to the economic planning authorities in Moscow.

After weathering the Polish and Hungarian Octobers of 1956, Khrushchev presided over a steady weakening of the Soviet bloc as a force in international politics. He had worked out a modus vivendi with Yugoslavia, but he was unable to "win back" what Stalin had lost. Khrushchev could do nothing to prevent Albania's breakaway and, by overreaching himself in pushing supranational economic integration, created the issue around which Romania's Gheorghiu-Dej was first able to assert his country's autonomy. Khrushchev did not develop an effective policy toward the West, and the root of his policy failure was at least partly in Eastern Europe or, more specifically, Berlin and the GDR. By repeatedly trying to compel Western recognition of the GDR and to achieve a solution to the Berlin problem on his terms, he contributed to the very Western solidarity that made such recognition so difficult to achieve.

Brezhnev-Kosygin and the Push for Integration

The Brezhnev-Kosygin regime that replaced Khrushchev in 1964 did not radically revise his policies toward Eastern Europe. In keeping with their overall preferences and priorities, the new leaders placed somewhat more emphasis than Khrushchev did on military integration and somewhat less on CMEA. In 1965, Leonid Brezhnev called for the "further perfecting" of the Warsaw Pact, by which he seemed to mean the creation of new institutional machinery to enhance supranational control. But he was unable to achieve anything in the face of Eastern European resistance. Meanwhile, Romania's victory on the supranationality question through its 1964 declaration of autonomy (which was quietly applauded by some of the other states) set back progress toward economic integration. On the East-West front, the new leaders could not prevent France, West Germany, and the United States from launching policies of détente, "small steps," and "peaceful engagement" designed to woo Eastern Europe away from Moscow or stop the People's Republic of China (PRC) from forging closer ties with Albania and Romania and even making overtures to the more Moscow-oriented allies. By early 1968, the new regime's record in Eastern Europe was probably even less impressive than Khrushchev's.

The August 1968 Soviet invasion of Czechoslovakia ushered in a new era in Soviet–Eastern European relations and marked the beginning of a sustained Soviet effort to make Khrushchev's policies both more effective and more palatable to the Eastern European regimes. The events of 1968 forced the Soviet leadership to pay closer attention to the bloc, whereas the military intervention gave the Kremlin new leverage over its recalcitrant allies, which could no longer doubt *Soviet* seriousness even as they reevaluated the worth of separate ties with the West.

The basic thrust of Soviet policy after 1968 was a new push for integration—across the board and "from the bottom up." To ensure that the pact would not again have to resort to military intervention to maintain control, the Soviet leadership sought to weave a tight network of economic, political, military, and cultural ties at all levels of state and society. At the same time, the loyal Eastern European regimes were given, in exchange for their support, a greater sense of participation and somewhat more of a say in *how* integration would occur.

In the economic sphere, Prime Minister Aleksey Kosygin introduced a package of integrationist reform measures at a special CMEA session in April 1969. The Kosygin package eventually became, in somewhat modified form, the 1971 Comprehensive Program for Integration, which is still a landmark document for bloc economic integration. The document called for joint action in three main areas: coordination of plans, cooperation on long-term target programs (LTTPs) in high-priority industries, and CMEA investment projects.

The new push for economic integration was complemented by integrationist reforms in the military sphere. The March 1969 meeting of the PCC resulted in the creation of three new institutions: the Committee of Defense Ministers, the Military Council, and the Committee for the Coordination of Military Technology. In addition to these high-level bodies, pact military establishments increased their ties with the Soviet military at the lower levels of command. During the 1970s, joint command-staff exercises, exchanges of military visits, and advanced training for Eastern European officers at Soviet military schools became more frequent and extensive.

After 1968, the pact also assumed a larger role in political and foreign policy coordination. Such coordination (which often did not include Romania) became more important with the onset of détente and specifically with the convening of two multilateral East-West forums, the Conference on Security and Cooperation in Europe and the Mutual and Balanced Force Reduction talks in Vienna.

Although the focus of the post-1968 program was on tightening of physical and administrative controls, the ideological factor was not neglected. Ignoring the cynicism about Marxism-Leninism that had taken hold in Eastern Europe, the USSR moved to tighten ideological coordination by setting up in 1973 a bloc conference of party secretaries responsible for ideology and culture. The conference sought to promote the emergence of a bloc-wide socialist consciousness and culture by, for example, forging new links among journalists, party activists, educators, and academics.

In pressing for greater bloc cohesion, Brezhnev continued to share Khrushchev's view that integration did not require complete uniformity. The Soviet Union thus permitted the individual Eastern European leaderships to work out, within certain well-defined limits, their own roads to socialism and prosperity. Hungary continued with its New Economic Mechanism, which it had launched in 1968. After Władysław Gomułka was ousted in 1970, the Soviet Union tacitly encouraged Edvard Gierek's consumerist approach to restoring stability in Poland. In Czechoslovakia, "normalization" was achieved in large part by encouraging the population to refocus its attention on private economic welfare.

Along with integration and tolerance of limited diversity, the third element of Brezhnev's Eastern European policy was an active détente policy toward Western Europe (which was of course motivated by other considerations as well). In the early 1970s, the Soviet Union at last appeared to have what it clearly did not under Khrushchev—an effective policy toward the West that served rather than undercut intrabloc requirements. Ever since the collective security proposals of the 1950s, Soviet leaders had sought a formula by which they could compel or cajole the West into recognizing the postwar European territorial and political status quo and then use this recognition to help permanently stabilize the domestic situation in Eastern Europe. Instead of a vicious circle in which "cold war" with the West helped to perpetuate the isolation and illegitimacy of the Eastern regimes, which in turn led to instability in the East, conflict with the West and the perpetuation of "cold war," Soviet leaders sought to initiate a virtuous circle in which relative stability in the East—underwritten, if necessary, by the direct application of Soviet military power—would facilitate détente with the West. This in turn would help to prop up, by political and economic means, Eastern stability and thus help to make further application of military power unnecessary.

Brezhnev probably believed that he had broken decisively with the pattern of the past and had initiated precisely such a virtuous circle. He was not naive about the potentially destabilizing effects of increased contact with the West or about the dangers of economic dependence on capitalist suppliers, banks, and markets. It is not accidental that Yuri Andropov's KGB was greatly strengthened in this period. But the world in general seemed to be going Brezhnev's way, and he probably genuinely believed that East-West détente on balance would have a stabilizing effect on Eastern Europe, both in political and economic terms. Bilateral treaties with the FRG and the Helsinki Final Act would legitimate the postwar order, which would be further bolstered by the economic gains expected from détente.

By the end of the decade, it should have been clear to the Soviet leadership that these calculations were profoundly mistaken and that the successes of the early 1970s were more apparent than real. Riots broke out in Poland in 1976. Although not as violent as those of 1970 that had led to the fall of Gomułka, they helped launch the movements and personalities that were to dominate the Polish scene four years later. Elsewhere in Eastern Europe, there was a general rise in dissidence, caused in part by closer links with the West and the inspiration to Eastern European human rights activists provided by the Helsinki Final Act. Economic growth had slowed, and nearly all the Eastern European countries began to face serious balance-of-payments and debt repayment problems.

In sum, Brezhnev's policies, which were sophisticated in design and which were implemented, at least in the early part of the decade, with considerable vigor, had done nothing to resolve the three dilemmas inherited from the Stalin era. Domestic legitimacy was as problematic as ever, as the rise of Solidarity demonstrated. Economic and other forms of bloc-wide integration continued to lag and were in fact set back further by the economic crisis in Poland, which made national economic planners more reluctant than ever to rely on their neighbors. Finally, Brezhnev's détente clearly had not succeeded in bridging the East-West gap in a way that had stabilizing rather than destabilizing implications for the bloc.

Crisis and Response

Despite the many warning signs, the Soviet leadership did not seriously focus on Eastern Europe's problems until it was forced to by the crisis in Poland that began in the summer of 1980. This crisis probably came as a profound shock to a Soviet leadership that had come to believe much of its own propaganda about trends in the bloc after 1968.

However surprised it might have been by the crisis itself, the Brezhnev leadership had few doubts about its ultimate response. It was determined not to allow the consolidation of a decisive change in Poland's internal order. The Gdańsk accords, which legitimized a degree of pluralism in Polish society, were clearly unacceptable to Moscow. In the course of the sixteen-month crisis, the Soviets pressured Gierek, Stanisław Kania, and then Wojciech Jaruzelski to retrench and crack down. Had Jaruzelski's imposition of martial law not finally stemmed the reformist tide, the Soviet Union probably would have intervened directly with its own military force, even though the international political costs of doing so would have been enormous.

The Soviet Union's instinctive explanation for the Polish crisis, in public at least, was Western "subversion," which in turn was linked to the increase in East-West tensions that had followed the 1979 North Atlantic Treaty Organization (NATO)–Intermediate Nuclear Forces decision and the Soviet invasion of Afghanistan. Echoing and indeed going beyond the accusations leveled against NATO during the 1968 crisis in Czechoslovakia, Soviet spokesmen accused the West of plotting to tear Poland away from the structure of "world socialism." As the crisis dragged on, Soviet analysis became somewhat broader and more realistic. Soviet authors began to acknowledge the existence of factors *in Poland* that made it vulnerable to outside pressures. These factors included the "mistakes" of the Gierek leadership and, more fundamentally, the failure of the Polish party throughout the entire postwar period to adequately follow socialist (that is, Soviet) models and to eliminate troublesome "vestiges" of the capitalist past, particularly the private peasantry and the special role of the church.

There was a great reluctance, however, to concede that such factors had any relevance for the other countries of the bloc and above all for the Soviet Union. It was only after the imposition of martial law and the relative stabilization in Poland that the Soviet regime began a serious analysis of what implications the crisis had for Eastern Europe as a whole and for the Soviet Union itself. In this period, attention shifted from Western "subversion" and circumstances unique to Poland to certain fundamental questions regarding the very nature of the socialist system.

Debate About Contradictions Under Socialism

Beginning in February 1982, the Soviet press featured a "sanctioned debate" among academics and party officials about the nature of "contradictions" under socialism. A number of Soviet writers rejected the argument that mere "vestiges of capitalism" could explain the crisis in Poland. Instead, they pointed to the importance of "contradictions inherent in and intrinsic to socialism itself." With the elimination of exploiting classes, these contradictions were by definition "nonantagonistic." Nevertheless, Soviet authors concluded that such factors as corruption, poor management, and the loss of contact by the party with the workers could result in some contradictions "acquiring the nature of an antagonistic contradiction."[3]

The implications of this debate for Eastern Europe were significant. If the outcome had been general agreement that the crisis was strictly the result of "capitalist vestiges," the message to Poland and the rest of the bloc would have been clear. Only thorough collectivization could solve the problem. But by concluding that corruption and other failings could in effect lead to antagonistic contradictions even in a socialist country, Soviet ideologues signaled that these "vestiges," although still to be deplored and eliminated in the long run, were not the real issue and that what was needed was some kind of reform in the Polish party and state apparatus.

Soviet theoreticians left open the possibility of domestic reform, but Soviet policymakers saw reform as only one and by no means the most important element of a broad strategy of "normalization." More important were such steps as rebuilding the Polish party; strengthening the Jaruzelski leadership and pointing it in the right direction; wiping out, by police methods if necessary, Solidarity and other "subversive" groups; and redirecting Poland's trade and economic cooperation away from the West and toward the Soviet Union and the rest of the bloc.

The Polish crisis coincided with a belated Soviet effort to restore momentum toward greater bloc cohesion and to redress the Eastern European drain on Soviet resources that Western analysts had long noted. The Soviet leadership was becoming concerned about Eastern Europe's failure to carry its fair share, as seen from Moscow, of bloc economic and defense burdens. In November 1981, just as the Polish crisis neared its climax, the Soviet Union decreed a 10 percent cut in oil exports to Eastern Europe, to take effect in 1982. Poland was exempted from this extreme measure but not from the general tightening. The Soviet Union had provided an estimated $4 billion in economic aid to Poland during the 1980–1981 crisis in an effort to promote stability. Such aid dropped precipitously after December 1981, however, and Soviet emphasis shifted to tightening the economic links between Poland and the Soviet Union.

Andropov, Chernenko, and the Economic Tightening

Brezhnev's successor, Yuri Andropov, was originally hailed in Eastern Europe as a man who understood the region's problems and who could be expected to countenance continued reforms. In the brief period in which he was active, however, Andropov did little more than press for better Eastern European economic performance and complain about the dangers of ideological deviance, especially in Poland and Romania.

Ironically, Konstantin Chernenko, a weak leader in the Brezhnev mold, accomplished more in this area than did Andropov, who was seen as more dynamic by Eastern Europe and the West. In May 1984, Chernenko was able to conclude a far-reaching, fifteen-year economic agreement that called for the closer integration of Polish and Soviet industry. The two countries pledged closer coordination of five-year plans, the development of "direct links" between Polish and Soviet firms, and closer cooperation in the scientific and technological fields. He later reached a similar agreement tying the Soviet and East German economies more closely.

On the multilateral front, Chernenko used the June 1984 CMEA summit to take up the questions of improved economic coordination and better East European performance. The meeting's final communiqué stressed improved planning and, no doubt in deference to Soviet concern about the increasing cost of energy extraction in the USSR, the need for energy conservation. The meeting also established the Permanent Conference of the Central Committee Secretaries for Economic Affairs, which was intended to facilitate the exchange of information about economic experiments in various bloc countries and, quite possibly from the Soviet point of view, provide a forum in which Eastern European economic experiments could be subjected to direct scrutiny by the CPSU. The June 1984 summit also announced plans for a CMEA 2000 science and technology program, although this was not formally adopted until December 1985.

For both Andropov and Chernenko, Eastern Europe's share of the defense burden continued to be the sore point that it had become in the late Brezhnev period. Soviet military planners were disturbed not only at the lack of growth in Eastern European defense budgets, but also at the resulting qualitative gap between armaments of the Soviet forces deployed in the theater and those of the non-Soviet Warsaw Pact armies. This issue had come to a head in late 1978, when Nicolae Ceauşescu publicly announced that he had withstood Soviet pressures to increase defense spending. After simmering at a low level for several years, the issue came to the fore once again at the annual meeting of the Defense Ministers' Committee in December 1983. Soviet Defense Minister Dmitri Ustinov called for increased Eastern European defense spending to counter NATO efforts.

In pressing the Eastern Europeans for better performance and greater cohesion, Andropov and Chernenko both relied heavily on the increased tensions with the West and with the alleged "war danger" emanating from the United States. The Eastern European regimes and peoples were told that the Soviet Union was in effect under attack by international "reaction" and that all Communists had a responsibility to rally to its side with moral and material support.

Continued Divisiveness Within the Bloc

Ultimately, however, rising East-West tensions proved to be a divisive rather than a unifying element within the bloc. No doubt emboldened by the absence of strong leadership in Moscow, the Eastern European regimes objected in varying degrees to the USSR's post-INF strategy. To earn the hard currency needed to pay off debts and sustain their economies, the

Eastern Europeans badly needed to preserve old and to win new export markets in the West. Thus, they were concerned at what appeared to be the onset of a deep East-West rift that could disrupt patterns of trade and economic cooperation.

The deployment of new Soviet short-range missiles in Eastern Europe, coupled with Moscow's war-scare propaganda, also caused concern in Eastern European publics and fostered the growth of independent peace movements that constituted an embryonic challenge to the Eastern European regimes. This was especially the case in the GDR, where the churches and many young people were affected by the behavior of their compatriots in the FRG.

The depth of these differences about policy toward the West was exposed in an unusual polemic that took place throughout 1984 in the Soviet and Eastern European press. The conflict began in January with the publication of an earlier speech by Hungarian Central Committee Secretary Mátyás Szűrös, in which he openly denied the existence of an "organized forum . . . that could formulate the communist parties' international interests and common strategy" and asserted that "certain current factors make it possible for relations between individual socialist and capitalist countries to develop even though a deterioration in East-West relations and a diminishment of contacts is the general trend."[4] Szűrös was promptly attacked in the Czechoslovak press, which stressed the need for absolute solidarity with the Soviet Union at a time of rising danger and warned that any "attempt to gain unilateral 'advantage' from the capitalist world and from its financial and other institutions merely harms the prestige of socialism in the eyes of the world."[5] Particularly remarkable and no doubt alarming from the Soviet point of view was the fact that the East German press promptly reprinted and thereby tacitly endorsed Szűrös's views. Before the polemic eventually died down at the end of 1984, Szűrös had been supported in different ways by the Romanians, Bulgarians, and the East Germans, but he had been decisively rebuffed by the Soviets and their surrogates in Prague.

Gorbachev's Approach

Gorbachev's approach toward Eastern Europe has gone through several stages. After taking power in early 1985, his main concern and that of his colleagues was to reestablish Soviet authority. The open polemics of 1984 and Eastern Europe's persistent failure to meet its economic obligations no doubt were enough to convince him that Eastern Europe had been allowed to drift in recent years and that what was needed were closer contact and renewed attention to the bloc.

The First Stage

In his first year in power, he met with the Eastern European leaders no fewer than three times: at Chernenko's funeral in March, at a special session in April to renew the Warsaw Treaty, and then at the Warsaw Pact PCC meeting in Sofia in October. In addition to these meetings with party leaders, Gorbachev made two other symbolically important appearances at multilateral gatherings of the bloc. In the summer of 1985, he addressed the first meeting of the newly formed Permanent Conference of Central Committee Secretaries of Economic Affairs, and in December he attended a Moscow meeting of CMEA premiers to oversee the formal launching of the CMEA 2000 science and technology program. In meeting with the bloc secretaries, he signaled his interest—both positive and negative—in the reform efforts in other countries. At the December meeting, he linked his ambitious plans for technological revitalization in the USSR with the long-standing Soviet goal of CMEA integration.

In this initial period of Gorbachev's rule, some Eastern Europeans were concerned that a strong new Soviet leader would move quickly to impose discipline and uniformity on the bloc. These fears were heightened in June 1985, when *Pravda* ran a major article suggesting that an increased role for markets and private enterprise could "destabilize the foundations of socialist economic management" and lead to the "violation of social justice." These fears proved unwarranted, however, and other articles soon appeared reiterating the admissibility of different roads to socialism. Even more telling was the actual practice of the Soviet leadership, which did nothing to stop or reverse reforms underway in Poland, Hungary, and Bulgaria.

It also became clear that Gorbachev had no plans to further his own domestic modernization program by trying to "squeeze" Eastern Europe. He did not, for example, repeat the one-time, 10 percent cut in oil exports that was decreed for 1982. Such an approach, he probably concluded, would risk destabilization and produce only modest short-term benefits to the Soviet economy.

Instead, he persisted in efforts launched in the early 1980s to gradually lower the level of subsidies and to bring trade into balance, and he spoke out against the poor quality of Eastern European exports to the Soviet Union. During his trip to Sofia in October 1985, he told Bulgarian factory workers that he and Todor Zhivkov had talked without "evading a few prickly issues," including the poor quality of Bulgarian goods to the Soviet Union, a matter about which the Soviets had long complained.

Responding to these pressures and aided partly by a favorable shift in the terms of trade as a result of the fall in the price of energy, the Eastern European countries began to close the trade gaps. The GDR had already begun to reduce its trade deficit with the Soviet Union in 1984. Hungary did so in 1985, and even Poland committed itself to eliminating its trade deficit with the Soviet Union by the end of 1988.

The Second Stage

The second stage of Gorbachev's policy toward Eastern Europe began in 1986, after control had been firmly established. During this period, Gorbachev continued to emphasize discipline and better performance, but he appeared to be increasingly attracted to Eastern European reform experiments and sympathetic toward greater intrabloc autonomy. He followed Brezhnev in praising the "diversity" of economic practice within the socialist system and hinted that the Soviet Union might adopt some Eastern European innovations. During his June 1986 visit to Hungary, he stated that the USSR watched "with attention and respect" Hungary's attempts to solve economic and social problems by innovative means, even though he stopped short of a blanket endorsement of the Hungarian reform. He also spoke highly of East German economic achievements and in particular of its system of industrial combines.

The Third Stage

This second phase of Gorbachev's policy was short-lived, however, and was soon overtaken by a third phase characterized by growing concerns about the close links between the fate of his own economic program and developments in Eastern Europe. The new emphasis was apparent by the time of Gorbachev's April 1987 visit to Prague and became especially pronounced after the June CPSU Central Committee plenum that unveiled major economic reforms in the Soviet Union. Although still willing to tolerate greater autonomy and interested in Eastern European reforms, Gorbachev seems from this point onward to have become much more aware of the need for bloc-wide restructuring. As he declared in *Perestroika,* "It goes without saying that no socialist country can successfully move forward in a healthy rhythm without understanding, solidarity and mutually beneficial cooperation with the other fraternal nations, or at times even without their help."[6]

Thus by the spring of 1987, Gorbachev had become considerably more forceful in pushing for change in Eastern Europe, both in private meetings with the leaders and through public pressure. He used his April 1987 trip to Prague to mount an indirect critique of the Husák regime and to take his case for "restructuring" directly to the Czechoslovak people. Soviet pressure for change no doubt played a key role in the retirement of Gustav Husák in December 1987 and his replacement as party head by Miloš Jakeš (Husák retains the largely honorific post of president).

Although Gorbachev's approach to Eastern Europe has evolved over time, it has not been marked by dramatic, bloc-wide initiatives. So far, the only major new initiative is the CMEA 2000 program, which was launched under Chernenko. It commits the member states to intensified cooperation in such high-technology areas as computers, microprocessors, robotics, and communications. Although the content of this program is modern and forward-looking, the form is rather traditional and not substantially different from the LTTPs of the 1970s. The program calls for more "direct links" between enterprises and ministries, greater exchange of information, and similar measures that have been tried in the past. It does, however, raise the political profile of intrabloc links in the technology sector and thus may give the Soviets greater leverage in working out technology-sharing arrangements and joint research projects with the Eastern Europeans.

The relative paucity of new, bloc-wide initiatives does not in itself imply a lack of dynamism in Soviet policy. Rather, it reflects a belief that the key to accomplishing Soviet goals is tighter integration based on real economic incentives rather than on a proliferation of sweeping bloc initiatives that are then not implemented. As Gorbachev has written, "We want the CMEA to have less administrative regimentation, fewer committees and commissions, and to pay greater attention to economic incentives, initiative, [and] the socialist spirit of enterprise. . . . We and our friends think that the CMEA must get rid of a surplus of paper work and bureaucratic muddle."[7] Soviet efforts to introduce a convertible ruble, which so far have been welcomed by some bloc countries but appear to be opposed by Romania and East Germany, are one manifestation of the increased interest in Moscow in creating new incentives.

Perhaps the most noteworthy aspect of Gorbachev's approach to Eastern Europe since the June plenum has been his apparent interest in defining new norms—both economic and political—for relations within the bloc. As he stated in his November 2 speech, "Relations among the socialist countries [need] to be better constructed on generally recognized principles." Such norms no doubt would be attractive to the Eastern Europeans because these norms would provide benchmarks for what is and is not permissible (or mandatory) in the area of economic reform and thus make Soviet policies and reactions more predictable. Adoption of such norms would be a reflection of and would in turn further enforce what appears to be a rising degree of tolerance in the Soviet Union for change and diversity.

So far, however, the "generally recognized principles" that Gorbachev has listed are rather vague and not all that new. They include

> unconditional and total equality; the responsibility of the ruling party for affairs in its state, and for patriotic service to its people; concern for the general cause of socialism, respect for one another, a serious attitude toward what has been achieved and tried out by friends; voluntary and varied cooperation; and the strict observance by all of the principles of peaceful coexistence. The practice of socialist internationalism rests upon these.[8]

Such principles are too general to serve as a guideline for policy, and some, although compatible in the abstract, are likely to conflict in the real world. "Concern for the general cause of socialism" is listed *after* "patriotic service" to a party's own people, but where these principles come into conflict, it is easy to see a Soviet leader invoking the latter to vitiate the former.

Apart from this commitment to new norms, Gorbachev seems genuinely committed to the improved consultation process begun in 1985. In his report to the Twenty-seventh CPSU Congress, he claimed that the "institution of multilateral working meetings of the leaders of the fraternal countries is taking shape." Whereas Brezhnev gloried in the "comradely atmosphere" and the absence of "the formalities of protocol" at his summer meetings in the Crimea, Gorbachev stressed frankness, the airing of differences, and the need for "working meetings."

It is of course impossible to tell whether these consultations will yield substantive results or whether they will degenerate over time into yet another example of pro forma cooperation. The most that can be said is that Gorbachev is certainly aware of the tendency for bloc consultations to evolve into mere formalism. As he wrote in *Perestroika,* "Beginning with the end of the 1970s, contacts between leaders of fraternal countries became more for show rather than for real business. There was less trust in them and their approach was more businesslike."[9]

Bilateral Relations

While hinting at bloc-wide norms and reform measures, Gorbachev and his colleagues have recognized the diversity of situations within the bloc and thus are devoting considerable attention to bilateral relations. Of the Soviet Union's bilateral relations in Eastern Europe, the relationship with Poland is the most important and the one that seems to have absorbed the greatest amount of Gorbachev's time and energy. Building upon the Chernenko-Jaruzelski agreement of 1984, Gorbachev has continued to press for closer integration of the Polish and Soviet economies. In 1986 and 1987, the two countries concluded additional intergovernmental protocols spelling out the development of new "direct links" between plants and organizations.

In the political arena, Gorbachev personally has gone out of his way to shower praise on Jaruzelski, and Polish-Soviet relations have improved steadily since Gorbachev's accession to power. The Soviet leader seems to have a genuine rapport with his Polish counterpart, but he probably also believes that a solid Moscow-Warsaw axis serves broader East-West and intrabloc objectives. In the East-West context, it provides tangible evidence of the futility of all Western attempts to divide or pressure the bloc. Within the bloc, full restoration of Poland to its traditionally favored spot as the most important country in the bloc is itself a symbol of "normalization" after the turmoil of the early 1980s.

In addition, the Soviet leadership may be looking to Poland as a testing ground for economic and social reform in the Soviet Union. As Hungary's economic performance has faltered and as East Germany has shown little interest in reform of any kind, Poland's role has increased. The Soviet media watched with keen interest in 1987 as Jaruzelski introduced a package of far-reaching reforms that combined decentralization with market incentives. At the same time, Gorbachev and his supporters must be disturbed by the temporary, although as yet not fatal, setbacks the Polish reform program has suffered, including the vote against it in the November 1987 referendum and the new waves of strikes in April and August 1988.

Although Gorbachev has aligned himself, at least on the theoretical plane, with those who recognize that reforms are necessary to ensure long-term stability, he does not seem to recognize that there may be, as many Western observers have argued, an inherent contradiction between domestic reform and the development of closer ties with the Soviet economy. This contradiction is most apparent in the case of Poland, which may have to delay progress on its stated goals of switching from "intensive" to "extensive" growth to meet its obligations to the Soviet Union. Meeting these obligations probably will require, among other things, more investment in Poland's energy-intensive steel and coal industries.

Although Gorbachev's policies may impede—unwittingly or otherwise—needed *economic* change in Eastern Europe, they may contribute to *social* and *political* developments that neither he nor the other bloc leaders would like to see. Gorbachev's efforts to use political and social mobilization as a weapon against the bureaucracy and to promote economic reform in the Soviet Union make little sense in the Eastern European context, where most countries already have a tradition of economic reform. Even though mid-level bureaucrats can, as in the Soviet Union, frustrate reform, the more persistent challenge has been to insulate economic reform from the political and social life of the nation. Eastern European regimes have struggled to maintain precisely those barriers that Gorbachev, for his own reasons and in his own peculiar circumstances, has concluded need breaking down. *Perestroika* thus could lead to instability, just as Khrushchev's de-Stalinization campaign of 1956 contributed to the upheavals in Hungary and Poland.

Glasnost' (openness) also has potentially destabilizing implications for Eastern Europe, even though access to more information is not in itself a danger to stability. Unlike in the Soviet Union, people in Eastern Europe generally have access to a wide variety of information about the outside world—in East Germany from West German television, in Poland from the widespread underground press, in Hungary from the somewhat more liberal official attitude toward what can be printed in the official press, and in all countries from Western radio broadcasts. What *glasnost'* could do, however, is broaden the range of topics that might be openly discussed and debated in the Eastern European media. This could lead to open discussion of that most sensitive of subjects—relations between Eastern Europe and the Soviet Union—and quickly provoke a backlash from a Soviet Union that is always alert to signs of "anti-Sovietism" and "Russophobia" within the bloc.

Gorbachev seems to think he can preempt such discussion by displaying frankness of his own. As he stated in a 1986 speech at a Warsaw factory,

> Let us have it straight—the heritage we have received is not easy. The relations between Russia and Poland over the centuries have been complicated by the struggle of the ruling exploiter classes of both countries. Both kings and tsars stirred up Poles against Russians and Russians against Poles. . . . But the best sons of Russia and Poland have always considered it as a cause of honor and conscience to fight together against tsarism and saw the meaning of their lives in the struggle against both Polish and Russian exploiters.[10]

In keeping with this spirit of frankness, Poland and the Soviet Union have set up a joint historical commission to investigate the past, and General Jaruzelski was allowed to comment on the history of Soviet-Polish relations in an article in *Kommunist* subsequently reprinted in the Polish press. But this kind of "frankness" is unlikely to appeal to the peoples of Eastern

Europe, who will recognize its instrumental purpose. It will not accomplish its apparent purpose of preempting debate or channeling it in a pro-Soviet direction, but it will whet Eastern European appetites for genuine frankness.

The World Outside the Bloc

Just as Eastern Europe cannot remain unaffected by the Soviet domestic reform effort, it inevitably has been caught up in the Soviet Union's renewed foreign policy activism. The Soviet leadership has looked favorably on Eastern European efforts to reestablish close links with the PRC, which the leadership sees, perhaps incorrectly, as a stalking horse for the USSR's own effort to rebuild party ties with the PRC. Moscow thus welcomed the 1986 visits to China by Jaruzelski and Erich Honecker. Moscow may also see some value in the partial restoration of ties between some Eastern European states and Israel.

Détente with Western Europe

But the main area in which Eastern Europe can contribute to Soviet foreign policy is in Western Europe. Like his predecessors, Gorbachev must find a way to make the bloc an asset rather than a liability in an active Soviet *Westpolitik.* At a minimum, this requires the maintenance of domestic stability. Another crisis in Poland or a blowup in some other country would raise tensions throughout Europe.

Beyond maintaining a minimum of domestic stability, Gorbachev shares his predecessors' view that he must make clear to the West his "bottom line"—to reiterate in no uncertain terms that there has been no change in the standard Soviet position that "socialist gains" are "irreversible" and that good East-West relations must be premised on Western recognition of this fact. The new edition of the CPSU Party Program, which Gorbachev no doubt had a role in shaping, reaffirms this point:

> The CPSU attaches great significance to the further development of peaceful good-neighborliness and cooperation among the states of Europe. Respect for the territorial-political realities which came about as a result of World War II is an inalienable condition for the stability of positive processes in this and in other regions. The CPSU is resolutely opposed to attempts to revise these realities on any pretexts whatsoever and will rebuff any manifestations of revanchism.[11]

Soviet attacks on "revanchism" are directed not only at West Germany for its alleged designs on the GDR but at the West in general for its past, and to some extent present, policies toward Poland. At the June 1986 congress of the Polish United Workers' party, Gorbachev praised Jaruzelski's imposition of martial law and once again stressed the international implications of what happened in Poland.

> The achievements in the socialist lands are irreversible. Attacks against the socialist order, or attempts to undermine this socialist order from the outside or to split one country or another from the socialist community, constitute an attack not only against the will of the peoples involved, but against the entire postwar order and ultimately against peace itself.[12]

While underlining the inadmissibility of all efforts to reverse Soviet positions in Eastern Europe, Gorbachev has been more adventurous than his predecessors in enlisting the Eastern European regimes in his policy of renewed détente toward Western Europe and in exploring new forms of bloc-to-bloc economic, political, and, even, military contacts. He pressed for the conclusion of a CMEA–European Community (EC) umbrella accord even though such an agreement could enhance the EC's access to Eastern Europe and undercut Soviet control. The accord, which was finally concluded in May 1988 after a prolonged deadlock involving West Berlin, will have only modest effects on trade, but it lends a degree of political substance to the "common European home" that has figured so heavily in Gorbachev's propaganda. Some bloc officials also have expressed the hope that the agreement will undercut the Coordinating Committee and facilitate Eastern access to Eureka and other Western European high-technology programs.

In the security area, the Soviet Union and its allies have been calling for direct NATO–Warsaw Pact contacts for the discussion of military doctrine. The June 11, 1986, "Budapest appeal" for new conventional arms control talks proposed creation of an "international consultative commission" composed of representatives from each of the blocs as well as from the neutral and nonaligned. Gorbachev also is encouraging the Eastern European states to cultivate their own bilateral relationships with the countries of Western Europe and has even partially endorsed the Hungarian contention that small and medium-sized countries in Europe can play a "special role" in building détente and maintaining peace.

The GDR and the FRG

Of these relationships, the one between the GDR and the FRG is clearly the most important and the one that in Soviet eyes needs the closest scrutiny. This relationship operates on two levels: the East German government deals with its counterpart in Bonn, and the East German Socialist Unity party (SED) and its various front organizations try to influence social and opposition groups in West Germany, most notably the Social Democratic party (SPD). In June 1985, the SED and the SPD reached agreement on a joint proposal for a chemical-weapons-free zone in Central Europe, which they then presented to their respective governments. This was followed in October 1986 by agreement between the parties on a proposal for a nuclear-weapons-free corridor in Central Europe. The USSR has endorsed both proposals and incorporated them into its own arms control policy.

East Germany's ties with the Bonn government are much more problematic from the Soviet point of view. Relations between the Soviet Union and the GDR were deeply strained in the aftermath of the INF deployments. While the Soviet Union sought to single out and punish West Germany for its role in carrying out NATO strategy, Honecker, instead of making good on his own earlier warnings of an INF-induced "ice age," spoke of the need for "damage limitation" and of keeping the intra-German détente alive. Honecker's actions, which were determined in part by his need for West German credits and technology, caused considerable irritation in Moscow, and Soviet pressure ultimately contributed to Honecker's decision to call off his visit to the FRG in the fall of 1984.

For now at least, the Soviet Union and the GDR have managed to patch up their differences about intra-German ties, as was demonstrated by Soviet acquiescence in Honecker's trip to the FRG in September 1987. The Soviet leadership (which in any case has moved toward its own "normalization" with West Germany) evidently now accepts, however reluctantly, the East German view that the visit served overall bloc interests by legitimizing and elevating the international status of the GDR—as was symbolized by the playing of the East and West German national anthems at the arrival ceremony—and by strengthening the forces of détente in the Federal Republic.

The New Political Thinking and Intrabloc Economic Development

Perhaps of more significance than the step-up in Soviet–East European efforts directed at the West are the implications of Gorbachev's foreign policy activism for domestic and intrabloc developments in Eastern Europe. As has frequently been pointed out, the "new political thinking," and in particular its emphasis on global "interdependence," lends at least some support to those in Eastern Europe who have argued the necessity of expanding ties with the West. That interdependence has broad implications for the way in which the Soviet elite sees Eastern Europe and defines its relationship to Soviet global interests.

Brezhnev was much enamored of the concept of a "world socialist system," which he saw as an emerging political, strategic, and economic unit. The USSR was one component of this system, the developed countries of Eastern Europe another, and the impoverished Communist states of Asia, Africa, and Latin America a third. Brezhnev wanted Eastern Europe to play a more active role in helping to build this system. He also called for the "restructuring of international economic relations," by which he meant, in effect, the striking of a deal with the other (capitalist) "world system" on a more equitable division of global economic power and a rewriting of the economic rules of the game. Western acceptance of barter, buy-back deals, and long-term agreements were seen in Moscow as partial steps toward Western acceptance of a legitimately socialist way of doing things. In the campaign to restructure international relations, it was expected that the nonaligned world would support socialist positions.

Gorbachev shares many of Brezhnev's long-term goals but has downplayed the concept of a world socialist economic system. To make such a system viable would mean a huge drain on Soviet resources and probably a widening gap between Soviet and Western levels of economic development. Instead,

Gorbachev has acknowledged that there is really only *one* world economic system, and he has announced his intention to enter it (on his own terms of course) and to seek a greater voice in its functioning. (This is in part the meaning of his proposal for a "comprehensive system of economic security" that is contained in his report to the Twenty-seventh party congress and was further developed in a January 1986 letter to U.N. Secretary General Javier Perez de Cuellar). Rather than forging an arrangement between the two "world systems," the Soviet Union now will seek to penetrate (and inevitably change the character of) such basically market entities as the General Agreement on Tariffs and Trade and the International Monetary Fund.

This subtle shift in how the Soviet Union defines its own position in the world economy has implications for the countries of Eastern Europe. On the positive side, these countries could have somewhat more latitude to develop their own ties with the West and could come under somewhat less pressure to aid the poorest Communist countries. On the negative side, the Soviet Union may become much more pragmatic and market oriented in dealing with Eastern Europe. Moscow would still press for bloc cohesion, but the emphasis would be on making all socialist countries, particularly the Soviet Union, efficient actors in the world economy. The USSR thus would be less willing to make allowances on ideological and political grounds for Eastern European economic weakness and inefficiency.

The New Political Thinking and Defense Establishments

The new political thinking also could affect the Eastern European defense establishments and the Warsaw Pact in general. On the operational level, most Western observers believe that in recent years the Soviet Union has been embarked on a determined effort to acquire a capability to defeat NATO in a purely conventional conflict. Such an effort not only requires preparing to meet the NATO conventional threat; it also means acquiring the ability to rapidly seize or incapacitate NATO's nuclear weapons, while retaining the option to rapidly "go nuclear" in the event the preferred strategy fails and NATO does respond with a decisive use of nuclear weapons. The mission that Soviet military planners have set for themselves is extremely demanding, and contributions from the non-Soviet Warsaw Pact militaries could well determine success or failure in a future conflict.

If the Soviet Union under Gorbachev continues to take this mission seriously, he is likely to continue to urge Eastern Europeans (especially Poland and the GDR) to expand and modernize their forces and to press for ever tighter military integration under centralized Soviet leadership. At the same time, however, Gorbachev may be realistic enough to conclude that Eastern Europe cannot be expected to make major additional efforts in the military field. The Eastern European armies probably are not regarded in Moscow as reliable. Even leaving aside questions of loyalty and reliability, after a decade of economic and demographic stagnation, Eastern Europe is likely to be a declining military asset in future years. If Gorbachev does indeed come to this conclusion, he may seek to modify Soviet strategy and to upgrade the role of arms control and propaganda in pursuing traditional Soviet security objectives. Proclaimed Soviet interest in "reasonable sufficiency" and "defensive defense" suggests some movement in this direction.

Whatever direction the evolution of Soviet military thinking takes, Eastern Europe is probably destined to play an increasingly active role in the new Soviet conventional arms control offensive directed at Western Europe. The Soviet Union is at least tolerating and perhaps encouraging Poland's recent forays into the conventional arms control area (the Jaruzelski plan) and can be expected to work out a conventional arms control strategy with the East German SED. Having tackled nuclear and chemical weapons in its talks with the SPD, the SED can logically be expected to move into the conventional area where it will try to influence SPD assessments of the East-West balance.

Beyond this kind of largely tactical cooperation designed to appeal to Western opinion, the possibility of a partial Soviet disengagement from Eastern Europe, although unlikely, cannot be ruled out. To decisively influence the West, to promote his denuclearization schemes, and possibly to save on resources, Gorbachev may contemplate large and possibly unilateral troop withdrawals from Eastern Europe. Such withdrawals would be fraught with major consequences for Eastern Europe and probably would not be undertaken unless there was a high degree of confidence in Moscow in the Eastern European leaders and their ability to maintain domestic stability.

The Loss of Romania, Yugoslavia, and Albania

A final aspect of Gorbachev's foreign policy as it relates to Eastern Europe concerns Romania, Yugoslavia, and Albania. The Soviet leadership has never reconciled itself to the "loss" of these three countries, and Gorbachev is no exception to this pattern. In contrast to his recent predecessors, however, he may see concrete prospects for making gains with these economically troubled former satellites.

Romania, of course, has never enjoyed full autonomy, but it has been a disruptive element in bloc security and economic forums and has irritated the Soviet leadership by taking independent stances on such international matters as the maintenance of diplomatic relations with Israel and participation in the 1984 Los Angeles Olympics. Moscow's main potential leverage over Romania is economic. Romania began importing Soviet oil in 1979, as its own domestic production failed to keep pace with domestic and export requirements. Subsequently, Soviet exports of other forms of energy, notably electricity and natural gas, have increased. Meanwhile, the share of Romania's trade with the West has declined, as Ceauşescu has pursued his crash program of paying off debt by limiting hard-currency imports. From the beginning of 1985 to the end of 1986, bilateral Soviet-Romanian trade increased by 47 percent, and Soviet experts and technicians have reappeared in force in much of Romanian industry. So far, this increased trade has not resulted in any change in Romania's foreign policy, but it has made Romania somewhat less vociferous in opposing intrabloc integration. This clearly is a gain for the Soviets on which they no doubt will attempt to build as the post-Ceauşescu leadership takes over.

Soviet-Yugoslav trade also increased dramatically in the early 1980s, as Yugoslavia began to import Soviet oil as a result of its own hard-currency problems. This trade may now have passed its peak, however, as the Yugoslavs reorient themselves toward Western export markets. The Soviets may be disappointed that increased trade did not lead to dramatically closer political ties and may now be ready to try a different tack. They cajoled the Yugoslavs into signing a new political declaration at the end of Gorbachev's visit to Belgrade in March 1988. Although the content of the declaration was satisfactory from the Yugoslav point of view and referred to, among other things, obligations in the U.N. Charter not to use force or to violate borders, the Yugoslavs would have preferred to leave well enough alone and to continue to base their relations with the Soviets on the understanding reached by Marshal Tito and Nikita Khrushchev in 1955, which included Soviet recognition of Yugoslav independence.

The Soviets also know that Albania is beginning to open up to the outside world, as was seen most recently in its establishment, in September 1987, of diplomatic relations with the Federal Republic of Germany. The Soviets have long held out an olive branch to Tirana and are certain to try, perhaps working through other Eastern European countries, to regain a presence. Here again, it would be difficult to point to concrete Soviet gains, but one can expect Gorbachev to continue low-key efforts designed to win favor in Albania without causing alarm in Yugoslavia or the West.

The Outlook

What Gorbachev would *like* to accomplish in his policy toward Eastern Europe is clear. All evidence suggests that he remains committed to the traditional Soviet goals of seeking both control and viability. Being somewhat more adventurous than most of his predecessors, he may risk a degree of control to promote viability. He is unlikely to go too far in this direction, however, because to do so is to put at risk much more than could possibly be gained. The potential upside benefits of a somewhat more dynamic Eastern Europe are too small to justify the downside risks of another 1956, 1968, or 1980–1981.

It is much less certain how successful Gorbachev will be in pursuing these traditional goals. As he tries to maximize the benefits and minimize the costs associated with continued dominance of the region, he must work within the patterns of cooperation developed during the Khrushchev and Brezhnev periods. Two of the six bloc leaders—Zhivkov and Ceauşescu—came to power during Khrushchev's rule and outlived the next three Soviet General Secretaries. Honecker came to power at about the time that Brezhnev was consolidating his preeminent position in Moscow. Jakeš is a recent appointment, but he is almost a decade older than Gorbachev and likely to be a transitional figure. Only in Poland and Hungary is the situation radically different. Jaruzelski, with whom, not surprisingly, Gorbachev has developed a close personal rapport, is roughly the same age and has experienced the same East-West and intrabloc crises as the Soviet leader. In Hungary, Károly Grósz, who replaced Kádár in May 1988, is a fifty-seven-year-old middle-of-the-roader whose election appears to have been welcomed by the Soviets.

The Road to Legitimation

Gorbachev also inherits an institutional structure that derives from the Khrushchev and Brezhnev periods. This structure has been unable to definitively solve any of the "dilemmas" created during the original period of bloc consolidation under Stalin. On the most basic level, the Eastern European leaderships are still struggling to achieve a modicum of legitimacy. Some, such as Kádár, have relied on economic performance and the promise of a rising standard of living. As living standards have stagnated, this path to legitimacy has become more difficult. In any case, even "success" in this area does not ensure legitimacy. The inculcation of consumerist values and the steady growth of economic contact with the West, both of which are essential to making such a policy work, inevitably remind Eastern European populations that their very economic "successes" represent little more than a laborious overcoming of the constraints imposed on them in the first place by the Soviet system.

The other route to legitimation that Eastern European leaderships have used, with varying degrees of success, is the nationalist one. Ceauşescu and, to a lesser extent, Gomułka, Jaruzelski, and even Honecker and Kádár asked for their peoples' support on the grounds that they knew how to pursue national interests within the severe constraints imposed by the bloc and thus by implication were able to protect the nation from an even greater and more onerous degree of Soviet domination. Such appeals can work up to a point, but they do not provide a basis for system or alliance legitimation, and they can hardly be acceptable to the Soviet Union as a final resolution of the legitimacy crisis.

Gorbachev can do little to confer added legitimacy on existing or prospective Eastern European leaders. Indeed, if he is not careful, he may make the legitimacy dilemma worse rather than better. By criticizing and demanding change, he can signal lack of support and increase the vulnerability of Eastern European leaders to domestic pressure. On the other hand, by identifying too closely with individual leaders (as he has done with Jaruzelski) Gorbachev risks tainting them in the eyes of their own publics. This factor will become more important as the Gorbachev euphoria fades and he becomes identified with the status quo rather than with the winds of change. All this is complicated by the impending leadership transitions in Eastern Europe.

Bloc Integration

Nor is it certain that Gorbachev will do any better than his predecessors in solving the dilemma of bloc integration. The Soviet leadership continues to press for "direct production ties" and increased investment flows within the bloc, thus trying to create, by intergovernmental agreement, patterns of integration that might have developed spontaneously had more private ownership and market mechanisms been preserved and had the laws of comparative advantage been allowed to operate. But more exhortation in support of horizontal linkages cannot solve the problem. What really is needed is either a decisive move toward supranationality (vertical subordination of the Eastern European economies to Soviet authority) or the development of the kind of bloc-wide, market-oriented integration measures that Hungarian and other economists have long advocated. Despite their growing interest in market measures and a convertible ruble, the Soviets are unlikely to accept the latter, and the Eastern Europeans will continue to resist the former.

East-West Split in Europe

Finally, it is unclear whether Gorbachev will be any more successful than his predecessors in overcoming the third traditional Soviet dilemma, namely, the East-West split in Europe, with all its perceived negative implications for the stability and prosperity of the Eastern bloc. The best that Gorbachev can probably hope for in his *Westpolitik* would be a renewed détente with Western Europe and some arms control agreements that marginally lower Soviet and Eastern European defense burdens. With its higher standards of living and greater personal freedoms, Western Europe will continue to exert a strong pull on the peoples of Eastern Europe and thus constitute, in Soviet eyes, an inherently destabilizing force. Moreover, even if the Eastern Europeans somehow manage to learn to make much wiser use of their economic ties with the West than they did in the 1970s, they may find that Western Europe is less interested than it was earlier in closer ties with the region. Banks and governments will be more cautious than in the past about lending to Eastern Europe, and Western European protectionism will adversely affect Eastern European access to markets (especially in the agricultural field).

The one exception to this pattern will be West Germany, which has both the political motivation and the economic and financial strength to substantially *increase* its involvement in the region. (Although even here there are limits. Bonn cannot, for example, finance a massive program to clean up the East German environment, much as it might like to both for political reasons and for the sake of its own environment.)

The Soviets are probably ambivalent and perhaps divided on the question of West Germany and its relationship with the East. On the one hand, they see West German involvement in the region as a two-edged sword: economically beneficial but possibly destabilizing politically. The Soviets and their allies will be wary of any political strings Bonn might attach to trade and aid. Soviet stubbornness on the Berlin issue in the negotiations leading to the CMEA-EC accord were one indication of a deep reluctance to allow the West Germans to translate economic power into political gains.

On the other hand, the Soviet Union may see increased opportunities to entice West Germany into the "common European home." The Soviets will continue to woo the Social Democrats and perhaps make efforts to court the West German Right, which has become increasingly disillusioned with U.S. economic and security policies and which has powerful political, economic, and even psychological reasons for intensifying links with the East. Bavarian premier Franz-Josef Strauss's visit to Moscow in December 1987 was one indication of a Soviet effort to reach out to and influence a broader spectrum of European opinion.

In addition to the structural dilemmas that Gorbachev inherits, a number of other factors make the future of Soviet–Eastern European relations especially hard to predict. To begin with, there is the question mark hanging over Gorbachev's own staying power in the Kremlin. If high-level officials in Eastern Europe believe that Gorbachev may lose his post or be forced to cut back on his reform plans, they are likely to hang back and pursue their own conservative course. Such a course is likely to postpone turmoil and upheaval in the short run but may make it more likely in the long term.

This, in turn, brings us to the final uncertainty hanging over Soviet–Eastern European relations. The real test of Gorbachev's Eastern European policy will not come until he confronts a major crisis in the region. With the exceptions of Andropov and Chernenko, both of whom were transitional figures who ruled only briefly, all Soviet leaders have faced either popular revolts in Eastern Europe or attempts by leaders to assert an unacceptable degree of national autonomy.

Although Gorbachev has raised expectations among Western analysts for dramatic change in Soviet foreign and domestic policy, there is little in anything that he has done or said to suggest that if confronted with a crisis of either kind, he would behave fundamentally differently from his predecessors. The outlook, then, is for continued Soviet control but no resolution of those underlying dilemmas that have made this control difficult, expensive, and a recurrent source of international tension.

Notes

1. "Report by Gorbachev at December 10, 1984, Ideological Conference," *FBIS Daily Report: Soviet Union,* February 19, 1985, p. 11.

2. See Herbert S. Dinerstein, *War and the Soviet Union* (New York: Praeger, 1959), pp. 174–177.

3. A. P. Butenko, "Once More About the Contradictions of Socialism," *Voprosy filosofii,* no. 2 (1984).

4. Mátyás Szűrös, "The Reciprocal Effect of National and International Interests in the Development of Socialism in Hungary," *Tarsadálmi szemle,* no. 1 (1984), in Ronald D. Asmus, *East Berlin: the Documentation of a Dispute,* Radio Free Europe, Munich, 1985.

5. Michal Stefaník and Ivan Hlivka, "The National and International in the Policy of the CPCS," *Rudé právo,* March 30, 1984, in ibid., p. 26.

6. Mikhail Gorbachev, *Perestroika* (New York: Harper & Row, 1987), p. 161.

7. Ibid., p. 168.
8. Seventieth anniversary speech, *Pravda,* November 3, 1987.
9. Gorbachev, *Perestroika,* p. 164.
10. *Pravda,* July 2, 1986.
11. *Pravda,* March 7, 1986.
12. *Pravda,* July 1, 1986.

6

The Soviets, the Warsaw Pact, and the Eastern European Militaries

Dale R. Herspring

The role of the Eastern European militaries in Soviet strategy has become increasingly important in the aftermath of the recently concluded Intermediate Nuclear Forces (INF) Treaty and of the talk in Moscow about possible changes in Soviet warfighting strategy. These forces make up almost half of the Kremlin's conventional strength in Central Europe and traditionally have been thought to play a key role in the Kremlin's plans for any North Atlantic Treaty Organization (NATO)–Warsaw Pact conflict. Western analysts have long believed that these militaries are critical to Soviet success in any war in Europe.

Nevertheless, at a time when the INF Treaty is focusing increased attention on the conventional balance of military power in Europe and hints of a possible restructuring of Soviet forces in the region are being widely discussed, there are increasing signs that the Eastern European forces may not be as useful to Soviet warplanners as was once the case. Their decreasing political reliability and military utility raise a number of questions for policymakers in Moscow. How should Soviet forces be modified to deal with the technical and political problems prevalent in the Eastern European militaries? Are more Soviet troops needed? Should greater reliance be placed on nuclear weapons? Are there control mechanisms that can be utilized to ensure Eastern European compliance with Soviet orders?

In conventional arms control negotiations, all the Eastern European political leaderships—with the possible exception of the East Germans—will want their forces included in any reduction plan. But the West is more interested in the reduction of Soviet forces and may well hold out for greater cuts in the Kremlin's forces. Although Moscow can always force the Eastern European

The views expressed in this chapter are those of the author and do not represent official U.S. government policy.

leaderships to obey on this issue, it would exacerbate relations at a time when Mikhail Gorbachev has enough problems in dealing with the region.

The problems of political reliability and technical insufficiencies are, however, indicative of a much deeper problem: Despite more than forty years of Soviet dominance in the region, Moscow has still not succeeded in either legitimating the local regimes or in overseeing the development of economic systems that can satisfy the basic needs of the populace. The one thing that seems to unite most of the peoples of Eastern Europe is a deeply held dislike for the USSR, and Kremlin decisionmakers must always keep the region's potential for political instability in mind. The costs of a military intervention at a time when Gorbachev is attempting to improve East-West relations would be catastrophic. But as he never tires of pointing out, the Soviet Union is beset by serious economic problems, and a reduction in Soviet forces—especially conventional forces, which are much more costly than nuclear—could have important implications for his efforts to get the stagnating Soviet economy moving again.

A reduction of Soviet forces in Eastern Europe would be fraught with serious political repercussions. What if this were seen in the region as a sign of the USSR's decline or, even worse, weakness? What would be the impact on the Eastern European populace? Would it bring about political instability? What if a cutback occurred at a time of political or economic instability in the area? Is there a limit to how many troops the Soviets could reduce in the region without causing problems (three or four divisions might have little or no impact, whereas ten or more could induce serious difficulties)?

A declining role for the Eastern European forces also has implications for any effort by Moscow to modify its warfighting strategy in Europe. Although details of a new policy of "military sufficiency" remain unclear—perhaps even to Soviet decisionmakers—any talk of going to a defensive posture in Europe has important implications for Eastern Europe. Assuming such a policy will mean smaller units primarily configured for defensive tasks, how will such a development affect Eastern European attitudes toward the West, military spending, and the maintenance of a high state of vigilance and discipline in its own military forces? Could such a policy incite others to follow the Romanian example of greater nationalism and military autonomy? Could such pressures be limited only to the military sphere?

The problems the Kremlin faces in dealing with these militaries are not new. Throughout the past forty years, Moscow has tried a number of approaches to ensure the political and technical reliability of its forces. Before looking at the evolution of Soviet policy toward the Eastern European militaries, however, something should be said about the concept of reliability. In essence, this concept asks whether the military in question (a) can carry out the tasks assigned to it and (b) will, if ordered, do so. The latter involves more than simply being prepared to do what one is told. All soldiers follow orders. The issue is with what dedication and steadfastness will the orders be carried out. The more an army—especially one made up primarily of conscripts—believes it is fighting for the nation's national interests, the more willing troops will be to fight and die.

Finally, there are different types of reliability. First, there is the willingness to defend one's own government in the face of internal threats. Generally, the police—and in Eastern Europe the security forces—protect the political system against threats from within the country. But in an extreme situation in which the police or security forces have failed to keep the situation under control, the armed forces may be the last defense against the regime's collapse. Second, reliability refers to the willingness of an army to fight against an external foe. How prepared are the troops to fight a particular war? Does it make a difference who the enemy is—is there a greater willingness to fight and sacrifice against one potential enemy than another? Are there limitations on the use of such troops? For example, must those fighting against a nontraditional foe be deployed differently from those fighting an enemy against which there are deep-seated historical animosities?

Third, there is the question of technical reliability, which primarily refers to a military's ability to fight an external conflict. If an army is prepared to fire on fellow citizens, we can assume it possesses sufficient forces to put down almost any type of internal disturbance. But in the increasingly complex and technological world of modern warfare, an army's ability to operate on the modern battlefield is heavily conditioned by the technical sophistication of the equipment in its inventory. The absence of an up-to-date command and control system may well doom an entire operation and, particularly in the case of an Eastern European army, severely limit its utility to the Soviets.

The Evolution of Soviet Policy Toward the Eastern European Militaries

The Early Years, 1944–1947

During the immediate postwar period, Moscow's priority in dealing with the Eastern European militaries was to neutralize them, particularly their officer corps. The basic message in the military sphere—as in the rest of Eastern European societies at this time—was "he who is not against us is with us." Efforts were made to bring individuals into the military who could be assumed to be more supportive of the regimes, but in the main the emphasis was on working with those who were not unalterably opposed to the new regimes.

This helps explain why in most of these militaries the process of politicization was not nearly as intense as it was to become in later years. The strong animosities on the part of Eastern Europeans who resented the Soviet imposition of alien governments and the Soviet fear of alienating the West combined to convince Joseph Stalin to adopt a go-slow policy in dealing with these countries. After all, these were armies that in one degree or another had long been hotbeds of anti-Sovietism. Consequently, even neutralizing them would mark a step forward. Politicization would come, but it could wait for a while, given that the alternative to neutralization would have been disbandment.

This general avoidance of politicization explains such anomalies as the low number (about 13 percent) of political education officers in the Polish military who were members of the party in December 1944 as well as the higher but still constrained number (56 percent) of party members among officers assigned to the Main Political Administration (MPA).[1] (These are two of the politically sensitive organs in any Communist military.) Some five years later, the mere idea that an individual could be a political officer and not a member of the party would seem absurd.

The situation did not change significantly in the immediate postwar period. For example, in 1946 the Polish political officer's school in Łódż was closed, and by 1948 Polish sources reported that only 50 percent of all political officer positions were filled.[2] Although the purpose of political indoctrination was to impart a basic understanding of Marxism-Leninism, even this was often not required at first in Eastern Europe.

Little thought was given at this time to the deployment of these forces against an external foe. Their equipment was antiquated (often of pre–World War II vintage), training rudimentary, and cadres unqualified, and neither the Soviets nor the Eastern European leaderships showed any concern with rescuing the armed forces from their emasculated condition.

Stalinism, 1948–1953

The imposition of Stalinism in Eastern Europe required the various countries to imitate fully the Soviet model. This included the armed forces. As a result, national command positions were immediately filled with Communists or pro-Communist officers. The "neutral" officers appointed to senior positions only a few years earlier were quickly shunted aside, and the process of recruiting officers from classes presumed to be more sympathetic to communism—workers and peasants—was intensified. Other areas of military life were also affected. Politicization was intensified (for example, attendance at meetings became mandatory), and Soviet doctrine, training procedures, and internal organization were introduced. Even the traditionally unique Eastern European uniforms were eliminated in favor of uniforms almost indistinguishable from those worn by the Soviets. In addition, thousands of Soviet military officers were assigned to Eastern European militaries as "advisers" and in some cases actually incorporated into the national armies as regular officers. The most conspicuous example was in Poland where Soviet Marshal Konstantin Rokossovsky became defense minister and a number of other Soviet officers assumed top-level positions within the Polish military.

Along with the Sovietization process, the Kremlin also began to build up Eastern Europe's military capabilities. By 1949, military conscription had been introduced throughout the region (except for the German Democratic Republic [GDR]), and by 1953 the Eastern European armies had expanded to 1.5 million men, organized roughly into 65 divisions.[3] Soviet equipment began to replace Eastern Europe's outdated weapons. Even though the Soviets saw little reason to trust the internal or external reliability of the various Eastern European militaries at this time, the Kremlin could at least take comfort in the fact that the basis for a more dependable military had been laid.

Post-Stalinism

The aftermath of Stalin's death was a period of major transition for the Eastern European militaries. Most of the more extreme forms of Sovietization were eliminated. Traditional Eastern European military uniforms and songs were reintroduced. Status-of-forces agreements were concluded with Poland (1956), Hungary (1957), Romania (1957), and East Germany (1957), thereby regularizing the presence of Soviet troops in these countries. Even so, the Soviets agreed to a Romanian request in 1958 and withdrew all of their forces from that country.

The most important form of "renationalization" in the Eastern European militaries was the recall of large numbers of Soviet "advisers" and military officers from the region's militaries. In Poland, Marshal Rokossovsky and most of his fellow officers were "thanked" for their services and returned to the Soviet Union in 1956. They were replaced by native Communist officers, many of whom had been purged and imprisoned during the Stalinist period.

At the same time the Eastern European militaries were being renationalized, the role of the political apparatus was again deemphasized. In Poland, for example, the post of deputy commander for political affairs at the company level was abolished and the time allocated for ideological indoctrination shortened. The Communist youth organization in the military was abolished, and the focus of party activity shifted from the political apparatus to the party organization. Because only half the officers and even fewer enlisted personnel were party members, the net result was to weaken party influence within the military.

The Warsaw Pact Is Founded—and Ignored, 1956–1960

Although ostensibly created as a loosely organized "socialist military coalition" to counter "possible aggression," the Warsaw Pact, formally established in May 1955, was equally important to the Kremlin as an institutionalized substitute for Stalin's personalized system of asserting hegemony over the Eastern European militaries. Article 5 provided for a joint military command, which was established in Moscow in 1956. Nevertheless, in military terms the pact remained a paper organization during this period. For example, the primary Soviet history of the pact lists only one major military exercise during the period.[4] As Thomas Wolfe put it, "The Soviet Union made no effort to weld the Warsaw Pact into an integrated military alliance" during its early years.[5]

One of the first things the Soviets agreed to—in light of the major economic problems facing these countries—was a reduction in Eastern European military budgets. The Soviets then accepted a cut of some 464,000 military personnel. The latter action had important economic benefits, and it also offered the Eastern European military leadership an opportunity to dismiss unqualified or undesirable officers and intensify the training of those remaining. As a consequence, the educational level of the region's officers began to rise.

On the technical front, the Soviets also continued their efforts to upgrade Eastern European equipment and weapons. Infantry units were motorized, new armored units were created, and tactical forces were modernized to enable them to operate in a nuclear war environment. T-54s gradually replaced the World War II–vintage T-34s, MIG-17s were added, and improved communication and transportation systems were introduced. Nevertheless, in terms of equipment, the Eastern European forces still remained far behind Soviet forces stationed in Central Europe.

Equipment problems were minor compared with the overall political reliability of the forces. The 1953 uprising in East Berlin was put down by Soviet forces because of the Kremlin's concerns about the reliability of East German paramilitary forces. During the Hungarian Revolution in 1956, some units fought against the Soviets "with valor, courage, and heroism reminiscent of the best traditions of Hungarian military history."[6] After Moscow suppressed the revolt, an army purge left large gaps in the ranks of the officer and noncommissioned officer corps. Hungarian divisions did not reappear in the pact's order of battle until the mid-1960s.

From Moscow's standpoint, events in Poland in 1956 represented an even more dangerous challenge (see Chapter 8). Not only was Poland strategically more important, but at the time, Soviet officers still occupied senior positions in the Polish military. When troops in Poznań refused to put down demonstrations in June and in some cases actually joined them, Polish authorities were forced to call in security forces from Warsaw. In October, shortly before Władysław Gomułka assumed power, Polish forces played a critical role in ensuring a "Polish solution" to the leadership question. Nikita Khrushchev and his compatriots arrived at Okęcie airport unannounced and uninvited, in an effort to oust Gomułka. At the same time, Soviet troops in Poland left their barracks and began to move on Warsaw. Polish security forces under the command of General Komar took up defensive positions around the city making it clear they were prepared to fight if necessary. According to Edward Ochab, at that time first secretary of the Polish party, Marshal Rokossovsky came to him and "admitted that his authority in the army was weakening, and that discipline was visibly going in some units. He also wasn't sure whether the orders of every commander of a large unit would be followed in a crisis."[7] In fact, his misgivings turned out to be well founded as "some Polish units . . . turned unreliable overnight, halting their march on Warsaw and preparing to defend the capital."[8] The very real threat of resistance by Polish forces at this critical juncture appears to have played an important role in Khrushchev's decision to back down and accept Gomułka as Poland's leader. For Moscow the message was ominous. Not even the presence of Soviet officers in the senior ranks of the Polish military could ensure its loyalty.

The Pact Is Upgraded

Despite these problems, the Soviets devoted considerable effort during the 1960s to improving the pact's and East Europe's military capabilities. A new strategy was adopted shortly after Marshal Andrei Grechko took over as commander of the pact in 1960. This new doctrine, called coalition warfare, assigned the Eastern Europeans (and particularly the East Germans, Czechoslovaks, and Poles) key roles in an East-West conflict. They would be expected to participate jointly with Soviet forces in rapid offensive operations against NATO.

To make this doctrine workable, Eastern European military equipment was further upgraded. The process of replacing World War II–vintage T-34s with the more modern T-54/55 was completed; MIG-21s and SU-7 aircraft as well as antitank missiles and self-propelled guns were introduced into pact inventories. Some forces were also supplied with nuclear-capable delivery vehicles (although the weapons systems remained in Soviet hands). Weapons standardization was pushed, a nascent East German aircraft industry was dismantled, and Poland renounced further work on advanced jet aircraft. Multilateral training exercises increased. Whereas there had been only one in the pact's first five years, there were nineteen between 1960 and 1968, and during this time the exercises began to take on increasing operational importance. Attention was also given to the improvement of the pact's top military organs. They began to meet on an annual basis and became involved with the operational details in such areas as training and exercises.

From the political standpoint, two events raised questions in Soviet minds about the reliability of the Eastern Europeans. In late 1964, the Romanians unilaterally reduced their term of service from twenty-four to sixteen months, and nationalist topics were emphasized in ideological indoctrination lectures. Bucharest began to argue that pact military expenditures were excessive, succeeded in reducing the size of the Soviet military liaison mission, demanded a consultative voice in matters related to nuclear weapons, refused to permit pact troop maneuvers on Romanian soil, declined to participate in joint maneuvers with combat troops in other countries, and finally proposed that the pact's military chief position rotate among member states. As a result, questions emerged about the utility of Romanian forces in the event of a war with the West.

Following on the Romanian deviation came an even more unsettling development insofar as the Soviets were concerned. In 1968, with the rise of reformist elements in Czechoslovakia, certain segments of the Czechoslovak military—concentrated to a large degree in the political apparatus—began to express open dissatisfaction with Moscow's domination of the pact's leadership councils and to side with Alexander Dubček in his efforts to "democratize" Czechoslovakia. (Previously, a letter sent to the crucial December 1967 Central Committee meeting had apparently contained an implied threat by the army to intervene on behalf of the preceding first secretary, Antonín Novotný, and certain units of the army were actually placed on alert, while a number of officers had planned to "intervene if the Party's deliberations went against Novotný."[9] The plot was reportedly neutralized by younger pro-Dubček elements in the officer corps). A document signed by officers at the Klement Gottwald Political-Military Academy was published that called for a more independent Czechoslovak foreign and defense policy. Clearly, the Czechoslovak army was split about defense and succession issues. Soviet concerns about the decreasing reliability of the Czechoslovak armed forces played an important role in the Kremlin's decision to intervene militarily.

Despite the army's inaction during the Soviet invasion (it was ordered not to resist), shortly after the Husák regime was installed, the Klement Gottwald Political-Military Academy was closed, and a large-scale purge of pro-Dubček forces followed. Not only did 57.8 percent of officers who were less than thirty leave the army at their own request, but the government was forced to rely on security and border troops to put down an anti-Soviet disturbance on the anniversary of the Soviet invasion. By 1969, the size of the army had dropped from a 1966 high of 240,000 to a low of 168,000, and by 1971 57.9 percent of junior officers had failed to reenlist.[10] As a consequence, personnel in some branches were at 10–30 percent less than normal strength. In the air force, for example, personnel was down 20 percent, which made it impossible during the early 1970s to hold proper training and evaluation exercises.[11] The Czechoslovak officer corps was devastated and deeply demoralized.

For Moscow the lesson from the Romanian and Czechoslovak cases was clear: Communist militaries, once they get out from under Soviet control, can turn on the Kremlin, even if they are staffed by good Communists who support their own government. It could be argued, however, that the period was not a total loss to the Kremlin. After all, the Soviets were able to convince five of their six allies (the Romanians opted out) to participate in the invasion of Czechoslovakia in 1968. This could be used as evidence that the Eastern Europeans were reliable in an intrapact policing role. But the importance of this event has been overestimated in the West. Ross Johnson put it best when he noted, "The invasion of Czechoslovakia demonstrated that the Soviet Union could mobilize some of its East European allies to interfere in the internal affairs of one of them; it did not demonstrate, however, that East European forces could contribute effectively to military operations against one of their number."[12] There were rumors, for example, that the East Germans aroused considerable resentment on the part of the local populace and had to be quickly withdrawn; that serious morale problems existed among Polish troops; and that the Hungarians had little heart for the exercise. With the exception of the Soviets, who had morale problems of their own, only the Bulgarians were enthusiastic supporters of the operation, which was carried out against a largely passive populace. Thus, even an apparent victory in Moscow's efforts to utilize the pact for its own ends left unanswered important questions concerning the reliability of Eastern European troops when ordered to carry out Soviet orders.

The Pact During the 1970s

Despite Soviet concern for Eastern European military reliability after the Czechoslovak and Romanian affairs, the Kremlin apparently still felt that the region's military contribution in the event of a future conflict with the West would be important. To counter some of the tendencies apparent in Prague and Bucharest and thereby improve pact unity, new modifications in pact structure were announced at the March 1969 meeting of the Political Consultative Committee (PCC). First, the Committee of Defense Ministers (CDM) was created as the pact's supreme military consultative organ. Second, the Military Council, subordinate to the pact's joint council, was established with responsibility for planning and quality control. Third, the Technical Council was created to help ensure that new types of weapons were more quickly integrated into pact militaries.

Military responsibilities therefore became more differentiated. Very broad political-military issues were discussed within the PCC, whose meetings usually included defense ministers and foreign ministers. Specific multilateral military issues were handled within the CDM, and the Joint Command oversaw the implementation of decisions taken at higher levels. The CDM met annually; the Military Council convened twice a year on the average—once during the spring and once toward the end of the year. (There is no information on how frequently the Technical Council met.)

Although the Soviets gave the East Europeans a greater role in pact decisionmaking—an Eastern European deputy minister of defense served as pact deputy commander and relayed directives from the pact chief to the national command—most observers agree that this change did little to dilute Soviet dominance over the pact's decisionmaking process. Key authority (especially in operational matters) remained in the hands of the Soviets.

One effect of Soviet preeminence within the pact was that the region's militaries were only indirectly involved in fiscal negotiations; the primary means any Eastern European military had of influencing the size of the military budget was through contacts with Soviet military colleagues. Thus, for instance, Hungarian officers spent most of their energy convincing their Soviet contacts of the need for more modern weapons systems. (Assuming the Soviets agree, and new demands are leveled on the Hungarian armed forces by the Warsaw Pact, the question of whether or not the Hungarian political system could afford such expenditures ultimately would become a political question for resolution between Gorbachev and Grósz [that is, would the shift of funds from the consumer to the military sector seriously undermine political stability in Hungary?]) The presence of Eastern European military officers on the Military Council, the Military Staff, and the Joint

Command of the Warsaw Pact gave them an excellent opportunity to make their wishes and needs known to their Soviet counterparts.

Another manifestation of the mounting effort at pact integration in the military sphere during the 1970s was the sudden increase in pact military maneuvers. During the first fourteen years of its existence, the pact held only twenty military exercises, but there were twenty-one in the period from 1969 to 1972, eleven of them in 1969 alone. This striking increase in exercises had a clear military rationale—to give pact forces extensive training on the multilateral level, a prerequisite for the efficient deployment of pact forces under the doctrine of coalition warfare. To work out problems in joint operations between different national forces as well as among various functional units (land, sea, and air formations), five air defense/air force exercises took place from 1969 to 1971, whereas only one had previously. Similarly, four rear-services exercises were held between 1969 and 1972.

Apparently satisfied that the ground had been laid for multilateral cooperation, pact officials let the number of such maneuvers drop off after 1972. But pact military cooperation of a new type, which has generally been overlooked in the West, began to emerge in the mid-1970s. This consisted of bilateral (and sometimes trilateral) cooperation between East European armies, in which the Soviet Union appeared to be only minimally involved. Such cooperation was particularly prevalent among the northern tier countries. For example, Polish officers attended the GDR's Friedrich Engels Military Academy, and Polish, Czechoslovak, and East German forces trained together without the presence of Soviet military units. They also utilize each other's facilities.

Despite all of the Kremlin's efforts, major problems did surface during the 1970s. First, although some Western commentators suggested at the time that modernization was proceeding apace in the Eastern European forces, the real situation was quite different. According to figures published by the Arms Control and Disarmament Agency, with the notable exception of the GDR, military expenditures in the region increased only gradually throughout the period and certainly not in sufficient amounts to cover even the minimal costs of expensive contemporary weapons systems. This failure to allocate sufficient funds to the military is borne out by an analysis of their actual holdings.

The Air Forces. Most writers on the pact point to the alleged acquisition by Eastern Europeans of MIG-23s and advanced Sukhoi aircraft during the 1970s as an example of how these military forces were being updated. But a careful review of Eastern European holdings as of 1979 (see Table 6.1) suggests that although the Soviets were moving ahead to introduce the latest aircraft into their own forces in the region, with a few notable exceptions little was being done to upgrade the Eastern European air forces with modern aircraft, such as the MIG-23 and Sukhoi aircraft.

The Armies. At a time when there was talk of new tanks and other equipment being introduced in the Eastern European inventories, the record shows (see Table 6.1) that the outdated T-54/55 remained the main battle tank in non-Soviet pact forces.

TABLE 6.1. Selected East European Air/Ground Holdings, 1979

Country	Air Force	Ground
Poland	MIG-17, 21; Sukhoi-7, some Sukhoi 20	T54/55
GDR	MIG-17, 21	T54/55
Czechoslovakia	MIG-17, 21, some 23s	T54/55
Hungary	MIG-21	T54/55
Bulgaria	MIG-17, 19, 21, some 23s	T54/55
Romania	MIG-17, 21	T54/55

Source: International Institute for Strategic Studies, *The Military Balance, 1979-80* (London: Institute for Strategic Studies, 1980), pp. 14-16.

The Navies. With the exception of East Berlin, which began a major naval buildup in the early 1970s, little was done by other pact leaderships to modernize their fleets. The vast majority of the Polish fleet was constructed in the late 1950s and mid-1960s, and there was almost no new construction in the Bulgarian and Romanian navies.

It could be argued that the delay between a push by Moscow and actual acquisition by the Eastern Europeans of the weapons was related to the considerable lead time required by most weapons systems. This does not, however, appear to have been a major problem in Eastern Europe. After all, the equipment was Soviet designed, and it was being introduced into frontline Soviet units at this time; if a high enough priority had been assigned to its acquisition in Eastern Europe, it could have been obtained.

The second major problem area for the Soviets at this time occurred in Poland. In 1970, riots occurred in Gdańsk, and although the circumstances are still unclear, the best available information indicates that the military was involved in the suppression of demonstrations by workers. Despite their involvement, the Polish military reportedly refused to go along with orders from one of Gomułka's representatives in the Gdańsk area to use overwhelming force to put down the demonstrations.

The event had two important consequences for the Polish military. First, it had a devastating and demoralizing impact on the Polish officer corps and was the subject of considerable soul searching and debate within the armed forces. Second, the event demonstrated that the military would not automatically follow the orders of the political leadership and convinced the High Command that the military should at all costs avoid involvement in internal Polish politics.

In 1976, price increases led to work stoppages by workers in and around Warsaw. According to Polish sources, the Polish military played a key role in Gierek's decision to back down quickly. Jaruzelski's now famous statement, "Polish soldiers will not fire on Polish workers," convinced Gierek of the need to avoid a confrontation."[13]

Taken together, these two events showed that far from being a reliable tool in the hands of the party leadership, the Polish military's utility in an internal crisis was limited. If it were to be employed, its use would have to be carefully orchestrated. Indeed, by the end of the 1970s, Moscow must have understood that the East Europeans were not ready to expend the necessary funds to modernize their armed forces and that serious questions existed concerning the reliability of at least one of the pact's key members.

The Pact During the 1980s

From the Soviet perspective, events in Eastern Europe since 1980 have increased the problems the Kremlin faces in utilizing the Eastern European militaries for its own ends. In fact, the difficulties faced by the Soviets reached the point where at least on the military front, the positive value of the Eastern European militaries may have been outweighed, or at least neutralized, by its negative aspects. This was true on both the political and technical fronts.

Poland and the Solidarity Experience. The actions of the Polish military since 1980 have been far from reassuring to the Soviets. During the August 1980 events, the Polish military remained neutral and refused to become involved in what was perceived as an internal political struggle. For example, Admiral Janczyszyn, commander of the Polish navy, is reported to have stated at the time that he would not permit the use of Polish troops to put down strike activity by Polish shipyard workers; instead, he called on the party's Central Committee to approve the Gdańsk accords.

Throughout the fifteen-month period preceding the declaration of martial law, the Polish military stayed in the background. Some Polish sources claim, for example, that Jaruzelski was offered the position of first secretary at the time of Gierek's ouster but turned it down. When he did accept it in February 1981, as the internal political struggle was heating up, any possibility of a compromise solution ended with the Bydgoszcz incident in March. At that time, in an effort to gain official recognition, members of Rural Solidarity had been occupying government buildings. Shortly after Polish labor leader Lech Wałęsa met with General Jaruzelski and hopes had risen about the possibility of a negotiated settlement to the country's problems, the police attacked those occupying the buildings, seriously injuring a number of them. The result was a further intensification of passions on both sides as Solidarity called for the punishment of police officials. Wałęsa reportedly described the affair "as an obvious provocation against the Government of General Jaruzelski; he plainly did not mean that Solidarity members had acted provocatively."[14] It is generally believed in Poland that the incident was staged by hard-line elements within the security services and the Polish leadership—perhaps with Soviet support—to prevent any accommodation between the government/party and Solidarity.

Throughout the remainder of the year, Poland fell still further into internal disarray. The party steadily lost cohesiveness, and there was increasing talk of a full-scale takeover of the party by liberal elements. Frustrated by an inability to get an increasingly beleaguered governmental/party apparatus to live up to its promises, Solidarity became increasingly radicalized to the point where Wałęsa's leadership of the union was in serious question at its September 1981 congress. In fact, he succeeded in maintaining control, but only by the smallest margin and only after making a number of concessions to more radical elements in the union.

Although we will probably never know exactly who was behind the declaration of martial law on December 13 (that is, to what degree it was a Polish decision or the result of intense Soviet pressure), contrary to the general Western perception, military involvement was minimal. Regular military units were often not even aware of the declaration of martial law. Furthermore, I am not aware of a single incident in which regular military units were involved in the use of force against civilians. The task of implementing the more onerous aspects fell on the shoulders of the security forces, in particular the dreaded ZOMOs. Military participation in the early days was limited to actions such as manning checkpoints on highways and at main urban intersections; conducting two to three soldier patrols in major cities; transporting ZOMOs around the country (by the air force); providing communications support to the media; or occasionally driving past key points in tanks or similar equipment in an effort to intimidate the populace. If the West misjudged events in Poland, it was not because the West underestimated the ability of the Warsaw leadership to utilize the military in an internal crisis; the West failed to recognize the tremendous buildup of security forces during the six months prior to the declaration of martial law.

At the point of crisis, Warsaw went out of its way to avoid utilizing regular military units in a confrontational manner. The leadership was too unsure of how the soldiers would react if called upon to use force against other Poles. In short, Polish leaders went out of their way to avoid testing the validity of Jaruzelski's 1976 statement that "Polish soldiers will not fire on Polish workers."

Since December 1981, the Polish military has been used in a variety of functions. First, in addition to General Jaruzelski and those immediately around him, a number of other senior Polish officers have taken on high-level positions. One even achieved the unprecedented position of chief of personnel at the Central Committee of the Polish Communist party. General Tadeusz Dziekan, formerly head of the Cadres Department in the Ministry of Defense, was named chief of cadres immediately after martial law was declared. This was a first for any Communist country and had obvious implications for the Soviet Union, something that was clearly not lost on Soviet political and military leaders. Second, members of the military have acted as troubleshooters. For example, colonels were assigned to provincial governors, who used these soldiers to help eliminate supply bottlenecks or to deal with other logistical problems. Finally, the military served on inspection teams to ensure that party and government bureaucrats throughout the country were carrying out the general's orders (they frequently were not). Many of these officers returned to their barracks after martial law ended in July 1983, but large numbers are still active in the civilian bureaucracy. A return to complete civilian rule would put the same civilians who brought about the 1980 crisis back into power, something the general seeks to avoid.

The Polish experience has a number of implications for the USSR. First, although the situation in Poland is clearly better than it was on December 12, 1981, to date Jaruzelski has not always done things as the Soviets would have preferred, even though Gorbachev seems by and large to support Jaruzelski's liberal (by Eastern European standards) approach to governing Poland. The Catholic church in Poland is the strongest in any Communist country, dissidents are dealt with less harshly than anywhere except perhaps Hungary, agriculture remains in private hands, the media is relatively open by Eastern European standards, and the universities retain more autonomy than is normal elsewhere. All of these factors could be held against the general should Gorbachev not succeed in moving the Soviet Union along the path of restructuring. In the meantime, the lesson of the Polish case is that Eastern European generals cannot necessarily be counted upon to do Moscow's bidding.

Second, although senior military officers and the security organs were able to hold the line this time, the Kremlin must continue to be concerned about stability in Poland in a crisis. After all, the 1981 takeover took place in the face of a largely passive populace. What if there is resistance next time and the internal security organs prove insufficient? What will the regular army do if called upon to use its weapons against fellow Poles?

Third, even though the impact of the events of 1980 may be receding into the background, their legacy lives on. As an ideal, Solidarity continues to have the support of the average Pole (and average Poles staff this largely conscript army). According to former Polish colonel Kukliński, the Soviet military and the Polish military leadership both worried about the state of the Polish army in 1980. To use Kukliński's phrase, it was "demoralized."[15] The Warsaw government has gone to great lengths since then to restore morale, but the Soviets see the Polish soldier (like most of his colleagues in other parts of the region) as loyal primarily to his own understanding of the country's national interest, something that very often directly contradicts the goals and interests of the Kremlin and the country's political leadership. A former Polish soldier probably put it best when he observed that "the political consciousness of the man who is entering the service now, who knows a little something of what went on during the Solidarity period is different. He is more difficult, more resistant to propaganda. It is difficult to convince him of friendship with the Soviet Union."[16]

This legacy is likely to remain a reality in the Polish army for some time. Not only must the Kremlin worry about how the Polish soldier will respond to internal problems, but his less-than-enthusiastic support for Soviet policies also has serious military implications. After all, Poland occupies a key position within the Warsaw Pact (fifteen divisions, perhaps with its

TABLE 6.2. Selected Eastern European Air/Ground Holdings, 1987

Country	Air Force	Ground
Poland	MIG-17, 21, a few 23s, SU-7, SU-20s, and SU-22s	T54/55, T-72
GDR	MIG-21, 23s, SU-22s	T54/55, T-72
Czechoslovakia	MIG-21, smattering of 23s SU-7, SU-25	T54/55, T-72
Hungary	MIG-21, 23s beginning to appear, a few SU-25s	T54/55, with a few T-72s
Bulgaria	MIG-17, 21, a few 23s, a few SU-15s	T-34, 54/55, a few T-72s
Romania	MIG-17, 21, 23s, IAR-93s	T-34, T-54/55, M-77, a few T-72s

Source: International Institute for Strategic Studies, *The Military Balance, 1987-1988* (London: International Institute for Strategic Studies, 1987), pp. 47-53.

own front). The loss or even weakening of this front would have the most serious consequences for Soviet military planners.

Modernizing the Eastern European Militaries. Despite some efforts at modernizing them, Eastern European militaries appear to be falling further behind Soviet forces in the region.

The Air Forces: At a time when Soviet forces in Eastern Europe are introducing MIG-29s and SU-29s, the Eastern Europeans remain far behind. As indicated in Table 6.2, the predominant aircraft in the region remain the MIG-21 and SU-7, although MIG-23s and SU-20s are beginning to make their appearances. Even these latter aircraft lag seriously behind frontline Soviet units in the region.

The Armies: After carefully analyzing the state of northern tier armies, one writer concluded that there are major disparities between Soviet and Eastern European forces. After looking at the Polish army, this writer stated, "At best, the Polish army would be hard-pressed to keep up with better organized and equipped Soviet forces and could not be expected to do well some of the very important things that Soviet units could do and Soviet doctrine requires."[17] The Czechoslovak army is in somewhat better shape than the Polish, but it, too, has serious shortcomings. "The Czechoslovak People's Army, like the Polish People's Army, seems ill-structured and ill-equipped to perform a first echelon role."[18] Even the East German army, which is the most modern in the region, is still inferior to Soviet forces, which are "receiving the newest equipment, tanks, self-propelled artillery and air defense missiles at a much faster rate than the NVA."[19]

The Navies: With the exception of the East German navy, all of the pact fleets have serious deficiencies. The largest, the Polish navy, is quickly sinking into obsolescence, the Romanian navy is small and outdated, and the Bulgarian navy is also in need of new ships and equipment.

To the Soviets, the situation among the Eastern European militaries must appear bleak indeed. The quality of their equipment, although improving, lags far behind that of Soviet forces. Figures from the Arms Control and Disarmament Agency do suggest that Eastern European military budgets are increasing, but this is not reflected in new weapons systems.

One option available to the Soviets would be to intensify pressure on the Eastern Europeans to purchase more modern weapons. Given the region's serious economic problems—Poland is only the most obvious and best-known case—such an approach could have a serious impact on these countries' economies if implemented. In view of the close tie between economic and political stability in the area, it could also have significant political ramifications. However much the Kremlin may prefer modern militaries in Eastern Europe, it is doubtful the Soviets are prepared to push the Eastern Europeans in that direction if the result is likely to be increased political instability.

Whether the Eastern Europeans—again with the exception of the East Germans—will agree to a significant increase in military budgets is also in doubt. By and large, the region's leaders and peoples appear to have other priorities, particularly the resolution of internal economic difficulties. A recent study by Keith Crane underlined this point:

> Assuming that budget changes are a good reflection of total actual expenditures changes, the record of East European military expenditures after the 1978 Warsaw Pact agreement provides a test of the extent of Soviet influence on spending levels in Eastern Europe. The results . . . indicate that with the exception of the GDR, the East Europeans failed to accelerate the rate of increase in their expenditure levels. The figures for real spending . . . show average annual growth rates of 1 percent or less for all countries except the GDR, considerably lower than the NATO targets of 3 percent. In real terms these increases were less than half the rate of the previous seven-year period for all countries, again with the exception of the GDR.[20]

Thus, despite pressures from the Kremlin, most of the countries of Eastern Europe appear to believe that their interests are better served by allocating scarce resources to nonmilitary sectors.

Another option available to the Kremlin would be to supply its allies with the necessary weapons free of charge. To date, however, the Soviets have not done so. As one Eastern European specialist on national security questions put it in a conversation with me, "We won't be supplied with the latest equipment for three reasons: first, the Soviets want to make money off the sale of weapons and we don't have the hard currency. Second, they don't think we will do our part in an East-West conflict and don't want to waste the weapons. Third, they don't trust us and are afraid some of our pilots, for example, will defect to the West with the latest equipment."

If the past forty years are any indication, the Soviets still have a long way to go before problems of political reliability are overcome. Even though none of these armies has yet been tested in a conflict against the West, their actions in Hungary and Poland in 1956, in the Czechoslovak crisis of 1968, and in Poland during the 1970s and 1980s all raise questions concerning their reliability at home, at least from the Kremlin's perspective. If the reliability of these forces cannot even be assured on the home front, how can Moscow have much confidence in their utility in a war against NATO—a conflict at least some of them might well see as a means to throw off Soviet domination of their countries?

Coping with the Eastern Europeans: The Kremlin's Response

While recognizing that there is little that can be done to get the Eastern Europeans to upgrade their weapons holdings and equipment, the Soviets have nevertheless refused to accept the trend toward decreasing political reliability. Indeed, they have adopted a number of measures aimed specifically at ensuring a greater degree of control over the East European militaries. In a crisis situation, the Kremlin does not want to be faced with the possibility of widespread disaffection in these militaries, which could lead to a 1980s version of a sitzkrieg or to open rebellion.

To help keep the Eastern European militaries in line politically, the Soviets have continued to push attendance by Eastern European officers at Soviet military schools. In 1975, for example, it was reported that 33 percent of Bulgarian officers "have studied in the USSR."[21] For senior, flag-rank officers, attendance at a senior Soviet military academy is mandatory, except in the case of Romania.

The Soviets have maintained a monopoly over access to most weapons systems by providing the Eastern Europeans with less sophisticated versions of the same equipment given to their own forces. For instance, an East European MIG-23 might be identical to a Soviet version but lack the advanced avionics equipment. There are even reports that countries in the Third World (for example, Syria) get modern equipment before the Eastern Europeans do.

At the same time, the Kremlin has minimized the region's ability to conduct combat operations without direct Soviet involvement. For example, there are reports that the amount of ammunition available to each Eastern European tank is limited to twenty-six rounds. Remaining stocks are held by Soviet forces, thus severely limiting the ability of national forces to operate against those of the USSR.

Moscow has also worked to isolate these militaries from Western influences. In the GDR, for example, East German soldiers are officially forbidden to have contacts with West Germans, and those who have close relations in the FRG are prohibited from attending officer schools. Nevertheless, a number of former East German soldiers have suggested that the former rule is often ignored in practice.

The Soviets have continued to insist on the use of Soviet operational concepts to prohibit the Eastern Europeans from developing anything resembling an independent military doctrine and have emphasized the use of Russian as the pact's operating language. Meanwhile, they have attempted to recruit East European military officers, especially those studying in the USSR, to spy for the Soviet Union by forcing them to sign what amounts to loyalty (to the USSR) oaths as part of their study in the USSR. (Those who refuse to sign are supposedly sent home with their military careers ruined.)

The Kremlin has introduced a major structural modification that more closely ties the Eastern European militaries to the Soviet Union. According to former colonel Kukliński, all of the Eastern European countries, except Romania, accepted the Statute of the Joint Armed Forces and Their Organs in Wartime, which almost completely subordinates the region's militaries to the control of the Soviet High Command during wartime. The statute is so secret, according to Kukliński, that "even the branch and military district commanders know only those provisions that affect them directly."[22] The practical result is that the ability of an Eastern European national command to obviate Soviet orders in a crisis situation is seriously undermined. If control of the troops automatically passes to Soviet command in a crisis, then Eastern European political or military leaders will find it very difficult to resist Soviet pressure for their involvement in a war with the West. Furthermore, it will also make it more difficult for individual units to resist their participation in such a war.

The Soviets have continued to ensure a Soviet monopoly over top-level pact command positions. Senior Eastern European officers are sometimes given command over military exercises, and they are present at a high level at Pact headquarters, but with the exception of the Polish front (traditionally believed to be under the command of a Polish general), all of the other wartime commands are Soviet. Even in the Polish case, there is some question whether it still exists in the aftermath of the Solidarity events.

The Soviets have worked to maintain close cooperation among the political organs of the various pact armies in order to provide a standardized view of world events while at the same time minimizing the impact of Western influences. At the same time, the USSR has utilized military exercises as an intimidating device to check signs of independence on the part of the Eastern Europeans. For example, in 1980 and 1981, Soviet maneuvers were held on or near Polish borders in an attempt to intimidate those in Poland who were pushing for openness and systemic autonomy.

Despite these maneuvers, a recent Rand study of fifty-nine former Eastern European servicemen indicated that the Soviets have been only marginally effective in attaining their goal of a more cohesive pact. In fact, if anything, political reliability appears to have gone down in recent years. For example,

Marxist ideology appears almost dead as a motivating factor, the various militaries are beset with internal tensions between officers and men, ideological indoctrination is often counterproductive, and anti-Sovietism remains deep-seated. As a Polish respondent put it with regard to the latter, "We talked about it ourselves. The ranks of officers involved in this were officers up to rank of captain. . . . They would not allow the Soviets to interfere in our affairs. . . . The soldiers said right away that they were going to turn the tank barrels against the Soviets."[23]

When asked what they would do in the event of a war with NATO, most of those interviewed in the Rand study believed that even though control mechanisms would ensure that the Eastern European forces would fight if ordered to, many felt the majority of soldiers would desist or desert at the first opportunity. Furthermore, if Soviet forces were faced with a stalemate or suffered serious reverses, the brittleness of this control would become evident, and it would eventually collapse and expose Soviet forces to possible defeat. Similarly, insofar as domestic reliability is concerned, the respondents concluded that Eastern European compliance with party orders would be conditional.

Indeed, recent events in Yugoslavia suggest that when it comes to issues such as civil unrest, senior military officers may have a mind of their own. According to West German press reports, the Yugoslav military came very close to intervening in Slovenian internal affairs during 1988 (see Chapter 11). According to these reports, the military commandant of the Ljubljana region, Colonel General Visnijić, met secretly with the Slovenian Interior Ministry to decide what actions should be taken by military authorities to ensure stability in the region should public demonstrations get out of hand. Visnijić, and his military superiors in Belgrade, reportedly believed that in intervening in civilian affairs they would be fulfilling their constitutional duty to protect the integrity and order of the country. As rumors of a possible military intervention began to circulate in Ljubljana, two journalists and an army warrant officer were arrested, were charged with betraying military secrets, and were placed in military custody. Military sources claimed that the secrets involved information dealing with the army's level of preparedness in the event of an attack, whereas civilian sources maintained that the three were arrested because they were about to publish minutes of the March 25 meeting of the Military Council. This meeting, held without the civilian leadership's knowledge, reportedly dealt with preparations for military intervention in Ljubljana.

Whatever the truth of the situation and its eventual resolution, the fact is that many observers in Yugoslavia and in the West believe that the Yugoslav army was and is prepared to intervene in internal civilian affairs under certain circumstances. Despite the obvious differences between Yugoslav and pact armies, the possibility of similar actions by Eastern European pact militaries in the event of civil unrest is certainly not lost on Soviet authorities. In a nutshell, this chapter suggests that the Soviets cannot be certain of East European support for their policies either against NATO or on the domestic front, except under very special circumstances.

The Declining Eastern European Militaries—Military Implications

Moscow's difficulties with the Eastern European militaries have a number of important implications for Soviet warfighting strategy. During the past twenty years, the Soviets have taken a number of steps to increase the probability that a conflict in Europe will remain conventional. Under Marshals Ogarkov and Akhromeyev the Soviet military introduced a number of measures aimed at increasing the pact's ability to fight a sustained conventional conflict. The Soviet goal is to prevent the use of nuclear weapons while at the same time prevailing over the West, first, by attacking and degrading NATO's nuclear assets and, second, by utilizing blitzkrieg tactics to achieve quick and deep penetrations into NATO territory. The Soviets intend to defeat the West before it can resort to the use of nuclear weapons.

Among the steps taken by the Soviets to enhance the credibility of their nonnuclear option are the following:

Creation of Theaters of Military Operations (TVDs) to facilitate the control of larger-sized forces under the command of a single TVD commander

Revival and updating of the concept of deep operations, including the creation of Operational Maneuver Groups, which would spearhead a breakthrough and thereby ensure a high rate of advance by pact forces

Placement of air forces under the control of the front commander to better enable him to deploy them in the event of a conflict

Modernization of Soviet ground and air forces through the introduction of more modern weapons and equipment and improved logistical arrangements for the resupply of Soviet forces in the event of a war in Central Europe

Despite these and other actions by the Soviets, Soviet warfighting strategy remains heavily dependent on the Eastern Europeans. Not only do they account for about 50 percent of pact forces in the Central European region, but their contribution may be decisive even if they are sometimes assigned secondary roles. For example, if they fail to protect adequately Soviet resupply lines, the Red Army's ability to sustain operations in the West could be seriously undermined. Furthermore, as Marshal Ogarkov has noted, the extent of damage and casualties in a war in Central Europe will be tremendous. The need to use Eastern Europeans as replacements for Soviet forces means that the former will in practice be indispensable to the Soviets. Nevertheless, the political and military problems associated with reliance on the Eastern European militaries present Moscow with a host of problems.

From a military-technical standpoint, Eastern European military deficiencies affect Soviet operational capabilities in three key areas. First, the antiquated nature of Eastern European equipment raises questions about the ability of Moscow's allies to keep up with fast-moving Soviet forces in the event of a conflict in Central Europe. One specialist, a former Polish officer, has estimated that given their current equipment, if Eastern European forces were assigned the same tasks on the same fronts as Soviet forces, they could only sustain an advance rate of 60 percent of the rate Soviet forces could be expected to maintain.[24] Given the importance of a quick decisive thrust westward in Soviet warfighting strategy, this could seriously lessen the scope and lethality of pact operations.

Similarly, technical disparities between Soviet and Eastern European forces exacerbate problems of interoperability, even though pact weapons are all Soviet in origin. In theoretical terms, Polish tanks can be substituted for Soviet tanks in a crisis, and Czechoslovak artillery can be cannibalized to keep Soviet systems going, but in reality, differences in equipment inventories have reached a point where Soviet and Eastern European systems are not interchangeable. In practical terms, Polish T-54/55s cannot be substituted for Soviet T-72s or T-80s without seriously affecting a unit's effectiveness. Parts from a T-54/55 cannot be used to repair a T-80. Finally, the Soviet tendency to surround Eastern European forces with larger Soviet units in order to ensure the former's political reliability creates resupply problems for the Eastern Europeans. Instead of being able to draw on large forces to replenish their losses, the incompatibility of much of the East European and Soviet equipment combined with the semi-isolation of non-Soviet pact forces means that replacement parts very often must come from deep in the rear.

The firepower of Eastern European divisions is also considerably less than that of a Soviet division stationed on the central front. This is not only a result of generational disparities in equipment but also of the lesser inventory in Eastern European units. That Soviet forces have many more artillery tubes than their East European allies and greater weapons accuracy means that Soviet forces present a much greater threat to NATO forces.

The Declining Eastern European Militaries—Political Implications

From the standpoint of political reliability, Soviet concerns are centered in three areas. The first is mobilization. Although there is little doubt that organizational machinery is in place that will ensure Eastern European forces are mobilized in a short amount of time—even without the approval of their national commands if necessary—the way in which they are mobilized could prove problematic. A surprise mobilization followed by the immediate deployment of troops to the front would have minimal impact on troop morale. But a mobilization that follows a slow buildup in tensions in Europe could be more difficult. The period preceding mobilization would focus public attention on the nature of the conflict and could make the issue of Eastern European involvement in a "Russian war" a matter of public discussion. Such a development would probably not adversely affect the outcome of a mobilization order, but a lengthy critical debate about the utility of such a conflict could intensify already existing anti-Soviet attitudes.

At a minimum, Eastern European enthusiasm for participation in such a war would be diminished.

A second area of concern is Eastern European willingness to support the Soviets in an external war in the face of serious reverses or defeats. It is generally agreed that Eastern European soldiers will follow orders as long as they are on the winning side, but the real test comes when they suffer serious losses. How will the unit behave if its forward positions are overrun? Fighting for a winner, even if one does not agree with its aims, is a low-cost operation. Continuing to fight when the other side has the upper hand and you are suffering serious losses is something else. In World War II, for example, the German soldier fought bravely to the end while his less well-equipped and less motivated Eastern European allies presented the German High Command with a constant flow of problems once the Soviet juggernaut began its relentless drive westward.

The third concern is the problem of maintaining stability in the rear. It could be argued that Eastern European civilians are not likely to present problems as long as the pact is winning, but in the event of a prolonged war that produces serious Eastern European casualties or exposes major weaknesses on the part of the Soviets, the situation behind the lines could deteriorate quickly. It could fuel the fires of instability, and by building on already existing feelings of nationalism and anti-Sovietism (by and large the two are intimately connected in Eastern Europe), it could result in guerilla warfare or large-scale violence in the form of riots or demonstrations. Both sets of circumstances would present the Soviets, who are dependent on sending supplies through this region, with serious problems.

The Eastern European Armies—A Balance Sheet

From an operational standpoint, Eastern European technical and political shortcomings primarily limit Soviet flexibility in Europe. Technically, for example, problems of interoperability, difficulties in keeping up with Soviet forces, and disparities in unit firepower mean that the Kremlin may be forced increasingly to rely primarily on Soviet forces. Indeed, the writings of senior Soviet military officers suggest that they may foresee reduced roles for the Eastern Europeans in a NATO–Warsaw Pact conflict. As a rule, major Soviet military writers such as Generals Gareyev, Kir'yan, and Zhilin all give the impression that the Eastern Europeans play a minimal role in Soviet warfighting strategy. In fact, in his major theoretical work on Frunze, probably the most important military book since the end of the 1960s, Gareyev devoted only one page to the pact. The message seems clear: Count first on Soviet forces in a crisis.

A decision by the Kremlin to rely more on its own forces will have important ramifications for Soviet force structure and deployments in the region. For example, the Soviets could be forced to take additional steps to facilitate the movement of troops from the Western regions of the USSR to the GDR in the event of a crisis (during the Solidarity period, much of the supplies sent to Soviet forces in Germany were transported by sea to avoid potential problems in Poland). Not only would such an action by the Soviets provide the West with a relatively clear and unambiguous warning indicator of impending hostilities; it would also raise the question of where such troops would come from.

Politically, problems with the Eastern Europeans mean that speed and success in any operation become even more important. A protracted, bloody conflict would not only increase the need to commit Eastern European forces to frontline tasks; it would also increase the problems the Soviets can expect to face in rear areas, especially if the Kremlin suffered serious reverses. In order to minimize such technical and political problems, the Soviets need minimal warning time prior to mobilization followed by a quick, successful, and decisive military campaign against NATO. But such a scenario may not be the most probable one. Although this does not mean that the Kremlin will not resort to the use of force in a crisis, it does suggest that Soviet military planners will have an additional potentially limiting element to factor into their decisionmaking process. The result could be a greater hesitancy to go to war.

Recently, there has been considerable talk about the emergence of a new Soviet doctrine, one that Gorbachev calls "military sufficiency." Based on what has been said to date, the major characteristics of the concept insofar as a conflict in Europe is concerned appear to be the presence of sufficient nuclear forces to deliver an unacceptable counterblow to the enemy and a reconfiguration of force structure in Europe so that conventional forces can repel an attack and deliver a counterattack but not carry out offensive operations or a surprise attack. The details of what this idea—if it is implemented—will mean in practice remain to be worked out, but assuming the Soviets are moving in the direction of a more defensive force structure in Europe, their problems with the Eastern Europeans may be *one* of the factors moving them in this direction. The USSR's serious economic problems, the impact of high technology on modern weapons systems (where the Soviets believe they are at a clear disadvantage), and an interest in playing to Western circles who favor better relations between East and West probably also play important, even determining, roles. Nevertheless, given the importance Moscow has traditionally assigned to massive forces in large-scale offensive operations and the likelihood that the Eastern Europeans will not do their job either militarily or politically, the Soviets may have decided that a rethinking of warfighting strategy was in order. They are clearly faced with a gap, which is increasing, between missions and their capabilities. If the Eastern Europeans are of only marginal utility, then even the numerical balance in Europe begins to look much worse to Soviet defense planners. In this case, the task is clear—either redefine the mission or be obligated to carry out a mission for which there are not sufficient assets.

Assuming the Kremlin does come up with a more defense-oriented strategy, with, as some predict, smaller forces, it would certainly lighten the economic burden on the Eastern European political leaderships. Smaller forces are also easier to maintain at a higher level of political and military efficiency. Assigning these forces to what would amount to home defense duties would be more popular within these countries. It could enable the political and military leadership to concentrate on tasks that are less expensive and that would use these forces on their own soil—something likely to get greater public support. Indeed, there is some indication that matters may be moving in this direction. In July 1987, for example, an article was published by a Polish colonel arguing that the redefinition of military doctrine requires the reorganization of the Polish armed forces to better enable it to carry out internal tasks.[25]

Any redefinition of Soviet strategy that involves the withdrawal of a significant amount of Soviet forces from Eastern Europe will have to be handled with considerable delicacy. The same is true of conventional arms limitations, about which there has recently been considerable discussion in the East. Leaving aside the complexities of any such negotiation—which may itself doom it to failure—the Eastern European factor is bound to impact on the Soviet negotiating position. A major change in the number of Soviet divisions stationed in Eastern Europe is bound to have an important impact in the region. Is it part of a major Soviet withdrawal from the region? Are the Soviets giving up in or at least ameliorating their demands for conformity with the Soviet Union?

Here I am not talking about the need for Soviet forces to police Eastern Europe. After all, Moscow has seven category-one airborne divisions, all of which could be in Eastern Europe in a minimal amount of time. The problem is one of perceptions. To what degree are Eastern European perceptions of Soviet power tied to the presence of Soviet divisions in the region? The answer to that question is not evident. The elimination of two or three divisions is not likely to have a major impact on Eastern European perceptions of Soviet power, but what about eight or ten? The bottom line is that the Soviets will have to keep this factor very much in mind when considering how to implement a policy of military sufficiency or of significant reductions of Soviet forces in the area. The potential instability if not volatility of the region leaves them little option.

Implications for the West

The role of the Eastern European militaries deserves special attention in any evaluation of the East-West military balance. For many years, there has been a tendency in the West in calculating the military balance to assume that quantity is what counts. Quality is too difficult to measure. After all, all soldiers will fight in a crunch and therefore must all be assigned equal weight. In fact, however, as this chapter has attempted to show, an Eastern European soldier is not the equivalent of his Soviet comrade. This is true not only in terms of the contribution he makes to the Soviet war effort but in his utility on the home front. There is an important, and growing, qualitative difference between the two soldiers.

Some Western analysts have suggested that Western policy should be aimed at increasing Soviet doubts about the reliability of their Eastern European allies. Indeed, Western policy toward the region has as one of its goals to convince Eastern European governments and peoples that it is in their interests to follow more independent domestic and foreign policies. Unfortunately, official Western evaluations of the likely response by Eastern European militaries in the event of a war, or of what actions the West might take to increase the likelihood of a less-than-enthusiastic response to a Soviet call to the colors, are not available in the public sphere.

Published literature abounds with suggestions that might advance Western interests by helping decrease Eastern European reliability. These include arguments favoring a more explicit declaratory policy informing the Eastern Europeans they will not be attacked if they opt out of a war, calls for increased contacts between Western and Eastern European militaries, and a push for the use of preemptive attacks into the Eastern European heartland in the event of a war. Unfortunately, it is not possible to ascertain to what degree these suggestions, or others, are taken seriously in official circles. Nor is it possible to determine the extent of agreement among Western governments on the utility of a more activist approach in this area.

Some on the Left argue that because Eastern Europeans are both militarily and politically unreliable, the threat facing the West is much less than is commonly believed. Certainly, the findings of this chapter suggest that Eastern Europe is much less important to the Soviets in an evaluation of the military balance than has been thought in the West. On the other hand, while recognizing the validity of many of the foregoing points, others maintain that prudent military planning requires the West to consider the Eastern Europeans to be as reliable as Soviet forces, even if in practice they may turn out to be less effective than their Soviet comrades. Calculations of the military balance are highly complex and involve myriad factors, some empirical, some less tangible. But insofar as this single indicator is concerned, current trends in the region do not favor the Soviets. This should provide at least some relief to those who believe the elimination of intermediate range missiles in Europe leaves the Soviet Union with a commanding lead in the area of conventional weapons. That a problem exists on the conventional front is obvious; that the Soviets have good reason not to be overly confident in their own calculations of the balance seems equally evident. This is particularly true when it comes to Eastern European forces.

East and West now appear to be entering a period of considerable flux in security relations in Europe. The Soviets claim to be revising their military doctrine, and there is a lot of talk about conventional arms limitations. The jury is still out on how serious and wide ranging the Soviets will be in both areas. Past Soviet practice would suggest caution in expecting major changes. But one thing is clear. In making their decisions on how to proceed in both areas, they will have one eye on their Eastern European allies, and it will not be a look of confidence. Rather, it will be one that asks the question, How far can we go given the problems we face in dealing with our friends and allies?

Notes

1. Ignacy Blum, *Z dziejów wojska polskiego w latach 1944–1948* (Warsaw: Ministerstwo Obrony Narodowej, 1968), p. 180.
2. Tadeusz Konecki, "Zawodowe szkolnictwo ludowego wojska polskiego w perwszym powojennym dziesiecioleciu," *Wojskowy przegląd historiczny,* no. 2 (1974), p. 341.
3. Thomas W. Wolfe, *Soviet Power and Europe, 1945–1970* (Baltimore, Md.: Johns Hopkins University Press, 1970), p. 43.
4. I. I. Yakubovskiy, ed., *Boyevoyoe sodruzhestvo bratskikh narodov i armiy* (Moscow: Voyenizdat, 1975), p. 273.
5. Wolfe, *Soviet Power,* p. 148.
6. Ivan Volgyes, "The Military as an Agent of Political Socialization: The Case of Hungary," in Dale R. Herspring and Ivan Volgyes, eds., *Civil-Military Relations in Communist Systems* (Boulder, Colo.: Westview Press, 1978), p. 152.
7. Teresa Toranski, *"Them"* (New York: Harper & Row, 1987), p. 73.
8. Alexander Alexiev and A. Ross Johnson, *East European Military Reliability: An Émigré-Based Assessment* (Santa Monica, Calif.: Rand, October, 1986), p. 53.
9. Galia Golan, *Reform Rule in Czechoslovakia* (Cambridge: Cambridge University Press, 1973), p. 183.
10. Robert W. Dean, "The Political Consolidation of the Czechoslovak Army," Radio Free Europe Research, Czechoslovakia/14, April 29, 1971, pp. 16, 20.
11. Condoleezza Rice, "Warsaw Pact Reliability: The Czechoslovak People's Army (CLA)," in Daniel Nelson, ed., *Soviet Allies: The Warsaw Pact and the Issue of Reliability* (Boulder, Colo.: Westview Press, 1984), p. 135.
12. A. Ross Johnson, "The Military in Eastern Europe—Loyalty to Whom?" (Paper prepared for the conference Eastern Europe—Stability or Recurrent Crisis? by the Department of State at Airlie House, Virginia, November 13–15, 1976).
13. Dale R. Herspring and Ivan Volgyes, "Political Reliability in East European Warsaw Pact Armies," *Armed Forces and Society* 6, no. 2 (Winter 1980), p. 279.
14. Kevin Ruane, *The Polish Challenge* (London: British Broadcasting Corporation, 1982), pp. 137–138.
15. J. Kukliński, "Wojna z narodem widziana od środka," *Kultura* (Paris), no. 4 (April 1987), p. 22. See also p. 41.
16. Alexiev and Johnson, *East European Military Reliability,* p. 57.
17. Richard C. Martin, "Disparities in Modernization Between Warsaw Pact Armies Opposite NATO's Central Region" (Paper delivered to the conference on Security Implications of Nationalism in Eastern Europe, U.S. Army War College, Carlisle Barracks, Pennsylvania, October 23–24, 1984), p. 10.
18. Ibid., p. 17.
19. Ibid., p. 19.
20. Keith Crane, *Military Spending in Eastern Europe* (Santa Monica, Calif.: Rand, May 1987), p. 49.
21. *Rabotnichesko delo,* September 21, 1975, cited in Ivan Volgyes, "Hungary," in Nelson, *Soviet Allies,* p. 102.
22. Kukliński, "Wojna z narodem widziana od środka," pp. 53–54.
23. Alexiev and Johnson, *East European Military Reliability,* p. 57.
24. Michael Sadykiewicz, *Organizing for Coalition Warfare: The Role of East European Warsaw Pact Forces in Soviet Military Planning* (Santa Monica, Calif.: Rand, forthcoming).
25. Longin Mucha, "Istota zmian," *Żołnierz wolności,* July 13, 1987. I am indebted to Ross Johnson for bringing this reference to my attention.

7

Human Rights and Civil Society in Eastern Europe

Robert Sharlet

Can the socialist convoy move faster than its slowest ship, the Soviet Union? Now that the USSR has begun to gather speed toward socioeconomic change, the effect has been salutary for all who desire change in Eastern Europe. The engine that propels the Soviet Union toward revitalization of the Communist system is Mikhail Gorbachev's metapolicy of *perestroika,* or systemwide "restructuring."

How far the official reform process will go in Eastern Europe remains an open question, but early returns are already coming in on its unintended impact on the informal sector, or "contra-system,"[1]—that is, the social substructure inhabited by diverse human rights groups. These groups dot the sociopolitical landscape from the Baltic to the Adriatic. Some are officially sanctioned (for example, certain churches), others are condoned within limits (for example, particular dissident political groups), and many others remain banned (such as disfavored religious "sects") or are actively suppressed in myriad ways (such as certain ethnic minorities).

Regardless of the degree of official tolerance, all these religious, ethnic, and political activists in quest of more human rights within the system are on the move and are challenging the status quo and testing the limits of official tolerance. In some instances, movement has been under way for some time (the Polish church and Charter 77 of Czechoslovakia); in other cases, existing human rights groups have been stimulated by the new winds of change from Moscow (the religious communities of Czechoslovakia and the political offspring of the East German churches). Other more spontaneous and inchoate eruptions of human rights protest are the direct, unwanted consequence of initial economic reform efforts; blue-collar unrest in Poland, Romania, Hungary, and Yugoslavia may be early warnings of what could happen when the party-states try to go farther along the road of reform-induced austerity policies.

The partly concealed, partly visible infrastructure for human rights activism was already in place in Eastern Europe when Gorbachev launched his reform program in the USSR. Much of the Soviet "package," such as limited entrepreneurial rights, is not new, even to the regimes in Eastern Europe. Other parts of Gorbachev's agenda, such as grass-roots pluralism, had already been experienced unofficially in the informal sectors of these same countries. In fact, the "human factor," so vital to the success of the Soviet reform movement, has long been cultivated and nurtured sub rosa by human rights activists in various parts of Eastern Europe. This, of course, is not exactly what Gorbachev has in mind, but this is what his Eastern European comrades will be coping with in the future. Clearly, the superlegitimating effect of change in Moscow has accelerated the reemergence of civil society in Eastern Europe by setting in motion or giving greater impetus to movements for change outside the official political establishment. The East Germans, Czechs, and Slovaks are responding to the Soviet impetus more rapidly than are their regimes; the Hungarian leadership is struggling to stay abreast of unofficial groups espousing reform; and the Jaruzelski regime in Poland is trying, perhaps vainly, to catch up with its own public, many of whose members have lived within a subterranean civil society of considerable sophistication since the imposition of martial law in late 1981.

Human Rights in the USSR Under Gorbachev

What have the Eastern European states and their citizens witnessed in the Gorbachev regime during its first years? Specifically, what signals has the Soviet Union been sending in the field of human rights? From the late 1970s to the mid-1980s, Soviet human rights and repression policies became increasingly harsher as East-West relations deteriorated, first with the decline of détente, then, in rapid succession from 1979 to 1983, with the Soviet invasion of Afghanistan, the declaration of martial law in Poland, and the shooting down of a South Korean passenger plane by a Soviet fighter. To each of the three events, the United States and its allies responded with embargoes, boycotts, and sanctions.

In the context of human rights, the Soviet leadership ratcheted up internal repression as its relations with the West progressively declined, and the cost-benefit ratio of domestic repression shifted dramatically in favor of the KGB. With key Western relationships at a low ebb, the authorities reasoned that the benefits of tighter internal control over dissidents and nonconforming citizens now greatly exceeded "foreign" costs in terms of the Soviet image and any additional Western sanctions.

The party line on repression remained in force from the late Brezhnev years through the short-lived terms of his two immediate successors and even well into Gorbachev's first year. In fact, former prisoners of conscience reported that the penal regime increased in severity under Yuri Andropov and under Mikhail Gorbachev at the onset. Upon taking office in early 1985, Gorbachev inherited a fully developed jurisprudence of political expediency. This included an array of administrative techniques for dealing with dissent, such as arbitrary bureaucratic deprivations; psychiatric internment for more difficult individuals; surreptitious "official" hooliganism to physically intimidate and deter certain dissidents; and the occasional decree of the Presidium of the USSR Supreme Soviet denaturalizing and forcibly expatriating a major personality for whom ordinary repression would attract too much attention abroad.

This special jurisprudence did not rely solely on prerogative actions; it also contained certain laws for enforcing the political status quo. These included laws on political crime (subversion and anti-Soviet sedition), on religion, and on ordinary crimes such as hooliganism. When the regime chose to proceed normatively against civic deviance, one or more of these laws were invoked to contain a wide spectrum of political, ethnic, and religious dissidents. In these cases, repression was processed judicially, either through a political trial or through a surrogate criminal trial serving as a crypto-political trial. In the latter variation on judicial repression, the target was framed for hooliganism, rape, or even arson or was sometimes selectively prosecuted for an often unwitting and unintentional technical violation of law. Whatever technique or method was selected by the authorities in individual cases, the purpose was the same—to politically neutralize a real or putative foe of the regime. Thus, an Eastern European leadership looking to the Soviet example in the first half of the 1980s would have found little reason or motivation to ameliorate its own human rights practices.

Throughout 1985 the Gorbachev administration continued to use this apparatus against myriad dissidents, nonestablishment critics, and nonconformists. Relations with the West were no better, and from the perspective of human rights advocacy, it looked like the business of repression as usual (and even a little worse) at home. This bleak picture, however, began slowly to improve as Gorbachev launched his peace offensive toward the West. Thereafter, in the latter half of the 1980s, a gradual amelioration of human rights policies coincident with a relaxation of repression was evident in the Soviet Union.

How might these course changes be construed in Eastern Europe? The principal sources for change are Gorbachev's major premises for domestic reform, the Twenty-seventh Congress of the Communist Party of the Soviet Union (CPSU) in 1986, the four Gorbachev-Reagan summits (1985–1988), and the ongoing politics of *perestroika* (or the struggle regarding Gorbachev's reform program).

In laying the groundwork for reform, Gorbachev has repeatedly proclaimed that dispute and conflict are normal and even healthy for a society and that "everything is permissible unless prohibited by law."[2] Under Gorbachev's leadership, the Twenty-seventh CPSU Congress set a new five-year course for foreign and domestic policy that inextricably links arms control with the United States to an ambitious agenda for restructuring at home. The latter includes three components: "*glasnost'*," or a policy of greater "openness" whose purposes are to enlist the press and intelligentsia as public persuaders of the larger, long-term objectives and to improve information flows within the system for better informed public policy; "democratization," or a policy of limited expansion of public participation in the policy implementation process designed to mobilize subelites (such as enterprise managers) and the mass public as leverage against a party-state bureaucracy generally reluctant and resistant to change; and "economic reform," or a policy intended to radically decentralize and partially marketize the foundering Soviet economy.

The first two program components have produced spinoffs in the area of human rights. *Glasnost'* and democratization have given more substance and vigor to heretofore severely abridged sections of the Soviet "bill of rights," especially in matters of speech, press, and assembly. The result is a set of de facto freedoms that is engendering a burgeoning socialist pluralism.

Summitry with the United States has also had an impact on the Soviet human rights performance. The USSR is mindful of the symbolic importance of human rights in the U.S. summit agenda and hence has taken steps to address these concerns in a visible way. Each summit from the Soviet side has been accompanied by the dramatic release of well-known prisoners of conscience of the stature of Anatoly Sharansky and Andrey Sakharov, the resolution of long-stalled family reunification cases, and an increase in exit visas for Soviet Jews, Germans, and Armenians. In addition, the priority of the peace offensive over the customary concerns about dissidence was, no doubt, a significant contributing factor in the leadership's decision to release several hundred political, ethnic, and religious prisoners of conscience from the Soviet camps, beginning in late 1986.

Finally, the politics of *perestroika,* or Gorbachev's efforts to get the major parts of his program approved by the Party elite, has probably dictated a greater degree of official tolerance than is usual for some of the unintended consequences of *glasnost'* and democratization. Most notable have been an upsurge of what would normally be seditious speech and writing by dissidents and others and a wave of nationalist demonstrations involving Armenians, Azeris, Balts, Jews, Tartars, and Russians. Any eventual resolution of the Armenian-Azerbaijani territorial dispute will no doubt be watched closely throughout the USSR, and in Eastern Europe as well, by other nationalities harboring irredentist claims.

The imperatives of *perestroika* combined with the impetus of the summits has significantly accelerated the emergence of civic alternatives to official reality in the USSR. For example, the Soviet contra-system (some aspects of which reach back to the times of V. I. Lenin and Joseph Stalin), which "matured" in the later Brezhnev years as a largely subterranean and sub rosa set of social alternatives to the planned economy and politicized society, is blossoming forth under Gorbachev into an increasingly condoned and partially legitimated civil society.

The contra-system, which attained its zenith under Leonid Brezhnev, comprises such loosely interconnected phenomena as the second economy and its bilegality and privatism; dissent in its political, ethnic, and religious variations; and a realm of alternate culture, including a parallel high culture, a youth counterculture, and modest endeavors toward independent education.

All of these phenomena tended to arise spontaneously as civic responses to conditions of chronic scarcity, restrictive censorship, and constraints on individual and group activity imposed by bureaucratic communism. Through surreptitious social networking and various subtle linkages, these congeries of contra-phenomena evolved in the 1970s into a kind of phantom reality, or contra-system. Motivation for involvement in one or another contra-component was invariably the individual's desire to enhance the quality of his or her life—materially, spiritually, or both.

The Gorbachev regime has progressively indicated that it is prepared to come to terms with large parts of the contra-system. The motives for this change in orientation are mixed. On the one hand, Gorbachev realizes that contra-behavior actually flourished under Brezhnev's policy of coexistence and that its more objectionable features did not fundamentally yield to years of police containment. On the other hand, Gorbachev seeks to reenlist millions of disaffected contra-citizens in the party's endeavor to build a better (read: official) society by liberating their energy and rechanneling it into lawful venues of action. To achieve his objective, Gorbachev has in the short term veered away from coexistence and tactically scaled back the emphasis on containment. Through his rhetoric, policies, and enabling legislation, Gorbachev has been signaling accommodation and cooptation as his preferred approaches to reconciling the contra-system to official reality.

Gorbachev's main problem is that his attempt to politically coordinate "from above" the transition from a contra-system to a qualified civil society is being outstripped by spontaneous social initiative "from below." This is a result of a revolution of rising political and legal expectations among the general public created by Gorbachev's rhetoric on the need for change. Many Soviet citizens, impatient with the slow pace of law reform in the critical areas of human rights, have begun in recent years to exercise promised rights without waiting for party-sanctioned de jure formulations. The authorities' response has been a zigzag policy of concession and repression. Some demonstrations are tolerated, but others are broken up; Sakharov is allowed to speak freely and boldly, but an attempt to form an opposition party is blocked; and the Russian Orthodox church is offered more autonomy, but other religious groups continue to be held in check. Nonetheless, this caution and ambivalence at the top have not deterred increasing numbers of ordinary citizens from continuing to press forward in testing the limits of *glasnost'* and in probing the parameters of democratization.

In conclusion, what can Eastern Europe—the elite as well as the person in the street—learn from observing the recent Soviet experience with human rights and repression? Basically, although there has been a great deal of motion, the Soviet Union has not yet embarked on a fundamental change of course in this area. At least four observations are relevant to Eastern Europe.

- Much of the movement on human rights in the USSR to date has been short term and tactical, usually with an impending summit or party conference in mind; when longer-term, strategic pronouncements have been offered, their language is frequently ambiguous and subject to party interpretation.

- Much of the progress has been in the form of policy change to compensate lagging law reform; this leaves the underlying legal structure on human rights still intact and raises the longer-range question of reversibility.
- Although repression generally has been relaxed and, in particular, political justice has been scaled back in the Moscow and Leningrad regions, the coercive apparatus remains unchanged and quietly continues to carry out the containment of dissent at a lower profile in the provinces.
- Even though the party line on religion is changing (subject to whether a particular religious persuasion is cooptable into the public business of *perestroika*), the leadership remains apprehensive and hesitant on the potentially more volatile contra-phenomenon of ethnic nationalism.

Civil Society in Eastern Europe

The new-style human rights activism in the USSR, both authorized and spontaneous, is having a differential impact on various parts of Eastern Europe, depending on the level of contra-system development in a given country. The variation is wide. Albania has only recently begun de-Stalinization, and only marginal youth ferment is observable. In Poland, however, the contra-system of the 1970s emerged as the civil society of the Solidarity period (1980–1981), retreated to sub rosa contraforms after martial law, and in recent years, through the passive acquiescence of the beleaguered regime, is again resurfacing as a civil society.

The other ships in the socialist convoy are deployed at various intervals between the Albanian and Polish extremes. Toward the rear is Bulgaria, with its less developed contra-activity. Ahead is Romania, with only a partially developed contra-system, although the largely ethnic Hungarian Transylvanian province is much farther advanced. In the middle are Czechoslovakia, Hungary, and East Germany. Cruising independently of the convoy just behind Poland, but generally in the same latitude and longitude, is Yugoslavia, a special case with considerable variations between its constituent republics—conservative Bosnia has a subsurface contra-system, whereas more liberal Slovenia has a relatively open civil society.

The course toward reemergence of civil society in the region, however, leads through rough waters. Given the economic reform cue from Moscow (or in Yugoslavia's case, from the dynamic of its own economic difficulties), the late 1980s and early 1990s are shaping up as a period of austerity in Eastern Europe. (A Hungarian prime minister has even spoken in praise of Thatcherism as a model of austere political economy.[3]) In Poland, Czechoslovakia, Hungary, Bulgaria, and Yugoslavia, restructuring is under way. East Germany and Romania, for different reasons, are holding to the status quo. Deep reform remains premature for Albania.

The basic agenda for economic reform entails cutting back traditional social welfare subsidies, tightening the linkage between productivity (qualitative as well as quantitative) and wages, introducing unemployment as a labor incentive, and, at least in Hungary, Yugoslavia, and Poland, contemplating or carrying out socialist bankruptcy proceedings for inefficient and unprofitable enterprises. Although the pace of reform varies from one country to another, depending upon the point of departure for change and the amount of political will available to push it through, the net effect will be the same—a dramatic revision of the consensual social contract between state and citizen. Food, housing, and fuel will become more expensive and jobs less secure. The mediocre but stable and predictable quality of life of the past is giving way to a more precarious and anxiety-inducing new lifestyle, as long-standing safety nets are lowered.

The imposition of austerity policies in the name of economic reform without significant social consultation is predictably generating blue-collar unrest. Although rare in the USSR, worker's protest is familiar in many parts of Eastern Europe. As a mass expression of inchoate economic dissent, it is potentially the most dangerous form of human rights activism for a regime. By contrast, religious and ethnic protest is usually relatively pacific (although the latter has the potential for violence), and political dissent, although high profile in its message, is customarily marginal in numbers involved and potential for disorder.

Blue-collar action is the most feared because it calls into question a Communist party regime's legitimacy, is least controllable by police power, and therefore sometimes necessitates large-scale, public coercion. Military force has been used against labor protests in Romania (1977) and Poland (1981). In Yugoslavia, the military has made veiled hints that it might be tempted to supersede the political establishment if ethnic and labor unrest could not be contained.

As economic austerity is politically imposed in the region, tremors increase in frequency and intensity, which suggests that political earthquakes may lie ahead in the next several years. In Yugoslavia, where strikes are neither prohibited nor legal, the number and longevity of work stoppages have increased. Romania, which has extreme austerity without even the rationale of restructuring, witnessed an explosive worker's eruption at Braşov in 1987. In Hungary, there have been scattered reports of anonymous symbolic violence against economic establishments in explicit protest against new wage policies. Poland in 1988 was the scene of the most dramatic blue-collar protests and the largest strike actions in the country since 1981. The strikes, mostly of the wildcat type, concerned narrow economic demands. Former Solidarity leaders who tried to politicize the events had little initial success, but in August 1988, after a second wave of strikes, the regime promised negotiations with Solidarity leader Lech Wałęsa. Even if held, the probability of a fruitful outcome is doubtful.

The microeconomic dissent of workers is a mixed blessing for the rise of civil society. The existence of such protest, whether large scale or small, peaceful or violent, is conspicuous testimony to the gap between state and society. In none of the East European states are there independent, legitimate, and fully effective upward avenues of communication between ruled and rulers. Even where there are some means of interest articulation, is anyone at the top listening? That strikes grow longer in Yugoslavia, that violence breaks out in Romania, and that workers occupy coal mines and shipyards in Poland suggest the answer is no. The notion of a civil society as a collective partner in vital social negotiations about public policy affecting the many is an idea whose time has not come in the European Communist states. Indeed, the congregation and clamoring of workers in the streets and shipyards bespeak an attempt, imperfect and frequently inchoate, to open a dialogue with the governing elite, to establish the right of the mass public to be heard and heeded. The standard regime response, however, is to brand such efforts illegal or at least contrary to the public interest (as construed by the elite) and to meet them with a mixture of tactical conciliation and selective repression. This suggests that the party elites are not prepared to concede any space to a conception of civil society that encompasses a sharing or division of power. As social developments unfold in Eastern Europe and contra-systems surface in civil societal forms, the powerholders try to demarcate a sociopolitical boundary beyond which they will not cede any turf.

Nonetheless, there is still ample room for the evolution of contra-phenomena into civil society, but as this happens, rotation of social leadership occurs. Historically, counterelite political dissent served as the catalyst, if not the continuing leadership stratum, of the earlier evolving contra-systems. Political dissidents in Poland, Czechoslovakia, Hungary, East Germany, and Romania (albeit only briefly in the late 1970s), demonstrated that there could be, although with difficulty, an unofficial alternative reality within a Communist system. Although these dissidents were always numerically small, they became role models for others by demonstrating that pervasive fear of the authorities could be overcome and by setting up the earliest *samizdat* networks, thus breaking the regime's long monopoly on information and communication. Even in Romania, the tiny band of political activists gathered around novelist Paul Goma, although quickly repressed, still managed to break out of social atomization and establish the precedent of independent communication, thus inspiring and emboldening their successors—ethnic and religious human rights activists. Political dissent was a catalyst for ethnic and religious dissent and thus for further contra-development beneath the surface of the nominally placid official society in Eastern Europe.

In the early stages of individual contra-system development, political dissenters played an essential role, if not among the founders of the system then among the group that first articulated a vision of an alternative to the status quo. The most notable of these groups were Praxis of Yugoslavia, KOR of Poland, and Charter 77 of Czechoslovakia. But as the 1980s wore on and years of repression took their toll, religious or ethnic advocacy (or both) gradually began to supersede political dissent in saliency and impact on the regime's social control agenda. Such activism, with its mass base, cohesive character, historical resonance, and universal appeal, is now perceived by the regimes to be potentially the most threatening human rights claims against the existing order. This appears to be the case, as will be demonstrated in the next section, in Poland (where the Catholic church had as much influence in the 1988 mini–labor crises as did the Solidarity leaders or the intellectual dissidents), East Germany, Czechoslovakia, Bulgaria (where political dissent has yet to emerge), Romania, and Yugoslavia.

The exception in Eastern Europe, where political activism still steers the contra-system *qua* civil society, is Hungary. Political dissent emerged relatively late in the post-Stalin period (because of the trauma of 1956), remained timid in the activist 1970s elsewhere, and has always been primarily confined to a relatively small group of intellectuals and literati in the capital. For many years, the party leader, Janós Kádár, skillfully coopted most of the intelligentsia (as expressed in the term *paraintellectuals*[4]) and successfully marginalized the smaller number of critical intellectuals. In recent years, however, as Kádár aged and the system reached the limits of his earlier reforms, the situation changed. Absent an indigenous ethnic problem (the external plight of the ethnic Hungarians in Romania is discussed elsewhere), and with only modest, fragmented religious activism, political dissidence came to the fore. This is especially interesting because the line between regime intellectuals and regime critics became blurred in the swirling leadership politics surrounding the succession to Kádár. Now that the succession is completed, the statements and initial actions of the new party leader, Károly Grósz, suggest that he hopes to monopolize reform initiatives at the leadership level. It seems likely that dissidents within and outside the party's ranks will soon again be at risk.

Where will this all lead in the 1990s? Clearly, small and large communities of political, religious, ethnic, cultural, and youth activists have staked out durable claims in the midst of foundering Communist systems in the European Communist states. This has been accomplished through the slow, steady reprivatization of enclaves of public space, which in turn have grown in scope and fused into contra-systems and embryonic civil societies. How are the regimes likely to meet the challenge to their social hegemony in the future? The sheer numbers of contra-citizens preclude police solutions except at the margins where occasional extremes arise. Most likely, Gorbachev's way, compromise between regime and society, will be the preferred solution of the future—not a grudging stalemate of forces as in Poland, but more likely, eventually, a partnership of sorts, a joint venture in sociopolitical power with the regime retaining a 51 percent majority. What, finally, might be the framework for such a historic compromise between communism and civil society in the future? It probably will be a type of socialist constitutionalism through which new rules of the game can be publicly codified along with, ideally, a mechanism for periodic renegotiation of the rules of power. Instead of the zero-sum solution of the Dulles doctrine of the 1950s, the actual scenario is more likely to be a non-zero-sum solution looking toward the twenty-first century.

Eastern European Case Studies of Dissent

During the last years of Stalin's rule, state control over society was the paramount feature of the Eastern European Communist systems. The party-state regimes left little space for contra-activity. Culture, education, and religion, along with many other aspects of prerevolutionary society, were under siege. Subsequently, as utopian experiments failed and party-state control began to wane, contra-systems slowly began to take shape in most parts of Eastern Europe. This took the form of small groups of citizens, unobtrusive at first, reclaiming segments of politicized society for their own material gratification or spiritual fulfillment. In the contemporary period, these contra-systems have begun to evolve into informal civil societies within Communist systems.

Political dissent, the most visible feature of the contra-system of the 1970s, has been gradually superseded in the 1980s by religious and ethnic dissent. Classic political dissidence, expressed by reformist intellectuals, appears now to be more peripheral, whereas mass-based, interclass expressions of ethnic and religious activism have moved center stage and become the new cutting edge of the contra-system, especially where the potential or reality of blue-collar economic unrest also exists.

Religious activism in Eastern Europe represents a significant manifestation of the contra-system in the region. Religion, whether it is state sanctioned or underground, tends to intersect with a variety of other contra-phenomena within a given contra-system. The Polish Catholic church, which is now the cynosure of contra-action in Poland, and religious activism and dissent in East Germany and Czechoslovakia are the focus of the following three case studies.

In three other states, Bulgaria, Romania, and Yugoslavia, the status of minority nationalities occupies a central place in the tableau of dissent. Ethnic advocacy, or merely the defense of the status quo, seems to preoccupy the regimes' attention more than do the indigenous manifestations of political dissent.

Poland

The Polish contra-system is the most highly developed in the European Communist states, in large part because of the temporal prestige and spiritual power of the Catholic church in Poland. The Polish pope, his several visits to his homeland, the experience of the Solidarity period, and martial law all have further strengthened the position of the church in society and vis-à-vis the Polish regime. One-third of all new priests ordained in Europe annually are Polish, and given the church's leverage with the regime, more than one thousand new churches have been erected since 1975, and hundreds of religious buildings are currently under construction.

The Polish church has achieved de facto "freedom of worship,"[5] which includes annual pilgrimages, some religious broadcasts, and the teaching of the catechism. The Polish episcopate operates a fairly large religious press, and the church's patronage extends throughout the alternate society of the contra-system as well. A leading Polish political dissident wrote in 1985:

> Nothing can change the fact that the Catholic Church is a great asset for the Poles. And not only because churches serve as headquarters for various committees aiding victims of repression, or because chaplains speak up on behalf of the wronged and the persecuted; and not only because church buildings ring with the free words of Polish music, and their walls are adorned with the works of Polish painters; not only because the Church has become an asylum for independent Polish culture. The Church is the most important institution in Poland because it teaches all of us that we may bow only before God.[6]

During the imposition of martial law, the church provided sanctuary for the Solidarity political underground until it resurfaced, for the parallel high culture, for independent education (or the "flying university"), and, to some extent, for the youth counterculture, which required space to perform its offbeat music. Similar arrangements exist in the rural areas. The church has also ordained secretly trained priests from Czechoslovakia and served as host to Catholic pilgrims from neighboring Communist states on the occasion of papal visits. Indeed, the Polish regime, given its weakness, needs the church to help maintain social peace. The regime must tolerate much of what the church does, although political pressure is steadily maintained on the higher clergy to keep the activist priests in line. On occasion, when the hierarchy cannot control a "political" priest, the police bring pressure to bear through an act of "official hooliganism." The execution-murder of Father Jerzy Popiełuszko by the secret police was an extreme case in point. On his most recent visit to Poland, the pope negotiated legalization of the Polish church's status in return for Vatican diplomatic recognition of Poland. When this agreement is consummated, the spiritual and secular power of the church in Poland will become even more formidable.

Now let us compare religious activism to the status of political dissent in Poland. The leading edge of the contra-system in the early 1980s, political dissidence, is now relatively subdued. There appear to be three reasons for its diminished status: (a) the former Solidarity leadership differs on how to react to the Jaruzelski regime on various issues; (b) their erstwhile followers appear to be suffering from some political fatigue; and (c) a generational change in the Polish working class is under way, which is decreasing the appeal of the veteran political dissidents of the early 1980s (except Wałęsa personally). As a result, the Solidarity leaders and their advisers have been overshadowed by the church hierarchy as the contra-leadership of society. In turn, the average Pole has taken refuge from the political arena in the socioeconomic and cultural activities of the contra-system. Privatism and political ennui are rife. Everyday life in a scarcity economy takes its toll and, by attrition, seems to have deflected public attention from the larger political issues. As August 1988 showed, this may have been but a pause in the recurring cycle of political dissent and popular unrest in Poland.

East Germany

In neighboring East Germany, the status of religion is different in several ways. The East German religious community is more diverse and pluralistic. Protestants greatly outnumber Catholics. There are several dozen other independent denominations, including Jehovah's Witnesses, Mormons, Christian Scientists, as well as a tiny Jewish community. The de jure status of the East German churches is more secure, although the Polish church enjoys a much stronger de facto position in society and the state. Even though the Polish church does receive more material benefits from the state, the Evangelical (Lutheran) church in the German Democratic Republic (GDR) is the most autonomous church in Eastern Europe. The minister does not draw his salary from the state, and the church is even permitted to operate its own hospitals.

Both East Germany and Poland try to coopt organized religion for their political purposes. The East German regime manages the church-state relationship more skillfully and tactfully, no doubt due in part to the proximity of West German fraternal churches. The party-state accepts the view that the church is neither for nor against socialism but is merely "a church in socialism." The political authorities, nonetheless, are able to use the church "as an escape valve for social unrest, the opening and closing of which still permits a degree of party control."[7]

Thus, the GDR regime tolerates, to a degree, the church's activity in the contra-community, especially among the countercultural youth and, to a lesser extent, among the parapolitical peace and environmental activists who flourish in East Germany. The church's work tends to exclude the emigration issue, the most salient issue for the thousands of GDR citizens who seek to emigrate to the Federal Republic of Germany (FRG). This is a troublesome question for the churches because emigration thins their ranks, carrying across the borders pastors, lay personnel, and parishioners in a kind of ecclesiastical "drain."

The major issues for the official East German churches in their contra-religious role are the political, socioreligious issues of peace, pacifism, conscientious objection to military service, and ecology. These concerns, revolving around the theme of antimilitarism, have drawn to the churches the youth of the country in increasing numbers, thereby offsetting the inroads in church attendance caused by secularization and emigration. As a result, the 1980s in East Germany have been a time of church-sponsored peace activism, including rallies, some quite large, and academic studies on the arms race.

How does the East German regime respond to the church's active role in the public arena? The religious community is closely monitored to ensure that it does not stray beyond the area demarcated for its activities by the authorities. For the most part, the regime's policy is one of coexistence tempered by mild containment. Thus, conscientious objectors have been subjected to short-term detentions, certain pacifist activists have been singled out for arrest, and dissident leaders are periodically expatriated to West

Germany. This unusual church-state concordat seems to be working, at least for now, because contra-religion provides a surrogate sphere for political dissent within fairly broad boundaries demarcated by the ruling elite.

Political dissent in the GDR is low keyed; it finds expression in the mass emigration movement and in church-led peace and environmental campaigns. The regime has not only accommodated itself to emigration but exploits it to gain badly needed hard currency through the annual "sale" to West Germany of hundreds of people serving sentences for trying to leave the country illegally. Because church-sponsored dissent deals with relatively mild, low-tension issues, it does not appear to be a major source of concern to the authorities at this time. If in the future, however, the church begins to lose control of its mixed constituency or, in order not to be left behind, decides to shift its focus to a more volatile issue (say, the Berlin Wall), tensions could rise between church and state. For now, classic intellectual political dissent, which has never been an important factor in the GDR, is presently subdued as a result of past expatriations, the attrition of time, and the absence of a compelling issue. Soviet pressures for *perestroika* combined with an impending succession process could, however, let in fresh issues through new windows of opportunity for political activism.

Czechoslovakia

Religion in Czechoslovakia, both permitted and contra, contrasts sharply with nearby Poland and East Germany. Church-state relations have been poor for years because the regime has consistently practiced containment and repression. For a long time, the result was a timid official religious community.

The Catholic church is by far the largest of the eighteen registered churches in the country. The next largest religious groups include the Czech Brethren, Baptists, Lutherans, Pentacostals, Seventh Day Adventists, and other Protestant denominations. Jehovah's Witnesses and Mormons are officially banned because of their proselytizing activities. The Roman Catholics are probably the most tightly controlled Catholic church in Eastern Europe outside of Albania. Until recently, the hierarchy had been weak and hesitant to challenge the regime, which resisted normalization with the Vatican for years. As a result, a majority of bishoprics have been vacant for many years, only two seminaries are permitted, and hundreds of parishes are without resident priests. Monasticism has been banned since 1950, and no new church construction has been approved for years. In signs of a possible thaw, the CSSR regime in 1988 (probably inspired by Gorbachev's gesture to religion) agreed to permit the Vatican to fill three vacancies, but with nonresident bishops.

Because the official church was severely restricted, a subterranean church or "church of the catacombs" arose in the 1970s and is today a thriving contra-institution in spite of constant surveillance and stern repression. The catacombs have their own part- and full-time clergy, including licensed priests working on the side, retirees, and hundreds of politically defrocked priests who had been punished for their religious activism. The parishioners include many youth and children, who ensure for Czech and Slovak Catholicism future generations of believers. In fact, for many of the dissident clergy and laity, "persecuted Christianity" seems to have a special attraction.[8]

The underground church meets secretly in small groups in which communion is administered, confessions are heard, and sermons are preached. Catechism is taught, Bible classes are held, at least three *samizdat* religious journals are circulated among the faithful, and even the tradition of monasticism is kept alive through secret orders. Most of the delicensed, underground priests and members of the secret orders lead a double life—holding down regular jobs by day while surreptitiously fulfilling the duties of their religious offices after hours.

These activities are illegal and punishable under Czechoslovak law. During the 1980s, the regime became especially diligent in prosecuting religious offenses, which reflected shifting priorities within its general repression policy. Compared to the emphasis on prosecuting political nonconformity after the 1968 Soviet invasion, and later after the creation of Charter 77, the present ranks of Czechoslovak prisoners of conscience tend to include more religious than political dissidents.

Although the regime tries to contain the subterranean church, an open, mass religious revival appears to be under way at the grass-roots level in Slovakia and in the Czech lands as well. Many people are turning to religion in search of spiritual sustenance, which neither the regime's policy of consumerism nor the moribund official ideology of Marxism-Leninism can supply. Expressions of greater religiosity were highlighted by the religious pilgrimages of tens of thousands of believers in 1985, on the 1,100th anniversary of the death of St. Methodius, the first Slavic archbishop and missionary. The numbers of people involved testify eloquently to this new wellspring of religion in Czechoslovakia. In the course of celebrations in the spring, summer, and fall, more than 150–200,000 Czech and Slovak pilgrims participated. In the spring of 1988, the authorities, probably to slow down the momentum of the mass religious movement, acted forcefully with arrests and water cannon to disrupt and break up two large demonstrations calling for religious freedom.

In addition to the established church and the church of the catacombs, a major new religious contra-phenomenon has emerged in Czechoslovakia. "The silent church"[9] may well present the most profound challenge since the Prague Spring to the long-closed Czechoslovak system. If we bear in mind the mass turnout for the first papal visit to Poland in 1979, the lesson of grass-roots religion in Czechoslovakia may be that "the organization and conduct of pilgrimages tend to provide the pilgrims with an experience of authentic participation, true communal feeling, self-reliance, and self-determination. All those elements contribute to a possible evolution of greater self-assertiveness that, born from a religious experience, could eventually expand into other, more secular areas of public activity."[10]

Emboldened by the spirit of the silent church, the cardinal-primate of Czechoslovakia recently issued a broad Charter of Believers in Czechoslovakia.

Although none of the points is unusual by Polish standards, they represent a radical appeal for greater religious freedom in Czechoslovakia. An even bolder petition, drafted by a layperson but endorsed by the cardinal-primate, had attracted several hundred thousand signatures by 1988. Together these documents represent a set of demands for secular approval, legitimation, and formal institutionalization of religious activities long underway in the contra-system in Czechoslovakia.

Czech and Slovak religious activism and protest have recently overshadowed political dissent as a problem for the regime in Prague, but the latter also remains important. Charter 77, the main association of political dissent in Czechoslovakia, celebrated its tenth anniversary in 1987 in spite of years of active police measures against it. Charter 77 has never acted as a political opposition. Instead, it has produced a considerable number of position papers presenting alternatives to a broad range of regime policies. Charter 77's *samizdat* output has been prodigious. But even its lower-keyed, nonconfrontational expression of political dissent often provoked the authorities, who reacted with familiar methods of containment. As a consequence, Charter 77 has probably had a greater impact on Western public opinion, and even on other Eastern European and Soviet dissidents, than on Czechoslovak society.

Chartist influence within Czechoslovakia has been limited for several reasons. Charter 77 has always been a small, predominantly intellectual group isolated from the mass public. Recent efforts to mount demonstrations were quelled by massive police power. Its focus has been issue oriented, and the issues addressed have frequently been abstract, philosophical, or otherwise removed from the daily concerns of the average citizen. Consequently, Charter 77 has never really aspired to or enjoyed any popular support that might challenge the regime; certainly nothing comparable to the appeal of the religious movement. Thus, in recent years the regime has begun to show much greater concern for the challenge to its hegemony arising from the religious sector of the contra-system. Charter 77 will remain a rich reservoir for an alternate vision of a civil society in Czechoslovakia, but for the party and security police in the late 1980s, its threat potential has receded.

Bulgaria

Bulgaria is the most dramatic case in point of minority nationalism overshadowing nearly mute political dissent. The ethnic Turks, who are the largest minority and constitute nearly 10 percent of the population, have for more than two decades been the target of Bulgarization by the ethnocentric majority. The Bulgarians have carried out several campaigns of forced assimilation against the Turkish minority since the 1960s. The current and most violent effort, which began in 1984, appears aimed at nominally eliminating the Turks as an identifiable group in Bulgarian society and obviating the intergenerational transfer of their ethnic identity.

This effort has entailed one of the most comprehensive antiminority campaigns in Eastern Europe. Turks are required to use Bulgarian, instead of Islamic, names; newborn babies are being registered with Slavic names. Turks are forbidden to speak their language in public on pain of fine, and Turkish-language newspapers and radio broadcasts have been eliminated. Turkish schools have been closed, and educational discrimination is practiced against Turks in Bulgarian institutions of learning. The Islamic religion, which the Turks as well as two smaller ethnic groups practice, is being systematically hampered by the state, which has, among other things, taken down tombstones with Turkish inscriptions and prohibited the circumcision of young males.

The authorities apply force to those who refuse to accept Slavic names, and in many locales, the Turks have attempted armed resistance to preserve their identity. Reportedly, hundreds of Turks and several dozen Bulgarian soldiers and police have lost their lives in the ensuing clashes. In spite of the regime's extraordinary effort to efface the Turkish nationality from the Bulgarian ethnic map, we can probably assume that many of the Bulgarian Turks have taken their culture and religion underground into the contra-system as a way of defending it against the majority.

In comparison with this raging ethnic conflict, documentable political dissent seems to barely exist in Bulgaria. There have been only a few modest manifestations in the past decade, mainly stimulated by events abroad. A brief anonymous statement called "Charter 78" appeared in 1978 as a faint echo of Charter 77 in Czechoslovakia. There was no followup. In 1987, the presence of the Helsinki Review Conference in Vienna elicited a critical document on human rights violations in Bulgaria signed by several brave citizens, all of whom suffered retaliation by the regime. Most recently, in 1988, the first unofficial human rights group, the Society for the Protection of Human Rights in Bulgaria, announced its existence. Even with more than two dozen members, only four dared sign its founding document—one has since emigrated, another is in internal exile, and the group's secretary is under house arrest.

The only activity that disturbs the placid calm of official Bulgarian society is a low-keyed environmental protest by regime intellectuals against Bulgarian transborder pollution. The problem preceded Gorbachev, but the more vocal unofficial response may be in part encouraged by human rights developments in the USSR. In any event, the Bulgarian regime in recent years has deployed a large part of its repression forces on the ethnic front, which it seems to regard as the only challenge to its authority.

Romania

Romania provides another case study of a country where ethnic activism prevails over political protest as a more serious problem for the authorities. The sizable ethnic Hungarian population in the Transylvanian region has been the object of continuing Romanian cultural pressure for years. There are Hungarian enclaves elsewhere in Eastern Europe as well, but nowhere do they fare as badly as in Romania.

The Hungarian minority has peacefully resisted Romanianization but has gradually lost ground to the majority culture. Pressure has also been brought to bear on other, smaller ethnic groups in Romania, but the Hungarians seem to have been especially singled out. Their Hungarian-language educational facilities have been cut back, from college to kindergarten, and Hungarian students have been subject to quotas at Romanian universities. Dissemination of the ethnic culture through Hungarian-language media—radio, television, and newspapers—has also been restricted. The purpose of Romanian policy is to cut off Hungarians from their past, isolate them from their cross-border brethren in Hungary, and thus promote assimilation. In essence, the regime is trying to sever the sources of historical memory.

The Transylvanian Hungarians have not remained impassive in the face of these mounting pressures. Underground *samizdat* bulletins have replaced the curtailed official Hungarian-language press. Certain Transylvanians, such as Károly Kiraly (a former high party official), have come forward to provide leadership in the struggle for ethnic survival. In recent years, Hungary has begun to come to the assistance of the beleaguered Transylvanians by offering rhetorical support from their religious and cultural communities and state-approved sanctuary for the increasing flow of Hungarian refugees from Romania. Most notable, however, have been Hungarian diplomatic interventions on behalf of their ethnic brothers and sisters in Romania, including a formal appeal in 1987 to the Helsinki Review Conference in Vienna to consider the matter. In effect, one of a number of long-suppressed, interstate ethnic differences has been allowed to resurface in Eastern Europe—probably with Soviet approval.

By contrast, political dissent in Romania has been a pale shadow of ethnic activism. Stimulated by the Helsinki process and by Charter 77 in Prague, organized political dissent first appeared in Romania in the late 1970s. For a brief period, a small group of intellectuals and professionals gathered around the writer Goma in Bucharest and unofficially advocated basic political and civil rights, including a free trade union movement. The authorities, however, showed little tolerance, and by the early 1980s, most of the dissidents were in prison, psychiatric hospitals, or involuntary exile abroad.

Since then, political activism in Romania has been minimal and largely focused on the desire of some citizens to emigrate to the West. For some, the motive is to escape the severe austerity of economic life in Romania, whereas others seek to gain freedom of religion abroad. Former leaders of banned political parties have recently petitioned to reactivate their causes but to little avail. Periodically, there is news of a lone individual or two carrying out an isolated, symbolic act in public, such as burning the collected works of Nicolae Ceauşescu—for which arrests predictably follow.

The only form of protest that temporarily preempts the regime's preoccupation with ethnic activism and religious dissent is the infrequent eruption of working-class unrest. Rooted in the country's harsh economic conditions, this type of protest tends to be spontaneous and leaderless. In such instances, the authorities see their immediate task as the short-term restoration of order or the regaining of control of the mines, factories, or streets where the protest is in progress. This usually involves a combination of conciliation and concession, but in the longer run, the regime fails to implement the concessions and repression takes hold. In 1987, for the third time in the past decade, large-scale blue-collar unrest broke out in Romania, and the authorities put their familiar containment techniques to work. Although mass economic dissent is at best episodic in Romania, each time it occurs the intensity of the protest increases, which raises the question of how long the regime can continue to buy social peace through a mixture of blandishment and force in conditions of such extreme austerity.

Yugoslavia

The final case study designed to illustrate the contemporary precedence of ethnic over political dissent is from Yugoslavia, the most multiethnic of the Eastern European states. The ethnic Albanians of the Kosovo autonomous region of the Serbian republic are one of the several restive nationalities of the Yugoslav federation. Albanian ethnic nationalism has been rising since the late 1960s, fueled by modernization, which has raised ethnic consciousness, and by the proximity of Albania across the frontier. Albanian activism reached a peak in 1981 when thousands of residents of the region took their cause to the streets.

Although subdued by force by the federal authorities and subsequently subjected to numerous political trials and wide-ranging job dismissals, the ethnic Albanian population continues to simmer and occasionally boil over in smaller-scale disturbances. Activism tends to focus on the demand for republic status for Kosovo, which would give the Albanians greater autonomy and parity with the major nationalities of the Yugoslav federation. When rebuffed in this demand, individual Albanians carried out sporadic reprisals against their Serbian neighbors throughout the 1980s. This has set in motion a Serbian exodus and, in recent years, an anti-Albanian backlash aimed at getting Belgrade to take more vigorous action to protect the Serbian minority in Kosovo. Restive Albanians, however, are just one of several ethnic problems (not to mention a variety of religious activism) confronting the politically fragmented and economically battered federal regime in Yugoslavia.

Political dissent is far less compelling than the seething cauldron of ethnic and religious activity within the Yugoslav contra-system. The reasons for this generally set Yugoslavia apart from the other European Communist states. What would be regarded as provocative political dissent in Bulgaria, Romania, or even the USSR before Gorbachev is frequently accommodated within the wider boundaries of permissible political speech in Yugoslavia. When political discourse does exceed the limits of repressive tolerance and becomes "dissent," it is often set within a regional context or focused on a discrete issue; hence, it is considered less threatening by the central authorities. What remains—traditional political dissent expressed by national and secular intellectuals—tends to be Marxist oriented (the Praxis group) or liberal in persuasion (Djilas). The scale of mainstream political dissent is small, its advocates are isolated and marginalized, and where administrative pressures fail to deter, vigorous political prosecutions for "hostile propaganda" under Article 133 of the Yugoslav Criminal Code await the dissident.

Nevertheless, the inflation-ridden Yugoslav economy and the gap between, for example, relatively prosperous Slovenia and bankrupt Montenegro and Macedonia intensify mass discontent and ethnic differences—a mixed and heady brew in multiethnic, Balkan Yugoslavia. This became strikingly clear when in spring 1988 regime-tolerated dissident publications in Slovenia attacked the then Yugoslav defense minister for selling arms to Ethiopia and illegally building a Dalmatian villa with ministry funds. The Serb-dominated High Command, spurred on by the rising tension between the nationalist Serbian party and the liberal Slovene party and without informing or consulting the federal party or government leaderships, inquired of the Slovene Interior Ministry if it could handle demonstrations and dissent. This was a clearly unilateral, perhaps illegal, and certainly intimidating military initiative. When the Slovene leadership protested, the military arrested two journalists and one warrant officer and charged them with disseminating military secrets. Despite mass demonstrations in Slovenia for their release, in summer 1988 they were tried and sentenced. In addition, International Monetary Fund (IMF)–forced deflationary measures led to strikes throughout the country. Thus, dissidence in Yugoslavia was rising and was more threatened by pro-Serb military pressure.

The political reality of multinational Yugoslavia is that ethnic advocacy, within and outside the establishment, has taken precedence over other forms of dissent and protest in the regime's priorities for social control. Although it would be a mistake to reduce Yugoslav political life to ethnic politics, it would not be an understatement to say that sub rosa and open ethnic conflict has long suffused the public arena. Given Yugoslavia's serious economic crisis, the situation could become even more volatile in the 1990s, especially if deeply felt ethnic issues fuse with mounting economic grievances as appears to be happening in the Serbian demonstrations.

Human Rights in Eastern Europe in the Era of Reform Communism

Overall, the pressures on the East European regimes to yield ground (or more of it) to contra-behavior on the road to the reemergence of civil societies in the next decade are likely to be greater than the leaderships' capacities to resist them. A constellation of such pressures from within and abroad, from West and East, are already in place and pushing the party-states to adopt some, or more, pragmatic tolerance toward the human rights of their long-deprived citizens.

From abroad comes a host of de facto human rights pressure groups. In the era of reform communism, Eastern Europe faces the unusual convergence of Soviet and U.S. political-economic pressure for change, including human rights improvement. The Soviet concern for human rights (including political and civil rights) is relativistic and pragmatic, whereas U.S. interest tends to be more universalistic and idealistic. Either way, both superpowers are amply equipped with sufficient means of political influence and economic leverage over the Eastern European regimes (with Albania still the exception) that in the longer run none will be able wholly to resist the pressures from East and West. Add to this the pressures from the IMF (on Yugoslavia and Poland), the human rights requisites for obtaining or retaining most favored nation trading status with the United States, the image-polishing needed to attract and maintain joint ventures from corporations operating in democratic societies, and the imperative of civil peace to ensure the flow of Western tourists as a source of hard currency.

Then there is an array of single-issue human rights lobbies in the West. These include the Vatican, which affords the Polish nation special protection (witness the pope's pointed remarks on the 1988 worker's protest) and shows concern for the spiritual needs of Catholics elsewhere in the region; the U.S. Jewish community, which not only espouses the rights of Soviet Jews but is attentive to the welfare of some of the smallest Jewish communities in Eastern Europe (such as in East Germany); the various ethnic émigré organizations in the United States and Western Europe, which have learned how to use the U.S. political process to maintain visibility for their Eastern European brethren's causes (for example, the Croatian émigrés); individual nation-states that act as protectors of ethnic kin (for example, the Turkish government and the Bulgarian Turks, Hungary and the Transylvanians of Romania, and the FRG and the GDR); Western artistic groups that come to aid of beleaguered fellow artists in the East (for example, the work of PEN and the *Index on Censorship*); general human rights organizations, which take up individual cases of prisoners of conscience (for example, Amnesty International, Helsinki Watch, USA, of the International Helsinki Federation, and the International League of Human Rights); and the Italian Communist party as well as the Western European socialist parties, which use their good offices to lobby for political dissidents on the Left.

Finally, the Eastern European party-states also face particular informational, internal, and regional pressures that cannot be ignored. All of these countries are exposed to Western radio, which has long since broken the informational monopoly in the East, and sections of nearly all the East European states are open as well to Western TV, with its subversive consumerist ethic. East Germany has long been permeated with West German television, and even certain parts of Albania receive Italian TV transmissions.

In addition, the ruling elites are constantly being confronted by inchoate expressions of deep discontent in their societies. Blue-collar strikes, stoppages, slowdowns, walkouts, or sit-ins are openly the most visible and volatile manifestations of this pressure from within. There are also reproduction "strikes" with adverse demographic consequences for the labor and armed forces and emigration movements that threaten a "brain drain" in East

Germany, Poland, and, to a lesser extent, Romania. Then there is the growing internationalization of dissent in the East as human rights groups in different countries coordinate their public statements and actions for maximum effect at home and media play in the West. Last, and cutting across the entire region, is the widespread problem of social apathy, especially youth alienation.

How will the regimes cope with all this? Clearly many of these challenges, such as inchoate protest, are not susceptible to conventional social control methods. Either because the challenge is too elusive or the international cost-benefit ratio is too unfavorable, we may be on the threshold of an era in which much of the nonviolent advocacy of individual and group rights is going to be beyond the effective reach of state police power. There will still be occasional trials, but the classic political trials of the 1970s and early 1980s (e.g., the Prague 6 of 1979) with their intellectual dissident defendants of stature may have already become obsolete because they have not really worked; their deterrent value is diminished and, in any case, misses most of the population; and the cost of trials in overseas image has now become too high. So the regimes are experimenting with alternatives to judicial political justice, such as "repressive tolerance" (developed into a fine art by the Hungarian authorities), decriminalization (ongoing in the second economies and probably forthcoming in reforming the restrictive legislation on religion), and a kind of desublimation by which the powers-that-be manipulate the unconscious of the mass public to deflect it from causes and politically charged issues (in recent years the Jaruzelski regime has permitted more soft porn in films and videos, which readily find a large audience).

Traditionally, an axiom of repression policy was to isolate the political dissidents from the working class, which was considered so much dry tinder awaiting a spark. In the future, now that religious and ethnic activism seems to have assumed social leadership in pursuit of a civil society, the major social control problem may be how to prevent an explosive fusion of blue-collar unrest with one or another religious or ethnic cause. In fact, it may already be too late and even impossible. A microcosm of the future is already present in Romania where Transylvanian protest includes ethnic Hungarian co-religionists who are also blue-collar workers. The security forces of Eastern Europe may some day look back with nostalgia to the time when their main problem was a small, discrete band of intellectual dissidents concentrated in the capital.

Notes

1. See Robert Sharlet, "Dissent and the 'Contra-System' in the Soviet Union," in Erik P. Hoffman, ed., *The Soviet Union in the 1980s* (New York: Academy of Political Science, 1984), pp. 135–146.

2. "Tezisy Tsentral'nogo Komiteta KPSS XIX Vsesouznoi partinnoi konferentsii," *Pravda,* May 27, 1988, p. 2.

3. On the eve of his visit to Great Britain, then Prime Minister Károly Grósz spoke of the "outstanding significance" of Margaret Thatcher's economic restructuring and said Hungary would need to follow suit as the "only way out." See Leslie

Collitt, "Hungary's PM Sets Off Down Thatcher's Path," *Financial Times,* May 4, 1988, p. 3.

4. See George Schöpflin, "Opposition and Para-Opposition: Critical Currents in Hungary, 1968–78," in Rudolf L. Tökés, ed., *Opposition in Eastern Europe* (Baltimore, Md.: Johns Hopkins University Press, 1979), Chapter 5.

5. Michael T. Kaufman, "Polish Church Awaits Pope, Bewildered by Its New Vigor," *New York Times,* June 7, 1987, sec. 1. The statement was made by a Polish bishop.

6. Adam Michnik, *Letters from Prison,* trans. Maya Latynski (Berkeley: University of California Press, 1987), p. 94.

7. Joyce Marie Mushaben, "Swords into Ploughshares: The Church, the State and the East German Peace Movement," *Studies in Comparative Communism* 17 (Summer 1984), p. 131.

8. Milan Simecka in *East European Reporter* 2, no. 3 (1987), p. 22.

9. *Radio Free Europe Research* 10, no. 40, Part 1 of 3 (October 4, 1985), pp. 13–15. The phrase is from a Czechoslovak *samizdat* religious journal.

10. J. B. de Weydenthal, "Religious Pilgrimages: A Step Toward Public Assertion," *Radio Free Europe Research* 11, no. 29, Part 2 of 4 (July 18, 1986), p. 2.

8

The Future of Poland: *Perestroika* or Perpetual Crisis?

Sarah Meiklejohn Terry

In mid-1985, approximately five years after the emergence of the independent trade union Solidarity and nearly four years after its suppression by the imposition of martial law, a well-connected Warsaw observer bluntly summed up the situation: "You might say we've emerged from our postcrisis period—and have entered our next precrisis period." He gave the regime no more than three years to stave off the next explosion of social unrest. Although that assessment predictably caught the listener's attention, it seemed somewhat overdrawn at the time. After all, Poland was then in its third year of modest economic recovery from 1982 lows; moreover, despite serious setbacks in the difficult process of regime-society reconciliation (most notably the October 1984 murder of the pro-Solidarity priest Jerzy Popiełuszko), the Warsaw leadership was actively seeking avenues for improving ties to the church and the moderate opposition. Not least important, the March 1985 promotion of Mikhail Gorbachev to the position of General Secretary of the Communist Party of the Soviet Union (CPSU) promised increased flexibility in Moscow's approach to Poland's endemic problems.

Three years later, the scenario of impending crisis seemed more credible, almost palpable. The economic recovery had run out of steam at performance levels still well below the precrisis peaks of the late 1970s. Moreover, the positive overall growth figures of the previous five years masked negative trends in a number of critical areas: most importantly, persistent shortages in the sensitive consumer sector, with the consequent adverse impact on social morale and productivity; the progressive decapitalization of industry and infrastructure due to lagging investments, with all of the negative implications for future economic growth; and a runaway ecological crisis, born of long-term neglect and misguided development policies, which Polish scientists feared was jeopardizing the biological future of the nation.

On the political front, the Polish United Workers party (PZPR), its ranks thinned and demoralized by the "one-two punch" of Solidarity and martial law, had effectively conceded its leading role to a military-dominated regime under the leadership of president and party First Secretary General Wojciech Jaruzelski. Repeated efforts by the regime to reestablish its credibility with society—most recently, the November 1987 referendum on wide-ranging reform proposals and the June 1988 elections to local People's Councils—fell far short of expectations. A public opinion poll conducted on the eve of the referendum by the general's official pollster found that 80 percent of those polled had wholly negative views of current policy and 60 percent said there were reasons for "a serious explosion [and] open social conflict," whereas only 7 percent thought planned economic reforms would succeed.[1] Filling the vacuum between regime and society was a growing number of independent organizations and uncensored publications—some with overtly political agendas—that were impervious to regime influence and increasingly defiant of official harassment.

None of this is to say that another political crisis is inevitable, although the waves of strikes in the spring and summer of 1988 were a clear warning that social tensions hover close to the flash point. Much will depend on Jaruzelski's ability to keep at least one step ahead of popular frustrations and assertiveness, while wrestling meaningful economic reforms through a recalcitrant bureaucracy. His success or failure will shape not only Poland's future but may well have an important, perhaps decisive, impact on the fate of *perestroika* (restructuring) elsewhere in Eastern Europe and in the Soviet Union itself, much as previous crises in Eastern Europe have contributed to the defeat of other Soviet reform efforts.

The Paradox of Progress: Recurrent Crisis

Poland emerged from World War II as the most ravaged and uprooted country in Europe. Its boundaries on either side were completely redrawn, with almost one-half of its prewar territory incorporated into the Soviet Union in the east and one-third of its postwar area annexed from Germany in the north and west. Poland's prewar population of an estimated 35 million had been reduced to less than 24 million, in part due to territorial changes, but mostly the result of deportations, concentration camp deaths, and war casualties. Massive postwar migrations, both into and out of the country and from one end to the other, added to the social turmoil. Overall economic losses were estimated at more than 40 percent of national wealth (in terms of fixed assets), which were more than for any other country. The enormity of the destruction was undoubtedly due to the fact that Poland suffered damages not only from military hostilities but also from systematic Nazi efforts to destroy Poland's cultural heritage, followed by rampant Soviet looting and "reparations" at the end of the war.

The PZPR did not come to power by popular mandate. Its prewar predecessor, the Communist Party of Poland, having begun its existence in 1918 by denying the validity of an independent Poland, survived on the fringes of Polish politics until its purge and dissolution on Joseph Stalin's orders in 1938. Even as he was forcibly imposing a Communist-dominated regime on postwar Poland, Stalin had few illusions that the Polish working class could be brought around to a pro-Soviet socialist stance. Wartime documents show that he saw the Polish population as overwhelmingly nationalistic and anti-Russian. His determination to incorporate Poland into a Soviet sphere of influence was dictated by strategic considerations: that it is the largest and most populous of the East European countries as well as the geopolitical linchpin of Soviet control over the region.

Against this background of devastation and political turmoil, the record of achievement during the first three and one-half decades of Communist rule must by virtually every index of socioeconomic development be regarded as impressive. In that relatively brief period, Poland was forcibly transformed from a predominantly rural/agricultural society into an urban/industrial one. In the same period, national income rose tenfold in constant prices, while industrial production increased more than fifteenfold, thereby making Poland the tenth industrial power in the world by the mid-1970s. Significant increases occurred in such key industrial sectors as steel, nonferrous metallurgy, coal mining, industrial machine building, transportation, and construction equipment. Overall living standards and the availability of consumer goods and services also increased substantially (if only erratically and at much slower rates than the economy as a whole), while striking advances were made in education and public health.

The paradox of Poland's postwar history is that the ruling Communist party has been unable to translate these not inconsiderable achievements into political legitimacy and stability. In the years since Stalin's death in 1953, the country has been wracked by social unrest and political crisis no less than five times—1956, 1968, 1970, 1976 and 1980–1981—so often, in fact, that Poles refer to each crisis simply by the month in which it began or reached its climax. Not only is Poland the least stable member of the Soviet bloc; it is the only East European country in which the grievances of the working class, the much-touted beneficiary of socialist rule, have served as a major catalyst of crisis on four of those five occasions.

"October"

The gradual decompression that followed Stalin's death in March 1953 culminated in Nikita Khrushchev's "secret" denunciation of the late dictator at the Twentieth Congress of the CPSU in February 1956. Although pressures for de-Stalinization varied markedly throughout the bloc, the timely (if unexpected) death of Polish party leader Bolesław Bierut, shortly after the Soviet congress, opened the way for a moderate Polish leadership inclined toward a more rapid elimination of Stalinist excesses. Whether this course proved "too little, too late" (or perhaps "too much, too soon"), the June "bread and freedom" riots in the industrial city of Poznań sparked a four-month period of turmoil and uncertainty. The crisis ended with the return to power in October of Władysław Gomułka—the postwar Communist leader purged in the Stalinization campaign of 1948—but only after a tense military confrontation with a Moscow leadership reluctant to see a reputed "national" Communist come to power in a strategic choke-point such as Poland.

Initially, Gomułka's return seemed to portend a more open and tolerant brand of communism. In economic policy, he promised a reorientation of priorities away from the Stalinist emphasis on heavy industry toward greater satisfaction of consumer needs; workers were assured a greater role through self-management councils; the pressure for collectivization was ended, and existing collective farms were allowed to disband; and more latitude was given to private initiative in small-scale industrial production and consumer services. In cultural and social life, the Catholic church regained a degree of autonomy in its religious and educational activities that was unprecedented for a Soviet-bloc country; social and professional organizations were also granted partial autonomy; and artists and intellectuals enjoyed an impressive degree of creative freedom. Finally, political life was enlivened by promises that representative bodies would have a greater role in decisionmaking, combined with a modest electoral reform offering voters a limited choice on their ballots, and by a reduction in censorship restrictions, which temporarily made the Polish press the liveliest in the bloc.

Within a few years, however, under external pressure from Moscow and stymied by an unreformed party bureaucracy at home, most of the gains of 1956 gave way to what came to be called the "small stabilization." The limited press and intellectual freedoms were the first to be curtailed. The changes in economic priorities also turned out to be short-lived, and proposed reforms of the central planning system never got past the drawing boards. Although pressures for collectivization of agriculture were not renewed, the private farm sector was systematically discriminated against in favor of the smaller but ideologically preferable socialized sector, while the scope for other forms of private enterprise were progressively restricted (although it remained broader than in other bloc economies). By the mid-1960s, the Sejm (Parliament) had fallen back into its former lethargic habits, as most candidates of independent mind were combed from electoral lists and the leadership ceased to consult the Sejm on vital policy issues—although here, too, the reversion was never complete. Even the modus vivendi with the church broke down under persistent pressures to limit its influence in society and the confrontation about which institution—church or party—should play the dominant role in the celebration of the Polish millenium in 1966.

"March" and "December"

By the end of the decade, the stagnation and general atmosphere of intellectual and political stultification that characterized the "small stabilization" produced two crises in quick succession. In March 1968, student and intellectual protests against censorship and cultural repression, inspired in part by the Prague Spring reforms in Czechoslovakia, provided the occasion for an indirect challenge to Gomułka's power engineered by the Partisans, a hard-line, nationalist faction of the PZPR led by Mieczysław Moczar and based in the military and security police. In the ensuing months, remaining liberal elements (especially those of Jewish origin) were forced out of the party and all important positions in public, intellectual, and cultural life. Gomułka survived this challenge—although only with the backing of Soviet leader Leonid Brezhnev, who was loath to risk a leadership shake-up in Poland while he still had his hands full with the Czech reformers.

Two years later, in December 1970, the Polish leader was not so lucky. Buoyed by his success in gaining final West German recognition of the Oder-Neisse boundary, an achievement that under most circumstances would have bolstered his popular support, he foolishly imposed sharp price increases on key food items shortly before the Christmas holidays. The resulting riots, which broke out first in the Baltic ports and spread later to other urban centers, led to Gomułka's replacement by Edward Gierek, the long-time party chief of the important industrial province of Silesia.

The early years under Gierek were in many respects a repeat of the post-1956 period: immediate concessions to key social groups together with promises of meaningful reforms, later retracted or whittled away as the new leadership consolidated its power. Just as Gomułka had done, Gierek reached a new modus vivendi with the church, announced a significant reduction in restrictions on private agriculture, eased controls over intellectual and cultural life, and in general promised a more open political style as well as an enhanced role for representative institutions, trade unions and worker self-management, and other professional groups. One area in which Gierek seemed to break new ground was in the industrial economy, where renewed proposals for reform of the central planning and management system were now coupled with a broad opening to credit-financed imports of Western technology as the main route to both improved economic performance and rising living standards. Yet by mid-decade, the political and cultural concessions had been retracted, the economic strategy was faltering, and the country was once again on the brink of crisis.

The root cause of Gierek's dilemma lay in his choice of a development strategy, which was in essence a failure to choose. Rather than make the tough decisions among competing priorities—in particular, between improving the lot of the long-deprived Polish consumer and pursuing rapid industrial expansion—he tried to do both. On the one hand, he ignored the warnings of economic advisers and embarked on an investment spree so ambitious and indiscriminate that by 1976, 50 percent of the country's industrial equipment had been installed during the previous six years. On the other hand, in an attempt to avoid another show of worker discontent, the new leadership team chose to heighten consumer expectations by allowing real wages to rise rapidly, far in excess of increases in labor productivity. Such a dual strategy would have been inconceivable without the massive influx of Western credits that suddenly became available in the heyday of détente and the oil price spiral induced by the Organization of Petroleum Exporting Countries (OPEC). Moreover, with food prices frozen well below costs and with other consumer prices also held at artificially low levels, this strategy predictably led to a surge in demand for meat, housing, and other scarce commodities. But precisely these sectors were given low priority in the regime's development plans.

The coup de grace to Gierek's development strategy was his failure to follow through on promised reforms in industry and agriculture. Proposals to streamline economic planning and management and to introduce incentives that would promote more efficient use of resources, improved product quality, and labor productivity quickly fell victim to resistance from entrenched bureaucratic interests and from Moscow and to the leadership's own indifference. Instead, the strategy of credit-financed investment came to be accepted as a substitute for essential structural changes, in the end intensifying rather than mitigating Poland's vulnerability to adverse global economic trends. Similarly, the reversion by 1974–1975 to a policy of deliberate discrimination against private farmers, especially in access to critical supplies and machinery, held down production in that sector, while investment funds poured into the smaller socialized sector were often wasted as a result of its gross inefficiencies.

Less tangible but no less relevant to Gierek's dilemma was the basic duplicity of his approach to political relations between rulers and ruled. The relative candor of the early Gierek years quickly gave way to renewed secrecy and arbitrariness as Poland's mounting economic problems were hidden behind a smokescreen of "the propaganda of success." In addition, he succumbed to the temptations of office, living lavishly himself and tolerating extensive corruption and abuses of power among his colleagues and subordinates. Thus, five years after taking office, the man whose dramatic flight to the strike-torn port of Szczecin in January 1971 paved the way for a settlement of that earlier crisis—the man whose rise to power was accompanied by pledges of greater openness and accessibility and by a condemnation of the aloof and autocratic style of his predecessor—was either unwilling or unable to engage in another "frank dialogue" with Poland's workers.

"June"

Just how empty Gierek's pledges turned out to be became apparent in 1976. Having promised that essential price increases on meat and other food items would be introduced only after "broad consultations with the working masses," the regime rushed the new prices through after apparently having "consulted" only with selected party officials and activists. So secretive were the preparations, in fact, that the Sejm learned of the extent of the proposed increases only hours before it was to enact them. (As one deputy caustically remarked later, "You see, our representative institutions really *are* democratic—even the deputies to the Sejm didn't know what was going on until the last minute!") The ensuing worker protests once again forced a rollback of the price increases, this time within twenty-four hours. Particularly grating to workers was the compensation scheme that was to accompany the revised price scale, which would have granted higher levels of compensation to those already enjoying higher incomes, thus adding insult to injury for a population already keenly aware of the rampant corruption and pervasive system of privilege from which the elite benefited.

The Slippery Slope to "August"

In retrospect, it is clear that the June riots were a final warning, a last chance for Gierek to change course if he were to avert the far more dramatic explosion of social protest four years later. What was needed was decisive action to bring the runaway economy under control and to reassure an increasingly sophisticated and alienated working class that the party was sensitive to its needs and aspirations. Yet, almost inexplicably, remedial measures were superficial and short-lived. Not only did the leadership survive intact, but, apart from the rollback of the price increases and a few hiccoughs in the implementation of other policies, the "June events" led to little more than a fleeting pause in the overall direction and substance of Gierek's policies. Apparently confident that the tactics of the post-1956 and post-1970 periods would again prove successful—that temporary concessions would suffice to defuse social unrest until the regime could regain its equilibrium—he not only underestimated Poland's looming economic crisis but totally misjudged changing social realities.

On the economic front, the so-called economic maneuver announced in December 1976 mandated a sharp reduction in industrial investments from the excessive rates of the first half of the decade, a shift in priorities in favor of agriculture and consumer-related industries, and an easing of restrictions on private enterprise in these sectors. In addition, talk of economic reform enjoyed a brief revival. All familiar promises from previous crises, they were not fulfilled this time either. Within a year, this latest effort finally to rid Poland of Stalin's economic legacy had been blunted. Moreover, by then the external support mechanisms that had allowed Gierek to pursue his dual strategy of rapid industrial expansion and rising living standards were gone. On the one hand, the plentiful Western credits of the early 1970s were inexorably being transformed into a hard-currency debt of $18–20 billion that now was falling due. On the other hand, the low prices for Soviet oil and other raw materials, which had partially shielded Poland and other bloc economies from the global inflation that followed the 1973–1974 OPEC oil embargo, were steadily rising toward world levels. Incapable of improving its own economic performance, the regime could meet its obligations to the West and East only by squeezing domestic consumption to maximize exports and by curtailing imports of goods essential both to industrial production and retail markets. As a result of the ensuing shortages and inflation—often hidden by the fact that official prices remained stable while the population was forced to shop for a growing list of "deficit goods" on the gray and black markets—real incomes for the great majority of workers began falling by the first half of 1977 at the latest.

Equally serious was Gierek's failure to appreciate the political implications of the profound changes in Polish society that the regime itself had played a major role in bringing about—changes not only in the consciousness of the working class but in the behavior of the intelligentsia and church. Among the workers, improved educational and skill levels as well as a growing awareness of the limits on opportunities for upward social mobility fueled frustrations about increasingly blatant elite privileges and corruption. In addition, the experience of past crises—in particular, the successful strike actions of 1956, 1970, and 1976—gave the workers an enhanced sense of class solidarity and confidence in their ability to challenge the political monopoly of the PZPR.

For the intelligentsia, 1968 had marked the end of "revisionism," or the illusion that the existing system could be reformed from within and that the party was capable of self-regeneration. Although they had failed to support the workers in the 1970 strikes, their growing disillusionment with the reversal of Gierek's early policies together with the impact of the June strikes brought many intellectuals into open opposition to the regime. Whether implicitly or explicitly, the emerging opposition led by such organizations as KOR (the Committee for the Defense of the Workers) adopted a strategy aimed at breaking the regime's monopoly of social organization and communication.

This strategy, first articulated by the exiled Polish philosopher Leszek Kołakowski in 1970, proceeded from the proposition that an "all or nothing" approach to the reform of communism in Eastern Europe was self-defeating. Accepting the fact, first, that Soviet proximity virtually guaranteed the survival of the present regime for the foreseeable future and, second, that this system was inherently incapable of reforming itself, Kołakowski nonetheless argued that monopolistic bureaucratic rule could and had to be resisted by exploiting contradictions in the system. "The rigidity of the system," he wrote, "depends *partly* on the degree to which the people living under it are *convinced of its rigidity*." By contrast, "a movement of resistance capable of limiting and weakening [bureaucratic rule] . . . will not lead to any perfect society, but . . . will create viable forms of socialist organization capable of offering its members a reasonable life."[2]

Thus, in the four years between the food-price riots of June 1976 and the birth of Solidarity in August 1980, the Polish population was treated to an unprecedented level of unofficial political activity and uncensored publications exposing the ineptitude and malfeasance of the regime and reeducating society in its tradition of resistance to unpopular rule. This in turn led to a proliferation of social action groups, which by 1978–1979 included the so-called Flying University offering independent courses on Polish history and politics; Committees for Free Trade Unions in major industrial centers; Farmers' Self-Defense Committees and the People's University (a rural counterpart to the Flying University); Students' Solidarity Committees and the Young Poland Movement; the Believers' Self-Defense Committee; and, the most conservative and nationalistic group, the Confederation for an Independent Poland.

Another crucial feature of Poland's changing sociopolitical climate in the second half of the 1970s was the new spirit of cooperation between the

Left intellectual opposition and the Catholic church. Since 1956, the church, especially as represented by the Znak parliamentary group, had pursued a strategy based on "a tacit compromise with the regime combined with nonacceptance of its ideology" and a belief, shared with Marxist revisionists, in the possibility of evolutionary change within the existing institutional structure. Even after the collapse of revisionist hopes in 1968, the church continued to believe that it "could accommodate itself to the . . . pragmatic course inaugurated by Gierek in 1971."[3]

For the church, the acid test of its relationship with the regime came in the confrontation over proposed amendments to the constitution in late 1975 and early 1976. Three amendments evoked particular controversy: first, the incorporation into the constitution of the "leading role" of the PZPR in what was now to be called the Polish Socialist Republic, thereby setting the party above the formal institutions of state power and providing a new source of legitimacy for its monopolistic position; second, the inclusion of a reference to Poland's "unshakable fraternal bond with the Soviet Union," which many saw as nothing less than a legalization of the Brezhnev Doctrine and an unacceptable limitation on Poland's sovereignty; and, third, a provision "inseparably" linking the rights of citizens to the "conscientious fulfilling of duties to the fatherland," which the church feared would provide the legal basis for political discrimination against believers.

The ensuing debate, which saw protests by prominent lay intellectuals as well as by the church, and which eventually forced the regime to modify the amendments, also marked a change in church posture. In retaliation for his abstention on the final vote approving the amendments, Znak leader Stanisław Stomma was stricken from the list of candidates in upcoming parliamentary elections. Denied a genuine opposition voice within the political system, the church found itself compelled to shift to a strategy of pressure from outside not unlike that outlined earlier by Kołakowski and to begin speaking out on a wide range of social and political issues. This convergence of the church's interests with those of the intellectual opposition led the latter to reappraise its traditionally negative attitude toward the former and to begin to see it not as the enemy of the Left but as a partner in the struggle against totalitarian power, thus setting the stage for their cooperation in the aftermath of the June riots.

With the benefit of hindsight, a lingering question is why the Kremlin did not react more quickly and decisively to the increasingly ominous situation in its most strategically sensitive ally. The answer is a complex one, and gaps remain in our knowledge of the details. Nonetheless, the most important factor appears to have been Moscow's complicity in the adoption and perpetuation of Warsaw's flawed economic strategy. As best described by one of Poland's most respected opposition writers, Jadwiga Staniszkis, Moscow had, and continues to have, a vested interest in reinforcing economic policies that were virtually guaranteed to produce recurrent crises:

> The present branch structure of the state [industrial] sector was forced on Poland in the 1940s and 1950s and is constantly reproduced as a result of

> Poland's specialization within CMEA. High demand for Soviet raw materials and energy (which has its basic source in the predominance of industries producing investment goods) not only forces Poland to invest in [development] of energy reserves in the USSR, but leads to a cyclical self-perpetuating deficit in trade relations with the Soviet Union. This deficit is used in turn by the Soviet side as an instrument for forcing further integration of the two economies . . . [in order to ensure] the structure of Polish exports desired by the USSR, even if this collides with the needs of the internal market and contributes to deepening economic disequilibrium.[4]

Although largely circumstantial, an accumulating body of evidence suggests that concerted Soviet pressure came to bear on the Gierek/Jaroszewicz team within two weeks of its assuming power. In a brief and little publicized trip to Moscow on January 5, 1971, the new duo was obliged to commit itself to continued cooperation in heavy and defense-related industries, which the ousted Gomułka leadership had only recently decided to downgrade because of their unprofitability and Poland's long-standing dissatisfaction with terms of trade within the Council for Mutual Economic Assistance (CMEA). (These included coal mining, ferrous metallurgy, heavy machine and aircraft construction, as well as shipbuilding and repairs—all of which weighed heavily in Polish-Soviet trade.) During this same meeting, the Poles apparently came under sharp attack for Gomułka's political deviations (especially his concessions to the church and private agriculture) and were admonished to bring domestic policy into greater conformity with the "general laws of socialism." Later, in the wake of the June 1976 crisis, the Soviets again contributed to the failure of the "economic maneuver" by repeatedly intervening to ensure continued "cooperation" in critical sectors.[5]

In addition to the overriding economic relationship, three other factors may have contributed to the apparent complacency shown by Moscow. The first was the importance of Gierek's role as a symbol of détente and as an intermediary in relations with West European leaders, a role that proved especially useful following the December 1979 Soviet invasion of Afghanistan. The second was the Soviet perception, based on the experience of the Prague Spring, that as long as the leadership of a ruling Communist party remained in loyal hands, the situation would be under control. In this respect, the Gierek/Jaroszewicz team seemed ideally suited to the task; the former was notoriously ambitious and eager to ingratiate himself with Brezhnev, whereas the latter had long been regarded as "Moscow's man in Warsaw." The third factor was Gierek's likely assurances to an apprehensive Kremlin that a policy of gradually squeezing out the opposition (as had happened after 1956 and 1970) was preferable to an all-out crackdown, which might succeed only in generating more popular support for dissident groups.

In fact, this latter ploy might have worked had it not been for two developments in 1978–1979: the precipitous deterioration of the Polish economy and the election of Karol Cardinal Wojtyła, the charismatic archbishop of Kraków, as Pope John Paul II. In the economy, mounting debt service payments to the West, combined with declining terms of trade with the USSR, forced Poland to increase exports (especially of coal and food products) at the expense of domestic needs and to curtail essential imports. Resulting shortages, most importantly in energy supplies, had a ripple effect throughout the economy, disrupting industrial production and transportation, damaging sophisticated industrial machinery (often imported from the West and not yet paid for), and generally creating chaos in the consumer economy. As a result, the leadership was deprived of its ability to placate the population. Following the unusually severe winter of 1978–1979, a local joke asked: "What does it take to create a disaster in Warsaw?" Answer: "Half a meter of snow, and thirty years of socialism!"

The impact of a tottering economy was matched only by that of the October 1978 election of the first Polish pope. This event, together with his tumultuous return visit to his homeland the following June, gave the still nascent coalition of church, intellectual opposition, and working class the psychological shot in the arm that provided the social cohesion and self-confidence for the emergence of Solidarity a year later. In the meantime, the Gierek leadership, heads firmly planted in the sand, turned a deaf ear to warnings, whether from inside or outside the party, of impending crisis. Already in mid-1977, a blue-ribbon panel of experts appointed to advise the leadership on socioeconomic problems by none other than the First Secretary himself warned that "only the most drastic" measures could turn the situation around. (Its report remained secret until the fall of 1980.)[6]

By the end of the decade, a striking consensus had emerged among opposition and establishment critics. On the side of the opposition, the most prescient and articulate appraisal came from the pen of Jacek Kuroń, a founding member of KOR and a leading figure in the intellectual opposition since the 1960s. In a brief but controversial article, "The Situation in the Country and the Program of the Opposition," Kuroń proceeded from the proposition that Poland was "threatened with an explosion of social anger on a scale greater than June '56, December '70, June '76 and March '68 taken together"—an explosion that could "very easily lead to a national tragedy (the probability of armed Soviet intervention)." The primary cause of the coming explosion, in Kuroń's view, was the "lowering of society's living standards that we are presently experiencing and that can only be compared to 1953." The possibilities for halting the decline "will be exhausted within the year," after which "a rapid worsening in living conditions will ensue."[7]

Kuroń's sense of alarm was shared by many in the establishment, as were the main points of his diagnosis. In the fall of 1978, a discussion group under the name "Experience and the Future" (Doświadczenia i Przyszłość, or DiP), composed mostly of party intellectuals, was formed with quasiofficial backing. When its first meeting in November proved too critical for regime tastes—foiling hopes that it could be used as a relatively innocuous safety valve for social discontent—official support was withdrawn, and DiP's organizers turned to soliciting from members written responses to a series of questions about the causes, depth, and possible ways out of

Poland's crisis. Its first "Report on the State of the Republic," based on answers to questions circulated in early 1979, was forwarded to the leadership in May. Dismayed by the lack of official response and the deteriorating economic and political situation, the organizers solicited the views of a somewhat wider audience in December; the second report, "Which Way Out?" was sent up in May 1980.

Despite the contrast in tactics—DiP's reports were aimed at directly influencing leadership decisions rather than generating pressure for change from below—its assessment of the situation was no less dire. Like Kuroń, respondents to DiP's questionnaires predicted an explosion of social anger:

> The expected decline in living standards over the next two or three years may prove more than society is psychologically able to bear. . . . Sooner or later there will be an explosion of the kind we have already experienced. It is a matter of secondary importance what specific event will trigger it. . . . The social cost of such explosions is always high. But in this case it could exceed anything we have experienced since the war.[8]

As might be expected, the bulk of the reports focused on official mismanagement and the economic and social manifestations of the mounting crisis. The bottom line, however, was the primacy of politics and the impossibility of resolving these deep-seated social and economic problems without fundamental changes in political processes. Among the most grievous defects in the existing structure were "the lack of mediating mechanisms . . . the stifling of spontaneous popular initiatives . . . the secretiveness of public life . . . [and] the tendency of the party to impose its decisions . . . [which] has clashed with deeply-rooted values in our society. . . . *In fact, for the last twenty years or so [social explosions] have been the only effective regulator of a system that has failed to create any other mechanism for correcting mistakes and replacing personnel.*"[9]

The Sixteen Months of "Solidarność"

The sequence of events that led to the formation of the independent trade union Solidarity in August 1980 began in an all too familiar fashion—with an increase in meat prices. The move was not wholly irrational. Under pressure from Western creditors to rein in Poland's runaway economy, the Gierek regime decided to begin by phasing out state subsidies on food, which were imposing an intolerable burden on the budget. Nonetheless, the reaction of the population was predictable. Bruised by four years of shortages and declining real incomes, distrustful of a regime that had made too many false promises in the past, the workers justifiably feared they would have to bear the brunt of the costs of the party's malfeasance.

On July 2, the day after the new increases were announced, the first of a wave of strikes that would radically alter the face of the country broke out. Although similar in origin to previous crises, these strikes soon assumed a character and scope that reflected the social and political changes of the preceeding thirty-five years. One difference was the strategy of the strikers, who used occupation, or sit-in, strikes rather than the street demonstrations of the past, which had brought only violence and injury. A second difference lay in the nature of the demands posed. No longer would the workers settle for satisfaction of their economic demands (for example, compensation for price increases or improved food supplies), which had proved all too transient. This time they also put forward a series of political demands intended to guarantee that any gains won would not again be whittled away by an arbitrary and monopolistic bureaucracy: most importantly, independent trade unions with the right to strike, freedom of speech and an end to censorship, release of all political prisoners and a prohibition of reprisals for a person's beliefs, full public disclosure of socioeconomic conditions, and the right of all social strata to participate in discussions concerning the reforms necessary to extricate the country from its current crisis.

A third difference was the almost spontaneous cohesion of the working class in response to the divide-and-rule tactics of the regime, which initially attempted to deal separately with each striking factory. By mid-August, when the wave hit the Gdańsk shipyard, scene of the most serious violence in 1970, an interfactory strike committee was formed representing hundreds of thousands of workers around the country. A fourth and crucial difference was the jelling of the worker-intellectual alliance. When KOR was formed four years earlier to provide assistance to workers fired or arrested in those disturbances, the workers for the most part remained skeptical and aloof. Now both KOR and Catholic intellectuals formed advisory groups to help the strikers (and later Solidarity) negotiate with the government and publicize their cause to the world outside.

In effect, what the workers with the help of their newfound allies were doing was putting into action the strategy of autonomous organization and social resistance that Kołakowski had articulated a decade earlier—not, as was so often charged both during and after Solidarity's brief sixteen-month life, in order to overthrow the ruling PZPR and "socialism," but in order to limit the party's monopolistic rule and make it more responsive to the needs and aspirations of the people. In fact, the union initially opposed even the concept of worker self-management, fearing that participation in enterprise management might only implicate the union in the regime's economic blunders without giving it real influence over policy. At the same time, understandably distrustful of the party's motives, the workers were quick to use their strike weapon whenever they sensed that the regime was stalling or trying to renege on the agreements signed. The contradiction inherent in this rejection of overt political ambitions, on the one hand, and the inescapably political implications of Solidarity's self-defined role as an external pressure group in a one-party system, on the other, was a constant source of tension within the organization, gradually polarizing the union as it became clear that the party had no intention of relinquishing its monopoly of power.

Indeed, the fact that Solidarity came into being at all was less a function of the PZPR's willingness to accommodate itself to the growing maturity and cohesion of Poland's working class than of the fact that the Gierek regime (as well as its overlords in Moscow) had simply been caught off guard. Apparently confident that its divide-and-rule tactics would work—Gierek himself did not return from his annual Crimean vacation in the USSR until the strikes hit Gdańsk—the government was ill-equipped to cope with a nationwide movement in which the strikers outnumbered an army that could not be relied on to shoot at compatriots. In this situation, any attempt to quell the strikes by force risked domestic chaos, which almost certainly would have been followed by Soviet military intervention.

Yet it is equally certain that the decision to seek a political solution—by signing the August 31 Gdańsk agreements that brought Solidarity into being (similar agreements were also signed in the second port of Szczecin and the coal-mining center of Jastrzębie in Silesia)—was viewed by the Polish leadership as an unpalatable and *temporary* retreat, which most of them *never* intended to honor. Indeed, the later revelations of Colonel Ryszard Kukliński indicated that a committee charged with drawing up contingency plans for the implementation of martial law was already set up on August 24, a full week before the agreements were signed.[10]

If it was not yet possible to crush Solidarity by force, one decision that could be made with little controversy was to remove those individuals most compromised by the crisis: Gierek, along with his closest and most corrupt associates. Beyond that, the party was divided into three factions: those who recognized the need for genuine compromise and reform (an estimated 1 million PZPR members, or about one-third of the party's total membership, joined Solidarity); at the other extreme, those who were never reconciled to any but the most cosmetic changes in political relations and whose open hostility to Solidarity was at best thinly veiled; in the middle, those who for varying reasons saw the necessity of some measure of dialogue and policy change but, guided by "geopolitical realities" (a not-so-subtle reference to the threat of Soviet intervention), paid lip service to the Gdańsk agreements but only until they could be whittled away. Because the first group, although numerous in the rank-and-file membership, was always a small (and dwindling) minority at leadership levels, the struggle within the party was primarily between the moderates and hard-liners (*betony*, or cement-heads, as the Poles call them). During the next sixteen months, the top leadership changed twice more but, despite challenges from the *betony*, remained under the control of the moderate group: in February 1981, when General Jaruzelski was named prime minister (while keeping his post as defense minister), and, in October of that year, when he assumed the top post as PZPR First Secretary from Gierek's immediate and rather ineffective successor, Stanisław Kania.

Clearly, a critical factor in the attitude of the Polish leadership was the reaction of the Kremlin, where the inclination to view Solidarity as the Marxist-Leninist equivalent of original sin was evident within a month of the Gdańsk agreements. The message was delivered in typically elliptical Soviet style, with no direct reference to the situation in Poland: in a *Pravda* review of a book on Lenin's trade union policy whose central theme was that there was no place for independent trade unions in a socialist society because the "objective" interests of the working class were fully represented by the party. But Moscow, too, misled in part by Gierek's casual behavior, had been taken by surprise and had to adjust its tactics accordingly. The question of whether the Brezhnev leadership might actually have been willing to use direct military force will be dealt with later. For the moment, suffice it to say that a Warsaw Pact invasion was always viewed as a last resort—not only because the Poles could be expected to put up fierce resistance, but because in the wake of the Soviet invasion of Afghanistan (then less than a year old) a similar move into Poland would have dealt a final blow to East-West détente. Instead, Moscow adopted a more manipulative strategy: "Never permit the Polish party to strike a genuine compromise with Solidarity, disrupt even temporary lulls that might allow the union to consolidate its legal and political status, and ultimately force the Poles themselves to end the threat to one-party rule."[11]

From these basic positions of the three key actors, a cyclical pattern of action and reaction emerged: (1) a confrontation between party and Solidarity resulting in a provisional compromise (generally a retreat by the former in the face of a strike threat that it could not contain); (2) a deliberate escalation of the polemical tone by Moscow, for fear that a period of genuine calm would allow Solidarity to solidify its domestic position; (3) a stiffening of the regime's resistance to the union's demands, prompted by Moscow's hard line and sometimes by *betony*-inspired provocations—all leading back to stage one and renewed confrontation between the PZPR and Solidarity. With each cycle, there was a progressive polarization in both organizations that weakened moderate elements in favor of hard-liners in the party and radicals in the union and made genuine accommodation less and less likely.

Throughout the Solidarity period, the church's position was complex and multifaceted, with strong moral support for the workers' demands partially offset by an overriding commitment to the physical and cultural survival of the Polish nation. These dual concerns forced the episcopate into a delicate balancing act in which it often had to play a mediating role, urging caution on the union at the same time as it was pressing the government to fulfill its promises and engage in a genuine dialogue with the people. Nonetheless, Solidarity leader Lech Wałęsa's strong ties to the church, together with Pope John Paul's outspoken defense of the union and of the right of his countrymen to social justice, gave it added leverage in the tug of war between regime and society. The assassination attempt on the pope in May 1981, followed the same month by the death of Cardinal Stefan Wyszyński, primate of the Polish church and a symbol of resistance to tyranny for more than thirty years, only heightened the traditional identification of church and nation in the popular mind.

These were the main actors in the Polish drama of 1980–1981, but they were by no means the only ones. In addition to Solidarity, whose 9–10 million members included a wide variety of white-collar and professional employees as well as industrial workers, an independent Rural Solidarity representing the country's 3 million private farmers was eventually formed, although only through the intervention of the church to overcome stiff resistance from the regime (and Moscow). Many official organizations—including the prestigious Polish Academy of Sciences, important professional groups such as the journalists' association, and a variety of other cultural and social groups—began electing their own leaders and redefining their policies and functions. Unofficial publications, already numerous in the pre-August period, continued to proliferate, some—such as the union's weekly, *Tygodnik solidarność*, and various regional bulletins—attaining a quasiofficial or legal status. Some parts of the official press also became distinctly more lively, running articles previously rejected by the censors and engaging in candid critiques of past policies. Even within the PZPR (and in contravention of traditional Leninist norms of party organization banning "factionalism"), reform elements in different regions began forming "horizontal links" among themselves to bring pressure to bear on the leadership.

This process was summed up in the word *odnowa* (renewal)—a concept to which all groups claimed to subscribe but to which they attached quite different meanings. To Solidarity, the church, and other new or newly independent organizations, it meant "democratic rebirth" and a "reintegration of society" in which the social vacuum that was the reverse side of the PZPR's monopolistic position, and that had left society alienated and powerless to influence its own situation, would be replaced by a more consensually based order—albeit one in which the Communist party was still primus inter pares. Although the most liberal elements in the party's rank and file shared this view, the dominant moderate (one might also say opportunistic) faction interpreted "renewal" to mean cleansing the party of its corrupt and incompetent elements so that it could perform its "leading role" more effectively, consulting with other social groups only as it saw necessary. The *betony*, on the other hand, never accepted the concept of "renewal" in any meaningful sense, paying lip service to it only until the opposition could be eliminated.

The turning point came in the summer and early fall of 1981 with the Ninth Extraordinary Congress of the PZPR in July, followed by Solidarity's First National Congress in September and early October. The former, already postponed several times and awaited with great anticipation, proved a bitter disappointment to those who expected the party to demonstrate its commitment to "renewal." Despite formal changes in party rules that provided a facade of democratization, the moderate-to-conservative leadership soon showed itself unable or unwilling to undertake essential economic reforms or engage in a serious dialogue with Solidarity. By contrast, Solidarity's congress was marked by a mood of bold self-confidence, reflecting both the progressive radicalization of the union's rank and file and a determination to break the stalemate caused by the party's paralysis. Although the leadership under Wałęsa continued to deny any political ambitions, heated debates during the congress raised sensitive issues—calls for free elections, worker self-management, unrestricted access to the media and, most provocative of all, an appeal to workers in other socialist countries to follow Solidarity's example.

Two weeks after his appointment as PZPR First Secretary on October 18, General Jaruzelski held an unprecedented meeting with Wałęsa and Archbishop Józef Glemp (Wyszyński's successor as Poland's primate) to discuss the formation of a "front of national accord" as "a permanent forum for dialogue and consultation . . . on the basis of Poland's constitutional principles." With the party in disarray and intimidated by intense pressure from Moscow, however, it soon became clear that the general was unable to offer Solidarity or the church anything more than an ill-defined and subordinate role and that the reference to "Poland's constitutional principles" was primarily intended to invoke the 1976 amendment concerning the party's "leading role." Thereafter, the situation deteriorated rapidly, with the third week in December looming as a critical challenge to the regime. On December 15, Jaruzelski was preparing to ask the Sejm for stand-by emergency powers, with approval in question; on December 17, Solidarity planned a one-day nationwide strike to commemorate the anniversary of the December 1970 strikes. Instead, just after midnight on Sunday, December 13, martial law was declared and Solidarity was suspended.

Two critical questions remain to be answered: First, how should we divide responsibility between Solidarity and the PZPR for the failure of "renewal" and the imposition of martial law? Second, was the threat of Soviet military intervention truly credible, or was it merely an exercise in blackmail to force the Polish military to resolve the situation itself? If the latter, does this mean that a different posture on the part of the Polish regime vis-à-vis Moscow, or a less assertive strategy on the part of Solidarity, might have allowed for the union's survival and a continuation of Poland's renewal?

The Jaruzelski regime's justification for the imposition of martial law as a desperate effort to rescue the economy from the Solidarity's disruptive strike tactics, and the "cause of socialism" from the union's excessive political demands, simply does not stand up to the evidence. The downward economic spiral, which continued through 1982, was due far more to Poland's liquidity crisis than to strikes. After years of overlooking the Gierek regime's mismanagement of its investment policy, by 1980–1981 Western lenders had finally gotten the message that the country was no longer creditworthy. In fact, strikes were responsible for only a fraction of lost work time, which was due mostly to Poland's inability to import essential industrial inputs as well as to dire shortages of consumer goods and time wasted in queues.

On the political front, the pertinent fact is that by November–December 1981, the underpinnings of the PZPR's monopolistic position were crumbling. The party itself was deeply split, with a significant minority of rank-and-file members and some at higher levels (apparently including ousted First Secretary Kania) preferring genuine political compromise. Already, earlier in the fall, the Sejm had forced changes in new laws on self-management and censorship in favor of Solidarity's position; and rumors concerning the session scheduled for December 15 hinted that some PZPR deputies would join other parties in opposing the government's request for stand-by emergency powers. A final ill omen was the rumor that the *betony* and security police were planning some kind of provocation against Solidarity in connection with the December 17 anniversary, which could have led to general violence.

None of this is to say that Solidarity's actions always fell within the framework of workable compromise. The increasing polarization of the rank and file, as well as the more provocative resolutions of the union's first national congress, reflected the growing political assertiveness of a mass organization frustrated by the stonewalling tactics of a ruling party determined not to relinquish its monopolistic position. On the other hand, the weight of evidence—both that available at the time and what can be gleaned from the Kukliński interview—clearly suggests that the party (badgered and intimidated in the most forceful fashion by Moscow) was intent from the very beginning on destroying Solidarity as an organized political entity.

Concerning the second question, Kukliński presented contradictory conclusions. On the one hand, he argued that had the Polish leadership demonstrated enough courage and dignity in defense of Poland's sovereignty (modeled on Gomułka's defiance of Khrushchev's demands in 1956), it could have stymied Soviet opposition to Solidarity (on the assumption that Moscow was unwilling to intervene militarily in the face of almost certain armed resistance). Kukliński further asserted that faced with an overt threat of Soviet intervention, Solidarity would have tempered its demands and made the defense of Poland's independence its first priority. Once again, these assumptions are not supported by the evidence. First, the nature of the threat both to Moscow and to the Polish party in 1980–1981 was wholly different and more fundamental than in 1956. The earlier crisis never involved the challenge of a mass-based organization demanding an institutionalized role in the political process. Moreover, it occurred at the height of revisionist optimism that the party was capable of reforming itself—a hope that had lost all credibility by 1980. Under the circumstances, it was probably inevitable that a significant segment of the PZPR leadership would see collusion with Moscow against Solidarity as preferable to a determined stand against Soviet pressure in defense of Poland's independence.

Second, even assuming the Soviets were unwilling to intervene directly, they had other options short of military action to bring Poland to its knees, such as the rumored threat of an oil cutoff in fall 1981. But the most convincing evidence came from Kukliński himself, who presented in excruciating detail not only Moscow's campaign of escalating military intimidation but also, and more importantly, extensive preparation for direct Soviet military involvement should the intimidation campaign fail to bring about the desired result, including the introduction of Soviet reconnaissance teams starting in February 1981 to select potential deployment sites for Soviet troops; the setting up of an independent communications network throughout Poland under cover of the Soyuz-81 Warsaw Pact maneuvers in March 1981;

the enhancement of the combat capability of Soviet divisions already stationed in Poland, also under cover of Warsaw Pact maneuvers; detailed plans for the deployment of Soviet, East German, and Czechoslovak divisions in Poland; and the dispatching of teams of Soviet military, KGB, and Gosplan functionaries as advisers to Polish military districts and headquarters. Kukliński also noted secret preparations to replace the Kania-Jaruzelski leadership at a particularly tense moment in November 1980, when Moscow sensed the Poles were stalling for time. He also claimed that Kania was removed as First Secretary when he refused to approve the use of force. Although many of these moves could be interpreted as part of the campaign to pressure Warsaw to impose martial law itself, they were also consistent with preparation for direct Soviet military involvement. Indeed, as Kukliński admitted at the end of his interview, "It is difficult for me to imagine circumstances in which [Jaruzelski] could say 'no' to the Russians, even if he deeply desired to do so."[12]

Beyond Solidarity and Martial Law

Martial law—or as the Poles called it, a "state of war" (*stan wojenny*)—was partially lifted at the end of 1982 and formally ended in July 1983, although only after many of its emergency provisions had been incorporated into the civil codes. Although a superficial kind of order has been restored, accompanied by partial economic recovery, none of the problems that led to the emergence of Solidarity or the imposition of martial law is any closer to resolution than it was in December 1981.

A House Divided

Politically, Poland remains a house divided against itself, in which a numerically weakened and demoralized party has proven incapable of bridging the chasm between itself and the mass of Polish society. In an uninterrupted six-year slide, PZPR ranks fell by one-third, from 3.1 million members in 1980 to 2.1 million in 1986, and many party organizations remain essentially dormant. The most dramatic changes have occurred in the younger age groups: a decline of approximately 90 percent in the eighteen to twenty-four age group, which comprises mostly candidate members but from which future elites are recruited; and a drop of almost 75 percent in the twenty-five to twenty-nine year age group, which was consistently the largest single five-year cohort in PZPR ranks from at least 1960 to 1980 and is the group from which the next generation of leading functionaries are intensively cultivated and trained. Together these two groups, which constituted one-fourth of total party membership in 1970, accounted for just under 7 percent of a much smaller party in 1986. The 40 percent decline in blue-collar members, from 1.34 million in 1978 to 800,000 in 1986, is also symbolically important.[13]

Equally problematic has been the critical weakening of the two factions of the party that might have had some chance of restoring its credibility in the eyes of the population: first, the genuine reformers, those who actively supported Solidarity and whose numbers were decimated by resignations and expulsions after martial law; second, the moderates, who have effectively been discredited in the popular mind by their complicity in martial law and in the subsequent political and economic stalemate. Ironically, the primary victim of this narrowing of the party's political base has been none other than Jaruzelski, who despite more than six years as First Secretary is still regarded as an outsider by the party apparatus. Indicative of the distance between the general and the apparat is the fact that he operates out of the Belvedere Palace, his official residence as president, rather than out of Central Committee headquarters. Indeed, it is reliably rumored that his secure communication lines to Moscow are also located in the Belvedere, under military rather than party control.

Another indicator of Jaruzelski's weakness in the apparat has been his choice of political confidants, none of whom comes from the professional party bureaucracy. Most important are five long-time military colleagues, who oversee security and general organizational matters: Generals Czesław Kiszczak, minister of internal affairs; Florian Siwicki, minister of defense; Józef Baryła, Central Committee secretary in charge of party organization; Colonel Michał Janiszewski, chief of staff of the Council of Ministers (with ministerial rank) and Jaruzelski's eyes in the government; and Colonel Stanisław Kwiatkowski, the First Secretary's chief pollster. The next contingent consists of four present or former journalists on the moderate-to-liberal fringe of the party, who appear to influence Jaruzelski's sociopolitical agenda: Mieczysław Rakowski, the former editor of the liberal party weekly *Polityka* who served as a deputy prime minister in the Solidarity and martial law period, after which he suffered a temporary demotion before being elevated to full Politburo status in December 1987 and to Central Committee secretary six months later; Jerzy Urban, long a thorn in the regime's side as a columnist for *Polityka* before signing on as government "spokesman," where his public image as Jaruzelski's "flak-catcher," or court jester, masks a more influential advisory role; Ludwik Krasucki, the reformist deputy editor of the party's theoretical monthly, *Nowe drogi,* and reputedly Jaruzelski's chief speech writer; and Wiesław Górnicki, a journalist with extensive Western experience but no official responsibilities. Among other key advisers—deputy chairman of the State Council (vice president) Kazimierz Barcikowski, Central Committee secretaries Józef Czyrek, Stanisław Ciosek, and Marian Orzechowski (foreign minister until June 1988)—none has a strong base in the apparat.

At the same time, the First Secretary has been notably unsuccessful (at least until mid-1988) in breaking the hold of the hard-line, heavy-industrial lobby over economic policy. Despite his non-Politburo status, the key figure in this lobby is Deputy Prime Minister Zbigniew Szałajda, who has responsibility for industry (including defense industry) and the State Committee for Science and Technology, which oversees coordination of economic and defense industry links with the Soviet Union. Among his chief accomplices have been Prime Minister Zbigniew Messner, who assumed that post from

Jaruzelski in November 1985 but who has proved a weak administrator, unwilling or unable to break with the bad habits of the past; first deputy chairman of the Planning Commission Franciszek Kubiczek, who inexplicably survived the October 1987 appointment of reformist planning chief Zdzisław Sadowski; and Central Committee secretaries Marian Woźniak and Tadeusz Porębski. (See "Postscript" for additional personnel changes in June and September 1988.)

That Jaruzelski has been able to survive, despite this unfavorable environment, is due to three factors. First, the People's Republic of Poland is no longer (or not yet again) a one-party Communist state, and the PZPR's continuing weakness means that only the military is capable of running the country.[14] Second, despite urgent efforts to reenergize the party (or conceal its parlous state), Moscow recognizes that it has no alternative to Jaruzelski; indeed, since the March 1985 appointment of Gorbachev as CPSU General Secretary, the Polish leader has been the beneficiary of repeated demonstrations of Kremlin support. Third, and somewhat ironically, from the perspective of the population at large there is also no alternative to Jaruzelski.

Nonetheless, the great majority of Poles emerged from the trauma of martial law emotionally exhausted but politically unreconciled. According to an independent public opinion poll conducted under the auspices of the Polish Academy of Sciences just a year after the lifting of martial law, the regime could count on the firm support of no more than 12–15 percent of the population; at the other end of the spectrum, the size of the confirmed opposition—those actively engaged in or cooperating with the political underground—was estimated at 15–18 percent. The remaining seventy-odd percent fell roughly into five groups:[15]

- "Law and order" advocates, who disliked the "chaos" of the Solidarity period and subscribed to the view (a favorite theme of officialdom) that Poles are "difficult to rule" and "need a strong government";
- Unskilled workers, who (although dissatisfied with certain aspects of the system) were basically apolitical and fearful for their material status and thus susceptible to regime pressures and manipulation;
- A broad group that continued to share Solidarity's values but saw the movement as a failed experiment—"A good try, but this period in our lives is over; now it's time to think about our and our children's future"—but a group that also placed the blame for martial law on the party and government rather than on Solidarity;
- The inactive or latent opposition—more alienated than the third group but still not actively engaged, although consumers of underground publications;
- The nonrespondents (20 percent of a random sample of 2,000 people), who whether out of opposition or fear of reprisal refused to respond to the poll or answered the most sensitive questions with "uncertain" or "don't know."

The first two groups together were estimated to account for less than 20 percent of the population, bringing total support for the regime (whether firm or grudging) to no more than one-third. From the leadership's perspective, the situation was all the more alarming in light of the age and social makeup of the remaining two-thirds, which showed that the alienated or overtly hostile majority was composed disproportionately of four groups: the cultural and professional intelligentsia, the peasantry (both traditional thorns in the regime's side), skilled workers (the presumed beneficiaries and co-managers of the socialist state) and, above all, youth. In other words, the nonsupportive majority was made up of those groups on which economic recovery and future stability would most depend.

The dilemma posed by the younger generations (generally defined as including those up to age forty) is particularly acute. For them, the sixteen months of Solidarity provided an intense political socialization or resocialization that could not be erased either by repression or by attempts at manipulation and cooptation. This was a period in which history was relearned and values formed. Nor were young intellectuals the only ones affected. Once the shock effect of martial law had worn off, political consciousness among young blue-collar workers again began to rise—a trend that has been followed anxiously by regime pollsters and confirmed by the increased participation of this group in a wide variety of educational and cultural activities under church and opposition auspices, especially in industrial centers such as the Nowa Huta steel complex outside Kraków.[16]

The determination on the part of Poles in all walks of life to insulate themselves from the encroachments of a monopolistic state was instinctive and pervasive, informed by heightened awareness of a tradition of resistance to alien and oppressive rule. Manifestations of this urge ranged from small acts of individual defiance in everyday life to the creation of the *drugi obieg* (second circuit), a broad-based social and cultural milieu independent of and in competition with official culture. By 1985, scores of uncensored newsletters and journals were said to reach some 3 million people on a regular basis (out of a total population of 37 million). Among the most popular book titles were a biography of the late Cardinal Wyszyński, the stubborn and revered primate of Poland from Stalinist days until his death in 1981; a scathing and revealing set of interviews with former party officials, titled simply "Oni" (They); and a five-hundred-page collection of statements commemorating the fifth anniversary of Solidarity, combining critiques of the current situation with appeals for renewed dialogue. Other unofficial phenomena included blacklisted journalists who circulated their views via cassette tapes and the proliferation of VCRs through which pirated copies of censored and foreign films found their way into the popular consciousness.

The Jaruzelski Compromise: Too Little, Too Late

The regime's response to these challenges has been at best indecisive, even schizophrenic, and at worst counterproductive. As a former Solidarity adviser reportedly quipped, "Jaruzelski is like a man with a choice between being on time for his train or being 10 minutes late, so he decides to compromise and is 5 minutes late." To the extent that he pursued a consistent strategy at all, it was one of attempting to buy off the undecided or only moderately alienated groups with a combination of limited cultural and political concessions, while isolating the actively hostile opposition by raising the costs of participation or association. Yet, caught between a party that refused to relinquish its monopolistic role and a highly politicized majority that refused to accept anything short of an institutionalized voice in the basic decisions of society, Jaruzelski's attempts to find a compromise solution repeatedly proved "too much, too soon" (if ever) for the party *betony*, but "too little, too late" for the population.

On the cultural and intellectual front, the regime sought to offset the influence of the counterculture by a selective easing of censorship restrictions that in effect acknowledged that its monopoly of the media had been broken and that it had to compete for the minds of the people. As a result, the still censored press remained livelier than in any other bloc country. Official publishing houses began accepting some books that would have been rejected a few years before—in the almost certain knowledge that otherwise they would be published by the underground, thereby further embarrassing the official cultural establishment. To compete with the VCR circuit, several provocative and sensitively executed films were released by the censors, including one on the Stalinist terror. Even more unexpected was official circulation of a film on the Solidarity period entitled *Without End;* it depicted continued resistance to martial law, although some suspected it was released because its underlying message was one of defeat and hopelessness.

On the political front, Jaruzelski's first move (and a symbol of his enduring dilemma) came even before the end of martial law, with the creation of the Patriotic Movement for National Renewal (PRON) in May 1982. Designed as a vehicle to bolster regime legitimacy by drawing leading intellectuals into a political dialogue with the leadership, it had difficulty from the outset attracting the participation of prominent independents, much less the attention of the population at large. For its part, the regime could do little more than trot out shopworn formulas about promised improvements in "socialist democracy" in the unchanged context of the "leading role of the party." By 1985, growing frustrations within PRON over its token role led at least one of its most visible members to threaten resignation. In preparation for parliamentary elections in October of that year, in another attempt to demonstrate that it genuinely wanted the Sejm to become an active forum for policy discussion, the regime initially seemed eager to recruit independent candidates for the unopposed national list—including an offer to allot 25 of the 50 unopposed seats (out of a total of 460) to lay Catholics if the church would endorse the elections.

Yet, as in so many other areas, the concessions were too limited to convince a wary public of the regime's sincerity. Changes in electoral procedures fell far short of the hopes of independents who wanted a more open nomination process and the introduction of contested single-seat constituencies, in contrast to the "list" system in which votes automatically went to those at the top of the list (the candidates preferred by the party) unless their names were crossed out. The result was widespread apathy and cynicism. Solidarity called for a boycott; the church, which refused Jaruzelski's offer of uncontested seats, remained silent on the elections; and few independents of any standing were willing to jeopardize their reputations by becoming candidates.

In the meantime, measures to curb and divide the opposition wavered between leniency and repression. Following the formal lifting of martial law in 1983, a partial relaxation was based on the hope that allowing moderate expressions of dissent within the limits of the existing institutional framework would mollify the majority of intellectuals while isolating the diehards. When that tactic did not work, the pendulum swung toward repression. One of the first moves against the mainstream opposition came in April 1985 with the expulsion of Bronisław Geremek, an historian and key adviser to Wałęsa, from the Academy of Sciences. Known as a moderating influence on the former Solidarity leadership, Geremek's expulsion was seen as a warning to other intellectuals that even moderate opposition would no longer be tolerated (and possibly also as a signal to Moscow that Warsaw could put its own house in order). Suppression of underground publications was stepped up, while a new law on higher education stripped universities of their remaining autonomy.

By far the most serious of the new repressive measures were amendments to the penal code and a new law on "special criminal liability," both passed in May 1985 with an unusual show of dissent by several Sejm deputies (who were then stricken from the list of candidates for the October elections). The arbitrary powers of the police had already been increased in 1983, when some features of martial law were incorporated into ordinary law. Now the new changes in the penal code broadened the range of punishable offenses. Previously, only leading a demonstration was punishable; now merely taking part (which in some cases meant simply being in the wrong place at the wrong time) could bring imprisonment for up to three months. Fines were also increased and could no longer be paid by groups or individuals outside the offender's family. The law on "special criminal responsibility" was even harsher, allowing in some cases for summary court proceedings, in which the defendant would not have the right to counsel and the only evidence that need be introduced was the police report.

A year later, it was clear that stepped-up repression against the opposition had succeeded only in increasing the number of political prisoners at the expense of the regime's image at home and abroad—where Jaruzelski was eager to find a way for Poland to break out of its international isolation and especially to gain U.S. approval for readmission to the International Monetary Fund (IMF). He also had to recognize that neither PRON nor the newly elected Sejm had increased the regime's credibility among the population at large. In addition, two events in the first half of 1986 visibly bolstered his domestic political position: the Twenty-seventh Congress of the CPSU in February, at which he was singled out for special attention by the new Soviet General Secretary, Mikhail Gorbachev; and the Tenth PZPR Congress in June, at which the Soviet leader endorsed Jaruzelski's program of "renewal" as consistent with his own program of "restructuring." Indeed, even earlier, Gorbachev's rise to power and the removal from the Soviet leadership of two powerful conservatives—Central Committee secretary and former Leningrad party chief Grigory Romanov and Moscow party chief Viktor Grishin—had allowed the Polish leader to remove two domestic rivals, Stefan Olszowski and Stanisław Kociołek.

Thus, the stage was set for another swing of the pendulum. In September 1986, Jaruzelski declared the first full-scale amnesty for political prisoners since the lifting of martial law three years earlier. He also made another attempt at creating a vehicle for dialogue with society, this time a purely appointive body called the Consultative Social Council. Yet neither initiative resolved his credibility problem. At the time, there were hints that several Solidarity moderates were (or would be) approached as potential members of the consultative council. Once again, however, the unwillingness of the regime to define a truly autonomous role for the new body foreclosed even token Solidarity participation and severely reduced the regime's ability to attract other prominent independents. In fact, in its first two years, the council provided a forum for some candid discussions of urgent public issues but with little discernible effect on major policy decisions. As for the opposition, the substitution of more subtle forms of harassment (confiscation of automobiles and other personal property used for underground activities) for summary trials and imprisonment was modestly successful in achieving Jaruzelski's main goals. It removed the most serious barriers to ending Poland's international isolation. It also led to a partial fragmentation of the opposition, with the moderate majority more inclined to give the regime a chance to demonstrate its good faith, while the hard-core minority remained both unmollified and uncurbed in its activities.

Nonetheless, the road to "normalization" continued to be strewn with unexpected pitfalls. Pope John Paul's visit in June 1987, his third return to his homeland since his election in 1978, dealt yet another setback to regime hopes for "national reconciliation" Jaruzelski-style. By all pretrip accounts, the pope was expected to take a relatively low-key approach, in line with a strategy of "small steps" leading to full legal status for the church and his hope of visiting both Moscow and Catholic Lithuania during the 1988 millennial celebration of Russian Orthodoxy. Instead, he embarked on an impassioned defense of human and political rights in general, and the legitimacy of the Solidarity movement in particular, thus severely embarrassing Jaruzelski and evoking bitter attacks from both Warsaw and Moscow.

By fall 1987, high-level party circles were again locked in debate about how to bridge the credibility gap. Reformers argued (although only behind closed doors) that the cooperation of the moderate opposition could be gained only by offering it some tangible concession. The boldest suggestion was to give the opposition its own political party, presumably with some representation in the Sejm and other forums. A less radical proposal called for allowing a coalition of more or less independent clubs or groupings to put up a limited number of candidates, but without formation of a coherent political party. In the end, motivated in all probability by fears that any tampering with the political structure would be seen as tacit admission of the PZPR's own weakness, the leadership opted for a watered-down compromise in the form of a popular referendum to elicit support for its reform program.

Had the referendum, which took place in late November, offered a genuine choice, it might have served its intended purpose. As it was, voters were asked whether they supported (1) a government-sponsored program of "radical economic recovery," which admittedly would entail a two to three year period of austerity, and (2) the introduction of a new "Polish model" for "democratizing political life." At best, the referendum was badly prepared; it required voters to cross out the "no" box in order to vote "yes." At worst, it was a self-inflicted "shot in the foot"—less than two weeks before the voting the regime announced a projected 100 percent increase in food prices and 200–300 percent increases in rents and energy costs. The result was neither victory nor defeat. Although a majority of those voting favored the government's proposals, negative votes and no-shows (the turnout was only two-thirds of eligible voters) ensured that the regime failed to gain the majority required to make the referendum results binding. Thus, whether by incompetence or design, the regime achieved an outcome that gave it a more or less free hand vis-à-vis its domestic constituency and its external creditors. With the former, it could claim the right to proceed with its program, albeit at a slower pace; with the latter, it could point to popular disapproval as a way of fending off excessively intrusive internationally conditioned recovery programs.[17]

At the same time, the exercise—which was greeted by most Poles with a mixture of cynicism and bemusement—cost Jaruzelski much of the goodwill he had garnered with his conciliatory line since the fall of 1986. He had also, yet again, given up the political momentum to the opposition which, in a move intended to demonstrate its conviction that the regime was incapable of fundamental change, announced the reestablishment of the Polish Socialist party (PPS). Such a move had been taboo since the forced merger of the remnants of a purged PPS with the Communists in 1948. In effect, early 1988, more than six years after the imposition of martial law, still found Jaruzelski "five minutes late for his train."

The Future of Poland: *Perestroika* or Perpetual Crisis

The consensus among official and unofficial observers alike is that the state of the Polish economy will continue to be a major factor limiting Jaruzelski's ability to overcome popular ambivalence and hostility. The four-year economic decline between 1978 and 1982, which saw real national income shrink by more than 25 percent, was followed by four years of steady recovery, averaging just short of 5 percent growth per year between 1983 and 1986. Nonetheless, in the latter year, national income used domestically was still almost 12 percent below the peak level of 1978, in per capita terms a full 18 percent lower. By 1987, it was clear that the recovery—which had been based, first, on the one-time gains of putting idle capacity back into production and, second, on several years of favorable conditions for agriculture—was running out of steam. Initial data suggest that overall economic growth slowed to less than 2 percent, with per capita growth at barely 1 percent. Even more worrisome is the fact that the critical choke-points in the recovery process still lie ahead.

Most familiar is Poland's outstanding hard-currency debt, which passed the $39 billion level by the end of 1987, against $25.5 billion in 1981 and up almost $6 billion from 1986. Although the latest figure is somewhat inflated by the current weakness of the dollar against other Western currencies in which the bulk of the debt is owed, most of the increase between 1981 and 1987 was the result of Poland's inability to meet interest payments, despite the fact that hard-currency exports exceeded imports every year from 1982 to 1987. A 1985 agreement provided some respite by postponing to 1990–1995 repayment of nearly $12 billion owed to Western governments. (Moscow also agreed to postpone repayment of Poland's less advertised ruble debt in the amount of 7 billion rubles, or about $11.5 billion.) On the other hand, neither the final lifting of U.S. sanctions imposed after martial law nor Poland's readmission to the International Monetary Fund in 1986 brought the breakthrough on the debt question that many anticipated.

A second choke-point is the progressive decapitalization of Polish industry, due in part to an inability to import spare parts for Western equipment installed in the 1970s and in part to sharp cuts in investments, which were sacrificed in a desperate effort to place a floor under the decline in consumption and which in 1987 were still 50 percent below the 1978 level. Western machinery still in service is often used well below capacity because of shortages of parts and inputs or is being damaged by the use of inappropriate raw materials. Moreover, cuts in total investments have made it impossible to begin the essential modernization and restructuring of Polish industry away from the inefficient energy-and-resource-intensive heavy industries that dominated repeated expansionist booms from the 1950s through the 1970s. A further negative indicator for the future is the revival of many of the mothballed projects from the 1970s, with the result that nearly three-quarters of a rising level of industrial investments in the 1986–1990 plan will go toward these same "smokestack" industries.

A third choke-point is the growing obsolescence of infrastructure investments, especially housing, transportation services, electric power networks, water and sewage systems, health care facilities, not to mention pollution controls. Traditionally viewed by centrally planned economies as "nonproductive," infrastructure investments have always taken a back seat to "productive" investments (expansion of industrial capacity), and infrastructure is now falling into disrepair faster than it can be maintained or replaced. A 25 percent decline in housing construction from the already inadequate "highs" of 1978 has turned a typical ten to fifteen year wait for an urban apartment into a nightmarish twenty years or more (unless one happens to belong to a privileged group or has access to hard currency). In other areas, more than half the equipment inventory of public transportation systems is obsolete or inadequately maintained, whereas the health care system suffers from chronic shortages of such basic instruments and medications as hypodermic needles, antibiotics, and insulin.

Of all these infrastructure problems, none is more alarming in terms of long-term developmental prospects than the deterioration of the environment. In light of the vacuous lip service given to environmental issues during the 1970s, one of the lasting contributions of Solidarity has been the increased public and official awareness of the acute ecological damage caused by the intensive development of large-scale heavy industry and the chronic neglect of environmental protection since World War II. The most serious problems include sulphur dioxide levels that rank among the worst in the world; high heavy-metal concentrations in water and soils; the lack of adequate wastewater treatment facilities; and a growing shortage of water available for all uses. Overall, the annual cost of environmental damage is reliably (and conservatively) estimated at 10 percent of national income. Without urgent corrective measures, which for the most part the country cannot presently afford, Poland will suffer a further erosion of its productive capacity as well as serious declines in the health and morale of its population.[18]

Jaruzelski's response to these economic challenges has been almost as halting, and so far as unyielding in tangible results, as his response to political problems. In early 1982, immediately after the imposition of martial law, a comprehensive package of economic reforms was enacted. The intention was to place state enterprises on a self-financing, self-management system to improve productivity, but the severity of the country's economic dislocations, combined with the revival of Gierek's investment follies, left this first reform largely on paper. Bolstered by Gorbachev's inauguration of restructuring in the Soviet Union, Jaruzelski announced a "second stage" of Polish economic reform at the Tenth Congress in June 1986, although a detailed program appeared only sixteen months later in October 1987. As described in the November referendum, the reform provided for a "radical curing of the economy," in principle permitting expanded scope for private and cooperative enterprise as well as joint ventures with Western companies. Even a cursory reading of the program, however, reveals the kinds of ambiguities and contradictions that have confounded past reform attempts, whereas doubts about the fate of the reform are likely to discourage potential foreign investors.[19]

Among the few bright spots on the economic scene was Warsaw's recent approval of two initiatives to aid the dominant private sector in agriculture. The first was a church-sponsored foundation that proposed to solicit hard-currency donations from Catholic, government, and private sources in the West to purchase farm equipment for resale in local currency to private farmers, with the proceeds to be used to develop clean and reliable water supplies in rural areas. Final approval of the foundation, which had been the subject of unsuccessful negotiations for more than five years due to the regime's insistence that it retain ultimate control over allocation of church-generated funds, appeared to reflect the regime's recognition that it lacked the resources to tackle the combination of water shortages and pollution that are jeopardizing future agricultural production. The second initiative, the Foundation for the Development of Polish Agriculture sponsored by the Rockefeller Brothers Fund with support from other U.S. foundations, was aimed at improving Poland's agricultural export potential. Although these are positive developments, in the foreseeable future they are likely to generate resources in the tens of millions of dollars, rather than the billions necessary to make a dent in Poland's debt problem.

On the last question, Jaruzelski has so far been reluctant to negotiate the kind of comprehensive recovery program that could release substantial IMF/World Bank funds, apparently in the hope that the mere fact of IMF membership plus his partial and unilaterally determined reform measures would be enough to loosen Western purse strings. But Western governments are proving equally reluctant to provide new credits without assurances that they will be better used than in the past. During a January 1988 visit to Warsaw, West German foreign minister Hans-Dietrich Genscher expressed Bonn's interest "in the stability of [the East European] countries and the well-being of their peoples" and promised to explore new economic aid for Poland; but the fact that he stopped short of committing his government to any immediate assistance clearly disappointed Polish leaders encouraged by Bonn's 1 billion DM credit to Hungary in late 1987. In early February, U.S. deputy secretary of state John Whitehead told his Polish hosts that Washington did not believe economic reform would be successful until Jaruzelski took steps to "win the support of a broad spectrum of Polish society" and that a resumption of U.S. aid would be considered only "when and if [an] IMF agreement is concluded" that commits Poland to specific economic reforms.[20]

Nevertheless, to see Jaruzelski's political and economic dilemmas solely in a Polish context, or as the combined result of the domestic situation and Poland's debt to the West, is misleading. Just as we saw in the 1970s, Moscow continues to play a crucial, even definitive, role in setting Warsaw's agenda and limiting its flexibility. This in no way means that in its specifics Gorbachev's approach to his Polish problem is the same as Brezhnev's. But it is to say that Soviet policy resembles less a coherent, internally consistent strategy toward managing a troubled and troublesome ally than a "wish list," some of whose elements are mutually contradictory and may well complicate rather than facilitate resolution of Poland's multifaceted crisis.

On the political front, support from the Soviet leader was undoubtedly essential in shoring up Jaruzelski's domestic position, first in late 1985 (removal of two *betony* rivals) and again in December 1987 (elevation of the moderate Rakowski to the Politburo). Soviet approval was probably also a factor in such conciliatory moves as the 1986 amnesty and the establishment of the Consultative Social Council. In addition, the 1987 promise to fill in the "blank spots" in Polish-Russian relations (for example, the Nazi-Soviet dismemberment of Poland in 1939 or the Katyń massacre of Polish officers in 1940) seemed to reflect a newfound appreciation of the need for dramatic gestures to overcome deep-seated Polish hostility.

At the same time, the signing of a wide-ranging declaration on "Soviet-Polish Cooperation in Ideology, Science and Culture" during Jaruzelski's April 1987 visit to Moscow signaled Gorbachev's resolve to intensify and fine-tune political and cultural relations, with Polish youth and media as prime targets.[21] The emphasis in the declaration on the need to revitalize and reassert the "leading role" of the PZPR, to engage broad sections of the Polish population in a web of contacts with Soviet organizations, and especially to inculcate in Polish youth "the spirit of socialist ideals and responsibility for [our joint] revolutionary legacy" will limit Jaruzelski's options in reaching out to a Western-oriented, fervently Catholic population already impervious to the relatively watered-down political indoctrination offered in Polish schools and media. (Indeed, the most rational explanation for the unexpected outspokenness of the pope during his visit, which took place several weeks after publication of this declaration, is that he perceived it as an unacceptable challenge to the church's place in Polish society and was signaling his determination not to concede the next generation of Poles to Gorbachev's restructured version of socialism.)

Conflicting Soviet goals are even more evident in economic policy. On the one hand, in pushing for restructuring at home and endorsing Jaruzelski's second stage, Gorbachev has demonstrated his belief that radical reform is the best prescription for both the USSR's and Poland's economic ills. In all probability, the new agricultural funds could not have been approved without removing long-standing Soviet objections to any policy favoring the private farm sector. On the other hand, a rising level of Soviet demands in bilateral trade relations and pressures for accelerated integration are among the most intractable obstacles to successful reform in Poland. Indeed, Moscow is now providing both ruble and limited dollar credits for the completion of a number of investment projects started in the 1970s and halted in the Solidarity period. These reportedly include the massive Katowice steel mill, several coal complexes, and shipyard modernization. The problem with these projects is that they perpetuate a pattern of development based on the same heavy, capital-and-energy-intensive industries that have proved unprofitable in the past. Thus, they can only impede the process of reform, are inconsistent with the need to restructure Polish industry to make it more competitive on world markets, and will exacerbate Poland's already tragic environmental problems. The primary rationale for these projects is that they fit very well with Soviet needs for large-scale infusions of the products of these traditional smokestack industries. The other side of the coin is the pressure on the Poles to participate in a new round of joint investments in heavy industry and resource development in the USSR, thereby diverting scarce investment funds from urgent domestic needs.

In addition, Poland and the Soviet Union have signed several ambitious agreements for new forms of cooperation, including joint ventures and direct links between existing enterprises and extensive coordination of technological research and development. So far, these initiatives have been slow to get off the starting block, due largely to problems in clarifying legal and financial details. However, should the Soviets continue to push these integration trends—and especially should their own reforms fail or end up as half-measures—the Poles have reason to fear that important parts of their economy will effectively become regional branches of Soviet industry. Whichever way it goes, the success or failure of reform in Poland will in large part remain hostage to Gorbachev's success in the Soviet Union.

Postscript, October 1988

In the six months since this chapter was first completed (March 1988), Poland has been wracked by two waves of industrial strikes, a shake-up in the top party leadership, and the resignation en masse of the Council of Ministers. As this is written, information concerning the composition of the new government is incomplete, and round-table talks scheduled for mid-October—the first tangible sign of a break in the stalemate between regime and opposition—have been postponed for at least two weeks. Given these uncertainties, only the foolhardy would venture to predict the future course of Polish politics. What follows is a more modest attempt to use the events of the first nine months of 1988 as a vantage point from which to assess the dilemmas facing all parties to Poland's intractable crisis.

In the wake of the referendum defeat, the regime scaled down its proposed price increases to an average of 27 percent (versus the original 40 percent). But this did little to placate Poland's workers, who, backed by the official trade unions (which along with Solidarity had denounced the original proposal), demanded full compensation in the form of wage increases. In late April these demands set off a two-week wave of strikes during which, at least for a few tense days in early May, the potential for a repetition of August 1980 seemed very real. If the constellation of forces behind this first wave was subject to some dispute,[22] the immediate consequence was not—namely, that neither side won. For Solidarity, the failure of the vast majority of Poland's workers to back the strikers or the call for the union's reinstatement must have come as a bitter disappointment. Despite Wałęsa's claim that the strikes "showed our strength as well as our helplessness" and that what was now needed was to develop new techniques of struggle, he had to recognize the possibility that Solidarity as a mass movement was a thing of the past—or at the very least that it was being torn between its original commitment to dialogue and nonviolence and the militant demands of a new generation of workers.

For Jaruzelski the message was even more sobering. On the social front, he knew full well that the quick termination of the strikes had done nothing to bridge the chasm of hostility and distrust separating regime and society and that the nonstriking majority was deterred more by fear and a sense of hopelessness than by any confidence that his policies would soon improve its lot or pull the country out of debilitating stagnation.[23] In addition, the church—the one institution that can provide a connecting link to the population—was deeply angered by the forcible suppression of the strike at the Nowa Huta steel mill near Kraków even as it (with the regime's apparent approval) was attempting mediation. On the economic front, the strikes left the much touted second stage of reform in shambles. Already in the first quarter of 1988, the price-wage spiral pushed inflation up by 45 percent. By June, government sources were admitting that the inflation rate for all of 1988 would be in excess of 60 percent, with unofficial estimates running as high as 100 percent or more.[24]

At the same time, this exposure of mutual weakness provided both the opportunity, and presumably the incentive, for both sides to reassess the rigid postures that have stood in the way of rapprochement. Significantly, and to the subsequent chagrin of the regime, the conciliatory gestures came largely from the moderate opposition. Even before the April–May strikes, Solidarity adviser Geremek had proposed an "anticrisis pact" between regime and opposition—a proposal that elicited no official response at the time. In the wake of the strikes, a major article by two other Solidarity advisers in the independent Catholic weekly *Tygodnik powszechny* implied a willingness to meet Jaruzelski halfway. After reviewing the economic situation and the numerous obstacles to reform, the authors warned that society must resist the "understandable" but "dangerous" temptation to view regime failures with "masochistic satisfaction": "Independent circles must do everything possible to avert a failure of changes presently being undertaken. Despite the risks associated with supporting the regime's program, there is no [realistic] alternative more beneficial for the interests of the country. Again, we must emphasize that a failure of the present reform attempts must lead to a prolonged impasse with negative consequences that are difficult to foresee."[25]

The authors lamented the fact that there was not only no cooperation between the authorities and independent circles; there was "not even a forum for contacts." They then went on to propose a ten-point anticrisis program both as a basis for building a consensus within opposition ranks and as a starting point for future negotiations with the regime. Two aspects of their approach were especially noteworthy: first, the moderate tone of their anticrisis program; and, second, the explicit and implicit importance attached to Gorbachev's reforms in the Soviet Union. Although the authors called for a wide range of changes in economic policy and management (none of which would be seriously disputed by the regime's own Consultative Economic Council), their social and political proposals stopped short of a demand for a reinstatement of Solidarity; instead they argued that economic reforms must be accompanied by a "democratization of the political system" sufficient to permit "the unrestricted functioning of public opinion . . . [which] would create minimum conditions for partial, albeit indirect, social control over the economy and . . . for the harmonizing of diverse interests."[26] On the second point, the authors noted the "favorable" climate provided by "the convergence of potential changes in Poland with Gorbachev's modernizing course"; but their more important subliminal message was that the opposition must tailor its demands to geopolitical realities in order neither to overstep the ill-defined limits of Soviet tolerance nor to provide Gorbachev's rivals with ammunition for scuttling his more modest reforms in the USSR.[27]

For his part, Jaruzelski's poststrike moves suggested that he intended to pursue his economic reform program more aggressively, but not that he was prepared to alter his posture vis-à-vis the opposition in any major way. A reshuffling of the party leadership in mid-June strengthened the hand of the reformers, but not decisively. In addition to Rakowski, new Central Committee secretaries included former foreign minister Orzechowski, with a reputation as a pragmatic troubleshooter, and Władysław Baka, government minister in charge of the Economic Reform Commission from 1981 to 1985 when, in what was widely perceived as a demotion, he was appointed president of the Polish National Bank. Baka also joined the other two as a full member of the Politburo. Among reform opponents ousted from the Secretariat or Politburo were Woźniak and Porębski.[28] At the same time, failure to force a similar shake-up on the government side, especially by removing Prime Minister Messner and his deputy and chief spokesman for the heavy and defense industry lobby, Szałajda, left economic reform in limbo.[29]

On questions of political reform, the picture remained blurred. On the one hand, the opposition's sense of urgency was clearly shared by many within the establishment. Geremek's notion of an anticrisis pact was picked up shortly after the strikes by Central Committee secretary Czyrek (although without acknowledging original authorship or proposing the terms of such a pact); and, at the end of June, several lower ranking officials attended two unpublicized meetings with opposition intellectuals. On the other hand, the regime's transparent eagerness to maintain the face-saving but dubious distinction between Solidarity and the "constructive" (especially Catholic) opposition had a manipulative ring, not only because of the episcopate's well-known ambivalence about active church involvement in politics, but also because any such involvement that excluded Solidarity would clearly weaken the cohesion of the opposition.[30] Moreover, even as these overtures to the church were being made, the decisive discussions were (characteristically) taking place within closed party circles, with little input from outside.[31]

Whether the product of overconfidence (premature expectations of Solidarity's demise?) or internal paralysis, the regime's indecisive response to the spring strikes soon bore bitter fruit in a second and more extensive wave of strikes in late August and early September, marking the eighth anniversary of the union's formation. In subtle and sometimes ironic ways, the recurrence of labor unrest has both sharpened the lines of confrontation and shifted the balance among the contending sides. The most salient reality of the new situation is that Solidarity and its leader, Lech Wałęsa, have reemerged on center stage. Despite the union's apparently diminished status after the spring strikes, Solidarity's reinstatement quickly became the common rallying cry and nonnegotiable demand of strikers from the coal pits of Silesia to the Baltic ports and shipyards. The fact that the strikes ended without formal relegalization of Solidarity was possible only because of Wałęsa's personal intervention—and only after the regime, in a concession it had dismissed out of hand for nearly eight years, agreed to "round-table" talks with the opposition that would include the question of the union's future status.[32]

Yet the new situation carries enormous risks for Wałęsa. The idea symbolized by Solidarity—namely, the right of the workers to an authentic and independent voice in the basic decisions of society—remains. As a cohesive and disciplined movement, however, it has virtually ceased to exist; and Wałęsa's mandate to negotiate in the name of the workers is clearly tentative and limited. Moreover, formal reinstatement of Solidarity—should it occur—would be only a first step, which in turn would place on the agenda the more intractable issues of reform and austerity. What responsibility would Solidarity be willing to bear for imposing sacrifices on its own constituency? Wałęsa's ace in the hole is growing recognition even within the party (and very likely also in Moscow) that failure to deal with the original generation of Solidarity moderates will leave the regime face to face with the new and militant generation of workers, untempered by the experiences of 1980–1981 and motivated by a sense that they have little or nothing to lose.[33]

Stung by the unexpected virulence of the second strike wave and the resurgence of support for Solidarity,[34] the regime had little choice but to accede to the round-table talks and to sacrifice its scapegoat-in-waiting, Prime Minister Messner and his cabinet. What is less clear is whether this will prove to be simply another temporary retreat or whether Jaruzelski is finally ready for genuine compromise. So far, the maneuverings that have accompanied formation of a new government and preparations for the round-table point to the former. The selection of Mieczysław Rakowski, named only three months earlier to the secretariat, to replace Messner was the first inauspicious move. Although long known as a proponent of far-reaching economic reforms, Rakowski still carries heavy baggage from the Solidarity period for his role in crushing the union, and he has continued to be one of the most vociferous opponents of talks with Wałęsa. In a recent memorandum, Rakowski rejected the concept of pluralism, suggesting that the term *przeciwnicy* (enemies or foes) was preferable to "opposition" because the latter term might inadvertently be seen as legitimizing hopes for a return to a "bourgeois democratic" (pluralistic) system.[35]

Although Rakowski's acceptance speech was more conciliatory in tone—he called broadening the political base of the government his "primary task" and said he hoped to form a "coalition" government within the next two weeks (by mid-October) that would include "moderate" opposition elements—his remarks were either naively optimistic or cynically manipulative. Both Solidarity and Catholic activists have made it abundantly clear that recognition of the union, as a demonstration of the regime's good faith and as a sine qua non of society's willingness to accept the sacrifices necessary for economic recovery, is a precondition of their cooperation. With the round-table talks not scheduled to *begin* until mid-October, it was a foregone conclusion that no independent figures would be willing to join the government until the successful outcome of the talks was assured. Had any been so inclined, he was quickly deterred by the leak of a letter reassuring officials in key enterprises that the party had no intention of reinstating Solidarity.[36]

In the two weeks since the new government was unveiled on October 13,[37] the talks have been twice postponed, and the mounting campaign of demands and charges by the regime against Solidarity—to the effect that the latter must remove alleged "extremists" from its delegation or that "scandalous excesses" under the union's banner (a demonstration by seven hundred youths in Gdańsk) are undermining prospects for dialogue—strongly suggests that the party is deeply divided on the question of holding talks at all and is seeking any excuse to void earlier promises.[38] In the meantime, the church, in yet another mediation attempt, has presented the government with three conditions for creating an atmosphere conducive to talks: that it end its propaganda campaign against the opposition; that it state clearly its intentions toward Solidarity; and that it reinstate the several score of strikers who were fired (in some cases conscripted into the army) contrary to promises made to church mediators in September. [39] At the moment, the outcome remains uncertain.

Nor does it appear that Jaruzelski is getting any definitive guidance or support from Moscow. In the wake of the spring strikes, he was clearly looking to Gorbachev's four-day state visit to Poland in mid-July to bolster his domestic position. In advance of the visit, there were widespread expectations that the Soviet leader would at long last acknowledge Soviet responsibility for painful events in Polish-Soviet relations. In fact, Gorbachev's references were disappointingly brief and vague, at times inexplicably insensitive to popular feelings. On questions of reforms, both leaders invoked the concept of "socialist pluralism," but there was nothing in the General Secretary's statements to suggest pressure on Jaruzelski to move beyond his own cautious course. In the end, the visit probably did the latter's image more harm than good, disabusing Poles of the hope that the "radical reformer" in the Kremlin would facilitate even more radical reforms in Warsaw.[40]

In the wake of the August–September strikes, Soviet commentary has been mixed, but for the most part low key and remarkably balanced. Although early reports were highly critical of Solidarity, once the strikes ended the press began to take a favorable view of an anticrisis pact, criticizing the foot-dragging of "conservative and bureaucratic forces" who "have become adept" at resisting change and implying that the strikers had finally forced the leadership to address "unresolved economic and social problems."[41] The most remarkable statement of all was an interview in *Le Monde* with Nikolai Shishlin, head of the international information section of the CPSU's Propaganda Department. Under the title "Union Pluralism Is No Heresy," Shishlin clearly implied that Moscow is tilting in favor of stability, regardless of the ideological compromises. "Of course we are following the latest developments [in Poland] very closely," he said:

> but we consider the Poles better informed about the situation in their country than we are and that it is up to them to take one decision or another. . . . If we do not have a solution ready-made for ourselves, we have even less of one for Poland where pluralism is so developed. . . . The latest talks . . . are good evidence of the realism [of the Polish leadership] of which we approve. . . . We are not afraid of a reemergence of Solidarity. . . . The men who participated in Solidarity are today in a position to play a more important role.[42]

Thus, the dilemma for Jaruzelski has, if anything, become more acute. Since 1981, his strength has been the perception—in Moscow and the West as well as among many Poles—that there was no alternative to him, that for better or worse he was uniquely qualified to steer a middle course between chaos and bloody repression (or worse, Soviet intervention) toward some vaguely defined "normalization." The crucial question today is whether he can muster the courage and foresight to move beyond his own prescription for pseudodialogue or whether he will continue to be a hostage to history—to his responsibility for the crushing of Solidarity. On the one hand, if he can recognize that Solidarity no longer poses the specter of a frontal challenge to the party's leading role, he can begin the delicate but essential process of genuine reconciliation and power-sharing. Alternatively, he can miss his train again, in which case it is unlikely that he will continue to be seen as the man who can resolve Poland's ongoing crisis.[43]

Notes

1. *The Washington Post,* January 7, 1988.

2. Leszek Kołakowski, "Hope and Hopelessness," *Survey* (Summer 1971), pp. 37–52 [emphasis in the original]; the article was first published in Polish in 1970 by the émigré monthly *Kultura* (Paris).

3. Jacques Rupnik, "Dissent in Poland 1968–78: The End of Revisionism and the Rebirth of Civil Society," in Rudolf L. Tőkés, ed., *Opposition in Eastern Europe* (Baltimore, Md.: Johns Hopkins University Press, 1979), pp. 86–87.

4. Jadwiga Staniszkis, "Polskie dylematy," *Aneks* (London), no. 48 (1987), p. 16.

5. Concerning events in the 1970s, see Sarah M. Terry, "June 1976: Anatomy of an Avoidable Crisis," in Jane L. Curry, ed., *Poland's Postwar Crises* (forthcoming), especially section IV.

6. Excerpts of the report were first published under the title "Raport doradców" in *Polityka,* no. 48 (November 29, 1980); two sections were reprinted in toto in

Przegląd techniczny, no. 23 (June 1981) and later translated under the title "Who Knew What?" by *Radio Free Europe Research* [*RFER*], RAD Background Report/241, August 25, 1981.

7. "Sytuacja kraju a program opozycji," *Biuletyn informacyjny,* no. 3 (April 1979); reprinted in Jacek Kuroń, *Polityka i odpowiedzialność* (London: Aneks, 1984), pp. 143–148.

8. Both reports were translated in Jack Bielasiak, ed., *Poland Today: The State of the Republic* (Armonk, N.Y.: M.E. Sharp, 1981); see pp. 77–78.

9. Ibid., pp. 15, 18, and 77 (emphasis added).

10. Kukliński, who was assigned to the planning committee, defected to the United States in November 1981. An extensive interview with him was first published in *Kultura* (Paris) (April 1987), pp. 3–57; lengthy excerpts were translated in *Orbis* 32, no. 1 (Winter 1988), pp. 6–31.

11. Andrzej Korbonski, "Soviet Policy Toward Poland," in Sarah Meiklejohn Terry, ed., *Soviet Policy in Eastern Europe* (New Haven, Conn.: Yale University Press, 1984), p. 82.

12. Kukliński interview, in *Kultura,* p. 57.

13. Derived from the annual statistical yearbooks (*Rocznik statystyczny* [Warsaw: Głowny Urząd Statystyczny, 1971–1987]).

14. Although the military no longer plays the pivotal role at the provincial and local levels that it did under martial law, in many regions the local power structure remains fragmented and fluid, with the military and security police sometimes wielding as much influence as the PZPR and local government.

15. Based on Władysław Adamski et al., *Raport z badania Polacy '84: Dynamika konfliktu i konsensusu,* published in a restricted edition by Warsaw University in 1986. The poll was conducted in the summer of 1984.

16. A separate survey of high-school students at about the same time revealed an overwhelmingly pessimistic image of the future. The dominant scenario was one of stagnation or worse, in which they would have little chance of getting jobs comparable to their qualifications, much less of being able to maintain the standard of living of their parents. At the same time, the students were determined to minimize the impact on their personal lives, and especially to get around the economic barriers: 40 percent wanted to open their own businesses; most favored a mixed economy with substantial privatization of industry as well as services and agriculture; and more than half hoped to go abroad, at least temporarily, to earn enough hard currency to exchange on the black market for the basics of a normal existence (most importantly, an apartment and car). Even among very young children, the residual influence of Solidarity remained strong. Before the September 1986 amnesty for political prisoners, the Polish version of "cops and robbers" was "Solidarity versus Jaruzelski" (or ZOMO, the much hated paramilitary police), with few volunteering to play Jaruzelski or the ZOMO. Indeed, the highest status a child could have among his or her peers was to have an interned parent.

17. Concerning the referendum, see, for example, Abraham Brumberg, "Poland: The New Opposition," *New York Review of Books,* February 18, 1988, pp. 23–27.

18. A secret report prepared in 1985 by the Central Committee's Academy of Social Sciences referred to Poland's environmental policy as a "clinical example of organizational and managerial pathology" and predicted that a continuation of the present rate of environmental degradation would result in "substantial increases" in disease rates, widespread shortages of water for all purposes, "serious perturbations" in agricultural production and declines in products fit for human consumption, and mass destruction of coniferous forests. "There can be no doubt," the author concluded,

"that we find ourselves on the brink of ecological disaster." Paweł Moczydłowski, "Próba podsumowania," in Przemysław Wojcik, ed. *Zagrożenia ekologiczne* (Warsaw: Akademia Nauk Spolecznych, 1985 ["for internal use only"]), p. 320.

19. See, for example, Hubert Gabrisch, "Die 'zweite Etappe der Wirtschaftsreform' in Polen," Reprint-Serie no. 110 (Vienna: Wiener Institut für Internationale Wirtschaftsvergleiche, April 1988); and Jan Chowaniec, "The 'Second Stage' of Poland's Economic Reform" (Cambridge, Mass.: Russian Research Center, Harvard University, January 1988, unpublished paper).

20. *New York Times*, January 17, 1988; and *Washington Post*, February 4, 1988.

21. For the full text, see Foreign Broadcast Information Service [FBIS], *Soviet Union Daily Report*, April 23, 1987, pp. F1–F5.

22. Although no one questions that genuine worker frustration was the root cause of the strikes, there were widespread rumors of provocations. According to one scenario, the regime itself instigated strikes in the spring, when Solidarity was unprepared and could be easily contained, in order to preempt a major strike action later in the year. A more credible theory is that opponents of reform within the leadership and apparat attempted to take advantage of the unrest to derail Jaruzelski's policies and disrupt behind-the-scenes contacts between regime and opposition; see notes 25 and 28.

23. If anything, social pessimism is greater today than in 1984–1985, immediately after the lifting of martial law, and again the young are most heavily affected. Young workers, for whom housing and other shortages are most acute, provided the backbone of the latest strikes; a poll in late 1987 showed that some 85 percent of Polish youth wanted to go abroad, one-third for good; and, in an unprecedented brain drain, approximately 10 percent of university graduates emigrate. (See Brumberg, "Poland: The New Opposition"; and *New York Times*, February 15, 1988.) Another indication of the popular mood was the embarrassingly low turnout for the June 1988 provincial and local elections. Despite changes in the electoral law that eliminated preferential listing and, in most cases, required voters to choose between contending candidates, the official turnout was only 55 percent (the opposition said this figure was inflated), with much lower turnouts in major cities. See *RFER*, Polish Situation Report/10, June 30, 1988, item 8.

24. Following the strikes, in an effort to control inflationary pressures, the government arrogated to itself extraordinary powers over the economy, in effect leaving Poland with three administrative systems—the pre-October 1987 unreformed system, the "second stage" promising extensive decentralization, and the new law authorizing preemptive central control. Despite the confusion, some good may come of these developments. One of the government's first moves under the new law was to announce the closing and reorganization of a number of unprofitable firms. Other actions included measures to improve the supply of consumer goods, ease restrictions on private and cooperative enterprise, and liberalize foreign trade regulations. See, especially, Urban's press conference on results of the mid-June Central Committee Plenum (*Trybuna ludu*, June 22, 1988); and Sadowski's speech on economic reform to the Sejm (*Rzeczpospolita*, June 18–19, 1988).

25. Ryszard Bugaj and Andrzej Wielowiejski, "Wobec malejących szans," *Tygodnik powszechny*, June 19, 1988. The article was originally presented to a meeting of Solidarity-connected economists on May 8, to which Deputy Prime Minister Sadowski had been invited; after initially accepting the invitation, he was forced by the strikes to withdraw. The article itself was published only after a lengthy confrontation with the censors and numerous deletions.

26. Ibid. In addition to market-oriented reforms and a major restructuring of investment priorities, Bugaj and Wielowiejski called for protection of living standards

and social services for poor and middle income groups, as well as aggressive policies to correct environmental deterioration.

27. Concerning the opposition's desire not to strengthen conservative opposition to domestic Soviet reforms, see "Towards a New Democratic Compromise," an interview with Adam Michnik, in *The Times Literary Supplement* (London), February 19–25, 1988; and *East European Reporter* 3, no. 2 (March 1988), pp. 24–29.

28. These were only the most prominent changes; for a full listing, see *RFER,* Polish Situation Report/10, June 30, 1988, items 1 and 3; and *Eastern Europe Newsletter* [*EEN*] 2, no. 13 (June 29, 1988). Woźniak and Porębski plus Włodzimierz Mokrzyszczak, who was also removed from the Politburo, were among those rumored to have been implicated in the strikes. Other changes, including the resignation of two men from the Secretariat who were close to Jaruzelski (Ciosek and Baryła), appear not to have been demotions but shifts related to the assumption of other important responsibilities; Ciosek was promoted to candidate member of the Politburo and Baryła remained a full member.

29. At the time, astute observers predicted that Jaruzelski was keeping Messner et al. in reserve as scapegoats for the next wave of unrest that was already being anticipated for the August anniversary of Solidarity's birth.

30. *RFER,* Polish Situation Report/11, July 21, 1988, item 55; and *EEN* 2, no. 11 (June 1, 1988). A report issued in early June by the official Consultative Economic Council echoed many of the concerns expressed by Bugaj and Wielowiejski (see note 25), similarities that were duly noted by a prominent proregime political commentator. See Konsultacyjna Rada Gospodarcza, "Zagrożenia gospodarcze i kierunki działan," *Życie gospodarcze,* no. 24 (June 12, 1988); and Daniel Passent, "Zagadka," *Polityka,* no. 26 (June 25, 1988).

31. A good example of regime myopia was the establishment of a group of some thirty academics, mostly long-time party insiders, set up to advise the Secretariat on possible political reforms. Although the initiative (which was not publicly announced) predated the spring strikes, they should have lent it a greater sense of urgency. Yet, observers close to the process reported that discussions at the first meeting in June were unable to break out of the contradiction between reinforcing the "leading role" of the party while reducing its monopolistic position in Polish society.

32. For coverage of the August–September strikes, see, for example, *New York Times* and *Washington Post,* starting August 18, 1988.

33. The tenuous nature of Wałęsa's hold over the young workers who made up the core of the strikers is indicated by reports that he was booed when he pleaded for an end to the strikes before relegalization of Solidarity.

34. That the regime had no intention of dealing with Wałęsa or Solidarity at the outset is clearly indicated by Interior Minister Kiszczak's denunciation of the strike organizers as outside instigators, even terrorists, and his statements to the effect that the strikes were undermining the "course and climate of national understanding" and that the "phantom of self-rule and anarchy is being born again." *New York Times,* August 23, 1988.

35. Mieczysław F. Rakowski, "Uwagi dotyczące niektórych aspektów politycznej i gospodarczej sytuacji PRL w drugiej połowie lat osiemdziesiątych" (a sixty-page confidential memorandum circulated within the leadership in November and December 1987). To his credit, the memorandum also contained many harsh criticisms of past policies and warned that, if the party cannot find the will to undertake fundamental reforms, "the future history of our [socialist] formation will be marked by shocks and revolutionary explosions." Although it is likely that some of his statements were

tailored to appeal to a conservative party apparat in advance of his own elevation to the Politburo, Warsaw insiders who know him well confirm that he remains bitterly opposed to any concessions to Solidarity (even to its most moderate spokesmen) and that the animus against the church expressed in this memorandum is quite genuine.

36. *Washington Post,* September 28, 1988.

37. The new cabinet retains several key political appointees—most importantly, Interior Minister Kiszczak, so far the main contact with Wałęsa and the opposition, and Defense Minister Siwicki. It also reportedly includes a strengthened cohort of economic reformers, but as yet no members of the opposition. See *Washington Post,* October 14, 1988.

38. See Reuters dispatches (both carried in *Boston Globe*), October 18 and 19, 1988.

39. See Reuters, October 11, 1988; and *New York Times,* October 28, 1988.

40. For coverage of Gorbachev's trip, see FBIS, *Soviet Union Daily Report,* July 11–19, 1988 (especially July 12), and *East Europe Daily Report,* July 12, 1988. In the absence of any explicit mention of Katyń or the 1939 Nazi-Soviet Non-Aggression Pact, Gorbachev's reference to "Stalinist repressions . . . affect[ing] many Polish Communists" was particularly offensive. Concerning skepticism in independent Polish circles about the relevance of reforms in the Soviet Union for Poland, see *RFER,* Polish Situation Report/11, July 21, 1988, item 4.

41. FBIS, *Soviet Union Daily Report,* September 8, 16, and 19, 1988.

42. Bernard Guetta, "Le pluralisme syndical n'est pas une hérésie," *Le Monde,* September 7, 1988.

43. One final uncertainty concerns the implications of Gorbachev's visit for Jaruzelski's political future. Initial reports differ. According to one, the rapport between the two was as good as on previous occasions; see *RFER,* Polish Situation Report/11, July 21, 1988, items 2 and 3. A second, however, reported that Gorbachev was more reticent in his expressions of support and that speculation is already circulating about Jaruzelski's replacement at a special party conference early in 1989; see *Christian Science Monitor,* July 14 and 27, 1988.

9

Reforming Communist Systems: Lessons from the Hungarian Experience

Charles Gati

Q: Why did Kádár wait till May 1988 to resign?

A: He was waiting so that he could return Hungary to the people in the same condition it was in 1956 when he took power.

For those familiar with Hungary only during the reform era of "goulash communism" that began in the mid-1960s, developments in the late 1980s, especially the forced resignation of János Kádár in May 1988, must have seemed strange if not altogether unbelievable. Yet so tense and troubled had Hungary become, and so pressed was its leader, that many Hungarians welcomed Kádár's ouster. They barely remembered that he was once the only popular Communist leader in Eastern Europe or that his reforms had served as a model for Soviet leader Mikhail S. Gorbachev's *perestroika* (restructuring). Indeed, the Kádár of the 1980s was not the same man whom Secretary of State George P. Shultz had once called a "wise man" to whom it was "well worth listening," a man whose "enormous capacity and leadership ability" Vice President George Bush had also found worthy of high praise.[1]

By the time Kádár was ousted at the May 1988 party conference, Hungary was in ferment. Consider these developments:

1. In its September 12, 1987, issue, *Dunántúli napló*, a party daily published in the southern Hungarian city of Pécs, devoted two pages to answers given by Politburo member János Berecz to questions posed by a group identified as Workers of the Mecsek Coal Mines. Although Berecz's answers contained standard party fare, the questions were most revealing of the issues occupying Hungarian society.

"With workers bearing the brunt of the economic crisis," asked one member of the group, "why aren't those incompetent leaders brought to account who squandered away [Hungary's Western debt of] $15 billion?" Another queried, "How come the socialist countries are getting poorer while nonaligned Austria and Finland have been getting ever richer?" The most provocative question was also the last: "If the party and the government are so sure that they enjoy the confidence of the people, why don't we have free elections under international supervision?"

2. At about the time *Dunántúli napló* published the miners' questions and Berecz's answers, workers set fire to several factories in the cities of Szombathely and Székesfehérvár. The handbill they distributed was blunt and brief. It read: "If you raise prices, we burn factories!"

3. Meanwhile, in Budapest, the full text of a manifesto issued by the so-called populist wing of the opposition[2] appeared in the prominent daily *Magyar nemzet* (November 14, 1987). Its key paragraph asserted:

> The Hungarian nation has drifted into one of the serious crises of its history. Its national strength is broken, its self-confidence and bearing are shaken, the bonds of its cohesion are tragically loosened, its self-knowledge is startingly inadequate. It anticipates a possible economic collapse. As an ethnic entity, Hungary is burdened by unprecedented divisions. Our nation does not possess a commonly accepted vision of the future.

4. Recalling the role they played prior to the 1956 revolution, Hungary's writers once again became active and outspoken. In 1986, members of the Writer's Union initially rejected the party's nominees for the union's leadership, although they subsequently accepted a compromise solution. In the fall of 1987, the union's official weekly, *Élet és irodalom,* even asked, however tentatively, why Soviet troops were still stationed on Hungarian territory.[3] The weekly also devoted almost two laudatory columns to the seventieth birthday of Miklós Vásárhelyi, mentor of the liberal or urbanist wing of the opposition. An uncompromising if soft-spoken man, Vásárhelyi also was once a close associate of Imre Nagy, leader of the 1956 anti-Soviet revolution.

5. The Hungarian Socialist Worker's [Communist] party (HSWP) was also subject to the rapidly growing tensions that characterized Hungary's political atmosphere in the 1980s. In party cells and in the Central Committee, questions were raised about the impossibility of effectively combining plan and market, of institutionalizing such vague concepts as "socialist pluralism" and "deep democratization," of finding solutions to—or even explanations for—Hungary's extraordinarily high rates of suicide, alcoholism, and heart attack.

Bitter debates on these and other issues increasingly centered on the effectiveness of Kádár's leadership. At an HSWP Central Committee meeting in the summer of 1987, several high officials—including Jenö Fock, the country's prime minister in the early 1970s—had already asked Kádár to step aside and accept a new, honorary position as the party's "chairman." After all, Kádár, who was born in 1912 and had been in power since 1956, *was* old, tired, and ailing. His prestige was all but gone, his policies seemed to have reached a dead end, and his speeches were convoluted.

For analysts the main questions are therefore these: What happened in Hungary, this showpiece of reform, tolerance, and "goulash communism," in the mid- and late-1980s? Perhaps more importantly, if the Hungarian experience with reforming a Communist system is (turning into) a failure, does that failure mean that *perestroika, glasnost'* (openness), and *demokratizatsiya* (democratization) elsewhere in Eastern Europe and in the Soviet Union face an uncertain future?

The Nature of Hungarian Reform

The process of reform in Hungary had its basis in the 1956 revolution. The crushing of that revolution by the Soviet Union taught the country's new, Moscow-installed leaders and, to a lesser extent, most Hungarians two lessons. One was that a small country located in the the shadow of Soviet power had no choice but to respect vital Soviet interests. The other lesson was that the new leadership should initiate policies that would reflect Hungarian interests as well in order to avoid similar outbreaks of public discontent in the future.

Thus, the Kádár regime has to accommodate Soviet pressure for bloc conformity and popular pressure for autonomy. To do this, Kádár promised Moscow a stable and loyal Hungary in exchange for Soviet tolerance for a measure of Hungarian autonomy. Implicit in that promise was a threat: Should Moscow refuse to grant Hungary a modicum of autonomy, "1956"—*another anti-Soviet uprising*—might occur again.

Kádár then promised the Hungarian people a moderate political and economic environment in exchange for popular acceptance of Hungarian solidarity with Moscow. Implicit in that promise was a threat: Should the people reject bloc solidarity, "1956"—*another Soviet intervention*—might occur again.

Kádár's compromise formula—an attempt to maneuver between Soviet demands and domestic sentiments and expectations—eventually found expression in his reformist course. By the 1960s, once the post-1956 terror had run its course, the reforms entailed a substantial reduction in the use of such terror, a measure of free expression for the country's recalcitrant intellectuals, and an improved standard of living. To a great extent, the reforms worked. From the mid-1960s to the late 1970s, Hungary experienced a period of relative normalcy and stability. Even though the half-loaf offered by the Kádár regime was far less than what the people of 1956 had sought, it was far more than they had reason to expect after the Soviet crackdown. Fatigued if not psychologically defeated, the generation that had produced the revolution thus adjusted to the new reality.

The trauma of 1956 was a necessary but insufficient precondition for Kádár's reformist course. Its implementation was made possible by additional circumstances. One was the close relationship between Kádár and the Soviet leadership, particularly between Kádár and Nikita Khrushchev. Kádár, who had spent several years in Stalinist jails, was one of the seven founding members, along with Imre Nagy, of the reconstituted HSWP *during* the 1956 revolution. At that time, he had called it "our glorious revolution."

A few days later, when a Soviet armored car returned him to Budapest, he was widely seen as a Soviet puppet, and yet he was also presumed by most Hungarians to be different from the available old Stalinists. Hence, at that time, Kádár was an invaluable, perhaps an indispensable, asset for the Soviet Union. With Moscow indebted to him for having signed on when there were few acceptable applicants for the job, Kádár could eventually pursue a reformist course in the knowledge that the Soviet leaders would likely tolerate, even if they did not fully approve, his policies.

Furthermore, the party that Kádár led after 1956 was *his* party. True, it was not always united; throughout the years, different factions contested many issues of substance and procedure. But precisely because the party Kádár had inherited was initially so small and weak, he could shape it in his own image. With his opponents—the Stalinist Mátyás Rákosi and the revisionist Imre Nagy—undone, Kádár was the reconstituted party's dominant force. Although some of his policies could be, and were, criticized from the Left—by József Révai in 1957, by Imre Dögei and others in the early 1960s, by the so-called worker's opposition in the early 1970s—Kádár's leadership was beyond serious challenge. Even his critics must have realized that because he enjoyed both Moscow's backing and a measure of popular approbation, Kádár was there to stay. Until the early 1980s, he led in the knowledge that the party would follow him.

The reforms were also made possible by Kádár's ability to focus on long-term goals and by his considerable political skills. For reasons having to do primarily with 1956, he was determined to make socialism work by avoiding the worst excesses of the pre-1956 Rákosi era. His deepest desire was to prove Rákosi wrong, to prove Imre Nagy wrong, to prove the Soviet Union wrong. Separately and collectively, they had spoiled his dream of building a viable socialist society. Kádár sought revenge by showing that he could do what they had failed to do: He would make Hungary a showpiece for *his* version of socialism; he would proceed neither by slavishly emulating the Soviet Union (as Rákosi had done) nor by naively confronting the Soviet Union (as, he thought, Nagy had done). Kádár's way was to play along when necessary and pursue his course when possible.

Two aspects of Kádár's political outlook were particularly appropriate for the job he had set out to accomplish. When it came to the Soviets he was—like most Hungarians—a cynic. He appears to have understood that although he could not rule without Moscow, he could govern only by keeping Moscow at arm's length. On August 17, 1968, three days before the Soviet intervention in Czechoslavakia, he said to Alexander Dubček, "Do you *really* not know the kind of people you're dealing with?"[4] Unlike Dubček and Nagy, then, Kádár had no illusions about the Soviet leaders on whom he relied and whom he handled with great care and considerable skill.

When it came to the ultimate goal of socialism, however, Kádár was an idealist. True, he did not want to duplicate the Soviet model, but he was not interested in capitalism either. The only "capitalism" he knew firsthand was prewar Hungary's—neither a shining example nor an appealing alternative. Hence, Kádár never contemplated anything but a fair, tolerant, and largely egalitarian socialist society, one that would also allow for a measure of self-expression and participation but would function under the aegis of the Communist party and within the confines of the Soviet bloc. In the paternalistic dictatorship Kádár envisaged and created, people would know what they could *not* do without being constantly reminded of what they *must* do.[5] The pace of change would be gradual. As Kádár once put it, "There was a time when we saw reality not as it was but as we would have liked it. We have cured ourselves of this delusion." "People do not exist," he said on another occasion, "so that we may test Marxism on them." Although a pragmatic tactician, Kádár retained his early idealism about socialism without entertaining any illusions about either the Soviet Union or its leaders.

All in all, the political circumstances that produced the Hungarian reform process in the mid-1960s included a still-apathetic public tired of fighting hopeless battles; a Soviet leadership that was rather supportive, and only occasionally critical, of the reforms; a party elite convinced of János Kádár's indispensability; and Kádár's skillful use of the opportunity "1956" gave him to realize his reformist version of socialism.

The Successes and Failures of the Reforms

Agricultural Reforms

Any discussion of the achievements of Kádár's reforms should begin with *agriculture.* By 1956, two out of three collective farm members had left the collectives, and against this background the party decided to initiate a recollectivization campaign in 1959. It was guided less by ideological than economic motives. Agriculture was not productive. Kádár's idea was to invest heavily in the countryside and persuade the peasants of the advantages of large-scale farming. Hence, the collectives were allowed to become something different from those of the pre-1956 era. They could elect their leaders, including the most enterprising members, often former kulaks, without excessive interference from above. They were offered substantial incentives in the form of government grants and loans. With prices for most agricultural products increasingly reflecting conditions of supply and demand, the collectives began to operate in a market-oriented environment. Because they were permitted to engage in nonagricultural activities (and compete with state-owned plants and service facilities in those sectors as well), they could also effectively utilize available labor, especially in the winter months, and in most cases, the leaders of the collectives could decide how to distribute the profits. The government also abolished mandatory plan targets and compulsory delivery quotas.

By the mid-1980s, the collectives owned more than two-thirds of Hungary's arable land, although their output was only about half of the total (51.1 percent). The contribution of state farms to the total output was 15.3 percent;

of the household farms (land owned by members of cooperatives), 18.4 percent; and of auxiliary and private farms, 15.2 percent. Thus, the ownership structure of agriculture in Hungary had become more diverse than any of the other Communist systems except Poland. Furthermore, as János Kornai has pointed out, the relatively small state-owned sector was "surrounded by a very large number of. . . . market- and profit-oriented cooperatives and private farms,"[6] and therefore it, too, had to adjust to the country's competitive agricultural environment.

To the extent that acceptance of market forces is a key measure of the reform of Soviet-type economies, Hungarian agriculture can be said to have been "reformed." It is also successful. Domestic food supply—and the system of distribution—is better than satisfactory; it is, despite comparatively high prices, the envy of all East Europeans. Moreover, Hungary has become a net exporter of food since the 1970s. It exports grain, meat products, live animals, fruits, vegetables, and, of course, wines to the East as well as to the West. There is considerable prosperity in the Hungarian countryside. The significant political consequence of Kádár's "Bukharinite" approach to agriculture has been the pacification of the country's peasantry.

Economic Reforms

In *industry*, the New Economic Mechanism (NEM), which was formally inaugurated in 1968, began to modify, although it did not radically change, Hungary's command economy. As in agriculture, compulsory plan directives were abolished. Taking their place was a complex set of such economic regulators as prices, interest rates, taxes, and wage guidelines. As the government's once-powerful Planning Office and the several ministries began to focus more on macroeconomic issues, managers obtained some freedom to shape policy within the context of economic regulators. Their newly found freedom to invest or otherwise spend according to their own priorities, taking into account local circumstances, also prompted managers to be interested in making profits rather than in merely trying to satisfy the central authorities by somehow "fulfilling" the plan.

Yet even before a general retrenchment got under way in 1972–1973, NEM was only a limited success. Most prices in the manufacturing sector were still centrally determined; indeed, prices seldom reflected either production costs (due to subsidies) or supply and demand. Most large industrial monopolies remained intact. In general, market forces were not given a sufficiently important role to create an efficient economic environment. Such a competitive environment was lacking at least partly because approximately half of Hungary's national income derived from foreign trade and more than half of that trade was conducted with the highly centralized, unreformed economies that made up the Council for Mutual Economic Assistance (CMEA), including the Soviet Union. As the market played no role in CMEA's commercial transactions, which were essentially barter deals made by governments, Hungarian industry was handicapped by the conflict between pressures for extensive growth inherent in trade with the CMEA and pressures for intensive growth inherent in trade with market-oriented (Western and to a far lesser extent domestic) economies.

The retrenchment of the 1970s took place because of the rise of the price of energy, domestic economic dislocations caused (partly) by the reforms, social inequities stemming from NEM's nonegalitarian features, and a vigorous campaign against "consumerism" and other "petty bourgeois" tendencies launched by Soviet critics and their Hungarian allies (the so-called worker's opposition).

In 1972, the party once again decided to provide "state protection" to six of the country's largest industrial firms, meaning that they would be saved from bankruptcy by subsidies irrespective of performance. In 1973, in a further revision of NEM, the previous trend toward decentralization was reversed when fifty of the largest enterprises were ordered to absorb a number of smaller factories. As the government renewed subsidies to large enterprises, it became obvious that economic efficiency and profitability once again mattered less than the party's view of the "importance" of a factory and its "essential" products. Although the party recognized that some of the country's smaller firms were doing well under NEM, it claimed that the large enterprises—still the backbone of Hungarian industry—suffered because of unfair competition by smaller firms that offered flexible assignments, greater challenges, and in some cases higher bonuses to their managers, engineers, and workers. In a sense, and ironically, NEM thus became the victim of its own (partial) success.

By 1979, the reform was on again. In part, the renewal of the reform process was prompted by a number of external economic shocks in the mid-1970s. Lacking flexibility, the Hungarian economy had proved unable to respond adequately either to the energy crisis or to the long Western recession. But economic considerations alone did not make all the difference. With Soviet leader Leonid Brezhnev ailing and the Kremlin deeply immersed in the struggle for succession, Kádár assumed that he had enough elbow room to neutralize the worker's opposition and undertake new reform measures. His calculation was also based on the relationship he had with Yuri Andropov, the Soviet ambassador to Hungary in 1956 and Brezhnev's eventual successor, who had played a role in choosing Kádár as Hungary's new leader after the 1956 Soviet intervention. In any event, a new reformist cycle was under way—as indicated by the removal in 1980 of three antireform officials from the Politburo, including Béla Biszku, Kádár's then de facto deputy (who had been removed from the Secretariat in 1978).

In economics, this post-1979 renewal of the reform process (NEM II) was a logical extension of NEM I. It also amounted to a rejection of policies pursued since 1972. According to Paul Marer:

> Recognizing that significant competition between producers is indispensable for an efficiently functioning market mechanism, a series of steps were taken: several trusts and enterprises were broken up into smaller units; setting up new small- and medium-sized business ventures in the socialized sector was facilitated; the scope of legalized private sector activities was expanded and

> restrictions on them eased; some competition in the foreign trade field was introduced; the size of the central bureaucracy was cut to provide fewer opportunities to meddle into enterprise decisions; new methods of appointing enterprise managers were introduced; and new financial institutions were created.[7]

The case of Hungary's largest enterprise, the Csepel Iron and Metal Works Trust, illustrated both the problems caused by the retrenchment of the 1970s and the seriousness with which the party approached the renewal process in the early 1980s. As of 1979, Csepel employed 20,000 workers; its annual sales amounted to about $500 million. As analyzed by Marer, "The trust became insolvent in 1979 and was given three years to become profitable. Since it continued to lose money . . . on July 1, 1983 it was broken up into 13 independent enterprises."[8] Hence, what was first enlarged before the reforms had begun in 1963–1966 and then again in the 1970s was reduced in the 1980s.

New laws enacted in the early 1980s also encouraged individuals to form so-called enterprise economic work associations. These associations or groups were made up of workers willing to do extra work on their own time, in the evenings and on weekends. Contracting with their employer for such extra work and using the facilities of the enterprise, workers would undertake assignments for which the enterprise lacked adequate labor. Another new measure was intended to help expand the private sector. Formerly, permission had been granted mainly for the opening of private repair outlets, boutiques, fruit and vegetable stands, and small Mom and Pop–type restaurants. Since the early 1980s, however, various types of private firms have appeared. Under some circumstances, they can now have as many as thirty employees on their payroll. But the legal private sector, unlike the so-called second economy, has remained small. Only 164,900 people were so employed in 1984 (compared to 104,000 in 1980.)[9]

The significance of NEM II has been as much the modest expansion of the private sector as the intended reform of the organization and functioning of large enterprises. The second wave of reforms has produced changes in industrial prices, created new banks to provide competition in financing investments, allowed enterprises to engage in direct foreign trade with non-CMEA customers, and even introduced a more flexible wage system. Alas, as is discussed later on in this chapter, what seemed so promising on paper frequently has not worked.

Political Reforms

As to *political* reforms, the system Kádár built was, and remains, a paternalistic dictatorship. Structurally, the Hungary he has left to his successors differs in no significant way from some of its Warsaw Pact neighbors. The changes that have been made, however, have affected the circumstances of the people and the elite alike.

On the popular level, the political atmosphere in the 1980s was certainly more relaxed than elsewhere in the bloc (except in Poland). Professional advancement in most fields was no longer a function of political considerations alone. Political opinion, unlike oppositional political activity, seldom resulted in either prosecution or persecution. Kádár's so-called alliance policy still held sway. As he explained its meaning a quarter-century ago, "It is necessary to remember what caused the difficult situation in 1956. . . . It began with suspicion. But every rational person must understand that a whole nation cannot be suspect. Our starting point is that the people are our people, that we are here for them, and when they put us [sic] in a responsible post they do so for the reason that we should work for them."[10]

Although the main reason for the regime's relative tolerance is still the memory of 1956, Kádár was, and his successors are, aware that "goulash communism" is an insufficient basis for legitimacy. This is why "democratization" was on the Hungarian agenda (as a slogan and as a hope) well before Gorbachev made it bloc policy. The party's agenda has long included an attempt to "redefine" (reduce) its role vis-à-vis society, and the party has given greater responsibility to the government in the implementation of policy. Consideration has been given to the possibility that the HSWP would lift its prohibition against the formation of "factions" in the party and thus make it more "democratic."

The problem is that for many Hungarians democratization means Western-style pluralism in general and a multiparty system in particular. Recognizing that, Prime Minister Károly Grósz explained in 1987, before his assumption of Kádár's mantle as the HSWP's general secretary, that it was only because of "bad luck" that Hungary ended up having a one-party political system—as if, in the absence of such bad luck, he would welcome organized opposition to the Hungarian Socialist Worker's party!

At the same time, the party *has* tried to make the one-party system more diverse. After decades of talk and planning, for example, Hungary held multislate elections for Parliament in 1985; voters had a choice among several (usually two) candidates. The choice was not between different ideologies or basic outlooks, of course; all candidates were approved by the HSWP and its arm, the Patriotic People's Front, and they all ran on the same platform. Furthermore, as the parliamentary session, although much more active than in the past, still lasts only a few weeks a year, a parliamentary seat carries limited influence.

Nonetheless, elections in 1985 were something more than the empty rituals they used to be. In some localities, they offered voters a chance to choose between opponents and proponents of the reform and to vote against several of the country's worst political hacks. For example, the *majority* of the candidates associated with the widely despised national trade unions—the company unions whose leaders had once made up the bulk of the hard-line, or dogmatic, worker's opposition—actually lost their legislative seats that year, and the results reportedly were closely studied at party headquarters. On the other hand, the public seemed uninterested and unimpressed. Hence, the regime's underlying purpose—to ease tensions by giving voters a sense of political participation and thus make up for accumulated economic woes—did not appear to have been achieved.

What have the reforms *done,* then? As the popular view is summed up by Budapest wits, the reforms have transformed Hungary into one of the freest barracks in the Soviet camp. That grudging assessment, combined with acknowledgment of improvements in living standards until the late 1970s, was about all that most would offer in praise of the Hungarian road to socialism at the end of the 1980s.

Hungary's Economy—Caught Between East and West

Having benefited from a favorable international economic environment for five years (1968–1972), the Hungarian economy began to experience serious problems at the time of the first energy crisis in 1973–1974. Although the price of Soviet oil did not immediately rise to world-market levels and hence the impact of the crisis was not immediate, the eventual impact—because of the misguided Hungarian response to external developments—turned out to be catastrophic. One consequence was such deterioration in the terms of Soviet-Hungarian trade that—to use a simple but vivid illustration—while in 1974, Hungary purchased 1 million tons of Soviet oil by selling 800 Ikarus buses to the Soviet Union; by 1985, 4,000 such buses bought the same amount of oil;[11] and by 1988, according to one Hungarian economist's informal estimate, the equivalent figure rose to about 5,000 buses.

Instead of restraining consumption and, especially, the rate of growth, the party decided to force the economy to grow quickly on the assumption that the external problems were only temporary. Growth was fueled by largely unproductive investments, whose share in the country's gross domestic product increased from 34 percent in 1970 to 41 percent in 1978[12] and which were paid for by foreign loans. In the critical years of 1973–1978, Hungary's hard-currency debt rose at an annual rate of 38.9 percent.[13] Meanwhile, consumption and investments exceeded production by an average of 2.2 percent a year in the 1970s.[14] Thus, the problems that would come to haunt the people and the party in the 1980s were not simply the "unavoidable" consequence of external developments. During the period of retrenchment, but also during NEM II, Hungary did not, and because of the CMEA connection perhaps could not, respond flexibly and effectively to changing international conditions.

The decision to borrow as much as Hungary did and to borrow on a short-term basis assumed incorrectly that the country could promptly repay its debt or that it could do so with cheaper dollars. Hungary's net Western debt rose from less than $1 billion in 1970 to $6 billion in 1980 and to more than $15 billion by the late 1980s. In per capita terms, this was more than Poland's Western debt! Indeed, when its reserves dropped to less than $500 million in 1982, Hungary was on the verge of rescheduling and thus joining Poland and Romania as the third East European "basket case." That unhappy alternative was averted only by the politically difficult decision to join the International Monetary Fund and the World Bank (Hungary was the second Soviet-bloc country, after Romania, to do so) and by convincing increasingly skeptical Western banks of Hungary's creditworthiness and the political benefits of its reformist course.

But the economy, even after 1979, could not effectively serve "two masters." A country so indebted to the West had to earn hard currency, but Hungary could adjust neither to the Western recession nor to the changing needs of Western markets. Much as the government tried to encourage exports to the West—by creating a special fund in the 1980s to aid companies with export potential, for example—the requirements of Western and CMEA markets still worked at cross purposes. Western markets demanded innovation, technologically advanced products, and high quality; CMEA markets did not. In at least one case, Moscow's preference for an *un*improved product forced a Hungarian firm to abandon plans to enter Western markets with an improved version because the cost of innovation and retooling for the Western customer alone was prohibitive. More recently, Soviet insistence on obtaining more Hungarian consumer goods, rather than machinery, has left Hungary with machinery it cannot sell because Western buyers also want the former but not the latter.

Finally, the most persistent problem with CMEA has been its old-fashioned trading mechanism. CMEA's long-term plans, barter deals, artificial prices, and inefficacious registration of trade transactions via the "transferable ruble" (which is neither transferable, even within CMEA, nor a ruble) give Hungary little or no flexibility. Handicapped in its reform efforts by its CMEA connection, Budapest has repeatedly proposed to make the transferable ruble convertible into at least "real" CMEA currencies. But the Hungarian proposal has not been implemented; in this respect at least, what would be good for Hungary is "too flexible" for its CMEA partners. Small surprise, then, that when a group of prominent economists recently called for a reduction in Hungary's involvement with CMEA and for association with Western Europe's Common Market, their proposal was promptly rejected. (It may be significant, however, that a summary of the proposal did appear in the semiofficial economic journal *Közgazdasági szemle*.[15])

Yet, although many Hungarians believe otherwise, the country's economic woes in the 1980s were not made, only exacerbated, by CMEA headquarters in Moscow. In his judicious essay on the subject, János Kornai stressed the *Hungarian* authorities' reluctance to take the "next steps" in the reform process, particularly in the industrial sector, and the bureaucracy's unwillingness to implement decisions already made. His observations are worth quoting at length.

Bankruptcies: "There are state-owned firms that go out of business, but their number is rather small . . . and the exit is decided by bureaucratic procedures. . . . No substantial positive correlation can be found between exit and persistent loss making or insolvency."

Resource allocation: "The all-encompassing system of formal material rationing and allocation has been dissolved, though a few goods are still centrally allocated. There are, however, informal quotas, licenses, or other restrictions."

Prices: "The majority of prices ceased to be administrative, at least nominally, after 1968. Most of such prices have still not become genuinely free market prices, either. Bureaucratic price control had different ways and means to exert strong, in some cases decisive, influence on price formation."

Credit: "Hungary [still] has a highly centralized monetary system. . . . Granting or denying credit is almost uncorrelated with the past or present profitability and credit worthiness of the firm. To some extent, the opposite relationship is true. The credit system is used frequently to bail out firms failing on the market."

Investments: "[Even now only] a small part of state sector investments, about one-fifth of the total, is really decided at the firm's level and financed exclusively from the firm's own savings. As for the rest, the firm must come to agreement with those who give external assistance; consequently the bureaucracy can have a decisive influence on the allocation of investments."

Size: "The size distribution of firms in Hungarian production is much more skewed in favor of large units than in developed capitalist economies. In 1975 in Hungarian industry the three largest producers supplied more than two-thirds of production in 508 out of 637 product aggregates. . . . The large firms are much more successful in lobbying for favors, particularly for investment resources."

Market: "The market is not dead. It does some coordinating work, but its influence is weak. The firm's manager watches the customer and the supplier with one eye and his superiors in the bureaucracy with the other eye. Practice teaches him that it is more important to keep the second eye wide open: managerial career, the firm's life and death, taxes, subsidies and credit, prices and wages, all financial 'regulators' affecting the firm's prosperity, depend more on the higher authorities than on market performance."

Inflation [1.6 percent, averaged annually, in 1967–1973, 3.9 percent in 1973–1978, 7.5 percent in 1978–1984, 12–15 percent in 1985–1986, and perhaps as much as 25 percent in 1987–1988]: "Central policy is ambivalent in this respect. While centrally decided price increases lead the inflationary process, there are official statements attacking managers . . . for forcing prices up. . . . The interminable series of partial upward corrections puts in motion the well-known *dynamic process* of price-cost-wage-price spiral. That can do much harm to the core of decentralization: to financial discipline and rational calculation based on prices and profits. Inefficiencies can be comfortably covered up by passing over cost increases to the buyer."

Kornai concluded, "Shortage, acceleration of inflation, deficits in the trade balance, the growing burden of indebtedness, liquidity troubles, or any other type of tension and unhealthy disequilibrium are good excuses for recentralization. They provide legitimation for suppressing market forces and reviving tight control, formal and informal interventions, and rationing of intermediate goods. This is a trap, because recentralization solidifies the deeper systemic causes that created most of the troubles."[16]

In a nutshell, the second wave of reforms since 1979 did not extricate Hungary from the problems imposed on it by external circumstances, including CMEA's constricting straitjacket, *and* made worse by the HSWP's faulty decisions. NEM II took the country in the right direction, but it came too late, and its implementation was haphazard. During the decade after the introduction of NEM II, the economy ceased to grow, both the level of investments and the standard of living declined, and inflation—compared to previous rates—skyrocketed. For most Hungarians, the reform has come to be identified with inflation and austerity. Whatever the long-term payoffs, they find no magic any more in the Hungarian economic miracle.

The General Crisis in Political and Economic Life

Whether Hungary experienced a systemic economic crisis in the late 1980s is arguable. That there is a popular perception and an atmosphere of general crisis are not. The country's mood significantly changed during the 1980s. The title of an article by Ivan Volgyes captured the atmosphere prior to Kádár's dismissal: "Hungary: *Before* the Storm Breaks."[17]

Important as the country's economic woes are, there is also a growing sense of popular uncertainty about Hungarian socialism—this "deceptive hybrid," as Bennett Kovrig called it.[18] What are Hungarians to make of the gap between the poor and the well-to-do? What are they to do about the differences between two supposedly socialist countries about the fate of the 2 million-strong Hungarian minority in Romania? What is the actual meaning of "deep democratization"? What does the future hold?

It became obvious by the mid-1980s that the reforms enacted since the mid-1960s had run their course. The old guard around Kádár had lost its ability to innovate, and Kádár himself had lost his once-considerable popularity. Although the political atmosphere could not be classified as revolutionary, it was—and remains—more tense than at any time since 1956. The dramatic change in the country's mood, and its leadership, had been fueled by six interrelated developments.

The Economic Factor

Of the uncertainties generated by economic change, inflation was the most worrisome for most Hungarians. The extent to which inflation was a function of the reform and, in particular, of free or freer prices is unclear. But because inflation accompanied NEM II, Hungarians did associate it with the reform process, and they responded the way people respond to inflation elsewhere. They did not save. They consumed and they borrowed. The private sector shied away from making long-term investments. Before the January 1988 introduction of new taxes and price hikes, there was widespread panic. The small corporate-bond market, one of the reform's innovations, collapsed. Those who could afford it bought jewelry, consumer durables, and hard currency on the black market. The economic cost of inflation was therefore very high; the spiritual cost—a pervasive feeling of fright—was, and is, probably higher.

Economic uncertainty was also fueled by constant talk of, and growing concern about the prospect of, unemployment. Two of the achievements of the prereform era were full employment and the steady purchasing power of the forint. Although no one had enough forints and few were fully satisfied with their jobs, the old practice of little pay, little work—as expressed in the East European maxim, "You pretend to pay us and we pretend to work"—had become part of the Hungarian way of life. But in the mid-1980s, there was already some unemployment and a considerable sense of uncertainty about jobs. The question was posed this way: What if the authorities really begin to implement the bankruptcy laws already on the books? With the economy both centrally planned and yet also subject to market forces, would Hungary end up with the worst of both worlds?

The Sociological Factor

One of the few socialist values most Hungarians had embraced—egalitarianism—was beginning to fade. Previously, only those belonging to the Communist *nomenklatura* had been compensated generously for their political usefulness and loyalty; but their privileges-in-kind, aside from the often-noticed black limousines, were largely hidden from the public. In contrast, the private entrepreneur of the 1980s—the so-called *maszek* of the *magán szek*tor, or private sector—was more conspicuous with his house, fancy car, and summer cottage, and he was more envied than admired. He was widely seen as a wheeler-dealer. That the leaders benefited from special privileges was old news, but the aura of deep suspicion about the *maszek* was new and pervasive.

Although the well-to-do were only a small stratum in society, their lifestyles stood in sharp contrast to the poverty of millions of Hungarians.[19] It was beginning to be difficult to see social justice at work in a system in which (as of 1982) 30 percent of the people at the bottom received only 18.6 percent, whereas 30 percent at the top received 44.2 percent of the total recorded income of the population.[20] In 1987, the average monthly wage in the country was about 6,000 forints (which, according to the unrealistically *low* exchange rate, was $130), whereas the official poverty level was set at only 20 percent less than that level at 4,800 forints ($105). By that official definition of poverty, more than one of three Hungarians—mainly the very old and the very young, members of large families, those without skills needed by the second economy, and the disabled—fell below the poverty line. Even if they had extra income from the second economy, and most probably did not, their circumstances were pitiful. Income distribution of this sort is deemed harmful and offensive even in most capitalist countries, let alone in a country whose designation is "socialist." Hence, the gap between professed ideals and reality created dissonance and social tension.

The Generational Factor

However grudging in its praise of Kádár's "goulash communism," the generation of 1956 could still find reasons to be mildly satisfied. Those who had made the 1956 revolution by and large accepted the half-loaf offered by the Kádár regime in the 1960s and 1970s. The actual accomplishments of the Kádár era mattered most, but members of the older generation also appreciated Kádár's widely perceived ability to outwit the Soviet Union. Rightly or wrongly (often rightly), they saw him as a clever, skillful, at times sly politician who did what he could to realize the revolution's "realistic" objectives. Many believed that he was "one of us," not "one of them." Although the Soviet leaders chose Kádár in 1956 to tame Hungary, his compatriots often presumed that he took the job in order to tame the Kremlin.

By the mid-1980s, Kádár could not "wink" at or otherwise signal to the new generation of Hungarians. He could no longer give the impression of having somehow outmaneuvered the Soviets. Now Gorbachev was the dynamic and radical reformer struggling against almost impossible odds to transform the Soviet system, while "uncle János" and the old guard in the Politburo argued against "the reform of the reform." As a result, the new generation could not share that once-prevalent feeling that Hungary was "the leader of the pack." In its eyes, perhaps even Gorbachev's Soviet Union was making progress—or at least taking chances. The Poles, although poorer, had more freedom. The East Germans, although less free, were richer. The Austrians, the West Germans, and the Finns were, of course, both free and rich. Meanwhile, Hungary was standing still: It had lost momentum, its leadership lacked vision, and uncertainties abounded. The regime could not answer the questions on most people's minds: "What have you done for me lately?" "What will the future bring?"

For the younger generation, more so than for the generation of 1956, the era of expectations came to an end in the 1980s. If young people had believed in the proverbial light at the end of the tunnel, their mood of confusion and pessimism might have dissipated. But in the second half of the 1980s, few Hungarians could see any light.

The Romanian Factor

The oppression and forced assimilation of 2 million ethnic Hungarians in Transylvania was (and continues to be) one of the most troubling political issues for 10 million Hungarians. As the number of refugees from Transylvania grew (the official figure in mid-1988 was 10,000), the public was almost as vehement in its expressions of fury with President Nicolae Ceauşescu of Romania as it was critical of Hungary's inability to make things better. It was not clear what any Hungarian regime could do under any circumstances, but in the tense atmosphere prevailing in the country *all* problems were blamed on the perceived incompetence and impotence of the Hungarian government. As in other areas of concern, impatient Hungarians asked why something was not being done.

The Gorbachev Factor

In terms of *perestroika* and *glasnost'*, Hungary has long been years ahead of the Soviet Union. Much of what Gorbachev is only thinking about has already been implemented in Hungary. Thus, what Hungary should now be doing—called the reform of the reform—would entail going well beyond Gorbachev. To give but two examples: For the sake of its economy, Hungary should gradually reduce its trade relations with members of the Soviet bloc and increase its Western exposure. For the sake of political stability, Hungary should move toward genuine political pluralism and eventually adopt a two-party system, even if both parties were to accept the country's "socialist" orientation and uphold its association with the Warsaw Pact.

These next steps have yet to be implemented, even though the Gorbachev phenomenon is encouraging Hungarians to consider such next steps. In this way, Gorbachev's "new thinking" has had and continues to have a profoundly destabilizing impact on the Hungarian political scene. The issue is further complicated by the seemingly unanimous belief of Hungary's attentive public that Gorbachev or his program or both are but a passing phenomenon in Soviet history. This is why Kádár and the cautious old guard around him in the pre-1988 Politburo preferred to postpone the introduction of "the reform of the reform"—not only because they feared the further erosion of socialist principles and worried about instability but because they were uncertain how long new measures would enjoy Soviet approval.

The Opposition Factor

Perhaps the most telling measure of the Kádár regime's fear of radical change is the party's preoccupation with and anxiety about the opposition and its growing number of active and passive supporters. Evidence of the leadership's mentality came to light in 1986–1987 when a lengthy, "strictly confidential" Politburo resolution dealing with the opposition was published first in a *samizdat* periodical in Budapest and then in the West.[21]

Although conceding that the opposition "does not threaten the stability of the internal political situation," the resolution nonetheless failed to distinguish between "enemy" and "opposition," resorted to the use of harsh formulations unseen in Hungary in years, and called for a variety of so-called administrative measures as well as for active propaganda at home and abroad to curtail the activities of the hyphenated "enemy-opposition." Two typical quotes from the resolution give a sense of the regime's mentality in the 1980s.

> The instruments of administrative restriction must be consistently applied against those who conduct organized, illegal political activity and maintain contact with subversive imperialist and hostile propaganda centers. The appropriate organs granting permission for foreign travel should strictly apply the pertinent legal regulations when dealing with those who are engaged in hostile activity. Administrative methods should be applied with due regard to political considerations and in a differentiated manner. . . . Let our propaganda

unmask the link that the leaders and members of the opposition have with the emigration and with Western subversive centers, and in this way seek the disintegration of the environment of enemy groups [and] their circle of sympathizers.

The apparent failure of the party to recognize that the opposition's "environment" is domestic, not Western, was an especially bad omen for prospective political reforms. This secret document certainly indicates that the regime was guided by fear of instability. The regime's reversion to old formulas negated the spirit of the post-1956 motto "he who is not against us is with us." The document surely made it easier to believe Budapest rumors about detailed plans being drawn up to prepare the security forces, the military, and the fire department for the troubled times ahead.

The Changing of the HSWP Guard

The HSWP's first party conference since 1957 was held on May 20–22, 1988, in Budapest. Although several resolutions were debated and adopted at that time, the central issue was power, particularly whether Kádár would resign (voluntarily), and, if so, whether the old guard in the Politburo would do so as well. For about six months prior to the conference Moscow had signaled its preference for Kádár to resign and for Prime Minister Károly Grósz to take Kádár's place. Admittedly, the Kremlin's public signals were subtle, even gentle.

Together with Romania's Ceauşescu, Kádár was the last East European leader to be called on to speak during the November 1987 celebration of the seventieth anniversary of the 1917 Bolshevik Revolution. Kádár was assigned the worst box in the Moscow theater during a performance for foreign Communist dignitaries. After he met Gorbachev on November 3, a meeting that was said to have lasted only fifteen minutes, *Pravda* reported the next day that they had had a "frank" exchange, using an adjective normally reserved to describe differences of opinion between Communists and non-Communists. The phrasing of the whole communiqué was somewhat strange, especially in comparison to the much warmer tone of similar communiqués issued after Gorbachev's meetings with other East European leaders. Moreover, in private conversations, Soviet officials expressed doubts about Kádár's dynamism, noting by way of explanation his "anecdotal style" and "unusual preoccupation with the past."

It was also evident that Grósz was Moscow's preferred successor to Kádár. As early as 1984–1985 Grósz had made several speeches in which he challenged the Kádár line on the issue of the HSWP's legacy. Although Kádár held that the HSWP, formed in 1956, was not responsible for its predecessor's policies in the Stalinist era of the early 1950s, Grósz in his speeches provocatively "accepted responsibility" for the whole postwar period. It is probable that Grósz was encouraged to state that position by the Soviets. Indeed, his 1985 promotion to the Politburo took place in the immediate aftermath of his all-too-obvious criticism of the Kádár line on the party's past. On a visit to Budapest in 1987, Yegor Ligachev singled out Grósz for praise at a time when Grósz, not yet prime minister, was only one of thirteen members of the Politburo.

Encouraged by Moscow, Grósz cautiously, but publicly, pressed for Kádár's removal. In the spring of 1988, for example, at a press conference in London, he alluded to certain "inevitable biological laws" from which no leader could escape. But the first critical confrontation was said to have occurred only a few days before the party conference, at a Politburo meeting on May 16, 1988, when Kádár reluctantly agreed to step aside and accept the new, honorary position as the party's "chairman." Three or four members of this old guard were to be replaced as well, including Miklós Óvári, who headed Kádár's secretariat; Sándor Gáspár, the trade union chief; and György Aczél, an ideologist.

But the 1,000 delegates to the May party conference apparently wanted a more radical break with the past. They rejected the proposal for gradual change, at least partly because of rising pressure within and without the party. By denying Central Committee membership to six old-guard Politburo members—Óvári, Gáspár, Ferenc Havasi, György Lázár, László Maróthy, and Károly Németh—the conference prevented their reelection to the Politburo. Under the circumstances, Kádár reportedly refused to rejoin the Politburo, and Aczél was denied his old seat. In the end, *eight* of the thirteen Politburo members were dropped. The old guard around Kádár, whose average age was sixty-four, was gone. By contrast, the average age of the remaining five members—János Berecz, Judit Csehák, Grósz, Csaba Hámori, and István Szabó—was only fifty-three.

The new Politburo elected at the party conference had only eleven members. The six new members were Pál Ivańyi (fifty-three), mayor of Budapest; János Lukács (fifty-three), a Central Committee secretary; Miklós Németh (forty), another Central Committee secretary; Rezsö Nyers (sixty-five), the "father" of NEM I who was ousted from the Politburo in 1975 for his reformist views; Imre Pozsgay (fifty-four), head of the Patriotic People's Front; and Ilona Tatai (fifty-three), manager of the Taurus rubber plant.

What was striking about the post-1988 Politburo was its youth and its inexperience. Aside from Nyers, who was returned to the leadership after an absence of thirteen years, no other member had served in this ruling body prior to 1985. Potentially more important was the elevation of Nyers and Pozsgay, the party's two bona fide radical reformers. Pozsgay, in particular, had even enjoyed some popularity; he was widely known as "Hungary's Gorbachev." Both Nyers and Pozsgay had openly and repeatedly called for "the reform of the reform," advocating such "next steps" in both the economic and political realms that would allow Hungary to resume its once-pioneering role in trying to reform a stagnating Communist system. They had stated many times that Hungary's economic problems could not be overcome without radical political change. Although not embracing the multiparty system "for now," they had favored Hungary's becoming the first Warsaw Pact country in which "socialist pluralism" was not a slogan but part of a broader, long-term accommodation with political reality. At least before they joined the Politburo, both had sought more than changes *in* the system; they had sought the reform *of* the system.

What seemed to matter most, however, was that Grósz had not been known to have shared some of Nyers's and Pozsgay's ideas. Nor had he displayed Gorbachev's commitment to radical reforms, only the Soviet leader's dynamism and public-relations skills. In the 1970s, Grósz had belonged to the HSWP's more orthodox wing (worker's opposition) and even as late as 1985 his political orientation appeared to resemble that of Yegor Ligachev, Gorbachev's conservative competitor in the Soviet Union. Indeed, Budapest wits referred to Grósz as a Ligachev in Gorbachev's clothes.

His past notwithstanding, the larger question is what Grósz is going to do *in power.* In this respect, early indications point to his desire to make Hungary *the* most reformist country in Eastern Europe, ahead of Poland and the Soviet Union. In doing so, he is guided by two considerations.

The first is Hungary's need to attract Western capital, without which—according to the seemingly unanimous view of the country's economists—the economy would face prospects similar to Poland's or Yugoslavia's by 1992 or 1993. To avoid rescheduling and to arrest the current inflationary spiral, Grósz and the new prime minister, Miklós Németh, have given the green light to new measures that would make Hungary once again the pacesetter among the centrally planned economies. As a result, Western firms and individuals, for example, will be allowed to purchase shares and develop controlling influence in Hungarian enterprises.

The second consideration is domestic pressure for political change, especially toward a multiparty system. To accommodate these pressures the government approved a new law on the right of assembly and association in late 1988 which was supposed to open the way for the formation of political parties by 1990. Grósz's new Minister of Justice, Kálmán Kulcsár, stated as his "personal opinion" in November 1988 that the Hungarian multiparty system would be more competitive than East Germany's and Poland's (where the existing small parties seldom if ever differ from the communist parties). Other officials insisted that "bourgeois pluralism" is out of the question. It is reasonable to assume that while the Grósz regime is not prepared to allow itself to be voted out of power, it is prepared to be very tolerant of political participation.

The Implications of the Hungarian Experience

If Hungary is to pursue truly radical economic reforms and introduce something more than "socialist pluralism" (even if it is less than "bourgeois pluralism"), will its experience prove the viability of reform or the inherent incompatibility of communism and democracy?

The prospects for successful reforms elsewhere in Eastern Europe and the Soviet Union cannot be judged against the background of Hungary's declining fortunes alone. Hungary is not a test case; reforms are not made in a laboratory or a classroom. Experiences, good or bad, cannot be simply transferred or avoided.

Indeed, the Hungarian reform is in many ways unique. It certainly could not have happened without the trauma of 1956. It might not have happened or lasted without János Kádár. It would have encountered far greater difficulties at the beginning without favorable international economic conditions. It would not subsequently have received essential Western assistance were Hungary not the bloc's sole reformer at the time. The country's small size, ethnic homogeneity, relative military insignificance, and arguably impenetrable language all set Hungary apart from its neighbors. The political, economic, and social conditions that had prompted and stifled NEM I, and then started NEM II, cannot be duplicated. By the same token, the successes of the Hungarian reform process can no more easily be emulated than its failures circumvented. Nevertheless, the Hungarian experience is very relevant; it is an important topic for discussion and debate in the Soviet bloc, particularly in the Soviet Union and in Poland.[22]

The Hungarian experience is *politically* relevant. Soviet reformers, for example, are apt to call attention to successes achieved in Hungary, no doubt to strengthen the case for their own proposals. Conversely, opponents of Soviet reforms often intimate, in effect, that there is not as much paprika in "goulash communism" as its proponents claim.

The Hungarian experience is *ideologically* relevant. Soviet and, to a lesser extent, Polish reformers must be able to argue that economic decentralization and other measures will not diminish the party's "leading role" and that Hungary is building socialism. Abel Aganbegyan, Gorbachev's economic adviser and a leading advocate of Soviet reforms, once told a story of how a Soviet citizen had pressed him about the nature of socialism in Hungary.[23] At a public forum, the questioner observed that he had encountered no queues during his recent visit to Budapest. What kind of a socialist country is it, he wanted to know in all seriousness, where people do not have to stand in line for food?

The Hungarian experience is *economically* relevant. Its successes, and to a far lesser extent its failures, have been widely noticed. The Hungarian reform is noticed by those millions of East European tourists who visit Hungary every year to shop. It is noticed by Soviet and East European reformers who want to import the spirit if not always the substance of NEM I and NEM II. Although the Hungarians prefer to deny that what they have done is a distinct "model" and especially that it is for export, they certainly welcome visiting Polish, Soviet, and Chinese economists and politicians who want to "study" the Hungarian road to socialism. One such admiring visitor in 1984 was Mikhail Gorbachev, then a Central Committee secretary in charge of agriculture, who spent a week studying Hungary's prosperous collective farms.

There are lessons to be learned from the Hungarian experience, but it is unrealistic to expect the simple "transfer" of its substance. Zvi Gitelman put it well: "If the achievement of lasting reform in one country is such a tenuous proposition, how much more so must be the prospects of its export and successful implantation in a different soil?"[24]

Nevertheless, partial adaptation of economic reforms remains a possibility. Agriculture and the privatization of parts of the service sector are cases in point, yet even in these cases, there is reason to be skeptical.

Whatever success agriculture enjoys in Hungary derives from food price fluctuation and the ability of producers to spend their extra income on a fairly wide selection of consumer goods. As the Hungarian experience suggests, however, price increases can never be fully made up by wage increases; price increases create anxiety; and price increases in one area of the economy inevitably stimulate inflation throughout the economy.

Partial adaptation of Hungary's modest political reforms is probably more feasible. The Polish Sejm is already more important (or as unimportant) as Hungary's Parliament; there is no reason why the Supreme Soviet could not be made into a deliberative forum. Holding competitive, multislate elections entails no risks either. At best, such political reforms would broaden the base of political participation.

Hungary's *glasnost'* is probably more extensive than what the Soviet Union has achieved. There are few limits to what Hungarians can say or write. In 1988, for example, several weeklies and monthlies frequently discussed the desirability of multiparty political pluralism. Such openness in the Soviet Union would please intellectuals, but others might become more confused about socialism than they would be enlightened by new information or new insights.

Although Hungarian society has certainly not become autonomous, the judiciary has not become independent, and localities have not become free of the central bureaucracy, the processes of decentralization and depoliticization have had an appreciable effect on the country's politics, economics, and social conditions. The party continues to play a decisive role; it controls the main levers of power. Yet its influence no longer penetrates all aspects of life. Professionals employed at party headquarters on Szechenyi rakpart—the so-called White House along the Danube—are reported to number less than four hundred. Compared to the "leading role" the party once played, its current "leading role" is a misnomer.

To transfer such processes and conditions to the Soviet Union would help tap dormant talent. But it would be the single most dangerous step or series of steps for Moscow to take. Hungary is a small country; informal networks, often established in childhood, have always helped make up for the absence of strong central authority. The Soviet Union, in its present form at least, cannot be governed effectively through such mechanisms. For the Soviet Communist party to have only ultimate power is for it to have insufficient power. Although the gradual introduction of a small dose of decentralization is probably feasible, replacing political criteria with professional considerations entails very considerable risks.

In more general terms, the Hungarian experience suggests that the reform process, because it is bound to be uneven, is destabilizing. The reform-retrenchment-reform cycle is unavoidable. Although it is not easy to undo structural reforms, the process of reform is certainly reversible. Nor is the reform ever done or completed; unexpected developments at home and abroad require prompt adjustments to new realities.

Above all, the Hungarian experience strongly suggests that every "good" measure will also have "bad" consequences, such as the following:

- Freeing the price of agricultural goods will bring food to the cities, but it will also start the inflationary spiral.
- Letting the private sector grow will improve the supply of goods and services, but the new entrepreneurs' high incomes will create pressures against "profiteering" and for "egalitarianism."
- Forcing unprofitable firms to go out of business will make for savings and efficiency, but bankruptcies will lead to unemployment.
- Allowing intellectuals and artists to express themselves more freely will help gain their support for the system, but their support will remain contingent on additional steps toward "democracy," not merely "democratization."

In short, reform, restructuring, openness, and democratization solve old problems and make new ones. Whatever else the Hungarian experience suggests, its most basic lesson is that there is no such thing as free goulash.

Notes

1. *New York Times*, December 17, 1985; Reuter, September 19, 1983.

2. There are two major groups within the Hungarian opposition. One is composed of the so-called populists whose considerable appeal stems from its supporters' fervent nationalism, concern for the plight of some 2 million ethnic Hungarians in Romania, a somewhat ambiguous attitude toward the "imperialist" East and the "decadent" West, and occasional anti-Semitism. In the 1920s and 1930s, the populist movement enjoyed widespread popularity among Hungary's young intellectuals, particularly in the countryside. The smaller opposition group, the so-called urbanists, has a liberal and pro-Western orientation, it welcomes modernity, and it is deeply concerned about democracy and pluralism. Its supporters are Budapest intellectuals, some or many of whom are Jewish. By acting with more leniency toward the populists, the Hungarian authorities have sought to drive a wedge between the two groups—with some success. For example, in late spring 1988, the authorities tolerated a huge anti-Romanian demonstration about Transylvania organized by the populists, while at the same time they roughed up a smaller group who pressed for Imre Nagy's rehabilitation. Thus, once again in the twentieth century, a Hungarian regime offers nationalism as an alternative to reform. For more on the populists, see Charles Gati, *Hungary and the Soviet Bloc* (Durham, N.C.: Duke University Press, 1986), pp. 60–72.

3. Pál Bodor, "Politikai szépirás" (Political belles-lettres), *Élet és irodalom*, August 7, 1987.

4. As quoted in Zdeněk Mlynář, *Nightfrost in Prague* (New York: Karz, 1980), p. 157.

5. There appears to be a curious historical parallel between Kádár's "paternalistic dictatorship" and the way Miklós Horthy, Hungary's right-wing regent in the interwar

period, construed his job and governed his country. The parallel extends to Horthy's dealings with Germany and Kádár's handling of the Soviet Union. See Gati, *Hungary and the Soviet Bloc*, pp. 169–170.

6. János Kornai, "The Hungarian Reform Process: Visions, Hopes, and Reality," *Journal of Economic Literature* 24 (December 1986), pp. 1687–1737. "Auxiliary" farms are cultivated by people whose primary job is in a nonagricultural field and who work on their gardens and small plots in their free time.

7. Paul Marer, "Economic Reform in Hungary: From Central Planning to Regulated Market," in *East European Economies: Slow Growth in the 1980s, Vol. 3: Country Studies on Eastern Europe and Yugoslavia* (Washington, D.C.: GPO, 1986), pp. 248–249.

8. Ibid., pp. 249–250.

9. Kornai, "The Hungarian Reform Process," p. 1705. The 1984 figure of 164,900 represented 4.2 percent of active income earners.

10. *Népszabadság*, March 21, 1964.

11. For the 1974 figure, see *Magyarország*, July 31, 1983. For the 1985 figure, see *International Herald Tribune*, June 18, 1985, as quoted in Bennett Kovrig, "Hungarian Socialism: The Deceptive Hybrid," *East European Politics and Societies* 1, no. 1 (Winter 1987), p. 122.

12. Paul Marer, "Hungary's Balance of Payments Crisis and Response," in *East European Economies*, p. 299.

13. Kornai, "The Hungarian Reform Process," p. 1721.

14. Marer, "Hungary's Balance of Payments Crisis," p. 299.

15. "Fordulat és reform" (Turn and reform), *Közgazdasági szemle* 34, no. 6 (1987), pp. 642–663. This publication included not only a summary of the original (radical) report but a professional/political critique of it by the HSWP Central Committee's Economic Working Group.

16. Kornai, "The Hungarian Reform Process."

17. Ivan Volgyes, "Hungary: Before the Storm Breaks," *Current History* 86, no. 523 (November 1987), pp. 373–376, 389–390 (italics added).

18. Kovrig, "Hungarian Socialism."

19. Of the voluminous literature on the subject, see, for example, Ágnes Bokor, *Szegénység a mai Magyarországon* (Poverty in today's Hungary) (Budapest: Magvetö, 1987).

20. Adapted from Kornai, "The Hungarian Reform Process," p. 1725.

21. The *samizdat* monthly where this document first appeared was *A demokrata* (The democrat). The full text, together with a much lengthier report submitted to the Politburo by the Central Committee's Science, Education, and Culture Department, was subsequently published in Paris in the émigré quarterly *Irodalmi ujság* (Literary gazette), no. 2 (1987), pp. 11–14.

22. For an excellent discussion and analysis of the Polish case, see Zvi Gitelman, "Is Hungary the Future of Poland?" *Eastern European Politics and Societies*, 1, no. 1 (Winter 1987), pp. 135–159.

23. Leonid Pleshakov, "Chelovek i ekonomika" (Interview with Abel Gezevich Aganbegyan), *Ogonek*, July 25–August 1, 1987, pp. 12–15.

24. Gitelman, "Is Hungary the Future of Poland?" p. 159.

10

Czechoslovakia Between East and West

H. Gordon Skilling

During the past seven decades, Czechoslovakia, located in the heart of Central Europe, has been a focal point of conflict. This conflict has occurred between East and West as well as among Western countries, which have rarely been united in their attitudes and policies toward this region. There has been a complex and changing interplay of opposing forces and tendencies—Soviet, German, French, British, and U.S.—that has at all times decisively affected the destiny of Czechs and Slovaks, as well as the other nations of Central Europe. The very existence of Czechoslovakia as a state and the extent of its boundaries were determined by the changing balance of international forces. Its domestic polity and society were influenced by outside factors that often interlocked with internal political movements so as to blur any real distinction between the domestic and external. In turn, the situation in Czechoslovakia affected the attitudes of Eastern and Western states to it.

From Independence (1918) to the Prague Spring (1968)

It is impossible to understand the present position of Czechoslovakia without examining the historical background, especially the critical years—1918, 1938, 1948, and 1968—each of which was a turning point. On these dates Czechoslovakia's official orientation shifted: in 1918, from overwhelmingly Western to anti-Western; in 1938, to pro-German as well; in 1948, after an ambiguous three-year interregnum, and again in 1968, to anti-Western and pro-Soviet. The attitudes of the population changed more slowly and subtly. There remained a deep undercurrent of pro-Western feelings and, after 1968, anti-Soviet feelings, but these were countered and distorted by official propaganda and pressure. Little wonder, given these sharp swings, that Czechs and Slovaks lost any real sense of national identity. Only in 1977, in the wake of Charter 77, was there a rebirth of consciousness and a sense of being part of a broader European and Western community, at least among the small circle of persons who expressed themselves independently in *samizdat.*

The Period Before World War I

Before 1918, Czechs and Slovaks did not possess their own state. Imbedded in an Austro-German and Hungarian environment, neither nation was fully satisfied with its lot and, by peaceful means, defended its national rights against German and Magyar discrimination. The Czechs, living within a system that was pseudodemocratic and in some sense foreign, were by and large "Austro-slav." They accepted the fact that there was no alternative to the Habsburg monarchy but strove to make it more democratic and to gain greater autonomy and national distinctiveness. To balance domestic pressures, the Czechs turned to Russia and France with romantic and cultural sympathy for both, but with no direct political implications. Both Tomáš Masaryk and Karel Kramář, who represented respectively a Western and neo-Slav, pro-Russian approach, were agreed in denouncing the Austro-Hungarian-German alliance. Slovaks had fewer opportunities for self-expression but were increasingly imbued with a consciousness of Slovak national identity. Their newly formed parties fought hard against Magyar repression, but many individual Slovaks succumbed to assimilation. Some, especially among the small Protestant minority, developed strong pro-Czech feelings. In the cultural realm, there were significant pro-Russian and pan-Slav tendencies.

World War I and Its Aftermath

During the war years, Tomáš Masaryk and Edvard Beneš, by dint of perspicacious efforts, gradually won over the Western allies to the ideas of the destruction of the Habsburg monarchy and the right of Czechs and Slovaks to establish an independent state. The attainment of independence in 1918 was not, as is sometimes claimed, a "gift on a silver platter"; it was the product of a combination of Western policies and allied victory and the supportive actions by Czechs and Slovaks at home and abroad. The Soviet Union could take little credit for this (although it later claimed exclusive merit), except for the impact on Czech and Slovak thinking of Lenin's espousal of the right of national self-determination and of the two Russian revolutions.

After 1918, Czechs and Slovaks escaped from Austrian and German power and became independent and for all intents and purposes an integral part of the West. The new state's political system was democratic, modeled on that of the United States and France; in contrast to its neighbors, Czechoslovakia's system persisted in this form throughout the interwar period. Its diplomacy, conducted by Beneš, was based on an alliance with France directed against the potential menace of a revived Germany and on an alliance with the pro-French Little Entente (Czechoslovakia, Yugoslavia, and Romania) against Hungarian territorial revisionism. After the rise of Adolf Hitler, Beneš, although still wedded firmly to the West, shifted the balance by recognizing the USSR in 1934 and concluding a military alliance in 1936. The Communist party of Czechoslovakia, which had initially opposed the very existence of Czechoslovakia as an imperialist state and nevertheless had won substantial support in elections, adopted, following the Moscow line, the policy of a people's front for the defense of the republic.

The Road to World War II

The Munich agreement in 1938 represented the culmination of Nazi aggression in Central Europe and of Western appeasement of Hitler's claims. The four Western powers forced Czechoslovakia, by ultimatum—a decision "o nas, bez nas, proti nám" (about us, without us, against us) as they put it in Prague—to accept the partition of its territory. This represented an open betrayal by France of its ally and an expression of callous indifference by Britain to the state it had helped to establish, which was by then considered "faraway" and "little known." The Soviet Union professed a readiness to honor its obligations to Prague (conditional on similar action by France), but its sincerity was not tested by Beneš by an appeal to Moscow for assistance. Confronted by this situation, Beneš rejected the idea of resisting by force of arms and capitulated (a decision later severely criticized by some). The surrender represented the breakdown not only of the entire concept of Beneš's diplomacy but also of the country's general belief in the West and in its ideas and institutions. Confidence in the Soviet Union was shaken by its failure to offer aid and by its subsequent acceptance of the Nazi occupation of Bohemia and Moravia in 1939. This event, following more or less inexorably from the Munich agreement, made the Czech lands an integral part of the Third Reich. The Slovaks, on the other hand, for the first time in their history, attained independent statehood, but this did not conceal the reality of German domination. Czechs and Slovaks, after twenty years of unity, were severed from each other, and Czechoslovakia disappeared from the map of Europe.

For Beneš, World War II was a reprise of World War I. Once again, he had to persuade the Western allies and the Soviet Union to recognize his wartime government and its goal of regaining independence. This time he had to contend with the rival Communist committee, headed by Klement Gottwald, in Moscow. During a visit to the Soviet capital in 1943, undertaken after overcoming British opposition to it, Beneš concluded a treaty of mutual assistance with the USSR and in a later visit, in 1945, came to terms with Gottwald about postwar conditions. In liberated Košice, in April 1945, a coalition government was formed, with Beneš continuing as president but with many key posts going to the Communists. In June, Beneš agreed to the cession of Ruthenian territories to the Soviet Union, thus breaking the territorial continuity of the republic but saving the Slovaks from a similar fate.

As in World War I, many Czechs and Slovaks contributed to the allied cause by serving in the Czechoslovak armed forces in the East and the West. Underground Communist and non-Communist resistance in the Czech lands was at first substantial but was crippled by severe repression after the assassination of SS "protector" Reinhard Heydrich by Czech soldiers who were parachuted in from England. Collaboration by pro-Nazi persons did not mirror the general hostility of the people to German rule. In Slovakia, the 1944 uprising conducted in unity by Communists and non-Communists gave testimony of the Slovak will to be reunited with the Czechs. The Prague uprising, in the closing days of the war, although much smaller in scope, was also a joint action by Communists and non-Communists and bore witness to the willingness of some Czechs to sacrifice their lives, if necessary, for independence.

Beneš based his policies on the realistic assumption that the USSR would be the dominant power in postwar Eastern Europe and on the naive belief that it would move toward greater democracy and would treat Czechoslovakia as a sovereign equal. The liberation of the Slovak and Czech lands, including Prague, by the Soviet armies was due partly to their rapid advance across Europe in battle with the German forces and partly to the Soviet-U.S. agreement on a dividing line in Western Bohemia that prevented U.S. troops going beyond Plzeň. This created the myth of the Soviet Union as the sole liberator and generated substantial enthusiasm among Czechs and Slovaks for the Red Army and admiration of the Soviet Union, which redounded to the advantage of the Communists in postwar politics. May 1945 was henceforth celebrated as a date more important than October 1918 in Czechoslovak history.

World War II brought about the restoration of an independent Czechoslovakia, its boundaries unchanged except for the loss of Ruthenia. Czechs and Slovaks were once more united, this time with the latter recognized as a distinct nation. The expulsion of the bulk of the Germans to Germany—an action pressed by Beneš and approved by East and West—and the transfer of many Magyars to Hungary made the state overwhelmingly Slavic. The victory brought what seemed to be the reestablishment of a democratic system, as Beneš had hoped, and a national democratic revolution, as Gottwald termed it, that would lead to socialism by a national road. The agreement of Communists and non-Communists on a program of radical reform and the withdrawal of Soviet troops seemed to open up the prospect of Czechoslovakia being a bridge between East and West and a synthesis of socialism and democracy.

The Rise of the Communists

Nevertheless, there were ominous signs of totalitarian tendencies in the government's banning of the Agrarian and Slovak People's parties and the expulsion of the German population after a century-long cohabitation with Czechs in Bohemia and Moravia. Slovak autonomy was drastically reduced by the Prague government, thus laying the basis of a centralized system. The elections in 1946 demonstrated great Communist strength in the Czech lands, but the Communists were resoundingly defeated in Slovakia by the newly formed Democratic party. Meanwhile on the international front, the conclusion of the Soviet-Czechoslovak military alliance was not balanced by a corresponding treaty with France, and this represented a decisive tip in the balance toward the East. Still more portentous was Joseph Stalin's July 1947 ban on Czechoslovak participation in the Marshall Plan. As Jan Masaryk, minister of foreign affairs, put it, the Czechoslovakians went to Moscow as allies and returned as satellites.

It was soon evident that the Communists were not satisfied with hegemony but aspired to total control. The takeover of power in Slovakia by Gustáv Husák in 1947 was a dress rehearsal for a similar coup in Prague in February 1948. When the non-Communists precipitated a crisis by resigning from the government, Gottwald, with the full backing of the Soviet Union if not on its direct command, frightened President Beneš into accepting a Communist-dominated régime. The non-Communists, having relied exclusively on Beneš, offered no substantial resistance, and the West was powerless to give support, even if it had been requested. As in 1938, Beneš's surrender was the product of international as well as domestic factors and was deemed by some to have been a failure of will and a fatal error. The suicide, or murder, of Jan Masaryk in March and Beneš's resignation in June symbolized the fact that Czechs and Slovaks, in spite of their democratic traditions and Western inclinations, had been fully absorbed into the Eastern European realm. The people's democracy had been transformed into a full-blown dictatorship of the proletariat under the command of the Communist party.

The "Terrible" 1950s and the 1960s Response

The "terrible" 1950s, as they were called, witnessed the transformation of the republic into a replica of the Soviet system, in accordance with what Gottwald grotesquely termed "the law of the increasing approximation of Czechoslovakia to the Soviet model." In compliance with the Communist theorem of the leading role of the party, the single ruling party transformed all governmental institutions and voluntary organizations into tools of its dictatorship, and the economy was remodeled on the Soviet command model. Non-Communists were dismissed en masse from their positions or driven into emigration. Leading Communists were liquidated in macabre trials on the Soviet pattern and under Stalin's pressure, leading to the murder of hundreds and the imprisonment of thousands. Churches, religious believers, and clergy were harshly persecuted, and the arts, culture, and scholarship were forced to accept socialist realism and the dogmas of Marxism-Leninism. In foreign policy Czechoslovakia became nothing more than an instrument of Soviet interests and displayed not even a hint of an effort to defend its own interests and ideas. The Soviet Union became "friends for all time," as the slogan went, and the West, especially the United States, became "public enemy no. 1."

Stalinism in Czechoslovakia, unlike in other people's democracies, continued after the death of Stalin and Gottwald in 1953. There were riots in Plzeň and a modest "new course" in that year, but terror continued in new trials, including those of Gustáv Husák and the Slovak "nationalist" Communists. The ordinary people were too frightened to resist, and their rulers were too subservient to Moscow to follow a more independent course. During the 1950s, the people, having lost heart as the result of the experiences of Munich, the occupation, and 1948, remained passive, and although many no doubt remained democratic at heart, they did not act on their convictions.

Czechoslovakia was almost the only Eastern European country unaffected by East-West détente and by Nikita Khrushchev's limited reforms in the USSR. During the critical days of 1956, the country remained an island of stability between its two turbulent neighbors and thus contributed to the Soviet Union's ability to survive the crisis and maintain its dominant position in Eastern Europe.

Beginning in 1957, under Antonín Novotný, the regime maintained an unswerving loyalty to Moscow and solidarity with the bloc and backed Soviet foreign policies to the hilt. The military alliance, renewed in 1963, and a five-year trade treaty for 1966 to 1970 placed Czechoslovakia in a position of almost total dependence on Moscow. Although giving verbal support for peaceful existence and for expanded economic relations with the West, Czechoslovakia did not basically alter its policies toward the latter. Apart from the abandonment of outright terror, the system remained unchanged during the late 1950s and early 1960s. A modest economic reform in 1958 was not followed by more radical change in the command economy in spite of growing economic crisis. The 1960 constitution was modeled on the Soviet pattern and openly endorsed the leading role of the party. There was sham de-Stalinization in 1961 when the ugly monument of Stalin was removed from the Letna height. Novotný remained supreme, and the only alternative leader, Rudolf Barák, was unceremoniously removed in 1962 for alleged embezzlement.

Yet beneath the surface there was a gradual and subtle revival of spirit and a steady decline in the legitimacy of the regime. There was a partial rehabilitation of some of the victims of the 1950s, widespread discussion of the urgent need for economic reform, and even modest political change. Slovaks evinced a growing hostility to the asymmetrical system that denied them equality and any semblance of home rule. In the cultural and scholarly fields, there was a growing rebellion against rigid conformity and a revival of independent and creative thinking. The half-hearted Stalinism of Novotný was unable to deal with this overarching crisis, and as a result of a revolt in the highest echelons, he was removed from office and replaced by the Slovak Alexander Dubček.

1968—The Prague Spring and Intervention

Another climactic year in Czechoslovak history, 1968, left a permanent legacy with which present leaders must still wrestle. What had seemed a possible turning point in the direction of a democratized and humanized communism led instead to a great step backward to a kind of neo-Stalinism reminiscent of the late 1950s.

During the Prague Spring, there was little or no change in the East-West balance or in Czechoslovakia's continuing association with the East. Dubček repeatedly asserted the need for absolute unity with the Soviet Union and the Eastern bloc and was not tempted by the examples of Tito's Yugoslavia, the People's Republic of China, Romania, or Albania. Czechoslovakia would remain loyal to the Warsaw Treaty and Comecon and seek reforms in these organizations only to strengthen them and to enhance its influence in the making of common policies. Foreign policy was to have "a new face," particularly "a more effective and especially Central European policy,"[1] but no new initiatives were taken. Neutralism was abjured. There was no change in Prague's hostile attitude toward West Germany. The condemnation of Munich ab initio remained the sine qua non, and the chief stumbling block, of any agreement. The possibility of financial and economic assistance from West Germany and world financial institutions was cautiously explored, but no massive foreign aid was sought.

The major reforms were not intended to terminate the Communist system but to change it substantially and to create a more democratic type of socialism. There was some public discussion of the second republic and a revival of the popularity of Masaryk and Beneš, but there was no thought of a return to the situation between the wars or of the creation of a Western-style political and economic system. Nevertheless, proposed changes were radical enough: the democratization of politics, but with the retention of the leading role of the single party; the invigoration of the institutions of government and administration and the democratization of the party; the reformation of the economy so as to combine central planning with a market; the recognition of Slovak equality and the creation of a genuine federal system; the rehabilitation and compensation of the victims of repression; the guarantee of freedom of the press and of intellectual and cultural life; the granting of freedom for interest groups and independent associations; and the revival of public opinion. There was some debate about ideas such as an opposition or even a multiparty system, but these were not in the party's program. The ultimate result, if unimpeded by foreign interference, would have been "an advance toward a more human social order embodying in some degrees the traditions of Masaryk *and* Marx and synthesizing the basic ideas of democracy and socialism in a manner not only new to Czechoslovak history but unduplicated elsewhere in the world."[2]

The Soviet Union demonstrated an increasingly negative attitude toward these plans, arguing that they would weaken Communist rule, undermine the bloc's military security, and loosen the bonds of Communist solidarity and unity. No doubt, the Soviets feared that in the end this would terminate Moscow's control of Eastern Europe and threaten the very existence of socialism in the entire region. Although firmly resisting Soviet pressures and defending the reform course, Dubček did not think of leaving the bloc or of resisting a Soviet intervention by force. When General Prchlík during the summer broached the idea of preparing a military defense for such a contingency, Dubček rejected it and clung to the naive belief that the Soviet

Union would not intervene by arms. Nor did he consider an appeal to the West or to the United Nations, and he was cool to the possibility—which did not materialize—of convening a conference of European Communist parties.[3]

The intervention, when it came, was a devastating blow to traditional Czech and Slovak attitudes toward the Soviet Union. It unleashed a wave of hostility such as had never before existed. Although Czechs and Slovaks had viewed the reform course somewhat differently, with the latter placing more emphasis on national objectives, they reacted in identical fashion with nonviolent, passive resistance toward the occupation forces. The revulsion toward Moscow was not limited to the non-Communist majority but embraced Communists, young and old, hitherto devoted to the Soviet Union and communism. The disillusionment was as profound as the disenchantment with the West at the time of Munich. The occupation was condemned by the National Assembly, the government and party organs, the trade unions, the intellectual elite, the party's rank and file, and many of the topmost party leaders. The resistance was not limited to the seven days of nonviolent demonstrations in the streets of Prague, Bratislava, and other cities, the broadcasting by underground radio, and the circulation of "free" newspapers; it continued for seven months in the form of political opposition by some Communist leaders and by workers, students, and intellectuals.

As in the case of Beneš in 1938, popular feelings ran high against Dubček, who under duress capitulated by signing the Moscow protocol that legitimized the occupation and with Lubomír Štrougal (later prime minister) and others accepted the bitter task of "ruling" the country and reversing the very reforms he had introduced. He did this reluctantly and sought in vain to preserve at least some vestiges of reform. Only a handful of leading party figures, notably Jaroslav Šabata, refused to approve the treaty legalizing the "temporary" presence of troops and condemned the policy of normalization pursued by Dubček. Another small group of leaders, such as V. Bil'ak and A. Indra, earned nothing but public anger and contempt based on the people's suspicion that they had invited the "fraternal" assistance and on the fact that they willingly collaborated with Moscow after August.

Throughout the Prague Spring, there was widespread sympathy and even enthusiasm in the West for Dubček's "socialism with a human face." Western governments, however, pursued a policy of cautious disengagement before August and took no decisive steps afterward. The Western response to the actual invasion was limited, as in 1938 and 1948, to verbal condemnation. The governments of the North Atlantic Treaty Organization (NATO) were concerned with the security implications of Soviet action, but they believed that détente could still be saved. As in previous crises, the powerlessness of the West to intervene decisively in Eastern Europe was again conclusively demonstrated.

1969 and After—Husák in Power

In April 1969, as a result of renewed Soviet pressures, Dubček was replaced by Gustáv Husák, who was associated with the reform policies but whose main purpose had been to gain autonomy for Slovakia in a federal system. Although he condemned the invasion, he gained the sympathy of the Soviet rulers by his actions in the postinvasion days and showed himself ready to submit to every Soviet demand. His policy of "consolidation" was designed to erase almost every trace of the 1968 reforms and to restore the status quo ante. The regime he inaugurated was an amalgam of features of Gottwald's and of Novotný's rule of the 1950s and 1960s and was to endure without serious changes in leadership or in policy for twenty years—a period as long as the entire life of the first republic. The continued presence of Soviet troops remained a constant reminder of the coercive hold of Moscow on its onetime friend and ally. Czechoslovakia seemed to be firmly and irrevocably sealed within the Eastern Communist bloc.[4]

After attaining supreme power, Husák purged Dubček, Černík, and Josef Smrkovský from the top ranks and absorbed into his team other Dubček associates, such as Štrougal, who was ready to turn his coat, and Bil'ak and Indra, who had been lukewarm supporters, if not opponents, of the 1968 course. In the following years, some differences of view could be discerned between the hard-line tendency of Bil'ak and Indra and the more moderate Štrougal. Husák, however, was not a moderate between extremes but a militant extremist in his own right. That not a single major shift in leading cadres occurred for twenty years was evidence of the unity of the leadership and the absence of strong competing factions.

Some observers abroad, and even some of the ousted reformers, such as Milan Hübl, entertained the illusion at first that Husák would eventually, after a spell of harsh repression, act in the Kádár fashion by moderating his course and introducing cautious reforms. Husák, however, always a hard-line dogmatic Communist and hardened by his personal experience as a political prisoner, pursued his harsh and vindictive course unchanged. The guideline was the 1970 Central Committee document, "The Lessons Drawn from the Crisis Development," which endorsed the Soviet intervention as "fraternal assistance" and condemned the Prague Spring as "counterrevolutionary" and Dubček as a right-wing opportunist. On the basis of this interpretation of events, the party, under the leadership of Miloš Jakeš, who ironically was appointed head of the party control commission by Dubček and had been in charge of rehabilitation during the Prague Spring, carried through a ruthless purge of some hundreds of thousands of party cadres at all levels, including the great bulk of the Communist intelligentsia active during the Prague Spring. True, there were no trials of topmost leaders, but lesser lights such as Šabata, Prchlík, and Hübl were imprisoned, and all those purged, including Dubček, were kept on the fringes of society, as manual workers or worse, for twenty years. It has been reported that Husák would have preferred a somewhat less draconic treatment than that favored by Jakeš, but the fact is that Husák was responsible for this policy of exclusion and continued it long after the five years of Kádár's similar policy.

Husák showed many of the elements of a "true believer," coupled with an absence of scruple and a taste for personal power, and he was devoid of any genuine Slovak nationalist spirit. After the war, his record in Slovakia was that of a ruthless seeker of power and the manager of the seizure of power in 1947 against the will of the largest Slovak party, the People's party. Although high in the Slovak leadership from 1946 to 1950, he held no position in the central party organs and was not directly responsible for the terror in the 1950s. When, in February 1951, it turned against him, he was imprisoned for many years as a "bourgeois nationalist." Like other charges, this was fabricated and did not confirm that he was imbued with strong nationalist feelings (as perhaps Vlado Clementis, another Slovak Communist leader, and others were). During the Prague Spring, Husák was the chief spokesperson of the Slovak party's federalist demands, which took precedence over the broader democratic program of the Czechoslovak party as a whole. In fact, he utilized Slovak nationalism as a tool to dampen the democratic tendencies in Slovakia and, after the occupation, to secure undiluted power in Slovakia and then in Prague. In 1970, he curbed his own great achievement, that of federalization, by reducing Slovakia once again to a region without real autonomy. The inclusion of many Slovaks in the Prague establishment and their numbers in the bureaucratic agencies of the new Slovak republic provided him for the first time with a social basis of support.

In 1975, Husák established a personal monopoly of power by combining the post of president with that of first secretary—the very "cumulation of functions" for which Novotný had been removed from office. Under Husák, Prague became once again an obedient satellite, ready to model itself on the Soviet Union and to support all the latter's foreign policies without question. Husák accepted the reality of the Brezhnev doctrine and by trade and military agreements incorporated Czechoslovakia more and more fully into the Soviet orbit. Even in the conditions of a more diversified bloc and of tendencies toward national communism, Husák gave no hint of following a distinctive line or seeking to defend Czechoslovak interests. This was no doubt a result of his lifelong devotion to the USSR, which had expressed itself during the war in the advocacy of postwar incorporation of Slovakia into the Soviet Union. Perhaps, too, Husák's actions reflected the fact that as a Slovak he possessed no feelings of Czechoslovak nationalism. Moreover, his team included other anational Communists, such as Bil'ak, a Ruthenian (Rusyn), and Bohuslav Chňoupek, a Slovak widely regarded as a longtime Soviet agent. Nor was there evidence of strong national sentiment among his Czech colleagues, such as Štrougal. In view of his own 1968 record, Husák was always threatened by possible attack by his extremist colleagues and had to counteract this danger by an exaggerated profession of loyalty to the Soviet Union. In any case, the continued occupation by Soviet forces rendered any autonomy of action difficult, if not impossible.

Czechoslovakia's Position in World Affairs

Czechoslovakia's relations with the West remained frozen for a long time, and normalization was slow and late in coming. Only in 1973, for instance, was a treaty with West Germany concluded that declared the Munich agreement null and void ab initio and opened the possibility of increased trade. Relations with the United States were hampered by the failure to reach a settlement of Czechoslovakia's claims for gold held by the United States since the war or of U.S. claims for property nationalized by the postwar Prague regime. The conclusion of the Helsinki Final Act in 1975 and the launching of the Conference on Security and Cooperation in Europe (CSCE) process seemed to mark a high point in the spirit of détente and to suggest a more open and friendly policy toward the West in Prague. Husák, however, like Brezhnev, saw in the Final Act a recognition of the European territorial and political status quo, including that of Czechoslovakia, and a removal of any threat of a reopening of the "Sudeten German" question. Czechoslovakia's commitment to the Helsinki process proved to be a boomerang, once Czechoslovakia and its violations of human rights became the targets at successive follow-up meetings of the CSCE in Belgrade, Madrid, and Vienna, and at the Ottawa human rights meeting. Faced with a remarkable unity of position by Western delegations, including the neutral and nonaligned, Czechoslovakia could only respond with shopworn arguments about "interference in internal affairs" and later with tu quoque attacks on Western violations of economic and social rights. The barrage of censure brought no change at all in Prague's failure to respect human rights or in its treatment of its own dissidents. This hard-line policy severely damaged Czechoslovakia's international image and marked it out as a pariah in the European community.[5]

Czechoslovakia's position in world affairs was damaged still further by the policies adopted in the economic sphere.[6] One of the first priorities of "normalization" was the dismantling of the economic reform barely initiated by Dubček and the restoration of the centralized command economy, although not in its fully Stalinist form. For some years, the economy still showed itself capable of steady growth, at a rate of about 5.7 percent annually. Agriculture, in particular, developed favorably. The regime was thus able to carry out a tacit "social contract" with the population, assuring stable prices, growth of real income, social security measures, full employment, and so on. The long-term negative features of the economic system produced, however, a slowing down of growth after 1976 (3.7 percent from 1975 to 1979) and then in the early 1980s what amounted to a serious crisis, with the gross national product (GNP) falling by 0.1 percent in 1981 and rising only by 0.2 percent in 1982. Agriculture also declined, and foreign trade balances with both the socialist and nonsocialist countries worsened steadily. The Set of Measures for Improving the Planning and Managerial System proclaimed in 1980 helped to generate a modest recovery in 1983 and 1984 (2.2 and 2.7 percent GNP respectively), but this declined by 1985 to a bare 2 percent, and the five-year plan had to be scaled down. The fact of the matter was that the command economy had not solved the chronic problems the 1968 reform had been designed to tackle: quantity at the expense of quality and efficiency; poor labor discipline; lack of material rewards and stifling of managerial initiative; piling up of unsold stocks; and serious shortages of some consumer goods.[7] Real wages were lower in 1985 than in 1978–1981, and serious inflation had set in.

Economic Stalemate

By 1985, the situation had become one of "stagnation, not dynamic development"[8] or one of chronic crisis, although not as catastrophic as in Poland and elsewhere and not yet so severe as to produce explosions of popular discontent. Although some of the causes were global in scope, the chief source of weakness was domestic and could only be met by economic and political reform. The dissident group Charter 77 forcefully pointed this out and called for public discussion of the problems and the alternatives. The stumbling block remained the "Lessons" of 1970 and its condemnation of economic reform. Only in March 1986 did Husák dare even to use the hitherto taboo word "reform." At last, in January 1987, the party's Central Committee approved the Principles of Reconstruction of the Economic Mechanism; six months later the Central Committee approved a draft law to assure enterprise autonomy. In March 1987, Husák, at the Central Committee plenum, stressed the need for economic reform and even spoke of the need for democratization and openness. Both these themes were echoed by Štrougal, the prime minister, who for some time had been pressing for an effective economic reform. Bil'ak, on the other hand, harped on the experience of 1968 and the continuing validity of the "Lessons," arguing that the changes now contemplated sought to strengthen socialism, not to undermine it, as in 1968. Miloš Jakeš, who had been head of the National Economic Commission since 1981, was more reserved and emphasized discipline and authority.[9]

By mid-1988, little progress seemed to have been made in implementing the planned economic reform, and the leadership was evidently seriously divided on the issue. Štrougal openly spoke before Parliament of three camps: those who refused change, those who favored it at a leisurely pace, and those who favored it immediately. He clearly favored the latter and declared that "the economic mechanism has essentially run out of its capacity for direction and motivation." His chief adviser, J. Sedlák, emphasized that "without political change, there can be no effective economic change."

Charter 77 and the Popular Mood

For some years after the occupation, a profound malaise gripped the entire country, and the great majority of people relapsed into what the internationally famous playwright and dissident Václav Havel called a state of anomie. Disillusioned by the experience of 1968 and by earlier disasters such as Munich and the Prague coup, most Czechs saw no prospect for early change and were not ready to risk their own futures through any kind of opposition or open criticism. The "social contract" assured them a meagre consumer society, without serious shortages or privations, and many supplemented this by earnings in the second economy. No one was satisfied with the way things were run, but anyone who publicly voiced concern could be locked up for damaging the interests of the state or for insulting the leaders of their own country and of friendly powers. There was a retreat into privacy and the pleasures of family life, a country *chata* (cottage) and an automobile for holiday travel. There was a growing awareness of environmental and health problems, even in official circles, as well as of the decline of the economy, but the absence of public discussion concealed the severity of these ills and frustrated proposals for change. There was perhaps some envy of the improved lot of the Hungarians, but as time went on, any hope that Husák would follow this path disappeared. Events in Poland in 1980–1981 aroused some hope but also skepticism that they would lead to any better results than those of 1968. When military rule was established, there was even a certain *Schadenfreude* that the Poles had suffered a fate similar to Czechoslovakia's and at their own hands. Meanwhile, official literature and scholarship declined to a low level, and outstanding scholars and writers vegetated on the margins of society and were only able to publish their work abroad or in *samizdat*.

Slovaks enjoyed somewhat better conditions of life, but the differences were not fundamental because the party's writ applied to the entire country. In 1968, the emphasis had been less on democratic reform than on national rights, and the attainment of federation seemed to represent a big victory. The whittling down of the reality of federalism did not alter the fact that many Slovaks could enjoy careers in Bratislava and Prague hitherto denied them.

Considerable economic and social benefits were derived from the federal policy of raising Slovakia to a level of development equal to that of the Czech lands. The mood was less one of malaise than of self-gratification and indifference to broader problems. The treatment of 1968 activists, although vindictive in some cases, was slightly more lenient, and some could resume their careers or publish their works after appropriate measures of contrition. Dissent was confined to a tiny group of persons, such as Milan Šimečka and Miroslav Kusý, who remained isolated in a sea of accommodation. Dubček worked as a machinist and artisan and apart from an outburst of protest in 1974 remained silent. He did, as he later revealed, address a number of private letters to the Central Committee and to other European Communist parties in 1975 and then in 1987.

Charter 77 and Human Rights

As time went on, there were modest but definite signs of a gradual awakening from the torpor of the early 1970s. The most notable ray of light in the gloom was Charter 77, a declaration of human rights issued in January 1977 and ultimately signed by some 1,300 persons.[10] By its own profession, Charter 77 was not a political opposition, because it had no program beyond the defense of human rights. Charter 77 grouped together persons of all political and philosophical orientations—Catholics, Protestants, reform Communists, a few democratic socialists, several Trotskyists, and others, such as Václav Havel, without a defined political position. Charter 77 did not claim to be a broad-based popular movement because most people were afraid to endanger whatever benefits they enjoyed by openly expressing sympathy, but its documents and statements were known to wide sectors through VOA and RFE broadcasts and German and Austrian television. In Slovakia, the declaration had little open support, except for a few individuals and M. Duráy, the head of a Hungarian committee for national rights in Slovakia.

Charter 77 functioned primarily as a kind of monitoring committee checking on the country's fulfillment, or nonfulfillment, of its obligations under the international human rights covenants and the Helsinki Final Act. Eventually it went beyond this into the field of politics, censuring official policies in all spheres and presenting alternative viewpoints on important issues. To its own surprise, Charter 77 survived for more than ten years and could claim to be the only voice of criticism among the mass of passive citizenry and to represent the unspoken opinion of the silent.

Abroad Charter 77 brought Czechoslovakia back on to the map of Europe, eliciting a warm initial response in an environment increasingly concerned for human rights. Although for many, Czechoslovakia remained a stagnant backwater of Europe and Charter 77 was forgotten and ignored, it gained increasing support from the attentive public, especially in West Germany, Britain, France, and, to a lesser degree, the United States. Support for its initiatives and protests against its persecution came from human rights organizations, some Western trade unions and social democratic parties, the Italian communist party, and such international bodies as the Council of Europe, the International Labor Organization, the United Nations Human Rights Commission and Committee on Human Rights, and, especially, the CSCE conferences. Western governments showed an increasing interest in Charter 77 as an alternative voice for Czechoslovak citizens and as a legitimate partner in talks with resident diplomats and other political and diplomatic representatives visiting Prague.

Charter 77 began to develop a kind of "foreign policy" of its own, although there were considerable differences among chartists on international questions. Some saw great virtue in Western strength and firmness and warned against appeasement. Others were critical of the West, for instance on Caribbean policies. Some were highly distrustful of Soviet intentions; others had greater hopes of change in the East. Charter 77 developed close relations with fellow dissidents in Poland and Hungary and with the Western European peace movements. The latter gradually came to understand the indivisibility of peace and human rights. At successive conferences of the peace movements, this basic tenet of the charter and its call for the end of the partition of Europe exerted considerable influence on the conclusions reached. A high point in the cooperation of civic initiatives in Eastern and Western Europe was reached in a joint submission to the CSCE conference in Vienna in 1986, signed by more than four hundred persons, including Poles, East Germans, Czechs and Slovaks, and Yugoslavs, and endorsed by ten organizations, including the Soviet Group to Establish Trust Between the USA and the USSR. This statement confirmed the inseparability of peace and human rights and called for a "pluralistic, democratic and peaceful community of European states, acting as equal partners." This would require, the statement said, the revival of the spirit of Helsinki and the use of the CSCE as a valuable framework of cooperation.

Other Signs of Reawakening

There were other signs of a reawakening of independent spirit among Czechs and Slovaks. Some were stimulated or promoted by Charter 77, whereas others developed spontaneously.[11] One was the wave of independent writing in *samizdat*—books, journals, and articles in the fields of history, economics, philosophy, poetry and belles letters, and drama. Of the many themes discussed one—the idea of Central Europe and of European unity—can be singled out as significant. A typewritten journal, entitled *Středni evropa* (Central Europe), appeared regularly. A number of chartists explored the concept of a united Europe and challenged Milan Kundera's pessimistic essay on the decline, if not the end, of Central Europe. Most eloquent was the appeal of Václav Havel, on the occasion of his receiving (in his absence) the Erasmus award in Rotterdam in 1985, that Western Europeans should not forget or abandon "the other Europe."[12]

Another sign of revival was evident among believers. Many Catholic and Protestant lay persons and dismissed priests and pastors were prominent in the charter movement. A Catholic dissent movement also developed, with its own widespread *samizdat*. After the election of Pope John Paul II, Cardinal Tomášek took a stronger stand against the regime by condemning the Pacem in Terris movement among the clergy and by issuing critical statements on the treatment of the church and believers. At the official Peace Assembly in Prague in 1983, he delivered a short but pungent statement on the interrelationship of peace and human rights. His relationship with Charter 77 also changed from hostility to warm sympathy. The petition for a visit of the pope, signed by many thousands and endorsed by the cardinal, was no doubt carried out with chartist help. A high point in Catholic activism was the pilgrimage of 150,000 people to Velehrad for the 1000th anniversary of Saint Methodius, to which the pope had been invited, and which represented, in the eyes of the Catholic chartist, Václav Benda, a turning point in state-society relations. Still more remarkable was the submission in December 1987 of a thirty-one point petition to the authorities, signed by some 100,000 persons and endorsed by the cardinal, that demanded the rectification of many injustices and called for the separation of church and state. The movement culminated in a nationwide pilgrimage to Svatý Vít cathedral in Prague in honor of the blessed Agnežka, soon to be canonized by the Vatican and a demonstration after high mass of some 8,000 in front of the cardinal's residence on the castle heights and under the very windows of President Husák.

Another current of independent activity manifested itself among young people, some of whom turned to religion as an alternative source of values and others to rock music and an underground youth culture. Although nonpolitical in their approach, young people showed a deep alienation from communism, and the consumer society that went with it, and sought an escape in a new lifestyle of their own. Many rock concerts were held in the suburbs of Prague and Brno at which dozens of bands played to thousands of fans. A spokesperson for this disaffected and rebellious community was the Jazz Section (JS), an agency of the official Union of Musicians that enjoyed the support of tens of thousands for their popular jazz festivals, later banned, and then for their production of publications on music, culture, and art in general. This challenge to the regime provoked the dissolution of the Jazz Section and the Union of Musicians and the sentencing to jail of Karel Srp, head of the JS, and his associates. His release in 1988 gave momentum to the efforts of the JS to regain an official status. It was clear that the regime and the official youth organization had little or no influence on young people.

Another ominous sign for the rulers was the growth of independent activity in Slovakia, which had hitherto seemed placid. There was a spreading wave of dissent among the Catholic youth and younger priests, many of whom were arrested for distributing *samizdat* literature and for participating in illegal masses in a kind of "underground church." Mass pilgrimages, attended by tens of thousands, were held every year at several places in the Slovak countryside. Kusý and Šimečka were joined by a number of other intellectuals. Discussion sessions were held, and protests of various kinds were issued. Most unusual was a statement signed by some thirty persons from cultural and artistic establishment circles that lamented the deportation of Jews from Slovakia in 1942 and requested forgiveness for the Slovak nation. An article in Bratislava *Pravda* (November 24, 1987), couched in old-style Stalinist terms, condemned this as a clerico-fascist action instigated by émigrés abroad.[13]

Gorbachev, Husák, and Jakeš

The coming to power of Gorbachev and his call for radical reform in the Soviet Union placed the rulers in Prague on the horns of a profound dilemma.[14] It was hard to expect that Gustáv Husák, who had for twenty years been fighting the ideas of the Prague Spring, would welcome Gorbachev's program, which struck notes not unlike those of the 1968 Action Program. Although Husák declared his full support of the Gorbachev line, began to mouth the slogans of *perestroika* and *glasnost'*, and called for democratization and public participation, there was little evidence that he wished to act on his own. Štrougal, on the other hand, urged the immediate introduction of economic reform and also stressed the need for closer integration of the Soviet and Czechoslovak economies. Bil'ak kept on rejecting any reevaluation of the 1968 events and exploited Gorbachev's proclamation that each country should follow its own path by warning against copying other models. Obviously, Gorbachev's bold plans aroused some fear and hidden opposition in ruling circles and even hopes that the plans would not go far or would ultimately fail.

Czech Reaction to Gorbachev

Among the people, Moscow's new course aroused mixed feelings. The public had been profoundly anti-Soviet and could hardly be expected to react with enthusiasm, or without deep suspicion, to the new sounds emanating from Moscow. The legacy of the Prague Spring was ambiguous and differed among generations. Older people, who had lived through 1968, could not help but remember the exhilaration of that time fondly; they also could not help but harbor a deep skepticism that anything good could come out of Moscow. Younger persons knew little of the real meaning of the Prague Spring and had lost faith in communism or belief in its reformability. Nonetheless, the general public, fed up with normalization and yearning for change, could not escape some hope that the events in Moscow would eventually influence the Prague scene. Gorbachev's visit to Prague in April 1987, however, poured cold water over these dreams and dispelled illusions of early change. Gorbachev made only fleeting and uncomplimentary references to 1968 and showed no sign of pressing Husák to speed up reform. The Prague leaders in turn seemed little affected by the visit and continued their circumspect course.

In chartist circles the reaction to Gorbachev was also a mixture of hopes and doubts. On the occasion of his visit to Prague, Charter 77, in its document no. 21 (March 23, 1987), welcomed his coming as an opportunity to deal with the deep crisis caused by the Soviet intervention in 1968 and called for the withdrawal of troops as evidence of the sincerity of his talk of freedom and democracy. Some reform Communists, whose number and influence in Charter 77 were declining, went further in a letter of April 5, 1987, addressed to Gorbachev. They warmly commended the "new thinking" and the "revolutionary path" he was taking and expressed a willingness to cooperate in restoring the traditional friendship of the two countries and in the restructuring of Czechoslovak society. Yet inwardly they had profound doubts that his course would be successful and that Prague would follow it. Other chartists, without former Communist ties, were even more skeptical. Charter 77 took bolder actions, such as the calling of a demonstration for peace on the anniversary of the U.N. Declaration of Human Rights, but it still had a limited public audience and no real contact with persons within party and state institutions. The group remained something much less than a political opposition and was unable to serve as a catalyst of a broader wave of dissent, as Solidarity and even the Hungarian opposition could do to a limited degree.

Apart from Charter 77, the stagnant waters were broken by hardly a ripple of movement, and Czechoslovakia seemed, in contrast to Poland and Hungary, a model of stability and order. The economic crisis was not catastrophic, as was the case in almost every other country in Eastern

Europe, and was hardly likely to produce explosive events. There was no ferment among establishment writers and scholars, no publications of books and plays raising sensitive historical issues, and no proliferation of independent groups and newspapers, as was occurring in the Soviet Union. There was only the lone voice of Miloš Kopecký, an actor, at the conference of the Union of Theater Arts, who was daring enough to call on the leaders to resign and give way to new persons who would identify themselves with a new course.[15] A request to form a society of friends of the United States was turned down by the authorities, as was the proposal to publish officially a paper with the distinguished name *Lidové noviny* (the title of a paper of the 1930s and the early postwar years), which had therefore to appear in *samizdat*. The most striking manifestation of changing moods was the increasing boldness of the church and of Catholics in manifesting their discontent with the present state of affairs and increased public activity in 1988 in the form of street demonstrations and the formation of new independent groups.

Husák's Removal

The picture of immobility at the top proved deceptive when at the end of 1987, Husák was removed from the position of general secretary and was replaced somewhat surprisingly by Miloš Jakeš, who had only joined the Presidium in 1977 as a candidate and did not become a full member until 1981. Perhaps behind the placid exterior of Gorbachev's visit were strong words of the need for change and a vying for favor by rival successors. It was impossible to know whether Jakeš had been proposed, or reluctantly accepted, by Gorbachev and difficult to tell whether Jakeš's appointment presaged an acceleration of reform or the reverse. Jakeš was cut of the same cloth as Husák and was perhaps even more hard-line in his attitudes. Like Husák, Jakeš had been associated in a subordinate capacity with Dubček, but unlike Husák, Jakeš had reportedly been one of those who sought to form a "government of workers and peasants" after the invasion. His career was that of a typical party functionary—he served under Novotný as head of the League of Youth, was deputy chairperson of the organ responsible for the local economy, and was deputy minister of the interior from 1966 to 1968. This, together with his work as head of the Commission of Party control from 1968 to 1977, suggested that his ties with the KGB were close. He had also studied for a year in Moscow in 1955, (ironically) at the same time as Dubček.

There were some mysteries surrounding the changeover. Husák had left Moscow early during the November celebrations and had stepped down only two months before the February anniversary. It seemed significant that Štrougal, who was most closely identified with reform and who visited Moscow one month earlier and had talks with Gorbachev, was passed over in the reshuffle. Equally significant were the continuance in the Presidium of Husák and Bil'ak and the absence of any other changes.

It seemed hardly credible that Štrougal, who had presided over the economy since 1970, and Jakeš, who had borne heavy responsibility in the economic field since 1981, would be capable of guiding a radical process of change. Many of the economists dismissed after 1968 were extremely skeptical that the "complex measures" riddled with ambiguities and contradictions would be adequate to establish a political environment of free discussion and wide participation regarded as a condition of successful economic reform.[16] Even an official economist, V. Komárek, expressed misgivings about the draft laws that were to accompany the "complex measures."

The December plenum did not promulgate a final version of the "Comprehensive Measures" but left this to a later decision by the government and assembly. Jakeš, after his election, referred to the reconstruction (*přestavba*) of the economy as the decisive question and called for broadened public discussion and participation, conducted, however, within the framework of the leading role of the party. He pointed to 1968–1969 as a lesson of what would happen if this were ignored. On the anniversary of the January 1968 change of leadership, *Rudé právo* underlined this, rejecting any comparison between *perestroika* today and the reform course under Dubček. The paper also condemned him as "unprincipled" and "capitulationist" when faced with antisocialist pressures. Jakeš, after his first visit to Moscow on January 11–12, 1988, reported an identity of views with Gorbachev that there was no need to revise the interpretation of 1968. Although the overall direction of the present Soviet and Czechoslovak programs were identical, each had its own specific features. The common objective was to "perfect socialism through restructuring and democratization." Jakeš laid great emphasis on the agreement reached to achieve an ever closer integration of the Czechoslovak and Soviet economies.[17]

The only person with a credible reform profile who might have replaced Jakeš was Štrougal, but he was widely distrusted as a turncoat and did not enjoy a high personal reputation. On a visit to Bonn in January, he expressed highly unorthodox views in a frank interview with a West German newspaper. He openly admitted the failure of the leadership since 1970 (including himself) to introduce an economic reform and also frankly spoke of opposition and serious differences of view within the government. Although criticizing Dubček as "weak," Štrougal expressed no very strong views on 1968 and even hinted that there might be a possibility, although again there were differences of opinion, of reconciliation with the ousted reformers.[18] His removal in 1988 indicated a hardening of the line followed by Jakeš.

The End of Dubček's Silence

Twenty years after coming into power in January 1968, Dubček emerged from a self-imposed silence of almost fifteen years with a long interview published in *L'Unità*, the Italian Communist organ, perhaps not accidentally just prior to Jakeš's trip to Moscow.[19] Dubček declared his warm and sincere support for Gorbachev's reforms, which although different from the 1968 course, contained the same basic ideas and thus confirmed their validity.

Dubček defended his own actions in some detail and saw no reason to reproach himself or to admit errors. He noted the announced support of reform by the current Prague leaders but the absence so far of concrete deeds. The military intervention in 1968, under the existing constellation of forces, could not have been avoided but would have been unthinkable under a leader such as Gorbachev. There was a need to "overcome the past," Dubček believed, to reevaluate the 1968 events, and to unify the party on the basis of a new program to be worked out through discussion by all who had something to say. Dubček declared himself ready to cooperate in any way but left it to others to decide how. He expressly noted that he was not a member or supporter of "unofficial structures," which had emerged only because they were unable to discuss their ideas publicly, and acknowledged that the various materials emanating from these structures were useful sources of information. Dubček strongly urged respect for human rights and endorsed the Soviet proposal of a conference on this subject in Moscow, at which official and unofficial representatives would be present. Interestingly, at various points, he spoke of Czechoslovakia as "belonging to Central Europe" and of its traditions of democracy, and he called for "new thinking about Europe" and the "building of a European house."

Czechoslovakia's Future

The future, even in the short run, is too opaque for predictions. It is too early to tell whether the Jakeš team will successfully carry through even a moderate economic reform while avoiding a feared spillover into the political realm. There is no desperate crisis making reform imperative at once, nor are there pressures from below that would push the regime into more decisive action. There is no evidence of independent thinking among party cadres at any level that would help to promote a change from above. In spite of some murmuring in Moscow academic circles of the need to reexamine 1968, this has been firmly ruled out in both capitals. No doubt both leaders still face the ghost of Dubček's "socialism with a human face," but there seems little likelihood of a future role for him or for his ideas of a democratic communism.

Czechoslovakia still remains a pawn on the Eastern European chessboard than can be moved toward decisive reform, paradoxically, only by Moscow, the onetime guarantor of the status quo. From the Soviet standpoint, however, the stability of Czechoslovakia, in the midst of crisis and turmoil in every other bloc country, is no doubt preferable to prodding local rulers to move more rapidly in a direction they do not favor and risk the unleashing of spontaneous forces that might escape control. The West, public and government alike, has watched Czechoslovakia with deep interest and often with exaggerated expectations but has not been able to exert great influence on the outcome. All that can be done is to study carefully the developing situation; to develop cultural, scholarly, and (eventually) economic ties; and to offer sympathy and moral support to those who express their thoughts bravely and independently.[20] But there seems little prospect that Czechoslovakia will emerge from the thrall imposed on it by the East in 1948, and again in 1968, or that anything resembling the Prague Spring will occur in the near future.

Notes

1. A. Dubček, *Rudé právo,* April 2, 1968.

2. H. Gordon Skilling, *Czechoslovakia's Interrupted Revolution* (Princeton, N.J.: Princeton University Press, 1976), pp. 849–850.

3. Ibid., pp. 295–296.

4. Vladimir V. Kusin, *From Dubček to Charter 77: A Study of "Normalisation" in Czechoslovakia, 1968–1978* (Edinburgh: University of Edinburgh Press, 1978); Vlad Sobell, "Czechoslovakia: The Legacy of Normalization," *Eastern European Politics and Societies* 2, no. 1 (Winter 1988), pp. 36–68.

5. H. Gordon Skilling, in Robert Spencer, ed., *Canada and the Conference on Security and Co-operation in Europe* (Toronto: Center for International Studies, University of Toronto, 1984), Part 2; also H. Gordon Skilling, in Robert O. Matthews and Cranford Pratt, eds., *Human Rights and Canadian Foreign Policy* (forthcoming).

6. For the following, Friedrich Levcik, "Czechoslovakia: Economic Performance in the Post-Reform Period and Prospects for the 1980's," in *East European Economic Assessment* (Washington, D.C.: GPO, February 27, 1981) Part 1, pp. 377–424; Friedrich Levcik, "The Czechoslovak Economy in the 1980's," in *East European Economies: Slow Growth in the 1980's* (Washington, D.C.: GPO, March 28, 1986), Part 3, pp. 85–108; Judy Batt, "The Past and Future of Economic Reform in Czechoslovakia," *East European Reporter* (London) 2, no. 4 (1987), pp. 24–26; and 3, no. 1 (1987), pp. 38–40. See also Kusin, *From Dubček to Charter 77,* pp. 124–134, 224–240; Sobell, "Czechoslovakia," pp. 43–49.

7. Batt, "The Past and Future," Part 2, p. 39.

8. Levcik, "The Czechoslovak Economy," pp. 96–97.

9. See *Rudé právo,* March 19, March 25, February 20, and March 20, 1987.

10. H. Gordon Skilling, *Charter 77 and Human Rights in Czechoslovakia* (London, 1981). For the later years of Charter 77, see H. Gordon Skilling, *Samizdat and an Independent Society in Central and Eastern Europe* (London: Macmillan, forthcoming).

11. For this and the following, see ibid., Chap. 4.

12. Text in English, *Praemium Erasmianum MCMLXXXVI* (Amsterdam, no publisher, 1987), pp. 44–48.

13. *Pravda* (Bratislava), November 24, 1987.

14. For the following, Sobell, "Czechoslovakia," pp. 49–68; *Eastern Europe Newsletter* 1, no. 15 (December 21, 1987) and 2, no. 2 (January 27, 1988); personal observations during a visit to Prague, April 1987. For charter documents and other materials, see *Listy* (Rome) (1987). Also see Husák, *Rudé právo,* November 3 and 9, 1987; Štrougal, *Pravda* (Bratislava), November 17, 1987; Bil'ak, *Pravda* (Bratislava) December 14, 1987.

15. *Rudé právo,* May 7, 1987, with many passages cut out. For full text, *Listy* 17, no. 4 (August 1987), pp. 5–8.

16. Charter documents no. 65 and 67, October 30 and November 11, 1987, containing responses to a questionnaire by dismissed professional economists (*Listy* 18, no. 6 [December 1987], pp. 40–46; also other comments by unofficial economists, ibid., and passim.

17. *Rudé právo,* January 4 and 12, February 12, 1988.

18. The interview was published in the *Frankfurter Rundschau,* January 22 and 26, 1988, and was reported in *Rudé právo,* January 22, 1988, with all the controversial passages omitted.

19. *L'Unità,* January 10, 1988; Slovak version, *Listy* 18, special number (January 1988).

20. William Luers, "The U.S. and Eastern Europe," *Foreign Affairs* 65, no. 5 (Summer 1987).

11

Yugoslavia: Worsening Economic and Nationalist Crisis

Viktor Meier

For decades, from the rupture with Joseph Stalin in 1948 to the years before Marshal Tito's death, Yugoslavia enjoyed considerable international prestige as an independent socialist country. Its system of self-management (chosen in 1950) was viewed by many observers as an exemplary model of a "third way" between capitalism and dogmatist socialism. Yugoslavia claimed to have "solved" its national problems, and Tito was one of the top leaders of the nonaligned movement. Many leftist-oriented intellectuals overlooked the negative sides of the Yugoslav regime in their admiration, especially for human rights policy, and some governments purposely overlooked these drawbacks for political reasons.

Today, Yugoslavia is in the midst of a deep crisis with no way out in sight. The country is struggling under the load of a 200 percent annual inflation rate and continually declining real incomes and faces a problem of deepening national divisions. Few still see Yugoslavia as a model for new economic, political, and social solutions. On the contrary, the country has become a negative symbol. Opponents of reform in socialist countries point to Yugoslavia to support their arguments, and those who ask whether socialism can be reformed at all cannot look to Yugoslavia for affirmative answers.

At first glance it seems that Yugoslavia's difficulties began at the time of Tito's death on May 4, 1980. Yet this is not the case. Its troubles had begun long before. In the year of Tito's death, Yugoslavia's net foreign debt had already reached almost $17 billion,[1] and by 1988, the debt burden had reached approximately $20 billion, with no prospect of it decreasing in the near future.

Yugoslavia's national problems were also evident at the time of Tito's death. In 1971, Tito had still been able to control the reformist Croatian crisis. But a half year before his death, he was confronted with organized demonstrations on a trip through the region of Kosovo, in which the majority of the population was Albanian, and a full-blown crisis in the Kosovo broke out at the end of March 1981. Since then, this crisis has developed into a political cancer for Yugoslavia. In other parts of the country, particularly in Serbia, it has provoked nationalistic reactions that have endangered the Yugoslav state.

Today it is evident that Tito used his authority to conceal many of Yugoslavia's problems and thus prevented the open outbreak of a crisis for a long period. This was precisely the way Emperor Franz Joseph dealt with the problems of the Habsburg monarchy. In both cases, the resulting crisis was all the worse. Tito can even be blamed for worsening conditions, particularly in the economy. In 1967, he abruptly blocked a general reform that had been decided at the Eighth Yugoslav party Congress at the end of 1964. (Tito's obstruction was even indirectly admitted at the Thirteenth party Congress in June 1986.[2]) Thus, the system of self-management initiated in 1950 never really was put into effect, and the system that did exist failed at the first shock from within the country and the world market.

In spring and summer 1988, however, there were two signs of a change in the leadership's economic views. On May 15, the Mikulić government was compelled by the International Monetary Fund (IMF) to put measures into effect of which at least one, the liberalization of many prices, led directly to some aspects of a market economy. A short time before this, Branko Mikulić had appointed a commission to work out proposals for an all-inclusive reform of the economic system. The commission did exactly this, and its proposals addressed macroeconomic policy as well as the structure of enterprises and property relations. The other source for systemic changes was the Serbian leadership under Slobodan Milošević, which even before Mikulić had submitted a reform plan. Milošević even suggested abolishing the enterprise system law of 1976, but otherwise his views remained state capitalist. In an interview with *NIN* in July 1988, he declared himself against a larger role for private property.[3] Mikulić, who was more flexible, said that the reforms must be basic ones. Considering that Mikulić had carried out an openly central planning policy as late as autumn 1987, uncertainty and mistrust arose as to whether he had genuinely changed his mind. He pleaded that his government should be judged by its present, not its past, policies.[4] Even so, we cannot yet know whether or not a process of reform has begun in Yugoslavia.

When analyzing the reasons for the failure of the Yugoslav system, in particular the economy, we must remember that the Yugoslav regime never permitted the release of the economy from political constraints, either under Tito or after his death. At all levels, the federal, republic, and municipal, functionaries feared that the party's retreat from the economy would mean the loss of political power. Typical of this attitude was a campaign personally led by Tito against managers and banks during the second half of the 1960s. Thus, the party stopped the positive economic development of the early 1960s. The oil crisis later did the rest. Following these events, Yugoslavia's economy was put in a straightjacket of absurd restrictions under the ideological influence of Edvard Kardelj and in the Law on Associated Labor of 1976 was downright atomized. As a result, the small and weak enterprises that had allegedly been created to enable the functioning of self-management were under regime control. The Yugoslav economy has to this day remained basically a function of politics, and attempts to change this have failed.

There is hardly another country in Europe with such diversity in its development, tradition, and culture as Yugoslavia. Although Communists are in power throughout the country, Yugoslavia is neither nationally nor politically united. Differences in development have never been eliminated by the socialist system, and, in fact, the socialist system has restrained progress in the more developed republics. As a consequence, the more developed republics have fallen behind their Western European neighbors, and the system has brought little progress to the lesser developed eastern and southern regions of the country. In 1985, the average monthly income of a Yugoslav was 30,541 dinars (at that time the equivalent of about $115); in Slovenia, it stood at 39,055 dinars and was rising; in Macedonia the average was only 23,021 dinars and was falling.[5]

The First Yugoslavia (1918–1941)

Interwar Yugoslavia, primarily because it was so dominated by Serbia, exposed its inner weaknesses when Adolf Hitler invaded it in April 1941, initially with little non-Serb resistance. These weaknesses had catastrophic consquences not only for the country itself, but also for Greece and for the position of the Western Allies in the eastern Mediterranean. This experience alone would justify the critical interest of the West in Yugoslavia's internal developments.

The Communists drew some consequences from Yugoslavia's problems before and during the war when they made their constitution at Jajce in 1943. A federal state with six republics was constituted, including two autonomous regions within Serbia; the borders were drawn partly on the basis of natural, partly on the basis of historic principles. But the population did not soon gain from this federalism. The only ones to profit were Communist functionaries, who based their personal power on party machineries in their own republics. Economic misery and police terror spread to all parts of the country and lasted for years. The principle of richer republics limiting their own progress in favor of the poorer ones became an openly practiced state maxim.

The south Slav peoples, who had moved together in the years before 1918 and eventually founded the Yugoslav state at the end of World War I, differed about the character and structure of their future state. Yet they shared a common interest and a common hope: Their new state, then called Kingdom of the Serbs, Croats, and Slovenes, should protect them from the menacing imperialism in their region and secure national development in peace and prosperity. Historically, the Serbs first embraced the Yugoslav idea because they felt that a small sensitively positioned state such as Serbia would not have the strength to stand its ground in the long run. But the

Serbs were not willing to give up their identity and statehood. Thus, they regarded the new Yugoslav state as a kind of enlarged Serbia.

In Croatia, the Yugoslav idea was first cultural in character. On the territory of the historic kingdom of Croatia, Slavonia, and Dalmatia, which was composed of diverse nationalities, a narrowly defined Croat national idea was bound to lead to conflicts, leading Croatians argued in the early nineteenth century. Later, during the "political" phase of Croatian Yugoslavism, the motive of protection against Hungarian and Italian demands predominated. The small Slovene nation hesitated until well into World War I and then decided that only by leaning upon Serbia and thus Yugoslavia could it save itself from being crushed between German and Italian imperialism.

When the Yugoslav state was founded, the Serbian conception prevailed. Serbia was already an established state with an army and a member of the victorious alliance in World War I. Its politicians knew what they were after, and they easily filled the framework of the new state with a concrete conception of Serbian hegemony. Thus, in Croatia, the initial positive attitude toward the new state soon changed to animosity and rejection. Croatia had never intended to give up its juridical or national identity; in this respect it demanded the same rights as Serbia. Slovenia, on the other hand, saw its interests materialized in the first Yugoslavia. For the first time in its history, Slovenia was a unified political organism. The Serbs respected this. Although the Slovenes did not agree with many aspects of the new state, Belgrade was then further away than it is today, whereas the Italians and Germans were dangerously close. As the great Slovene clerical leader Monsignor Korosec used to say, even the worst Yugoslavia was better for Slovenia than none.

The Crisis of the Second Yugoslavia

It is still too early to analyze reliably the reasons the second Communist Yugoslavia fell into a deep crisis so quickly. Spain, which was also forced to rearrange its system after the death of an authoritarian leader, managed the economic and political transition well; today it is a modern, stable, and democratic European state because it was able to depend upon well-prepared and well-functioning institutions at the time of Francisco Franco's death. In Yugoslavia, this was not the case. The Yugoslav Communists under the leadership of Tito and Kardelj continually showed their contempt for "legalism;" they claimed to be revolutionaries and not bourgeois lawyers. Shortly before his death Tito proclaimed a system of so-called collective leadership in the most important bodies of the state and the party.[6] This was forced upon an already overcomplicated political system. After much discussion, in the spring of 1981, the principle of "one-year mandates" for many important offices was added to the principle of collective leadership. As a consequence, the political institutions of the country became inhibited in their functioning and to a large extent faceless. Indeed, one aspect of the political crisis in present-day Yugoslavia is whether the common state, in the minds of its member nations, still has the significance and role it had at the time of its creation and whether it can still offer protection, a secure national life, and prosperity to all its members.

The economic crisis has not strengthened feelings of solidarity among the different republics and nations. On the contrary, the economic difficulties have led to new feelings of mutual dislike and blame. Today, Slovenia and Croatia feel they are being exploited more than ever before, and the lesser developed republics feel more than ever neglected. Efforts to reform the federal constitution in support of a "unified Yugoslav market"[7] seem illusory at best.

The lack of reform to date under the Mikulić government has followed from its dogmatic economic policy. The fate of the Stabilization Program is a case in point. At the Twelfth party Congress in June 1982, the League of Communists accepted a so-called long-term economic stabilization program that provided for far-reaching reforms, which included the introduction of a market economy and a wide range of freedom for private initiative. This program was designed by economic experts who knew their field and were authorized by the state presidency and was presented as a means to make the system of self-management function, not as a revival of capitalism. None of the experts proposed changes in the system of property rights. Party functionaries let themselves be persuaded, and the program was hailed within the government and in the public as the only possible way out of the crisis. Nevertheless, the program was not officially published as a party document; it was only announced in the introductory speech at the Twelfth party Congress.[8]

Implementation of the Stabilization Program would have demanded far-reaching reforms in the Yugoslav economic system. The Law on Associated Labor of 1976, which reflected Kardelj's ideological influence and to a great extent proved to be just as impracticable as the political system designed by him, should have been either abolished or basically revised. It would have been necessary to free business enterprises from political constraints at all levels. The government should have set up a free-market system, but this would have meant that the Communist regime would have lost much influence and power.

The government of Milka Planinc, which took office in May 1982, tried to work along the lines of the Stabilization Program. Highly qualified experts, such as the economist Alexander Bajt from Ljubljana, advised the government in this matter. The recommendations of the International Monetary Fund were also taken into account, although they did not always completely fit the complex Yugoslav reality. The government became increasingly aware that basic reforms could not be postponed much longer if there were to be any chance of getting out of the crisis. It seemed prepared to pay the political price. But as soon as the Planinc government was ready to go through with its plans, it encountered insurmountable opposition from those parts of the regime unwilling to give up political power for any reason.

The opposition to Planinc was concentrated in the state Presidium, where the dogmatic Bosnian Branko Mikulić had been put in charge of economic problems.

Only later on in May 1986, when Mikulić succeeded Planinc, did it become evident that the opposition planned an economic-political counter-revolution away from a market economy toward a planned economy. Mikulić dismissed or isolated advisers who defended a market economy and relied upon followers of "economy by agreement," a doctrine originally developed in Zagreb (although no longer promulgated there). It aimed to substitute market economy principles with a network of "social agreements." Although twenty years ago this system had been progressive in comparison to a pure command economy, by 1986 it was the most reactionary of the Yugoslav economic theories. (In fact, Yugoslav newspapers later frankly expressed their suspicion of ill-intentioned and dogmatically inspired manipulation by Mikulić and his associates.[9])

Within six months, the Mikulić government was forced to realize that its policy of "planned (controlled) inflation" had failed. It had to adjust interest rates and the dinar exchange rate to the real situation, as the IMF had demanded, as well as induce enterprises to employ more realistic accounting systems. But the government was still unable to move away from the principle of an administratively controlled economy. The program proposed by Mikulić in the fall of 1986 and the so-called anti-inflation program of the fall of 1987 were based on an administered freeze of prices and wages. In both cases, the public responded with strikes and demonstrations, first in the more developed republics and later in the lesser developed republic of Macedonia. The Slovene representatives openly voted against Mikulić's program in the Belgrade Parliament at the beginning of November 1987, together with a number of Croatian representatives, and declared that the plan would soon prove ineffective.

The National Problems

Those who still adhere to the tenets of socialism believe that the struggle in Yugoslavia is not between western and eastern republics or nations but between progressive and reactionary elements within the League of Communists.[10] This belief is perhaps engendered by a wish that the League of Communists (the party and with it all the socialist-oriented elements) should now as before alone determine Yugoslavia's future and hold the monopoly of power. Even in the early phase of the Mikulić government, there were many indications that opinions on government policies were by no means determined along national lines. Indeed, administrative measures taken by the government encountered opposition in Slovenia, Croatia, and Serbia. Even today, many opinions on economic or other issues are formed within an all-Yugoslav framework, but polarization on a republic level has increased rapidly and has become predominant in the shaping of economic policies.

Hardly anything has contributed so much to this polarization as the 1986 Foreign Exchange Law. For many years, Yugoslav enterprises were permitted to retain a portion of their foreign exchange earnings from exports. With this amount they were able to import goods according to their desires, but they could also sell their foreign currency on a "gray market" if they wished and thus increase their profits. This system was changed at the beginning of 1986 by the Planinc government, through the influence of forces that later dominated the Mikulić government and tried to push back the country in the direction of a planned economy. The International Monetary Fund was also responsible for this change through its support for economic calculations based exclusively on dinars. But the IMF proposed a centralized foreign exchange market, not a centralized administrative distribution of foreign currency incomes. When Mikulić came to power, the idea of a currency market was completely forgotten. The International Monetary Fund, which did not consult with representatives of Slovenia or Croatia, did not treat this question very precisely in its agreement with the Yugoslav government in spring 1988. It did not compel the Mikulić government to reinstate the customary foreign currency retention quotas for exporting firms, which had previously strengthened the authority of the republics and autonomous regions, but the government did decide to open a genuine foreign currency market. In the beginning, this did not work badly, even though the government frequently had to help stabilize it with newly borrowed credits. In the longer view, however, this problem is still unsolved.

After posing strong opposition at first, the Slovene representatives in the Yugoslav Parliament agreed to vote for the new foreign currency law at the end of 1985. They did so because its advocates had managed to bring this issue to a decision on a party level first, where the principle of democratic centralism still retained a certain meaning. Even the Slovene representatives felt bound by "solidarity." It was probably the last time in the history of postwar Yugoslavia that a consensus that had been reached on a party level through democratic centralism could in this manner be transferred to the state sector. Thus, a centrally administered foreign exchange control was established, giving the federal government strong administrative power that it used chiefly against the western republics.

In Slovenia, whose 10 percent of the Yugoslav population accounted for about 20 percent of the gross national product and produced 30 percent of all exports, these new measures were viewed as a raid of the lesser developed republics on Slovenia and, to some extent, on Croatia. At the end of 1987, a struggle broke out in the open. At the recommendation of their Central Committee, the Slovene representatives in the Belgrade federal Parliament agreed to the budget and to the Resolution for Economic Development of 1988 only on the condition that the Foreign Exchange Law be revised in a form acceptable to them. They partially succeeded. The Slovenes had a strong case because the Foreign Exchange Law had made exports to countries with convertible currencies more difficult. In summer 1987, Yugoslavia stood at the brink of insolvency, and this reoccurred in spring 1988. In late fall 1987, when Yugoslavia had to begin negotiations through the International Monetary Fund for a general moratorium on its foreign debt, interest repayments on its foreign debt had reached more than 45 percent of the yearly foreign currency earnings of the country.[11]

The Political Consequences of the Economic Crisis

Political polarization in the country ran parallel to the economic disputes. Beginning in 1958, dissatisfaction with income distribution in Slovenia spread from the population to the Communist functionaries. In the years of the Croatian crisis (1970–1971), political disagreements arose in Slovenia as well. In the course of time, the specific circumstances of the 2-million-strong Slovene nation made themselves felt: their Central European civilization and their position on the borders of two Western countries, Austria and Italy. The Slovenes did not compare their situation to Bulgaria or Romania but to their neighbors in the West. They longed for a form of socialism that would permit a standard of living in line with objective possibilities; not a socialism that only allowed for a "fair distribution of poverty," as Slovene leader Milan Kučan put it.[12]

This concept of "different socialism," which Slovenia and party leader Kučan supported, called for political democratization in addition to market economy policies. Kučan labeled this the creation of a "civil society" not totally state dominated. This term included the dissident alternative Slovenian youth movements as well and was directed at certain groups within the Yugoslav army that sharply attacked "alternative" ideas taken over from the West, such as the introduction of civilian service in place of military service. Slovene socialism is searching for "dialogue." (The present Slovene leaders do not intend their "different socialism" to be interpreted as separatism; on the contrary, they are convinced that Slovenia can improve its conditions only if conditions in the whole of Yugoslavia improve. This is the spirit in which Slovene conceptions of socialism are meant to influence economic policymaking and Yugoslav foreign policy toward the West.[13])

The political polarization that resulted from these Slovene concepts was the consequence of unconcealed and partly irrational hostility toward them coming from other republics (in particular Serbia) and from the ranks of Yugoslav unitarists. Part of the Serbian press considered the Slovenes Enemy Number Two after the Albanians long before the nationalist and dogmatist Serbian faction of Slobodan Milošević came to power in Serbia in the fall of 1987.

This new situation was very different from the interwar period when Slovenes and Serbs usually stood together and their "enemy" was in Croatia. Now the Slovenes no longer shared Serbian attitudes toward the Kosovo and the Albanian "threat"; on the contrary, they opposed Serbian calls for repression there. To Slovenes, the nationalist tirades coming from Belgrade, with which unconcealed traits of old Serbian hegemony were mingled, were beginning to pose a danger to Slovene interests and a threat to the existence of the Slovene nation. This danger seemed all the greater because it also came from parts of the Yugoslav army, in which the Serbs and Montenegrins made up about 60 percent of the officer corps.[14] (The Yugoslav army still insists that Serbo-Croat remain its sole language.)

This feeling of national threat gave rise to a discussion in Slovenia, particularly among intellectuals, about Slovenia's future direction. Although even in these circles no one directly questioned Slovenia's being a part of Yugoslavia, they nevertheless demanded that the nation's independence and its contacts to the West be guaranteed in the common Yugoslav state. As the Slovene author Kermauner said, "Certain people in Yugoslavia should take care that one day the Slovenes will not feel they are 'in Yugoslavia,' but will feel instead they are 'under' Yugoslavia."[15] In spring 1987, Slovene intellectuals published a "national program" in the periodical *Nova revija,* in which they stressed that Slovenia had not given up its right of self-determination when it joined Yugoslavia.

The Slovenes have emphasized their ties to the West through an organization of regional cooperation in the area of the eastern Alps called Alpen-Adria. This organization includes Bavaria, parts of Austria, of Italy, of Yugoslavia (Slovenia and Croatia), and recently even of Hungary. In Slovenia, much more political importance is often attached to this organization of regional cooperation than it really can have. Furthermore, the Slovenes now consider Slovene minorities living in Italy and Austria as part of a "common Slovene cultural area." This is not a matter of irredentist demands, as it was in the past, but of an intention to demonstrate that Slovenia has a foot in the West as well.

In March 1988, the crisis in Slovenia reached a new high point. Insofar as we know, on March 25 the so-called Military Council met in Belgrade under the chair of then minister of defense Branko Mamula and declared that agitation was going on in Slovenia against the army and the Yugoslav state to the point that a counterrevolutionary atmosphere reigned there. By direction of the Military Council and without the knowledge of party and government authorities, on the following day the commandant of the Ljubljana military district visited the Slovene minister of the interior to inquire what the Slovene leadership would do if, after arrests among the dissident Slovene intellectuals, "the people would go into the streets." The Slovene minister broke off the discussion and informed his political leadership. The head of the Slovene party, Kučan, and the Slovene representative in the Yugoslav state Presidium, Stane Dolanc, refused to discuss such a problem. On March 29, in a sharp speech in the Presidium of the Yugoslav federal party, Kučan rejected such "autocratic" judgments about the situation in Slovenia and the conclusions drawn from them. He also pointed out the international consequences of such military measures. Thus, the threatening military intervention against Slovenia was prevented for the time being, but the background of the whole affair still remains unclear. The army took its revenge a little later when it arrested (and later convicted) three Slovene journalists and a noncommissioned officer and put them before a military court, charged with having betrayed secret military documents with the intent to publish them. It seems that these documents also had to do with Slovenia.[16]

As to political democratization, the dividing lines for a long time were by no means strictly identical to republican borders. There was even less East-West contrast within the country than with respect to economic reforms. Croatia, along with Bosnia-Hercegovina, had long been under repressive rule whereas relative liberalism was already blossoming in Slovenia. Croatia did not begin to experience a period of political relaxation until the summer of 1986 following personnel changes among the leadership. (The newspapers and periodicals from Zagreb, *Vjesnik* and *Danas,* are, together with those from Slovenia, among the most liberal in Yugoslavia.) Macedonia had for a long time enjoyed a relatively liberal atmosphere. Only after the conflict with the Albanians living in that republic escalated did conditions there worsen somewhat. For years, newspapers and periodicals from Belgrade were remarkably liberal in their coverage of Yugoslav internal affairs, in particular *Politika* and *NIN.* The press in Belgrade had, however, always been strongly dependent on the party leadership of the republic of Serbia, which for a time seemed to respect the traditional liberal atmosphere that existed in Belgrade among intellectuals.

This changed fundamentally with the Eighth Plenum of the Central Committee of the Serbian Communist party at the end of September 1987. There a group led by party chief Slobodan Milošević succeeded in politically isolating Ivan Stambolić, then head of the republic of Serbia, and eventually pushed him and his followers out of office. Milošević's group made clever use of the resentment in Serbia about events in the Kosovo. They linked national emotions to political dogmatism and thus were able to mobilize the complete Serbian party apparatus, especially the functionaries outside Belgrade, against the liberally inclined capital. This purge of the party and state authorities was carried out under the slogan "Through differentiation to unity."[17] At the same time, a purge and *Gleichschaltung* (making uniform) of the Serbian press occurred, urged on by slogans that had not been heard in Belgrade since the Stalinist era and that claimed the first duty of the press was to "mobilize the masses for their duties."

The Cancer of Kosovo

The question of the Albanians in the Kosovo has poisoned relations among the Yugoslav nations like no other problem since World War II and is at the core of Yugoslavia's political crisis. In interwar Yugoslavia, the problem of the ethnic Albanian majority there was not so clear. Then, only the Serbian, Croat, and Slovene nations were important. The Montenegrins were considered minor relatives of the Serbs, the Macedonians were to be freed of their "Bulgarian errors" and made into good Serbs, the Albanians were suppressed, and the Moslems in Bosnia and the Sandžak were considered, at best, a religious group but were never acknowledged as a nation.

After 1945, the political spectrum was broadened as a result of wartime ethnic slaughter. The Macedonians became a republic, and the Montenegrins could shape their national consciousness as they wished within their own republic. The Moslems in Bosnia were long uncertain of their position as a nation, but Bosnia-Hercegovina formed its own republic and the Moslems there voted in the 1960s to become a nation of their own. (As more than 40 percent of the population, they are the largest group in Bosnia-Hercegovina. They speak Serbo-Croatian, but as they possess their own cultural heritage, they can be classified neither as Serbs nor as Croats.)

The problem of the Albanians in Yugoslavia was, and is, complex. The two southern areas of Kosovo and Metojia, which today form the autonomous region of Kosovo (Albanian: Kosova) in the republic of Serbia, were in the Middle Ages the center of the historic Serb Kingdom. The Serbian orthodox patriarchate was in Peć. Only a few kilometers away from Prizren lie the ruins of the monastery in which Czar Dušan, the great Serbian ruler from the middle of the fourteenth century, lay buried. In 1389, a great battle took place in Kosovo Polje, near Priština, now the Kosovo's capital, in which the Serbs were defeated by the Turks and ceased to exist as an independent nation for more than four hundred years.

At that time, the majority of the inhabitants of Kosovo were Serbian. (Traces of old Albanian settlements can be found only in the area around Prizren.) The Albanians did not arrive in large numbers in the Kosovo until the late Ottoman Empire, in the eighteenth or nineteenth century. They were largely Roman Catholics from northern Albania, but they converted to Islam after their arrival in the Kosovo. Even in 1944, the Albanians in the Kosovo made up only 60 percent of the population; the rest were Serbs, Montenegrins, Turks, gypsies, Vlachs, and Slavic-speaking Moslems. Many Turks emigrated to Turkey in 1953–1954. In the 1981 census, the Albanians were about 1.23 million, or 77.5 percent, and the Serbs and Montenegrins together were 237,000, or 14.7 percent of the population.[18] For decades, the Albanian population in Yugoslavia has had a very high birth rate (24 per thousand in the Kosovo, according to *Politika* estimates, which was higher than in other parts of Yugoslavia[19]). Altogether the Albanian population in the whole of Yugoslavia in 1981 numbered 1.73 million as compared to a population of 3 million in Albania.

The Albanians in the Kosovo, Macedonia, and Montenegro did not voluntarily join Yugoslavia. (The Albanians are an Indo-European ethnic and linguistic group. They regard themselves as descendants of the ancient Illyrians. Their language is Indo-European but very different from the Indo-European languages in Europe.) As they were predominantly Moslem, it was more difficult for them to develop a national identity and the idea of a state of their own under the Ottoman Empire than it was for the Christian peoples of the Balkans. The Albanians felt threatened by the new Balkan nations in the nineteenth century. Thus, their first political organization, the League of Prizren, formed in 1878, wanted to keep the Ottoman Empire in Europe as long as possible and merely to demand autonomy within its framework. In this fashion, they hoped to maintain the unity and integrity of the Albanian nation as long as possible.

After the first Balkan War in 1912, present-day Albania became an independent state with support of the European powers, but Kosovo and other regions that had long been objects of Serbian national aspirations were annexed to Serbia and Montenegro. The Albanians of Kosovo defended themselves by force of arms, and in 1912 and 1913 many Albanians were killed in massacres. Under the banner of Serbian hegemony, the new Yugoslav state at first took no heed of the Albanians in the Kosovo as a nation. They were discriminated against by administrative measures, and neither Albanian schools nor Albanian institutions existed. Albanian Catholic priests were shot by Serbian gendarmes, and Albanian was not spoken by the state authorities or in the law courts. The result was that the Albanians of Kosovo and western Macedonia welcomed the Italian occupation in April 1941 as a sort of liberation. They were even more satisfied when two months later Benito Mussolini united the largest part of Kosovo and western Macedonia with already Italian-occupied Albania into Greater Albania. As Svetozar Vukmanović-Tempo, one of the leading Yugoslav Communist functionaries working there at the time later wrote, the Albanians in Yugoslavia for the first time were a recognized nation.[20] The situation in Albania proper was completely different, however; there the population considered the Italian occupation (begun in spring 1939) a foreign occupation and a national oppression.

The Communists would probably have never succeeded in creating a powerful organization in Kosovo during World War II if it had not been for the course of the war after 1942, particularly the return to Kosovo of former refugees who had taken refuge in Albania, developed Communist ideas, and were sent back by the Albanian Communist party. (This is an important point because under the influence of the Serbian campaign against everything Albanian, these people, above all Fadil Hoxha, the "grand old man" of the Albanian Communists in the Kosovo, are being accused today of having come back to the Kosovo as Albanian agents and pursued nationalist and separatist policies there.[21]) Had these people not left the question of the borders open at the conference of Bujan in January 1944, it would have been even more difficult for the Communists to pacify the Albanians after the war. Then, all sides believed that future close cooperation between Yugoslavia and Albania under similar Communist regimes would blur the question of the borders.

When the nationalist Albanians of Kosovo tried to prevent their reincorporation into Yugoslavia at the end of 1944, again with armed force, Tito introduced military administration there. Yet the real Serb political settling of accounts with the Albanians, the return to forms of national oppression, came only later in the 1950s. Tito's minister of the interior and head of police, Alexander Ranković, a Serb, was responsible for this, although Tito certainly knew of it. In 1953, some Albanians were forced to declare themselves Turks and to emigrate to Turkey. The Serbian-controlled police terrorized the Kosovo in the winter of 1955–1956 under the pretext of searching for weapons, in the course of which about 30,000 Albanians were physically mistreated and about 100 were killed.[22] A number of trials took place, some even of Albanian Communist functionaries. The outside world heard little about these events at the time. When Ranković was dismissed in 1966 and the Kosovo police came partly under Albanian control, observers wondered why two years later Albanians were demonstrating in Priština and in other places. The answer can be found in events of the 1950s. Today, Serbian publicists around Milošević are attempting to rehabilitate the police who took part in these events.

Communist Yugoslavia thought that it had solved the question of Kosovo in 1944 when it established the autonomous region Kosovo-Metojia (later Kosovo) within the republic of Serbia. The Vojvodina in northern Serbia, a second such region, had a Hungarian minority, but its majority was Serb. The autonomous regions became politically more important as Yugoslav federalism developed. In the constitution of 1974, the autonomous regions were almost equal to the republics, except they did not have state character and were slightly less represented in the top federal, state, and party bodies. There was a general agreement that the autonomous regions were to be viewed like the republics, as "constitutive factors" of the second Yugoslavia.

The existence of two regions within its territory put Serbia in a special situation. It felt constrained in its normal functioning as a republic, but on the other hand it did not want to be only a "small Serbia"—that is, a Serbia without its autonomous regions. The Albanian nationalist demonstrations in Kosovo at the end of March and the beginning of April 1981 marked the flare up of this issue. The government of Serbia was forced to realize that it had no legal right to intervene in the Kosovo. This caused vehement Serbian demands to revise the republican as well as the federal constitution, so that Serbia could have the "right to function as a unified republic." In early summer 1988, when the debate about the reform of the federal and Serbian constitutions reached an acute stage, the Serb leadership under Milošević intensified its agitation (for a limitation of the powers of the autonomous regions) to a degree not previously known in Yugoslavia. On July 9, 1988, Serbs from the Kosovo, probably at Milošević's initiative, tried to demonstrate in Novi Sad, the capital of the autonomous region of the Vojvodina. The purpose of this maneuver was to put pro-Serb pressure on the Vojvodina leadership because the Kosovo leadership always cited the Vojvodina's opposition when it opposed the same demands from Serbia. In the Vojvodina the idea of autonomy is embraced by the Serb majority there. However, on October 6, 1988, Milošević succeeded, by means of an organized mass demonstration in its capital, Novi Sad, to force the Vojvoidina leadership to resign. Thus the "autonomist line" was defeated there.

The key problem that kindled Serbian emotions and allowed them to become irrational and fanatic was, and is, the emigration of Serbs and Montenegrins out of the Kosovo. According to the Serbs, they and the Montenegrins were systematically forced by the "Albanian nationalists" to sell their homes and emigrate to Serbia, and in the course of a systematic campaign to create a "pure ethnic Kosovo," they were threatened and physically attacked, their wives and daughters allegedly raped, their harvests destroyed, and their cattle slaughtered. This campaign, according to the stereotyped Serbian version, was possible because the republic of Serbia is prevented from direct intervention and the federal authorities do not act upon Serbian complaints.

A realistic view of the situation indicates that there were occasional excesses against Serbs and Montenegrins and that Serbs sometimes did not have an easy life in the midst of an Albanian majority. Emigration out of the Kosovo, begun many years ago, increased after 1966. A letter in the August 22, 1982, issue of *NIN* stated that according to the Statistical Office of Serbia, the emigration of the Serbs and Montenegrins out of the Kosovo between 1961 and 1981 (before the turmoil) was 112,620.[23] Two years later, in the fall of 1984, *NIN* reported that about 20,000 Serbs and Montenegrins had left the Kosovo since the "counter-revolutionary events" of 1981. *NIN* also reported that the number of émigrés in 1983 was 4,377.[24] By 1988, the number should have dropped to about 3,000 yearly. The number of Serbs remaining in the Kosovo has thus declined.

These statistics show that 1981 was not such a blow to the Serbs and Montenegrins in the Kosovo as Serbian agitation maintained. Indeed, the causes of the emigration must be viewed realistically. Even if the excesses are not taken into consideration, there are still enough reasons for Serbs to emigrate from the Kosovo, according to a Serbian politician in the regional government in Priština.[25] Albanians and Serbs do not share the same culture or religion, their customs are different, and many Serbs refuse to live in alien surroundings. The Serbian elite has diminished, as has Serbian intellectual life in general. In addition, real estate prices in Kosovo are three times that of elsewhere in Yugoslavia, so that a Serb who emigrates to other parts of the country can buy more land.

The Danger of Serbian Hegemonism

The fears and emotions of the Serbs in the Kosovo were manipulated and used by people in the Serbian leadership in a struggle for power. In summer 1987, the Serbian party leader and present leader of the ruling group in Serbia, Slobodan Milošević, mobilized the Serbs in Kosovo in his struggle against the Albanian party leadership under Azem Vlasi in the Kosovo and against his political rivals in Serbia, led by the former head of the republican presidency, Ivan Stambolić. Milošević also used the Serbs in the Kosovo to blackmail the Yugoslav federal authorities. His aim was to make the Kosovo a federal issue and to force the federation to solve it according to Serbia's wishes. Milošević's Serbia was, and is, in favor of "energetic action" by the police and the army and, if possible, de facto abolition of the autonomy of the regions, especially with respect to the police. Milošević hoped to gain this through revision of the federal constitution and federation pressure to revise Serbia's constitution.

After the victory of Milošević's faction in Serbia in September 1987, the rest of the Yugoslav federation saw clearly how the Kosovo could endanger

Yugoslavia. Today the question is not what Yugoslavia should do with the Kosovo, but rather what the Kosovo did to Yugoslavia, as the Zagreb periodical *Danas* remarked before the Eighth Plenary Session of the Serbian Central Committee.[26] The question of Kosovo, according to *Danas*, created dangerous feelings of frustration and a backward nationalism in Serbia that reflected the style of old Serbian epic poetry.

On October 25, 1987, the Yugoslav state Presidium decided on federal intervention in the Kosovo. Special police units were ordered to Priština, and the participation of federal officials in the Administration for Security and Justice of Kosovo was begun.[27] This intervention made the question of Kosovo a federal issue, but in another fashion than the Serbian extremists had wanted, for it was directed in the first place against the political agitation of Milošević and his associates. Suddenly this agitation ceased. Kosovo calmed down somewhat, and the local Albanian party leadership, headed by Azem Vlasi, which had given in so much to the Serbian agitation that it therefore did not enjoy high prestige among the Albanian population of the Kosovo, pulled itself together to demonstrate stronger resistance.

The federal intervention in Kosovo did not change the Serbian agitation. Milošević's activities worried the other regions in Yugoslavia and affected Yugoslavia's relations to foreign countries. Milošević tried to win allies in the other republics for his course. The people around him even attempted to present their dictatorial approach as a course of action for the whole of Yugoslavia.[28] Many people saw in such attitudes a revival of Serbian hegemonism and centralism similar to the period before World War II. The previously liberal newspaper *Politika* became a mouthpiece for Serbian frustration and aggressiveness against the outside world. The Federal Republic of Germany was written about as if it had revived the anti-Serbian policies of Nazi Germany in World War II.[29]

Milošević is now concentrating on winning the army leadership to his side. Former general of staff Gračanin was appointed president of the republic of Serbia in place of Ivan Stambolić, who was dismissed. Although Gračanin is not a political personality, he has readily echoed Milošević and his associates. Another general, Tito's former minister of defense, Ljubičič, has long been a member of the Serbian leadership. After the "purge" in *NIN*, articles appeared stating that the Yugoslav army was the only institution in the country that showed the courage to learn from mistakes.[30]

The Political Dimensions of the Yugoslav Army

This raises the issue of the army's position in Yugoslavia. The Yugoslav army is a political one: Article 240 of the constitution specifically assigns to the army, among other tasks, the protection of the "social order as established by the Constitution." Its representatives are members of the top state and party authorities. The former minister of defense, Admiral Mamula, long tried to keep the Yugoslav army supranational, but this became increasingly difficult, especially because of the majority of Serbs and Montenegrins in the officer corps. After the 1981 turmoil in the Kosovo, trials with obvious anti-Albanian features were held in different garrisons. When in 1986 and 1987 demands arose in Slovenia for the introduction of civilian service and the use of the Slovene language in the army, charges were promptly raised against Slovene recruits for alleged "national agitation." Following a grave incident in the barracks of Paračin in the summer of 1987, when a soldier of Albanian nationality shot four comrades and then committed suicide, Mamula was also forced to go along with anti-Albanian statements; in January 1988, ten Albanian soldiers were tried for allegedly assisting the assassin at Paračin. The present minister of defense, General Kadijevič, appointed in May 1988, is considered a professional officer. But there are political ties going back to Tito's time among the army, police, and politics, through the army's secret intelligence service, the KOS, that are very difficult to penetrate and that often make it unclear whether this or that action should be ascribed to the army or to politics.

The interplay of Serbian nationalism and hegemonism with Serbian-inspired centralist tendencies in the army gives more reason for great concern in the other Yugoslav republics. A centralist coup of the army would not solve any problems in Yugoslavia, as the army has neither a program for the economy nor for the solution of the national question. It would only greatly intensify these problems. Those elements would prevail in economic policymaking that now, through antimarket policies, are mainly responsible for the failure of every effort to stabilize the economy. Yugoslavia would then definitely be split into a western and eastern part; nationalist persecution and excesses against certain nationalities, especially Albanians, would then probably become real; and a new political beginning thereafter would be extremely difficult. Apart from this, the last bit of Yugoslavia's international prestige would be lost.

The alternative to this negative development would be a Yugoslavia that functions according to its actual character. Because the differences among the parts of the country are so large that common solutions sometimes can hardly be found within the framework of the federation or result only in conflicts, the alternative is for the republics to go their own way in numerous questions even more than they do already. This would give rise to a "confederative" legal system. Real autonomy for Kosovo could find its place therein as well. The term *confederative* often causes great clamor, at present especially in Serbia,[31] but its critics only expose their hidden centralist and hegemonic intentions. They try constantly to change the Yugoslav constitution to strengthen the federation, but this attempt is not especially successful. Slovene politicians explicitly declare that "more federal life should not in the least imply more rights for federal authorities."[32]

In the early autumn 1988 these mutually intensifying economic and political crises reached even greater intensity. Inflation continued to rise: By November 1988 it was 217 percent annually, although the Yugoslav agreement with the IMF, concluded on March 25, 1988, was followed by a Yugoslav commitment to lower inflation. (However, Yugoslav actions following a May 1987 Yugoslav-IMF agreement to lower inflation to 95 percent actually caused inflation to double by 1988.) This resulted in a drastic further fall in the standard of living. For example, some 60 percent of Yugoslav workers live at or below the minimum guaranteed income. The living standard has fallen by nearly 40 percent since 1982, and is now back to the mid-1960s level. Real wages fell 24 percent in 1988 alone. Is it any wonder that this produced strikes, demonstrations, and an intensifying crisis?

It was thus the easier for Milošević, who to the Serbs had become their charismatic leader, to make use of this widespread economic dissatisfaction to intensify their agitation to limit the autonomy within the Serbian Republic of the Vojvodina and Kosovo regions. He did so by arranging constantly greater Serb demonstrations, directed against what the Serbs alleged to be Albanian mistreatment of Serbs in the Kosovo and Albanian nationalist influence on party and government institutions there, which demanded limits on the autonomy of the Kosovo and the Vojvodina, and massive purges in their leaderships, and Serbian constitutional changes to expand Serbian police power in these provinces.

By early October 1988, however, it became increasingly clear that Milošević's objectives went much farther: They were to use Serbian-inspired centralization at the federal level to increase Serbian power in Yugoslavia. In the amendments to the Yugoslav federal constitution, to which the republics and autonomous regions had agreed, and which were proclaimed on the national holiday, November 29, 1988, Milošević and other centralist elements did not succeed in overthrowing the basic principle of the Yugoslav federal state, "consensus." The effort of the Serbian leadership, therefore, had to be to gain a majority role in the federal authorities through the control of the two Serbian autonomous regions, the Vojvodina and the Kosovo, plus the support of other "friendly" republics.

After the October 6 "victory" in the Vojvodina a similar overthrow of the leadership was tried in Montenegro. During the demonstrations the slogan "Montenegro is Serbia" appeared. The Montenegran leadership resisted the pressure, with the support of the federal party leadership, but it was clearly weakened. Probably the Montenegran population was also sympathetic to Milošević. The federal party leadership first showed its resistance to Milošević, who threatened to overthrow republic and regional leaderships through mass demonstrations.

Milošević suffered a political defeat, albeit perhaps only a temporary one, at the seventeenth plenum of the Yugoslav party central committee in Belgrade from October 17–19, 1988. In a so-called "vote of confidence" with respect to members of the federal party leadership, a leading associate of Milošević—Ckrebić—failed to get an (expected) vote of confidence. However, the Yugoslav central committee gave Milošević a weapon against the Kosovo leadership by declaring that the latter carried the "main responsibility" for the alleged worsening of the Kosovo situation and of the relations between the two nationalities there. Despite expectations, the plenum did not otherwise announce any new reform measures. On the contrary, in order to lower popular unrest, the Mikulić government de facto suspended the salary limitations agreed upon with the IMF.

As was expected, Milošević did not allow himself to be discouraged by his setback, but continued his agitation, especially vis-à-vis the Kosovo leadership. Its removal, he believed, would clear the way for the centralist constitutional reforms within the Serbian republic, which were scheduled to take place after the federal constitutional reforms. Milošević felt justified by the declarations of the party central committee and the central party leadership to demand the resignation of the Kosovo party leadership in Priština, and above all of its two most important members, Kaqusha Jashari and Azem Vlasi, in the name of the "democratic centralism" that the party still recognized.

His attempt ended with demonstrations in Priština between November 17 and 20, 1988, of up to 100,000 Albanians to protest the forced resignation of their leaders and the intended centralist reforms in Serbia, which, they thought, would practically end the autonomy of the Kosovo. These demonstrations were remarkably well organized. They showed that it was no longer possible for the Yugoslav federal leadership to try to "quiet" Milošević at the expense of the allegedly weaker Albanians or Slovenes. The enormous demonstration in Belgrade on November 19, 1988, for which Milošević assembled a million Serbs, therefore did not become a victory celebration but rather a manifestation of disorientation.[33]

Two roads still lay open for Yugoslavia in 1988: the road to democratic rationality and the road to emotional, hegemonic, and violent solutions similar to those that ruined the first Yugoslavia. In the opinion of most of the other republics, the change in Serbia did not enhance, but also did not destroy, the prospect of democracy and rationality. Moreover, many officers in the army are aware of the danger of a military coup. The present, second Yugoslavia is more complex than the first, within the economy as well as its national structures. However, among the "new" nations there is one, the Albanians, that is not of Slavic origin and on account of this only partially feels it belongs to a state defined as the "State of the Southern Slavs" that addresses the "Slavs" in its national anthem. Thus, the present situation is different and more complex than it was before 1939, but clearly dangerous.

Yugoslavia's Foreign Policy

As to Yugoslav foreign policy, hardly anyone in Yugoslavia wishes to completely give up the framework of the Yugoslav state. The orientation of the state toward the outside world seems to have remained unaffected by the inner confusion. Yugoslavia's neutrality and nonalignment are in accordance with the wishes of the population and are contained in the fifty-fifty formula Winston Churchill and Joseph Stalin devised in 1944 when defining the "reciprocal influence" of East and West. Yugoslavia's present position is therefore an established component of the order of postwar

Europe. The struggle today is whether Yugoslavia's nonalignment should be oriented more toward Europe or, as under Tito, toward the Third World.

After 1948, while Tito felt militarily threatened by the Soviet Union, Yugoslavia accepted Western aid and even established an indirect connection to the North Atlantic Treaty Organization through agreements with Greece and Turkey. Following the reconciliation with Khrushchev in 1955, Tito for a short period embraced the idea of an equally matched partnership in a newly arranged "socialist family." But after his disappointment in respect to the 1956 Hungarian events, Tito shifted his activities to the nonaligned movement. He seemed to regard this movement mainly as an instrument to keep the newly arising states of the Third World from committing the "capitalist error" and to lead them to socialism. He probably hoped that the Soviet Union would then take him seriously. But Tito took up an attitude of real nonalignment only after the Soviet intervention in Czechoslovakia in 1968. He then sharply opposed the Soviet theory that nonaligned countries were a "natural ally of the socialist camp."

Mikhail Gorbachev's visit to Yugoslavia in March 1988 showed that hardly anybody in Yugoslavia considered promoting an "Eastern orientation" there. Soviet interests in Yugoslavia, similar to those of the Western world, seem small and limited to the upkeep of the country's nonaligned position. Yugoslavia's internal order has never been object of the division of "influences." For more than forty years, the West has considered a Communist regime in Yugoslavia compatible with the European postwar system. The Soviet Union may therefore one day have to accept a non-Communist Yugoslavia or a strong decentralization of the Yugoslav state. Domestic discussions of foreign policy therefore do not focus on the question of "Western or Eastern" orientation, but rather upon the question of whether the hitherto existing policy of nonalignment with its strong bonds to the Third World is still up to date, or whether a stronger orientation toward Europe may not be more adequate. Yugoslavia's foreign policy is in this sense incorporated in the advancing polarization within the country, as the demand for an orientation toward Europe is voiced with increasing impatience, especially in the western republics.

Notes

1. "Bilten Narodne Banke SFRJ," *NIN*, March 24, 1985.
2. Speech by Vidoje Žarković, *Politika*, June 25, 1986.
3. *NIN*, July 3, 1988.
4. Interview for Radio Sarajevo, *Politika*, July 9, 1988.
5. *NIN*, June 9, 1985, cited from *Südost-Europa* (Munich), nos. 7/8 (1985).
6. *Borba*, November 10, 1978.
7. "Najvažnije promene u ustavu," *Politika*, December 30, 1987.
8. Introductory Speech by Dušan Dragosavać, *Politika*, June 26, 1982.
9. *NIN*, in *Frankfurter Allgemeine*, July 25, 1987.
10. Stane Dolanc, *Tanjug-Bulletin*, January 4, 1988.
11. *Frankfurter Allgemeine*, December 22, 1987.

12. *Frankfurter Allgemeine,* May 12, 1987.
13. Interview with Milan Kučan, *Frankfurter Allgemeine,* November 3, 1987.
14. Ibid.
15. *Frankfurter Allgemeine,* October 19, 1987.
16. "Wie der General den Slowenen Hilfe anbot," *Frankfurter Allgemeine,* June 14, 1988.
17. *Politika,* September 25 and 26, 1987 (Eighth Session of the Communist Control Committee of Serbia).
18. *Kosovo—Faits et chiffres* (official publication).
19. *Politika,* December 6, 1987.
20. Svetozar Vukmanović-Tempo, *Memoari* (Belgrade) 1 (1971), p. 332.
21. See "Separatistička koncepcija", *NIN,* November 8, 1987.
22. Hajredin Hodža, *Afirmacija albanske nacionalnosti u Jugoslaviji* (Priština, 1984), p. 71.
23. "Zablude . . . , " *NIN,* August 22, 1982, p. 10.
24. *NIN,* September 23, 1984.
25. *Frankfurter Allgemeine,* December 2, 1986.
26. "Najveća avantura Jugoslavije," *Danas,* August 25, 1987.
27. *Frankfurter Allgemeine,* October 27, 1987.
28. Former Army General Pantelić to the Party Committee in Belgrade, *Frankfurter Allgemeine,* January 22, 1988.
29. "Uputstvo za upotrebu Srbije," *Politika,* December 15, 1987.
30. "Armija i kriza," *NIN,* January 10, 1988.
31. "Uputstvo za upotrebu Srbije," *Politika,* December 15, 1987.
32. Milan Kučan, see *Frankfurter Allgemeine,* September 17, 1987.
33. "Die Universität als 'Kopf der Schlange,'" *Frankfurter Allgemeine,* February 12, 1988.

12

Conservatism and Nationalism in the Balkans: Albania, Bulgaria, and Romania

J. F. Brown

The Balkan Historical Background

Nations seeking states make one of the dominant themes of modern history. But this theme has almost invariably had its corollary: The state, once found, disappoints the nation. This is usually so for two closely interacting reasons: (1) the state is not big or rich enough; and (2) not all the nation is inside it. National fulfillment then becomes nationalist frustration. The new political map is dotted with irredenta. The emergent states grow up in an atmosphere of mutual hatred and suspicion.

Nowhere is this truer than in the Balkans, among the states that emerged from the dismemberment of the moribund Ottoman Empire in the last century. The process began with Serbian independence early in the nineteenth century and ended with the establishment of the Albanian state early in the twentieth. In between, Greece, Romania, and Bulgaria acquired independence.[1] All these states owed their independence to three factors: (1) Ottoman decline; (2) their own exertions; and (3) great power diplomacy. In 1918, after all the Balkan states had achieved independence of sorts, they were exposed to a new factor in international relations—the Wilsonian principle of national self-determination—which gave priority to ethnographic considerations in the formation of states. The principle was based on a simple U.S. notion of justice, which, however, more than met its match in the European complexities to which it was applied. It solved some problems, aggravated others, and created new ones.

The independence, once achieved, was preciously prized and doggedly defended. But the new situation in the Balkans was just as unsettling as the old, was ripe for mischief, and was beckoning interference. The daunting domestic concerns of the new states were usually neglected for the sake of defense or external ambition. New "little imperialisms," to use Hugh Seton-Watson's expression, replaced the big old ones. Neighbors were mostly covetous enemies. To achieve their aims the new states courted different European powers, which saw these states almost solely in terms of their own interests. With the United States withdrawn, the Balkans and Eastern Europe as a whole quickly reverted to what they has been for more than a century: the proverbial cockpit for national antagonisms and international imperialism.

Albania, Bulgaria, and Romania were all parties to this historical process, although in the end each was affected differently by it. They were all part of that century-long imperialist melodrama called the "Eastern question." Albanians, Bulgarians, and Romanians, ethnologically quite different peoples, formed an unbroken arc of critical strategic importance stretching from the Adriatic to well beyond the Russian frontier. This arc lay between Turkey and Greece to the south and Serbia and Austria-Hungary to the north, often a no-man's-land where rival ambitions probed and clashed.

All three nations spread far beyond the limits of the states allotted to them by the leading European actors in the "Eastern question." The boundaries of these states were often fixed as arbitrarily as any in Africa in the next century. Before the Congress of Berlin in 1878, for example, the "accepted minimum Albanian ethnographic limits" included not only Kosovo but also large parts of Macedonia and northern Greece. (The city of Janina had an Albanian majority, although the surrounding area was mainly Greek.) But when Albania was finally established in 1912, it was a rump state, barely including Shkodër in the north and Vlorë in the south, stretching eastward to Lake Ochrid. The same Congress of Berlin also deprived Bulgaria of Macedonia, which had been an integral part of it in the great days of the medieval Bulgarian kingdoms, which Russia had forced the Porte to cede to it by the treaty of San Stefano immediately before Berlin, and to which most nineteenth-century ethnographers thought it unquestionably entitled. Less than twenty years earlier, in 1859, the union of Romania had come into being without Transylvania, which Romanians regarded as the cradle of their nationhood, and without Bessarabia. In both of these regions, whatever the historical disputations, Romanians constituted the clear majority.

All three countries were born dependent on greater powers, and all three grew up dependent. Albania lacked even the most rudimentary polity and economy, and its very existence was threatened by Greece and the brand new Serbia-dominated Yugoslavia. Albania's immediate objective was simple: survival. For this Albania came to lean more and more heavily on Italy and in 1939 fell easy victim to Benito Mussolini's imperialist posturing. Bulgaria's considerable young energy was largely squandered in vain efforts to recover the territories it considered its birthright. In both world wars, it did recover them for a while and then lost them again. It also lost much of its reputation in the process. But, for all its considerable historical misdemeanors, I also feel that Bulgaria has never been judged fairly by world opinion. Nor, for that matter, has Albania. Both have suffered from what Noel Buxton once called "the unthinking excitement of pro-Serbian feeling"[2] and from the modish philhellenism that pervaded the West in the nineteenth and early twentieth centuries. It was hardly surprising, then, that Bulgaria, driven by irredentism for more than a half century, turned neither to an unsympathetic West nor to its "natural" protector, Russia, but to the one power most likely to satisfy—Germany, first in its Hohenzollern and then in its Hitlerian incarnations.

Romania, too, was a dependent young country. But here its similarities with Albania and Bulgaria end. With its considerable natural resources, Romania has been incomparably richer. Its diplomacy, too, has always been skillful and often successful, whereas Bulgaria's has been disastrous and Albania's nonexistent. Indeed, Romania's dealings with the bigger powers have been a model of small-state leverage. When Romania achieved statehood it consisted only of the two principalities, Moldavia and Wallachia. But after World War II, the old Regat became Greater Romania, with Transylvania and Bessarabia "redeemed." In 1940, after King Carol had maneuvered his country into a cul-de-sac from which there was no escape, Hitler forced Romania to surrender northern Transylvania to Hungary. Bessarabia and Northern Bukovina were taken by the Soviet Union, which meant that the USSR, for all its new face-lift, was back to the same old bad habits from which Romania had suffered so much. But after World War II, Romania recovered northern Transylvania, much the most valued of its lost territories. Bessarabia and Northern Bukovina stayed with the now all-powerful Soviet Union. But few Romanians fretted about this for long. There was nothing to be done about it, and Transylvania was the jewel in the crown anyway.

Romania was lucky, whereas Albania and Bulgaria were not. But all three were part of the hit-and-miss game the great powers played, the objects not the subjects of international relations. The apparent winners could never be sure that the game had finally ended in their favor. The resulting uncertainty often bordered on paranoia, of which there are scores of examples in the last century of Balkan history. Two very recent examples will illustrate this.

In 1958, Mehmet Shehu, then prime minister of Albania, referred to Kosovo in a speech and said that "at present" Albania was making no claims for its restoration. In 1986, twenty-eight years later (and five years after Shehu's death), the Yugoslav official news agency, Tanjug, carried a special commentary devoted to Shehu's remark, maintaining that it clearly revealed Tirana's irredentism.

The second is even more poignant. Larry Watts, one of the sharpest-eyed Romania-watchers, was told by two acquaintances of proven credibility that Brezhnev's successor, Yuri Andropov, was considered by the Romanians to be so pro-Hungarian that when his selection as Soviet leader became known, special meetings were held in several Transylvanian towns to discuss means of repelling the Hungarians in case they came.[3]

The Communist Background

By the end of World War II, the situation in the Balkans had completely changed. Albania, Bulgaria, and Romania became Communist states. Their previous close ties with the West were severed as East-West relations became frozen in the cold war. The Soviet Union, which for the first twenty years of its existence had played practically no role in Eastern Europe, now dominated it exclusively, and this domination was of a kind never experienced in history. It involved the transmogrification of the subject into the image of its master. Russian domination under the czars had never been like this. But, as Joseph Stalin told Milovan Djilas, the rules of international relations had now changed: Domination now meant the imposition of identical political, social, and economic systems bound together by ideological conformity and underpinned by Soviet power. The empire into which Albania, Bulgaria, and Romania were now herded was also very different from the Ottoman Empire from which they had all once emerged. Although never benign, the Porte had been indifferent, often casual, even easygoing. The Kremlin pressed a totalitarian model that brooked neither exception nor delay. But the same model was supposed to fit *eight* captive countries spanning a range of national difference even wider than in Western Europe. The hat that fit the German Democratic Republic (GDR) was supposed to fit Albania; the straightjacket that suited Bohemia should have suited Moldavia. The whole concept, based on ideology and paranoia, was impractical. Almost immediately the indestructible differences that were the quintessence of Eastern Europe began to reappear, like grass growing between flagstones.

Nowhere did these differences appear more quickly than in the Balkans. The most dramatic example was Yugoslavia, where the triumphant Communists, who had freed their country from the Germans by their own exertions, now proceeded to free it from the Soviets in 1948. But differences also appeared in, and among, Albania, Bulgaria, and Romania that were profoundly to affect their future development, especially the course of their foreign policies.

Like the Yugoslav party, the Albanian Communist party largely fought its own way to power, whereas the future Bulgarian and Romanian regimes had trailed in the Red Army's wake. Albania's first Communists had mostly been the sons of wealthy landowners or merchants from more advanced southern parts of the country. Some, like Enver Hoxha, party leader for forty-four years, acquired their communism through education in Western Europe. To many of the educated younger generation in the Balkans, as elsewhere, communism seemed to provide a shortcut away from the past to a more equitable future. But try as they might to repudiate their history, they could not escape its legacy. In the weltanschauung they now espoused, nationalism was shrugged off as an irrelevance. But nationalism was to persist as one of the most powerful dynamics in Balkan history, interacting with communism in a potent, new chemistry. The Communist regimes of Albania, Bulgaria, and Romania were all strongly affected by it, and many of their policies would be incomprehensible without reference to it. This was the most immediately apparent in the case of the fledgling Albanian regime. The Yugoslav Communists, who had helped found the Albanian party in 1941, now considered Albania as their dependency, just as their

Serbian predecessors would like to have done. Triumphant now after their heady wartime victory, historical fulfillment seemed theirs for the taking. But just as the Soviets provoked nationalist resentments in Yugoslavia after 1945, so the Yugoslavs did exactly the same in Albania. The results were almost identical: As the Yugoslavs broke with Moscow in 1948, so the Albanians broke with Belgrade. They exchanged domination by a neighboring enemy for protection by a distant patron. Whatever reservations many Albanians—Communist and anti-Communist alike—may have felt about the Soviet Union, at least it was not Yugoslavia.

Enver Hoxha was never slow at finding enemies, at home or abroad. To a well-cushioned Westerner, many of his actions suggested paranoia. But in the Albanian context paranoia is often but caution writ large and is indispensable for safety, even survival. At any rate it served Hoxha well. It enabled him to be what history will remember him as: a nation builder, the man who changed Albanians into Albanian citizens—oppressed citizens, certainly, but citizens just the same.

Ahmed Zogu (King Zog), the tribal chieftain, later monarch, who dominated Albania in the interwar years, had already begun to give his country an international profile and a degree of national unity. But he had hardly finished the job of nation building before the Italian invasion forced him to leave his country forever in the spring of 1939. During the war there was little united resistance against, first, the Italian and, then, the German occupying forces. Whatever resistance there was often fought, as in Yugoslavia, against itself. But something of great historical and symbolic importance happened to Albania during the war. It was joined with Kosovo and the predominantly Albanian parts of Macedonia into Greater Albania. The irredenta was redeemed; Albania, although not free, became ethnically whole. Like the puppet Slovak republic (also under Axis patronage), it was brief, but its effects were lasting. It gave a strong stimulus to the pride of a previously despised small nation.

Albanian national sentiment received a further boost with the rejection of Yugoslav patronage in 1948, the first of several crises Hoxha skillfully exploited. The propagandist par excellence, he projected a mutual identity between himself and his country. His fate was wedded to Albania; its survival rested on his. In domestic affairs he ruthlessly imposed a rigid centralism. Society became heavily militarized. A simplistic Communist belief was the only one tolerated. Religion was suppressed. Albania, Hoxha proclaimed, was the only religion for Albanians. His whole rule was virtually a prolonged state of siege; paranoia was transmuted into patriotism. His means may have been dubious, but no one can deny that when he died in 1985 Albania was a nation-state—and that achievement will last.

The Bulgarian Communist experience was older, fuller, and more eventful than the Albanian. Indeed, no other Communist movement in the Balkans could compare with the Bulgarian in numerical strength, forceful personalities, intellectual capacity, or what the initiated called "revolutionary tradition." But in World War II, the Bulgarian Communists were never able to conduct anything like the mass resistance the Yugoslav Communists managed to do under Marshal Tito. The Bulgarians' efforts were puny in comparison, and it was this difference that partly explained why the Yugoslav Communist regime after the war enjoyed so much more prestige than did the Bulgarian. It would, of course, have done so in any case. Yugoslavia was on the winning side, and traditional pro-Serb Western sentiment now rubbed off onto the heirs of Karageorge: Tito's partisans! The Bulgarians had once again chosen the wrong side and added insult to injury by occupying portions of Greece as well as Serbia. The prestige of the Yugoslavs, by contrast, seemed assured; inside the Communist movement it was now second only to that of the Soviets.

The early postwar Bulgarian experience was not much different from that of several other East European countries. Not only was the Communist regime imposed by Moscow, it was also divided along familiar lines: between "home Communists" and "Muscovites," or between those whose formative political experience had largely been confined to their home ground (or underground) and those for whom exile in the Soviet Union had been decisively influential. Home Communists were considered more susceptible to native vibrations, whereas Muscovites, some of whom knew little and cared less about their land of birth, were considered more responsive to proletarian (that is, Soviet) internationalism.

The struggle for power in Bulgaria between these two factions also took on a familiar pattern. After uneasy cooperation before the seizure of power, the home Communists fell foul of Stalin. The Muscovites gained control, ruthlessly purged their opponents, and set about transforming their country in the Soviet image. Nowhere was this sequence more grisly or more thorough than in Bulgaria. But after Stalin died, the Muscovites went into eclipse. "Legitimacy" was now the mode, as dictated by Nikita Khrushchev, and they were clearly an impediment to that or, at least, more of an impediment than the home Communists who were now taking over.

In Bulgaria, the return of the home Communists was associated with the rise of Todor Zhivkov, who became party leader in 1954. In a classic power drive, which included the essential Soviet backing, he put his authority beyond serious challenge by 1962. Since then, he has not just remained master in his own house but has also become dean of the Warsaw Pact party leaders, a Balkan institution, and a small but seemingly standing fixture in the European international order. By 1988, he had ruled Bulgaria longer than anyone since liberation in 1878. Although his legacy might be debatable, there can be no denying the impact he has made on his country or the astonishing transformation it has undergone during his leadership.

The Romanian Communists had nothing like the tradition of the Bulgarians. Nor could they conjure up a mythology of wartime resistance like the Albanians. The Romanian Communist movement had been the weakest, not just in the Balkans but in the whole of Eastern Europe. The movement's real weakness had lain not so much in its infinitesimal numbers or in its negligible intellectual qualities but in the ethnic composition of its leadership, which in the Romanian context was considered alien. Many of its leaders between the two world wars were either Jews, Hungarians, or Bulgarians, and its policy on international issues often ran counter to Romanian national aspirations. The party, for example, advocated the cession of Bessarabia to the Soviet Union. The nationalistic mass of the population considered it not just un-Romanian but also anti-Romanian.

When it came to power the Romanian Communist regime was already dominated by Muscovites, a cosmopolitan mélange carried over from the interwar period. But from then on, events took a bizarre turn. The leadership group, of which Ana Pauker was the most colorful and, for a time, the most powerful member, was purged in May 1952 (almost a full year before Stalin's death), apparently a victim to Stalin's last bout of anti-Semitism. This leadership was replaced by the home Communist faction, led by Gheorghe Gheorghiu-Dej. A former railway worker, Gheorghiu-Dej had been nominal party leader all through the Muscovite ascendency, having been retained apparently to give the leadership a much needed homegrown look. Once the home communists were firmly in power and had survived the shocks of de-Stalinization, they joined the now modish pursuit of legitimacy. They did this by invoking the spirit of nationalism, and it was while doing this that the unexpected metamorphosis of Romanian communism took place. It became a national Communist movement that with nerve and skill questioned the basic principle of Moscow's bloc leadership and reclaimed as much independence from the Soviet Union as possible.

The psychological groundwork for Romanian boldness was laid in 1958 when Soviet troops, stationed in the country since World War II, withdrew, part of a Khrushchev gambit in his maneuverings with the West. It probably gave the Romanian regime and the population the confidence necessary for the encounters to come. The dispute that put Bucharest and Moscow inseparably at odds centered on Soviet attempts to get the Romanians to abandon their comprehensive industrialization drive and concentrate on the exploitation of their raw materials and on light industry and agriculture. The aim was to rationalize Comecon, which in turn was one aspect of Khrushchev's efforts to reorganize the whole Soviet alliance. Romania rejected Khrushchev's plans and the principle of supranationalism that lay behind them. Romania's own interest came first, and the alliance as a whole was not to be considered greater than its parts. Romania set out its own principles in the famous April Declaration of 1964, which, although it did not declare Romania's independence, gave notice that Romania's satellite status was over.

The Romanian people responded, not so much with support for the regime but with backing for its nationalism. The high point of mutuality between rulers in Romanian Communist history was reached in August 1968, when Romania not only refused to take part in the Soviet-led invasion of Czechoslovakia but also roundly condemned it. However nervously many Romanians many have looked across the Pruth, they supported their leader in what was one of Romania's finest hours.

The leader was now Nicolae Ceaușescu, and for several years after he succeeded Gheorghiu-Dej in 1965 Ceaușescu embodied the hopes of many

Romanians for an enhancement of national dignity and a better way of life. But it has been one of the tragedies of Romanian history that he so quickly dashed these hopes. In my book on Eastern Europe, I have summed up Ceauşescu as follows:

> No European leader in the second half of this century has so personified the debilitating effects of power. An intelligent man, an extraordinarily hard worker, a patriot, not personally cruel . . . , once well intentioned—he has remained so in a perverse sort of way—his name has yet become synonymous with many of the iniquities associated with historic tyranny. A willful refusal to take advice; a toleration for nothing but sycophants; a nepotism ever-growing in dimensions; an intolerance visibly hardening as absolute power corrupted absolutely; a self-defeating impatience clamoring for instant success; an inconsistency and unpredictability; a conglomerate of convictions and prejudices; a pretentiousness reflecting little but bad taste; a suspiciousness bordering on paranoia; a wife Elena, who encouraged the bad and stifled the good in her husband; a self-promoting personality cult, the sheer ludicrousness of which insulted, humiliated, angered, or amused most Romanians—it was for these characteristics that Nicolae Ceauşescu would be remembered by most of his countrymen.[4]

One must allow for a certain hyperbole here, but even the most sober reappraisal would cause little to be altered. Ceauşescu began his rule amid hope and goodwill. Twenty years later, he had forfeited everything except the independence of his own misrule. In retrospect it seems that all those defects just described were parts of a degenerative syndrome that became discernible with the passage of time. There may well be sociological explanations for part of Ceauşescu's behavior: his nepotism, for example. Ceauşescu's wife, Elena, is the second most powerful figure in the country; his son, Nicu, who combines depravity with nastiness—but not with intelligence—is, according to some, being groomed for the succession. (The Kim Il Sung comparison is often made.) One of Ceauşescu's brothers holds a key post in the defense ministry, another in the interior ministry; Elena's clan, the Petrescus, is also well represented in ministerial and party positions. "Socialism in one family" is a fair enough characterization of this plebeian dynasticism. The more sociologically solemn term is *familialization,* the peasant instinct of withdrawing into the fastnesses of the family in times of uncertainty. But sociology only goes so far with the Ceauşescus. Their degeneration has been such that moral, mental, and psychological factors should be taken into account when trying to fathom it.

The Soviet Stake

Bulgaria and Romania began their Communist histories as Soviet satellites. Communist Albania, dominated by Yugoslavia, began more as a Soviet subsatellite but graduated to satellite status after 1948. They all formed part of the Soviet Union's newly acquired East European empire. This empire was valuable to Moscow on many counts—military, strategic, economic, political, diplomatic, ideological, and psychological. Although all three countries were valuable to the Soviets, they were not of equal or similar value.

Romania must at first have been considered the most valuable prize of the three. It was on the historic trail leading eastward to the Balkans and to the Aegean. This was familiar territory; the Russians had invaded the Romanian principalities fourteen times in their history. But Romania's more immediate and practical use to Stalin lay in its considerable economic wealth, which he proceeded mercilessly to exploit. In fact, no other part of Eastern Europe, except what was to become the GDR, was robbed more cynically or systematically by the Soviet Union in the immediate postwar years. In other respects, however, Romania was of less value to Moscow. Strategically its value was insignificant. Bordered on all sides by Communist states, it was not crucial to Soviet defense or offense and has remained the least important of all the Eastern European states in terms of Soviet strategic considerations. In time this very lack of strategic importance proved a blessing because it enabled Romania to defy the Soviet Union the way it did. Moscow would never have allowed a more strategically important satellite to slip the steel hoop.

Bulgaria, on the other hand, although economically much less important, has had real strategic value. It borders on two volatile Western allies, Greece and Turkey, and—important after 1948—on Macedonia, one of the most vulnerable parts of Titoist Yugoslavia and in which Bulgaria had always had a strongly acquisitive interest. Subsequently, as the domestic situation in both Greece and Turkey became more erratic and as each of these two Western allies began to fear each other more than any of its nominal adversaries, Bulgaria's value to Moscow increased accordingly. So, it might be added, did Bulgaria's own potential leverage in its relations with Moscow. Just how much Bulgaria has used it, if at all, is a matter of some debate. But the squirmy subservience shown to Moscow has probably always had its element of calculation and has brought its own reward. Bulgaria has done quite well being where it is and always ready to oblige Moscow.

But even Bulgaria could not match the strategic importance of Albania. Albania controlled access to the Adriatic, and the bay of Vlorë (Valona) had great potential as a naval base. Indeed, the strategic significance of Vlorë, and the danger of it falling into the wrong hands, had originally prompted Italian interest in Albania. Nor could the Yugoslavs ever be indifferent to who controlled Vlorë. Now, after 1948, it was in Soviet hands, and they steadily made it into a key naval base. The Soviet Union was now at the mouth of the Adriatic, some 50 miles from the heel of Italy.

But the value of Vlorë was not just that it could bottle up the Adriatic; it enabled the Soviet navy to establish a standing presence in the Mediterranean, something the European powers, through their worrying about the Turkish Straits, had been trying to prevent for two centuries. In early 1958, the Soviets began building a permanent operating base at Vlorë to service submarines. Very soon four submarines and a tender were on station there, thus permitting Soviet vessels to move regularly into the central and eastern Mediterranean. By 1969, this force had expanded to four auxiliaries and up to a dozen submarines and was joined occasionally by Soviet Black Sea forces and ships in transit to or from the Baltic, Northern, and Pacific fleets. The Soviet navy's first major Mediterranean exercise was staged out of Vlorë in 1960.

Albania, therefore, was becoming an ever-appreciating Soviet asset. But then, in 1961, the Soviets lost it. They lost it because they ignored Balkan history and underestimated the strength of Albanian nationalism and the will of Enver Hoxha. Khrushchev's persistent efforts to reach reconciliation with Yugoslavia and his increasingly friendly overtures to Greece, Albania's two predatory enemies, together with his barely disguised attempts to get rid of Hoxha himself, drove the Albanians into the welcoming arms of the People's Republic of China (PRC). Albania now became the PRC's first full-fledged satellite, out-Maoing the Maoists when it came to ideological primitivism and ferocious anti-Sovietism. Khrushchev had to let Albania go. For all its importance it was still not worth the military and, above all, the political risks of trying to keep it by force.

After the withdrawal from Vlorë in 1961, the Soviet navy, denied shore access, could no longer sustain a permanent presence in the Mediterranean. It has never permanently recovered this loss. It did so for a while when it had access to Alexandria. But Leonid Brezhnev fell foul of Anwar Sadat as Khrushchev had fallen foul of Hoxha, and in 1976 the Soviets had to leave Alexandria, too. If the Albanians ever gave the nod, it is difficult to see any Soviet leader, however relaxed East-West relations may have become, passing up the chance to return to Vlorë. Its strategic value may have lessened, but it would be a prize just the same.

But if there were ever a return to Vlorë, it would for the Soviets have almost as much symbolic as military value. It would mean they were beginning to recover at least some of the ground in the Balkans they had steadily lost in the decade and a half after 1948. The reversal in the Soviet position in the Balkans was indeed startling. After World War II, the Soviets controlled four countries: Albania, Bulgaria, Romania, and Yugoslavia. The civil war in Greece seemed to be going the Communists' way. True, Stalin never helped them much, but he would hardly have been too self-denying had they won. As for Turkey, it was being subjected to intense Soviet pressure but was resisting demands aimed at putting it irretrievably inside the Soviet orbit.

Then the Soviet position began to deteriorate. Thanks to U.S. help, and their own steadfastness, the Turks warded off Soviet pressure. The Greek Communists were to lose the civil war—again largely through U.S. action. In 1948 came the greatest blow of all—the Tito-Stalin break and the defection of Yugoslavia—which not only affected the Balkans but was to have worldwide repercussions. In 1961, Albania finally defected, and by 1964 it was evident that Romania was no longer the satellite it had once been. All that was now left of Soviet power was Bulgaria. Balkan history after World War II provides a useful corrective to those who see the last half century solely in terms of inexorable Soviet advance and aggrandisement.

Domestic Development and Western Ties

The Western diplomacy of the East European Communist states has passed through several phases. They can be categorized as follows: (1) *nonexistent* diplomacy, before, and for a time, beyond Stalin's death; (2) *proxy* diplomacy, in the second half of the 1950s and the early 1960s, when Soviet regional initiatives in Europe were made by a satellite immediately involved instead of by the Soviet Union in propria persona; (3) *sanctioned* diplomacy, when, beginning in the early 1960s, some states, with Soviet permission, developed bilateral relations with Western countries, often with a strong economic component; (4) *autonomous* diplomacy, usually beginning in the 1970s, when some states, without expressed Soviet objection, developed a broad range of relations with Western countries; (5) *independent* diplomacy, conducted most notably by the Romanians since at least 1967 and, much later and only on occasion, by Hungary and the GDR in 1984.

The foregoing progression was anything but clear and smooth. In fact, it was dim and stuttering. The phases overlapped; one country could be in more than one phase at one time. Which phase it was usually depended on relations with the Soviet Union and sometimes on the West's interest in the country concerned. Some countries—Czechoslovakia, for instance—have hardly made any progression at all. The English journalist Bernard Levin was right when he once said that Bohuslav Chňoupek was no more the Czechoslovak foreign minister than he was. It is a progression, therefore, that must be handled with care. But it is a servicable guide to a process that has led to a genuine interaction between some East European states and the West, and it is most unlikely that this process will be reversed.

Romania

If Eastern Europe's relations with the West were to be seen as a race, then Romania was out of the starting blocks before the rest of the runners were on their marks. (Yugoslavia as usual was excepted). Romania's determination to get started was largely a measure of its deteriorating relations with the Soviet Union in the early 1960s. But the European diplomacy conducted by the Communist regime in Bucharest soon began to show striking similarities with that of its monarchist predecessor, as did the principles on which the diplomacy was based. Paul Lendvai, in his book on nationalism and communism in the Balkans, quoted a 1936 statement by Nicolae Titulescu, the great interwar Romanian foreign minister, and then followed it with one by Nicolae Ceauşescu in 1967.

> *Titulescu:* We shall never renounce for the sake of any of the Great Powers, or of all the Great Powers together, the principle of equality of states, that is, the sovereign right to decide our own fate and to refuse decisions concerning us in which we have been involved without our consent.

> *Ceauşescu:* The small and medium-sized states refuse to play the role of pawn in the service of the interest of big imperialist powers any longer. They rise

> against any form of domination and promote an independent policy. By vigorously defending their legitimate rights and interests, the small and medium-sized countries can still play an outstanding part in international life, can considerably influence the course of events.[5]

The main powers in Ceauşescu's day have not all been the same as in Titulescu's, but the international environment has not been very different nor have the dangers confronting the minor powers. The philosophy governing their two foreign policies and the strategy behind them have been virtually the same. The continuity is clear, and it can be pushed back further than Titulescu, back to Ionel Brătianu and the precarious but successful maneuvering after World War I. But Ceauşescu's field of operation has been much bigger than that of his "bourgeois" predecessors. Theirs was European; his has been global, involving very closely the two non-European great powers, the United States and the PRC.

The real architect of Romania's new foreign policy was neither Ceauşescu nor Gheorghiu-Dej, his predecessor as party leader, but Ion Gheorghe Maurer, an intellectual with wisdom who took Romanian traditional diplomacy and transferred it to a world setting. He also gave Romanian Communist diplomacy the necessary respectability and "seriousness." He served his regime with style and dignity as well as with ability. Romania was lucky to have a man so well suited to meet its need. But as the Ceauşescu regime deteriorated, he became increasingly estranged from it. He left it in 1974, ostensibly because of injuries sustained in a motor accident several years earlier. But that, apparently, was mainly an excuse. He joined the growing number of Romania's "early retirees" who had had their fill of the Ceauşescus—*père, mère, et fils.*

But however great Maurer's merits and however serious Ceauşescu's failings, it is the latter to whom credit must be given for the successful conduct of foreign policy during so many years. Ceauşescu rallied the nation behind this policy, which it was to support until the decay at home began to vitiate the success abroad. He also took on the Soviet Union, frontally when need be, and this was the mainspring of the entire policy. Ceauşescu also carried Romania's name (and his own) around the world, visiting countries of all sizes in all parts of it. (He even vied with Tito as Europe's top political tourist.) He would have liked Romania to join the nonaligned group of nations, but that was incompatible with the country's bloc commitments, which he could not openly flout. So he consoled himself with associate or observer status in practically every developing-country group that would have him—and in his early years he was quite a prestigious catch on the Third World circuit. Like Tito, Ceauşescu can be criticized for his incessant globe-trotting. It was often more ego trip than anything else, not to mention the time and money involved. But it had a genuine purpose: to make Romania a more difficult target for Soviet wrath by becoming a world champion of medium, small, and developing states. For a time it also appeared that a Bucharest-Belgrade axis was developing, two medium-sized Communist states with similar defensive concerns regarding Moscow and similar European and world interests. They even combined in the joint production of a military aircraft, which, happily for all concerned, never had to fire a shot in anger. But after peaking in the middle 1970s, Romanian-Yugoslav cooperation descended gently to a plateau of formality. The construction of the Iron Gates dam project on the Danube remains its lasting monument.

Ceauşescu also knew, however, that neither Third World declarations nor any special relationship with Belgrade was a substitute for real diplomacy. Maintaining and expanding Romanian independence of action essentially lay in beneficial relations with three countries: the PRC in the East and the Federal Republic of Germany and the United States in the West. (France under Charles de Gaulle was a fleeting, flamboyant fourth. But the general's ignominious retreat back to Paris from a visit to Bucharest in May 1968 to face the student revolution was an appropriate reminder to Romania, and everybody else, that France's reach was exceeding its grasp.)

It was in relations with the Federal Republic that the first major Romanian break with the Soviet-coordinated Western policy occurred. Romania defied Soviet dictates and broke bloc unity by establishing diplomatic relations with Bonn in January 1967. This began a cordial and profitable relationship for Romania that has continued to the present.

More recently, both the West German government and the public have been repelled by the growing instances of Ceauşescu's misrule, but the presence in Romania of a large ethnic German minority has compelled West Germany to react with caution. Before World War II this minority numbered about 700,000. Today, mainly as a result of migration and loss of territory, there are less than 250,000 left. An estimated 80 percent of these Germans—which virtually means everybody except the aged—want to leave. In 1978, an agreement between the countries provided for the emigration of 12,000 a year. As compensation for what the Romanian government spent on the education and social welfare of each emigrant, the West German government agreed to pay DM 8,000 (about $5,000) per person to the Romanian government. (This sum was far exceeded in the case of many emigrants. What was meant, at least by Bonn, to be a humanitarian act has often become a disreputable racket in human cargo, with tidy profits pocketed by unscrupulous middle people.) The West German government has continually pressed Bucharest to let more people out. The most recent effort was made in December 1987, when Foreign Minister Hans-Dietrich Genscher visited Bucharest. He apparently got no definite answer. It was typical of Ceauşescu, however, that when Genscher suggested that food packages might be sent from West Germany to Romania to ease the food shortages there, he got a definite "no." What food shortages?

The deepening economic relationship with West Germany has been valuable to Romania; but in its quest for more independence from the Soviet Union in the 1960s, Romania had a greater need for diplomatic than economic sustenance, and this the Federal Republic could not provide. Neither could France, which for much of the interwar period had been Romania's main diplomatic support. Bucharest, therefore, had to look elsewhere and soon came up with as disparate, but as powerful, a pair of backers as the global constellation had to offer: the PRC and the United States.

The Chinese connection was joined in 1964, by Premiers Maurer and Chou En-lai, shortly before the famous April Declaration of the Romanian Communist party. The U.S. connection began in earnest with a visit by President Richard Nixon in 1969. The value to Romania of Red China and the United States was obvious. But Romania, for its part, was not without utility to these newly found patrons. For both, Romania had considerable anti-Soviet nuisance value and helped Peking by weakening Moscow in the struggle that was developing in the world Communist movement. More locally, in the Balkans, Romania seemed to have great potential for Peking, and was perhaps another Albania in the making. For the United States Romania was of some assistance in the larger East-West rivalry as a small asset embedded in the Soviet alliance that was embarrassing to Moscow and a possible example for others. For Washington, too, the regional aspect was important. First Yugoslavia, then Albania, now Romania—in progression, perhaps? At any rate, another zero-sum plus for the West in southeast Europe.

Romania, therefore, was a catch for the United States—modest, perhaps, but not one to be thrown away. Romania's value in the 1960s was enhanced by its singularity. It was then alone among the Soviet Union's East European allies in trying to win the West. In just a few years, with détente in full swing and virtually all the East European states trailing their skirts, Romania's attractions correspondingly diminished. Poland, the GDR, even Hungary, aroused more interest. But, for the present, Romania had the field to itself, and the liaison with the United States began. It was all the more successful because it was conducted with discretion. Both realized that it had limitations set by adversarial alignments and geopolitical realities. The United States certainly respected the constraints on Romania more than the PRC did. U.S. diplomats never embarrassed the Romanians the way even the sophisticated Chou En-lai did in June 1966 when, at the end of a visit to Bucharest, he unsuccessfully tried to get Ceauşescu to sign a communiqué, parts of which would have seriously upset his tightrope act with the Soviets.

On his visit in 1969 President Nixon was, by contrast, the soul of discretion, as was President Gerald Ford when he stopped in Romania in 1975 on his way to the European security summit conference in Helsinki. The two presidential visits highlighted the U.S.-Romanian cordiality, along with the visits by Ceauşescu to the United States in 1970, 1973, and 1978. These top-level visits were only the most striking in a whole series of exchanges between the two countries. But one of the most tangible—although eventually controversial—marks of U.S. goodwill was the granting of most favored nation (MFN) status to Romania in 1975, only the second country to receive it after Poland in 1960. Materially, MFN has not been decisive for Romania, but it did enable the United States in 1985, for example, to take a more than 24 percent share of Romania's total trade with Western industrialized countries. The attraction of MFN, however, lies as much in its political symbolism as in its economic value, and it is keenly sought after by most East European countries.

But by the time MFN was granted in 1975, some U.S. leaders were already having misgivings about Romanian domestic policy. As in the case of Poland in 1960, when the reward for good conduct was eventually granted the conduct had already begun to deteriorate. Ceauşescu's personality cult was already established; so were what some Romanians were soon describing as his "Caligulan eccentricities." This all went along with the steady reversal of what a few years before had seemed to be a more liberal attitude to human rights. Indeed, in a very short time, it was clear that all the earlier hopes of liberalization had been illusory. Western, particularly U.S., attitudes to Ceauşescu's Romania therefore began to harden. The "Romanian deviation," a once laudatory expression for Bucharest's rejection of Soviet dictates, now came to signify its contempt for Western standards of public decency.

Romania's favored position came first under scrutiny and then under fire. The annual renewal of MFN status, once a formality, now became a hotly debated, touch-and-go issue. Those for its retention argued that Ceauşescu, for all his sins at home, was still independent of Moscow on many key issues—Afghanistan, for example, in 1979–1980 and the intermediate nuclear forces (INF) controversy in Western Europe in 1983–1984. Therefore, warts and all, he remained a realpolitik asset. As for human rights, deplorable although Ceauşescu's behavior had become, a loss of MFN might reduce all hope of mitigation. He had, after all, withdrawn his notorious 1983 emigration tax, which "fined" every potential emigrant according to the amount the state had paid on his or her education. Ceauşescu did this, so the argument went, because he feared losing MFN. The threat to take away the carrot was a stick in itself.

These arguments were rejected by those who maintained that any support for Ceauşescu had now become immoral and was tarring the United States with the same brush he had so liberally applied to himself. Besides, it was self-defeating politically because whatever realpolitik use Romania may once have had was now exhausted. Its government was now despised, not admired. As for independence from Moscow, economic necessity, it was alleged, was now steadily pushing Romania back toward dependence.

The clamor for the United States to change its policy was growing when Ceauşescu himself effectively ended the dispute by bowing Romania out of it. He announced in February 1988 that Romania would not seek a renewal of MFN status when it expired the following July. The move came after particularly intense U.S. pressure for an improvement in Romania's human rights record. It surprised almost everybody, particularly in Washington, where both advocates and opponents of MFN for Romania suddenly found themselves combatants without a cause.

The move was also vintage Ceauşescu, typifying several facets of his style and personality. First, his timing, reflecting a characteristically Romanian touch of the theater as well as an undoubted flair for diplomatic one-upmanship. Second, Ceauşescu's own egotistic posturing—the *nemo me impune lacessit* bravado. Third, his nationalism: Romanians will never be supplicants. Fourth, the *Bauernschlauheit,* elevated to the international plane: Even after formally renouncing MFN, he apparently still hoped to make some deal with Washington enabling him to keep some of the privileges while evading the conditions. Finally, his lack of realism, demonstrating its power to transcend all his actions. This was shown both in his attempt to make patriotic capital at home out of his grand gesture abroad (with a people now thoroughly fed up with his flag waving) and in his provincial overestimation of whatever leverage he may have had with the United States.

So much, then, for what renouncing MFN revealed (or confirmed) about Ceauşescu. How much would it hurt Romania economically? The Romanians would need to find other Western takers for the exports that had previously gone to the United States, and in 1988 they owed a sizable sum in foreign debt repayments. But in a relatively short time the losses could be absorbed or made up. More important, what could it mean for Romania's future relations with the United States and for Ceauşescu's relations with his own subjects? In the former case, the outcome might not be so grim as some have predicted. The Romanian regime still showed itself anxious to maintain the Washington connection, and there was certainly no sign of any compensating gravitation in the direction of Moscow. (Economic relations with Moscow had been improving for several years, but this was largely due to increasing Romanian vulnerability in raw materials, including oil, of which Romania had once been a significant producer.)

In domestic affairs the impact was insignificant. What happened in Romania at the end of 1987 and during 1988 had nothing to do with Washington or the West in general. In November 1987 there occurred serious rioting in the Transylvanian city of Braşov, Romania's second largest industrial center after Bucharest. This was followed by disturbances in several other cities. The main reason was miserable living conditions.

Order was eventually restored with little difficulty, if with some severity. But no sooner had Ceauşescu seen the effects of his misrule on parts of Romania's urban population than he began a massive reorganization calculated to disrupt life in many parts of the countryside. It acquired the name of "systematization" and involved the planned destruction of over half of Romania's villages and their consolidation into new "agrogorods." As it had been modestly conceived in the early 1970s, the idea of rural consolidation had some economic merit, but as it developed in Ceauşescu's imagination it acquired the characteristics of a Pharaonic nightmare. It certainly meant the biggest transformation of the Romanian countryside since collectivization. Indeed, this was even bigger. Collectivization had at least left the villages physically intact. As the "systematization" campaign got underway, Romania began to attract the worst publicity in its entire history, partly because many villages inhabited by members of the Hungarian and the German minorities were due to be affected. But Ceaușescu showed little or no sign of being affected. It seemed it would take only a massive resistance by the Romanian peasants themselves, recalling perhaps the great revolt of 1907, to deter him fully.

Certainly on his policy toward the Hungarian minority in general he remained likely to be totally impervious. The history of this minority and of Transylvania, where most of its members (now about 2 million) live, was for centuries tied to the history of Hungary. Until 1918, Transylvania was an integral part of Hungary, and its Hungarian inhabitants were the dominant race, despising totally the more numerous Romanians who had also lived there for centuries. Just how long they had lived there and whether they were there before the Hungarians became much more than a mere historical debate. Beginning in the nineteenth century the Transylvanian question was caught in the tidal wave of nationalism, involving power, territorial claims, prestige, even honor. Scholarship went by the board unless it produced the "right" results. Since 1945, it has been just the same as it was in "feudal" or "bourgeois" times.

After World War I, Transylvania was awarded to Romania, ostensibly on Wilsonian principles but also because Hungary lost the war and Romania finished it on the winning side. Between the wars, like Bulgaria with Macedonia, Hungary used dubious means to try recovering what it considered its birthright. This led Hungary into the arms of Hitler and, although it recovered part of the prize in 1940, Hungary lost it again at the end of the war. Transylvania reverted to Romania as Soviet communism swept over the whole of Eastern Europe, and only the wooliest of Hungarian romantics—a dwindling band—now imagined Transylvania's status would ever change again. Hungarians' attention was now directed, not on irredentism, but on the condition of their countrymen and women living in Romania. For about ten years under Romanian Communist rule the Hungarian minority did not fare badly. At least they were no worse off than the Romanians, and some observers (and many Romanians) even argued that they were a relatively privileged section of the community. The deterioration of their situation dates from the Hungarian Revolution in 1956 when many of them strongly sympathized with their compatriots in Hungary. Savage repression by the Romanian authorities followed, and there then began the steady dismantling of the administrative, institutional, and educational system that had preserved the separate identity of the Hungarian minority. That process of dismantling is still going on and is causing mounting resentment in Hungary and considerable unease in the West generally. State relations between Hungary and Romania, never fraternal at the best of times, have suffered seriously because of it. But no real concessions and very little flexibility can be expected from Ceaușescu. Like the Bulgarian leaders, his ultimate aim is the unitary state, and however unpopular he may otherwise be, his Romanian subjects support him in this, as the Bulgarian people support their leaders. Indeed, the strength of Hungarian feeling on the subject is at least matched by that of the Romanians, who generally think

Hungary is at long last getting the just deserts of history. If Ceauşescu were more illiberal toward the Hungarian minority, Romanians would not mind.[6]

Bulgaria

Nothing presents a sharper contrast with the heresy of Romania's foreign policy than the orthodoxy of Bulgaria's. Whereas the distinctiveness of Romanian policy lies in its pursuit of good relations with any Western country that is willing, the distinctiveness of Bulgarian policy lies in its close relations with Moscow. No other East European country has so reveled in its "ever-deepening relations with the great brotherly Soviet Union."

But it would be mistake simply to condemn Communist Bulgaria as a "model Soviet satellite," more loyal than the situation requires and with never a thought for its own national interest. Such a condemnation would rest more on rhetoric than reality, more on what the Bulgarians have said than on what they have done. Bulgaria may have followed the Soviet Union "through thick and thin," as Zhivkov and others like to remind us, but it has picked up some tidy rewards on the way in the form of Soviet credits, subsidies, and preferential supplies of raw materials. Moreover, there was apparently no sustained Soviet attempt, as there was in the case of Romania, to prevent Bulgarian industrialization in the interests of Comecon specialization. In the 1960s, therefore, Bulgaria (like Romania) became a comprehensively industrialized state. In its foreign relations, Bulgaria seldom performed a service for Moscow from which it did not derive some advantage. In the Balkans, for example, particularly in the early 1960s and again in the early 1980s, it was active as a Soviet proxy, proposing sundry desirables such as peace, nuclear disarmament, and cooperation. But in doing so it was furthering its own, as well as Soviet, national interest. Moreover, the very fact that Bulgaria was engaged in international diplomacy at all, however restricted and in whatever capacity, has raised it from the provincial backwater in which it has customarily languished.

Bulgaria's relations with its Balkan neighbors have played a key role in its international activity. Bulgaria is more isolated than any other Warsaw Pact country, not geographically, but diplomatically and psychologically. One of its neighbors, Romania, is an unreliable member of the Warsaw Pact, the alliance to which it belongs. The other three, Turkey, Greece, and Yugoslavia, have in varying degrees had adversarial relations with the Soviet alliance. Moreover, all four are Bulgaria's historical enemies (Romania less so than the other three). This may have deepened the sense of isolation, thereby providing a further reason for Bulgaria's dependence on the Soviet Union but at the same time inducing as activist a role as circumstance would allow in order to lessen the vulnerability this isolation might cause.

Bulgaria's role in the Balkans is also a factor in the shaping of domestic public opinion about its foreign policy as a whole. Although many Bulgarians find the demonstrativeness of the regime's devotion to Moscow demeaning, relations with the Soviet Union are of less emotional consequence to them than are relations with Greece, Turkey, or Yugoslavia (Serbia). It is on their deportment with these three traditional enemies that politicians are judged. This is quite a different angle of vision from which to view Bulgaria's foreign policy and one that puts it in a considerably less murky light. Zhivkov has certainly given nothing away to any of the three countries concerned. On the Macedonian issue, for example, he has been as nationalistic as the situation permits; he has constantly irritated the Yugoslavs by claiming the Macedonian people and their history to be Bulgarian, but he has been careful at the same time not to make the same claim for Macedonian territory. In the case of Turkey, he has not been above stoking the baser instincts of Bulgarian chauvinism, as with the steps to force the assimilation of the large Turkish minority in the country in 1984–1985. Indeed, Bulgarian policy in the Balkans for the last quarter century can be described as one of "surrogate nationalism," which mitigates, compensates for, distracts from, the obeisance to Moscow.

Bulgaria, therefore, in its Western policy has concentrated on the Balkans, but not exclusively. Almost from the very beginning of the West German *Ostpolitik,* Bulgaria has been surprisingly susceptible to its attractions—surprisingly, not from any longer perspective of Bulgarian history, but from the shorter perspective of the period of Communist rule. Before 1945, Germany had been the most dominant foreign power in Bulgarian affairs, at least from 1914 onward. After 1945, Bulgaria passed under Soviet control and assumed its role as "model satellite." Because Soviet–West German relations for the twenty years after 1945 were mutually antagonistic, it was only to be assumed that Sofia's attitude to Bonn would also be antagonistic.

For many years it was. But when West Germany began revising its own policy toward Eastern Europe, Bulgaria began revising its policy toward West Germany. The first sign of this came in the Bulgarian response to what became known at the Erhard "peace note." Bonn's *Ostpolitik* began to gather pace under Konrad Adenauer's successor, Ludwig Erhard, and his foreign minister, Gerhard Schröder. In 1966, Erhard sent a letter—the "peace note"—to the Soviet Union and all its East European allies (except the GDR) urging a new start in relations between them and the Federal Republic. Erhard's overtures were firmly rejected by all except Romania and Bulgaria, which chose not to reply (or, at least, no reply from either of them was ever published). The import of their silence was clear: They were willing but not able. Romania's attitude was no surprise; this was two years after the April Declaration. But Bulgaria's was. It was the first rustle of Bulgaria's own *Westpolitik.* Bulgaria was not defying the Soviets but was not exactly deferring to them either.

Only a few months later, in January 1967, Romania established diplomatic relations with Bonn, against Moscow's express wishes. There were indications that Bulgaria would have liked to have done the same. But dodging issues was one thing, breaking ranks quite another. Bulgaria stayed in line. Very soon, however, with the onset of détente in the 1970s, West Germany was no longer out of bounds, and Bulgaria joined the rush for diplomatic relations and for its share of the bounty that followed. Bulgaria's Western interest was not confined to the Federal Republic but was mainly centered on it. The rewards were considerable. The "economic miracle" many visitors thought they saw in Bulgaria by the end of the 1970s certainly owed something to the benefits of détente—increased trade and generous credits—of which the Federal Republic was the biggest single provider. The West Germans' share of total Bulgarian trade might be tiny compared with the 60 percent share the Soviets took. But in 1985, they were taking nearly a third of Bulgaria's total trade with Western industrial countries; included in that were the types of sophisticated import on which Bulgaria's competitive future would depend.

Bulgaria developed a relatively close and beneficial relationship with the Federal Republic, and like the relationship several other East European states developed with Bonn, it shaped its own contours and generated its own momentum. It was never part of a Soviet-manipulated exercise, like so many previous East European foreign policy ventures had been. If proof of this were ever needed it was supplied in the summer of 1984 during the tension between Moscow and East Berlin regarding the GDR's relations with the Federal Republic. Bulgaria played no hero's role. It did not take on the Soviets, as the East Germans, Hungarians, and Romanians came close to doing. In fact, Bulgaria said nothing. But the significance of this silence was the same as it had been eighteen years before in response to the Erhard peace note. True, Bulgaria soon did what the Soviets told it, and Zhivkov called off his planned visit to West Germany (after a visit by Politburo member Mikhail Gorbachev), just as Erich Honecker had to call his off. But Bulgaria had made its point, which in a situation like this amounted to defiance—and it was recognized as such.

Bulgaria's relations with other West European countries also expanded under the sign of détente, but the extent of these relations should not be exaggerated. It remained limited by the standards of other East European countries, except for Czechoslovakia, which was still traumatized by the impact of 1968. But too much could not be expected. Bulgaria was the smallest country in Eastern Europe, except for Albania, and historically there was a lot of ground to be made up in relations with the West. Relations with the United States expanded but not by very much. In 1985, U.S. trade took up less than 6 percent of Bulgaria's total trade with Western industrial countries, less than that of any advanced West European country, including Austria. Even at their best, Bulgarian-U.S. relations have never been more than lukewarm. If the Bulgarian ethnic community in the United States were not so small (about 100,000) relations might have been warmer or at least more intense. As it is, no U.S. secretary of state, let alone president, has ever visited Bulgaria, and the highest level official Bulgarian visit to Washington was made in 1974 by deputy premier and Politburo member Ivan Popov.

Popov was a technocrat, and therefore it was not by chance that he was selected to go to the United States. He was one of the small but growing number of Bulgarian technocrats—officials, managers, scientists, an impressive group by all accounts—who fanned out across the industrialized

West in the 1970s. The impact of what they saw could eventually be the biggest single benefit Bulgaria ever derived from the whole détente process. They did not return to their homeland convinced capitalists, but they seemed strongly impressed by Western technology, standards, and methods and were in no doubt about their relevance to Bulgaria. Nor did the contrast between Western and Soviet "state of the art" fail to register. These travelers now constitute the basis of Bulgaria's technical elite and are not without influence on political decisionmaking.

Bulgaria derived much from détente, but it would be a mistake to assume that the country gave nothing in return. Nor were its offerings restricted to attar of roses and fine tobacco, the sum total of Bulgarian excellence in the minds of many Westerners. The offerings consisted of some of the finest examples of early and medieval Bulgarian art and civilization, arranged in exhibitions under the auspices of Lyudmila Zhivkova, Todor Zhivkov's daughter.

If Nicu Ceauşescu gave nepotism a bad name, Lyudmila Zhivkova made it almost respectable. She was a feisty personality, with a wide range of interests, some of them exotic. But what really distinguished Lyudmila was her cultural nationalism. What she tried to do with her magnificent cultural-historical exhibitions and archeological excavations, not to mention the massive celebrations she promoted in 1981 to mark the 1300th anniversary of the founding of the first Bulgarian state, was to convince Bulgarians of the value of their heritage. Many of them apparently needed convincing. Throughout their modern history, Bulgarians have labored under a crippling national inferiority complex born of frustration, slights—real or imagined—and a bad international reputation. More recently, the Marxist-Leninist indoctrination young Bulgarians endured inside and outside the classroom often belittled or ignored the national component in their country's history.

Backed by a doting father, Lyudmila set about altering this, and she struck a responsive chord in the Bulgarian population. In Western Europe and the United States, her exhibitions made a considerable impression and at least made a small dent in the prevailing ignorance. They showed not just Bulgaria's debt to European civilization but also her contribution to it. Zhivkova had spent several months as a postgraduate student at Oxford University and was a frequent visitor to Western European capitals, only going to Moscow when it was absolutely necessary. Already minister of culture and a Politburo member, she might have become Communist Bulgaria's Margaret Thatcher had she not died suddenly in 1981 at the age of thirty-seven. The Soviets never liked her. She was too Bulgarian and too European. Besides, she was spontaneous and unpredictable, two of the grisliest adjectives in the Soviet Russian lexicon. But the Bulgarian people did like her. They turned her funeral into the biggest demonstration of national feeling since the death of King Boris in 1943.

But while Lyudmila Zhivkova was striving to enhance Bulgaria's reputation in the West, the Bulgarian secret service appeared to be doing just the opposite. The allegation by Ali Ağca, the man who shot Pope John Paul II in 1981, that the Bulgarians had hired him captured world attention and gave Bulgaria the kind of spotlight it could well have done without. Whether this new notoriety was deserved or not has remained open to question. The Bulgarian defendant in the ensuing trial, Antonov, was acquitted in 1986 with a verdict equivalent to "not proven." His trial was a Roman judicial spectacular, and most Europeans took much of the evidence against him *cum grano salis.* But as the case developed, both inside and outside the courtroom, it threw some light, however dim, on the unsporting activities of the Bulgarian secret service that were all too demonstrable—gun running, drug smuggling, terrorism, sundry murders, to mention just a few. Nobody claimed that such activities were the exclusive preserve of the Bulgarians. But their disclosure ensured that Bulgaria emerged from the whole episode a certain loser. If Bulgaria were not guilty of trying to kill the pope (in the interests, of course, of the Kremlin—the "model satellite" syndrome), it was guilty of practically everything else, which made the charge of attempted pontificide plausible anyway! Bulgaria may have been not guilty as charged, but it had shown itself to be a criminal all the same.

Bulgaria showed itself even more criminal in the fall and winter of 1984–1985 when the Sofia regime ordered the compulsory, assimilative, name changing of the Turkish minority. This minority numbered between 700 and 800,000, about 10 percent of the whole population. They were ordered to shed their Turkish names and assume Bulgarian names. At the same time, they were declared not to be Turkish at all but descendants of ethnic Bulgarians who had been "turkicized" during the five hundred years of Ottoman rule. So it was now time to "bulgarize" them back again. Many resisted but were repressed with severity. Nothing can explain this preposterous barbarism except the hankering after a national, unitary state—the modern European obsession—and the determination to use any methods to achieve it.

Bulgaria had really put itself in the dock this time. But if, by rights, it got too much dreadful publicity for the papal assassination attempt charge, Bulgaria got far less than it deserved for the Turkish minority. The world reported the action and condemned it. Bulgaria appeared in a very bad light. But the Bulgarian leaders had calculated on the bad light soon lifting, and they were right. The big international scandal that the incident warranted did not materialize.

To those who remembered Vice President George Bush's remarks about Bulgaria in his "differentiation" speech in 1983, they now seemed just as prophetic as they had been indignant. Bush clearly "differentiated against" Bulgaria on two counts. It not only continued "to flagrantly violate the fundamental human rights," but it, and the GDR, acted as "proxies for the Soviets in the training, funding and arming of terrorists," as well as supplying "advisors and military and technical assistance to destabilize governments in the developing world." There would be neither grace nor favor from the United States, said Bush, unless the Bulgarian leaders altered their ways. They showed no signs of doing so.

Finally, as if Bulgaria has not had enough unwelcome attention, it is worth pointing out a feature of its development that could bring it even more. For a quarter century, Bulgaria has been the gateway to Europe for more than 1 million Turks. These are not its own Turks (who, officially, are no more) but citizens of Turkey who work and live in different West European countries. (The Turks are very much back in Europe, but in the other half and in a less exalted status than in days of Ottoman yore.) They use Bulgaria as transit territory: In a single year about 2.5 million Turks move in transit to and from Turkey, with some obviously going more than once. The overwhelming majority are on lawful business, and the last thing they want to do is loiter in Bulgaria. But a few are less innocent. They are part of a new criminal conspiracy with heroin as its basis, with Sofia as its headquarters, and presumably, with links to the Bulgarian secret service. Some of the witnesses at the Antonov trial in Rome were denizens of this underworld, and we have probably not heard the last of them or their sort. Largely thanks to them, Sofia, always a dignified provincial city, has become a metropolis of crime.

Albania

For many years, the apparent nonexistence of relations between Albania and the West seemed so established as to make pointless any speculation about them. Everybody said that for Albania's sake, this should not go on for ever—and left it at that. But Enver Hoxha seemed bent on showing that it could. Western imperialism along with Soviet revisionism were the two cardinal sins in his canon, and there was to be no truck with either.

But it was never quite as simple or as bleak as all that. Albania, after all, maintained diplomatic relations with several West European countries, including Italy, France, and Austria, and with very many countries throughout the world. (At the beginning of 1988 the total number was 110.) Relations with several Muslim countries in the Middle East and North Africa have always appeared to be relatively close. Albania was now officially atheist (religion was officially abolished in 1967), but two-thirds of its citizens had been Muslims, and many must have covertly remained so. It is this Islamic heritage that seems to explain the closeness of this tie. (In 1987 even a Saudi Arabian prince touched down in Tirana but not, presumably, in search of its night life.) Reluctantly, but out of necessity, Albania has also always maintained an embassy in Belgrade. (Yugoslavia has always been Albania's biggest trade partner.) Through all the vicissitudes of its communist life span, Albania has remained a member of the United Nations, its representatives incorrigibly antiimperialist, its permanent delegation lodged deep in the bowels of New York's Tudor Village.

Thus, Albania did not isolate itself totally, even from some Western countries. But if the "the West" is taken as a philosophical, historical, and political concept, then Albania wanted nothing to do with it. But things, indeed, had to change, and even before the end of the Hoxha era, they showed signs of doing so.

The change was hastened by the termination of Albania's client-patron relationship with China. This had been good while it lasted. China appeared only to have demanded what Hoxha was ready to give anyway: unstinting support against the Soviet Union. In return, the PRC gave Albania vital succor. Estimates of how much vary. Michael Kaser put total Chinese financial aid at about $885 million between 1959, when it began, and 1975.[7] But the sum total of Chinese aid was hardly measurable in any currency. As Louis Zanga pointed out, thousands of Chinese experts helped build industrial projects in Albania, including the powerful radio transmitters that made Radio Tirana's soporific foreign language broadcasts so audible. There was a Sino-Albanian shipping company and a weekly Tirana-Peking flight connection. Albania also became dependent on Chinese supplies of military hardware, either of its own manufacture or dusted-down models of Soviet provenance.[8] Some estimates have put total Chinese aid at $5 billion.

China was the longest-standing patron in Albania's history, longer even than Italy between the wars—and much less predatory. But on July 11, 1978, a date that could be a turning point in Albanian history, the Chinese announced that they had cut off all aid to Albania. Vitriolic insults had been traded between the two countries for more than a year, ostensibly regarding a major point in China's global ideology but actually because China was changing both its domestic and foreign policy. Most unnerving for Albania were the improving relations between Peking and Belgrade. Yugoslavia, therefore, popped up yet again as the Albanian bugbear. It is hard to exaggerate the role Yugoslavia has played in Albanian history, or at least, the role in which Albanians—often with good reason—have cast Yugoslavia. No matter how many corridors Albania has run down, it has never been able to hide. Yugoslavia has loomed at the end of every one.

It was time, therefore, for Albania to move on. But where? Hoxha was adamant: not to the West with cap in hand. He elevated "self-reliance," a constant slogan, from a virtue into part of his mythology. Nor did he just preach "self-reliance", he legislated it. An amendment to the constitution in 1976 expressly forbade the present and future Albanian governments from raising international loans. But, again, reality was not as stark as Hoxha's obsessiveness might have suggested. Total "self-reliance" would have meant suicide for the Albanians—perhaps through eating the grass Hoxha once threatened Khrushchev they would do. Behind the posturing, what Hoxha seemed to have had in mind was a strategy that, taking "self-reliance" as its cornerstone, would include three other components: intensified economic relations with the Third World; business (not client) relations with China; and expanding nondependent relations with the West. Relations, therefore, could be expanded with every part of the world except two: the United States, and the socialist sixth and its myrmidons.

This strategy got off to a fair start. To begin with, Albania's own contribution was by no means negligible. Although poor, Albania was not exactly a pauper. It had enough oil deposits for its own consumption, with a bit over going to Italy, Greece, and Yugoslavia, and considerable reserves of natural gas. Albania was also the world's third largest producer of chrome and its second biggest chrome exporter, mainly to the West. Albania had good reserves of copper and nickel and, again, was a big nickel exporter. The country's own energy supplies came mainly from hydroelectric power, which it also exported to Greece and Yugoslavia and even to Austria. Albania also exported agricultural produce; tomatoes, for example, did pretty well in Bavaria against more established competition.

Albania therefore could back its strategy with something of value. Trade with the Third World had also increased considerably and with China had settled onto a steadily rising curve, although nothing like what it was before 1978. The resumption of any economic relations at all after the termination of Chinese aid surprised many observers. But it was mutually beneficial. Albania needed parts and servicing for equipment already received. China's interest was more political: Keeping the tap dripping might make Tirana hesitate about edging back toward Moscow.

But however important distant parts might have been, it was Albania's window to Western Europe that promised the most. Hoxha opened the window a little, however reluctantly, before he died in 1985. With Greece, for example, with which relations had always been bedevilled by territorial and ethnic disputes, there were promising contacts at the beginning of the 1980s. With Italy, contacts had always been relatively correct. They were strengthened, at least symbolically, by the inauguration of a thrice-monthly ferry service between Durrës and Trieste in 1983. This is still losing money (all Italy's), but Italy's profit was political, not financial. French business delegations also began coming to Albania, but it was with West Germany that the most rewarding opportunities obviously lay. Contacts apparently began in the late 1970s, and in 1984 none other than Franz-Josef Strauss descended on Tirana, representing himself, Freistaat Bayern, and the Federal Republic of Germany—probably in that order.

After Hoxha's death, the pace of Western contacts quickened and the scope broadened. Ramiz Alia, Hoxha's anointed, has undemonstratively but assiduously begun to change Albanian policy at home and abroad. Relations with Greece, for example, had improved beyond all recognition by the end of 1987. The Papandreou government in Athens came in for much criticism at home for its share in this. Conservative and clerical circles tried to keep the old wounds open, but they could not stop what may become a permanent healing process. The forty-seven-year-old state of war that still technically existed between the two countries was finally lifted in 1987, and this led to a visit to Tirana by the Greek foreign minister with a large delegation. By 1988, Andreas Papandreou was scheduled to come to Tirana, and Adil Çarçani, the Albanian premier, was invited to Athens.

Albania seemed ready for reconciliation with Greece. With other Balkan countries there have been no such signs of bilateral improvement. (Turkey is here excepted; relations have been good since independence.) There have been some efforts to lessen tensions with Yugoslavia. A cultural agreement, delayed since 1984, was finally signed in 1988, and Yugoslav tourists were allowed in a few at a time. But Kosovo alone prevented any real rapprochement. Massive Serbian agitation regarding Kosovo began in 1988. In 1989, when the Serbs commemorate the 600th anniversary of the Battle of Kosovo, tension will even increase. On the field of Kosovo in 1389, the Ottomans broke Serbian power, and this defeat, in what was once the heartland of Serbia, has gone down in legend and emotion as the greatest event in Serb destiny, tragic, glorious, and mystical.

But, while still remaining selective in bilateral relations, Albania became a convert to multilateral regional cooperation in the Balkans, something from which Albania had excluded itself for more than twenty years. In December 1987, Albania attended an all-Balkan conference on the environment and in February 1988 participated in a regional foreign minister's conference sponsored by none other than the Yugoslavs. This was a welcome development and could be important. Albania now considers itself better off "inside" than "outside" the Balkan club.

But the biggest break of all came with the establishment of diplomatic relations with West Germany in October 1987. This was immediately followed by a visit to Tirana of Hans-Dietrich Genscher, the West German foreign minister. Work began on a program of economic cooperation and, very soon after Genscher's departure, the ubiquitous Franz-Josef Strauss, not to be outdone, turned up again in Tirana, this time with a check for DM6,000,000 (about $3.5 million) as an earnest demonstration of West German good intentions.

Very soon after this, the GDR raised the status of its embassy in Tirana from chargé d'affaires (a status in place since 1961) to full ambassadorial level. This move was less a harbinger of some future Albanian rapprochement with the Soviet bloc as a whole than another case of the East Germans aping their neighbors. This resumption of normal diplomatic relations with Albania, although a surprise, did not come totally out of the blue. As Bonn's contacts with Tirana increased, so did East Berlin's. This, presumably, was not done behind Moscow's back, still less against its wishes. Besides, this contact could have obvious advantages for the Soviets. But that might be for the future. For the present, this was a case of "autonomous diplomacy" on the East Germans' part. As for the Albanians, they stand to do quite well outside of the dual relationship.

With other Western countries there have been no breakthroughs, but there is progress. There have been informal meetings with Great Britain to try to break the deadlock arising from the Corfu channel incident of 1946, when two British destroyers were struck by Albanian mines with considerable loss of life. As a result, Britain impounded some Albanian gold. This was the kind of dispute on which Hoxha was pathologically stubborn. Ramiz Alia is more supple, and it should not be long before British diplomats return to Tirana after an absence of a half century. Whether U.S. diplomats will return so soon is doubtful. This would mean a momentous break with the past for which Alia is not yet ready.

He is not even ready for the kind of gesture that might make a real breakthrough in relations with Italy, Albania's "natural" Western partner.

In December 1985, six Albanians broke into the Italian Embassy in Tirana and asked for asylum and passage to Italy. They have been there ever since, getting no closer to Italy than watching Juventus Turin on Italian television. As a result, Albanian-Italian relations have been almost frozen. The situation is a microcosm of the East-West standoff, of the classic struggle between liberalism and Leninism. But with a minimum of will and wit, the Albanian government could solve or at least finesse this problem. Albania needs Italy to help it into the European economic system and into the world generally. If Albania lets six citizens holed up in the Italian Embassy get in the way of this, the country cannot complain if nobody takes it seriously.

The Outlook

All three countries under review face a difficult and uncertain future. The problems they face, although different in degree, are broadly similar and could bring serious consequences if they are not solved or at least tackled with some resolution. For all three, part of the uncertainty centers on leadership. In Albania, the transition from Enver Hoxha to Ramiz Alia in 1985 proceeded with an apparently enviable smoothness. This was largely because Hoxha settled the question of his succession several years before he died. Mehmet Shehu, prime minister since 1954 and the recognized number two person in the regime, had evidently expected to succeed him. Hoxha, however, decided against Shehu and in favor of Alia. Whether he had the good of the country in mind or was nursing some personal grudge against his old, fearsome comrade-in-arms is unimportant. Hoxha would never have recognized the distinction anyway. Once he made his decision, Shehu had to be disposed of. In a classic Stalinist frame-up, spiced with his own paranoid inventiveness and with vestiges of Balkan blood feud, Hoxha physically destroyed Shehu in December 1981, either through murder or forced suicide, and dispersed his powerful supporters. Without this carnage, Alia would never have been able to control Shehu once Hoxha died. With the dirty work already done for him, Alia had little problem settling into office. But it still remains to be seen whether he has the authority and the ability to lead Albania out of the Communist Dark Ages. He has at least made a beginning.

In Bulgaria, with Zhivkov at seventy-six, a change of leadership must be in the offing. When it does come, it will certainly lack the blood-soaked prelude that occurred in Albania, but some Bulgarians worry that so far there seems to have been no prelude at all. There have been several putative "crown princes" in the last twenty years, but Zhivkov has seen fit to reduce them all. There are now several potential successors with talent and experience. The most recent heir-apparent, Chudomir Alexandrov, was unceremoniously cut down in July 1988, after a lengthy run during which he made a strong impression as a modern, reform-minded aspirant. He certainly seemed to be riding the crest of the Gorbachev wave, which may well have been one reason for his undoing. Another—much more serious—may have been that he not only chafed at Zhivkov's political longevity but actually tried to shorten it. Rumors were indeed rife in Sofia that Alexandrov had led a conspiracy against Zhivkov. But Zhivkov, mindful of the recent palace revolution in Budapest, met the danger with masterful determination. He might be prepared to accept the new recipe for system regeneration that Moscow had drawn up, but he was, at the same time, going to show everybody—Soviets, Bulgarians, and anyone else interested—that he was not going to be hanged, drawn, and Kádáred. Even so, Zhivkov would be doing his country a service if he designated his successor soon and gave him security of tenure.

Whereas Albania has recently had a change of leadership and Bulgaria is expecting one, in Romania everybody is hoping for one. Few, however, would wager on it happening very soon. Ceauşescu celebrated his seventieth birthday in 1988 amid megalomaniac celebrations and mounting popular discontent. He suffers from cancer of the prostate, an affliction he has contained for several years through medical attention and his own toughness. It could kill him or force him out of office any time. But it appears to be the only thing that will, so long as he keeps control over his security apparatus and the army stays loyal or at least neutral. (Several military coup attempts have been rumored during the last several years, but if they have amounted to anything at all, they have apparently not been serious enough to shake the regime.) If, for any reason, Ceauşescu were to go, then his family would go, too, and with considerable fleetness of foot. Whatever arrangements he might make for their future, they would quickly follow him unlamented into the past. His successor will probably not be a uniformed general, still less a Soviet proconsul, but an experienced senior apparatchik charged with shedding the Ceauşescu incubus and keeping the party together. It could be Gheorghe Pana, a veteran with a wealth of experience, who has achieved the rare distinction under Ceauşescu of retaining his dignity as well as his rank. Pana has elements in common with Miloš Jakeš, Husák's successor in Czechoslovakia. Neither seems fitted to lead his country in a new era, but each might bring it with less than mortal injury out of the old one. Such men cannot make history, but they might do a creditable job tidying up after it.

Whoever the new leaders are in Bulgaria and Romania, they will face the most serious problems, but there can be none more awesome than the one facing Hoxha's successor, Ramiz Alia. This concerns the very survival of his nation, and the threat this time comes not from Yugoslavia but from a still more pervasive enemy: starvation. The Albanian population is the fastest growing in Europe. It is now about 3 million; by the end of the century it will be 4. Albania is a small country with large parts of it uncultivable. It can sustain such a population increase only if it grows (and distributes) more food. Albania will not do this until it gives its peasants the right incentives through extensive privatization. There have already been a few signs that Alia is aware of the problem, but what he has done hardly scratches its surface. Much more must be done urgently, and while he is about it, Alia could do worse than scrap some of Albania's useless heavy industry, built according to Stalinist prescription. But nothing on the domestic scene should divert attention from reform in agriculture. Alia must also continue to expand contacts abroad and get as much Western help as possible. The constitutional proscription of foreign loans, even if it stays on the statute book, need not be an insuperable obstacle. As it is, Albania takes small commercial credits from abroad, and for pragmatism it might take a lesson from some Muslim countries. The Sharia forbids charging or paying interest, but these countries still manage to live a pretty normal international financial life. In sum, what Albania needs is progressive deEnverization. The house that Enver Hoxha built can only be saved if its builder is repudiated.

In Romania's case, it seems that change depends on Ceauşescu's departure. Although the debris of his rule will still remain, the whole context of Romanian public life will have changed and its atmosphere lightened. Nor would it seem that Romania's problems, however acute, are insoluble. Over time their seriousness might be mitigated enough to make them containable, and this need not involve giving up the degree of independence Ceauşescu has gained. The country is ripe for *perestroika,* and if Romania were to begin "restructuring," the West could then maintain and increase its economic aid without the current pangs of conscience. If, for example, Ceauşescu's obsessive determination to pay off Romania's hard-currency debt by the early 1990s were moderated, the West would cooperate by agreeing to a generous rescheduling, and this would have a considerable effect on living standards. It would have an instant effect on morale, too. Few nations are as resilient as the Romanians. They would get over Ceauşescu as they have gotten over other blights on their history.

Bulgaria's immediate problems appear less pressing than those of either Albania or Romania. Already in 1987, Bulgaria announced its own version of *perestroika,* a typically gargantuan program that may have been Zhivkov's way, not of copying Gorbachev, but of preempting him. Subsequently, this reform program was considerably toned down perhaps through opposition, perhaps through poor preparation. The Bulgarian economy has fallen precipitiously off the plateau of prosperity it appeared to reach in the late 1970s. The standard of living has been seriously affected. Food and energy shortages, although less severe, are now as familiar in Bulgaria as they are in Romania. In 1986, the economy made a quite impressive recovery, which was at least partly maintained in 1987. But, considerably more so than the Romanian, the Bulgarian economy is vulnerable in raw materials, and the outlook is unpromising.

All three countries, therefore, are facing uncertainty at home. But they must also be looking with uncertainty and even some apprehensiveness toward Moscow, awaiting the first real signs of any shift or quickening in the new leadership's relations with them. It is still too early to be definitive, but there have already been signs that might point permanently to new paths. The least discernible change so far has been with Albania. Gorbachev appears to have extended an olive branch in much the same way Brezhnev did, and Ramiz Alia appears to have spurned it in much the same way Hoxha did. This could go on indefinitely.

Bulgaria will probably have to fend more for itself under Gorbachev. It formerly enjoyed an informal Soviet equivalent of "most favored nation" status, but there have recently been signs that this might be coming to an end—not because of any special Gorbachev animus against Bulgaria but because of a tougher Soviet policy generally toward economic relations with Eastern Europe. Bulgaria's geostrategic location, however, remains as crucial as ever, and the country could well come in useful to Moscow again in any new strategy toward Greece and Turkey the Soviets might initiate. If so, there would be more opportunities for the Bulgarian leaders to exert the leverage they have always had with Moscow.

With Romania, Gorbachev suffered his biggest rebuff to date in Eastern Europe when, during a visit to Bucharest in 1987, Ceauşescu made it plain to him—and to a disappointed Romanian public—that *perestroika* was unsuitable, un-Romanian, and unsocialist. Gorbachev may have to wait—and may be content to—until Ceauşescu's fate or his folly finally catches up with him. Gorbachev may not have to wait long.

Moscow's future bilateral relations with these three countries are intriguing enough. But even more intriguing would be Moscow's designs on, or for, each of them in any multilateral policy, any overall Balkan policy, the new leadership may be brewing. Has the Soviet Union permanently resigned itself to its losses in the Balkans, or will it evolve a new, noncoercive approach designed at least partly to recover its former position? Will a Gorbachev Doctrine rise to match the Reagan Doctrine or will the adversarial context of East-West relations that spawns such strategies melt away? It would be unwise to assume too early that it will; in which case a new Soviet *Balkanpolitik* might be expected to unfold. It would be directed primarily at Yugoslavia, but neither Albania, Bulgaria, nor Romania could remain unaffected by it.

In the meantime, all six Balkan states—Greece, Turkey, Bulgaria, Romania, Albania, and Yugoslavia—have been showing welcome signs of multilateral cooperation. The Balkan foreign ministers conference in Belgrade and other signs of cooperation are welcome developments, renewed efforts at rapprochement that go back almost sixty years. These developments should be followed with interest and sympathy but, for the moment, without undue optimism. Until the existing bilateral differences at least begin to be settled, then multilateral conferences, however cordial, may not be so much a solution for Balkan problems as a diversion from them.

Notes

1. Montenegro, which has played a role in Balkan history out of all proportion to its size, was never subjugated by the Turks but was only recognized as an independent state in 1878.

2. Quoted in J. Swire, *Albania—The Rise of a Kingdom* (New York: Arno Press and *New York Times,* 1971), p. 162.

3. Larry Watts, personal communication.

4. J. F. Brown, *Eastern Europe and Communist Rule* (Durham, N.C.: Duke University Press, 1988), p. 276.

5. Paul Lendvai, *Eagles in Cobwebs: Nationalism and Communism in the Balkans* (Garden City, N.Y.: Doubleday, 1969), p. 273.

6. Amid all the mutual hatred, it is a pleasure to record that in the famous Jiu Valley coal miners' strike in Romania in 1977, Hungarian and Romanian strikers stood shoulder to shoulder against the authorities. But this was a rare occasion indeed. It would be instructive to know the approximate ethnic breakdown of the Braşov rioters, particularly whether Romanians, Hungarians, and Germans (Saxons) showed a degree of unity there. The size of any Hungarian participation would be especially interesting. Braşov has traditionally had strong Hungarian and German communities.

7. Michael Kaser, "Trade and Aid in the Albanian Economy," in *East European Economics Post-Helsinki* (Washington, D.C.: GPO, 1977), pp. 1327–1328.

8. Louis Zanga, "China Stops Aid to Albania," *Radio Free Europe Research Background Report,* July 13, 1987.

13

The German Democratic Republic

William E. Griffith

Of all the Communist countries of Central and Eastern Europe, the German Democratic Republic (the GDR, or East Germany) has risen the farthest and fastest. Although its cities were mostly bombed into destruction during World War II, and what was left of its factories was largely dragged away to the Soviet Union as reparations, it is today the most prosperous Communist country in the world and one of the top twenty world industrial powers. Much of this recovery is the result of its industrial traditions; but perhaps more is due to the fact that its citizens are Germans, endowed with discipline, organizational talent, bureaucratic efficiency, and a work ethic rare in Communist countries.

Yet the GDR is the smaller, less naturally endowed, much more politically dependent, and less affluent of the two German states, and it is now in increasing political, economic, and technological difficulties. The attempts by its Communist rulers to create a "socialist German nation" have failed. Indeed, since the early 1970s, some 80 percent of all East Germans have watched *West* German television news nightly. Moreover, East Germany has close to a two-currency system. The West German deutschmark is preferred, indeed essential, to get repairs done.[1]

Since 1961, the Berlin Wall has surrounded West Berlin, a city of 1.9 million in the midst of East Germany that is officially still under the military occupation of the United States, Great Britain, and France, but is actually in most respects a de facto part of the Federal Republic of Germany (the FRG, or West Germany). The two most serious post–World War II East-West crises in Europe were about two unsuccessful Soviet attempts to cut back this allied role and the city's Western democracy. But despite the Wall, the Iron Curtain, and the East German border guards' order to shoot to kill those East Germans who try to flee to the West, in 1987, 3 million East Germans legally visited West Germany, of whom more than 1 million were under the retirement age of sixty-five and almost all of whom returned.

The Council of Mutual Economic Assistance (CMEA) and Warsaw Pact members are "penetrated," perhaps now less than before, by the Soviet Union. The GDR is doubly penetrated: politically, militarily, and economically by the Soviet Union, but also economically, culturally, by the mass media, and through them politically as well by West Germany. Moreover, there have recently been three episodes of GDR opposition to Soviet policies: the then Socialist Unity party (SED) First Secretary Walter Ulbricht's resistance in 1971 to Soviet pressure to conclude a compromise Berlin Agreement with the three Western powers; the Soviet refusal to allow his successor Erich Honecker to visit West Germany in 1984 because he opposed the USSR's then violently anti–West German policy; and Honecker's resistance to instituting Mikhail Gorbachev's reforms in the GDR. The old saw, "The German Democratic Republic is neither German nor democratic nor a republic" is thus in part false. The GDR is neither democratic nor a republic, but it is as German as it dares and only as Soviet as its Communist ruling elite thinks it must be in order to maintain themselves in power.

More than in any other country in the region, East Germany is politically schizophrenic. If the East Germans thought that they could reunite with the Federal Republic without precipitating a Soviet invasion, they probably would; but because they believe that the Soviets (despite Gorbachev's current nonintervention promises) probably would invade, the East Germans are making the best of their situation, which is not as bad as it used to be. Their belief in the possibility of such invasion is strengthened by the more than twenty Soviet divisions, some 350,000 troops, and about 5,750 tanks stationed in East Germany. In addition to their war-fighting capabilities, this Group of Soviet Forces in Germany (GSFG) ensures Soviet control over East Germany. The GSFG also so blocks off Poland from the West that Moscow can either invade Poland from the west as well as from the east or, if it wishes, allow Poland to become less repressive than East Germany, as it has, without the latter's stability being overly threatened.

The GDR's Beginnings

During World War II, the German Communist leaders in exile in Moscow planned, presumably under Soviet direction, minimally to sovietize rapidly the Soviet zone of Germany and maximally to sovietize all of it. After the USSR's defeat in World War I and near defeat in World War II, no leader of any strong Soviet Union has wanted, or probably again ever will want, a strong, united Germany. Many Germans in both German states believe, and almost all hope, that this is not true, but they are victims of illusion. Joseph Stalin's immediate postwar policies reinforced the fear, hatred, and frustrated superiority with which the Germans have historically viewed the Russians. He underestimated the U.S. reaction to his sovietization of Eastern Europe (as Vojtech Mastny writes in Chapter 2), so that when the United States decided to stand on the Elbe, he so intensified sovietization that the cold war began in earnest, initially with the first Berlin blockade and then with the Korean War. Meanwhile, the Social Democrats had been forcibly merged with, and taken under control of, the Communists in the Soviet zone. Moscow used de-nazification there to bring about a major socialist revolution. However, when Stalin began his post-1948 blood purges, Ulbricht only minimally followed suit.

Ulbricht was a Communist, but a German one. His highly developed instincts for survival and power made him so conform to Stalin's every whim that he seemed to many in and outside Germany to be a Soviet agent. He had also lived through Stalin's bloody reign of terror in Moscow in the 1930s, when one-third of the German Communist leadership was slaughtered, but probably more as a conformist than an instigator. Certainly Ulbricht was a Marxist-Leninist; certainly he had an authoritarian, indeed a tyrannical personality. But his opposition to Leonid Brezhnev's desire for a Berlin compromise in 1971 and his resultant removal showed, as his successor Honecker has also done, that each was willing to differ with Moscow when he thought that Moscow, not East Berlin, had changed its policies and that his own interests were at stake. However, Honecker's differences were less offensive because, unlike Ulbricht, he did not directly and openly challenge Soviet authority and Moscow was weaker in 1984 than when Ulbricht opposed a strong Brezhnev in 1971.

It is in this context that one can best understand the past and the present of the German Democratic Republic. Its leaders want power, for themselves and for their country. They know that they cannot ensure the former unless they are allied with and supported by the Soviet Union, for they have few if any illusions about their subjects' sullen toleration of them, although they hoped in 1984 to get some popularity by opposing Moscow on its anti-German policies. They thought until the 1962 Cuban crisis that Soviet power would make them strong and West Germany (and the United States) weak. But thereafter, especially after the 1971 Berlin Agreement, they knew they could not rely on such a Soviet victory.

The GDR and the High-Technology Revolution

At the same time, they also came to realize that the developed world was entering the new high-technology revolution and that this gave East Germany the greatest chance of any Communist state to take the lead in it and thereby to offer the Soviet Union what it could not become itself: a Communist source of high technology. But it was one thing to realize this and quite another to do it successfully. As it turned out, the GDR has been increasingly unsuccessful in this effort.

The GDR has failed to compete successfully with the West technologically for three reasons. First, the GDR's research and development base is too small to enable it to be competitive with the West and Japan. Second, its bureaucratic system discourages innovation and prevents increased cooperation with the West to limit lags in its development. Third, Comecon's (the USSR's) attempts to overcome this handicap by intrabloc division of labor failed because the GDR's Comecon partners could not meet East German quality standards. These Comecon attempts and Soviet demands in the 1980s for more GDR exports (even if of higher quality manufactured goods) were dragging GDR technology down by making it less possible to export for hard currency to Western markets. Indeed, by the late 1980s, East Germany had so lost in export competitiveness that even other Comecon countries tried to buy Western, rather than East German, technology when they could. Despite the improvement of political relations between the two German states, the trade between them, after previously rising, declined in 1986 and 1987, primarily because of declining East German export competitiveness and greater GDR trade with the Soviet Union. In part for these reasons, but also because of West German economic growth and emphasis on export competitiveness, including in high technology, East German per capita gross national product (GNP) in 1986 was only 55.5 percent of West German, whereas in 1983 it had been 76 percent. Thus, the gap between East and West Germany was growing, in favor of the latter. Nor surprisingly, West German credits to East Germany were rising rapidly also.[2] Thus, East Germany could not alone recover export competitiveness; Soviet foreign economic policy hindered, not helped it to do so; and West Germany had ample resources and, if anything, rising political will to do so.

To recover its export competitiveness the GDR had to either limit the areas of its research and development or maintain closer relations with West Germany, which alone had the money and the political motive to help the GDR with credits (guaranteed either by the Bonn government or by Hermes, a semi-public export guarantee institution) and with technology. In return, the GDR had to pay in political currency: more East Germans visiting West Germany and more East German dependence on, and accepting more influence of, the FRG.

Honecker's GDR

East Germany included the core of Prussia's combination of work ethic, respect for authority, ambivalence in attitudes toward the West, and little experience of democracy. The GDR's 1961 construction of the Berlin Wall had staunched the flow of refugees, especially of skilled personnel, to West Germany. The coming to power in Bonn in October 1969 of a Social Democratic party–Free Democratic party (SPD-FDP) government seemed to promise that the GDR would achieve one of its principal foreign policy objectives: diplomatic recognition on a global scale.

When Honecker succeeded Ulbricht in 1971 he began a deceptively contradictory policy: consumerism plus delimitation (*Abgrenzung*) against West Germany. He did so because he feared that the massive travel of West Germans and West Berliners to the GDR, for which the 1971 Berlin Agreement provided, would so increase envy of the FRG and discontent about the GDR that he had to bribe and cut off the East German population from infection by West Germany.

Consumerism and high technology, as the Third Reich and Imperial Japan had shown, did not necessarily require complete political pluralism and an open society; they could be reconciled with some degree of political delimitation. But whereas the GDR's predecessors, Imperial and Nazi Germany, had been in the front rank of technology, East Germany was technologically inferior to the United States and Japan and even to West Germany. The GDR therefore had to have access to their higher technology. Moreover, West Germany offered such access on uniquely favorable terms. There were those in Moscow, as well as in East Berlin, who argued that Soviet technological advance required access through East Germany with that Western country, West Germany, that had the geographical location, economic tradition, technological competence, and the political motives to give that access, even against the opposition of its senior ally, the United States.[3]

This policy proved increasingly successful. After 1961, when the Berlin Wall went up, average East Germans, and even more the managerial and professional classes, who enjoyed under Honecker what the late Peter Ludz called "consultative authoritarianism," felt that they had no alternative but to adjust to the inevitable, and so they did.[4] Some 3 million East Germans had fled to West Germany before then, a far greater percentage than in the other Communist country, Cuba, that allowed its dissidents to emigrate. After 1961, delimitation and the ruthless East German security police (the *Staatssicherheitspolizei,* usually called the *Stasi*) took care of the rest. Finally, after 1975, when Moscow and Washington became involved in Angola, East-West tensions rapidly increased, so that the Soviet pressure for détente that had unseated Ulbricht no longer weighed on Honecker.

What did, however, were the unfavorable consequences for East German high technology that East-West tension brought with it. These were double and reinforcing in nature. On the one hand, Brezhnev's rule increasingly brought stagnation in the Soviet Union. Although this made Moscow more dependent on East Germany for technology and thus increased East German leverage there, it also had an opposite, and from the Soviet viewpoint, more devastating effect. It rapidly eroded East German confidence in Soviet power, especially technological power, and modern German history predisposed East Germans, like West Germans, to measure power by level of technology. In the 1980s, increasing crisis in Poland, stagnation in post-1968 Czechoslovakia, disturbing domestic reforms in Hungary—all these made East Germany more important to the Soviet Union and East Berlin more aware of that fact.

Moreover, Honecker and his associates became increasingly confident that the Berlin Agreement and the resultant influx of West German tourists were not destabilizing the GDR and that consumerism, consultative authoritarianism, and the security police had the situation well in hand. As Bonn's attitude toward East Berlin became less hostile, the GDR profited increasingly from a variety of West German deutschmark payments, ranging from the West Berlin transit traffic to Bonn's ransoming East German political prisoners at very high prices. When Soviet-U.S. tensions increased, Bonn's SPD-FDP government helped keep Western Europe an island of détente, a policy that the CDU/CSU-FDP coalition (Christian Democratic Union/[Bavarian] Christian Social Union–Free Democratic party) continued after it took over power in late 1982.

East Germany increasingly reciprocated this West German policy, for several reasons. The GDR's elite was increasingly confident of its own and its state's stability. The elite had also become more confident that Helmut Kohl was continuing Helmut Schmidt's *Ostpolitik.* By 1984, Honecker was dealing with a Soviet leadership that was weak, old, and divided, just the opposite of the Brezhnev leadership in 1971. Kohl knew that Konstantin Chernenko's health was so bad that there would soon be a new Soviet leader, for whom Kohl could afford to wait. He needed West German credits and technology more than Ulbricht had in 1971. He was negotiating with the SPD, with some success. Finally, he knew that a minority of the Moscow ruling elite agreed that the GDR, and indeed the USSR, should not engage in such a confrontation course with Bonn, which would fail to stop intermediate-range nuclear forces (INF) deployment or reverse it. Rather the GDR should move toward détente with the FRG, for much the same reasons that Gorbachev later did.

The Bonn–East Berlin Rapprochement

Like the other East European countries, the GDR took advantage of the eagerness of Western banks to loan the funds they received after 1973 from oil-producing countries, but it borrowed much less than Poland and Hungary and kept its Western credit rating high. Moreover, the West German banks received what amounted to West German governmental guarantees for their loans to East Germany. Soon Bonn began to offer increasingly large credits to East Berlin in expectation of improvement in travel between the two German states. Moreover, Bonn was the most opposed of any North Atlantic Treaty Organization (NATO) state to limitations on nonmilitary technology transfer to East Germany, never considered revising the Treaty of Rome's guarantee that trade between the two German states (*innerdeutscher Handel*) would be tariff free, and only occasionally raised or lowered (in 1982–1985) the interest-free credits to East Germany (the "swing") according to East German political concessions. However, by the late 1980s, the "swing" amount had greatly increased. Nevertheless, the GDR found it necessary to use it only very little.

Thus, when the East-West controversy broke out in Europe at the end of the 1970s about NATO INF deployment, East Germany, and much more overtly Hungary, resisted Soviet pressure on the issue. Although a minority in the Moscow political elite did not believe that Moscow would succeed, Leonid Brezhnev, his successors Yuri Andropov and Konstantin Chernenko, and the majority of their associates were determined to try to stop NATO INF deployment and were increasingly encouraged by the large-scale anti-INF peace movements that rapidly developed in Great Britain, the Netherlands, and especially in West Germany. (The West German movement inspired a small equivalent response in East Germany that was strengthened by the extreme militarization of East German society and centered among the youth of the Evangelical church, but GDR repression and discrimination against church members kept it under control.)

In December 1983, the West German Parliament endorsed INF deployment, which began immediately thereafter. In response, Moscow counterdeployed more intermediate- and short-range missiles in East Germany and Czechoslovakia. Honecker thereupon declared that East Germany did not "enjoy" this counterdeployment and that there was a "community of responsibility" between the two German states that war should never again begin on German soil.

The extent of East German objections to this Soviet policy was implicitly but clearly shown by the GDR's reprinting excerpts from several articles by Mátyás Szűrös, international secretary of the Hungarian party Central Committee, in which he declared that equal priority should be given to national and to international (Soviet) priorities and that socialist countries should therefore compromise on them (rather than countenance a Soviet "leading role"); that small countries in both parts of Europe should play a greater role in preserving détente; and that the (Soviet-formulated) "general laws of the construction of socialism" should be "creatively reinterpreted." Because Hungary also needed West German credits and technology and had no anti-German tradition but an anti-Russian one, and because Moscow had tolerated János Kádár's reformist policies, these positions were perhaps less surprising than the East German reprinting of much of them. Still, with a very few exceptions, the SED leadership only reprinted and did not originate such articles—another example of Honecker's careful and, as it eventually turned out, successful maneuvering.

As long as Chernenko was in power, Soviet hostility to both German states continued to intensify, to the point where in September 1984 Honecker felt compelled to "postpone" his scheduled visit to the Federal Republic. He did this, in my judgment, primarily because of the Soviet pressure to do so. But he had other reasons as well. He knew he could afford to wait (because Chernenko was old and ill), and he probably thought that Moscow would return to détente sooner or later; his desire to improve relations with West Germany was shared, for historic and economic reasons, by Hungary and also by Romania and Bulgaria; the SED was negotiating with the SPD, within the context of the SPD's "second phase of *Ostpolitik*"; and the year before, at a conference in East Berlin on Karl Marx, the SED had joined with the SPD in maintaining that preserving peace must take priority over social change.[5]

Honecker probably thought that by waiting he would get Bonn to upgrade its protocol status when the visit did occur and knew that Bonn blamed Chernenko, not him, for the postponement; he profited from the GDR's good economic situation; and he successfully strengthened his domestic power position, more than once reasserted his general support for détente, and continued contacts and negotiations with Bonn after he had postponed his visit there. The good relations between the two German states were also shown by the fact that during 1984 East Berlin received some 2,933 billion DM (about $1.55 billion) in West German government–guaranteed credits more than it had in 1983, and these credits continued to rise, if more slowly, thereafter.[6] In return the GDR eased its restrictions on travel to West Germany.

When Gorbachev came to power in early 1985, he soon moved rapidly toward détente with the West, abandoned his opposition to INF deployment, and negotiated an INF treaty with the United States whereby both INF and the total Soviet SS-20 deployment were to be destroyed. Gorbachev also made Soviet policy less unfavorable to the two German states. Thereafter, Soviet policy toward West Germany improved, and Honecker was no longer under Soviet pressure to be hostile to Bonn. The INF treaty provoked conservative criticism within the West German CDU and CSU. Kohl's decision shortly before the Honecker visit to endorse the treaty, as well as to dismantle the West German Pershing I-A missiles helped prepare the atmosphere for the visit and for Soviet-U.S. arms control negotiations. Honecker made a similar contribution just before the visit by releasing some prisoners and easing border tensions.

When Honecker visited West Germany in September 1987, Bonn had already agreed to upgrade the protocol of the visit from what it had been prepared to agree to in 1984 and also to discuss with him international issues such as arms control. For example, although it was not officially a "state visit" but only a "working" one, and his host was therefore Chancellor Kohl rather than President Richard von Weizsäcker, the ceremonies were at a state-visit level. That Kohl and Honecker inspected a West German guard of honor at the Bonn Chancery while both national anthems were played, seemed to many West Germans to symbolically make the partition far closer to permanent, one of the things Honecker wanted the most. The visit also helped improve his image abroad and in the GDR and identified him more closely with détente. From his viewpoint, all this overshadowed the fact that East as well as West German television broadcast the speeches of Kohl and Honecker, and the former forcefully stressed Bonn's commitment to its eventual goal of German reunification.[7]

The visit also further symbolized that Gorbachev was prepared to give the Communist Central and East European states more autonomy provided that certain essentials were maintained: rule by the Communist party; some, albeit less, control over their media; and coordination of foreign policy with him on important issues, rather than automatically following the Soviet line. Thus, Honecker did not defy Moscow as much as Ulbricht had, including by first postponing his trip to West Germany, and Gorbachev, not he, changed his policy on détente and on West Germany.[8]

Honecker and Gorbachev

Why, then, were East German relations with the Soviet Union again strained, on a quite different issue, by 1988? The immediate cause was the East German resistance to Gorbachev's reformist policies, which, Honecker feared, would destabilize him and Communist rule in East Germany. This was not new in East German–Soviet relations. Ulbricht had opposed Nikita Khrushchev's reforms in 1956 and Brezhnev's desire for a compromise Berlin Agreement in 1971. Honecker was initially so fearful of the latter's destabilizing results that he instituted consumerism plus delimitation. The more West

Germany penetrated East Germany by credits, technology, television, radio, and massive inter-German travel, and the more the Soviet Union was looked down upon in East Germany (as it had been in Prussia), particularly after Gorbachev's decision to pull the Soviet troops out of Afghanistan, as an underdeveloped, backward, Slav country, the more Honecker had to be concerned about his and his party's future. So had Ulbricht when Khrushchev combined domestic reform with international détente, especially with the United States and West Germany. Honecker may think that both are necessary to prevent the Soviet Union from becoming a second-rate power, but the East German leadership has historically never been so convinced that they can do the same. Finally, Honecker, like Ulbricht before him but far more successfully, resisted rapid Soviet policy changes that gave total priority to Soviet interests and, he thought, endangered East German stability and his own power position.

In the late 1980s, Honecker had more justification for his concern than before. Although the East German peace movement, like its West German counterpart, had declined sharply after INF deployment, Honecker faced more popular pressure from several sides at once. There seemed in 1988 to be five such sources of pressure: Gorbachev; the West German model of freedom, prosperity, and détente, which so many more East Germans came personally to experience; the general popular malaise in the GDR; alienated youth and intellectuals; and their complex interaction with the East German Evangelical church.

Honecker disliked, even feared, the impact of Gorbachev's reformism in the GDR. Two public events will suffice to characterize it. First, in June 1987, assembled on the GDR side of the Berlin Wall to hear a British rock concert on the other side, a group of GDR youth shouted, "Hurrah for Gorbachev!" and "The Wall must come down!" Second, on April 10, 1987, Kurt Hager, the leading GDR party ideologist, said in an interview in, of all places, the mass-circulation Hamburg illustrated weekly *Der Stern,* "Just because your neighbor is repapering his house doesn't mean that you have to do the same," and two days later this was reprinted in the official SED daily *Neues Deutschland.*

As time went on, and Gorbachev consulted his Central and Eastern European allies more regularly and reiterated in public his intention not to force them to follow the Soviet model, and if appropriate to learn from them, East German criticism of Gorbachev's reforms declined, but Soviet–East German relations were still strained. Moscow had two contradictory objectives. It wanted to use the GDR to influence the SPD, but it was uneasy about West and East Germans negotiating with each other, particularly about ideological issues. Moreover, until Gorbachev came to power and began to cut back on some of Brezhnev's commitments in the Third World, the GDR had been perhaps the USSR's most helpful ally there, notably in intelligence, police, and propaganda functions. However, like the Soviet Union, East Germany by the early 1980s had begun to downwardly reevaluate the Third World. East Berlin will probably follow Gorbachev's lead in his Third World cutback just as it generally has on other foreign policy issues.

Honecker and the SED, on the other hand, liked Gorbachev's lessening of foreign policy pressure on them and favored a more efficient Soviet economy. But they feared the impact in the GDR of the totality of Gorbachev's reforms because they thought that the GDR had already been reformed and therefore needed no more reforms and, more important, because they felt seriously challenged by another problem of overriding urgency. They must, they were convinced, thoroughly restructure and improve the high-technology sectors of their export-oriented economy in order to regain their export competitiveness in Western markets. In order to do this, they had to get more West German credits and other payments, for which they would have to make political payments in return, which they wanted to be as small as possible lest the payments destabilize their rule. In this critical situation the SED leadership was convinced that implementing Gorbachev's reforms would dangerously increase the risks of destabilization. That Gorbachev probably shared their concern presumably explains in part why he did not exert more pressure on the GDR to imitate his reform policies.

The SED probably underestimated the impact of West Germany on, for example, the more than 3 million East Germans who visited West Germany in 1987. Not all of this impact was entirely positive, although most of it probably was. East Germany remained much more "German" than the Federal Republic, whose prosperity had enabled even its workers to take summer vacations south of the Alps and where Western influence, especially U.S. mass culture, probably became greater than in any other non-English-speaking European country. Thus for some East Germans, the less attractive aspects of Western mass culture—drugs, crime—were affronts to their still Prussian virtues.

But this was overridden by West German freedom and prosperity. Moreover, that Mikhail Gorbachev and Ronald Reagan had signed the INF treaty, a clear and visible sign that East-West détente was breaking out all over, delegitimatized what remained of the GDR's anti-U.S. and anti–West German propaganda. True, these GDR visitors had been seeing West German television news every evening, but to see West Germany in person and to hear about it from their West German relatives (of whom there were still millions) intensified West Germany's impact on them. Most important, whereas other Central and East Europeans compared their own poverty with the relative prosperity of Hungary, the East Germans always compared themselves with West Germans, always to their own disadvantage, and increasingly so as they saw West German television and visited West Germany.

GDR Economic Problems

All this contributed to the general popular malaise that characterized East Germany in 1988. One of its principal causes was economic. In brief, the GDR was in increasingly serious danger of falling behind in high technology but was unlikely, largely for political reasons, to undertake the necessary measures, either sufficiently or soon enough, to meet the challenge. The global rush forward of high technology required that the GDR import more of it from the West (including Japan and the other newly industrialized Pacific Rim states), and in 1988 the GDR seemed reluctantly, but insufficiently, prepared to use Western, primarily West German, credits to do so. But it faced two obstacles—Soviet economic demands and its own reluctance to undertake basic economic reforms—and one potential, unique opportunity—the Federal Republic—about which it was ambivalent.

Not that the GDR did not early recognize the coming key importance of high technology; in theory it did and continued to do so. Furthermore, in 1971 it had restructured its industry into only partially decentralized "combines," which did aid the GDR's economic growth. After a brief period in the early 1980s when the GDR borrowed heavily from Western banks, it paid back some of its debts to reestablish a good credit rating and thereby cut back on its imports of Western technology. This slowed the modernization of its own technology, just as the high-technology revolution was intensifying.

By then, the GDR was also feeling the results on the Soviet Union of the world decline in petroleum prices, after they had first risen in the 1970s. By the mid-1980s, Moscow wanted East Berlin to pay off its deficit in Soviet–East German trade and export more and better quality goods to the West in order to buy high technology there. This contradiction, which applied equally to Hungary, was made worse for the GDR by two other factors: the GDR's reluctance to undertake the necessary economic restructuring required to improve its rate of domestic innovation in high technology (see Chapter 3) lest the SED's political supremacy be endangered, and the GDR's special trade and credit relations with the Federal Republic. Since 1949, these legally have been relations of "inner-German trade" and at Bonn's initiative were confirmed by the Treaty of Rome, which founded the European Community. As a result, trade between the two German states is conducted not in hard currency, as the GDR must do with all other Western countries, but in "units of account" based on the West German deutschmark, settled yearly between the two governments; the GDR also pays no tariffs or taxes on its trade with West Germany.

Until the late 1970s, the GDR has been reluctant to trade too much with West Germany lest it become politically too dependent on it, but recently, especially since Gorbachev came to power, Soviet objections on this point have lessened, and West German credits to the GDR have greatly increased. In return, the GDR in 1987 alone allowed more than 3 million East Germans to visit West Germany. Even so, East Germany has tried to divide its Western imports among various countries, but the commercial and financial attraction of trade with the Federal Republic will continue to increase, especially after 1992 when West European unity becomes greater. West Germany, which is expected to profit the most from this, will thereby probably strengthen its position as the economic center of the European community.

In contrast, GDR consumerism was still present, but less so. Total imports and exports declined, but East German dependence on trade with the Federal Republic grew, as shown by the widening intra-German trade deficit. Thus, in sum, the GDR's economic future, like that of the rest of Communist Central and Eastern Europe, looked in late 1988 to be one of further decline.[9]

This trend increased the East German perception of West Germany's prosperity. Honecker was resisting Gorbachev's reforms. He and most of his colleagues were so old that they could not long remain in power, and jockeying for succession was therefore under way, although still well below the surface. Even in the SED, and overwhelmingly outside it, Marxist-Leninist ideology and the Soviet Union were delegitimized. Egalitarianism was increasingly seen by some of the GDR elite as an obstacle to economic growth and socialism to necessary export competitiveness, and "socialist nationalism" had dwindled down into nationalism whose main targets of scorn were Poles and Russians.

The aspect of this malaise most difficult to estimate, just as in West Germany, has been the extent to which it reflected in part a revival of German nationalism or at least a sense of culturally belonging together—the *Kulturnation* that for so many centuries has been the only unifying concept of being German. When Honecker (and Kohl) first spoke of the German "community of responsibility" (*Verantwortungsgemeinschaft*), pledging that war should never break out again on German soil, they meant in part that they wanted the two German states, and all of Europe, to remain an island of détente amid superpower confrontation and Third World proxy wars. But although certainly not intended by Honecker, the great majority of their German hearers felt that it was more: the public reassertion that although Germans lived, indeed had to live, in two separate states, they all belonged to one German nation. Earlier, Honecker, and Ulbricht before him, had said that there was not one German nation but two: socialist and capitalist. Now Honecker seemed to abandon this in favor of one German "community of responsibility." He probably considered this, like the new, massive intra-German travel, which in fact cut so many holes in the Berlin Wall, a necessary although risky price that the GDR had to pay to the Federal Republic for the credits and technology.

Events in early 1988 showed that however relaxed the relations between the two German states might have become, the domestic stability of the GDR, although relatively firm, was likely to come into question from time to time. In addition to the three reasons analyzed previously, the interaction of youth and intellectual alienation with the complex policies of the GDR's one major non-Communist organization, the Evangelical (Protestant) church (only about 10 percent of the GDR population is Roman Catholic) contribute to these fluctuations. Because this throws much light on the actual situation in the GDR, Evangelical church developments need analysis in some detail.[10]

One preliminary important point: The dissident movement in the GDR, like others, was carried on by a minority of disaffected youth, students, and intellectuals. It was politically leftist in character and included Christians and perhaps more non-Christians. East Germany's youth, as elsewhere in Communist Central and Eastern Europe, and especially students, has primarily been influenced by the general Western youth movement and especially by the alienated pacifist and ecological youth movements in West Germany. Disaffected East German youth dislike the conformism, discipline, and

FIGURE 13.1. East German and Soviet Net Material Products (NMPs) and Gross Industrial Output

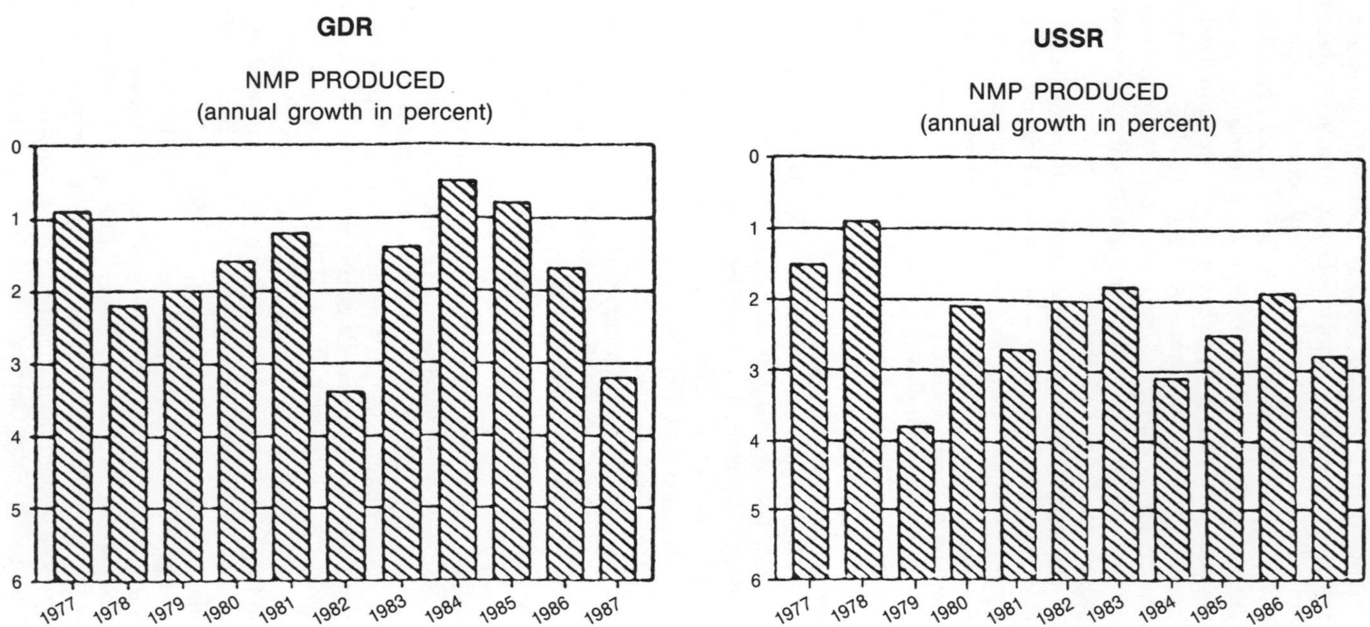

GROSS OUTPUT OF INDUSTRY
(annual growth in percent)

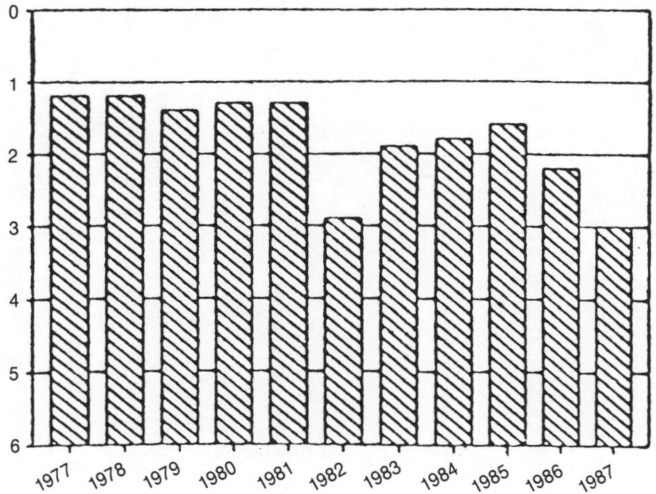

GROSS OUTPUT OF INDUSTRY
(annual growth in percent)

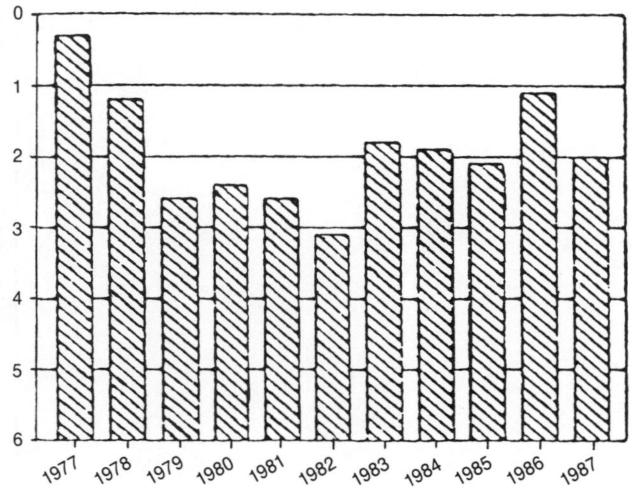

Source: Jan Vanous, ed. *PlanEcon,* 3, nos. 31–32, p. 2; 33, p. 2.

FIGURE 13.2. East German Trade with West Germany

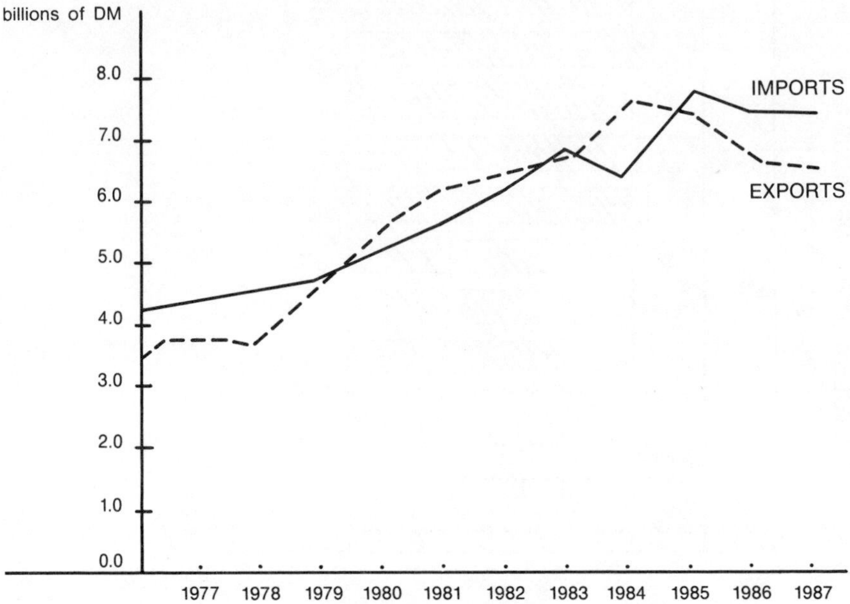

TABLE 13.1. East German Trade with West Germany (in millions of DM)

	1979	1980	1981	1982	1983	1984	1985	1986	1987
Exports	4,589	5,580	6,051	6,639	6,878	7,744	7,636	6,844	6,650
Imports	4,720	5,293	5,575	6,382	6,947	6,408	7,901	7,454	7,406
Balance	-131	287	476	257	-69	1,336	-265	-610	-756

Sources: East Germany, 1987-88 (London: The Economist Intelligence Unit, 1988); Statistisches Bundesamt Wiesbaden, FRG.

dullness of East German life, and although they may not admire the bourgeois affluence of the Federal Republic, many of them want to emigrate there because it is so much more tolerant of them than the GDR is. Rock music and blue jeans are the proud symbols of their nonconformism, so much so that both became reluctantly tolerated in the GDR and in the Soviet Union.

These East German dissidents must either conform or emigrate legally to West Germany (as perhaps up to 250,000 East Germans have, according to church estimates).[11] They still may well be exported there against their will or at worst imprisoned for dissident activity. Most sullenly conform but some do not, and they recently, Christian or not, increasingly turned for shelter, support, and solace to the Evangelical church.

GDR Evangelical Church Dissidence

The church's complex policies and dilemmas on dissent and emigration to West Germany have a long historical background. The church's founder, Martin Luther, turned against the peasant revolt and supported those princes who found it attractive, for whatever reason, to support him; and the horrendously destructive Thirty Years War (1618–1648) ended with subjects having imposed on them the religion of their rulers. Nowhere was this more true than in Prussia, whose Lutheran pastors were the king's firm supporters. This tradition, and the German nationalism that Lutheranism adopted in the German Empire, led far more Protestant than Roman Catholic clerics to conform to, support, or even praise Adolf Hitler. Only a small minority, the Confessing church (*Bekennende Kirche*) actively rejected Nazism.

After 1945, this made the Evangelical church in both German states reject communism and German nationalism. This was no great problem for the church in the democratic Federal Republic, where the churches' financial support came in the form of the "church tax" (*Kirchensteuer*), which all had to pay unless they formally left one or the other church, something relatively few did. Thus, the West German Evangelical and Roman Catholic churches are among the wealthiest in the world and officially as well as informally give important financial support to other churches in the GDR.[12]

The Evangelical church in East Germany gets little money from the state, (in the form of subsidies for pensions and charitable activities, for example). Church schools are forbidden, as is influence on education or GDR compulsory military training. Its members, like all Christians, could not join the atheist SED and were actively discriminated against by it both personally and professionally. Some of the more anti-SED lower clergy thought their hierarchy unrealistic and were harassed by the security police for their support of political dissidents. The Evangelical hierarchy tried to steer a course midway between collaboration and open resistance, thereby combining some of the Lutheran tradition of loyalty to the state with more of the self-sacrificing opposition of the Confessing church. In the early 1970s, the church decided that it had to be the "Church in Socialism." This meant that although it would not oppose the state as such, the extent of church involvement in society would probably encompass taking stands on social issues. This the Communist state would have to take into account. In practice, this meant walking a tightrope between opposition and collaboration, and thus antagonizing both the SED and the dissidents, especially those who had decided to emigrate but were not allowed to do so.

Before the Berlin Wall, most East German oppositionists fled to West Germany. After it, there were several GDR waves of intellectual and student dissidence. As Bonn's *Ostpolitik* got under way and was increasingly reciprocated by Honecker, the less oppositional GDR intellectuals realized that they had some more leeway, and they would on occasion write letters of protest to Honecker. This trend reached a critical point in November 1976, when a well-known East German balladeer, Wolf Biermann, was deprived of his East German citizenship while he was giving concerts in West Germany because the SED thought his ballads subversive. More and more the SED imprisoned few if any dissidents but allowed, or forced, them to emigrate to West Germany, sometimes with permission to return but mostly without. The East German dissidents grew in number and daring as they heard, mostly from West German television, how much *glasnost'* (openness) Gorbachev was encouraging in the Soviet Union, how much more there was in Poland and Hungary, and how stymied Honecker's relations with Gorbachev were in this respect. Thus, the SED's problems became fourfold: to continue improving its relations with West Germany; to try profiting, which it did by emphasizing some parts of German history, from increased German national cultural consciousness in both German states; to prevent its differences with Gorbachev from becoming so serious that he would put much more pressure on the GDR to liberalize; and to prevent these three from destabilizing the GDR domestically.

True, as Chapter 14 shows, Bonn favored stability, not destabilization, in the GDR. Gorbachev knew that the division and consequent weakening of Germany was the Soviet Union's most important gain in World War II, and he dared not risk its loss. He also knew that reforms were safer in Hungary than in East Germany, so he could not expect Honecker to go as far as Kádár had. True, the East German popular revolt on June 17, 1953, crushed by Soviet tanks, was never repeated. Nor is it likely to be, and if it were the Soviets would crush it again. My purpose here is to show what the true feelings of most East Germans would be if they dared to express them.

The best recent example from which to judge is the developments in 1988 centering around the GDR Evangelical church. Not that the majority of GDR dissidents are Protestant or even Christian; they seem to most experts not to be. Many are attracted by the Evangelical church, however, because it is the only GDR organization not controlled by the SED. But because the GDR Evangelical church's ties with the Evangelical church in West Germany are so close, and because its activities and therefore those of the dissidents who have become linked with it or sought its shelter are all the more covered by West German television, the principal source of news and analysis in the GDR, the analyst is in danger of overestimating and indeed oversimplifying the role of the Evangelical church. The reality of opposition in the GDR is much more complicated.[13]

Why, by 1988, were East German intellectual and student dissidents so linked with the Evangelical church, and what was the church's attitude toward them? The main reason has already been mentioned: The church was the only effective non-Communist organization in the GDR. There were other reasons. There was the example of the West German Evangelical church, many of whose activist members had made up the single largest group in the West German peace movement. There was the example of the Roman Catholic church in Poland, Hungary, Czechoslovakia, and Lithuania and of Gorbachev's détente with the Russian Orthodox church. As in West Germany, many of the younger Evangelical clergy were critical of the church hierarchy for what they saw as its excessive willingness to compromise with the SED and therefore not support the dissidents. These young oppositional pastors were joined by young oppositional Evangelical laypeople to form the Church from Below (*Kirche von unten*). By 1987, this loosely organized movement, which saw itself as a critical supporter of the church leadership and which the SED found especially objectionable, was having its own meetings in the yearly East German Evangelical Congresses. Finally, because the Evangelical church had in effect compromised with the SED by declaring itself the Church in Socialism, it soon became more involved in GDR politics, if only in its continuing struggle to keep as much independence as possible.

On January 17, 1988, several hundred dissidents, of whom the best known was the balladeer Stephan Krawczyk, tried to take part in the annual East German demonstration on the anniversary of the murder of Karl Liebknecht and Rosa Luxemburg in 1919 (this has always been the largest ceremonial demonstration). What brought down on them the SED's fury, and their arrest, was that they carried a banner on which they had written one of Luxemburg's most famous and certainly her most anti-Leninist saying: "Freedom is always freedom for one who thinks differently" (*"Freiheit ist immer die Freiheit des Andersdenkenden"*). Krawczyk was later indicted for high treason.

There followed a wave of protests in both German states by intellectuals, especially by writers, and also Evangelical prayer services (*Fürbittgottesdienste*) in all the major East German cities and many smaller ones. The Evangelical church leadership declared that it would try its best to have those who had been arrested released, and the church engaged as its lawyer Dr. Wolfgang Vogel, whose legal practice had for many years concentrated on the negotiations that helped Bonn buy out GDR political prisoners. The church also declared that it had advised against dissident participation in the demonstration, which it felt would set back necessary GDR reforms; that it would do its best to get those arrested released, as was its Christian duty; but that it continued to advise against emigration. The Church from Below called for silent demonstrations in the churches and staged some in East Berlin and elsewhere. The East German and Soviet media denounced those arrested; the West German media denounced the arrests. Then, at the beginning of February, many of those arrested, including Krawczyk, were suddenly allowed to leave for West Germany, as an alternative, as he said there, to long prison terms. It is probable, as the church said, that there were differing views in the SED Politburo on this subject. There were even reports that Honecker initially failed to get a majority for his more moderate line but that he eventually did, and therefore the dissidents were exported, not imprisoned.

One may speculate whether these differences reflected differing SED estimates of the situation in Moscow, where there were signs that although Gorbachev's personal position was growing stronger, his policies were far from popular within much of the *nomenklatura,* and he had felt it advisable not to remove Boris Yeltsin, the radically reformist First Secretary of the

Moscow city party organization. We do know that twice before, in 1953 and 1956, there were serious differences in the SED Politburo that reflected factional struggles in Moscow. In 1953, Rudolf Herrnstadt and Wilhelm Zaisser were removed after the June 17 revolt, in part because they had been close to Beria. In 1957, Schirdewan and Wollweber were removed, probably because during the 1956 Hungarian crisis they had been close to moderates in the Soviet Politburo. The SED leaders, like those elsewhere in Communist Central and Eastern Europe, must try to anticipate who is winning in Moscow.

Such events at a time when fear declines, rises again, and then declines once more often reveal much of what men and women really think and feel. The first example of Christian dissident sentiment is from a speech by the physicist Hans Jürgen Fischbach, a member of the Evangelical synod of Berlin-Brandenburg, during the First Ecumenical Christian Congress held in Dresden on February 12–15, 1988, after those arrested had been released. Dr. Fischbach had been one of the initiators of a resolution discussed, but by agreement not voted on at the church's Görlitz synod on September 18–22, 1987. Like Dr. Fischbach's speech in Dresden, the resolution attacked "delimitation" (*Abgrenzung*) by the GDR not only toward West Germany but toward its own citizens. The Görlitz synod had been preceded by several discussions between church leadership and the state, in which the latter made clear its fundamental objection to the church accepting and sheltering the "marginal groups" (*Randgruppen*)—peace movement adherents, ecologists, and antimilitarists—many, if not most, of whom wanted but were forbidden to emigrate to West Germany.

Dr. Fischbach's Dresden speech was similar to the Görlitz resolution, but its context was different, for the Dresden meeting was the first in the history of the GDR attended by all Christian denominations, including the previously politically inactive Roman Catholic church, and he spoke there during the month after the Krawczyk arrest and expulsion. The meeting's beginning, including Dr. Fischbach's speech, was public and broadcast on West German television. Dr. Fischbach said inter alia:

> The Wall was not only a hard restriction, one that we had to accept, on our freedom to travel—after all, there are more important things than travel—but it far more deeply affected and deformed our self-understanding, our feeling for life, and our social behavior than I had myself previously realized. Our inferiority complex, our unjustified general discontent, our "poor cousin" mentality toward visitors from the other side (*von drüben*), our lust for Western products, our helplessness and inability to communicate with foreigners, and our false fixation on the liberal consumer society west of the Wall, which we have stylized into an ideal—all of these have become clear to me as symptoms of a syndrome. . . .
>
> The delimitation line goes right through the middle of us. It was implanted in us at school. We are professionally what we have to be. At home we try to be what we want to be. This enforced double existence makes us and our society sick. Thus the symptoms of the delimitation system include fear, lack of independence, lack of adulthood, lack of perspective, shyness before re-

> sponsibility and substitute satisfaction through consumerism. Are these not also roots of alcoholism? This results in poverty of culture and art, relatively unproductive intellectual achievement, and uninnovative technology. The flood of applications to emigrate and the years of need of those who apply show the connection of internal and external delimitation. . . .
>
> This devil's circle can only be overcome if it is broken through. . . . Gorbachev has begun to do this with his courageous policy. . . . Because we do not have the same economic compulsion as the Soviet Union does, the GDR tries to participate actively in the détente process but simultaneously to hold fast to internal and therefore necessarily to external delimitation. The January events have shown, however, that this illogical concept cannot succeed. . . .
>
> We must reject the principle and practice of imposed delimitations, I think, on the basis of the Bible, just as we reject the principle and practice of unjust domination.[14]

February 13, the second day of the ecumenical meeting, was the anniversary of the destruction of Dresden by Allied bombers in 1945, with immense loss of life. The largest church in the GDR, the Kreuzkirche in Dresden, was jammed for a prayer service. Posters were unfurled, such as "Peace, justice, and realization of human rights in the GDR." After the church service there was a demonstration, largely made up of those who wanted to emigrate, which was finally broken up by the police.

The second example is from an interview with the Evangelical bishop of (East) Berlin, Gottfried Forck, broadcast on February 15, 1988, by the Deutschlandfunk, the official foreign broadcasting station of the *West* German government in Cologne:

> *Interviewer:* More and more people come to the churches in the weeks since January, in Berlin, in Dresden—one gets the impression that the Evangelical Church, nolens volens perhaps, is becoming a political factor in the GDR. How do you see this?
>
> *Forck:* Yes, I think that this is the case, and that this is also the fear of the state authorities. They see perhaps in the background a development like Poland, and they would naturally like to avoid this. It is also not a light burden for us that we are undertaking, for many men and women, especially young ones, come to the churches who do not want to be Christians, but who want to see their interests represented and who come to the Church because it is the only institution in the GDR which has a certain independent freedom. We are glad to take on all their wishes, but we can only do it on the basis of the Bible.[15]

After the confrontations in Berlin and Dresden, SED Politburo member Werner Jarowinsky secretly demanded of the church that it withdraw entirely from domestic political activity. The church presiding bishop, Werner Leich, then met with Honecker, after many unsuccessful attempts to do so. Leich pleaded for (1) more openness of the authorities with GDR citizens, especially about applications to emigrate, attempts by the state to persuade citizens not to emigrate, and a minimal delay before permission to do so if persuasion did not work; (2) a civilian substitution possibility for military service; and (3) a clear statement about equal educational opportunity for all. The next evening, in an interview over West German television, Bishop Leich said that he considered Honecker's reaction positive but that "the Church's behavior has to contribute to the desired stabilization of inner peace in the society, which has been and is threatened."[16]

Thereafter the security police used force at least once against churchgoers, and more censorship was imposed on church publications. More important, perhaps, were the signs of differences of view among the church leadership. Some said that the church could not allow non-Christians to use its facilities for political activity; others stressed the church's duty to help all those in need, be they Christian or not, and the continuing criticism of its hierarchy by GDR dissidents.[17]

Conclusion

As Chapter 14 further illustrates, the GDR is quite different from the other Communist states of Central and Eastern Europe. Not only because its leadership in 1988 was resisting Gorbachev's reformism, if somewhat less strongly than before; so was the leadership in Prague. Not only because dissidence had increased and centered in and around the Evangelical church; so did it in the Roman Catholic church in Poland. Not only because the GDR was having increasingly serious economic and foreign trade problems and falling economic growth[18] and was in danger of further erosion of its export competitiveness; so were Czechoslovakia and Hungary. No, the single most important, overriding difference was the GDR's complex relationship with the larger, richer, freer part of the divided German nation. Even though neither the Bonn government nor its citizens want the destabilization of the GDR, they do want a degree of change in it, however gradual, that Honecker and probably any strong SED leader have to consider too dangerous. So, he probably thinks, would be an East German version of Gorbachev's reforms. But, unlike Ulbricht's 1971 defiance, Honecker wants consultation, not defiance or, as Palmiro Togliatti once put it, "unity in diversity"—that is, mutual acknowledgment of mutual interdependence, with the Soviet Union being first among equals but without a "leading role." Nevertheless, in late 1988 Gorbachev was still accepting Togliatti's view.[19]

The GDR is not the same as it was under Ulbricht. For most of its citizens, it is less unacceptable than it was. The enormous increase in legal travel to West Germany alone would guarantee that. Nor do its people lack pride in the GDR's considerable economic achievements, and its people's pride in being German is no longer openly affronted by the SED but catered to, if only symbolically. Moreover, in the past few years the situation of GDR writers and other cultural intellectuals has improved, and those who have emigrated to West Germany are no longer so defamed.[20] Nothing has happened culturally that can be compared with the flood of cultural and even ideological *glasnost'* in the Soviet Union or in Hungary, but something has happened. At the end of 1987, in an East Berlin round table sponsored by the main GDR research institute on West Germany, many of Gorbachev's ideas were repeated, with emphasis on the priority of the high-technology revolution in peaceful competition with capitalism.[21]

In summer 1988, the official GDR philosophical journal published several articles, one of which called for further "revolutionary restructuring" of the economy and other sectors of society, including the use of some market mechanisms. Several others positively summarized the reforms under way elsewhere in Communist Central and Eastern Europe. Nevertheless, these articles were careful to repeat Honecker's view that the GDR need not, and should not, automatically copy other reform initiatives.[22]

But such articles were few and far between and little read except by the SED intellectual elite and Western experts. Yet this was the way that liberalization began in Poland and Hungary after Stalin's death and in Czechoslovakia in the mid-1960s. It was still too early in late 1988 to foresee how far these intermittent departures from orthodoxy by a few GDR party intellectuals would go and what would be the result.

With respect to GDR foreign policy, in late 1988 its relations with the Soviet Union were strained by Gorbachev's reforms, but basically they were still ones of mutual need. Its relations with West Germany were certainly better, but the real question was which of the two German states profited the more from them. Bonn had made some, but not decisive, concessions to East Berlin. Tactically and psychologically, Bonn was more vulnerable to GDR pressure, especially on inter-German travel. The GDR had had some influence on the West German Left, but the reverse was also true. Indeed, as has been set forth, the GDR was likely to become increasingly dependent on West German credits and high technology, no matter how much it did not want to. Indeed, because it did not want to, it was likely, for this essentially political, not economic, motive, not to profit technologically as much as it could from credit and technological ties with West Germany. But neither could it afford to put too much emphasis on exporting second-rate technology to the Soviet Union, which would make it fall still farther behind the West in high technology.

The advanced age alone of Honecker and many of his associates makes change in the ruling elite inevitable and soon. That their criticism of Gorbachev's policies is no longer as overt as it was and that popular pressure for reforms is growing make it likely that sooner or later they or their successors will feel compelled to move farther toward imitating Gorbachev's *glasnost'* than they have. The GDR's immediate future will probably see more of the same cycles of dissidence, repression, and renewed dissidence, but the gap with the Federal Republic, against which East German citizens will continue to measure the state, will increase, to its disadvantage and to the discontent of its citizens. Even if Gorbachev and his reforms survive but neither wholly succeed nor wholly fail, which in late 1988 seemed likely; even if the succession to Honecker goes smoothly; even if the differences between East Berlin and Moscow continue to be compromised; even if, as is probable, East German dissidence is kept under control; and even if East Berlin's relations with Bonn, and East-West détente, remain as good as they were in late 1988, relative economic and technological decline seems the GDR's most likely near future.

Notes

I am grateful for comments by Ronald Asmus, Wolfgang Berner, and A. James McAdams.

1. J. F. Brown, *Eastern Europe and Communist Rule* (Durham, N.C.: Duke University Press, 1988), pp. 230–262 (the best and latest overall analysis). Also see William E. Griffith, *The Ostpolitik of the Federal Republic of Germany* (Cambridge, Mass.: MIT Press, 1978); A. James McAdams, *East Germany and Détente* (New York: Cambridge University Press, 1985); and A. James McAdams, "Inter-German Détente: A New Balance," *Foreign Affairs* 65, no.1 (Fall 1986), pp. 136–153.

2. David Childs, "East Germany to the 1990s: Can It Resist Glasnost?" Special Report no. 1118 (London: The Economist Intelligence Unit, December 1987), p. 7; *The Military Balance 1987–1988* (London: International Institute of Strategic Studies, 1987); Bundesministerium für innerdeutsche Beziehungen, *Materialien zum Bericht zur Lage der Nation im geteilten Deutschland* (Bonn: Bundesministerium, May 1987), pp. 478–480. For West German credits to East Germany, see Klaus Schröder, "Die Ost-West-Beziehungen vor neuen Herausforderungen," *Osteuropa*, no. 3, (1988), pp. 189–204, at pp. 191–192. For the recent decline in East-West German trade, see Carl Graf Hohenthal, "Im innerdeutschen Handel muss noch viel geschehen," *Frankfurter Allgemeine Zeitung*, June 11, 1988, p. 12.

3. William E. Griffith, "Superpower Problems in Europe: A Comparative Assessment," *Orbis* 29, no. 4 (Winter 1986), pp. 735-752; Ronald D. Asmus, "The Dialectics of Détente and Discord: The Moscow–East Berlin–Bonn Triangle," *Orbis* 28, no. 4 (Winter 1985), pp. 743–774; A. James McAdams, "The New Logic of Soviet–East German Disputes," *Problems of Communism*, 34, no. 5 (Sept.-Oct. 1988), pp. 47–60.

4. Peter Christian Ludz, *Die DDR zwischen Ost und West* (Munich: Verlag C. H. Beck, 1977).

5. See McAdams, "The New Logic of Soviet–East German Disputes," p. 14.

6. See the tables in Klaus Schröder, "Die Ost-West-Finanzbeziehungen vor neuen Herausforderungen," *Osteuropa*, no. 3. (1988), pp. 291–292.

7. Karl Wilhelm Fricke, "Der Besuch Erich Honeckers in der Bundesrepublik Deutschland," *Europa Archiv* 42, no. 23 (December 10, 1987), pp. 683–690.

8. McAdams, "The New Logic of Soviet–East German Disputes."

9. Jürgen Nötzöld, K. Schröder, A. Inotai, "East-West Trade at the Crossroads," *Aussenpolitik* (English ed.) 37, no. 4 (1986), pp. 400–412; Hanns-D. Jacobsen, "Technologiepolitische Handlungsspielräume und die Aussenwirtschaftsbeziehungen der DDR," in Ilse Spittmann and Gisela Herwig, eds., *Das Profil der DDR in der sozialistischen Staatengesellschaft* (Cologne: Verlag Deutschland Archiv, 1987), pp. 120–132.

10. There is little good English-language analysis of recent developments with the GDR Evangelical church, except the excellent analyses by Barbara Donovan of Radio Free Europe. In 1988, *Deutschland Archiv* (Cologne) carried many articles and much documentation on this issue, especially by Gisela Helwig and Theo Mechtenberg in 21, no. 4 (April 1988) and by Gisela Helwig in 21, no. 8 (August 1988).

11. *Der Spiegel,* September 5, 1988, pp. 102–103.
12. Gerhard Rein, "Die Krise in der Gesellschaft und die Kirchen: Zur Situation der Evangelischen Kirchen," *Das Parlament,* August 26, 1988, p. 10.
13. For background see Dietrich Staritz, "Die SED und die Opposition," in Ilse Spittmann, ed., *Die SED in Geschichte und Gegenwart* (Cologne: Edition Deutschland Archiv, 1987), pp. 78–97.
14. Translated from *Deutschland Archiv* 21, no. 4 (April 1988), pp. 450–451 (reprinted from a tape recording of his remarks published in the *Frankfurter Rundschau,* February 29, 1988).
15. Translated from *Deutschland Archiv* 21, no. 4 (April 1988), p. 453.
16. Translated from ibid., p. 342.
17. "Die DDR-Kirche ist Verbündeter der SED", *Frankfurter Allgemeine Zeitung,* August 18, 1988, p. 4.; and "Innerkirchliche Spannungen in der DDR," *Neue Zürcher Zeitung,* August 20, 1988.
18. Deutsches Institut für Wirtschaftsforschung (DIW) (West Berlin), *Wochenbericht,* no. 30 (1988), summarized and analyzed in Barbara Donovan, "Economic Slowdown in the GDR," *Radio Free Europe Research,* August 8, 1988.
19. Cf. McAdams, "The New Logic of Soviet–East German Disputes." Also see Fred Oldenburg, "The Impact of Gorbachev's Reform on the GDR," Berichte des Bundesinstituts für ostwissenschaftliche und internationale Studien (Cologne), no. 25 (1988), and Barbara Donovan, "The GDR and Gorbachev's Reforms," *Radio Free Europe Research* (Munich), April 6, 1988.
20. Some cultural liberalization was evident in the critical atmosphere that prevailed at the Writers' Congress in East Berlin. See Harald Kleinschmid, "Experimentierfeld für *Glasnost?" Deutschland Archiv* 21, no. 5 (May 1988).
21. "Systemauseinandersetzung und Sicherung des Friedens," *IPW Berichte,* no. 12 (1987), pp. 1–12. Also see an attempt to define a dialectical relationship between ideological struggle and ideological coexistence in Burkhard Koch, "Streit der Ideologien im nuklear-kosmischen Zeitalter," *IPW Bericht,* no. 3 (1988), pp. 22–27.
22. See the articles in *Deutsche Zeitschrift für Philosophie,* no. 7 (1988), especially the one by Alfred Kosing, summarized and analyzed by Barbara Donovan, "SED Ideologist Calls for Reform," *Radio Free Europe Research,* August 8, 1988.

14

West German Policy Toward Central and Eastern Europe

Wolfgang Berner and
William E. Griffith

Relations between the Federal Republic of Germany and the six smaller states of the Warsaw Pact—the German Democratic Republic (GDR), Poland, CSSR, Hungary, Bulgaria, and Romania—have improved in recent years. This trend was not changed by the replacement in early October 1982 of Helmut Schmidt's SPD-FDP coalition (Social Democratic party–Free Democratic party) cabinet by Helmut Kohl's CDU/CSU-FDP administration (Christian Democratic Union/[Bavarian] Christian Social Union–Free Democratic party), despite the CDU/CSU's original opposition to the SPD's *Ostpolitik* in the 1970s. Indeed, Kohl's continued rapprochement with the countries of Eastern Europe, especially with the GDR, made some CDU/CSU and journalistic conservatives criticize him for going too far in this respect.[1]

So did many in Paris, and some in Washington, London, and the other countries of the North Atlantic Treaty Organization (NATO). Their main target of attack was not Kohl, who successfully and simultaneously improved relations with Washington and Paris and pushed European unity forward. Nor was it his foreign minister (and Schmidt's), Hans-Dietrich Genscher, although he was often attacked by conservatives in West Germany, France, and, to a lesser extent, the United States for allegedly being insufficiently firm vis-à-vis the East. Their main concern was the West German Left. There the SPD's "new *Ostpolitik*" centered on a "security partnership" with Moscow and thereby rejected the NATO security consensus, whereas the new Greens were overtly neutralist. The net result was that the CDU and CSU conservatives attacked Kohl because they thought he was not nationalist enough, while Kohl's allies at home and abroad feared that perhaps Genscher, and certainly the West German Left, were nationalist and neutralist. Relations within the Atlantic Alliance are therefore affected by relations between the two German states, as most Germans in both of these states are aware.

West German Ambiguities: Between Self-Assurance and Frustration

The German question is the most complex, most important, and most emotion laden in Europe. The Germans are a dynamic, technologically advanced, and industrious people. The two German states are the only ones in Europe that are parts of a centrally located, often divided, historically powerful, and increasingly self-assertive nation. The German question has become even more complex because the two German states, which for almost forty years have confronted each other on the East-West military frontier, are now moving from confrontation to reassociation. The Germans are again divided, remain so because nuclear weapons have frozen European boundaries, and therefore are frustrated and searching for the identity of which they were deprived by Germany's total defeat in 1945.

Moreover, in their grasp for world power during the two world wars, the Germans struck such fear and trembling into all their neighbors that their self-assertion still, nearly a half-century afterward, could again unite their neighbors against them.[2] This instinctive fear of Germans often comes to the surface quite unexpectedly. In Eastern Europe it compels the GDR to exercise some preemptive self-limitation (like the similar precautions habitually practiced by West Germany's official representatives) because East Germans are disliked by all their socialist neighbor countries given their proverbial German efficiency and their achievement-conscious arrogance.

Some Historical Background

While the other West European states colonized beyond the seas, and Russia colonized Siberia, Germany colonized its immediate eastern neighbors, often by force and about as often by invitation. German peasants, artisans, and professionals were initially welcome additions to their more underdeveloped eastern neighbors. But as the two greatest German states, Prussia and Austria, expanded forcibly to the east, where the German minorities who were already there or whom these Germans brought with them became ruling minorities, and as modern nationalism arose with the French Revolution, these German minorities and the largely Slav majorities they came to rule increasingly turned against each other.

Austria was consciously a Catholic multinational state and therefore did not try to germanize its minorities as long as they remained loyal to the emperor (*kaisertreu*). But Bismarck's Prussia and then Imperial Germany were Protestant, authoritarian, and contemptuous of, and determined to germanize, as many of their Polish subjects as they could. Indeed, the Polish partitions strengthened authoritarianism in Russia, Prussia, and Austria, a heritage that long made all three the enemies of democracy in Europe. For many centuries the average German could not (and some still cannot) imagine applying to the Poles Thomas Jefferson's prescription, "Self-government is better than good government."

Military skill, industrial competence, popular discipline, and conviction of cultural superiority twice pushed Germany in the two world wars to try becoming a world power. Imperial Germany was militarist and expansionist, but Hitler's Third Reich incarnated mass murder, torture, and enslavement. Both were "out of phase," for imperialism was going out of fashion, and both so subjugated the rest of Central and Eastern Europe that by 1945 Europe, Asia, and North America were united by their fear and loathing of the Germans and the Japanese. How, then, have West Germany and Japan become two of the three most powerful economies in the world and the two most important, albeit hardly the two most beloved, allies of the third, the United States?

Modern German History

Germany has had two great modern statesmen, Otto von Bismarck and Konrad Adenauer. Bismarck designed a political system that, if not run by a genius like himself, was almost destined to disaster. Adenauer began in 1945 surrounded by total defeat, while Bismarck strode from victory to victory. But the greatest difference between them reflected the religious and class splits caused by the Reformation and industrialization. For Bismarck, Germany was the saturated center and should be the mediator of the European state system. Adenauer's ideas were formed after Protestant Prussia had conquered and, he thought, wrongly dominated his beloved Catholic Rhineland. He wanted in the early 1920s what he achieved after 1945—a Rhineland separated from Prussian rule, remaining within the Reich, but with a special economic relationship with France. He was not then or later very interested in the countries to Germany's east; for him, Germany's western Catholic neighbor France was, and remained, his priority.

When Adenauer became West Germany's first chancellor in 1949 (at the age of seventy-three), his minimal and lasting objective, and indeed that of all his successors, was "Never back to Potsdam"—that is, the Federal Republic should never again be subject to a Soviet veto. His maximal objective was that Western Europe become politically, economically, and militarily united, with the Federal Republic regaining therein a status equal to France and Britain.

These were his priorities because they always had been and because, cold realist that he was, he knew that there was no possibility that the Soviet Union would agree to a non-Communist united Germany. (We now know that the wartime German Communist planning in Moscow confirmed this.) But he also knew that popular demand in the Federal Republic to make reunification a major priority was very great and that his principal opponent, the SPD leader Kurt Schumacher, gave it absolute priority. However, Adenauer was sure that West Germans so feared the Soviets, so wanted again to be masters of themselves and to regain prosperity, and were so appalled by total defeat and, for many of them, by the Nazi crimes, that he could get popular support for security, especially for West Berlin, through continued U.S. military presence and reconciliation with France. Prosperity, he believed, would return with free enterprise plus the Bismarckian welfare system, and he could afford to make unilateral concessions to France, for example on the Saar and the Coal and Steel Community, knowing full well that they would be returned with interest as the Federal Republic became more prosperous and more respected. He steadily maintained that the West would become so strong via NATO and European unity and through a "policy of strength" that the USSR and the GDR would feel themselves compelled to accept German reunification. (Whether he believed this or not is less certain.) When they did not, but instead built the Berlin Wall, this policy had failed.

It would be wrong, however, to think that Adenauer had no *Ostpolitik.* In 1958, and again in 1960, he had reunification plans secretly drafted. The first proposed an "Austrian solution" for the GDR, and the second proposed separate referenda in both German states on reunification. Nikita Khrushchev not surprisingly rejected both because they would have changed the status quo in favor of the West, while he was simultaneously, but eventually unsuccessfully, trying through the second Berlin crisis (1958–1962) to change the status quo in favor of the USSR and the GDR.

The most important single caesura in West German policy in general, and toward the East in particular, was Walter Ulbricht's construction of the Berlin Wall in August 1961 and, as most West Germans saw it, especially West Berlin's then mayor Willy Brandt and his adviser Egon Bahr, the unwillingness of President John Kennedy to prevent it or to get it torn down. This reflected, as had the first Geneva East-West summit conference in 1955, the increasing hesitation of the United States to give priority to German reunification, or more accurately to Bonn's views about it, over negotiations with the Soviet Union on arms control. This change was the inevitable result of Moscow's obtaining sufficient destructive nuclear capability to end the invulnerability of the United States to attack.

Adenauer tried to counter this erosion of the West German position by establishing diplomatic relations with the Soviet Union at the end of that year. However, he showed no inclination to do the same with the Communist Central and Eastern states and indeed prevented it by the Hallstein Doctrine, which declared that Bonn would not have diplomatic relations with any state that also had them with the GDR. (When Yugoslavia established relations with the GDR in 1958, Bonn immediately broke off diplomatic relations with Belgrade.)

Adenauer and most West German conservatives were worried by what they considered to be Kennedy's excessive willingness to compromise with Khrushchev during the second Berlin crisis, and they therefore encouraged Charles de Gaulle's veto of Kennedy's attempts. Hence, the distrust in the West German Left and Right of U.S. policies increased, but because both agreed that the Federal Republic had to have U.S. troop presence and nuclear shield, little immediately came of it; the more so because Bonn-Washington tension diminished after Kennedy's victory in the Cuba crisis made the second Berlin crisis disappear. As the superpowers moved toward détente, beginning in the late 1950s, despite, for example, the 1968 Soviet invasion of Czechoslovakia, Bonn slowly but surely moved in the same direction: the SPD faster and farther than the FDP, the CDU more slowly than the FDP, and the CSU the least of all.

Nevertheless, *Ostpolitik*, even at its height in 1969–1972, was not the most important element in West German foreign policy, nor did foreign policy decide West German elections. Personalities and economic policies did that. The Berlin Wall, which symbolically cut the two German states in half more clearly than anything before or since; the events in Poland and Hungary in 1956 and in Czechoslovakia in 1968; the gradual, intermittent, but still significant partial easing of repression in most Communist Central and Eastern European countries; the economic, and gradually also the political, assimilation of the 12 million German expellees into West German society; and for them and for all others in both German states, the sheer passage of time, the persistence of the status quo, and the peace, prosperity, and growing prestige of the Federal Republic and its citizens' pride in it—all these created, furthered, and gradually legitimatized the shift in West German *Ostpolitik* from confrontation to reassociation, above all with the GDR.

The SPD's Ostpolitik

West German *Ostpolitik* became much more active, gained a much higher priority, and included the GDR, when for the first time since 1949 the SPD came to power, in coalition with the FDP, in October 1969. The previous CDU/CSU-FDP "grand coalition" had already begun to prepare the way for this change, notably through the establishment of trade missions in some East European countries. Brandt's SPD won the 1969 election primarily on economic, not foreign policy, issues. Its new *Ostpolitik* was, ironically, also made more acceptable by the 1968 Soviet invasion of Czechoslovakia, which confirmed, as the Berlin Wall had earlier, that Moscow was determined to maintain its influence in Communist Central and Eastern Europe. The SPD's *Ostpolitik* had for some time also been supported by both West German churches and by much, if not most, of the West German intellectuals and the media.

What the SPD's *Ostpolitik* amounted to was the negotiation of renunciation-of-use-of-force agreements with the Soviet Union and Poland, a treaty with Czechoslovakia that annulled the 1938 Munich Agreement, and a "basic treaty" with East Berlin that increased and codified state-to-state contacts. Brandt succeeded in several respects. First, he did not recognize the post-1945 boundaries de jure; he successfully used with Moscow the argument that this could only be done by a four-power-sponsored peace conference and that until then the four allied powers retained certain residual rights in Germany (as Moscow wanted to retain for itself). Second, he therefore did not recognize the GDR de jure, and thus the two German states established permanent missions (*ständige Vertretungen*) rather than embassies, with the GDR mission in Bonn accredited to the chancellor's office, not to the foreign ministry (although the West German mission in East Berlin was accredited to the GDR foreign office). This meant that the leading governing party in Bonn, be it the SPD or CDU/CSU, not the foreign minister (who since 1969 has been FDP), controlled the West German bureaucracy that dealt with the GDR. In practice, therefore, because the same party has not held both the chancellorship and foreign ministry for such a long period, the basic treaty institutionalized a further cause of bureaucratic and political tensions in any such Bonn government.

While these treaties were being negotiated, the four powers (in practice six because the two German states were de facto, although not officially, part of the negotiations) were also negotiating a new Berlin agreement. This turned out on balance to be generally favorable to Bonn and the West because it made travel, transit, and access to and from West Germany and West Berlin to East Germany and East Berlin more secure, although the Soviets refused to agree that East Berlin was only a part of Berlin (and not the capital of the GDR), and West German presence in West Berlin was decreased, but not decisively so. In the process of the negotiations (as has been set forth in Chapter 13), the Soviets got Ulbricht removed because their interests in détente with the West and confrontation with the People's Republic of China took priority over their support of the GDR's fear of infection from West Germany.

Moreover, Brandt and the Western powers made ratification of the treaties with the Soviet Union, Poland, and Czechoslovakia and of the Berlin Agreement, and the convening of a conference on European security (which Moscow had long wanted in the hope of getting a multilateral ratification of the status quo) and another on mutual troop reductions, all dependent on the completion of the treaty between the two German states, whose contents included Bonn's ability to negotiate for West Berlin as well. Thereupon, after the CDU/CSU narrowly failed to unseat Brandt by a vote of no confidence, the treaties were ratified. The CDU/CSU, with only a few exceptions, abstained.

Of these results the clearest, and most to Bonn's advantage, has been the defusing of the Berlin situation, although East Berlin (presumably with Soviet agreement and perhaps sometimes with Soviet encouragement) has intermittently tried to erode the level of relations between West Berlin and the Federal Republic and the Western status in Berlin. Conversely, Bonn has from time to time tried (with allied tolerance and sometimes with allied support) to improve its position in West Berlin. The net result has been that the status quo established by the Berlin Agreement has been little changed.

Yet what might have happened in Berlin if the West Europeans, with increasing, if largely unpublic, support in Eastern Europe, had not succeeded in keeping Europe an island of détente during the second period of Soviet-U.S. tension (from 1975 on)? Moscow wanted it kept so, for the USSR was, as it turned out, overengaged in Third World crisis areas and wanted thereby to increase U.S.–West European tensions. The desire in Bonn, and among almost all West Germans, that this new East-West confrontation not produce a third Berlin crisis contributed to the general West European, and especially West German, lack of support for U.S. confrontational policy and to the similar lack of support by at least the GDR and Hungary for the Soviet confrontational policy as well. It is to the analysis of this complex, new situation that we now turn.

From Brandt to Schmidt to Kohl

The main point to understand about these chancellors is that their *Ostpolitik* was much more alike than it was different. Brandt fell because Herbert Wehner, the SPD's most politically acute leader, decided that Brandt could not win the next election. Wehner then used the discovery that one of Brandt's personal assistants, Günter Guillaume, was an East German intelligence officer to have Brandt replaced with Helmut Schmidt, whom Wehner correctly calculated could win, as he did.[3]

Schmidt's *Ostpolitik* was substantially the same as Brandt's, but he gave it somewhat lower priority as compared to relations with Giscard d'Estaing's Paris, which he handled very well, and Jimmy Carter's Washington, which he handled, as did Carter, unnecessarily badly. Schmidt's first foreign policy priority was economic: to prevent a worldwide depression with its catastrophic consequences for export-dependent West Germany. When East-West tension spiraled after the 1979 Soviet invasion of Afghanistan, Schmidt, like Giscard, successfully kept Western Europe an island of détente. His *Ostpolitik* priority for relations with the GDR and against East European revolts was highlighted by his lack of strong reaction against Wojciech Jaruzelski's December 1981 crushing of Polish Solidarność. This having been said, Schmidt was nevertheless the greatest post-1945 West German leader after Adenauer.[4]

1984

What then happened between the Soviet Union and East Germany has been analyzed in Chapter 13. To recall it briefly, Budapest and East Berlin resisted Soviet pressure to respond militarily to NATO intermediate-range nuclear forces (INF) deployment, lest it endanger their improving relations with Bonn and thereby their access to West German credits and technology transfer. Erich Honecker finally and reluctantly felt compelled, primarily as a result of Soviet pressure, to "postpone" his scheduled visit to Bonn. Gorbachev's accession to power in early 1985 began to soften Soviet pressure on East Berlin and Budapest and to improve relations with Bonn.

Thus, East and West German policies remained anticonfrontational, and Gorbachev changed Soviet policies toward them. But why did the West German CDU/CSU, which had so opposed the SPD's *Ostpolitik*, take it over when they came to power in 1982? Most West German conservatives responded to the support of *Ostpolitik* by the West German population because it allowed so much more travel from West Germany and West Berlin to East Germany and East Berlin, and because it seemed to help keep

Europe an island of détente amid rising Soviet-U.S. tension. When that tension began to decline again, West German support of *Ostpolitik* seemed to most West Germans to be successful, so they supported it even more. Other factors also favored CDU support of *Ostpolitik:* its popularity in the West; the CDU's concern, and indeed that of all West German political leaders, about West Berlin; and its previous endorsement by the FDP, without whose support the CDU/CSU could not recover power.

Before the CDU returned to power in 1982, its change from opposition to support of *Ostpolitik* was slowed down at first by Honecker's delimitation policy and because its moderates on this issue were initially a minority. Their principal leader was the late Alois Mertes, by then the CDU's most important foreign policy spokesman. Another was Richard von Weizsäcker, then mayor of West Berlin and now the West German federal president.[5] To the east of West Germany, the Eastern bloc seemed reconsolidated after the December 1981 Polish military coup, and thereafter not only West Europe but the United States wanted to resume détente with Moscow. Finally, the CDU returned to power in coalition with the FDP, so that Genscher, a great *Ostpolitik* supporter, remained Kohl's foreign minister as he had been Schmidt's.

The Kohl-Genscher Ostpolitik

A good case can be made—and Josef Joffe has made it persuasively[6]—that Bonn really wants stability in Communist Central and Eastern Europe, most of all in East Germany, and that this view is generally shared by the West German body politic. One argument for this view is that there can be no change in East Germany unless there is change in all of Communist Central and Eastern Europe and that this will not be possible unless and until there is major change in the Soviet Union, which is at best a long-term prospect. Moreover, spontaneous change from below, or even such change from above as has occurred in Romania, to say nothing of Yugoslavia and Albania, would not only be repressed by Moscow but would set back by one or two decades—as it did in Hungary, Czechoslovakia, and Poland—genuine, gradual liberalization in domestic and foreign policy, at least in East Germany.

The *Ostpolitik* of the Kohl-Genscher coalition, and in some respects that of the SPD, has not been the first priority of West German foreign policy. The first priority is the security relationship with the United States, the reconciliation with France, and, based on this, rapid progress toward the unity of Western Europe. To give only one example: It is very unlikely that Kohl or Genscher will allow the Soviet protests to interfere with the development of military cooperation between France and the Federal Republic.

Bonn officially opposes differentiation among the Communist Central and East European states, whereas Washington advocates it, but Bonn does differentiate in practice, to Moscow's and Warsaw's displeasure. Bonn maintains East Germany as a silent quasimember of the European Community and extends it billions of deutschmarks in credits. In 1988, for purely political reasons, the Bonn government exceptionally guaranteed a 1 billion DM credit to Hungary, thereby consciously saving Budapest from defaulting on its Western debts and giving a strong signal that Bonn supported reforms financially in Communist Central and Eastern Europe. In return, the cultural status of the large German ethnic minority in Hungary was greatly improved. Conversely, Bonn has not given credits to Poland, in large part because Poland refuses to give any cultural minority rights to ethnic Germans in Poland and obstructs emigration to the Federal Republic of those who wish to do so. (That at least some of these have not too strong a claim to be Germans, if only because many, especially in Silesia, are close to bilingual and bicultural, complicates the issue even further.) It is probably no accident that Bonn's policies toward its pre-1945 Central and East European allies, Hungary, Bulgaria, and Romania (if Bucharest were not so unforthcoming toward emigration of ethnic Germans) are more favorable than toward its pre-1945 opponents. The converse is also true: Hungarians, Romanians, and Bulgarians are historically pro-German, whereas the others are not. Moscow's relations with Bonn are improving, but anti–West German polemics are not entirely absent from the Soviet media.

There have been also differences, and more obvious and publicized ones, in the Kohl-Genscher coalition on *Ostpolitik.* They are primarily between Kohl and Genscher and between the CDU and the FDP. There were also until recently differences between Kohl and the Bavarian premier Franz-Josef Strauss, but after Strauss's visit to Moscow in December 1987 he toned down his opposition to *Ostpolitik,* and his death in 1988 greatly decreased such tensions.

Although the CDU is a biconfessional party, about equally divided between Catholics and Protestants, and is in part a people's party because it has within it a Catholic minority of the West German trade union movement, it has been largely dominated by Rhineland Catholics, beginning with Adenauer. Like him and most other German Catholics, the CDU has long been Francophile, since 1945 pro-U.S. and anti-Soviet, and at least in theory committed to German reunification. In fact, however, the CDU has given priority to West European unification and to NATO.

Conversely, the FDP, the heir of the nationalist People's party and of the liberal Democratic party of the Weimar Republic, is almost entirely Protestant and by now largely North German. In the postwar period, it has been less interested than the CDU in, although basically supportive of, Western European unity; like Bismarck, more in policy toward the East; and in East-West détente in general. The differences between the CDU and Strauss's CSU until recently centered on *Ostpolitik,* to which Strauss was much more opposed than the CDU became, and differences still continue with respect to policy toward South Africa.

Especially with respect to the FDP, domestic electoral considerations often are decisive in foreign policy. The CDU came to support *Ostpolitik* despite the fierce opposition of its conservative wing. The FDP, so small that it is permanently threatened with loss of its seats in Parliament by falling under the required 5 percent of the vote, was especially subject to these considerations before elections. Then, it had to project itself as different from all the other parties, especially the one with which it seemed likely to form a governing coalition. This explains much, although not all, of Genscher's strong support of détente.[7]

The West German Left—the SPD and the Greens—broke with the NATO consensus on INF deployment after the fall in 1982 of the Schmidt government. The SPD, historically a pacifist party, whose support comes from Protestants and ex-Protestants and which would probably be the majority party if Germany were to be reunified (East Germany is 90 percent Protestant), became in the 1970s increasingly influenced by the peace and ecological movements. The Greens—who came out of these movements and their forerunners (the new leftists of the 1960s), had gone on the "long march through the institutions" and had become civil servants, teachers, or, if not, dropout "alternatives"—gave priority to peace and ecology and were against the work ethic and economic growth.

After Schmidt resigned in 1982, the SPD, led in opposition by Willy Brandt and Egon Bahr, developed "the second phase of *Ostpolitik*." Although it did not reject NATO, European unity, or nuclear weapons on West German soil, it did give priority to an intensified *Ostpolitik*, decoupled from NATO's and especially of France's and the United States's. Its overarching concept was the replacement of NATO's strong emphasis on the Soviet threat with a "security partnership" with the Soviet Union, in order to protect its principal goal, peace, against what it saw as the principal threat, nuclear war. This security partnership required, the SPD maintained, a "structural inability to attack" through a purely defensive military strategy; Western unilateral initiatives toward nuclear-free and chemical-free zones in Europe, especially on both sides of the East-West German border, and ultimately toward European denuclearization; a European "second pillar" in NATO, under Franco–West German leadership, to deal with the United States on equal terms; and party-to-party negotiations with the ruling parties in the Soviet Union and Central and Eastern Europe toward these ends.

Thus, the SPD was even more for "stability" in Communist Central and Eastern Europe than the governing coalition and gave priority to it over contacts with dissidents there. The SPD placed more emphasis on maximum freedom of maneuver for West German foreign policy, while remaining in NATO and the European Community, than, as Kohl and Genscher did, on coordinating foreign policy with Paris and Washington.

These SPD policies were less anti-NATO and anti–European unity than those of the SPD's first post-1945 leader, Kurt Schumacher, but they were also far less anti-Soviet and anti-Communist. They were viewed by domestic and foreign opponents, especially in France and the United States, as nationalist and neutralist in their results, even if not in their purpose. They were one, but not the most important, reason the SPD was badly defeated by the Kohl-Genscher coalition in the 1987 West German parliamentary elections. (The main reason was that Kohl was identified by the voters with prosperity, whereas the SPD voters were divided between the working class, which was less radical, and the Greenpeace and ecological radicals of bourgeois origin, whose ideology and social origins made them disliked by the working class.) Since the SPD's 1987 electoral defeat, its foreign policy has gradually become somewhat more moderate, in part because its new leader, Hans-Jochen Vogel, a former close associate of Schmidt, is more moderate and because its electoral defeat has made him and the previous leftist leader, Oskar Lafontaine, the minister-president of the Saarland, more concerned about appealing to middle class and trade union voters in the political center.

By 1988, the Greens, who were strongly anti-U.S., favored West German withdrawal from NATO, urged rapprochement with the Soviet Union and Central and Eastern Europe, but also supported dissidence there, were caught in electoral stagnation and fierce factional struggles between "fundamentalists" and "realists." Their radicalism made it unlikely the SPD could return to power in the near future with or without the Greens' support; thus, by 1988 the SPD's "second phase of *Ostpolitik*" remained ineffective.[8]

Recent Developments

As time passed, East Germany remained stable and the Soviet Union remained opposed to German reunification. By the late 1980s, when East-West détente had again set in, most West Germans, according to public opinion polls, did not expect but hoped for reunification; would accept neutrality to get it; but would not accept less political freedom for that goal. (That they would accept neutrality in theory probably reflected their lessened fear of Soviet aggression more than any real expectation of reunification in the near or foreseeable future.[9]) West German politicians probably reflect their constituents' views when they put more emphasis on the possibility and desirability of gradual, peaceful change to the East.

What we cannot yet know, but soon may, is whether Gorbachev's *glasnost'* (openness) will help liberalize, or help explode, one or more of the states of Communist Central and Eastern Europe. In the longer run, if the 1987 level of visits between the two German states continues, this will help preserve the sense of German national consciousness. Because the Germans' neighbors, east and west, are far from enthusiastic about German reunification, the stress of the main West German political parties on the necessity of change in Europe as a precondition for it is one that will not soon be surmounted. The USSR would have to become much weaker than it likely soon will, another precondition that is even less likely soon to be surmounted. Finally, "Germany," and then without Austria, was historically "unified" only from 1871 to 1945. Indeed, the eighteenth-century English spoke of "the Germanys." For all these reasons, German reunification is most unlikely in the near future.

Perhaps what Willy Brandt once defined as the minimum goal of *Ostpolitik,* "the maintenance of the substance of the nation," will again, as before 1871, be defined only as the German *Kulturnation* (cultural nation). Perhaps this, too, will be further eroded by the growing economic unity of Western Europe. But Poland was partitioned from 1795 to 1918, and Polish nationalism remained; and other nationalisms, such as the French, have survived imperialism and defeat. In any case, "the German question" will long be with us and not the least with the Germans' neighbors to the east.[10]

The recent intensification of rapprochement between the two German states has further influenced the attitudes of West German opinion leaders and government officials. This became strikingly evident in connection with Bonn's upgrading of the protocol of the Honecker visit of September 1987, compared to the one scheduled but "postponed" in 1984. Another example was the updated foreign policy program drafted by a commission nominated by the executive committee of the CDU and, after revisions, adopted by it in June 1988. The program modified the party's future course in foreign and security policies, with specific reference to the European Community (*Europapolitik*) and inter-German affairs (*Deutschlandpolitik*).[11] The program did not chart really new ground. Rather, it eliminated the five-year gap that had existed between the previous declaratory aim of CDU *Ostpolitik*, to reestablish a reunited Germany, and the party's much more pragmatic, moderate present course. It confirmed explicitly what has been in fact the CDU/CSU policy line since October 1982—that the treaties with the USSR, Poland, and Czechoslovakia were among the documents on which the party's *Deutschlandpolitik* was based.

The new program showed the CDU leadership's greater pragmatism: "As long as the East-West conflict prevents us from overcoming the division of Europe and of Germany, we are called upon to do whatever is possible and reasonable today in order to mitigate the East-West conflict in Germany and in Europe and to contribute to overcoming it." The first draft version[12] was even clearer: "The overcoming of the division of Europe and Germany depends on the previous overcoming of the East-West conflict. This means that the solution of the German question is impossible for the time being. Therefore the Germans are called upon to do whatever is possible and reasonable today in order to mitigate the East-West conflict in Germany and in Europe and to contribute to overcoming it." (The original, unrevised draft version often provides more reliable insights into the discussion among CDU policymakers and their most prominent foreign policy advisers than the version revised and edited by the party's executive committee, where the archconservatives proceeded to modify it, as the preceding quotations show.)

Thus, the Christian Democrats have moved closer to the *Ostpolitik* of the Brandt-Scheel and the Schmidt-Genscher cabinets. Genscher himself intends to be the guarantor of continuity in this field and has done so successfully. His moderating influence is shown by the fact that CDU/CSU right-wingers claim that they have detected large numbers of "Genscherists" among their own party's Bundestag deputies as well as in the chancellor's office, and it is not unusual for SPD spokesmen to praise Genscher in public for his policies, which they claim are really theirs. Indeed, there is much common ground in foreign and inter-German policy among the "traditional" parliamentary parties of the Federal Republic—CDU/CSU, SPD, and FDP.

The only parliamentary party that does not share this is the Greens. They reject the constitutional commitment to work for the restoration of national "unity in freedom"; they demand the Federal Republic's withdrawal from NATO; and they favor an equidistant, neutralist West Germany between the United States and the Soviet Union. The other parties, on the contrary, subscribe in general to the reestablishment of national unity as a long-term policy goal, to West German NATO membership and cooperation with the United States in security matters (including, in particular, the protection of West Berlin), and to permanent integration into the community of Western democracies, as shown by the FRG's unreserved adherence to the European Community and to NATO.

While the Social Democrats had electoral problems with their "second phase" of *Ostpolitik,* so did the Christian Democrats with their draft program. Many CDU/CSU conservative voters opposed its leadership's effort to move toward more realism and flexibility about FRG-GDR relations and German reunification. Their views were denounced by expellee organizations, right-wingers from other interest groups, and anti-Communist journalists as a treacherous sellout.

Conclusion

"Betrayal" is the standard accusation hurled against West Germany's parliamentary parties and their more prominent representatives. Many Greens originally left the Social Democrats because they felt "betrayed." The charge of political "treachery" is also leveled by the Greens at the extraparliamentary "New Left" and by violence-prone ("autonomous") radical groups at West Germany's miniscule Communist party, East Germany's Communist regime, and Central and Eastern European ruling parties in general. They all felt "betrayed" by the politically dominant "old established forces." This protest potential presently has gained some right-wing reinforcement.[13] However, it is unlikely to succeed, either on the Left or the Right, in the foreseeable future.

With the ratification in 1988 of the Soviet-U.S. treaty for the dismantling of the intermediate nuclear missiles of both, in Europe and in Siberia, the attention of the Bonn government turned toward the probable renewal, in a larger context, of negotiations on conventional force reductions in Europe. Although the Communist states of Central and Eastern Europe did not seem likely to play a major role in these, Bonn certainly would do so. Bonn was also likely to try using these negotiations and at least the desire of Hungary, and to some extent of the GDR, to have them result in fewer Soviet troops on their territory and to get some support to its east to lower the Soviet military potential arrayed against it without imperiling major U.S. troop presence in the Federal Republic. In this context, West Germans, conservative and leftist, were also trying to play a larger, but certainly indirect, role in further limiting any possibility that short-range nuclear weapons on West German territory would be used, contrary to Bonn's will, against targets on its soil or that of the GDR.[14] Thus, in nuclear and conventional reduction negotiations, it seemed likely that Bonn, East Berlin, and Budapest would share certain common interests.

But the greatest problems between the Federal Republic and the United States are, and will probably remain, economic. Most of them, fortunately for Bonn, concern foreign trade problems outside the Communist world and therefore are formally negotiated between Washington and the European Community. But with Gorbachev's desire, as well as the desire of Honecker and Károly Grósz, for more West-East technology transfer, the issue of West German technology transfer and credits to the Soviet Union and the Communist countries of Central and Eastern Europe is likely to remain a recurrent problem for Bonn in its relations with Washington. In this respect, at least, protectionism and West German policy toward Communist Central and Eastern Europe are organically connected.[15]

Notes

1. This chapter draws especially on William E. Griffith, *The Ostpolitik of the Federal Republic of Germany* (Cambridge, Mass.: MIT Press, 1978); and on Josef Joffe, "The View from Bonn: The Tacit Alliance," in Lincoln Gordon, ed., *Eroding Empire: Western Relations with Eastern Europe* (Washington, D.C.: Brookings Institution, 1987), pp. 129–187.

2. Edwina Moreton, ed., *Germany Between East and West* (Cambridge: Cambridge University Press, 1987.)

3. Arnulf Baring, *Machtwechsel* (Stuttgart: Deutsche Verlags-Anstalt, 1982), is by far the most complete and authoritative history to date.

4. Wolfgang Jäger and Werner Link, *Republik im Wandel: Die Ära Schmidt, 1974–1982* (Stuttgart: Deutsche Verlags-Anstalt, 1987); and Christian Hacke, "Traditionen und Stationen der Aussenpolitik der Bundesregierung Deutschland," *Aus Politik und Zeitgeschichte*, B 3/88, January 15, 1988, pp. 3–15, at pp. 11–12.

5. See Clayton Clemens, "The CDU/CSU and West German Ostpolitik, 1969–1982" (Ph. D. diss., Fletcher, 1986), on which we have primarily relied. It is expected to be published soon by Duke University Press.

6. Joffe, "The View from Bonn"; cf. Renata Fritsch-Bournazel, *Confronting the German Question: Germans on the East-West Divide* (Oxford: Berg Publishers, 1988); and Richard Lowenthal, "The German Question Transformed," *Foreign Affairs* 63, no. 2 (Winter 1984-1985), pp. 303–315.

7. One of the best recent sources of Genscher's views is his speech at the Potsdam (DDR) meeting of the Institute for East-West Security Studies, New York, June 11, 1988, of which the English text was published by the German Information Center (New York) in its *Statements & Speeches* 11, no. 10 (June 13, 1988), pp. 1–7.

8. William E. Griffith, "The Security Policies of the Social Democrats and the Greens in the Federal Republic of Germany" in *Security Perspectives of the West German Left: The SPD and the Greens in Opposition* (Cambridge, Mass.: Institute for Foreign Policy Analysis, 1989), pp. 1–20. In addition to the literature cited there, for the theoretical origins of nondeterrence defense policy, see Egon Bahr and Dieter S. Lutz, eds., *Gemeinsame Sicherheit—Idee und Konzept*, vol. 1: *Zu den Ausgangsüberle-*

gungen, Grundlagen und Strukturmerkmalen Gemeinsamer Sicherheit (Baden-Baden: Nomos, 1986); for negative views, see Walter Laqueur and Robert Hunter, eds., *European Peace Movements and the Future of the Western Alliance* (New Brunswick, N.J.: Transaction Books, 1985), especially pp. 273–401.

9. See Jonathan Dean, "Directions in Inner-German Relations," *Orbis* 29, no. 3 (Fall 1985), pp. 609–632, at pp. 619–621. See also Gerhard Gerhegen, "Perspektiven und Begrenzungen: Eine Bestandsaufnahme der öffentlichen Meinung zur deutschen Frage," *Deutschland Archiv* 12 (1987), pp. 1259–1273 and 4 (1988), pp. 391–403; and Gerd Langguth, "Wie steht die junge Generation zur deutschen Teilung?" *Politische Studien*, no. 289 (September-October, 1986), pp. 524–542. For background, see Gebhardt Schweigler, *West German Foreign Policy: The Domestic Setting*, The Washington Papers, no. 106 (New York: Praeger, 1984); and Gebhardt Schweigler, *Grundlagen der aussenpolitischen Orientierung der Bundesrepublik Deutschland* (Baden-Baden: Nomos, 1985).

10. Reinhard Meier, "Die allmähliche Auflösung der deutschen Frage," *Europa Archiv* 29, no. 21 (November 10, 1984), pp. 644–654. During the 1980s, Dr. Meier was the correspondent of the *Neue Zürcher Zeitung* in Bonn. See also Lowenthal, "The German Question Transformed"; Moreton, *Germany Between East and West;* Fritsch-Bournazel, *Confronting the German Question;* and Ronald D. Asmus, "West Germany: Old Questions Posed Anew?", *SAIS Review* 5, no. 1 (Spring 1985), pp. 211–225. The most authoritative recent statement of West German policy on the GDR and on Eastern Europe is the speech at the yearly meeting of the Deutsche Gesellschaft für Auswärtige Politik by Dr. Wolfgang Schäuble, minister of state in the Federal Chancery. The text is reprinted in *Europa Archiv* 43, no. 14 (July 25, 1988), pp. 414–420.

11. *Unsere Verantwortung in der Welt.* Christlich-demokratische Perspektiven zur Deutschland-, Aussen-, Sicherheits-, Europa-, und Entwicklungspolitik, Beschluss des 36. Bundesparteitags der CDU, adopted June 14, 1988 (Bonn: Konrad-Adenauer-Haus, CDU-Dokumentation 19, 1988).

12. *Unsere Verantwortung in der Welt.* Diskussionsentwurf der vom Bundesvorstand eingesetzten Kommission, CDU-Dokumentation 6/1988 (Bonn: Konrad-Adenauer-Haus, 1988).

13. Hans-Georg Betz, "Romantic Anti-Capitalism in Germany" (Ph.D. diss., MIT, 1987).

14. Volker Rühe, "Perspektiven der Friedenssicherung in Europa," *Europa Archiv* 42, no. 23 (December 12, 1987), pp. 675–682; Thomas Enders and Peter Siebenmorgen, "Überlegungen zu einem sicherheitspolitischen Gesamtkonzept der Bundesrepublik Deutschland," *Europa Archiv* 43, no. 14 (July 25, 1988), pp. 385–392; Jonathan Dean, "Will the Two German States Solve the Problem of European Security?", *SAIS Review* 8, no. 7 (Summer-Fall 1988), pp. 173–190.

15. The West German position on COCOM is set forth best in Hanns-D. Jacobsen, Heinrich Machowski, and Klaus Schröder, "The Political and Economic Framework Conditions of East-West Economic Relations," *Aussenpolitik* (English ed.) (no. 2, 1988), pp. 138–149.

15

French Policy Toward Central and Eastern Europe

Dominique Moïsi

Does French policy toward Central and Eastern Europe still exist? This question, however provocative, is nevertheless justified. The judgment that Eastern Europeans have with respect to France—a growing mixture of disillusion and resignation—is indicative of a new climate underneath the traditionally well-controlled language of diplomacy. During the last visit made by Foreign Minister Jean-Bernard Raimond to Budapest in March 1988, the Hungarians openly expressed their frustrations with the limited role played by Franco-Hungarian exchanges. In Poland—a country traditionally favored by France in Eastern Europe—the French language is losing ground. There it has become the third Western language after English and German, a sad irony for France, whose "mission to civilize" was largely based on the defense of a historical and cultural legacy incarnated by a language, for which it is now bravely fighting a rearguard battle in the world. To add insult to injury, it is not the French but the Poles who want to diversify West Germany through French influence. Between the French ideal and the German reality, Eastern European countries have been forced to choose, and France has lost, largely by default.

Is this diagnosis too extreme or does it correspond to reality? France's Eastern European policy, or rather the lack of it, is the inevitable result of an inability to choose between realpolitik and emotions, without the correct means with which to apply either or both. The history of the relations between France and Central and Eastern Europe is a long one, but the legacy of the past—although sometimes an asset—can also be a burden because it is largely dominated by memories of constant disappointment on the part of its East European partners.

The Legacy of the Past

Central and Eastern Europe have always been important in French diplomacy, for geographic and historical reasons. Because it was separated from France by Germany, Eastern Europe in its various incarnations always seemed to be a natural ally of French diplomacy in its attempt to resist the German threat on its borders. Conversely, countries such as Poland hoped they could count on France to resist the pressures from more aggressive and dynamic neighbors. Yet the Franco-Polish dynastic alliance did not prevent the three partitions of Poland in the late eighteenth century. Combining the wrong political culture with the wrong geography, Poland was unable to resist the greed and territorial appetite of three stronger neighbors, Russia, Prussia, and Austria. The ancien régime of these monarchies, by violating their own foreign policy traditions and permitting the drastic alteration of the European balance of power by allowing the disappearance of one of its key actors, Poland, helped pave the way for the excesses of the French revolutionary ambition. This process was well described by Albert Sorel in his book *Europe and the French Revolution.*[1] France, immersed in its revolution, was utterly unable to prevent the Polish state from disappearing. For the nations of Central and Eastern Europe, the French revolution and the Napoleonic wars marked the awakening of their national aspirations, a phenomenon well symbolized in Ljubljana by the statue honoring the emperor-liberator Napoleon Bonaparte as the inheritor of the French Revolution.

The principle of the *alliance de revers* (alliance with the neighbors and rivals of one's enemies) was used by France as part of its attempt to change or to consolidate the European system, depending on whether France was a revisionist or a status quo power. But Eastern Europe was never considered alone nor treated with the necessary consistency between aims and means.

In the nineteenth century, France's policy toward Eastern Europe seemed caught between realpolitik and emotions. Until the revolution of 1848, the defeated France that emerged from the Congress of Vienna behaved as a prudent status quo power, thereby following Charles de Talleyrand's aim to regain for France the legitimacy within the European concert that Napoleon's adventures had compromised. Emotions for the plight of the Polish people, incarnated by the romantic figure of Frédéric Chopin and played upon by the opponents to the bourgeois monarchy of Louis-Philippe, could count for little when opposed to the prudent and noninterventionist strategy of the Orleanist regime, to the great disillusionment of the Poles. With the coming of Napoleon III to power, France switched from a status quo to a revisionist policy, which seemingly allowed a reconciliation between emotions and realpolitik. The defense of the national aspirations of the Italians or the Poles—although much less visible and important in the Polish case—was played upon by the new Bonaparte until another nationalism, Germany's, led to the demise of his own regime through military defeat.

The desire of the Third Republic to contain Germany led France to alliance with Great Britain and then with Russia, an *alliance de revers* that could only clash with support for oppressed nations such as Poland or minorities within the Russian Empire such as the Jews. Confronted with the growth of German power, France and the United Kingdom had to transcend their near-collison at Fashoda and leave aside their colonial rivalries to come to terms with each other and to ally themselves with the tsar, thereby abandoning the Poles, Jews, and all other minorities within the Russian Empire. French realpolitik required abandonment of French emotions.

The new world order that emerged after 1918 allowed France to reconcile its conflicting goals. France sought to establish a system of *alliance de revers* against the revisionist claims of a defeated Germany, while supporting the principle of national self-determination. A third value—the commitment to democracy—was less well respected, given the very nature of the regimes that existed in Eastern Europe, with the notable exception of Czechoslovakia. That many of these regimes tried to copy the institutions of the Third Republic was a cultural tribute to France's prestige, but also a sure recipe for disaster, given their socioeconomic conditions; the disaster extended to France as well.

But the absence of Russia (now the Soviet Union), the differences between France and Great Britain, and the divisions among the Eastern European countries themselves prevented this reduced version of the *alliance de revers* from resisting the revisionist policies of Adolf Hitler's Germany. The new order that emerged in Eastern Europe, in part under French patronage, had two fundamental weaknesses: It could survive only if Germany and the USSR remained weak and hostile to each other and only if Poland, Czechoslovakia, and Yugoslavia (or rather Serbia) were pro-French (Hungary and Bulgaria were pro-German and Romania waffled, as usual). Moreover, France's strategy, hampered by the weakness of a decaying Third Republic, proved contradictory. The divorce between the defensive strategy of France incarnated by the Maginot Line and the diplomacy of support to the Eastern European countries is still used today in military schools as the best example of discrepancy between strategy and diplomacy. Such a conceptual incompatability led first to the betrayal of Czechoslovakia in Munich and then to war in support of Polish independence when it was too late. If France was a symbol of freedom before 1918 in Eastern and Central Europe, it became after 1918, through the Little Entente, much more than that, a true continental "balancer" and the guarantor of Eastern European independence. France did not, and indeed could not, maintain its position in Eastern Europe, and its failure to do so mortgaged and presaged its failure after 1945.

From Grand Design to Patchwork

Charles de Gaulle's attempt to resuscitate France as a world power after 1945 turned Eastern Europe into a useful card but not an important interest. As Pierre Hassner justly emphasized, there was a major difference between de Gaulle's vision in 1945 and his goal in 1958.[2] In the aftermath of World War II, his primary consideration in recognizing the new and emerging Moscow-oriented status of Eastern Europe was to enlist the support of the Soviet Union for France's anti-German policy and to increase French bargaining power with the Anglo-Saxons. When de Gaulle returned to power in 1958, he attempted to act as a go-between among West Germany, Eastern Europe, and the Soviet Union.

In December 1944, the Franco-Soviet alliance, purportedly against Germany, corresponded to de Gaulle's attempt to reinsert France diplomatically into the international system by having it play the arbiter between the Anglo-Saxons and the Soviets, whose differences were already beginning to appear. This French ambition was disappointed because Moscow did not support France's international claim to be a major partner in the concert of victorious powers. Only slowly and reluctantly did France accept the position that its defeat in 1940 and the enormously increased power of the United States and the Soviet Union had condemned France to the status of a medium power and to the necessity of substituting for the independent policy of a great power the alliance-oriented policy of a medium power. Yet in comparison with nonnuclear West Germany and with weakened Great Britain, France remains the only West European power with an extra-European sphere of influence (in Francophone Africa).

The irresistible rise of the cold war in Europe and France's need to resist Soviet destabilizing tactics with the economic, political, and (ultimately) military help of the United States condemned Georges Bidault's dream of having France play a third role between East and West and a triangular game between the USSR and the United States. However, the passions underlying the European Defense Community (EDC) debates in France, especially between 1952 and 1954, illustrated France's psychological difficulty in switching from the German to the Soviet threat. In 1954, the alliance between the Gaullists and the Communists, added to the divisions of the Socialists, led to the rejection of the EDC Treaty in France. The treaty's purported threat of denationalization of the French army, coupled with the rearmament of West Germany, seemed far greater than the real presence of Soviet divisions, whose danger seemed further removed and abstract compared with the impending prospect of German soldiers within a European army. During most of the Fourth Republic, the cold war did not allow France a specific policy toward Eastern and Central Europe. It was completely absorbed into the global context of East-West relations. The only specific French concern was to integrate West Germany into the West. France's policy toward Eastern and Central Europe was therefore always secondary to Franco-German or Franco-Russian policy[3] and really still is.

The Suez crisis in October 1956, used as a diversion by the Soviets to crush the Hungarian revolt, constituted a severe psychological blow for France's image in the world in general and specifically in Eastern Europe. France, by allowing itself, together with Great Britain, to practice gunboat diplomacy in an anarchistic attempt to reestablish its neocolonial status, and in its attempt to hold on to Algeria, was betraying once more its responsibilities toward Eastern Europe and more generally toward its European role.

In 1958, the return of de Gaulle to power in the midst of the Algerian drama coincided first with the Berlin and Cuba crisis and then with the onset of détente. This proved to be the ideal context for de Gaulle's principles. The two pillars of his policy were (1) firmness toward the Soviet Union and solidarity with the United States in acute East-West crises, and (2) dialogue with the Soviet Union and enlargement of France's diplomatic margin of maneuver vis-à-vis the United States through a policy of calculated differentiation. The validity and limitations of this policy were demonstrated from 1962 to 1969. De Gaulle's trip to Moscow in June 1966, coming so shortly after France's departure from the North Atlantic Treaty Organization (NATO) integrated military command, was wrongly denounced by many as a reversal of alliances. The two actions were perfectly complementary in the context of the policy of "détente, entente, and cooperation" that de Gaulle wanted to establish and that stemmed from a French desire for a central international role transcending France's regional limitations. How could Eastern Europe be integrated into this diplomatic and strategic context?

The Historical Dimensions of de Gaulle's Policies

To understand de Gaulle's approach to the question of Eastern and Central Europe, one must realize France's fascination with its own history, which thus gives a high priority to the historical dimension of politics. Inheritor of a prestigious past and a long tradition as a nation-state, France naturally seeks in others what it looks for in itself—a sense of continuity and tradition, with eternal goals beyond the transient nature of different regimes. De Gaulle's view of history—his personification of nations—has had a long-standing impact on the way France perceived and still perceives the Soviet Union. Tempted to see eternal Russia under the Leninist mantle, France voluntarily neglected, for cultural and for political reasons, the ideological nature of the Soviet regime and of the other Eastern European states. Ideology was not supposed to interfere with history or immediate, détente-oriented political concerns. De Gaulle's famous and ambiguous statement about a Europe from the Atlantic to the Urals was a total rejection of the ideological nature of the East-West divide. (This concept now comes back at us like a boomerang when Mikhail Gorbachev speaks of a "European Common House".) From this perspective the desire to restore the completeness of Europe and the need to recognize the national legitimacy of the East European longing for true independence were part of de Gaulle's Atlantic-to-Urals dream. (For the Soviet Union such a historical approach could be accepted within limits, as long as the USSR was integrated into the geographical scope of the European scheme and as long as its control of Eastern Europe was not threatened.)

For de Gaulle, an approach so different from the traditional "geography of values," which was rendered possible by the U.S. nuclear umbrella, could alter the nature of the international system in Europe. Less integration in Western Europe would encourage less control of the Soviet Union in Eastern Europe. Could not France's distance from NATO be presented as an indirect appeal to the people of Eastern Europe to try the same with Moscow? De

Gaulle's trip to Moscow in June 1966 was followed by a series of visits to Poland in 1967 and to Romania in 1967.

Unfortunately, de Gaulle's only followers in the East proved to be the "oriental despot" Nicolae Ceauşescu in Romania. The entrance of Soviet tanks into Prague to crush a Communist- and intellectual-led movement, described flippantly by Michel Debré, then French foreign minister, as "a traffic accident on the road to détente," led to the de facto abandonment of de Gaulle's grand design and all the more so because May 1968 had drastically reduced France's internal margin of maneuver by exposing the fragility of French society and the weakness of its economy. Debré's unfortunate comment could only be perceived in Eastern Europe as a second betrayal (after 1956) by France of its responsibilities toward Central and Eastern Europe.

The Effects of West German Ostpolitik

France's original approach to détente was completely superseded in the late 1960s and early 1970s by West Germany's *Ostpolitik*, symbolized by the treaties signed between the Federal Republic and its Eastern neighbors and by the superpower dialogue on arms control. Georges Pompidou's numerous meetings with Leonid Brezhnev were part of a global process of détente and were based on the recognition of the status quo in Eastern Europe. Pompidou's goals were much less romantic than de Gaulle's. Pompidou wanted to transform France into a modern industrial country. His vision of Europe was oriented more toward the West and the European Economic Community (EEC) as was made evident by his successful rapprochement with Great Britain. Under Pompidou, France's approach to Eastern Europe was a mixture of the interest and benign neglect a country gives to a secondary stake that might or might not be used in a global strategy game. In contrast, West Germany's direct interest in East Germany and willingness to normalize relations with Poland and Czechoslovakia made the West German vision more intense, more concrete and imbued with societal interest that transcended the reflections and emotions of a small group of politicians and intellectuals.

France has one important common interest with the Soviet Union: that Germany not be reunited and dominate them both. After 1945, both initially were hostile to Germany, but the cold war made them even more hostile to each other. As West Germany grew stronger, Giscard d'Estaing and François Mitterrand intelligently embraced it lest it go nationalist or neutralist or both. (That they exaggerated the danger of this was analytically incorrect and politically desirable.) They also joined Bonn in pushing for Franco-German cooperation and leadership in West Europe.

France had two assets that West Germany did not: its nuclear status and its occupation rights in West Berlin. Mitterrand also shared Helmut Kohl's desire to have good relations with the United States. France knew that West Germany was economically far stronger and politically determined to intensify its contact with East Germany and thus with the Soviet Union in order, as

Willy Brandt once put it, "to maintain the substance of the German nation." Therefore, the closer French relations are with West Germany, and as long as France maintains and uses its position in West Berlin, the more France can contain any developments in Bonn contrary to its interests. The same is true a fortiori with respect to the EEC and to Franco-German leadership in it. Moreover, France has indirect, if only negative, influence on the GDR, if only because of West Berlin, and not only via Bonn. All this means that France, via Bonn and West Berlin, does have some, however minimal and negative, influence on Moscow, East Berlin, and Eastern Europe.

From East European Independence to Interdependence

The support given by French diplomacy to the Conference on Security and Cooperation in Europe (CSCE) process led France to encourage an independent role for the East European states, in accord with the French traditional opposition to bloc-to-bloc discussion. Yet concern for Eastern Europe as such, although not negligible with the initiation of the concept of the (human rights) Third Basket, was clearly secondary and stemmed from the fear of a renewed superpower condominium caused by a consolidation of détente.

When Pompidou's Western concentration was replaced by Giscard's vision of interdependence and convergence between East and West, Eastern Europe was naturally less absent from France's considerations. Giscard dreamt of an attenuation of the ideological competition with the Soviet Union and believed in the weapons of peace—trade and reinforcement of the détente process through East-West exchanges. This dream particularly encompassed Edward Gierek's Poland, and it was an infatuation shared by others, bankers above all, that helped lead to the Polish economic disaster.

The deterioration of détente, especially after the Soviet invasion of Afghanistan, and the resultant negative image of the Soviet Union caught Giscard d'Estaing off guard. Unlike Jimmy Carter, who had discovered in a week the true nature of the Soviet Union even if he never fully adjusted to it, Giscard d'Estaing tried to preserve his essentially positivist, nontragic vision of the world. He was denounced by Mitterrand as the "messenger boy" of the Soviet Union after he imprudently met with Brezhnev (the first Western leader to do so) after the invasion of Afghanistan in a misplaced attempt to extract some concessions from him.

Mitterrand's Rehabilitation of Socialism

With the coming of Mitterrand to power in 1981, a certain romantic vision of foreign policy returned, one that had been absent in the Pompidou and Giscard period. Mitterrand shared de Gaulle's faith in France's special mission in the world and even gave the impression in the early period of his presidency of transcending it by fusing France's destiny with that of socialism. If de Gaulle guided France's destiny using a classical realist vision of a balance of power concerned only with nation-states, Mitterrand's ultimate goal seemed initially to rehabilitate socialism in France and then in the world.

From 1981 to the end of 1983, from Mitterrand's election to the high point of the Euromissile crisis, France's hard-line policy vis-à-vis the Soviet Union, a so-called "deintoxication cure," was the product of strategic, domestic, and cultural considerations. In the late 1970s and early 1980s, the two superpowers engaged in a major test of political will and diplomacy regarding intermediate-range nuclear forces (INF) deployment. Mitterrand was worried about the evolution of the balance of power in the world, particularly in Europe, at a time when the Soviet Union appeared to have a strategic edge and when the Federal Republic of Germany, in its identity crisis, seemed to be flirting with Gaullism and pacifism. For Mitterrand the realist, France had to be aware of its new responsibilities. Furthermore, socialist France had to prove its Atlantic reliability in spite of the Communist presence in the government.

At a deeper cultural level, largely because the French intelligentsia had to make up for its long infatuation with the "motherland of socialism," the French were more negative toward the Soviet Union than were most of their European partners in the late 1970s and the 1980s. In cultural terms, the impact of the gulag revelations and the Soviet Union's aggressive anti–human rights behavior transformed the French intellectual context and subsequently the Left itself. Because the Left stressed the very basis of the Russian Revolution, with its antipluralist totalitarian elements, in explaining the nature of the Soviet system (as opposed to its subsequent Stalinist degradation), the implication was bound to affect the French view of the "mother" of all modern revolutions, the French revolution. French intellectual and sociocultural trends in the 1970s thus converged in a new, more public adherence to democratic values and in a questioning of traditional left-wing revolutionary ideology. The Soviet model was rejected, and in its place the United States emerged as a positive reference point because of its social dynamism and democratic culture.[4]

A policy of firmness toward the Soviet Union could have included a true concern for Eastern Europe. Unfortunately, as was demonstrated early in the December 1981 Polish crisis, what emerged was a discrepancy between France's harsh words and its conciliatory deeds. In an interview he gave to *Newsweek*, the then French foreign minister Claude Cheysson perfectly summarized the tenets of France's attitude toward the Polish crisis—a realistic assessment of the nature of the crisis coupled with a refusal to take steps that would lead nowhere (according to him).

> We have made a more fundamental analysis than the Americans of the Polish situation. We believe it is a further demonstration of the logic of the totalitarian system which simply cannot accept free expression. That system was forced by its nature to crush liberty and muffle the Church. Minor measures like increasing interest rates on loans to the Soviet Union won't have the slightest influence on the unfolding drama. Secondly, we are more dependent on the Soviet Union for trade. Above all, since we are not as strong as the

> United States, and since our national defense depends on our credibility, we simply cannot afford to make a threat that is not realized—as happened with the American embargo on grain in Afghanistan.[5]

In December 1981, France was clearly closer to the firm U.S. policy toward Poland. But from December 1981 to March 1982, as the Jaruzelski regime seemed to consolidate itself, as emotions faded, and as concrete measures succeeded verbal denunciations, France seemed to move closer toward the Federal Republic's softer policy, in deeds if not in speeches. It seemed as if France were returning to Cheysson's original assessment: "It is a Polish internal affair that must be solved among Poles. We do not see for the moment any trace of a threat of foreign intervention. . . . Of course, we are not going to react." Pierre Hassner used the following formula to describe the French attitude to Poland: "The French talk like the Americans, but act like the Germans; Americans believe in sticks, the Germans in carrots and the French in words." The West Germans, on the other hand, gave more generously to the Polish people. This generosity was probably encouraged by a sense of guilt but also from West Germany's more pragmatic approach toward Eastern and Central Europe.

The abrupt character of Cheysson's first reaction, in contrast to the impressive pro-Polish demonstration of fifty thousand people, marked a gap reminiscent of de Gaulle's isolation in the late 1960s when he declared an embargo on the sale of weapons to Israel. This gap had to be bridged because criticism came from the traditional Right as well as (and mainly) from within the new majority, led by the CFDT and the Rocard wing of the Socialist party. Therefore, on Wednesday December 16, 1981, three days after the Warsaw coup, Mitterrand denounced it without ambiguity. But in his New Year's greetings he said that "everything that will help us overcome Yalta is welcome." (In Yalta, a decision to hold free elections in Poland was taken, and a compromise was reached on the fate of the Lublin versus the London Polish governments.) Although meant to alleviate any future suffering of Policy society, the president's remarks helped perpetuate the myth that the fate of the Polish people was sealed at Yalta; his remarks also had the dubious advantage of creating a false analogy between the control exercised by the two superpowers on their respective sides.

Against this background of sustained verbal indignation and global firmness vis-à-vis the Soviet Union, the French natural gas deal with the USSR took place. The gas decision seemed to contradict France's previous policy. Furthermore, the presentation of the deal to the French public was not well prepared. Prime Minister Pierre Mauroy's unfortunate comment, "One must not add to the sufferings of the Polish people those of the French people lacking gas," added a touch of indecency to a decision that could perhaps have been justified in political and economic terms.[6]

Ambiguous French actions could also seem contradictory. For example, France was the country in Western Europe to reduce most of its diplomatic contact with Jaruzelski's Poland, but it was also the first one to receive him officially.

Normalization of Relations with the USSR

The trend toward normalization of official bilateral Franco-Soviet relations was begun by East-West normalization but was accelerated in some measure by Gorbachev's smile and facilitated by his choice of Paris in October 1985 for his first official visit to a Western country. France could only be pleased that the Soviet Union had singled it out of respect for French firmness on the Euromissiles and out of pleasure for France's critical stance on Reagan's Strategic Defense Initiative. In France, the 1970s and early 1980s discovery of the evil nature of the Soviet Union gave way slowly in 1985–1986 to growing hopes that the "evil" could be reformed. Would the Soviet Union significantly improve its record on human rights, moderate its global ambitions, and reform its economy or society? Questions that were unthinkable in the past were now being raised, although with massive doses of historical skepticism. Meanwhile, without waiting for final answers, France could always resume dialogue and normalization.

This process of normalization with the Soviet Union was accompanied by slow normalization with Eastern European regimes. Hungary, the model of economic reform (whether it is judged to be a myth or a reality), was the first Eastern European country to benefit from a French presidential visit, and János Kádár went to Paris in 1984. Normalization with Poland culminated in 1985 with the visit of Wojciech Jaruzelski to France and that of foreign undersecretary Jean-François Baylet to Warsaw, in which he was not allowed to meet with representatives of the Polish opposition or to make symbolic gestures toward Polish society. This was a stark contrast to the attitude of other Western ministers, described by some as a "diplomatic Dien Bien Phu."

With the coming of cohabitation after the parliamentary elections of March 1986, normalization with the East was consolidated and extended. For the first time, an East German head of state, Erich Honecker, was received in France by one of the three Western powers that had responsibility in Germany and in Berlin. This visit, made possible by the September 1987 meeting between Erich Honecker and Helmut Kohl, was an illustration of Mitterrand's willingness to work for reconciliation between the French and all the Germans, notwithstanding the East-West divide. This concern could, however, not suppress the French need to reaffirm the differences existing between the two systems so as to reassure the West Germans about the purity of French intentions. Mitterrand insisted that it was unthinkable, that "les Européens s'accordent sur la paix, s'ils se séparent sur la liberté."

France's Central and Eastern European Policy—
The Test of Reality

The fate of Central and Eastern Europe was sealed twice in the twentieth century. At Munich, France failed. At Yalta, it was absent. Such handicaps could only be difficult to surmount. But in a favorable context, before the 1968 Prague coup, de Gaulle played an original card and played it rather well. It was a time when people hoped for an alternative to partition and dreamed that ideological bridges could be crossed by rapprochement between the two systems. But the encounter between an exceptional man, de Gaulle, and exceptional circumstances proved illusory and short-lived. Without de Gaulle, French words were bound to carry less weight.

The present crisis of France's Eastern and Central European policy—as demonstrated by France's declining share of economic markets, the declining presence of the French language, and the reduced consideration or hope stemming from French words—is largely the result of the increased lack of adaptation of France's approach to the new conditions of the Eastern European scene in the Gorbachev era. In contrast, the Federal Republic of Germany seems to be reaping the profits from its recent judicious policies in spite of its past. At a time when Eastern Europe seems characterized by the awakening and greater self-assurance of modernizing elites, the Federal Republic of Germany can use fully the benefits of its more dynamic economy, more conciliatory political tone, and more direct and widespread historical and cultural presence. Moreover, France's traditional allies—Poland, Romania, and Yugoslavia—are clearly in severe crisis—which is relative and stalemated in Poland, total and absurd in Romania, economic and ethnic in Yugoslavia—whereas West Germany's "allies"—the German Democratic Republic, Hungary, and Bulgaria—are comparatively better off.

France's economic dealings with the East were always characterized by the relative lack of dynamism of its entrepreneurs. In a country such as France, where raison d'état, political and diplomatic vision, and ideological debates are so crucial, the economic dimension of the relationship (although always present and even important for a country with declining external competitiveness and a corresponding need for markets) ultimately proved to be secondary. In fact, the French economy, because of its structural weaknesses, needs to use all the resources of the state to gain markets, and even so it cannot escape a trade deficit.

But even if France's lag in economic matters in Eastern Europe can be understood, its cultural withdrawal, the result of the priority given to the Third World by France in the postwar period, is less acceptable. The defense of Francophonie for the Africans prevailed over France's larger European identity. In broadcasting, as pointed out by Jacques Rupnik,[7] the merger of the eastern program of Radio France Internationale with its southern program directed toward Africa meant in fact the absorption of the East by the South. Moreover, in the present debate on security in France, Eastern Europe is largely absent or more than ever a function of France's triangular relations with the United States and the Soviet Union, on the one hand, and with the Federal Republic of Germany and the Soviet Union, on the other.

Gorbachev's deft combination of reform at home and imaginative diplomacy abroad has crystallized West European ambiguities. In their reactions to his proposal on arms control or in their debates on the possibility for reform within the Soviet system, the West Europeans reveal their inner divisions, their deep attachment to stability, and their profound yearning for change.

Sometimes both are present, as in the German case. Beneath pretended unanimity each European country has to struggle to reconcile conflicting priorities.

The prospect of a denuclearized world is thus seen very differently in Paris than in Bonn. The Kremlin's increasingly dynamic arms control policy and Washington's renewed openness in the matter are perceived in Paris as a challenge to France's security and its self-image, given the close link in France among independence, security, and absolute reliance on nuclear deterrence. Bonn's generally positive reply to Gorbachev's proposals corresponds to deep hopes for an alteration of one of the bases on which European stability, but also Germany's division and its inferior status, has rested. Germany's hopes are France's fears.

What could be the impact of François Mitterrand's reelection on French policy toward Central and Eastern Europe? Will his choice of Michel Rocard as prime minister make a difference? After the Jaruzelski coup, Rocard, a man closer to the sensitivities of the second Left, wanted to send boats to pick up Polish refugees on the Baltic shores. At the end of 1988 the reinforcement of détente, and especially Bonn-Moscow détente and London's turn in the same direction, encouraged Mitterrand to do the same.

Most probably those personal factors will have little impact on key French foreign policy orientations. It is difficult for France today to have an *Ostpolitik* perspective. France at the time of de Gaulle's grand design had a vision and was essentially a revisionist power intent on changing the existing order. France has become essentially a status quo power intent on preserving its international status and clout and its foreign policy consensus. France, rightly or wrongly, feels threatened by the evolution of an international system that would put pressures on French nuclear choices. France also fears that technological, diplomatic, and psychological development will endanger the country's independent, medium-size nuclear forces.

If there is fear, there is also hope stemming from Mitterrand's strong desire to contribute to the emergence of a unified Western Europe. But there may be a contradiction between his rhetorical claim to transcend Yalta and his sincere willingness to give priority to Western Europe. France's ultimate priority is Western Europe.

Whatever cracks exist in its "grandeur," France is the only truly political entity that could play a decisive role in the construction of a politically unified Europe, provided France surmounts its economic weakness. Because West Germany, as a result of its past, its present division, and economic triumph remains essentially an economic power; because Margaret Thatcher's Great Britain is still torn between Atlanticist and European faithfulness; and because Italy is an economic miracle embedded in a political quagmire, only France can play a pioneering political and security role. In the first presidency of President Mitterrand and even with the process of cohabitation, a new consensus has been formed in France around the values of Europe.

The Pompidou and Giscard d'Estaing presidencies may in the eyes of historians appear as a brief interlude between the Gaullist and the Mitterrand era. In Mitterrand's style, in his historical and literary approach to politics, and in his length of power, he has proven to be the most Gaullist of de Gaulle's successors. Only a man of his generation who lived through World War II as a mature adult can have a full openness to the European ideal that transcends the often technocratic imperatives of younger politicians. It is now Mitterrand's responsibility, by performing the necessary foreign policy shift from Europe to New Caledonia, to prove he embodies de Gaulle's realism.

Mitterrand's failure to do so would mark Europe's own decline because no other nation can play France's role. Ultimately, such a unified Western Europe would be the best hope for Eastern Europe as well.

Given Gorbachev's presence and initiative, a Western European *Ostpolitik* is more necessary than ever. Ideally this *Ostpolitik* should combine Germany's pragmatism with France's antitotalitarian criticism. Only then perhaps can the French trend of political idealism from Chopin to Solidarity be rendered effective. The alliance between French words and German deeds is more than ever a necessity for both countries and for Europe.

Notes

1. Albert Sorel, *L'Europe et la révolution française,* 8 vols. (Paris, 1905).
2. Pierre Hassner, "The View from Paris," in Lincoln Gordon, ed., *Eroding Empire: Western Relations with Eastern Europe* (Washington, D.C.: Brookings Institution, 1987), pp. 194–197.
3. Ibid., p. 195.
4. Diana Pinto, "Social Cultural Trends Versus Culture" (Prepared for the colloquium on European-American Relations, Talloires, September 6–10, 1987).
5. *Newsweek,* March 1982.
6. Dominique Moïsi, "France and the Polish Crisis," *SAIS Review* (Summer 1982), p. 101.
7. Jacques Rupnik, "La présence radiophonique française dans les pays du Centre Européen. Un bilan et quelques suggestions" (unpublished manuscript, June 1985).

16

The United States and Eastern Europe: A Window of Opportunity

Michael Mandelbaum

In September 1938, at the time of the Munich crisis about Czechoslovakia, Neville Chamberlain, the prime minister of Great Britain, made a radio address in which he said, "How horrible, fantastic, incredible it is that we should be digging trenches and trying on gas masks here because of a quarrel in a faraway country between people of whom we know nothing." Fifty years later, his words have a certain unhappy resonance for U.S. policy toward the region of which Czechoslovakia is a part. Although much has changed, the continuities are pronounced enough that Chamberlain's observation is a not altogether inappropriate epigraph for U.S. policy toward Eastern Europe in the 1980s.

One change is for the better. The U.S. public now knows more about Eastern Europe and its quarrels than the British did about Czechoslovakia or its neighboring countries. Air travel has made it possible to visit the region; television brings pictures of Wenceslas Square in Prague and the monument to the 1970 strikers at the Lenin shipyard in Gdańsk into U.S. living rooms. The United States has, moreover, a large number of citizens of Eastern European origin. To the descendants of those who emigrated at the end of the nineteenth and the beginning of the twentieth centuries have been added several waves of refugees fleeing the political disasters that began at Munich and that have occurred with dismal regularity ever since.

There are, however, similarities between the late 1930s and the late 1980s. Now, as then, most of the countries of Eastern Europe are dominated by a hated imperial neighbor.[1] Now, as then, the people of the region look to the West for deliverance or, if not that, then support for such resistance as they can muster. Before World War II, Britain and France were the liberal great powers in which the Eastern Europeans vested their hopes; since then, the United States has filled this role. The United States now, like Britain then, has sympathized with the Eastern Europeans' plight but has been able to do very little to change it. By now, of course, the inability of the United States to free East Germany, Czechoslovakia, Hungary, Poland, Romania, and Bulgaria from Soviet control has long been established. The year 1956 was the crucial moment, the failure of the West to assist the Hungarians in their revolt the telling event.

Nevertheless, the U.S. failure in 1956 and afterward to fight for Hungary or Czechoslovakia or Poland has not earned the contempt associated with the British and French surrender of the Czech Sudetenland to Hitler at Munich. The reluctance that seemed cowardly fifty years ago is no more than simple prudence in the age of nuclear weapons. A serious Western effort to break the Soviet grip on Eastern Europe, it is widely believed, would lead to World War III and thus to nuclear conflict. Nuclear war, instead of liberating the Eastern Europeans, would destroy them, and millions of others.

Because the United States can do nothing to alter the basic political arrangements in Central and Eastern Europe and because the Soviet empire there is guaranteed by nuclear weapons, the region tends to be peripheral to the concerns of those responsible for U.S. foreign policy. Eastern Europe is unpromising, remote, and the object of little attention. For U.S. leaders, it is a series of small, faraway countries about which they can *do* nothing. These countries make their way briefly to the top of the U.S. agenda when their people rise up against the Soviet Union and are crushed. Such episodes serve as reminders of Soviet iniquity, then pass into the domain of scholars and middle-level diplomats. This lack of interest represents a U.S. failure to appreciate the important role that Eastern Europe actually plays in the country's foreign policy, and this is particularly unfortunate because in the late 1980s and early 1990s, circumstances in these countries and in the Soviet Union offer an opportunity for the United States and the West to exert never-before-available influence in the region.

The Importance of Eastern Europe

Why is Eastern Europe important for the United States? One purpose of U.S. foreign policy is to foster liberal political values and spread democratic practices. Eastern Europe is governed by Communist parties that forbid them. The Communist regimes of Eastern Europe are neither the only ones in the world nor, by most standards, the worst. Károly Grósz's Hungary and Wojciech Jaruzelski's Poland are less repressive than Fidel Castro's Cuba or Mengistu Haile Mariam's Ethiopia, not to mention Mikhail Gorbachev's Soviet Union.

The Eastern European regimes (except Yugoslavia), unlike other Communist governments, have been imposed by another country. In the USSR, the People's Republic of China, Vietnam, and Cuba local Communists won power through revolutions that they made or wars that they fought, or both. The Communist regimes in Berlin, Warsaw, Prague, Bucharest, and Sofia were put in power and are kept there by Soviet military forces. Even if the regimes in Moscow, Beijing, and Havana are not legitimate by Western standards (they have not been freely elected), they are certainly authentically Russian, Chinese, or Cuban. The ultimate power over Eastern Europe, by contrast, rests with foreigners. To the injury of oppression has been added the insult of imperialism.

Eastern Europe therefore represents a worse violation of democratic standards than do other Communist governments in the sense that the gap between the governments that exist in Eastern Europe and those that would exist if the people of the region were free to choose is wider than it is elsewhere. Although all Communist governments violate the political standards in which U.S. citizens believe, these standards are not equally embedded or embraced everywhere. Democratic government and liberal economic practices are associated with historical experiences and social structures that the countries ruled by indigenous Communist parties have generally lacked.

The USSR, for example, has a very weak democratic tradition. China was a huge peasant country with a long history of hierarchical administrative rule when the Communists won power there. Vietnam, Cuba, and Ethiopia all had few of what the history of the West suggests are the prerequisites for democracy. The countries of Eastern Europe, on the other hand, by and large (and with important exceptions) do have these historical and social prerequisites. They are would-be democracies as the others are not. They have a special claim on U.S. sympathies as the nations most like the West that are prevented from governing themselves along Western lines.[2] The democracy movement that appeared in the Soviet Union in the 1970s—consisting of people actively working for Western-style democracy—was small. The number of those who sympathized but were unwilling to say so openly was no doubt larger but probably not, in the context of Soviet society, very large. In Poland, by contrast, the ranks of those with such attitudes spread across the entire nation.

The differences between Eastern Europe and the other Communist regimes affect the course of political development in these countries. Where Communist regimes have roots in the societies they govern, indigenous reform movements have appeared and have had some success. Yugoslavia abandoned many important features of the Stalinist model of political and economic organization. China has moved sharply away from it as well under Deng Xiaoping. The Soviet Union and Vietnam have only begun such changes. How far they will go remains to be seen, but this will depend on the interplay of political forces within each country.

In Eastern Europe the pattern has been different. Rather than peaceful evolution, the region has seen explosions of economic and political discontent that have been repressed by the Soviet Union or its proxies in 1953, 1956, 1968, and 1981. The ultimate check on political change is external; internal forces cannot fully work themselves out. These explosions, in turn, affect the second, more important set of considerations around which U.S. foreign policy revolves. What makes these regimes illegitimate and unstable also constitutes a threat to U.S. security.

The central purpose of the foreign policy of the United States for four decades has been to contain the power and influence of the Soviet Union. The heart of the confrontation between the two great nuclear powers is Europe. The policy of containment was first devised to prevent the Soviet Union from extending its domination to the western part of the continent. Forty years later, Europe remains the glittering prize in the great global rivalry. It is economically the most valuable, culturally the richest, and strategically the most important contested piece of territory on the planet. In recognition of its status, Europe plays host to the world's heaviest concentration of military forces.

Issues other than the political control of Europe have preoccupied the United States and the Soviet Union since the early 1960s. Although such issues may have been more contentious, they have not been more important than the European question. The military competition, the subject of protracted negotiations, is an outgrowth of the political rivalry. The two sides are armed, as the saying goes, because they are rivals, rather than the other way around.

Although the Third World has been less stable and more susceptible to coups, revolutions, and wars of various kinds, including proxy wars between the United States and the Soviet Union, the stakes for both sides are much more modest there than they are in Europe. Both world wars began as political disputes in Eastern Europe; if there were to be a third such conflict, it, too, would be over Europe. The United States and the Soviet Union will not go to war with each other over Angola or Afghanistan. They will fight over Germany.

If Europe is central to Soviet-U.S. relations, the status of Eastern Europe is the heart of the conflict between them there. The U.S. mission on the continent is to protect Western Europe. The United States and Western Europe have regarded the Soviet Union as a threat because it has subdued, occupied, and dominated Eastern Europe. The forcible imposition of Marxist-Leninist rule in Eastern Europe led to the formation of the North Atlantic Treaty Organization (NATO) in 1949. Eastern Europe is a potential staging area for a Soviet drive westward. More importantly, Eastern Europe embodies what the United States is dedicated to preventing in Western Europe. The fears that the Soviets will behave in aggressive fashion toward Germany and France arise in no small part from the fact that Moscow has already committed a kind of aggression against Poland and Hungary. They stand as concrete examples of what the Soviet Union would do to Western Europe in the absence of countervailing power. The periodic political explosions in Eastern Europe reinforce the sense of threat because they have the potential to ignite a wider conflict between the two large military blocs and because, even short of that, they illustrate in dramatic fashion the determination of Moscow to control its neighbors.

Eastern Europe, to summarize, is important for the United States because Soviet domination there is the basis of the U.S. commitment to Western Europe, which is the heart of U.S. foreign policy. The cold war began because of Soviet action in Poland, Hungary, Czechoslovakia, and Germany. It cannot end until this is undone.

U.S. Goals

The initial postwar U.S. aim in Eastern Europe was liberation. The logic was plain. Freeing Eastern Europe from Soviet control would give the people of the region what they wanted—national independence—and would reduce the Soviet threat to Western Europe. The crushing of the 1956 Hungarian Revolution by the USSR put an end to any serious expectation that Eastern Europe could be liberated. No U.S. government since then has accepted Soviet domination of Eastern Europe as legitimate. This was hardly possible because whatever Washington's wishes, the people of the region have never been resigned to eternal subjugation to Moscow. From the Hungarian episode, however, the United States drew three conclusions, on which policy toward Eastern Europe has since rested: (1) because the Soviet Union exercises military control there, only changes that Moscow is prepared to tolerate are feasible; (2) what Moscow is prepared to tolerate has changed and may be changing now, but it still falls considerably short of what the West and the people of Eastern Europe desire; and (3) it follows, therefore, that Western policy must aim at incremental rather than sweeping improvements in the region.

On the basis of these conclusions the United States has constructed an Eastern European policy of "differentiation." It treats different countries of the region differently, despite their common membership in the Soviet bloc, and rewards them to the extent that they deviate from Soviet orthodoxy either in foreign policy or in the way they govern themselves.

Romania has charted a modestly independent course from the Soviet Union in foreign policy and has been rewarded by U.S. trade preferences and high-level political attention. Bucharest condemned the 1968 Warsaw Pact invasion of Czechoslovakia, and Nicolae Ceauşescu, Romania's leader since 1965, served as an intermediary in the rapprochements between the United States and the People's Republic of China and between Israel and Egypt. The act of independence most visible in the West was Romania's refusal to join the Soviet bloc's boycott of the 1984 Olympic games in Los Angeles. Nevertheless, on the whole, Romania's independence in foreign policy has brought disappointing results. It has gone hand in hand with increasingly harsh rule within the country. So far had conditions deteriorated within Romania that the U.S. Congress opposed the continued extension of most favored nation trading status to Bucharest, and finally Ceauşescu withdrew his request for it. By the end of the 1980s, Romania had come to contest Albania's distinction as the most repressive country in Europe.

The regime's fidelity to Communist orthodoxy at home was one reason that Moscow was willing to tolerate a measure of independence in its foreign policy. Nor was Romania's example of independence followed in any significant way by the other satellite regimes, even though other members of the Warsaw Pact did occasionally distance themselves from the Soviet Union in cautious ways on particular issues, especially on economic matters. For instance, in the early 1980s, the government of the German Democratic Republic was unhappy with the Soviet deployment of SS-20 missiles, which prompted the Western democracies to deploy comparable weapons in Western Europe. This in turn may have contributed to the change in Soviet policy on this issue that Mikhail Gorbachev introduced.

But the results of Eastern European independence in foreign policy have at best been modest. They have had little impact on the basic East-West conflict. There was no evidence that Romanian policy had a major effect on Soviet behavior. Bucharest's apostasy may have annoyed the Soviet Union and pleased the United States, but its actual importance was confined to Romania, and in the greater scheme of things—even in Eastern Europe—Romania is not an important country.

If all the countries of Eastern Europe were to pursue foreign policies independent of the Soviet Union, this would have important and, for the West, favorable consequences. Taken to its logical conclusion everywhere in Eastern Europe, independence would mean the dissolution of the Warsaw Pact. The abolition of the basic military arrangements in Eastern Europe, however, is unlikely in the near term. In fact, of all the institutions and practices that the Soviet Union has imposed on the region since 1945, the Warsaw Pact will probably be the last to disappear. This is not because of its military value. In the nuclear age a third German drive to the east would be suicidal. The Germans certainly know this, and the Soviets seem to be ready to acknowledge it. Nor is the Soviet Union likely to mount a direct military assault on Western Europe. NATO, too, has nuclear weapons, and responsible officials in Moscow certainly understand the implications.

Moscow may be willing to remove some of its forces from Eastern Europe, including East Germany, as a gesture of political accommodation toward the West. Large detachments will remain, however, because they are necessary to perpetuate the division of Germany, and for the Soviet Union a divided Germany and the control of one of its parts are high priorities. The USSR has powerful historical memories of a united Germany and is unlikely to permit the restoration of one of the political conditions in which the two great wars of the twentieth century began.

Nuclear weapons afford Moscow something close to absolute protection against a replay of 1914 and 1941; indeed, its occupation of part of Germany actually subverts the security of the Soviet Union because it causes instability and animosity on the part of Germans that would not otherwise exist. Even if the leadership in Moscow comes to recognize this, however, it is not likely to take all of its divisions out of East Germany. If it did, the East Germans ultimately would merge in some fashion with the Federal Republic to form what would be in economic, cultural, and political terms the most powerful state in Europe. This is a prospect that no Soviet leader will regard with equanimity; nor, it must be said, would the leaders of Western Europe be particularly enthusiastic about it.

Finlandization is the term sometimes used to describe the status for Eastern Europe for which it is feasible to aim. Finland is a neighbor of the Soviet Union, a former imperial possession and adversary in war, that is independent, democratic, and capitalist while maintaining good relations with Moscow and following formally a neutral foreign policy. Although a desirable status for Eastern Europe, it is not, in the short term, a feasible one because Germany cannot be Finland. It is too large, too powerful a presence in Europe to float harmlessly between East and West. Finland, Austria, Switzerland, and Sweden are neutral but also of modest weight politically. Germany cannot be the second and so will not be the first. What, then, is the appropriate goal for Western policy?

It is to promote, in Soviet policy toward Eastern Europe, the separation of ideological conformity from military security. The Western aim in the short term ought to be to help create circumstances in which, while the formal structure of the Warsaw Pact may remain intact,[3] the nations of the Eastern bloc will be increasingly able to order their internal affairs as they choose.[4] (International orthodoxy combined with domestic autonomy is the formula that the realities of the nuclear age and of European politics make the best achievable one for Eastern Europe in the foreseeable future.) The foundation of independence in their own affairs for the countries of Eastern Europe would be the establishment of democratic political systems. Insofar as the wishes of the people of the region can be determined, this is what they want.[5] Freely contested elections among legally constituted political parties would guarantee the kind of open society that flourishes in the West and to which the people of Eastern Europe aspire. A democratic political system provides the basis for a capitalist economic order and for personal liberty. Unfortunately, political democracy, like international independence, is unlikely in the foreseeable future in Eastern Europe. If the Warsaw Pact will be the last vestige of Soviet domination of Eastern Europe to disappear, the single-party regimes that Moscow has forced upon these countries will be the next-to-last.

The regimes were initially established to ensure Soviet control; they are increasingly unsuited to that purpose. They were also supposed to be showcases for Soviet-style socialism, glowing advertisements for the virtues of the Soviet system. They have become, instead, telling examples of the failures of Marxism-Leninism in practice. They retain, however, a significance for the Soviet Union itself.

The claim to rule of Soviet party leaders rests on the ideology of which they are the bearers and interpreters. The power of Marxism-Leninism, in turn, depends in part on its universal character. Eastern Europe is by far the most important concrete piece of evidence of its universal validity. The Communist regimes there give the rulers in Moscow some basis for saying, and perhaps for believing, that the creed on which they depend for their legitimacy is something more than a parochial Russian creation. Without Eastern Europe, Marxism-Leninism would stand exposed (or more clearly exposed) as a cover for old-fashioned autocracy within the empire and for imperial ambition abroad, a set of political dogmas empty of meaning for all except those whose power it justifies.

The regimes of Eastern Europe are not, to be sure, models of Leninist propriety. In Poland, the Communist party scarcely functions; the military dominates the upper echelons of the regime. Romania is an unsavory combination of brutality, corruption, and nepotism, an example of socialism in one family. Nonetheless, each government keeps up the pretense of orthodoxy. Ceauşescu and Jaruzelski, whatever else they are, are each the leader of his country's party. Neither political system could be mistaken for a Western one. For the Soviet leaders to allow the development of parliamentary institutions where once communism had governed would weaken the basis of their own power.

Complete independence and genuine democracy are unlikely in Eastern Europe in the foreseeable future because the Soviet Union will not permit them. What ought to be, and indeed to a large extent is the aim of U.S. and Western policy to foster, therefore, is social and economic pluralism.[6] Pluralism of this sort includes private ownership of property and commercial and productive assets; a wider role for money; independent associations of all kinds ranging from economic guilds to clubs of stamp collectors; institutions that do not depend on the government, notably religious ones; and the free circulation of ideas and information—none of which is officially permitted, although all exist to some degree, throughout Eastern Europe. All this is possible even where governments are not democratically constituted, such as in Mexico, Jordan, and Taiwan. Social pluralism and economic pluralism distinguish totalitarian from authoritarian regimes.

Social pluralism and economic pluralism are also forms of liberty. They provide pockets of independence within which people can, in the words of the Polish philosopher and Solidarity activist Adam Michnik, "live freely in a country that is not itself free." They are also preconditions for formal political liberty. They redistribute power from the government to the society. Social pluralism creates independent bases for political activity; economic pluralism gives citizens leverage over their rulers. The promotion of social and economic diversity in Eastern Europe and the creation of centers of activity independent of the Communist regimes may therefore be understood as ways of building pressure for the kind of political system that the people of Eastern Europe want. This diversity would, if it could take root throughout the region, ease dramatically the conflict at the heart of U.S. foreign policy.

U.S. policy has, in fact, promoted social and economic pluralism. The policy of differentiation has rewarded those countries in Eastern Europe that have diverged from the Soviet path in domestic as well as in foreign policy. As Romania has been the exemplar of the second, Hungary, with its economic reforms and relatively tolerant society, has been the prototype of the first. In promoting economic and social pluralism in Eastern Europe, the United States is aligning itself with trends that are already well under way. Throughout the region, the grip of the regimes on the societies has steadily weakened. It is weakest in Yugoslavia, where the various regions have considerable independence from the center, and in Poland, where the Catholic church functions as an alternative center of authority and the proliferation of underground publications gives the country a virtually free press. Elsewhere the regimes are less powerful, in part because they are less legitimate, than in the Soviet Union. The tradition of social and political activity independent of the state, of what students of political philosophy call "civil society," is stronger in Eastern Europe than in the Soviet Union.

The pace at which civil society has asserted itself has varied from country to country in the region and within each country over time. Now, developments in Eastern Europe and in the Soviet Union offer an opportunity for the West to help accelerate the process. Those developments have their roots in the failure of the Communist regimes to make themselves acceptable to those they govern.

The Problem of Stability

The Communist regimes of Eastern Europe have tried for four decades to overcome the circumstances of their births. They have sought political legitimacy but have never achieved it. They have continued to be regarded as creations and puppets of a foreign power, unlike the Soviet, Chinese, Cuban, and Vietnamese regimes. Since 1945, the people of Eastern Europe have come to identify more, not less, strongly with the West, a point that the periodic uprisings against Soviet domination have vividly demonstrated.

The most recent of these episodes, the Polish mass movement centered on the free-trade union Solidarity, underscored the failure of communism in Eastern Europe. Solidarity was made up of Poles in their twenties, thirties, and forties, people who had grown up under communism, who had never known any other system at firsthand, and who had been immersed in the party's propaganda all their lives. Solidarity was, moreover, a workers' movement that opposed the party that claimed to represent the interests of the working class. If the "revolution" that brought the Communists to power in Poland was made for anybody's benefit it was for Lech Wałęsa, the son of a peasant who became an electrician at the Lenin shipyard in the Baltic city of Gdańsk. In response to the gift that Stalin bestowed on them, however, Wałęsa and millions like him have not been grateful, loyal, or docile.

Because the Eastern European regimes could not win the active enthusiasm of the people, they settled for keeping control of them. Denied legitimacy, these regimes were forced to aim for something less—political stability. The chief instrument for promoting stability was, of course, armed force, ultimately the army of the Soviet Union. Still it was Napoleon Bonaparte who, commenting on the difficulty of holding power by force alone, remarked that a man may make a throne of bayonets, but he cannot sit on it. Metaphorically, the Communist governments of Eastern Europe sit, uncomfortably, on thrones of bayonets.

Each has tried to cushion its perch. Some have attempted from time to time to identify themselves with nationalist feeling by deviating from Soviet policy in one way or another (Romania is the outstanding example), but the room for maneuver is limited, and even Ceauşescu seems to have squandered whatever credit he accumulated at home by his repressive methods of governance and disastrous record of economic management.

Beyond the threat—and the use of—force, therefore, the Eastern European governments have relied on economic performance to promote political stability. Besides perpetuating themselves in power, the regimes have sought to raise the standards of living in their countries. Providing more food, better housing, and a modest assortment of consumer goods has been the only achievement to which the regimes could aspire that the people of the region would regard favorably.

In the Soviet Union in the years after Stalin's death, a kind of informal "social contract" was established between the rulers and the people: political passivity in exchange for steadily improving material circumstances. A similar arrangement came into being in Eastern Europe, but because the governments there enjoyed far less legitimacy than in the Soviet Union and because they tended to measure their own circumstances against conditions in the West, the Eastern European social contracts have been much more fragile. Unlike the Soviet Union, Eastern Europe has been the scene of political uprisings since 1945, and in almost every case they have begun as public protests against economic conditions.

Despite the periodic revolts, for much of the postwar period the economic performance of these regimes was in some ways respectable. Standards of living rose steadily across Eastern Europe. But the region's economies drew on sources of economic growth that were ultimately exhausted and could not be replenished.[7]

In the 1950s, these regimes exploited labor reserves. Throughout Eastern Europe people moved from farms into the factories of the city, where they worked much more productively. In the 1960s, their links with the Soviet Union enhanced the performances of their economies. In the 1970s, the governments of the region received economic infusions from the West through trade and credits—mainly in the form of commercial loans—and also, in the special case of the German Democratic Republic (GDR), through grants and access to Western markets provided by the Federal Republic. In the 1980s, however, there was no longer a labor surplus, the connections with the Soviet Union were economically disadvantageous, and further loans were unavailable because Hungary, Romania, and especially Poland had had great difficulty in repaying the money already borrowed. Poland all but defaulted on its foreign debts.

At the end of the 1980s, therefore, none of the Eastern European economies, with the partial and perhaps temporary exception of the GDR, was performing well. Some were doing better than others, but in all the countries of the region growth was slow, static, or, as in the cases of Poland and Romania, worse. None was able to compete with the West in the production of high-technology goods. In several, food shortages and power outages were common. With the level of economic performance low, the potential for political explosions was correspondingly high and signs of discontent multiplied. There were strikes in Romania, Hungary, and Poland and political protests in East Germany. Political unrest was likely to persist, and to grow, unless and until the regimes could find a way to restart the process of economic growth.[8]

With the available external sources of growth exhausted, the only way for these regimes to right their economies was to change their basic economic institutions and practices. The countries of Eastern Europe suffered from the same fundamental problem as the Soviet Union. The economic system imposed on them by Joseph Stalin, with its central direction and use of administrative commands rather than market signals, had become obsolete. To avoid chronic economic stagnation, to keep from falling farther and farther behind the West and the dynamic economies of East Asia and Latin America, Eastern Europe requires substantial economic reforms of a liberal character.

Eastern Europe needs to make far more extensive use of the market mechanism in order to apportion resources more productively. There is far too much emphasis, for example, on heavy industry. For the same reason, Eastern Europe needs to introduce real, market-determined prices. This would have broad effects, such as reducing the wasting of energy. There is a need to encourage individual initiative and entrepreneurship, for which there is little room in the Stalinist economic order, perhaps by broadening the private sector in services and construction and then fostering the spread of individual ownership and private management to other economic areas.

There is a need to promote efficiency by permitting economic competition. Competition comes from abroad as well as from competing firms at home. Eastern Europe is already more extensively connected to the world economy than is the Soviet Union, but the countries of the region need to open themselves even more.

Even if they could introduce the changes necessary to make their economies more Western and therefore more efficient and creative, East Europeans, in order to lift themselves out of the economic rut into which they have fallen, would still require Western technology, Western capital to purchase it, and access to Western markets to sell what they made as a result. The need for such reforms is widely understood in the region.

The West therefore is in a more powerful, or at least influential, position in dealing with the regimes of Eastern Europe than ever before. They depend on economic well-being to purchase political tranquility. Economic performance requires both internal changes that the West favors and direct Western participation. The United States can make the first a condition of the second.

The economic reforms that Eastern Europe requires would have political consequences. They would move the countries of the region further along the path of social and economic pluralism. Where market forces are more important, economic bureaucrats and party officials have less power. As the private sector expands, the social space beyond the direct control of the state broadens. To the extent that a Communist country multiplies its ties with the rest of the world, it widens the channels through which it receives ideas and information from abroad. The necessary conditions of economic effectiveness are also the elements of political change that U.S. and Western policymakers should promote in Eastern Europe.

It has, however, been the Soviet aim for forty years to thwart such changes. Now, as forty years ago, the Soviet Union has the power to stop them. Why should Moscow be willing to permit them? In his statements on Eastern Europe, Mikhail Gorbachev has sounded better disposed to economic reform and social change than his predecessors were. There are reasons to believe, moreover, that he means what he says. He and his associates have embarked on an ambitious campaign of reform in the Soviet Union. His program of *perestroika* (restructuring), he has made clear, takes precedence over everything else. A political explosion in Eastern Europe, especially if it provoked Soviet or Soviet-inspired intervention along the lines of 1968 and 1981, would interfere with and perhaps even derail Gorbachev's reforms. Twenty years ago the invasion of Czechoslovakia squelched the economic changes that Prime Minister Alexei Kosygin had proposed in the Soviet Union. Political upheaval in the region, insofar as it appeared to be inspired by Gorbachev's more permissive policies, could even threaten his own position. Gorbachev and his colleagues might therefore be willing to pay a considerable price in deviation from Communist orthodoxy to avoid such upheavals.

In fact, since Stalin's death Moscow has tolerated increasing deviation, although unevenly and always reluctantly. Almost from the beginning of Communist rule in Eastern Europe, the Soviet Union and its client regimes have confronted a trade-off between orthodoxy and stability. The price that they have paid to purchase stability, measured in departures from the orthodoxy that Stalin established, has risen over time. The pattern may not be pleasing to Moscow, but it is certainly familiar.

Moreover, Gorbachev is encouraging change in his own country. He, too, is talking of introducing market procedures, of price reform, and of permitting a private sector in the Soviet economy. It will therefore be easier for him to regard with equanimity, or at least more difficult for him to try to stifle, similar changes in fraternal socialist countries.

Economic Conditions

An effective U.S. policy toward Eastern Europe must begin with an understanding of U.S. aims there. Although the most promising policy instruments are economic ones, those aims remain political.[9] The U.S. economic stake in the region is small. The Western European interest is larger, but even West Germany conducts only a fraction of its foreign trade with the Communist countries to the east.[10]

The United States ought to use the economic leverage that the confluence of circumstances in the region provides to promote economic changes that will have significant social and political consequences. These are changes that will make the countries of Eastern Europe more Western and less Communist. Such changes would be small but tangible steps toward the transformation of the political arrangements in Eastern Europe, which in turn are ultimately the basis for the U.S. military presence on the continent, are the likeliest cause of World War III, and stand as the greatest obstacle to a genuine rapprochement between East and West.

It may be objected that by contributing to improvements in the performance of the economies of the region such an approach risks making it easier for the regimes to control the societies and that it is therefore a form of complicity in the Soviet oppression of Eastern Europe. One by-product of such an approach might well be a more stable Eastern Europe, if stability is defined as the absence of dramatic political upheaval. That is the reason, after all, that it may be attractive to the ruling Communist parties and to Moscow.

Stability per se is not a U.S. interest. Indeed, the United States has an interest in a certain amount of instability insofar as this brings with it greater liberty. In Eastern Europe the one has historically followed the other in some places. Hungary and Poland are freer than their neighbors because they have been prepared to resist Moscow. By their exertions they have compelled the Soviet Union to permit economic and political latitude that it would not voluntarily have surrendered. The approach proposed here builds on that historical experience. It proposes to use the threat of instability to win further liberty. This is a way of using the certainty that turmoil will occur without change to achieve such change. The ultimate goal is not a more stable or even humane communism but steady progress toward Western political and economic forms.

Thus, Western economic participation in Eastern Europe should take place only with strings firmly attached. The regimes should be required to implement liberal economic reforms as the condition of loans, grants, joint ventures, and privileged access to Western markets. There is an economic rationale for such conditions. Without them the economies of the region will not improve. That was the clear lesson of the 1970s. The ultimate purpose, however, is political. Along with these economic requirements ought to go more strictly political conditions of certain kinds, such as the release of all political prisoners and the loosening of restrictions on travel and information.

There are precedents for these more political conditions. The freeing of all those detained for political offenses was the price that the Warsaw government paid for the resumption of diplomatic relations with the United States in 1987. Poles and Hungarians are more or less free to go wherever they wish, and more East Germans have been able to visit the Federal Republic in the last several years. The Poles have a virtually free unofficial press, censorship is much more modest in Hungary than in the Soviet Union, and almost all East Germans can receive television broadcasts from the Federal Republic. Thus, these conditions involve affirming and extending what already exists in much of Eastern Europe.

There also are precedents for the economic conditions that ought to accompany Western economic assistance to Eastern Europe. Developing countries with large external debts, such as Mexico, Argentina, and Brazil, have received loans from the International Monetary Fund (IMF) on condition that they make economic changes of a liberal character. Indeed, Poland, Yugoslavia, and Hungary have dealt with the IMF on these terms. They, like the Latin American countries, went deeply into debt in the 1970s when Western commercial banks sought to recycle the huge inflow of dollars they were receiving from the oil-producing states. Like the Latin American debtors, they used the money unwisely and, with the recession of the early 1980s, were unable to keep up their payments. The international financial community proceeded to restructure these debts, using the IMF as an umbrella organization.

The conditions imposed by the IMF are not an altogether happy precedent. They have had the effect of lowering living standards. In general, creditors have demanded that the debtor countries reduce consumption to make resources available for repayment. A common feature of an IMF package of loans and conditions is the removal of subsidies on food. Throughout the world, and especially in the Communist bloc, food subsidies may be economically wasteful, but they buy social peace.[11] The Eastern European regimes therefore have reason to be wary of reforms that will impose short-term hardships on their populations.

On the other hand, hardship is already the lot of the people of the region. Sweeping reform offers the only hope for improvement in the long term; in the short term there is no alternative to hardship. The association of the West with liberalizing reforms, even though their immediate effect is to make life harder, might make them more palatable in Eastern Europe. General Jaruzelski of Poland has proposed economic changes but cannot secure the cooperation of the Polish population in putting them into practice because his regime is so deeply distrusted. His program might achieve popular credibility if the West were to take an active part in it.

There is another, more distant precedent for a Western program of conditional economic assistance to Eastern Europe. In 1947, the United States launched the European Recovery Program, better known as the Marshall Plan, to revive the economies of Europe after the devastation of World War II. Washington offered to include Eastern as well as Western Europe in the plan. The Eastern European regimes, for all their Communist loyalties, were tempted; but Stalin rejected Marshall aid for them. U.S. economic assistance was desperately needed, but Stalin feared—no doubt rightly—that it would open the way to Western influence and then to Western practices and institutions.

Four decades later, it is politically sensible for the West to table an offer with some of the same features as the Marshall Plan. This time the man who occupies Stalin's position, Mikhail Gorbachev, because he is both more confident that the Soviet Union can retain control in the region and less confident that the people of Eastern Europe will ever embrace socialism, may be prepared to approve it.[12]

If the West should propose a program of conditional economic participation in Eastern Europe, there is no guarantee that the Soviet Union would permit it to go forward. Gorbachev seems more liberal than his predecessors, but the limits of his permissiveness are yet to be established and may be too narrow to be compatible with reforms that are desirable from the Western point of view. Hungary has gone farther than any other Eastern European country in diluting central control of its economy, perhaps farther than Gorbachev would like to see others go. Yet the Hungarian economy plainly requires more dramatic changes still in order to avoid stagnation.[13]

Even if Gorbachev is agreeable, the local leaders may balk at the changes that Western economic assistance would require. The Czech, Romanian, and East German parties have been distinctly cool to Gorbachev's reforms. They have signaled in various ways that they do not regard *perestroika* as necessary or even advisable in their own countries. The advent of Gorbachev has created a situation unusual in the postwar history of Eastern Europe, in which the leadership of the imperial metropolis is more liberal than the ruling parties in the satellite countries.[14] Even if Moscow decrees reform, the local rulers can delay, question, implement in halfhearted fashion, and generally obstruct it.

It may, finally, be too late for such reforms. Eastern Europe may be doomed to further political explosions whatever the West offers to do. The strikes in Poland in late April and August 1988 may be harbingers of a larger uprising there and perhaps elsewhere in the region. The Western economic role that is plausible and the changes in Eastern Europe that are politically feasible and upon which the future performance of the economies most heavily depend may turn out to be far too modest to reverse the deterioration of the Eastern European economies.

Officials and members of the intelligentsia in the Soviet Union and Eastern Europe have been heard to say that Gorbachev represents "the last chance for socialism." History may demonstrate, however, that the kind of political and economic order to which Gorbachev and the Communist leaders of Eastern Europe are committed, no matter how broadly interpreted and extensively modified, is simply incompatible with social tranquility and economic prosperity in the twenty-first century. The last chance for Soviet-style socialism may already have passed.

All these considerations are beyond the power of the United States and the other industrial democracies to influence. But in contemplating a program of conditional economic assistance to Eastern Europe there is one thing that the West can and must do. It must coordinate national policies more closely than has been the practice in the past. Coordination is especially important between the United States and the Federal Republic of Germany.

Western Cooperation

The United States remains significant for Eastern Europe. As the leader of the Western military coalition, it has an important say in the security arrangements in Europe. Moreover, it looms large in the hearts and minds of the people of the region. Partly because it is the military bulwark of the

West, but also because of its history and its powerful liberal ideology, the United States stands as the symbol of liberty for people who are deprived of it. It is also the symbol in Eastern Europe, as in much of the rest of the world (including the Soviet Union), of modernity—the birthplace of technical advances, the originator of the consumer society, the cradle of popular culture. For many in Eastern Europe, the United States is also a branch of their own countries because it has been the destination of so many emigrants from that part of the world.

The role of the United States in the world and in Europe has, however, changed since the days of the Marshall Plan. Then, only the United States had the resources to promote economic recovery. Now, the Western Europeans have recovered and prospered. In fact, by one important measure the United States has come, in the last decade, to be the least wealthy of them. A lopsided imbalance between expenditures and revenues in the 1980s has made it the world's largest debtor.

The United States cannot hope to sustain a Western initiative toward Eastern Europe by itself. Such an effort must be a multilateral undertaking. Because of its own political prominence and economic success and because Washington is hardly in a position to provide large-scale loans and grants to any other country, the natural, indeed the indispensable, partner is the Federal Republic of Germany.

Germany has a long and, to say the least, checkered history in Eastern Europe. For centuries German culture was the most influential in the region. In the last decades of the nineteenth century and the first part of the twentieth, German capital brought the industrial age to this part of Europe. It is not an overstatement to say that Germany, or rather Germans, were the bearers of modernity to what is now called Eastern Europe, including the Balkans, and to define Eastern Europe as historically a sphere of German cultural and economic influence. The large German communities scattered throughout the region, and in the USSR as well, were themselves agents of cultural change and economic advance.

The efforts of the German state that Otto von Bismarck created to assert political control to the east and southeast in 1914 and again in 1939 brought disaster. It was the second German bid for an empire to the east that opened the way for Soviet domination of Eastern Europe.[15]

At the end of the war, Germany was defeated, occupied, divided, and deprived of its former influence. The redrawn map of Europe pushed its eastern border well to the west of where it had been in 1939, giving to Poland and the Soviet Union one-quarter of the territory that had been Germany in 1937. The overwhelming majority of the Germans living east of that border, almost all of whose families had been there for centuries, were evicted.

Slowly but steadily throughout the postwar period, and at an increasing pace since the inauguration of the policy of *Ostpolitik* in the late 1960s, West Germany has reasserted itself in Eastern Europe. Although its political role has remained a small one, its economic presence has expanded. That presence has become increasingly acceptable, indeed welcome in the region. The memories of the German occupation in World War II are bitter, but they are fading. Each year fewer Poles and Czechs remain who lived through the nightmare of those years. All Eastern Europeans, by contrast, have extensive personal experience of Soviet domination. The West Germany of today is attractive by comparison. Indeed, the West Germany of today is not, in the eyes of most Eastern Europeans, the political descendant of the Nazi regime. Rather, it is the easternmost outpost of the West, the political community with which they identify. Stalin and Brezhnev, Konrad Adenauer and Willy Brandt have, along with the passage of time, transformed Eastern European attitudes toward Germany.

West German policy in Eastern Europe centers on East Germany. This is hardly surprising. Germany is a divided country; relations with the GDR are, for the Federal Republic, an internal not an international matter. The Federal Republic has set itself the task of overcoming this division. Its strategy for doing so changed sharply in the early 1970s. Until the late 1960s, Bonn tried to isolate the GDR, insisting that the regime in Berlin was an illegal one and that the only suitable goal for German policy was reunification.

Brandt's policy of *Ostpolitik* proceeded from the realization that reunification was impractical in the foreseeable future and sought, therefore, to preserve the substance of the German nation within two German states by trying to foster the "reassociation" of the two societies. This involved multiplying contacts between the two Germanys, a prerequisite for which was better political relations between Bonn and East Berlin. The Federal Republic has followed this policy since the 1970s.

Within this political framework economic ties have expanded. West Germany has increasingly provided East Germany with credits, markets, and access to the rest of Western Europe. By virtue of its special economic relationship with the Federal Republic, the GDR is in some ways effectively a member of the European Economic Community. West German television reaches virtually all of East Germany. Germans move back and forth across the inner-German border in ever-greater numbers. The Federal Republic's policy of trying to subvert rather than assault the division of its country can therefore claim a record of partial success. But that policy has sometimes put Bonn at odds with Washington, where policy toward Eastern Europe takes a different shape. The differences between the two approaches will have to be overcome in order to forge an effective Western policy toward the region.

Whereas German policy toward Eastern Europe has a national emphasis, the United States customarily adopts a regional perspective. The Federal Republic's dealings with Warsaw Pact countries other than the GDR are geared to the German issue. In 1987, Bonn guaranteed a DM 1 billion (about $550 million) loan to Hungary partly in appreciation of the benign conditions in which its ethnic German minority lives. Relations with Warsaw have been troubled by a dispute about how Germans in Poland are treated or indeed whether any remain there.

For Germans to care more about Germans than about Poles or Czechs is emphatically not a reprise of the terrible events of the 1930s and 1940s. It is not abnormal. To the contrary, any freely elected government will be subject to pressure to attend to the interests of its own people, even if they happen not to be living within its borders. The government of the United States is not notable for showing greater concern for foreigners than for Americans. The difference in perspective does, however, have several consequences for policy.

West Germany seeks to pursue an undifferentiated policy toward Eastern Europe or at least to differentiate among the countries there according to how they treat Germans, not by how liberal or independent they are. Bonn reckons that intra-German relations can only be as good as relations between and among the countries that surround and control the two Germanys. U.S. policy proceeds from a different premise. It seeks to reward some countries and punish others—or at least deprive them of such rewards as are available—according to their international independence and internal liberalism.

This difference is closely related to another one. The Federal Republic is strongly disposed to good relations with Eastern Europe and especially with the Soviet Union. Bonn is committed to good relations across the board on the grounds that political tension elsewhere can interfere with good relations between the two Germanys. The process of reassociation can be cut off by Moscow. Thus, the Soviet Union holds West German *Ostpolitik* hostage to good German behavior, or so West Germany believes. Successful *Deutschlandpolitik,* the Federal Republic's formula goes, depends on regional détente; and regional détente requires global détente.[16]

The Federal Republic has given higher priority than the United States to good relations with the Soviet Union for the sake of its German policy. This is an approach for which there is a strong consensus across the political spectrum in Germany. But it can make for conflict with Washington. In the early 1980s, Bonn (along with the other Western Europeans) was reluctant to punish the Soviet Union for its invasion of Afghanistan or for the crackdown on Solidarity in Poland. This reluctance created friction with the United States, which championed punitive measures in both cases. In dealing with the Communist world West Germany believes in carrots while the United States often favors sticks.[17]

Thus, West Germany is likely to be less enthusiastic than the United States about attaching conditions to economic assistance to Eastern Europe. The record of West Germany's economic involvement with the region shows no inclination to do so. Bonn has received some concessions for aid to the GDR, notably in permitting travel between the two Germanys, but it has not sought to induce liberal economic reforms. East Germany is not a particularly liberal regime in economic or political terms, even by Eastern European standards. The differing interests and correspondingly divergent assessments of how best to serve them has led to an emphasis on different goals in Eastern Europe. U.S. policy has stressed liberty; West Germany has imputed greater importance to stability.

This is in a sense unfair to the West Germans. They are not indifferent to the claims of liberty. They certainly do not endorse Soviet domination of Eastern Europe. The ultimate aim of their policy of reassociation is the promotion of national unity in cultural terms and greater liberty in East Germany. Still, Bonn's preoccupation with the German question and its conviction that only in conditions of political tranquility in Eastern Europe can it pursue its German policy successfully do lead Bonn to a strong preference for stability there. This preference found unfortunate expression in a remark by Helmut Schmidt during a visit with Erich Honecker. When asked to comment on the internal coup in Poland in December 1981, Schmidt said that he and Honecker regretted that the measure had been necessary.

To launch a successful Western initiative toward Eastern Europe will require a convergence of U.S. and German policies that will not be easy to achieve. It is for the United States to acknowledge that change in Eastern Europe will come gradually; that the kind of economic engagement that the Federal Republic has practiced for two decades can have salutary political effects over time; and that Western policy can most profitably seek to promote internal transformation rather than external independence in the region. It is incumbent on West Germany to recognize that the West does have some leverage on the Communist bloc, more now than ever before, and that it is therefore both appropriate and feasible to demand economic reforms in exchange for economic assistance. Indeed, it is arguable that even if the West Germans maintain what seems to the U.S. public an unseemly devotion to stability in the other Europe, they still ought to favor such changes because without them the economies of the region are doomed to stagnate and the societies are doomed to recurrent instability.

Soviet leaders suffer, now as in the past, from a certain amount of anxiety about their imperial possessions to the West. It ought to be the Western, including the West German, aim to exploit rather than simply to assuage that anxiety. A Western economic program for Eastern Europe would likely be primarily a West German–U.S. effort, although the participation of the other Western Europeans and perhaps also the Japanese and other East Asians would be desirable. Such a program might usefully proceed under the auspices of some international organization, preferably one whose concerns are economic. The Organization for Economic Cooperation and Development may *not* be a good candidate because it lacks operational capacity, but it is an example of the kind of body in which such an effort should be formally lodged in order to make it easier for the Eastern European regimes to accept. Western policy toward Eastern Europe is likely to achieve political results to the extent that it does not appear to be explicitly political.

Conclusion

The main theme of the postwar history of Eastern Europe is the struggle between the people of the region and the rulers of the Soviet Union. It is, in this sense, a rather old-fashioned imperial drama, a fight for national liberation of the sort that has become familiar in the modern age and especially in the twentieth century. Each of the two principal parties to the conflict has an ally. The people of Eastern Europe can count on unlimited sympathy and limited support from the West; the advance guard of the Soviet Union is made up of the Communist parties of Eastern Europe.

The struggle for Eastern Europe has been waged in two different arenas and is an uneven contest in each. It is a struggle for control of the machinery of the state. Because this ultimately belongs to the superior force, the Soviet Union enjoys a decisive advantage. It is also a contest of beliefs, of values, of loyalties, with its locus in the societies of Eastern Europe. Here the Soviet Union is overmatched. The effort to build Soviet-style socialism has failed. Popular allegiance to the values of the West is strong and growing stronger; Western social forms are becoming stronger despite the wishes of the regimes.

The two conflicts affect one another. In the short term those who hold formal power can impose the practices that they prefer and repress those that they dislike. In the long run, however, the society will assert itself independently of, indeed in opposition to, the wishes of the authorities. The predominant social forces in Eastern Europe will wear down the regimes, like the tide relentlessly eradicating a manmade structure jutting out into the sea. This historical process is well under way. It will proceed with or without the direct participation of the West; but the United States and the West now have an unusual opportunity to help it along, to the benefit of the people living not only in Eastern but in Western Europe and in North America.

Notes

1. Yugoslavia is certainly part of Eastern Europe but is not dominated by the Soviet Union, nor is Albania. Thus, much of the analysis of this chapter does not apply to these two countries. Some of it, however, is relevant. Yugoslavia is an important country for the United States precisely because it did break with Moscow after the war. Yugoslavia is experiencing serious economic and nationalities difficulties that threaten its stability and therefore has a claim on U.S. attention and resources. See Chapter 11.

2. In the interwar period, when the Eastern Europeans were independent of foreign control, none was a model democracy, as Vojtech Mastny's chapter in this volume notes. Nor, of course, is the hypothetical assertion that if they were free to determine their own destinies, they would adopt parliamentary political forms and liberal capitalist economic institutions subject to testing. Still, there is reason to think that this would occur, at least in Germany, Hungary, Poland, and Czechoslovakia, should the Soviet army miraculously disappear. These countries had some democratic experience before the war, imperfect although it was. All had liberal economies, with private ownership and market rules.

The circumstances that destroyed the fledgling democracies, moreover, are no longer present—or would not be if the Soviet threat vanished. In the 1920s and especially the 1930s, the countries of the region were under enormous pressure from aggressive powerful neighbors, which made it difficult for democratic systems to flourish. They were plagued by ethnic conflict; each country contained large minorities.

The largest of them, the Jews and the Germans, are now gone. Poland is for the first time entirely Catholic and Polish speaking. Other ethnic and border disputes remain, but none so acute as those of the interwar years; and the lessons of that period might be expected to encourage moderation.

During the last forty years, moreover, democratic systems have thrived in the Western part of Europe, serving as examples for the countries to the East. The systems that the Soviets imposed have served as the opposite kind of examples. In 1945, many in the region were well disposed to the Soviet Union and to its political and economic system. After four decades of communism, the system and its progenitor retain almost no sympathizers.

If Poland, Hungary, and Czechoslovakia were not stable democracies between the wars, neither were Germany and Italy. The Allied occupation had something to do with their postwar conversions to democratic forms, of course, but other Western European countries later moved in the same political direction without the same pressure. Spain, Portugal, and Greece were certainly no more Western than the countries of Eastern Europe in the 1930s; but for the presence of the Soviet Union, Poland, Czechoslovakia, and Hungary would not be less Western than the Southern European countries in the 1980s.

3. Although the West will probably have to accept the existence of the Warsaw Pact, this does not mean accepting its present troop levels and military doctrine. It is an appropriate and perhaps a feasible goal of arms negotiations to reduce the numbers of Soviet troops in Eastern Europe and to change the way they are deployed, equipped, and trained so that they are less capable of conducting offensive military operations.

4. Charles Gati has called this a "Greek solution," drawing a rough parallel with Greece's status, which combines membership in NATO with considerable latitude in domestic (as well as foreign) policies. ("Gorbachev and Eastern Europe," *Foreign Affairs* [Summer 1987]). Because NATO is a coalition of sovereign states and not an instrument of imperial control, *all* of its members have the internal latitude that it is the appropriate near-term aim of Western policy to promote in Eastern Europe. The members of NATO also have the freedom to pursue independent foreign policies, and on many issues they are publicly at odds with one another, something that is at present highly unusual for the Warsaw Pact.

5. The best evidence of the real political preferences of the people of Eastern Europe comes from the surveys taken by Radio Free Europe–Radio Liberty. See, for example, the *East European Area Audience and Opinion Research* reports of January 1982, January 1983, and December 1986.

6. This is not to say that the United States should oppose political pluralism in Eastern Europe or should refrain from expressing support for it in countries, such as Hungary, where it is widely discussed.

7. The following analysis draws heavily on Chapter 3 in this volume.

8. Yugoslavia was less tied to Stalinist economic methods but still in acute economic difficulties because its system of economic organization was still not Western enough and because of national conflicts, which were sharper there than anywhere else in Eastern Europe.

9. For a survey of the other tools available to promote U.S. and Western interests see Chapter 17.

10. The GDR is a special case for the Federal Republic, in economic and political terms.

11. The fundamental economic problem in Eastern Europe is not, of course, that food prices are too low but that the economies are so irrationally structured that

salaries are too low and agriculture is too unproductive to feed the population without subsidies.

12. In the last, tense days before the crackdown on Solidarity in Poland, and in retrospective analyses of that episode, it was suggested that an offer of large-scale Western economic aid to Poland in exchange for a pledge not to crush the free trade union might conceivably have been accepted by Moscow. No such offer was ever made, and there is of course no way of knowing what effect it would have had. For a discussion of this issue, see Lincoln Gordon, "Interests and Policies in Eastern Europe: The View from Washington," in Lincoln Gordon et al., *Eroding Empire: Western Relations with Eastern Europe* (Washington, D.C.: Brookings Institution, 1987), p. 119ff.

It is possible that a similar proposal in less pressured circumstances that does not require Soviet tolerance of an active, visible, powerful, quasiformal opposition movement and that would be considered by Mikhail Gorbachev would find favor in Moscow.

13. There is some evidence that Gorbachev wishes to follow a "centrist" policy in Eastern Europe, encouraging more liberal measures in the most conservatively governed countries, such as Czechoslovakia, while reining in the most liberal regimes, such as Hungary. If so, the result may be the worst of both worlds for Moscow, with the Czech regime failing to change enough to engage the energies of the Czech people while the Hungarian economy stagnates.

14. Young East Germans, staging a protest at the Brandenburg Gate in East Berlin, chanted Gorbachev's name. In Prague, the Soviet leader was received by a genuinely enthusiastic crowd, surely the first time something like this had ever happened in the history of the Soviet empire in Eastern Europe.

15. German complicity was not simply the indirect and unintended consequence of losing the war in the East. The first stage of Soviet imperial conquest came in 1939 and 1940 as the direct and explicit result of the Nazi-Soviet pact.

16. On German policy, see Josef Joffe, "The View from Bonn: The Tacit Alliance," in Gordon et al., *Eroding Empire*, pp. 182–187.

17. As Pierre Hassner has put it, the Germans believe in carrots, the Americans believe in sticks, and the French believe in words. Timothy Garton Ash has speculated that the origins of *Ostpolitik* have something to do with this feature of German diplomacy toward the East. It began in Berlin, where the Federal Republic is unusually weak because authority is still formally vested in the occupying powers. Ever since, West German governments have operated from a presumption of weakness that is at least arguably excessive.

17

U.S. and Western Policy—New Opportunities for Action

Mark Palmer

Western policy toward Eastern Europe should set aside philosophical debate about extremes. Direct Western military intervention is next to impossible, as is a massive uprising throughout this region that would "liberate it" from the Soviet Union. The Soviets under any leadership, including Mikhail Gorbachev, will intervene again with military force if necessary. But it is also true that the West will not accept that this part of the world is a permanent part of the Soviet empire, forever forced to live under one-party dictatorships; and Hungarians, Czechs, Poles, and others will not permit a "stable" Europe to be built at their expense—as the events of 1956, 1968, and 1980 demonstrated.

The objective of Western policy is clear: to enable these six nations (Bulgaria, Czechoslovakia, Hungary, Poland, GDR, and Romania) to recover their historical heritage and become an integrated part of Europe and the modern world. The central issue is Western skill, creativity, and level of effort in trying to achieve this goal. Between the extremes of passivity and force there is an extraordinary terrain, and in it the opportunities for Western engagement are growing at an unprecedented rate. The Communist party and body politic of virtually every Communist country in the world are beginning to recognize that in the twenty-first century how open, free, and information oriented a society is and how market oriented and high tech its economy will determine whether a nation stagnates or achieves an appropriate standard of living and national strength.

With the possible exception of Romania, the Eastern European members of the Warsaw Pact are increasingly conscious of the need for fundamental change and for growing ties with the West. These countries are acutely aware that nations with which they were more or less equal four decades

The views stated herein are exclusively those of the author and not official positions of the U.S. government.

ago, such as Austria and Finland, have opened gaps that now seem unbridgeable and nations once far behind, such as Korea, Singapore, and, more recently, the people of Taiwan, are passing them in terms of modernization. Increasingly the historical question asked in Eastern Europe is not when socialism will triumph, but whether the socialist countries will slide back into the standard of living of the Third World; whether, like Argentina, nations that were once considered developed will now be considered developing. This growing sense of near desperation opens a broad vista of opportunities for the West.

The key issue is whether the West has the will, energy, and financial resources to realize these opportunities. The current level of Western effort is far from meeting the challenge of Western strategic interests. The two world wars broke out in this region; it remains profoundly unstable and the most likely cause in Europe of World War III (although the possibility of any war in Europe is quite remote). The roots of one out of every eight Americans are in Eastern and Central Europe. Yet, no U.S. president has ever visited four of the six nations. The United States is not alone in devoting inadequate effort. Western Europe is and will remain not just closer, but of more economic and political importance. Yet only in the last few years has there been much in the way of high-level political dialogue. Perhaps the single most important and active Western country of all, the Federal Republic of Germany, has only a limited program of cultural activities and centers and is only just beginning a dialogue with the democratic forces (as opposed to the party leaders) in the East.

What is possible? Viewed from Hungary, practically the only constraints are Western imagination and resources. But some will respond that Hungary is not a valid example, that the possibilities for the West in Czechoslovakia and Romania, for example, are far more constrained. This is partially true, but even today there are opportunities the West is not realizing because of lack of effort. If one looks at the next fifteen to twenty-five years—and it is only within this context that a sensible policy can be pursued—then in these countries as well there is reason to believe that major Western involvement is possible. It was just fifteen years ago when Hungary was at or near the bottom of the list of countries with which the United States could conduct a set of programs. Rapidly expanding opportunities are already evident in much of the region.

If we take a view and a context that encompass the next fifteen to twenty-five years, the types of policy the West initiates and pursues should build institutions, programs, and extensive connections of such deepening mutual interest that they will not be shaken by the inevitable setbacks in individual countries or in the overall East-West climate. The West should be designing a comprehensive network of relationships that makes the borders irrelevant. The West should also be striving for détente in the East, a change in the security equation, and a massive increase in the Western physical and spiritual presence. The concern of the Eastern European governments should be with the welfare of their peoples, not with control or the preservation of a military psychology. Western private and public efforts should be wholly integrated into every fiber of these countries' lives. Western political leaders and political parties should be deeply engaged with the leaders and politics and democratic forces of these countries, our churches and believers with their churches and believers, our students with their students, our militaries with their militaries, our environmentalists with their environmentalists, our companies with their companies.

What could such a program of action look like? This chapter sets out a few ideas, but it is primarily designed to stimulate thought and the ideas of others. The strength of the West is that initiatives come from many sources. The important point is not that we set into concrete a specific list of programs; rather, what is needed is an explosion of effort across a broad front from every element of Western society. In many cases, these efforts will be independent of each other, but in all cases there will be an overall common sense of direction. Three areas for action are discussed herein: economic, sociopolitical, and security.

Economic Action

A clear concept of Western economic participation in Eastern Europe could realistically set as a goal that within the next twenty-five years, the six countries will become mixed economies with a much greater role for the market and greater economic involvement with the West. This goal has obvious political as well as significant economic interest for the West, but in its attempts to achieve this goal, the West has been making one strategic error. By introducing Western financial resources into the region primarily through large-scale, syndicated, untied loans to the region's central banks (and therefore to governments and parties), the West actually may have reduced the pressure for economic reforms and movement toward sensible economic policies. (In this respect, the right-wing criticism of Western policy for "prolonging the lives of these regimes" has some validity.) The West has also burdened the most reform-oriented countries with a level of debt that imperils their ability to carry out reforms and to meet even the minimal needs of their peoples. The Japanese are the most recent offenders in this regard, having dumped some $4 billion into Hungary in the last several years, but the West Germans also are continuing this pattern. U.S., British, French, and other governments and banks have an undistinguished record as well, particularly during the 1970s.

Therefore, the first step on an economic action agenda should be for Western governments, the International Monetary Fund (IMF), and the World Bank to develop a new approach. We need to develop a set of tactics designed to help achieve the strategic goal for these economies set forth in the preceding paragraph. We should tie IMF/World Bank/other credits to a set of specific reforms: radical reduction of the role of ministries and of party and government apparats; establishment of transparent and consistent *economic* criteria and mechanisms in place of politically motivated subsidies and favors for individual sectors and firms; incentives for individual managers and workers; liberalization of foreign investment laws and practices; and expansion of the cooperative and private sectors. We also need to alter the ways in which the West interacts. Instead of giving large-scale loans to national banks, we should make smaller, targeted loans to the growing network of decentralized/commercial banks in these countries and then require that these banks make their loans on the same basis as in the West. Direct Western financing for individual companies and joint ventures would also prove useful, but to do this, Western banks must reevaluate their role and their long-term interests in lending to these countries.

Direct Western Investment

The most important component of an economic agenda is direct Western investment. Joint ventures are one vehicle. Another is a mutual fund to invest in the shares of companies in those countries where this is possible. Eastern Europe should be encouraged through this process to move from its still dominant Stalinist concentration on large enterprises and heavy industry toward a diversification of its manufacturing base with greater emphasis on consumer goods, agricultural commodities, and tourism. An increased role for small business—whether state or private—would be an important stimulus to improved economic flexibility and efficiency. The heavy emphasis given to militarily relevant production should be cut back, in part, through this change in the way the West interacts with the countries of this area. By dumping hundreds of millions, even billions of dollars into the hands of central banks and central governments, the West is simply reinforcing the Stalinist model. A younger generation of enterprise managers, bankers, and economists in some of these countries is enormously frustrated with the West for not insisting that they be allowed to keep the hard currency that they earn, to make independent investment decisions, and to change the structure of investments.

In addition to reform-oriented performance criteria, demand management also is important for any IMF or other program. But austerity is not a solution in Eastern Europe any more than it is in Latin America. The "Latin Americanization" of this region, which is evident in growing inflation, the influence of the military, and the political drift, should not include attempts to make the people pay for the mistakes of the Communist parties. If sensible politico-economic strategies are pursued, debt relief and stimulus rather than stagnation should be the objective. Although I think that any proposal of a Marshall Plan for some Eastern European countries is forty years too late and is not realistic or desirable, the West should be willing to consider debt relief in the context of genuine and far-reaching reform.

Western Business-Sector Involvement

A second component of an economic agenda will be much stronger encouragement of Western companies' involvement in Eastern Europe. The United States, for example, has a commercial attaché in only three of its six embassies in this part of the world. Western European governments are only slightly better organized to promote the sale of Western goods and the establishment of joint ventures. There are fewer than two hundred Western joint ventures in all of Eastern and Central Europe. Of course, these countries must radically reduce barriers to foreign investment to become as attractive as the newly industrializing countries. Similarly, the Eastern European countries do an extremely poor job of marketing their goods in the West; the quality of their goods also leaves much to be desired, but structured reform will help. Overall, the economic interaction is still minimal. Only 2 percent of European Community (EC) imports and 0.06 percent of U.S. imports come from Eastern Europe. (The interaction is much more significant as a percentage of the Eastern Europeans' gross national products.)

There are many concrete steps the West can take, and there is reason for hope. In Hungary, for example, from 1986 to 1988 the number of U.S. companies with offices in Budapest increased from seven to twenty, and the number of Western joint ventures in Hungary exceeded one hundred. The world fair, now planned to be held simultaneously in Vienna and Budapest in 1995, is an excellent example of the kind of bridging that is desirable and a U.S. company, Bechtel, has a contract to help set up the fair.

Another example of a regional, institutional initiative is the management center in Budapest. This is the first Western management institute in any Warsaw Pact country, and it trains Hungarian, Soviet, Polish, Czech, and other managers in Western marketing, personnel, and other management approaches. Originally a Hungarian-U.S. initiative, the center has drawn in other major Western countries and will provide a place for discussion of economic reform as well as increased East-West trade and investment.

Technology Cooperation

A third component of an economic agenda is the question of technology cooperation. The Coordinating Committee (COCOM) should continue to play a strong role, particularly as long as the qualitative edge of Western military technology is required to offset the quantitative military superiority of the Soviet Union and the East. Enforcement of those areas of high technology that are of genuine strategic importance must be tightened. This will be of increasing importance as the overall integration of Eastern Europe with the West increases. However, the concomitant for successful enforcement of genuinely important items is that they be relatively limited in number. Western countries, including the United States, must ensure that license decisions are made more quickly and that the list of COCOM-restricted items is kept to a reasonable minimum. This process is under way and has already yielded results.

Trade Barrier Policy

A fourth component is trade barrier policy. The EC, Japan, and the United States should review, from a political, security, and economic point of view, such matters as the tariff treatment accorded individual countries. How much "differentiation" is necessary, and what are the criteria? How much integration does the West want and how fast? In general, the West should be prepared to reward movement toward more open and liberal societies with most favored nation treatment. The West must also be clear about its minimum expectations: freedom of travel, no political prisoners, movement toward civil societies. Western attitudes toward government credits also should be influenced by these criteria. At the same time, when they are met, Western countries should be forthcoming. Poland and Hungary meet these criteria in part, and EC responsiveness to their desires to reach EC-Poland and EC-Hungary trade accords is appropriate. (The U.S. government has been urging greater openness in Eastern, Central, and Western European capitals and has argued that any accords be consistent with the General Agreement on Trade and Tariffs.) Similarly, a greater openness on Japan's part to exports from these countries would have significant results. Countries that do not meet these standards should not receive favorable treatment. We hope that our Western partners will come to accept this point of view.

Many meaningful and regular policy discussions should take place among Western countries and could include Japan and other Asian countries whose role in the region is growing. A semiannual meeting of policy-level officials on all aspects of the West's relations with Eastern and Central Europe should be established.

Sociopolitical Action

The objective here is similar to that in the economic realm. The peoples of Eastern and Central Europe want the kinds of political institutions taken for granted in the West. Eastern Europeans want newspapers that print news, not propaganda; trade unions that represent workers, not a single political party; universities that are free to develop ideas and innovation; and governments elected by the people. Clearly, it is up to the peoples of this region to insist upon progress toward pluralism and openness. But the range of possibilities for the West to play a secondary role is broad and extends from traditional diplomatic exchanges to innovative private initiatives. Overall, the point is massively to increase the amount of interchange and presence.

Unfortunately, the policy of differentiation has led to a rather limited amount of official political dialogue and presence, and this bears reexamination. Although economic differentiation is necessary, it is not at all clear that high-level visits by Western leaders do more to legitimize existing regimes than to encourge change. Much depends upon how the visits are conducted. The recent pattern of Western European and U.S. leaders insisting upon seeing church and democratic opposition figures as well as the party leadership in Poland, Hungary, and Czechoslovakia does encourage change. It should be sustained and broadened.

Tour by a U.S. President

One objective could be for a U.S. president to tour all six countries during a single visit and therefore make up for the fact that no U.S. president has been to most of them. The United States is probably more popular in this area than in any other part of the world. A visit by the president would be warmly welcomed by the people and those inside and outside Communist parties who want to bring about political and economic change. His speeches and the events that could be organized during such a trip would have real value in bringing greater attention to an expansion of overall ties with Eastern and Central Europe. (Similarly, Western European leaders should accelerate their visits and dialogue with all elements.) In particular, the West should focus visits on the next generation of political leaders—in five of the six countries the current leaders are in their sixties or seventies.

Expansion of Direct Political Ties

A second objective would be to expand party-to-party and other directly political (nondiplomatic) ties. As the past thirty years in Eastern Europe have demonstrated, debate and change can come from within the Communist party as well as from outside it. This was evident in 1956 in Hungary, in 1968 in Czechoslovakia, and is obvious today in a large part of this region and in the Soviet Union. Therefore, greater Western party involvement with the parties in the East is beneficial if done in a realistic manner. Western political parties do no favors for reform elements in the East by allowing themselves to be manipulated on security issues. Western parties should be candid in their discussions and insist upon contacts with the entire spectrum of forces in these countries. At a time when the very definition of socialism is being debated, it is useful for Social Democrats and others to engage in a dialogue on the meaning of democracy and justice; on the nature of mixed economies; and on the means to higher standards of living through individual initiative, free-trade unions, and reduced bureaucracy.

Similarly, the West should strengthen its ability to help the democratic movements in Eastern and Central Europe. Some in West Germany, Austria, France, England, and the United States are helping in concrete ways. Groups such as Solidarity, Charter 77, the democratic reformers in Hungary, and others deserve assistance. Just as the Soviets and the parties of Central and Eastern Europe have long helped Communist movements with political training, printing presses, and money, so can the West help democratic movements in Central and Eastern Europe in tangible ways. This is not interference in internal affairs; it is simply helping the political modernization of these countries, even as they want the West to help with their economic modernization. The two are inseparably linked, as even Communist parties now recognize. At a time when democratization and multiparty systems are fairly openly discussed in this region, the West must not unilaterally restrain itself from participating actively in this process. It is, for example, striking that most Western embassies have no contacts with the democratic forces that represent much of popular public opinion. It is equally striking that most Western countries have no equivalent to the West German party foundations and the U.S. National Endowment for Democracy, which enable countries to participate in the political process on an international scale. The United Kingdom, France, Spain, Japan, and others should set up such foundations with government funds but independent boards designed to promote democratic political growth.

Interest-Group Contact

A third objective is a reevaluation of the West's relationship with trade unions. To the extent that legitimate, independent trade unions begin to emerge, the United States and other Western countries on a case-by-case basis should review their policies of not having contacts with trade unions in socialist countries. This is a longer term question but one worth some active consideration. The West should also work with other interest groups such as environmentalists and professionals in functional areas: science, narcotics, terrorism, and so on.

Teacher Programs and Student Exchanges

A fourth objective is a relationship with the younger generation. Here the West has truly extraordinary assets. The worldwide hunger to learn Western languages, in particular English, is very palpable. The West can set as an objective sending 1,000 English teachers a year from the United States and the United Kingdom to teach in high schools, colleges, and summer camps in Central and Eastern Europe. It is obvious that such teachers take with them not only language but a set of values and an attitude toward change that is of very great importance. Such a program would cost about $1 million a year and would be a real bargain.

The West would also be served by truly massive exchanges of young people. That there are now some 20,000 students from the People's Republic of China (PRC) in the United States demonstrates that bold thinking in this area is not unrealistic. Why not strive to have 2,000 students a year from Eastern and Central Europe studying in the West? The focus in particular should be on programs for high school students and undergraduates and on placement in U.S. and European homes. This not only reduces the cost very significantly but adds a deeper and more durable tie to the West. Local costs can be paid by the receiving side to eliminate the problem caused by hard-currency shortages. Similarly, the West could strive to have at least 2,000 young Germans, Italians, Finns, British, Canadians, and Americans spend a semester or more in Eastern and Central Europe. In fact, in 1988 there were more than twenty U.S. universities that had exchange programs with Hungary, and several hundred U.S. students a year go to Hungary for courses in medicine, economics, and other subjects.

The central challenge in many of these areas is to generate adequate financial resources. Western governments must review their priorities and the cost-effectiveness of their programs from a long-term security, political, and cultural perspective. Bringing gradual détente to the East and reintegrating one or more of these countries into Europe and the modern democratic world would be a fundamental improvement in the security situation the West faces and would be worth larger shares of Western government budgets. The amount of money is very small in any case in comparison to other areas of expenditure, as the $1 million price tag for a very large-scale teacher program shows.

Nongovernmental Resources

A fifth objective is a major push to generate greater resources from nongovernmental sectors. Foundations are increasingly interested in this part of the world and can be persuaded to support more programs. For example, the Rockefeller Brothers Fund has established a foundation in Poland to help private agriculture. Companies that are active in this region also can be persuaded to support youth exchanges and other activities, such as the management center.

Citizen Activity

A sixth objective is to generate activity on the part of those living in the West who originate from Eastern and Central European countries. In some cases, these people are already active in a constructive manner. Obviously the inner-German set of ties is extraordinary. Some Polish-Americans have been very important in preserving and expanding ties in Poland. Even those who fought in the 1956 revolution come back to Hungary regularly and are engaged in trade promotion and the promotion of democratic values there. One outstanding example is George Soros, the New York financial wizard of Hungarian origin whose Open Society Fund contributes more than $3 million a year in Hungary to promote cultural, educational, human rights, and other value-oriented programs and who is now active in Poland, the PRC, the Soviet Union, and elsewhere in the socialist world. There has been a tendency in certain quarters to consider "ethnics" and "émigrés" as out-of-touch bomb throwers. But they can be the most natural and capable promoters of a deepening fabric with these countries. Western governments should encourage this development, for example, between U.S. Czechs and Slovaks and Czechoslovakia. There are many other cases in which the ties are very underdeveloped.

Culture

A seventh objective is increased cultural contact. It is sad but true that some of the great U.S. orchestras go regularly to Vienna but never bother to make the three-hour drive to Budapest. U.S. art exhibits are similarly limited. In general, Eastern and Central Europeans are recipients of second- or even third-rate Western cultural groups because there is so little hard currency to be made. Yet, when a Luciano Pavarotti appears in the Budapest or Prague opera house, the whole nation knows and cares; clearly the impact is much greater than when he appears in Paris or London for the umpteenth time. Similarly, there are very few Western trade promotion centers. One way to proceed, as the United States is now doing in Budapest, is to establish America Houses or British, French, and German centers in each capital. In the case of the America House in Budapest, this combines trade, travel promotion, exhibits, and all of the elements of a cultural center, including a theater and library.

Religion. The religious connection is of growing importance. Western churches could be encouraged to send pastors and priests to preach and teach. There should be more help for the reestablishment of church-run secondary schools and even universities and greater help for religious summer camps inside Eastern Europe and in the West. The revival of religion, which is evident in many countries and in particular among their young people, can be helped in these and other tangible ways.

Education. Another idea is to establish an international university in Hungary. This would bring faculty from Western and Eastern countries together to teach an international student body. Here again the central question is finance and, in particular, the start-up funds. There already is a chair in U.S. studies at Budapest's Eötvös Lorand University. Why not chairs of French, German, Italian, British, and U.S. studies at the most prestigious universities throughout this region?

Sports. Sport has one nice element to it. This is an area where the Eastern European countries are in some ways more advanced than the West and therefore can give something. It is important that the overall relationship be two way and not that of a supplicant. The discipline and training methods of the Bulgarians, Romanians, and East Germans offer much for the West. In fact, in some specific areas there already has been much learned from them. The West might consider setting up some joint sports training facilities or at least more invitations/exchange with existing institutions.

Media. Information media are the means to get to the largest audience. It is important to get the leading Western thinkers and ablest people onto Eastern European television. Zbigniew Brzezinski's 1987 trip to Budapest and Warsaw and his lectures and appearances on local television are a good example. The role of the radios—Deutsche Welle, BBC, VOA, RFE/RL—is key because they provide a surrogate free press. The West can increase the impact of Western television—West German television is already the main source of news and views in the GDR. The West should spend money to put up a satellite devoted to direct television broadcast into the homes of all countries in the region—there is now only very partial coverage and none in local languages except German.

Security Action

Security issues have caused the greatest concern in the postwar era, and yet paradoxically the West has talked the least about them with individual Eastern European countries. Only recently, for example, have there been any exchanges between Western militaries and the militaries of these countries, and these contacts are still very thin. Only very recently has there been any serious dialogue on arms control. Western thinking on the political and strategic consequences of various conventional, chemical, and nuclear arms control steps in this region is still relatively superficial.

First, the West has to develop its own concept of the security situation it would like in these countries. This concept should focus heavily on reducing the threat of a blitzkrieg being launched from them. Reduction to equal numbers of tanks, artillery, and soldiers in the zone from the Atlantic to the Urals is obviously a desirable objective. Additional steps could change the deployment and nature of the residual forces to eliminate the possibility of a surprise attack. The West also should move further with steps to enhance transparency and early warning. For example, stationing Western observers permanently at key transportation links throughout Eastern and Central Europe would help. The West also should reconsider, broaden, and "legitimize" the role of military attachés—the only Western military now permanently present inside this region. They can be seen as enhancers of openness and confidence and facilitators of military dialogue, rather than "spies."

The West must think through the desirability of total Soviet withdrawal of forces from one or more of these countries or the radical reduction in their presence in one or more. Western thinking should include military consequences as well as the effect on internal political dynamics. What would it mean in both military and political terms, for example, if Soviet forces were withdrawn from Poland and Hungary? Should the West be prepared to pay a price for such a move or for other elements in a package? What should this price be? Even the democratic opposition would like to see a major U.S. response if the Soviets were prepared to deliver very significant reductions and withdrawals. What level of Soviet withdrawals and demobilization would justify, for example, a significant reduction of the U.S. ground force presence in Western Europe? Clearly, the United States needs to keep a substantial force. But what level of Soviet cuts would make Washington comfortable pulling back 25 to 50 percent of the U.S. ground forces in Europe?

The West should intensify and institutionalize contacts on security issues, including a regular practice by Western foreign ministries of sending their chief arms control people for consultations and of receiving them in Western capitals. In at least some cases this can be placed on an annual basis. The West should promote regular conferences that bring together foreign ministry, military, institute/academic, and other elements on questions like conventional forces. The West has to move beyond thinking of Vienna and Geneva as the only places for meetings. Holding meetings in Warsaw and Budapest as well as in Washington, Bonn, and London will help the strong Eastern European yearning to be considered part of Europe, not something stuffed behind an artificial wall. The West can make its points even more forcefully in their capitals than in neutral places.

The West should encourage the kinds of institutional tie that the New York–based Institute for East-West Security Studies (IEWSS) has initiated.

The IEWSS has in residence each year midcareer people from Eastern and Central Europe, Western Europe, and the United States for joint in-depth work on key security issues. The alumni of this program are in key positions in the politico-security establishment of the East and are among the best promoters of new ideas and cooperation. Similar efforts between Western universities and institutions would be productive.

The military in each country may be of enhanced political importance in the future. Poland is only the most obvious example. The visit by the chair of the Joint Chiefs of Staff, John Vessey, to Romania was as unprecedented as it was important. We need to build a fabric of ties between our militaries. The United Kingdom, Austria, Finland, and Switzerland now have annual exchanges of their chiefs of staff with Hungary. This sort of practice can be expanded to all of the countries of this region. The United States has begun with modest exchanges of military historians and military sports teams in some of these countries and is willing to have higher level contacts. Now that the U.S.-Soviet military dialogue is developing, the door is more open in Eastern and Central Europe.

Visits to military units are in a sense already happening with the observers at exercises provided for under the CSCE process. But there could be a much broader picture developed here, including a dialogue on doctrine. Visits to each other's military schools would ensure that new generations of officers and soldiers are not being instilled with a spirit of enmity and suspicion. Why not lecturers at each other's military academies and institutes? Where possible, there could be ship visits and unit visits. In the longer term, the West should not rule out the thought of some joint exercises. These initially could be command-post exercises designed to deal with a terrorist desiring a nuclear weapon or with some malfunction in nuclear warning systems. Gaming could be one very useful way to reduce the chance of accident or miscalculation—perhaps the most likely cause for war in the future. We have developed the concept of risk reduction centers between Washington and Moscow. Perhaps some risk reduction discussions between the governments of Eastern Europe and the West could be useful.

From Words to Action

The questions might be asked—Why is the West not already doing all of these things? Who will ensure that they do happen in the future? There has been no adequate mechanism for keeping track of what the West as a whole is doing in this region and no adequate dialogue on policy and concrete steps. Some sort of a clearinghouse should be established to monitor and encourage overall Western activity, including private as well as government programs. Perhaps the EC could take the lead in this regard. It is crucial to institute at least semiannual meetings of the political and economic policy-level officials from key Western countries responsible for relations with Eastern and Central Europe. The hosting of such meetings could rotate among the seven industrial democracies or be centered in Brussels. The important element is that we create an action-oriented means of communication and consultation.

Conclusion

It is time for the West to perceive this region as a "new frontier," one in which a new level of effort and perseverance will yield substantial results in the long term. The built-in rigidities and inefficiency of communism will not yield quick results. Basic reforms will come slowly, there will be reversals, and some countries will be more ripe for change than others. The West may not get all that it or the peoples of the region hope for. But there is no alternative—either for them or for us. Stagnation for the East and passivity on the part of the West are not viable policies. They will only lead to further explosions and inherent instability at the heart of the most heavily armed region in the world, where the two most powerful military forces in history confront one another. The time has come for a new era of cooperation between Eastern Europe and the West.

18

Central and Eastern Europe, *Perestroika,* and the Future of the Cold War

Seweryn Bialer

The Soviet bloc in Eastern Europe includes six countries with a combined population of more than 100 million and a civilian gross national product (GNP) close to two-thirds that of the Soviet Union. These six countries—Poland, the German Democratic Republic (GDR), Czechoslovakia, Hungary, Romania, and Bulgaria—are different from each other in size, culture, history, political orientation, and level of economic development. Very few statements made about the bloc hold true for all these countries. They are valid for each only to a different degree. Yet one can treat all six countries, within limits, as a separate entity, primarily for four reasons.

First, these countries are part of a Soviet empire created by Joseph Stalin in the late 1940s and held ultimately by force by all his successors. The post-Stalin thaws and reforms did not change the limited domestic sovereignty of these countries; the subordination of their foreign policy to the needs of the imperial power; their integration in a military alliance, the Warsaw Pact, whose military policies were dictated by expansionist Soviet policies; and the direction of their foreign trade and international economic activity toward the giant in the East or toward each other.

Second, all these countries (with the partial exception of Bulgaria) have been a part of Western civilization and have been tied to the basic cultural institutions of Christianity in their Roman Catholic, Protestant, or Orthodox forms. The duality of Russian history, Asian and European, and the subordination of the Russian Orthodox church to the state were alien to the evolution of the bloc countries, particularly in the last three centuries.

Third, all these countries developed fierce nationalisms among their populations at large and among their educated strata and political elites. These nationalisms were fueled by initial identification with the West as the front line of Christianity against the onslaught of the Mongols, Tatars, and Turks and then by the pressure of growing Russian might. Later these countries were caught between the conflicting interests and expansion of the great central European powers, Germany, Austria-Hungary, and Russia. In modern times their independence was always in question, and they preserved their cultural identity by an immense and costly struggle against assimilation. Their nationalisms were authentic, uncompromising, and primordial forces that created tight bonds between their elites and their populations. Their fate was to be constantly involved in the conflict among the great European powers and between them and Russia.

Finally, these countries share the distinction of belonging to the same political-economic species—the Communist systems—imposed on them by force by the Soviet Union. Although often different in degree and form, all these countries today share similar and profound problems that are rooted in the patterns and results of their evolution in the last forty years under communism and in the systemic crisis that besets the Soviet Union, the imperial power itself.

The Specific Characteristics of the Soviet Empire

Because of what the East Europeans were, who they are, and how their development and spiritual predispositions differ from those of their imperial metropolis, Soviet rule in Eastern Europe has faced several negative factors that together are unique among modern empires. The most important are the following:

- The East European client states of the Soviet Union are not Third World countries. They are not underdeveloped peripheries dominated by a technologically and economically superior power—a carrier of material civilization and progress. On the contrary, almost all are economically more advanced than the Soviet Union or than the Russian Republic alone. The classical imperial "white man's burden" is in this case reversed—economically and technologically, the East European client states have, involuntarily, to carry it.
- Regardless of whether they are right or wrong, and to what degree, East European countries, elites and populations alike, perceived Russia and now perceive the Soviet Union as culturally inferior to themselves. President Charles de Gaulle, in his dream of an independent Europe, included the Soviet Union to the Urals in his concept, but the educated strata of Eastern Europe consider themselves European and their Soviet tutors culturally inferior. Only now, under Mikhail Gorbachev, do they think his *perestroika* (restructuring) an attempt to Europeanize Soviet socialism, in whose success, incidentally, most of them do not believe.
- Because of their historical experience, the nations of Eastern Europe are skilled at adapting to unfavorable national situations without giving up their national identity and values. Periods of national apathy in their relations with the Soviets are replaced by periods of great energy in their quest for liberation, whenever the slightest chance of improvement

appears on the horizon. This skilled adaptation leads only to superficial acquiescence, and the periods of general apathy do not reflect conditions of genuine stability but only of waiting for better opportunities to reassert themselves. It looked at times as if the West had abandoned Eastern Europe, but Eastern Europe has never abandoned the West.

- The East European countries possess broadly developed counterelites, a large stratum of educated, skilled people who can replace if needed the existing ruling elites. Their ruling elites are heterogeneous in character, divisive in terms of power and alliance formation, and split even on fundamental issues of social order and legitimate rule. In critical times many barriers between the ruling elite and the counterelite are erased by a common orientation, mutual dependence, and personal acquaintance. Even conservatives within the ruling elite seek greater political independence from Moscow and greater economic autonomy from the Council for Mutual Economic Assistance (CMEA).

The Soviet Union thus faces with its East European clients irredentist nationalism of a special kind and virulence. It is a nationalism of various sources and carriers and of diverse dimensions that overlap and reinforce each other. We do not know any one example in the history of modern empires where the superiority of the metropolitan power in fact, and especially in the perception of its subjects, depended so uniquely and overwhelmingly on military power, seldom applied but always present. The ideological glue that tied the elites of these countries and some part of their populations to the metropolitan power in the initial decade of the empire has by now for all practical purposes dissolved, thus leaving the ultimate source of subjugation—Soviet imperial aspirations backed by superior military might—more naked than ever before.

Another aspect of Soviet–East European relations is also unique and important. The metropolitan power itself, the Soviet Union, is not an ethnically homogeneous nation. It encompasses fifteen union republics, eighteen autonomous republics, twenty-three autonomous provinces, and forty-eight autonomous regions, each ethnically different from the others. Whether the Soviet Union is a multinational state or a continental empire need not be discussed here. What is clear, and sufficient to know, is that relations between the Russians and other Soviet nations are not those among equals. The Russians ultimately rule the Soviet Union. The multinational character of the Soviet Union and the ethnically unequal distribution of power therein are of major importance for Eastern Europe. Irredentism from any source in the East European empire feeds irredentism in the Soviet Union, and vice versa. This limits the room for maneuver of the Soviet leadership in dealing with Eastern Europe. In sum, more is at stake here than "only" the fate of Moscow's outer empire.

Finally, there is another crucial factor in the relations between the Soviet Union and Eastern Europe. The Soviet Union created and consolidated its East European holdings at the same time as the progressive disintegration and final dissolution of all other empires occurred. Eastern Europe therefore remains the only large and, in classical terms, imperial sphere in the world. But in the last twenty years, after the western empires ceased to exist, a continuous, growing spirit of ethnic and political assertiveness and of political participation has swept the globe. The equally growing and powerful global trend of economic, technological, and scientific interdependence feeds rather than counteracts the spirit of national self-identification. One of the sources of this ethnic and political assertiveness is the desire to participate freely in global affairs, not to be left out of the global technological revolution—that is, in permanent economic subordination to the technologically powerful nations. Inside the Soviet Union, Gorbachev's *perestroika* is a recognition and a sign of the main tendency of the time we live in. Yet nothing is more unnatural for our times than the type of imperial ties established by the Soviet Union in its relations with Eastern Europe. How can one expect that the powerful trend of global political participation will not assert itself, indeed, is not already asserting itself, within the East European countries? The trends and forces of the remaining decade of the twentieth century have again forcefully put on the agenda the issue of the Soviet East European empire.

The Systemic Crisis of Eastern Europe

The emergence of Gorbachev as the leader of the imperial power and his efforts at radical reforms did not create or even aggravate the complex systemic and policy problems facing Eastern Europe. These problems exploded in Poland five years before Gorbachev took power, with the establishment and then the suppression of Solidarity. Gorbachev's *perestroika* and its international repercussions put, however, the challenges facing Eastern European countries in a new perspective and added urgency to the entire East European problem.

The Crisis of Legitimacy

The fundamental systemic problem of the East European countries is that of popular legitimacy, or rather the lack of it. This goes back to the first years of their existence as Communist states. Communism and the sovietization of these countries were established by very small native minorities through employment of Soviet force, military and security, or through the recognized, perilous eventuality of its use. In discussions with Soviet colleagues about Eastern Europe they often ask, "Why do you put such stress on history, on the past about which we disagree, when we should rather consider the problems of today where we have a common opinion on many issues?" The answer is that we in the West do it not for the dubious pleasure of rubbing in again the initial and brutal Soviet misdeeds in Eastern Europe, but because the past has tremendous, central influence on the present. The origins of the Communist states in Eastern Europe are the "original sin" of the Soviets and their local cohorts, and it projects into the present, will project into the future, and cannot be erased without fundamental changes.

The regimes in Eastern Europe lack popular legitimacy in two respects: Their populations do not accept Soviet domination over their nations as natural, just, or irreversible, and they do not accept the right of their native rulers to rule. Authentic Communist revolutions, such as in Russia, China, Yugoslavia, Albania, Cuba, and Vietnam, were able to acquire legitimacy because their socialist goals were from the beginning, or in the case of the USSR at a later time, identified and fused with native nationalism and national interest. The unauthentic revolutions in Eastern Europe and the Communist regimes that they established were never and are not now fused with native nationalism. Their legitimacy base is very shallow. They can broaden and deepen it only if they visibly oppose Soviet domination and give up their monopoly of power for a broad national coalition.

The extent of popular legitimacy in any country is best tested in periods of crisis and upheaval. In this respect the legitimacy of Soviet rule for the Russians, but not for the Tatars or Lithuanians, for example, was tested in the crucible of the Nazi-Soviet war and passed the test. At no time did any of the regimes of Eastern Europe, except Yugoslavia and Albania, pass such a test. Whenever a crisis, or hard times, set in, their popular legitimacy was found wanting. Moreover, this was true not only in broad social strata, but in the Communist party itself and even in a large part of the ruling elite.

In the early 1950s, the Western fear and the hope of the Soviet Union and their native East European viceroys were largely similar. The West feared and the Soviets hoped that time, economic success, social reforms, indoctrination, and, in particular, generational changes would make communism in these countries genuine and irreversible. The forty-odd years of Communist rule in Eastern Europe have showed the hopes and the fears to be unjustified. The Communist control over these countries has increased immensely, but the legitimacy of the regimes remains questionable. Most importantly, public opinion polls and simple observation indicate that generational change works, all in all, not for the Communist rulers but against them. The young workers and intelligentsia are in the forefront of the opposition to these regimes and are the most contemptuous of their Soviet "older brother." Time did work against Communist rule in Eastern Europe. The events in Poland in the 1980s and the present situation in Hungary have made this clear even to the Soviet political elite. Thus, time is working against Soviet domination of Eastern Europe and against the Communist monopoly of power there.

The Communist rule of the East European regimes is based on internal and external, actual and potential coercive power. The extent of their legitimacy, however, is based on their ability to assure dynamic economic performance and improvement in the popular standard of living. In the last decade, and especially at present, the economic situation and performance of these countries are by any standard inferior. The economy, rather than acting as a base of their legitimacy, however inadequate, constitutes the most important challenge to the safety and stability of their Communist rule.

The Economic Crisis

All the East European countries are in an economic backwater when compared to the "old" and "new" industrialized capitalist countries, which conduct almost 70 percent of world trade. Against this yardstick, the level of development, consumption, and performance in Eastern Europe is decisively substandard. Some of these countries, such as the German Democratic Republic and Czechoslovakia, were among the ten most industrialized countries of the world before World War II. The others reached the goals of the first Industrial Revolution during the initial two decades of their development under communism. Yet none of these East European countries has accomplished the goals of the second Industrial Revolution (saturation of relatively inexpensive consumer durables and a high-quality standard of living—for example, better diet, quality housing, and private cars). None has yet entered the third Industrial Revolution of information, communication, and global economic and technological interdependence.

Romania is an economic basket case by any standard. Poland is in economic chaos: The standard of living and level of production were lower in 1988 than they were ten to fifteen years earlier, and Poland's indebtedness to the West is of astronomical proportions. Hungary entered a period of stagnation and financial crisis in the 1980s; its per capita foreign debt is higher even than in Poland. The Czechoslovak economy is growing slowly, but it is increasingly falling behind capitalist industrial nations. East Germany is smug and arrogant as far as its economy is concerned vis-à-vis its East European and Soviet comrades; yet the GDR's relative prosperity is inferior to West Germany's and is secured by one-sided, indirect subsidy on the order of $2 billions yearly from the Federal Republic of Germany (FRG).

From the time Gorbachev came to power, and to a large extent even before, the economic problems facing Eastern Europe did not derive from the extent of Soviet permissiveness with regard to autonomous economic policies or from Soviet dictation. In the 1970s, the Soviet Union gave a free hand to Edward Gierek's "socialism on Western credits," even after 1976 when worker unrest in Poland demonstrated its bankruptcy. Today, the leeway East European leaders have to move in the direction of "market socialism" and even political liberalization is quite extensive and far from what would be considered unwise and troublesome in Moscow. Moreover, that Yugoslavia, an East European socialist country that is not a member of the Soviet bloc, is in an economic and political crisis resembling those in the Soviet satellites shows that their deep-seated causes are not directly "made in the Soviet Union."

The bad economic situation in the Soviet bloc and the resulting danger to its sociopolitical stability are primarily the result of three types of crises that beset these countries: the socialist economic order, the Communist political order, and the socialist international integration.

The Socialist Economic Case. The failure of the socialist economic system in Eastern Europe is clear beyond any doubt. Whereas in the post-Stalin era the key economic issue for the East European countries was formulated by the Soviet leadership as Moscow's acceptance of "different roads to socialism," at present it is the search for "different roads *from* socialism." Although the crisis of the Communist economic system in Eastern Europe has common sources, it has three expressions: the crisis of the traditional economic system, the crisis of "market socialism" reforms of the system, and the crisis of the necessary political preconditions for radical economic reforms.

The crisis of the socialist economic system is best exemplified by countries that are the two extremes: East Germany and Czechoslovakia on the one extreme and Romania on the other. The GDR went through a cycle of managerial reforms that modified its Stalinist economic model and strategy of growth. Czechoslovakia has the traditional Stalinist economic system in its purest form. Romania adds to it a dimension of irrationality, even madness, that is associated with personal dictatorship of the most extreme form.

Despite the obvious differences between the relatively prosperous GDR and the catastrophically poor and declining Romania, they both share basic systemic economic traits—reliance on central planning, centralization of economic power, and the only partially hidden supremacy of the maintenance of political power over economic growth and progress. The Nicolae Ceauşescu personal dictatorship in Romania pushes the irrationality of the socialist economic system to its outer limits. The GDR restrains the disastrous effects of the traditional socialist economic model partly as a result of major help from the FRG and partly as a result of the work ethic of its workers and managers, which even the Communist system was unable to destroy. Yet for all those differences their growth as compared to their potential is critically diminished by their adherence to the Stalinist economic model.

Hungary is the archetypal example of the crisis of marketizing, liberalizing reforms of the socialist economic system. The radical reform of the Stalinist economic structural model and strategy of growth, initiated and presided over by János Kádár, was successful in the 1960s and 1970s. Yet in the 1980s it reached its systemic limits and was further worsened by changes in the global economy and the European market. Hungary thus convincingly demonstrated the limitations of the reform model unless it went beyond the limits imposed by the nature and social policies of the socialist political system. The still politically determined macroinvestment decisions, the "back door" centralization, the fear of acceptance of unemployment and of bankruptcy of the firms and enterprises that lagged behind the national average, and the resistance to making costs of production and productivity of labor and capital the determining indices of success were the prime causes of Hungary's economic stagnation in the 1980s.

Poland in the 1980s was a classical example of an economic catastrophe caused mainly by the unwillingness of the Communist authorities to accept the necessary political preconditions of a radical economic reform. The economic reform plans of General Wojciech Jaruzelski's government are basically rational and do not differ substantially from the economic reforms proposed by Solidarity. The reform's implementation, however, requires support from above and from below and a change of economic strategy. Although in late summer 1988 the position of the Polish government toward Solidarity was modified, at least in theory, in the direction of dialogue with the union, and the government's determination to fight bureaucratic resistance was reinforced at the August 1988 Plenum of the Central Committee, the outlook for economic improvement remains grim. The situation in Poland demonstrates clearly that even ultimately beneficial economic reforms cannot be carried out by a political regime that entirely lacks mass support, is unable to overcome its ideological fixations, and cannot purge the party-state bureaucracy of those who are reformist in their official pronouncements but conservative at heart.

The Political Crisis. The countries of the East European Soviet bloc are also in a chronic political crisis, which is partly the effect of and partly the cause of the economic crisis. Due to the shallowness of the regimes' legitimacy, economic difficulties in these countries tend to become translated into social unrest and political instability. Moreover, the disaffection of the populations, and even parts of their elites, with Communist rule has acquired a weight of its own, independent of its economic causation. Thus, the political crisis in Eastern Europe concerns not only the policies of their governments but the very nature of their political structures and political processes. It is truly a crisis of the socialist system of political rule.

The political crisis of the Communist regimes in Eastern Europe, aside from its economic roots, is intensified by other factors that add to its virulence and chronic character:

- Among all generations in Eastern Europe, the reference point by which they evaluate their own sociopolitical and economic situations and life-styles is not their past, but conditions in Western Europe and in non-European newly industrialized countries. Travel and exchanges between East and West have so grown, especially among the middle class, and the penetration of these countries by Western communications media (including videotapes) has reached such intensity and across-the-board saturation that the technological revolution sweeping the world, and especially the "leisure revolution" in the West, serve as compelling but unattainable models for their own aspirations. The deep frustration that accompanies this phenomenon is not difficult to imagine.
- The negative perception by the population of these countries, and especially by their middle classes, of their Soviet "big brother" contributes to the political crisis in two ways. The revelations about Soviet stagnation and past crimes that emanated from the Soviet Union reinforce these populations' negativism about their own regimes, which after all developed from the same tree. Gorbachev's *perestroika* and verbal radicalism

about the nature of socialist rule thus lead, particularly in such countries as Czechoslovakia, the GDR, and Romania, to an astonishing and ironic development—a comparison of Soviet "freedom" with their own "enslavement."

- The longevity of a political regime tends, up to a point, to increase its stability, to make it look "natural" and "normal." This point, however, has already been crossed in Eastern Europe. The length of Communist rule in Eastern European countries and the frequency of reforms that promised major improvements and change and produced neither have made the population of these countries lose all hope that traditional or untraditional Communist regimes can solve the vital problems that these countries are facing. The result in these countries is political polarization, which has two consequences. In Poland, the population or large elite minorities ask for fundamental *political* changes; and in Hungary, the serious reformers are caught between the conservatism of a large segment of the party and state bureaucracy that they lead and strong popular pressures for crossing the political parameters of reforms that are even as liberal as those instituted by János Kádár.

The political crisis in the Soviet bloc countries is potentially destructive in them all, but its intensity and explosion threshold vary from country to country. Poland, the largest and most important East European country, is at one end of the continuum—the most explosive—and the German Democratic Republic is at the other—the most tranquil. Separate chapters in this book deal with specific countries. In my own review of the political crisis in these countries I will therefore touch only, and briefly, on those aspects I consider particularly important.

The GDR is by almost any measure the most politically stable Soviet client state. Yet the economic factors that mostly account for its relative stability—its closeness to the FRG; its enormous subsidies from their western countrymen; its membership, for all practical purposes, in the CMEA and the European Community—determine the relative shallowness and artificiality of its stability.

The population of the GDR is perfectly aware of the economic, social, and political situation in the FRG. Its entire population is able to, and three-fourths do, watch West German television. Several million East Germans and West Germans from all walks of life visit each other yearly. It is not Eastern Europe and the Soviet Union, or even their own past, to which East Germans compare their situation, but to West Germany—one of the most prosperous countries in the world, the third global economic giant, and the key Western European military and political power. Economically behind and relatively technologically backward, the East German population, although submissive by tradition to authority, is nevertheless frustrated by what it could be and is not. Whereas for Poles absolute pauperization creates deep political instability, for East Germans an inferior situation relative to the FRG produces seeds of instability.

The frustrations of the East Germans have economic as well as political sources. As the frontline state facing the North Atlantic Treaty Organization (NATO), the GDR contains a much larger and more visible Soviet military presence than do all the other satellite countries taken together. Politically, East Germany is more dependent on the Soviet Union than other Soviet client states are because its military importance is most central to the Soviets and because it is the smaller part of a truncated central nation of Europe. The East German party and political elites were in the past very servile with regard to Moscow. Today they are the most arrogant. But they were not, and are not, trusted by the Soviets. The Soviets were always afraid of the powerful pull of the idea of German unification on the East Germans. Today, the Soviets think, their fears are amply justified.

On the other side of the political stability-instability continuum in Eastern Europe is the People's Republic of Poland. In the short run, the introduction of martial law in December 1981 seemed very successful. It preempted the necessity and inevitability of Soviet military intervention and destroyed the organized, national base of Solidarity. What it created, however, was, as we can now see, not political stability but apathy, tiredness, and indifference to the Jaruzelski government. Poland is a country where a semblance of civil peace is safeguarded by the church, where the government has no nation to rule, and where the nation has no government to which it offers even minimal allegiance.

In 1988 the temporary stability in Poland, or rather the absence of confrontations between the existing Polish "civil society" and the government, gave way to an increase in the frustration of the population because of the drastically worsening economic situation (the collapse of the second phase of the official economic reform). The increased social dissatisfaction and its expression in a wave of strikes in May and August led finally to the recognition by key Polish government leaders of two basic truths: that one cannot conduct an economic reform without the support of the working class; and that there is no alternative left to the government, short of a civil war, except to start stabilizing politically the situation through negotiations with the opposition about power-sharing. Negotiations between the Polish government and Solidarity had, in November 1988, not yet begun. If they do, they may not succeed. But that the government has even in theory agreed to them underlines the basic instability of the Polish government and the sociopolitical situation in Poland.

The Crisis of Socialist Integration. The conditions of Eastern Europe can be defined finally by the crisis of socialist economic integration. It is truly amazing, but easily explainable by the prevalence of the Stalinist economic model, that in the forty years of its existence the European "socialist commonwealth" has not developed a common market and convertible currency of its own. The economic relations between the Soviet Union and Eastern Europe and among the Eastern European countries are very important, and at the same time destructive, to all these countries.

More than one-half of the bloc's foreign trade is exchanged within the socialist community. Most of the raw materials and energy resources necessary for East European growth come from the Soviet Union. In turn, Eastern Europe finds in the Soviet Union a ready market for its traditional industrial products and consumer goods. (The era, however, when East European consumer goods could be dumped on the Soviet market regardless of their quality seems to be coming to a close.) Until the early 1970s, most of the goods necessary for increased productivity and technological progress were acquired through mutual exchange, although their contribution to the modernization of these countries is, of course, highly questionable.

The economic relations among the socialist countries of Europe gradually became irrelevant to their key economic problems. All these countries, although at different levels of underdevelopment, were circumscribed in their domestic economic activity by the Stalinist economic model. Even Hungary's marketizing reforms could still be described as one form of a command economy (as the great Hungarian economist János Kornai argues and the experience of the 1980s proves). Their economic relations with each other could not alleviate their domestic economic backwardness and counteract the restrictions of their Soviet economic model, which accounts so much for their stagnation. Two measures are particularly necessary—to spur domestic productivity by imports of advanced technology and to begin sharp competition between economic units.

From this point of view, East European economic relations with the Soviet Union were and remain simply irrelevant to the countries' economic problems. It is true that through the acceptance of shoddy goods (without any chance of being sold for hard currencies) for goods of higher quality than domestic Soviet products, trade with the Soviets provided short-range economic relief for their outdated factories. In the longer range, however, it forced the Soviet Union and most of the East European countries into conditions of technological stagnation and underdevelopment. This is equally true for today and for the future. It is almost certain that the Soviet economic *perestroika,* which has not yet gotten off the ground, will not become more relevant to the critical issues and needs of East European economic development in the foreseeable future.

The capitalist markets of goods and capital are the only external source to alleviate East Europe's economic crisis. Hungary's expanded relations with, and adjustment to, capitalist markets were a crucial factor in improving its domestic performance and promoting its relative prosperity in the 1970s. Unfortunately, the international capitalist market conditions of the 1980s, and probably in the foreseeable future, were not conducive to the repetition of the Hungarian pattern. Technological progress in the West has speeded up. The competition for markets has sharpened in a major way. Protectionism has increased and promises to increase still more. On a purely commercial basis, the East European opportunities of the 1970s will hardly be repeated in the foreseeable future.

I do not want to give the impression that the near-term situation in Eastern Europe is prerevolutionary. Yet it seems likely that in the coming years, explosive conditions may develop in one or another country of the

Soviet East European empire. But what is as important, even without explosions, is that this region will remain unstable, plagued by unrest and popular and intraelite conflict. Several not easily changeable conditions argue for the realism of this outlook: The idea of communism, the corrupted form of the idea of justice has suffered an irreversible bankruptcy; the legitimacy of each regime is probably less viable today than in the 1960s and early 1970s; the Communist elites have lost their élan and are corrupt, split, and fearful of the future; leadership successions are on the agenda of many of these countries; the private freedom that developed in many of these countries provides a basis to fight for political freedom; stability through improved economic performance is and will remain extremely difficult; the example of an exciting and dynamic world that passes them by has entered the consciousness of the population and particularly the youth; the conditions for an alliance between the traditional intelligentsia and the industrial working class have improved; and the drastic decline of the East-West conflict, especially in Europe, makes it difficult to keep up indefinitely a siege mentality. Under these conditions the direction and substance of Soviet policies toward Eastern Europe, and the very influence of Gorbachev's *perestroika* on this region, as a catalyst or obstacle to change becomes of prime importance.

Gorbachev's *Perestroika* and Soviet and East European Dilemmas

The internal stability of the Soviet party-state and the strength of the Soviet international position as a global power are at the very roots of the goals of Gorbachev's *perestroika.* The internal stability of the Soviet Union was shaken by the nearly two decades of economic and technological stagnation, social alienation, and corruption and by the breakdown of centralized authority during the long period of Leonid Brezhnev's rule. The Soviet position as a global superpower has been undermined by the one-sidedness and limitations of its foreign policy resources and the overextension and rigidity of its international security and foreign policies. From both points of view—domestic stability and international position—the preservation of its East European empire remains among the key goals of the Soviet party-state. Moreover, for reasons to be explained later, developments in Eastern Europe and in Soviet–East European relations are of central importance to the fate of *perestroika* in the Soviet Union. Needless to say, conversely, the evolution of *perestroika* in the Soviet Union is of central importance for Eastern Europe.

To paraphrase Winston Churchill, Gorbachev was not elected to the position of the General Secretary to preside over the dissolution of the Soviet East European empire. As in the case of his domestic course and his security and foreign policies, he recognizes without any doubt the necessity of radical changes in Soviet East European policies. The problems that he faces, however, in this respect are at least as difficult as in the other areas of *perestroika* and "new thinking." These problems are threefold: First, how will his policies of radical reforms influence developments in Eastern Europe, and will Eastern Europe leave to him the determination of the boundaries of changes that the region will undergo in the foreseeable future; second, how far *can* he change Soviet policies toward Eastern Europe without seriously endangering his power position and his "alliance for progress" at home; third, how far does he *want* to change Soviet policies toward Eastern Europe while preserving Soviet domination in the region?

The change of course in Moscow—*perestroika, glasnost'* (openness), and new thinking—cannot but have a profound effect on the situation within Eastern Europe. Today some of these influences are already visible. Conservative East European party leaders are enraged and discouraged. They are fighting a rearguard battle to prevent *perestroika* and *glasnost'*, these dangerous imports from the USSR, from crossing their borders. The East German and Czechoslovak leaderships ill conceal their hostility to Gorbachev's course and their foreboding of worse things to come. They repeat ad nauseam that their countries do not need *perestroika* and that they have very little to learn from the Soviets.

The East German party newspaper, *Neues Deutschland,* reprinted Nina Andreyeva's notorious article from the March 13, 1988, issue of *Sovetskaya rossiya,* inspired by Yegor Ligachev and an all-out attack on Gorbachev's line and an open attempt to rehabilitate Stalin. Ironically, the East Germans published the article on April 5, the same day that *Pravda* published a long article, authorized by the Soviet Politburo, as a stinging rebuttal and condemnation of the March 13 Andreyeva letter.

The liberals within the party, the party intellectuals and intelligentsia, and the "progressive" part of the economic administration in the East European countries feel encouraged and uplifted by the surprising winds of renewal from Moscow. They hope that they will now be able to propose liberalizing political, social, cultural, and economic reforms directed against dogmatic Communist orthodoxy and legitimized as a lawful pursuit by the changes in the "fatherland of socialism." They make it clear to their Western friends and colleagues that they regard the Gorbachev phenomenon as their last chance to civilize East European socialism.

In Hungary, where the aging János Kádár became conservative, defending the existing political and economic model as the limits of permissible reform, the party opted for further change. Kádár has for all practical purposes been retired and replaced by Károly Grósz. Almost the entire top leadership echelon has been replaced, and the doors have been opened wider for young, liberal, and more radical reformers to enter the second stratum of the party-state leadership. Romania, under the highly oppressive and dogmatic dictatorship of Nicolae Ceauşescu, has become even more isolated within the "socialist bloc." The Soviets barely hide their deep distaste for his Romanian brand of socialism.

On the popular level, the message of renewal emanating from Moscow is reaching the East European industrial working class. Their initial skepticism toward the authenticity of *perestroika* still exists in part, but today it is as much focused on whether *perestroika* will succeed as on whether it is a serious effort in the first place. The credibility of the conservative East European party leaders among their own populations is even lower than before, and the unspoken assumption that they cannot do more for the independence of their countries because of Soviet restrictions has become even hollower than before. In a situation that seems almost surrealistic in the light of the past, East German and Czechoslovak, let alone Romanian, leaders are attempting to cut off their people from Soviet news on the progress of *perestroika.* News from the Soviet Union is highly selective, even about speeches by Gorbachev. Television programming from the USSR is heavily censored.

In Poland, the country where the radicalization of the industrial working class is greater than anywhere in the region, the leaders of the Solidarity movement are split on the authenticity of *perestroika* but united in the judgment that it provides a strategic opportunity to press the Jaruzelski government into sharing power with the workers' organization. Lech Wałęsa probably best expressed the mood of the workers' leadership when he remarked, just before Gorbachev's visit to Poland, "What a shame that Brezhnev did not die five years earlier." Even the leaders of the official Polish trade unions, created as a counterforce to Solidarity, seem emboldened enough to take a strong stance *against* the party leadership in defense of the workers. Their leader declared during the industrial strikes in August 1988 that if the government used force to evict the workers from the mines and shipyards they had occupied, the official trade unions might declare a general strike.

This is not the first time in post–World War II history that events in the Soviet Union acted as catalysts of radicalization in Eastern Europe. The death of Stalin in 1953 and Nikita Khrushchev's subsequent anti-Stalin campaign found a wide response in Eastern Europe, such as the worker unrest in East Germany; unrest and the transfer of power in Poland to Władysław Gomułka, a leader who had been accused of nationalism; Imre Nagy's "new course" and the subsequent revolution in Hungary; and the purge of the secret police and super-Stalinist leaders in all East European countries. The Soviet Union's anti-Stalin course and reforms liberalized the East European regimes and their relations with the Soviet Union somewhat. But the supremacy of the Soviet Union as an arbiter that would decide what would and would not be permitted in its sphere remained unchanged, and, as in Czechoslovakia in 1968, this was unhesitatingly backed with Soviet military power. Domestic liberalization and economic reforms in most East European countries were a step forward from the brutality of Stalin's oppression and the dogmatism of the Stalinist system. The hopes and promises of freedom that Moscow's anti-Stalin course had evoked in Eastern Europe, however, remained unfulfilled. The Soviet tanks in Prague that reversed the Dubček experiment also ended the hopes for liberal change and independence for the other countries of the Soviet empire.

The hopes and promises created by Gorbachev's *perestroika* in the Soviet Union and in Soviet–East European relations may also end in bitter disappointment, either through the collapse of *perestroika* or through the unwillingness of the new Soviet leaders to change radically their attitudes toward their East European empire. Yet the situation in the late 1980s is substantially different from that of the Khrushchev period in the Soviet Union, within the East European countries, in Soviet–East European relations, and in the general international climate. Today and in the years to come, the promise of change and the perils of unfulfilled hopes are much greater than during the anti-Stalin campaign of the Khrushchev years.

The crisis of Soviet communism today is much deeper and the radicalism of the steps taken to overcome it much greater than at the time of Stalin's death and Khrushchev's rule. Khrushchev's great achievement was to abolish mass terror in the Soviet Union. This fundamental change created the foundation for reforms without which Gorbachev's *perestroika* could not even have begun. But Gorbachev's achievements, not to mention his plans, go well beyond anything Khrushchev did. Khrushchev tried to destroy Stalin's ghost; Gorbachev is in the process of destroying Stalinism as a system of action and thought. Gorbachev's *perestroika* domestically and his new thinking in foreign and security policy question and reevaluate almost every aspect of the Soviet Union's domestic and foreign behavior. Moreover, the structural changes pushed through by the new Soviet leadership have only started. It is impossible to predict how far they will go if Gorbachev retains and consolidates his power.

In Eastern Europe, the frustration of the political public with the existing state of affairs is deeper than it was in the mid-1950s. Moreover, the definition of the political public has broadened immensely to encompass not only the intelligentsia but the very core of the East European nations—a dominant segment of the industrial working class and the youth. The disparity between the hopes and desires and the reality that these nations face is greater than at any time in the past. In Eastern Europe, the bankruptcy that the Communists are facing is no longer only that of Stalinism but that of socialism as a system of rule and economic organization. The malaise of the socialist system is clearly visible even within the ruling parties. Experience since the end of Stalin's tyranny has led the East Europeans to lose hope that the system can sustain more than marginal improvements. The question that they are now facing, therefore, is ultimately not how to improve the system but how to change it. The economy was the ultimate source of the partial legitimacy of these basically unauthentic regimes, and, given the basket cases of Romania and Poland at the one extreme and the major difficulties of Hungary and Yugoslavia at the other, the East European intelligentsia has concluded that the socialist economic system is basically nonviable and that there are confining limits to marketizing reforms. This view, based on theoretical analysis and empirical studies, is shared instinctively by the working class, based on practical experience.

As I will discuss in greater detail, the relations between the metropolitan power and its East European client states differ substantially today from those of the early post-Stalinist period. The recognition by Khrushchev and Brezhnev of the legitimacy of "different roads to socialism" left the East European countries with a very limited margin of autonomy and a very small space for fundamental innovation away from the Soviet model. Only three and a half years into Gorbachev's rule, this space for innovation already seemed much greater, and the threshold of direct Soviet political intervention, let alone military response, to reforms much higher than at any time in the past.

If this evaluation is true, the already existing, or potentially expanding, realistic influence of *perestroika* on irredentist and nonconformist developments in Eastern Europe is of great consequence. The much more liberal approach of Gorbachev to "different roads *from* socialism" improves the chances for the emergence and expansion of major reformist movements, initiated by the party elites or originating in the nonparty intelligentsia in coalition with the industrial working class.

Historical experience suggests that autonomy and partial freedom to act are for radical reform (or revolutionary) movements in their initiation and gestation phase of cardinal importance for their expansion and consolidation. To put it simply, most such movements do not get off the ground. But by now increased liberalization, the potential for hesitation, the consideration of the costs and consequences of intervention on the part of the Soviets, as well as possible lack of Soviet support—or even discouragement—for the use of harsh preventive measures by the native elites substantially increase the chances for the survival and consolidation of radical reform movements in the East European countries.

The international setting against which the drama of *perestroika* and its influence on the East European empire are played out also differs substantially from the conditions of the mid-1950s. The Soviet Union is in retreat in the international arena because it is overextended in relation to its international resources. Its domestic goals of renewal have acquired overwhelming priority over external aspirations in the minds of the new Soviet leadership. If Soviet military expenditures have to increase by the year 1990, Gorbachev's economic reform will not get off the ground. The USSR therefore needs agreements with the United States on arms control. The Soviets have decided to assume a lower profile in their dealings with the Third World. They are engaged in a diplomatic offensive to gain friends among the capitalist nations and to seek reconciliation with China. They hope to receive help from the West to counter their economic woes. What the Soviet Union wants to avoid now, even if it requires a high price, is a confrontation with the United States and therefore a reversal of the Soviet diplomatic offensive.

It is very likely that the *internal* repression of a reform movement in Eastern Europe, the extreme form of which was the declaration of martial law in Poland in December 1981, will meet, in the present conditions of growing radicalization and polarization, with greater resistance than in the past. It will also most likely be blamed on the Soviet Union and will make its diplomatic offensive much less effective. Internal repression will also have a very negative effect on economic help from the West for Eastern Europe, which is an important condition for its stability. A Soviet military intervention in Eastern Europe, which may come if all internal efforts to stop mass unrest fail, will have far more destructive consequences on the Soviet Union than those brought about by the Soviet invasion of Hungary in 1956 and of Czechoslovakia in 1968. Intervention will certainly destroy the new détente with the United States. It will dramatically reduce the credibility of the new thinking, the prerequisite of better relations with the West. It will halt or reverse the process of normalizing relations with the People's Republic of China. At best it will set back the progress of *perestroika* at home and may even destroy it. The Soviets remember very well that the reforms promoted by Aleksey Kosygin after the ouster of Khrushchev in 1964, and Libermanism in general, ended for all practical purposes after the invasion of Czechoslovakia in 1968.

That *perestroika* will bring winds of change to an already restless Eastern Europe is almost certain. That these changes will attempt to move beyond the limits of *perestroika* in the Soviet Union is very probable. The key question about Eastern Europe for the West and for the Soviet Union is whether the changes that *perestroika* encourages will be evolutionary and gradual or spontaneous and explosive; whether they will aim to achieve what is possible in the new circumstances, which is more than what was possible in the past; or whether they will rush out of control and end in explosion.

The forces of *perestroika* and *glasnost'* unleashed by Gorbachev are difficult to control in the Soviet Union. Many of the things happening in the Soviet Union are unintended consequences of *perestroika,* which Gorbachev certainly did not have in mind when he started his radical reform. The flare-up of national aspirations among the non-Russian peoples of the Soviet Union, particularly in Transcaucasia and the Baltic states, are the most visible expression of how difficult it is to control radical change. The uncontrolled growth of the so-called horizontal associations, those not controlled by the state, which already number more than 30,000, is another example. Workers' unrest in the USSR, which is likely in the near future if their increased political participation and expectations are not matched by material improvements, may provide another instance of unintended consequences of Gorbachev's reforms.

Yet radical reform movements in Eastern Europe, encouraged by *perestroika,* will be infinitely less controllable and more radical than in the Soviet Union. Many factors argue in support of this proposition. The most important of these are the following:

- As was mentioned, the political and cultural tradition of most East European countries differs significantly from the Russian and Soviet tradition; their cultural and life-style identification with the West is indisputable; and their political affinity for the West is very high and increasing.

- Nationalism in these countries is very strong and still increasing. Contrary to the countries of Western Europe, where unifying supranational institutions (for example, the European Community) have had a mellowing effect on traditional nationalism, the integrational efforts of the Soviet Union are resented and rejected and in the end feed native nationalisms. Most importantly, in contradistinction to the Soviet Union, China, or Cuba, where communism and nationalism became fused, in Eastern Europe communism and nationalism are countervailing forces, and the strength of the latter is undoubtedly rising among the population and even the elites.
- The material and spiritual aspirations of the populations of these countries, and particularly of the intelligentsia and the professional strata, are much higher and growing faster than in the Soviet Union. The industrial workers of these countries do not have the seemingly endless patience of the Soviet worker, and their intelligentsia, even when it belongs to the party, has not been integrated into Communist political culture.
- Some of these countries, for example Hungary and Poland, have already moved, in their economic, political, and cultural spheres, far beyond the actuality and promise of *perestroika* and *glasnost'* in the Soviet Union. The Hungarian economic reform in action and the Polish reform in plan are not likely to be matched by the USSR in many years. The private freedoms in most East European countries are unmatched by the Soviet Union. Hungary is thinking about evolution to a semi-multiparty system, and in Poland an authentic counterelite and counterregime institutions act openly and engage in negotiations with the government.
- Many East European countries are facing or are in the midst of successions that are not limited to the top leader but to large elite groups. Experience shows that successions are periods when Communist elites are split and the conditions for reform emanating from the party and allied nonparty people are most propitious.
- In almost every country of Eastern Europe, the youth is the stratum most alienated from the regime and from the very ideas of socialism. In every East European country, including relatively prosperous East Germany, the party has major trouble in recruiting young members. In the most important East European country, Poland, youth is in a state of far-reaching social alienation and prone to outbursts of anomic violence. To a lesser degree this is true in the other countries of the Soviet bloc as well.

To sum up, Gorbachev's *perestroika* is apt to find fertile soil in Eastern Europe. Yet the aspirations that *perestroika* does express in Eastern Europe will tend to go beyond the perimeters pursued by Gorbachev in the Soviet Union. The movements that will challenge the existing regimes in Eastern Europe will be more spontaneous, much more radical, and much less controllable than in the Soviet Union. It also seems likely that neither repressions nor concessions will be able to defuse the radicalism of East Europeans' edition of *perestroika*. Finally, there exists a consensus among the reform-minded party leaders and activists in Eastern Europe, as well as among a part of the opposition to the regimes, that Gorbachev's *perestroika* provides probably the last chance of trying to resolve the East European problem without major bloodshed. The ultimate consequence of the failure of Gorbachev would be tyranny and civil wars.

Eastern European Developments and *Perestroika:* Short-Term Options

The extent of Gorbachev's political strength at home is far from certain. The question therefore of how far he can afford to change Soviet East European policies, especially in the case of major unrest, is a very relevant one. Gorbachev and his supporters constantly reiterate their goal to make *perestroika* irreversible. By doing so they admit that *perestroika* is still reversible and that the political power of Gorbachev and his supporters is limited. They are probably right to stress that such a reversal would be "fatal" for Soviet prospects of stability and growth at home and global power status abroad. But a nonreformist alternative to Gorbachev's radical program still remains a politically viable option. Nevertheless, the price of such a reversal increases with every month and probably already now would lead to bloodshed. Therefore to prevent a reversal, to stay on the course of *perestroika,* Gorbachev's policy options are circumscribed and his actual policies are definitely centrist.

The depth of Soviet elite and popular commitment to the preservation of the empire in Eastern Europe beyond obvious Soviet security needs is great. The issue of how far to go to permit change and accept different roads from socialism in this region is one of the two most sensitive items on Gorbachev's political agenda; the other is the national question in the Soviet Union. Gorbachev cannot afford risky and too liberal moves in his imperial policy, let alone face a "loss" of a satellite country. Such a loss will have a catastrophic impact on his political fortunes at home.

The Brezhnev Doctrine, as everything that the "old man" did, is not popular in the Soviet leadership circles and in the alliance for *perestroika* that Gorbachev has forged. The Soviet leadership has not declared officially and openly that the Brezhnev Doctrine is dead. Yet Gorbachev's speeches on East European themes, and his behavior during his visits to East European countries, aim, inter alia, to create the impression that events like the Soviet invasion of Czechoslovakia in 1968 are out of the question for the present and the future. Young Soviet party intellectuals speak openly, boldly, and with an inner certainty that one can only envy, that a Soviet military intervention in Eastern Europe is simply unthinkable. Many of their older and experienced comrades, when they are pressed, surprisingly say the same, although, it seems, with somewhat less certainty. When trying to convince their interlocutors, and reassure themselves, they eloquently use two basic arguments. First, the Soviet policy approach to Eastern Europe has really changed, and the Soviet leadership is conscious that the international consequences of applying the Brezhnev Doctrine will be far worse than attempts to enforce East European conformity by extreme means. Second, they emphasize, sometimes angrily and bitterly, that they will no longer permit East European countries to exercise a veto on Soviet domestic *perestroika,* which would be the most likely outcome of Soviet application of extreme measures against one or another of the recalcitrant East European clients.

Yet despite these impressions, it is far too premature to pronounce the Brezhnev Doctrine null and void. True, it is almost certain that the emergence of a new Alexander Dubček to radically reform Czechoslovakia would be tolerated by the Soviet leadership and probably even welcomed. Czechoslovakia is a country with a highly developed sense of the possible and of moderation as a means of national survival. The chances that a reformist leadership in that country would not lose control over developments and would steer a course within the parameters of Soviet permissiveness are high. Yet realistically, one should expect at this stage of Soviet *perestroika* and new thinking, and in the conditions of the highly defined limits of Gorbachev's power, that a revolution of the Hungarian type of 1956, or a situation such as existed in Poland in the fall of 1981, will be confronted head on by gradually but rapidly escalating response and resistance by the new Soviet leadership.

That Gorbachev will have to employ extreme measures, including military intervention, if he is faced with an extreme situation of a moving away from the traditional political model of socialism in an East European country, is based not only on the domestic sensitivity of the issue of freedom for Eastern Europe. Political logic and historical experience argue that the lack of decisive Soviet action in one East European country will only encourage forces of radical change in other parts of the empire. Moreover, the Soviet position as a superpower declined visibly when the extent of Soviet domestic difficulties became better known. Soviet withdrawal from Afghanistan, negotiation on withdrawal of proxy troops from Angola, the lowering of commitments in the Third World, and major concessions in arms control negotiations leave one with no doubt that the Soviet Union has entered a period of weakness and retreat in the international arena. The Soviet aspirations to be an influential global power, the equal of the United States, however, have not diminished. In fact, these aspirations are at the core of *perestroika* and provide the broadest base for Gorbachev's coalition among the power-holders in the Soviet Union. This too argues that a radical challenge in an East European country that cannot be contained by local forces will result in extreme Soviet steps. Gorbachev's Soviet Union is at present too weak in the international arena to show the ultimate weakness of being unable to control a recalcitrant satellite on its western borders where the USSR faces the forces of NATO.

Discussion of whether under Gorbachev, as of now, the Brezhnev Doctrine is alive or dead is therefore far from only an academic exercise. Developments in Poland may soon, within a year or two, provide a practical test for the assurances emanating from Moscow that the pattern of Soviet intervention in Eastern Europe is broken once and for all. The compromise with Solidarity toward which the Polish government may be moving, probably partly under Soviet pressure, is very frail, not at all institutionalized, and far from tested. It can be reversed and broken by either side at any point of tension. Moreover, it is not at all clear whether the leaders of Solidarity, particularly Wałęsa, can speak in the name of the working class and deliver industrial peace in return for major political concessions by the government.

The most inflammatory issue for the Polish workers, in contradistinction to many intellectual advisers of Solidarity, is not political freedom as such but the catastrophic economic situation. The most active part of the industrial working class, the young workers in their twenties and thirties, was the moving force of the strikes of April–May and August 1988. Solidarity supported it, according to the maxim "I am your leader, therefore I will follow you." The prospects of economic improvements in Poland are very low. The frustrated mood of the mass of young workers makes them prone to anomic violence rather than political reform. It is also not certain, if the need arises, that the Jaruzelski government will be able to pull off the kind of relatively low-cost martial law operation it did in 1981. This operation was performed by security forces with military units on the sidelines. The behavior of the Polish military, if it were to be used directly against the workers, is uncertain. Yet the use of the military may become necessary if an effective general strike breaks out, which did not happen in 1981. In light of this, it is easy to understand why some of the Polish political elite would in principle like some kind of a partial power-sharing deal with Solidarity. The Polish and Soviet leaders need stability in Poland in the next year or two, even if the price to be paid for it is high. But nobody really knows whether an explosion in Poland can be avoided. The only force in Poland that can possibly prevent one is the Catholic church.

Nobody can be sure whether the strong Soviet reassurances that the Brezhnev Doctrine is dead and will not be resurrected are true. However, the very fact that such Soviet reassurances are given by people with authority is of major importance on its own. Their importance is not so much for the West as for the peoples of Eastern Europe and their political elites. Many people discount these reassurances as propaganda directed at the West to improve the general atmosphere of East-West relations, as helpful to *perestroika*, and as a reflection of the Soviet hope that developments in Eastern Europe will not require in the foreseeable future a test of Soviet guarantees of nonintervention.

It is highly ironic, however, that in Eastern Europe, the laboratory where the truth of the decline and fall of the Brezhnev Doctrine ultimately will be tested, the actual impact of the line disseminated by the Soviets in this respect could, and probably will, be the reverse of the intention of its authors. The point is that, in the shorter run especially, perception of reality and the reality itself have an interchangeable, identical impact on human behavior. If the message from Moscow continues to be that Soviet military intervention in Eastern Europe is unthinkable, then parts of the intelligentsia, of the workers, of party people in one or another East European country will start to believe in the truth of this message and try to act accordingly. It was not the fear of native security forces that acted as the basic pacifier of the peoples and parties of Eastern Europe and as the moderating force of their reforming programs and movements. This function was, rather, a result of their belief in the ultimate danger—the employment of overwhelming Soviet military might against their countries. The peaceful and reassuring message from Moscow may therefore, instead of producing stability, have the reverse effect: to encourage and radicalize movements that strive to change the system and to gain national independence. Instead of being a self-fulfilling prophecy, the premature Soviet pronouncement of the death of the Brezhnev Doctrine may in fact become a self-destructive prophecy. By saying it, the chances of its remaining true decline.

Soviet Policy Toward Eastern Europe

The question of how much Gorbachev can change relations with Eastern Europe, considering his power position at home, is one about the near future. Probably a more important question, which is about the next decade, is, How far does Gorbachev want to change Soviet relations with Eastern Europe? In trying to answer this question, I take as axiomatic points of departure the following three propositions:

- Gorbachev does recognize that the former Soviet approach to Eastern Europe is no longer viable and is outright dangerous.
- Gorbachev considers the international dimension of Soviet–East European relations to be of much greater importance than his predecessors did.
- The entire course of Gorbachev's policies at home and abroad testify to the flexibility of his approach and to his ability to learn, to improvise, and to change.

Gorbachev's judgment about, and policies toward, Eastern Europe evolved parallel to the development of his domestic *perestroika* and foreign policy new thinking. At the beginning of his rule he was most anxious to resume and strengthen Soviet control and leadership over Eastern Europe, which had weakened during the last years of Brezhnev and thereafter. Yet the General Secretary gradually recognized that the hard and dogmatic policies of his predecessors toward Eastern Europe were potentially as dangerous to the Soviet Union's future role in this region and its international position as were the stagnation and dogmatism at home. He concluded that a new Soviet policy toward Eastern Europe was needed, one that would be more accommodating to the East European Communist elites, more liberal and flexible politically, and more differentiated in order to take account of the relative importance of, and the different conditions in, each of the East European countries.

His greatest change, as with his foreign policy in general, was rhetorical. In his frequent speeches on Eastern Europe he seemed eager to admit past Soviet "mistakes" in relations with these countries and to assert that a new era in Soviet–East European relations was starting, which would show greater Soviet respect for independence of these countries and their closer but "equal" ties with the Soviet Union. Soviet revisionism with regard to past Soviet–East European relations and the promise of "equality" in those relations at the present and in the future was startlingly presented in a Soviet document prepared for the first Soviet-American Conference on Eastern Europe, which took place in June 1988 in the United States, and which is well worth quoting. The head of the Soviet delegation to this conference, Academician Oleg Bogdanov, stated that "everyone has to follow very strictly the principles of sovereignty, non-interference and mutual respect. The Brezhnev Doctrine is completely unacceptable and unthinkable. . . . We gave too much advice before to our partners, and it was actually very damaging to them. It's time to keep our advice to ourselves. We cannot take responsibility for all of Stalin's mistakes, [but] we are responsible to change our performance now."[1]

In his frequent visits to Eastern Europe, Gorbachev took pains to stress that what was acceptable to the peoples of Eastern Europe in their domestic political and economic organization and cultural policies was acceptable to the Soviet Union. At the same time he often tried to distance himself from unpopular policies of local leaders. In Czechoslovakia, for example, his spokesman, Gennady Gerasimov, when asked in 1987 what was the difference between Dubček's program of 1968 and Gorbachev's *perestroika*, answered enigmatically, "Nineteen years." In Romania, Gorbachev pointedly praised the process of democratization in the Soviet Union and extolled the general virtues of democratic order. In those visits Gorbachev wanted to gain sympathy for the Soviet Union's reform programs and to convince the local populations that the Soviet Union is not the cause of the unpopular policies of their own governments.

Although the nature and direction of Soviet declarations on Eastern Europe are readily apparent, it is much more difficult to evaluate the extent of actual changes in Soviet policies toward its satellites. It is clear that across the entire political spectrum of the East European countries, from the Left to the Right, their leaderships and high party and government officials feel much more freedom to speak out in disagreement with their older brother and to underscore that they feel much more independent from Moscow than before. On the Right, East German leaders behave with arrogance toward the Soviet Union and its problems. They openly say that they need no *perestroika*, whereas the Soviet Union can learn much from their experience. During 1988, Erich Honecker wrote a number of protests in official letters addressed to Gorbachev about articles that appeared in the Soviet press; in the spring of 1988, Honecker even confiscated three issues of the Soviet weekly *Novoye vremia* (published inter alia in German) for containing an article advocating a reduction in the size and deployment of Soviet conventional forces facing NATO, and for reprinting an anti-Stalinist Soviet play. On the Left, the Hungarians openly discuss the inadequacy and the insufficient radicalism of the Soviet *perestroika* model for their own country and, in an unheard of development, stress that the domestic and international interests of Hungary need not always be identical with those of the Soviet Union or, for that matter, with those of the other countries of the Soviet commonwealth. (Incidentally, on the other side of the globe, Fidel Castro, engaged in his own "cultural revolution" and appalled by Gorbachev's course, stated flatly that he did not consider Hungary to be a socialist country.)

In his practical policies toward East European countries, Gorbachev has given them a large margin of autonomy over their internal affairs and over the extent of their dealing among themselves (for example, tense Hungarian-Romanian relations) and with the West. The consultations between the Soviet Union and its East European allies regarding common foreign and security policies have increased visibly and are not entirely, as in the past, pro forma. There is evidence from both the Soviet Union and Eastern Europe that Gorbachev and high Soviet officials responsible for relations with Eastern Europe, let alone Soviet ambassadors in these countries, are much more sensitive to East European sensibilities and interfere much less in domestic party issues, particularly in personnel changes and leadership successions (which probably means that the KGB must be more active in this respect through its own hidden channels). This does not indicate less Soviet interest in what is happening in Eastern Europe. If anything, Soviet interest and concern have clearly increased (one example is the appointment of a special assistant to Gorbachev on East European affairs, a high party official, Shakhnazarov).

From the beginning, Gorbachev's East European policies have had one overriding goal—to ensure stability in the region, to provide a breathing space for the Soviets and room to maneuver by ensuring tranquility there for domestic *perestroika* and the new détente with the West. Initially, and to a large extent even today, he tried to promote such stability by gently pushing reforming regimes, such as Hungary, to the Right and conservative regimes, such as Czechoslovakia, to the Left. Recently one has the impression that this stabilizing policy makes the pushes less gentle and expresses greater worries about the danger to Gorbachev's domestic and international course that may emerge from Eastern Europe from the Left and from the Right.

If this impression is correct, there are a number of reasons for the change and for greater Soviet concerns. To start with, the policy of "gentle push" was not successful. The Hungarians, for example, instead of leaving Kádár in the leadership or selecting his own choice of a centrist successor, changed the leadership and political elite wholesale, in a more liberal direction.

Czechoslovakia at the same time replaced Gustáv Husák with another, although younger, conservative, Miloš Jakeš.

In this new Soviet sensitivity to events in Eastern Europe, and their tendency to exert greater pressure, the Soviet leadership clearly distinguishes among the East European countries in the extent of their concern and involvement. Soviet leaders dismiss Romania as a marginal and hopeless case; as one Soviet official said, "Let them do whatever they want to do." They think Czechoslovakia is of secondary importance because it is reasonably prosperous and reasonably stable. They do not expect major challenges from the Czechoslovak leadership, whom they regard as relatively timid. They regard the Czechs and Slovaks as sufficiently "civilized" to reject open revolt and largely moderate in the way they will express their aspirations. The three East European countries on which Soviet concern and increased activism centers, for somewhat different reasons, are Hungary, East Germany, and Poland.

As mentioned, in Hungary the departure of Kádár, who was trusted and admired by the Soviets, took place with a swiftness and radicalism surprising to the Soviets and not to their liking. The very probable radicalization of Hungarian economic reform does not seem to concern Gorbachev. What does matter, however, is the accelerating discussion in Hungary of the sociopolitical model of socialism. The Hungarian intelligentsia, party activists, and leaders are thinking dangerous thoughts about the viability of a socialist multiparty system, the right to create factions within the Communist party, and developed civil society. A majority of the Hungarian party leadership and membership seems to feel that without radical political changes, future economic progress, and therefore political stability, is in question. Furthermore, the aforementioned changes parallel the Hungarian effort to come closer to West Europe—the only available source of economic help to start a new and politically necessary cycle of expansion of the Hungarian economy. In the Soviet eyes, Hungary has embarked on an enterprise whose consequences can be only dimly perceived.

Gorbachev and Eastern Europe—The Scope of Soviet Commitment

Gorbachev's first three and a half years in power proved amply his ability to learn to adapt and improvise his domestic and international policies. Yet we really do not know how much of his rhetoric about the "new freedoms" for Eastern Europe will survive the challenges that Eastern Europe is apt to produce to Soviet domination in the near future and to Soviet evaluation of what is fit and proper in the internal developments of its "allies." Gorbachev may have the good sense to see the incompatibility of his domestic and foreign policies with the aim of preservation, if need be by force, of the Soviet empire, even if the Soviet role there will be much relaxed.

It is my contention, however, that not only in the short term, but also in the medium term of the coming decade, the odds are heavily weighted against Soviet acquiescence either to the loss of an East European country as a member of the Warsaw Pact or, even more important, to the actual abolishment of Communist rule in any of these countries. There are two reasons Gorbachev cannot afford the collapse of an important link in the chain of East European satellite countries, let alone the dissolution of the empire, even if he came to the conclusion, for which there is no evidence, that the continuation of a Soviet East European empire is untenable in the long range with the success of *perestroika* at home and the winding down of the cold war abroad.

The first reason in support of this proposition has already been mentioned. As the movement in some East European countries, which has already started, toward establishment of non-Communist regimes gains momentum, it is unlikely to proceed in such a gradual and incremental way as to preclude a strong and ultimately decisive reaction from the Soviet Union. The historical traditions of such countries as Poland, for example, with their polarization of political forces that do not really look for compromise and where it may already be too late to achieve a compromise, argue against gradualism and incrementalism. In such a country, with such a catastrophic economic situation, where the ruling circles are split and often unrealistic and the intelligentsia and working class frustrated, impatient, and often maximalist, confrontations and explosions are more likely than a prolonged evolutionary process away from the abyss. But, in contrast, Soviet acquiescence and lack of determined responses with force are most likely in situations where each single step from dependence and communism is by itself not a sufficient reason for intervention and where gradualism and incrementalism may thus win the day.

The second reason against Soviet acquiescence to basic systemic changes in Eastern Europe, even if Gorbachev is aware that in the longer run the Soviet East European empire is doomed to extinction and that in the meantime it is a heavy burden on Soviet efforts at *perestroika* and international détente, is of even more fundamental importance. It has to do with the sources and the continuing scope of Soviet commitment to an East European empire and more precisely with the close interaction of developments in this empire with the Soviet domestic situation and foreign policy.

In the history of Soviet expansion there was no greater or more important achievement than the establishment of the Eastern European empire. Along with the USSR's internal empire—the non-Russian republics of the Soviet Union—Eastern Europe is today the only surviving empire in the world. Many of the Soviet domestic, foreign, military, and economic policies can be explained by their goal of preserving hegemony there. In turn, Eastern European policies stem from their countries' ties to, and expectations of, the Soviet Union. The existence of this domain—along with partial control of countries such as Cuba and Vietnam—was and is perceived by the Soviet leadership as the basis for the future expansion of Soviet rule and of communism and as the confirmation of the historical trend toward the inevitable victory of socialism over capitalism. Soviet leaders from Stalin to Brezhnev, despite some differences in specific policies toward the region, have been steadfast in their total determination to preserve this empire.

Eastern Europe serves a number of important purposes. It is a security belt of allied buffer states on the Soviet Union's western borders that defends the homeland and provides a beachhead for actions against the West. Eastern European armed forces are important additions to those of the Soviet Union and constitute more than one-third of the mobilized armed forces on East European–West European borders. The Eastern European economies together supplement the military and civilian sectors of the Soviet economy. These countries also serve as sources of technical expertise and as conduits through which advanced Western technology finds its way eastward.

Nations such as East Germany, Czechoslovakia, and Poland help the Soviet Union to pursue its foreign policy objectives in the Third World. They bolster the Soviet presence among potential allies or clients. They also play an essential role in Soviet foreign policy toward Western Europe, both as hostages that moderate Western European policies toward the Soviet Union and as intermediaries that make Soviet foreign policies more palatable to Western Europe.

Yet neither security interests—Eastern Europe as a buffer zone and as a military and economic counterbalance to NATO—nor the usefulness of Eastern Europe for advancing Soviet global ambitions suffices to explain the depth of Soviet determination to maintain its hold over the empire regardless of the cost. Considerations of security and utility alone do not require the present high level of Soviet control over social and political developments in Eastern European countries. The explanation lies beyond pragmatism. Soviet rule provides one of the ideological foundations of Great Russia and Communist party control within the Soviet Union and also contributes decisively to the credibility of Soviet foreign policy.

Victory in World War II was the central legitimizing experience of Soviet rule at home and is associated with, even focused on, control over Eastern Europe. As the major spoil of that war, the empire serves to legitimize the Kremlin's rule at home. In particular, the empire helped to form a bond of common interest between the government and its Great Russian and other Slavic populations. The creation of the empire made permanent the unification of the Ukraine and Belorussia with the eastern parts of Poland, which were annexed by the USSR in 1939. The empire's creation also led to the division of Germany, the historic threat to the Eastern Slavs.

The domination of this empire is expected and supported by Russian party and nonparty members alike. When in 1981 the Polish situation was developing in a way that threatened Soviet rule there, a member of the Russian academic establishment, a liberal in Soviet terms, told me, "You will probably hate me for what I have to say to you, but I will say it nevertheless: If tomorrow Soviet forces enter Poland I will applaud them, and I can assure you that is a very widespread feeling in my milieu." Echoes of this attitude prevail among diverse parts of Russian society. To some members of the public, the Eastern European empire represents the fulfillment of the dream of the unification of the Slavs under Russian power and influence abroad. To many it provides the desired confirmation and reinforcement of the cherished belief that the USSR belongs to Europe and is a dominant part of the continent's structure of power. For all, it contributes to a feeling of security and pride.

The continuing domination of Eastern Europe also confirms the basic ideological proposition that the establishment of Communist rule is irreversible. Soviet rule in the USSR and Communist domination in Eastern Europe represent, in the party's view, the victory of a historical process and the inexorable trend of the future. Even after Stalin's death, the Soviets insisted on the monopoly of power by Communist parties in Eastern Europe. They have not permitted autonomous organizations of a political character to exist for long, let alone to challenge the parties' monopolies.

East European Development and *Perestroika:* Medium-Range Connections

The question of the margin of freedom open to Gorbachev in his East European policies, to a man who takes great risks in the policies he promotes but who is very cautious as a politician, earlier posed in short-range terms, has also to be considered in a longer-term analysis. It remains a central question even if one assumes that Gorbachev will immensely consolidate his power in the years to come; will be able to preserve the sociopolitical and cultural dimensions of his *perestroika,* with sufficient control preserved for Moscow; and will have a measure of success in his restructuring of the Soviet economic model and a quantitative improvement in Soviet economic growth. Even then, the interconnection between the situation in Eastern Europe and Soviet policy there with the Soviet domestic situation and foreign policies will remain inexorably tied with respect to power, interest, ideology, and perceptions.

When I said previously that the question of the importance and evolution of Eastern Europe for the Soviet Union goes much beyond security concerns, I did not intend to denigrate the importance for the Soviet Union of security concerns. These concerns loom very large, not only in the perception of the Soviet armed forces, where they are of central importance, but also within the party leadership, the political public, and even the Soviet population at large. After all, the trauma of historical danger from the West is associated directly with the status of Central and Eastern Europe. Whether this region, despite all doubts about its genuine loyalties to the Soviet Union, is a Soviet military bridgehead against the West (even if only defensive) or a neutral zone similar to that of Finland or Austria remains a central security question for various powerful groups in the Soviet Union and for the general Russian popular psyche.

If the question of Eastern Europe were for the Soviets only a security question, one could contemplate the retention of the Warsaw Pact and the deployment of large Soviet troop contingents in Poland, Hungary, and

Czechoslovakia, let alone East Germany, along with the gradual evolution of the East European countries away from the Communist system and close Soviet dependency. But even then, the time needed for such change would be long, the process dangerous, and the outcome uncertain. Neither the Communist party nor the Soviet armed forces have any experience with a close security alliance with another nation that envisages Soviet tolerance and the equality of both sides. The entire Soviet experience in this regard, before World War II and more recently in the Third World, argues for the instability of, and Soviet unease with, such arrangements.

In the Soviet mind, whether party, military, or popular, an alliance is regarded as an unequal arrangement in which the Soviet side exercises control. For the run-of-the-mill Soviet party leaders and military commanders, the security and stability of their military alliance with Eastern Europe are guaranteed not only by overwhelming Soviet military preponderance but by actual Soviet military control over the territory and forces of the main Warsaw Pact countries and, what is particularly important, by the Communist nature of their "allied" regimes, which provides unity of purpose and tight control over the populations of these countries. It is too much to expect that this type of approach will change as a result of a few years of Gorbachev's *perestroika* and new thinking even if Gorbachev himself, a big "if," does not share this attitude.

The direct connection of potential East European developments with the development of the Soviet Union under *perestroika* is also particularly important with respect to the domestic Soviet national question. Embarking on his present course, Gorbachev must have been aware that the "renewal" that he proposes for the Soviet Union will require major changes in the relations between the dominant Russians and the other nations of the Soviet Union. He may have been unprepared, however, to encounter so many unintended consequences of his liberalizing policies in this particular field so early on his course. The ugly and brutal conflict between Armenia and Azerbaidzhan over the province of Nagorno-Karabakh is not readily open to mediation and reconciliation. This conflict demonstrates the explosive potential of many decades of accumulated grievances, frustrations, and emotions, which by touching upon the very roots of communal existence—religion, national identity, and cultural traditions—are the least likely to be open to rational reasoning and compromise solutions.

Although the Armenian-Azerbaidzhani conflict is not contiguously aimed at Russians, it in fact concerns them directly because, in the eyes of the other Soviet nations, the Russians bear the ultimate responsibility for all existing arrangements between the nations of the Soviet Union. In other areas of the country the escalation of openly expressed aspirations by non-Russian nations is directed against the problems of injustice, callousness, and domination imposed by the Russians. These developments are present in virtually every union or autonomous republic and are especially strong in the Baltic states of Estonia, Lithuania, and Latvia; in Georgia; in the western Ukraine; and probably also in the Muslim areas of Soviet Central Asia.

One element of these national and mass protests for redress of grievances is particularly noticeable and important; it unites against the power of Moscow large parts of the party elites with the traditional intelligentsia and youth, a powerful and combustible mixture that cannot be ignored or satisfied with token concessions. It is clear by now to Soviet leaders and to outside observers that the Soviet national question is potentially the single most difficult challenge on Gorbachev's agenda to an evolutionary, gradual solution. Once again the course of Soviet history is taking revenge on Marxism, which stresses social distinctions and working class solidarity as opposed to what has proven to be the main force of the twentieth century—the differentiation and conflict of nations.

Gorbachev and his associates clearly have no ready-made prescriptions for solving the national question to the satisfaction of all. The Central Committee Plenum planned for February 1989, the first to be devoted to this set of issues, will at least provide some departure points for a comprehensive policy in this respect. The program of *perestroika*—with its stress on the decentralization of power, especially economic power, and on a greater scope for local participation and initiative—overlaps in part with the aspirations of the non-Russian communities. Yet this partial overlap of interests, which accounts for the considerable support for Gorbachev among the new party establishments and the old intelligentsia strata in the non-Russian republics, is counterbalanced by another requirement of *perestroika,* one absolutely central to Gorbachev's plans and urgent needs. During the last years of Brezhnev and the interregnum that followed, there was a breakdown in the flow of authority from Moscow to the peripheries and in the flow of accurate information from the peripheries to Moscow. The new Soviet leadership is determined to restore more centralized relations between Moscow and the peripheries in the interests of the cohesion of the Soviet party-state and even as a precondition for the partial devolution of power. *Perestroika* is a gigantic enterprise that requires cohesion in the central leadership and in its political institutions. Moreover, Gorbachev and his associates are far from voluntarily imitating the kind of federalist arrangements tried in Yugoslavia, which are at present shaking the very foundations of that socialist multinational state.

All signs point to the conclusion that the question of relations among the diverse national-administrative entities of the Soviet Union will lead to conflicts, dangerous escalation of aspirations, divisions within the Soviet power establishment, and many unexpected turns of events. If this is true, developments in Eastern Europe and Soviet policies toward East European countries acquire major *domestic* significance for the Soviet leadership. To put it simply, the extension of freedom and change in Eastern Europe, which from the point of view of the Soviet Union's international interests would be very positive and could, although with difficulty, even be reconciled with Soviet security interests, will most probably not be accepted from the *domestic* Soviet point of view. *Perestroika* in Eastern Europe and in the Soviet Union is indivisible, and this reinforces its limitations and the margin of safety for its changes, as perceived by the Moscow leadership.

Another element in the East European situation that may have major influence on *perestroika* in the Soviet Union, and is already becoming intertwined with Soviet domestic developments, is the evolution of the traditional intelligentsia in most countries of Eastern Europe, particularly in Poland and Hungary. In the Soviet Union the traditional Russian intelligentsia is only beginning to recover its old libertarian orientation and values in the favorable climate of *perestroika*. After decades of alienation, conformity, and enforced silence, it now constitutes the left wing of Gorbachev's coalition and, through *glasnost'* and historical revisionism, plays an important role in his struggle against conservative opposition and bureaucratic resistance.

Although serving Gorbachev's political purpose, the Russian intelligentsia is not entirely controlled by him. The pressure of its members for the further radicalization of his course toward freedom and cultural and professional autonomy from the state already frequently goes beyond the limits that he and his associates consider prudent and timely. Gorbachev's enemies are the conservatives in every walk of life, but he is clearly worried that the "exaggerations" of his supporters on the Left provides the ammunition for his conservative opponents.

After decades of silence, isolation, and timidity, the bulk of the Russian intelligentsia needs a model that will infuse it with new ideas and reinforce its traditional but long-forgotten themes and values. The main source from which the Russian intelligentsia draws in putting pressure on the Gorbachev regime is the tradition of the democratic Russian intelligentsia of the early and mid-1800s. This intelligentsia preceded the revolutionary intelligentsia, whose moral relativism became responsible for so much of Russia's later misfortunes. Through direct contact, writings, closeness to the West, and innovative ideas, the intelligentsia of the East European countries—Poland, Czechoslovakia, Hungary—exert a growing influence on the Russian intelligentsia (and on some of the non-Russian, as in Lithuania and Georgia). The freedom that Gorbachev is expanding in the USSR is still increasing. But it is not too difficult to foresee and to predict the restrictions that will be imposed on this process, the limitations on the emerging Soviet "civil society" that the future holds in store. The East European intelligentsia, with its Westernizing orientation, political radicalism, and powerful ideas, will most likely exert a major influence on the equivalent strata in the Soviet Union.

The domestic complications for the Soviet Union, connected with the changes that are emerging in Eastern Europe, may limit the declaratory liberalism of Soviet policies in this region and can also be expressed through the central dimension of Soviet reality at the present and in the future—ideology and the power situation. Gorbachev's *perestroika* downgraded the role of traditional Communist ideology in shaping Soviet policies and moved away from its purely Stalinist interpretation. Although ideology is far from dead in the Soviet Union, the basic motivating force, the normative basis of Gorbachev's *perestroika*, is Russian patriotism and nationalism. The core of Gorbachev's coalition, the strength of which will make or break his program and determine his power position in the longer run, is not the creative intelligentsia but those elements of the party apparatus, of the mass party, and of the various functional elites and bureaucracies who have hitched their fate to Gorbachev's star for patriotic reasons.

This core of Gorbachev's coalition is centrist in nature. It is primarily attracted to *perestroika* by its economic component—reform to make the Soviet Union modern. Although the coalition's members recognize the necessity of democratization or *glasnost'* in an instrumental way, they are far from enthusiastic about them and want to keep them in well-defined limits. To keep the Union of Soviet Socialist Republics intact and to hold onto the Soviet empire in Eastern Europe are for them self-evident Russian goals. This is especially true for the substantial part of the professional military that supports Gorbachev. The danger of the national disintegration of the Soviet Union or of its "losing" its East European empire, to which Gorbachev does not respond with full force, probably describes the only situation in which a conservative-military coalition to oust Gorbachev could come about and be victorious.

Thinking About the Unthinkable

Eastern Europe has always been either a forgotten region in international relations or a region of central importance. In 1945–1949, it became the centerpiece of a fast developing superpower conflict, the cold war, which is by now approaching its fiftieth anniversary. In the decade of the 1970s, the issues of the Eastern European region were overshadowed on the one hand by European détente and on the other by Soviet-U.S. conflict outside of Europe. In the late 1980s, and most probably in the 1990s, the East European region again became a major focal point of international relations.

Whether forgotten or in the center of attention, the sensitivity of the East European regions in international relations was always a function of two factors: the particular focus of superpower rivalry and the behavior of the East Europeans. Today, because of both factors, Eastern Europe is very much in the forefront of the international agenda. The changes in Gorbachev's Soviet Union may have created new conditions for East European evolution away from dependency and communism that may be either explosive or incremental. The declining spiral of superpower rivalry, which is much more profound and probably longer lasting than that of the early 1970s détente, redirected the attention of both superpowers to the core causes of the cold war, in which Central and Eastern Europe holds pride of place. If the détente of the late 1980s is to change radically superpower relations, East European developments are of central importance. The cold war started over Eastern Europe and can end only if the key issues of this region are settled.

At the present and in the coming decade, the key issue of Eastern Europe, under which all other issues can be subsumed, is no longer the question of Soviet permissiveness in liberalizing the Communist regimes of their clients and in redefining market-oriented economic reforms. Assuming that

Soviet *perestroika* and new thinking will continue to evolve in their present direction, Soviet acceptance of both processes, even far-reaching ones, is virtually assured. What is at stake today, if the Cold War is really to end, is more fundamental—the transformation of the East European monistic regimes into pluralistic democracies to an extent that no existing Communist regime has yet achieved in practice and the abolition of the master-client ties that prevail in Soviet–East European relationships in domestic and foreign policy issues.

In the first decade of the cold war, U.S. policy toward the Soviet Union proclaimed two goals—containment and rollback. The first goal was pursued with determination and consistency. The second goal was no more than an ideological chimera, even when U.S. domination of the international arena was absolute. The policy of rollback was never operationalized and collapsed even conceptually with Soviet intervention against striking East German workers in 1953 and the Soviet invasion of rebellious Hungary in 1956. The development of the Soviet Union into a major nuclear power, even before strategic parity between the Soviet Union and the United States was reached, forced the concept of rollback into oblivion because of the near certainty that it would lead inexorably to a Soviet-U.S. war.

It is historically ironic but politically logical that today, when relations between the Soviet Union and the West have so dramatically improved, the end of the cold war, which both sides want so much, is practically impossible without a Soviet rollback in Eastern Europe. This rollback, which the United States also wants, cannot be forced, however, by the strength of U.S. arms; it can only be the result of a gradual but profound change within Eastern Europe and within the Soviet Union.

The crisis of the Soviet system, which constitutes the fundamental cause of Gorbachev's *perestroika* and new thinking and coincides with the systemic crisis of the East European Communist regimes, may lead in the coming decade to what was unthinkable for more than four decades—the end of Soviet imperial rule in Eastern Europe as the precondition for dramatic transformation of at least some of the East European regimes. The odds against such change taking place are still prohibitively high. The convergence of circumstances that may make it possible will be complex and to a large extent internally contradictory.

The optimal conditions under which the emancipation of Eastern Europe in line with the wishes and will of its peoples may become possible include the following *domestic* factors:

- The countries of Eastern Europe should experience major sociopolitical domestic tensions that will promote the responsiveness of the ruling elites, and particularly of the leadership, to the needs of political change under the threat of an explosion that will sweep them away, even if, ultimately, major internal security countermeasures or Soviet military intervention contain the explosive forces at work.
- The level of tension that might enforce a political change from the leadership would require a radicalization of major units of the working

class, their presence in a number of industrial centers and geographic areas of key importance, their merger with the antiregime intelligentsia, and the resultant fusion of labor and intelligentsia leadership elements.

- Political instability in East European countries that inexorably escalates toward explosions and confrontations is not in the interest of the West, the native anti-Communist forces, and the Soviet Union, which may under such circumstances be forced into costly military interventions. This means that the sociopolitical tensions in these countries should stop short of spreading major unrest, let alone a national explosion; such restraint will require the presence of an antiregime leadership recognized by the workers and intelligentsia.
- Political stability (understood as the absence of explosions) that is combined, however, with major tensions that promote change is probably possible only if a major mediating role is assumed by existing or newly created prestigious non-Communist institutions. Existing institutions that would promote change and gradualism could be the church or an emergent national parliament in which the representation of workers and intelligentsia is strong.
- In the past the threshold of change that might secure development toward democratic pluralism was represented either by a revolutionary explosion, as in Hungary in 1956, or by an internal party reform, as in the Dubček regime in 1968. Today both are unacceptable—the first because it will most probably lead to the same outcome as in 1956 and the second because a liberal party reform by itself does not reflect sufficient meaningful response to the depth of the systemic crisis and to the radicalization of the aspirations of broad social strata in Eastern Europe. In the late 1980s and in the 1990s, the initial threshold of meaningful political change required, and will require, practical steps that ensured institutionalized political power-sharing between the existing political elite and the forces of national opposition to Communist rule and dependency on the Soviet Union. The most likely power-sharing scheme would combine the legalization of an independent trade union movement with large representation of non-Communist forces in the national parliament and in regional and municipal representative bodies. Such a power-sharing plan would recognize and preserve the leading role of the party in policy decisionmaking while creating an institutionalized non-Communist veto over these policies. Such an arrangement, in fact a political stalemate, would hopefully ensure gradualism of political evolution in the countries of Eastern Europe and a redefinition of "socialism" that the ruling parties of Eastern Europe would consider the necessary condition for their tolerance of institutionalized oppositional forces.
- The domestic development in Eastern European countries that will promote movement toward an increasing democratic pluralism would require under the best of circumstances a consensus within the party leadership and political elite that they can preserve their leading role

only if they are willing to share power with the forces of opposition. Such a consensus can, however, be attained, and renewed with every gradual step toward democratic pluralism, only if the Communist leadership and political elite are politically split and disunited and their conservative forces gradually purged and politically deactivated.

- Economic difficulties in Eastern Europe may act, and in the past often did, as a stimulus for change; yet the level of economic hardship in some East European countries today is too high, prolonged, and difficult to master even through economic reforms. Rather, it creates an explosive potential that is a threat to gradual political change. These economic difficulties cannot be solved or ameliorated for any intermediate period of time by help from outside (although such help is necessary). The East European countries have not only to embrace real economic reform that will make eventual outside help productive, but also to change their economic strategy in both the short and intermediate range. (Economic reform deals with changes in the economic structure and mechanism, whereas economic strategy concerns various dimensions of economic policy such as the flow of investments and credit, price range, and wage policy.) The economic strategy of the leadership of these countries should abandon for now utopian dreams about high technology, redirect their investment to consumer sectors, abolish punitive tax policy toward private enterprise, and concentrate on export production in the areas of their relative advantage.
- Turmoil and pressure for political change in Eastern Europe have focused most often in the past on one country. This isolation of reform activity in one country, and the hostile response from other countries in the region, made easier and more effective Soviet conservative pressure. Today there exists a real chance of simultaneous, if not equally intense, pressure for change in most of the region. Such conditions would reinforce the reformist forces and minimize the effectiveness of probable Soviet counterpressures.

The optimal conditions for far-reaching political change in Eastern Europe would, of course, require developments in the Soviet Union that are conducive to the emancipation of the region. These will have to include the continuation and radicalization of *perestroika,* partial economic success for its basic goals, the containment of social disorders in the Soviet Union that are the unintended consequence of *perestroika,* and a gradual redefinition of the Soviet concept of security.

With the ouster of Gorbachev and the failure of *perestroika,* the chances for radical political change in Eastern Europe would be reduced to nil. The determined continuation of *perestroika* is the sine qua non of the process of freeing East European countries from imperial ties. Until now Soviet *perestroika* proceeded parallel to the process of education and radicalization of Gorbachev and his associates. The continuation of this process and the consolidation of Gorbachev's power may produce in practical policies the change in Soviet attitude toward Eastern Europe that is proclaimed verbally. Some Western analysts of the Soviet Union argue that even Gorbachev's ouster and the retreat of *perestroika* may preserve the key principles of new thinking in Soviet foreign and security policies. This seems unlikely, but even if the assumption of continuity of Soviet foreign policy without Gorbachev and *perestroika* proves valid, the direction of Soviet policies toward Eastern Europe will be the first to change back to the previous model and the last to be changed as a part of a new model.

The partial success of *perestroika* in the economic field, which is also the condition necessary for its survival, will still further moderate Soviet foreign policies in general, including the USSR's attitudes toward Eastern Europe. Partial economic success in practical terms would include visible improvements in the standard of living in the major Soviet metropolitan areas, particularly with regard to agricultural products; improvement in the intensive factors of growth, such as the productivity of labor and capital; and increased investment of old and new industrial capitalist countries in the Soviet bloc. Such partial economic success, which is possible, will not only strengthen and institutionalize the policies of *perestroika* but will also increase the relative costs of its reversal. Such partial success will radically increase the threshold of Soviet intervention in Central and Eastern Europe and simply make such an intervention less likely.

As I argued, the connection between nonorthodox events in Eastern Europe and sociopolitical turmoil in the Soviet Union makes Soviet policy toward Eastern Europe a domestic problem more than ever before. The centrifugal processes in Eastern Europe and within the Soviet Union feed on each other. If Gorbachev cannot steer toward gradualism, the autonomous aspirations of Soviet nations, the demands of the industrial working class, and the increasingly liberal pressure of the creative intelligentsia, the best that he can afford is to make a radical break with the past in Soviet–East European relations. His, and *perestroika's*, survival depends on his ability to change the Soviet sociopolitical system gradually and without major explosions. So does his policy of increased autonomy and freedom in Eastern Europe.

One of the most important elements of the new thinking in Gorbachev's foreign policy concerns the changed understanding of the logic of national security. Through major doctrinal pronouncement, the idea of total (and unilateral) security is being replaced by the concept of common security. This conceptual change makes possible for the first time a radical cut in nuclear weapons by the two superpowers. Yet with regard to Eastern Europe, as was noted, the concept of Soviet security includes the element of Soviet control that can be assured only by the Communist nature of the East European buffer states.

The central question concerning Soviet–East European relations is whether the changes in Soviet perceptions of the general concept of security can be expanded and adjusted to East European realities. To put it differently, is it possible for the Soviet Union to separate Soviet security needs in Europe from the impulse to control its East European empire? That the Soviet Union has legitimate security interests in Eastern Europe is beyond question. These security needs could require the presence of Soviet armed forces on East European soil (primarily in East Germany) for a very prolonged period.

Until and unless conventional radical arms control in Europe becomes a reality, and the cold war confrontation winds down, Soviet legitimate security interests may even require the preservation of the Warsaw Pact as a counterweight to NATO. Nevertheless, can these security interests be reconciled with a high degree of independence of the East European regimes in their domestic political and economic systems and, within limits, in their relations with the West?

Conceptually, such a change would constitute a logical follow-up of the concept of common security adapted by the Soviets and would be in line with the change of their military doctrine in Europe toward active defense. The separation of Soviet security from Soviet control in Eastern Europe cannot be ruled out in the future, although one has the impression that this kind of development will be among the last items on the East-West agenda of arms control. The term *spontaneity* with regard to domestic developments in Eastern Europe has too long been associated with the image of "hostility" toward the Soviet Union. This association does not have to be true if the Soviet Union accepts the archaic nature of its East European arrangements, which were initiated by Stalin, which in the long run are detrimental to Soviet renewal at home and long-lasting détente abroad, and which would provide a sound basis for the eradication of the very roots of the cold war.

In the light of our discussion, the odds against a gradual and nonconvulsive solution to the East European "question" and the peaceful resolution of the systemic crisis in this region are very great indeed. But for those who know Eastern Europe, there can be no doubt that the alternatives for the region in the coming decade are either major domestic changes toward democratic pluralism, which will go much further than even the most optimistic scenarios of the Soviet *perestroika*, or chronic instability, turmoil, and even revolutions.

The Soviet Union and the West are at present, and I hope will remain, in a situation in which the interests of both coincide in many respects. With regard to Eastern Europe, instability is clearly neither in the self-interest of the West nor in the interest of the Soviet Union. Yet stability in Eastern Europe can be achieved only by profound domestic political changes that the Soviets may dislike but should not veto by threats or actual use of force. The transition from the pseudosterility of coercive compliance to the real stability of normative acceptance and participation, even if it is gradual, will be full of tempestuous events. These should not provoke the Soviet Union to direct interventions or imposition of "internal [security] invasions." The subdued turbulence will only return later, with even greater intensity and more radical objectives.

The process of transition of Eastern Europe to much more representative systems and significantly revised types of relations with the Soviet Union would also require active support from the Western Alliance. There are many principles that should inform the policies of the United States and its allies in facilitating the process of change in Eastern Europe. These were aptly discussed by Mark Palmer in the preceding chapter. It should be clear that proper Western policy may help the process of non-violent change but that the process and its outcome will be decided by the social and political forces already at work in the Soviet Union and in the East European countries. On paper, the long list of conditions necessary for success in attaining change looks quite discouraging. But this is not surprising. After all, every major change in modern history was accomplished against heavy odds. It is only proper and reassuring that the historical fate of nations is not decided by accountants who calculate the odds, but by brave people and wise leaders.

Notes

1. Oleg Bogdanov, "East-West Relations and Eastern Europe," *Problems of Communism* 37, nos. 3-4 (May-August 1988), pp. 55–56.

Index